STATE
◆
SOCIETY
AND
CORPORATE
POWER

A trilogy of books based on articles from the *Journal of Economic Issues*, edited by Marc R. Tool and Warren J. Samuels and published by Transaction Publishers.

The Methodology of Economic Thought

The Economy as a System of Power

State, Society, and Corporate Power

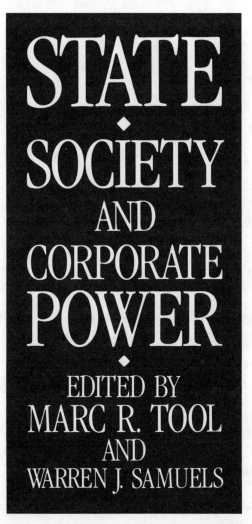

STATE
◆
SOCIETY
AND
CORPORATE
POWER
◆

EDITED BY
MARC R. TOOL
AND
WARREN J. SAMUELS

SECOND EDITION, COMPLETELY REVISED

Transaction Publishers
New Brunswick (U.S.A.) and Oxford (U.K.)

Library of Congress Catalog Number: 88-29185
ISBN: 0-88738-759-4
Printed in the United States of America

Library of Congress Cataloging-in-Publication Data

State, society, and corporate power / edited by Marc R. Tool and
    Warren J. Samuels.
        p.   cm.
    "Selected papers from the Journal of economic issues"—Pref.
    ISBN 0-88738-759-4
    1. Institutional economics.   2. Power (Social sciences)
3. Corporations.   4. Trade regulation.   I. Tool, Marc R.
II. Samuels, Warren J., 1933-
HB99.5.S74   1989
330.1—dc19   88-29185
                                                                CIP

Contents

Introduction

For centuries, Western scholars have persistently been absorbed by a range of issues and problems concerning the question: how does and should the state deal with private economic power? This volume of selected papers from the *Journal of Economic Issues* (JEI) on the relationships between the state, society, and corporate power continues and contributes to this inquiry agenda.

This is a heavily revised and much extended collection of material that originally appeared in an earlier publication by Transaction Publishers entitled *The Economy as a System of Power*.[1] It is the third in a series of revised, republished JEI articles currently available from Transaction. The first concerned *The Methodology of Economic Thought*, the second retained the original title of *The Economy as a System of Power*.

Continuing a concern introduced in the first of the series and developed in the second, this third book carries the institutionalist analysis of the acquisition and use of economic power into new and critically significant subject areas: law and economics, the public control of economic power, and international implications of public and private use of power to influence the flow of real income on a global scale. However, since the volumes stand independently it is desirable to reiterate comments from the introduction to *The Economy as a System of Power* that introduce the institutionalists' research program in the areas indicated:

> Institutional economists, from the beginning, have seen power as inherent and essential to any social order. Where power is perceived as the capacity and opportunity to exercise discretion over the rules that organize social life, it is obvious that judgments reflecting use of power organize the social process and determine how the institutional structure of that social order is determined, modified, and replaced. Power-reflective judgments have defined the extant institutional fabric of the economy, the polity, and the social order generally. Institutions . . . are *prescribed* and *proscribed* patterns of correlated behavior and attitudes. The prescribing and proscribing are done, obviously, by discretionary agents—people with power. In sum, power means discretion over other people's behavior. Prescribing and proscribing judgments delimit

behavior in ways that reflect the agents' priorities and purposes: they may or may not reflect recourse to democratic criteria of choice.

The state, public government, is unique in that by constitutional specification or otherwise, it possesses sovereignty—the primary and enforceable power to prescribe and proscribe behavior. Its acknowledged and utilized powers of mandamus and injunction reflect this locus of authority to determine the structural fabric of the society. Though the state, including democratic forms, embodies primary power centers, other institutional and individual power loci often exist and flourish as well. In this volume, the possession and use of corporate power, especially in relationship to the state as a representative of society, will be of special concern. These relationships include state control of private power, state aid to and abetting of private power acquisition, state indifference to possession and use of private power, and even state deference to, or control by, private centers of power. The society's economic wellbeing depends finally on how power, public and private, is acquired and used. What goals are sought? Whose interests matter? What criteria of judgment are reflected in private and public power decisions and choices? How can power, public and private, be held accountable?

A neoclassical Chicago school approach in the relatively new field of law and economics has gained some following in the last three decades in its ideological advocacy that law courts and judges use neoclassical microeconomic analysis to inform their judgments about how, and to what ends, private-public sectoral relations should be conducted. In this view, the state's judicial power should be used to serve the utilitarian and pecuniary ends of individuals in private market and non-market centers of economic power with the expectation (or at least the claim) that the public interest is therewith better served. Given their archaic presumption that the exercise of state power is always an impairment of freedom, where freedom and authority are dichotomized, such views correlate with a diminished role for the state, deregulation of social controls, and deferential treatment of private property rights.

But the institutionalists in Part I of this work cannot abide the Chicago school's implicit apologia for the private exercise of corporate power. They follow a long institutionalist tradition of advocacy of a selectively activist problem-solving state. They see governmental institutions as the only institutional vehicles with which the community, as a community, can rewrite the agenda of governmental action to modify institutions to enhance the flow and equity of real income. The state's responsibilities for agenda creation and rule and law modification is continuous, evolutionary, and primary. Institutionalists argue for a democratically managed economy. They see freedom not as the absence of governmental restraints, but as continuing discretion over restraints. They would define freedom, then, as an expanding area of discretion over the rules that organize our common lives as a community.

Consider private property rights, as several chapters do: we are all aware, that private ownership of property, is a socially prescribed and proscribed area of discretion concerning the use and disposition of an item. The community has always set limits and constraints to whatever is privately owned. More than three centuries ago Lord Chief Justice Hale observed that when private property is "affected with the public interest, it ceases to be *juris privati* only."[2] Unlimited discretion over personal or corporate property is never, and can never be, permitted; one way or another, the community (or those in control of it) always determine which restraints will be imposed and why. Accordingly, the state and its courts have continuously recurring obligations to review such areas of discretion over property to ensure that the public interest is being served. Does the private owner of a plant have the right to pollute? Does the owner-seller of real property have the right to discriminate invidiously? Are private property rights inviolate? Of course not; not now and not ever! Papers in this collection till this field.

The chapters in Part II raise similar fundamental questions in the area of social control of corporate power. Given the corporate revolution and the rise to hegemony of the corporate conglomerate or megacorp, only the ill-informed or the ill-intended can presume that, in the absence of governmental involvement, unfettered market forces can hold achieved power centers publicly accountable. The works herein review options of antitrust constraints, regulation of enterprise (as with public utilities) and planning. In all areas, the fundamental quest is to turn actual or potential private vice (price gouging, service denial, waste mismanagement) into public virtue (pricing review, full access to service, environmentally safe operation).

As domestic megacorps have become multinational power centers, the scope and scale of problems of public control of private power have enormously increased. As the concluding chapters of Part III make clear, the level of international interdependence is so high that the issues of control have become truly global. A moment's reflection on Chernobyl should convince the non-believers. But in the absence of international governmental institutions, control instruments must be pursued by ad hoc negotiated agreements and arrangements among allegedly sovereign states.

So the material herein serves to reset the research agenda and policy approach for dealing with the exercise of economic power, and again demonstrate the relevance and viability of the institutionalist perspective in finding ways to hold achieved power to democratic accountability. That the quest is interminable, no serious observer will deny.

As in the other two books in this series of *JEI* papers newly published by Transaction Publishers, the primary concern of the co-editors is to stimulate inquiry into what has been and remains a troubled and significant area of concern. No synthetic summaries are attempted; none are required. The inquiry agenda remains open. But introductions to the individual papers will be found at the beginning of each of the three sections.

As noted in *The Economy as a System of Power,* the *Journal of Economic Issues* will continue to publish articles on the persistent and important questions and issues of economic power raised in these chapters. You are cordially invited to continue the dialogue begun with these works through recourse to future issues of the *JEI.*

Marc R. Tool
Warren J. Samuels

Notes

1. Warren J. Samuels, ed., *The Economy as a System of Power,* (New Brunswick, N.J.: Transaction Publishers, 1979).
2. From his *De Portibus Maris,* 1 Harg. Law Tracts 78. Quoted in *Munn vs. Illinois,* 94 U.S. 113, 1876. Henry Steele Commager, *Documents in American History,* Volume II, 4th ed., (New York: Appleton-Century-Croft, 1948), p. 92.

PART I

POWER AND THE INTERRELATIONS BETWEEN ECONOMIC AND POLITICAL SYSTEMS

Introduction to Part I:
Power and the Interrelations Between
Economic and Political Systems

In the lead chapter by Robert B. Seidman, the ideological divorcement in the field of law and economics between Chicago neoclassicists (Seidman's "classicists") and institutionalists, alluded to in the introduction to this volume, is addressed head-on in consideration of the nature and significance of *contract law*. His primary goal is to examine critically presumed dichotomies of the following sort:

> Social engineering and planning are perceived as the very opposites of the free market; intervention is the opposite of nonintervention. The legal expression of social engineering is perceived as a set of commands directed by the state to various citizens. The legal expression of the free market is perceived as facilitative law, of which the law of contract is the archetype. As social engineering is the opposite of a free market, so command law is the oppositive of facilitative law.[1]

It is Seidman's purpose to demonstrate that these dichotomous pairings rest on unreal assumptions about how contract law operates.

For the classicists, contract law is noncoercive; it merely requires that persons freely making agreements live up to their terms. Seidman shows this to be a shallow contention. The classicists' underlying propositions affirm that, with facilitative law, persons define their own norms of conduct, competitive markets assure equivalence of power, the state is value neutral and limits its role to conflict resolution. In consequence, "facilitative law insures 'voluntariness.'" For Seidman, however, "the net result of contract law is to transfer to the economically superior classes in the community the most significant powers of the state, all under the fictional disguise of notions of 'freedom.'" His anticlassical perspective rests on contrary propositions: facilitative law does permit parties to set their own norms of conduct, but that same law ensures that the more powerful party

3

will impose his desires upon the weaker, that the perfectly free market will
not protect the weaker, that the state uses its power to enforce the contract
against the weaker, and that the state cannot be value neutral. Therefore,
the state's enforcement of a private bargain is as much a form of state
intervention as more direct commands from the state to citizens. In consequence, facilitative law ensures that the state will delegate its power to the
more powerful party to the exchange. The chapter concludes with exploratory applications of this theoretical analysis in the African countries of
Kenya and Ghana.

S. Todd Lowry demonstrates that the Chicago School's approach to law
and economics is flawed in still other respects: Lowery begins his formulation of bargain and contract theory through an analysis and critique of the
Coase theorem. This theorem "states that individual bargaining will result
in similar allocations of resources regardless of the presence or absence of
legally enforced rights or liabilities if there are no transactions costs." It
postulates that there is a "natural plateau of socially uniform, rational
behavior generated by individual bargaining." It "accepts the rational two-
party bargain as the basic unit of social welfare and treats this plateau of
two-party bargaining as the potential measure, or definition, of social cost."
It reflects rationality and is the route to economic efficiency. It assumes the
absence of external intrusions on the bargain and the presence of competitive market influences. In consequence, Coase relies "on subjective individual rationality as a means of minimizing social costs" and would
"substitute unregulated bargaining for the legal system's use of tort liability
to optimize resource allocation in unique or imperfect market situations."

In Lowry's view, however,

> the concept of the competitive, two-party bargain as conceived by the Coase
> theorem falls short of providing an economic formulation to parallel the new
> legal analyses being developed in the modern theory of contract. Although
> the two-party bargain may superficially resemble the two-party contract, the
> burden of this article ... [is] to show that [that] bargain is a regressive,
> adversary transaction in which individualistic self-interest is paramount and
> that either party's gain is the other party's loss. On the other hand, the con-
> structive process in which mutual advantage is structured through the build-
> ing of relations with reciprical content is an essentially social phenomenon
> and must be deduced from a primary commitment to social values. ... Two
> party contract in legal theory is being increasingly distinguished as a phe-
> nomenon where parties with long-term planning objectives are primarily
> concerned with structuring relational arrangements to provide a continuum
> of stability productive of reciprocal mutuality.

He argues that

... the bargaining transaction is essentially divisive and zero sum, and that it must occur in a contained zone structured by a relational system. [Moreover,] the relational structure necessary to an organized economy cannot be derived from an aggregation of bargains, but must be understood as a social construct developed in a setting of widely accepted social values and goals.

That is, a market-deferential, methodological individualistic view must give way to a discretionary, relational contract view reflecting normative social judgments.

Ian R. Macneil continues deliberation on the adequacy of the neoclassical model in the exploration of relations, in this case, between the law of contracts and economics. The conclusion to which his analysis leads is that the neoclassical model is unable "to deal with unilateral power, except for its bilateral aspects ... whenever unilateral power is diffuse, complex, or changeable *within* the structure of exchange."

Macneil defines power "as the ability to impose one's will on others irrespective of their wishes." Unilateral power permits a person "to subject another to some particular effect without the other's consent," as with property rights. Bilateral power appears "when the possibility of exchange exists by which two parties can release each other from some of the restraints imposed by their respective unilateral powers," as in potential employer-employee negotiations. Bilateral power is "the foundation of the economic model and of classical contract law (and thinking)." From it emerge "freedom of contract, maximization of efficiency (or wealth) and much else." But it is Macneil's major contention that "bilateral power undergoes a transformation upon exercise, a transformation largely ignored in standard microeconomic analysis, but necessarily not ignored in contract law." When agreements are made, when bilateral power is actually and mutually exercised, necessarily in a time sequential setting, "each party acquires *new unilateral* power." Both buyer and seller acquire new powers to impose sanctions on each other, to meet contract terms. Accordingly, "even in the most paradigmatic of contracts, bilaterial power is converted into unbalanced unilateral power." The remainder of the paper develops these themes with special reference to the restraint of power hypothesis and to the Richard Posner efficiency hypothesis. Arguments and evidence tend to support the former hypothesis over the latter.

The chapter by Arthur S. Miller shifts the focus from the dichotomous views of law and economics of Chicago neoclassicists and institutionalists, to a consideration of the actual, emergent structural character of the American economy. Has America become a corporate state? If so, what are its legal foundations? Where is power, "the ability or capacity to make or influence decisions of national importance," held? In response, Miller contends that "a proper definition of the American version of the corporate state, when developed, will have to encompass at least the following: (1) evidence that some sort of merger, actual or tacit, has taken place between political and economic power; (2) a legal nexus between the two; (3) a consequence of some type of corporate body that both encompasses the two and is greater than the arithmetical sum of the two; and (4) a diminution of the social and legal role of the individual *qua* individual." He finds that historical evidences generally confirm the emergence of a corporate state; the above mentioned attributes have been realized.

He sees the present structure as a gradual culmination of trends traceable throughout national history. Private "law and the legal system were employed by the business community during the nineteenth and early twentieth centuries to further its interests." Public law contributed as well: The Supreme Court declared corporations to be persons in the eyes of the law and therewith were entitled to protections of the Fourteenth Amendment. A "corpus of public law . . . insulated companies from the pressures of a rising trade-union movement, Populism, and Grangerism."

A government-corporation symbiosis has emerged in the twentieth century; supercorporations, jointly, and intimately interdependent with a positive government, have generated a corporate state. This *positive state* is characterized by "the change from a Constitution of limitations to one of powers . . . the advent of a system of overt economic planning . . . the alteration of governmental framework . . . the politicization of law and the legal process," and "the progressive blurring of the line between public and private government-business relationships." Miller offers a "living law" analysis of this "emerging synthesis" which asks: "*who* makes the decisions, *how*, and with what *effects*? We have, in sum, a new social order, appropriately termed the corporate state, American style."

Robert Delorme introduces a fresh and significant view of the relations between the state and the economy derived from one of the most extensive empirical investigations of governmental involvement in an economy ever undertaken, that of France from 1872-1980. He traces the origins and evolution of long-run state intervention, including spending, and other public interventions, for the central government, local government, and (after 1945) social security. He finds that the ratio of public expenditure to gross domestic production ranges from around 14 percent in the early decades of the period, to around 48 percent in recent years. The central theoretical concern is to explain this long-term growth of public expenditure.

In quest of explanatory approaches to account for the phenomena observed, Delorme considers and rejects "determinant" (such as quantitative time series), "individualistic" (such as public choice), "constraint" (such as corporate state), and Marxist (such as state capitalism) models of inquiry; they are all, in different ways, reductionistic or causally one-sided, and therefore inapproporiate. Instead, Delorme pursues an approach which adapts the method to the research object. "Instead of having an object [of research] adapted to a given method we end with a method adapted to a constructed object." No method is *a priori* illegitimate or legitimate. The method followed addresses "interdependencies and their dynamic nature;" he sees "the state on a methodological level as a relation in movement." "The state is that through which public interventions take place. These reflect the relations between the state and the sectors to which they are directed. The notion of dynamic interdependences is given substantive content . . . It is the study of the evolution of public spending under the angle of the relation between the state and the main fields of intervention."

The inquiry takes the form then, first, of a inductive systematic study of "public interventions in major economic and social fields of activity." And second, extensive consideration of, and the generation of ordered answers to, the following questions: "Why the public nature of intervention and not a private form, either individual or collective? Why the expenditure nature of the intervention and not a qualitative form or a quantitative one other than spending? What are the causes of the evolution of public expenditure for each function?" Central is the recognition and insistence that there must be an inquiry process of "reciprocal adaptation between the method and the object, between the abstract and the concrete" It is an adaptive process that remains open; it is never finally ended. The need for the further development of a theory of state insertion is acknowledged.

The examination of John R. Commons's theory of the democratic state, in the next chapter by John Dennis Chasse, may well contribute to such a theory. Commons was, in all accounts, continuously engaged in reformist activities, and held, with conviction, that the state's role must be democratic. Chasse considers at length this theory of the state and offers an appraisal thereof. Common's concept of the state consists of an "evolutionary interaction of three interrelated processes." "First, a collective effort to control the use of violence as an incentive creates the state—a hierarchy of officials, each subject to some earthly authority; second, these officials control violence by enforcing rights and duties, necessarily 'liberating and expanding' the powers of the citizen, and enforcing a particular distribution of liberty and property; third, an evolving public purpose determines the working rules that guide the officials, and hence the distribution of liberty and property." With regard to the first, the state must protect against the use of violence by one citizen against another, and by officials of the state against citizens. With regard to the second, while the state must obviously enforce the laws and control behavior, the state can "also 'liberate' and 'expand' the personality:" liberate through enforcement of "remedial rights" and expand through enforcement of "substantive rights." With regard to the third process, the public purpose or interest can be identified and pursued through the use of state power to support dispute-settlement arrangements, collective bargaining under governmental aegis, and the provision of "going concern" continuity. Reasonableness and humanity can be reflected in such use of state power.

Commons rejected the conservative advocacy of the minimalist state and authoritarian deference to an absolutist state. A democratic state that evolves to admit larger fractions of its members is responsive and accountable in its use of power, and that continuously encourages the modification and updating of problematic institutions, offers the best hope for successful reform of the economy. In all cases, persuasive approaches were to be supported over coercive ones. The negotiation of reasonable settlements to economic and political differences is both desirable and feasible. The state can and should play a facilitative role in such determinations.

Steven R. Hickerson narrows the focus of inquiry to a consideration of the economic power of legal counsels. We gain therewith additional insights into how the corporate state emerged and is operated, (as discussed by Miller), how difficulties arise when legal counsels of large corporations are confronted by those that would implement Common's view of the democratic state (as presented by Chasse), and how and why the public sector has expanded over the years, (as described by Delorme).

It is Hikerson's contention that those comprising the legal profession have the potential power to influence, and often shape, decisions, that they have "differential participation in decision making through effectual control or manipulation of property rights, income, or 'other rights of economic significance.'" Their "underlying ideology is that of those who control, or at least routinely use, legal services to achieve their specific aims." "The institution of legal counsel stands at the forefront of the confrontation between power and its field of responsibility." Through an historical review, Hickerson establishes that the "'law-job' is a functional category of activity that is . . . continuous and developmental . . . that the institutions created to perform these legal tasks are discontinuous and replacemental . . . and that the role of legal counsel with repect to power is contextual. . . . The nature and scope of the legal expert's work are dependent on the extant cultural milieu and the dominant institutions thereof."

"The adversarial process is a significant part of the field of responsibility that power must confront and is itself structured to the strategic advantage of recurrent (mainly corporate) litigants." But there is nothing sinister or conspiratorial about the role of legal counsel in relation to power. It is simply "a product of the mechanisms which function as instruments of corporate institutional hegemony." Drawing on constructs formulated by William Dugger (see *The Economy as a System of Power,* in this series), Hickerson examines corporate hegemony in this context:

> Through subreption the key "institutions of representation" have become a virtual annex of corporate enterprise. . . . Through contamination, the values and ideology of corporate institutions are transferred to the institution of legal counsel and are subsequently reflected in the pattern of claims which successfully secure representation. Through contamination in conjunction with emulation, the mark of success (prestige and status) in the practice of law comes to be closely associated with performing the key advisory roles required by corporate enterprise. . . . Through mystification the institution of legal counsel plays a key role in the manipulation, support, and distortion of symbolic legal principles which emanate from, and in turn help to legitimize, the corporate way of life.

At issue, either explicitly or implicitly, in several of the preceding papers has been the nature of the existence of economic coercion. The exercise of power is always in some sense coercive. What uses of power that coerce are permissible? What uses are not permissible, and on what grounds? Warren J. Samuels, co-editor of these volumes, offers an incisive consideration of such questions through the presentation and analysis of a fairly extensive exchange of correspondence in 1923 between Robert Lee Hale, an institutionalist, and Thomas Nixon Carver, a traditional neoclassicist. The exchange remains as vital and significant today as it was originally.

In Samuel's view,

> the exchange of views between Hale and Carver represents a straightforward juxtaposition of neoclassical and institutional conceptualizations of coercion in a market economy. Carver's neoclassical position generally maintains that coercion is either fundamentally absent from or severely constrained in a market economy, especially one that is competitive and exhibits relatively

easy entry. Power, and therefore coercion, would comprise only command price, which competition prevents. In a market system there is voluntary exchange, consent, and individual(ist) choice within individual opportunity sets. Hale's institutionalist position generally argues that coercion is inevitable and ubiquitous in every economy, not excluding the market economy. There is generalized, systematic, and structural coercion. Coercion—both personal and, especially, impersonal—exists thorugh the aggregate exercise of choice, through the control over resources and participation in the economy. Coercion is consequent to the exercise of choice based upon one's opportunity set and involves effects visited upon others; coercion is involved in the ongoing formation of the structure of opportunity sets. Voluntary exchange takes place only within the system of mutual coercion.

Where Carver sees only the state (and perhaps unions and cartels) as coercive, Hale finds both the state and the market to be coercive. For Hale, the laws of property coerce people to work for factory owners; "the income of each person in the community depends on the relative strength of his power of coercion, offensive and defensive;" and "the channels into which industry shall flow . . . as well as the apportionment of the community's wealth, depend on coercive arrangements." Carver predictably rejects the market coercion thesis and considers governmental rules as contra-freedom. He does, however, acknowledge the potentially weaker bargaining position of labor and the probable superior power of the rich to impose their will. The exchange of ideas between Hale and Carver is lively, engaging, and instructive. It discloses well the nature of major philosophical and analytical differences in perspective of neoclassicists and institutionalists.

In chapter 3 Richard Posner's economic views are illustrative. In the chapters by Margaret S. Hrezo and William E. Hrezo, they become the central focus as the Hrezos describe his "economic model of the common law, assess its implications for judicial decision making . . . and attempt to apply the model to an area of . . . policies affecting the environment and workplace health and safety."

Risk assessment via cost-benefit analysis has become a major evaluative criterion for much U.S. economic policy. The undergirding theory for such analysis is provided by the Chicago neoclassical perspective, especially as reflected in Richard Posner's use of the microtheory model to inform judicial decisions. As many are aware, an extensive indoctrination campaign has been under way during the last two decades to instruct and persuade judges to incorporate this model as their main referential grounding for judicial decision making. As the Hrezos make clear, such adoption represents a massive reductionist exercise in that all other considerations beyond the conscious or intuitive calculation of economic costs and benefits are passe. Wealth maximization becomes the singular determining criterion of judgment. Noninterference with the basic workings of a free market system, a system of voluntary exchange, results "in the shift of resources to those uses in which the value to the consumer, as measured by the consumer's willingness to pay, is the highest." Highest efficiency is achieved therewith; wealth is maximized. Where judges must rule on losses incurred reflecting "wasteful, uneconomical resource use," Posner's model is presumed to provide guidance for a judicial judgment by "predicting the effect of legal rules and arrangements on value and efficiency in their strict technical senses and [on] the existing distribution of income and wealth." For Posner, such is what many judges actually do and what all judges ought to do. "The assignment principle allows the legal system to mirror the market by using opportunity costs to reward efficient resources use and the maximization of wealth."

The Hrezos offer a summary and critique of the Posner model and explore probable consequences were it actually to dominate judicial decision making. Interestingly, through a content analysis of some 518 federal court decisions actually made between 1978 and 1983 regulating environmental and workplace health and safety, they find that cost-benefit and cost-sensitive concerns (the Posner approach) appear to be reflected in only a relatively small number of cases (44 cases or 8.5%).

At this juncture, the focus on law and economics turns to considerations of property, property rights, and economic power. A normative inquiry by Stephen E. Barton examines property rights and human rights in a context of regulatory reform. An aspect of the Reagan revolution of the 1980s was to "reform" the regulatory process. "Particularly in vogue [were] proposals to increase the role of private property rights, either by eliminating regulations or by changing them so that property owners can more closely approximate market behavior." In this paper, Barton reviews and criticizes "the theoretical basis of the privatization approach to regulatory reform, using the example of zoning." He then argues that "certain weaknesses in regulatory processes can be overcome through extending the scope of human rights, rights entirely removed from the domain of the market."

The privatization campaign is rooted, of course, in the belief that "private property is essential to individual freedom and to democratic government, and that government interference with private property rights is suspect as a step toward despotism." Property is the basis of freedom; "the market is an expression of that freedom;" market efficiency is the "embodiment of free choices of sovereign consumers and producers."

Barton then considers and rejects various contemporary arguments which reflect this basic ideological affirmation: questionable externality jusitifications for government intervention; the Coase rule argument against modification of private property rights; replacement of zoning rules with modified property rights to minimize transactions cost; the question of whether the erosion or attenuation of property rights should be addressed by making such regulatory processes as zoning regulations more closely resemble private property rights. Implicit in such arguments are unexamined value premises. Pursuit of these conservative agendas can only extend exclusionary tendencies and exacerbate social conflict. "Private property rights are a form of power created by government but insulated from democratic control by their private status. Instead of dispursing power and limiting the leviathan State, private property can serve to harness the power of government to create great accumulations of wealth and power."

Judgments concerning regulation for Barton, then, should be rooted in the pursuit of universal and inalienable human rights. Human-rights-based judgments tend to equalize power and insulate the political domain from the differential effects of private market power. Human rights can make regulatory processes more effective. The paper concludes with an exploratory application of these ideas to the area of land use regulation.

In the chapter by R. Larry Reynolds, an effort is made "to bring into focus the role of property rights from an institutionalist perspective, and to offer an explanation of how these property rights are specified and how they can be altered to resolve economic problems."

In Reynolds view,

> every society must have a system that defines and enforces property rights. This system is dynamic and may be the result of planned or unplanned behavior patterns. The structure of the rule system that defines these property rights and the institutions that enforce them play a large role in determining the relationships and activities in the society. . . . [Moreover] policy choices invariably involve restructuring the system of property rights. . . . These claims to property are granted by society and are not 'natural rights'.

Reynolds considers and rejects the neoclassical view of property; it connotes individualistic holders of property having bundles of rights, that are socially sanctioned, normatively grounded in utility, and operationally validated with claims to efficiency. An institutionalist view connotes creation and use of institutions which socially (often politically) specify areas of discretion concerning the retention and use of the item owned, are normatively grounded in instrumental value theory, and are operationally validated by an instrumental assessment of the consequences invoked by their use. "Rules defining property rights ought to reflect human nature and values (which change), technology, and the institutions" in a processual context of circular causation. Those who possess rule-making authority, the political-economic loci of defacto power, determine whose property interests shall be served and to what degree. The discretion conferred by property ownership may itself be a major instrument for further enhancement of both power and property. The ultimate sanction on use of achieved power is political control exercised directly or indirectly by the community generally.

In a short chapter, Ann Mayhew offers admonitions concerning the analytical use of the idea of "property rights." Aware that in the current literature there is something of a contradiction between those who use the idea of property rights to make "a foolish and illegitimate extension of concepts of microeconomic theory to social organization and institutional change," on the one hand, and those for whom "the concept of property rights is a useful tool for exploration of social processes," on the other, Mayhew offers three cautionary observations. First, the *descriptive* "task of discovering and accounting for changes in property rights is important and can be revealing about wider social processes." J.R. Commons, for example, argued that "the courts extended the meaning of property [in the late 19th century] so as to include not simply 'the use value of physical things' but also the 'exchange values of anything,'" thereby aiding and abetting the emergence of industrial capitalism. Such descriptive analysis renders a useful and more accurate characterization of the actual economy.

Second, it may also "be revealing and powerful to use the concept of property rights in ways that the natives do not, in order to draw useful analogies." One may, for example, use "the analogy between property in land and property in jobs in order to defend a social change." Here the property rights idea is not mainly or merely descriptive, it is a vehicle of advocacy, a device with which to push for economic or social reform. So much is legitimate. "What is not legitimate is to pretend—wittingly or unwittingly—that some things are property when they are not, and that some kinds of property are the same as other kinds of property when they are different." The effect is to introduce unexamined notions of morality, to invite uncritical affirmations that "exclusive property will be managed more efficiently," and/or to indulge "the temptation to extend the analogy to motives in the manipulation of the relationships or things that are described as property." Institutionalists should be wary, then, of falling into the neoclassical trap of analytical deference to property rights thereby "enshrining social patterns in a moralistic terminology."

Admonitions concerning analyses of property and property rights of a related sort are provided in chapter 13 by Walter C. Neale. In particular, he disputes the contention that the referential content of the term "property" is everywhere the same or that a "bundle of property" rights has a universal core of meaning.

> The idea of property in land is not one idea but a great many ideas. It is not about property but about a great many relationships of people to the surface of the earth and to other people. And it is not about parcels of land, but about the ways in which people exploit the earth. . . . Evidence from Asia and Africa shows that the ideas about property current in economic literature may be fatally ethnocentric and positively wrong-headed. . . . *Property,* is certainly a possible focus of interest—*if* the word is taken as a rubric from investigations into how different peoples and groups use and dispose of things and parts of nature and other people. . . . What is not established . . . is that there is such a thing as property in general or a universal institution of property.

We may ask, however, under what conditions or circumstances can one person say what some other person may do with something—what Karl Polanyi called "the appropriational movement of goods." "To view 'complexities of property' as 'mere variations' on a clear and universal core evades the problems raised by the role of social organization and by perceptions of the possible, of right and wrong, and of power by substituting logical speculation for fact." *Property* is an English word and derives its referential content from a cultural history very different from that of other peoples and other times. A presumption of its pancultural explanatory relevance

> makes it easy to oversimplify complex situations by creating a homogeneous whole made up of substantively different but logically fungible parts. . . . It makes more sense to view the power and privileges of people as deriving from the relationships among people and groups and the roles of people and groups in societies, and not from an anterior or superior idea of property, whether that idea be one that is universally immanent or one that is out there waiting to be discovered.

Neale then illustrates the significance of these admonitions through a brief consideration of land tenures in India under British rule and of the absence of property in land among the Tiv of central Nigeria. Land revenue was the organizing idea in the Indian culture; property was not. A conception of place and use of the earth among the Tiv was derived from kinship, not from ownership. Cultural history confers meaning and significance to patterns of human relationships, including conceptions of whether there is, or what is, property.

In concluding the first section of this volume, Barry Price and Roslyn Simowitz return to our own cultural history. Their main concern is to distinguish between the Libertarians' retention of a Lockean natural rights view of property and a political theory of property. It is their belief that both the explicit and the tacit deference to the natural rights theory has facilitated recent conservative deregulation efforts beginning with the Carter Administration. Price and Simonwitz argue that the Libertarians have held an "ideological edge" over defenders of government regulation.

In the real world of policy and its implementation, "when government regulates it redefines existing property rights. Property rights guarantee an individual that he or she can use an item largely independent of the will of interference of others." Regulations thus do reduce or modify property holders' discretion in some measure. Libertarians maintain that a person has a natural right to property: "He or she appropriates this property originally by carving it out of the state of nature, and subsequently alters this pattern of original acquisition through inheritance and voluntary exchange." Price and Simowitz provide a persuasive critique of this convenient piece of conjectural history and suggest its displacement with a political theory of property. The latter encompasses the following elements: "Property is inevitably a social, legal, and political institution. . . . It is the choice by society to allow individuals to use and dispose of these items. . . . Unless the community sanctions and enforces the individual's right to property, it remains nothing more than a subjective claim." "The decision about how to allocate property rights dictates who must pay whom and, therefore, who gains and who loses;" and "what constitutes a 'volunary exchange' is invariably a source of political conflict." The distinction between the two views, as it relates to debates over deregulation, can be summarized as follows: "So long as one sees property as something individuals create on their own, independent of and prior to entry into a political community, one can easily concede that limitation or restriction of property rights through government regulation is inherently suspect." However, if "one understands the state's role in creating property and investing it with much of its value, one is likely to see government redefinition of existing property rights through regulation as perfectly legitimate." This political view of property rights provides an alternative ideological perspective with which the public sector's regulatory efforts can be sustained or extended and the community's concern for "fair play" can be met.

Note

1. All quotations in these introductory comments throughout the volume can be found in the chapter by the author being discussed.

1

Contract Law, the Free Market, and State Intervention: A Jurisprudential Perspective

Robert B. Seidman

It frequently is argued that the more the state plans, the more power is placed in the hands of the planners (1, pp. 761, 766). Social engineering begets power, and Lord Acton long ago warned us that power tends to corrupt.

The classical response has been the celebration of the free market economy. Social engineering and planning are perceived as the very opposites of the free market; intervention is the opposite of nonintervention. The legal expression of social engineering is perceived as a set of commands directed by the state to various citizens. The legal expression of the free market is perceived as facilitative law, of which the law of contract is the archetype. As social engineering is the opposite of a free market, so command law is the opposite of facilitative law.

We examine here these supposed dichotomies. We argue that they are based upon an unreal set of assumptions about how contract law operates. We first examine the theoretical issues posed and then turn to a brief analysis of two sharply contrasting colonial African economies, those of Kenya and of Ghana.

Facilitative Law: Theoretical Analyses

Many sorts of law on their face are rules expressing how the lawmaker expects the targets of the law to behave, on pain of sanction.

Criminal and tort law fit this model nicely. A rule is promulgated; if a person violates the rule he is punished, either directly as in criminal law, or through the imposition of a judgment for damages.

Many other sorts of rules, however, seem to be cut from a different bolt of cloth. Contract law does not require people to do anything. It merely prescribes that if certain agreements are entered upon, and broken, the courts may be required to levy a sanction. General corporation laws do not require anyone to enter upon a corporation. They provide a facilitative form. If parties wish to enter into a corporate relationship, the law prescribes some of the consequences. Because role occupants are not required to enter upon particular contracts, or to enter into particular organizations, the facilitative form seems to free the role occupant of coercion and to release him from the shadow of overarching power.

Is it true that facilitative law frees the role occupant from coercion? We shall denote the two contrary answers to this question as the classical and the anticlassical views.

The Classical Perspective

The classical paradigm asserts that facilitative law does free the citizen from state coercion. Long ago Sir Henry Maine said that the movement of all progressive societies heretofore has been from status to contract. By this Sir Henry meant that "the Individual is substituted for the Family, as the unit of which civil laws take account. . . . Starting, as from one terminus of history, from a condition of society in which all the relations of Persons are summed up in the relations of Family, we seem to have steadily moved towards a phase of social order in which all these relations arise from the free agreement of individuals" (2, pp. 168–70).

Jurisprudential theories were developed which gave ideological support for the theme of contract. Thomas Hobbes said that the definition of injustice "is no other than the nonperformance of Covenant." Nietzsche, perhaps sarcastically, was even more extravagant: "To breed an animal that is able to make promises—is that not precisely the . . . task which Nature set for herself as regards man" (3, p. 12)?

Contract is a device for social cooperation. In a highly complex society, people must do many different things. Manufacturers must buy from suppliers, employ labor, sell to customers; landlords must rent to tenants; submanufacturers must contract with manufacturers; wholesalers and retailers and customers must interact with each other to keep the vast engine of the economy moving.

Without planned organization of the interchanges necessitated by the division of labor, it seems preferable for every man to seize his own opportunity. Through contract, the parties to an exchange define the norms of conduct for the occasion. The market becomes a giant communication system, by its "Invisible Hand" advising individuals the sort of norms to demand and accept in order to maximize their personal benefit.

From the point of view of the parties to the contract, they merely exercise a personal freedom to conduct their affairs in accordance with their emergent needs and desires. They exercise freedom by themselves determining the norms to which they will be bound.

The notion that contract law embodies "freedom" is closely intertwined with the ideal type of the market economy. If perfect competition prevails, then, by definition, no individual has the power to affect market price. The availability of other potential bargaining partners, who offer their services or goods on terms and conditions defined not by themselves, but by the Invisible Hand of the market, protect the parties each from arbitrary power in the other.

What ideal type of legal order is apt for this ideal conceptualization of the economic order? (See, generally, 4.) Unless one can exclude others from interfering with his possession of things, he will not purchase them. The law of property and of torts purports to guarantee rights of peaceable possession. Unless there are guarantees that the law of marginal utility will not continue to operate *after* a bargain is struck, promises for future performance become mere pious intentions. The law of contract purports to ensure that promises, once made, will be kept.

The classical view implies a model of the state as a value neutral framework whose task it is to ensure only that in case of dispute these bodies of law are enforced. It presupposes a sharp discontinuity between the private sphere, between state action and state nonaction. The former consists of intervention and social engineering; the latter consists of adjudicating disputes arising in the private sector. In this view, the laissez-faire ideal of the state is the very opposite of social engineering. State inaction is markedly different from state action.

We can summarize the classical perspective in a series of propositions. (1) Facilitative law permits the parties to an interaction to determine their own norms of conduct. (2) The perfect competitive market ensures that neither party has power over the other. (3) The state is a neutral, impartial framework within which bargaining can take place peaceably and conflict can be resolved peaceably. (4) The state, by limiting its function to conflict resolution, does not engage in ordering the society; there is, therefore, a sharp discontinuity between state inaction and state action. (5) Facilitative law therefore ensures "voluntariness."

The Anticlassical Perspective

The anticlassical paradigm is at issue with the classical on all but the first of these propositions. Facilitative law does permit the parties to the transaction to determine between themselves the norms defining their interchange. Through it, the state delegates to the contracting parties a portion of its sovereign power. The two parties legislate for themselves in the act of bargaining; they lay down rules; the state proceeds to enforce them. "From this point of view the law of contract may be viewed as a subsidiary branch of public law, as a body of rules according to which the sovereign power of the state will be exercised in accordance to the rules agreed upon between the parties to a more or less voluntary transaction" (5, p. 69).

Parties to bargains are seldom of equal bargaining strength. To the extent that they are not, contract, however it may appear to the parties, is not a matter of freedom of choice, but of command. Is it significantly different to say to a man, "I will pay you a wage if you will work for me?" rather than, "You will get no wage unless you work for me"? Two hundred years ago Lord Chancellor Northington expressed it succinctly: "Necessitous men are not, truly speaking, free men."

At law, to treat unequals notionally as equals is in fact to elevate the stronger to a position of domination. In a bargaining situation, the stronger imposes upon the weaker the norms of conduct which he desires. There is no "equality" between African laborers and a giant copper mine or plantation. An African who must raise cash to pay a poll tax, or go to jail, has no freedom to decline to work for cash wages.

The power to create norms of conduct, that is, to legislate, plus the use of state power to enforce them are two of the three familiar attributes of government. The net result of contract law is to transfer to the economically superior classes in the community the most significant powers of the state, all under the fictional disguise of equality and freedom. Facilitative law and "voluntariness" begin with notions of "freedom." They end by subjecting the weaker party to the power of the stronger. Facilitative law manipulates the weaker party, as does planning law or social engineering. The principal difference lies in who does the manipulating.

Classical theory meets this claim by reliance upon the Invisible

Hand of the market to determine "objectively" the terms and conditions of any particular interchange. The anticlassical model argues not only that the perfectly free market never, in fact, appears in the real world, but also that it is theoretically impossible for it to exist. The model of perfect competition assumes that all preferences can and must be expressed through the market. "Before the principle of marginal utility nothing is sacred" (6, p. 28). If there are effects of economic activity which are not taken into account in setting prices, that is, externalities, to that extent the market mechanism does not function (7, p. 17).

All laws and customs are externalities in this sense. They impose constraints on bargaining, constraints that do *not* fall before the principle of marginal utility, for they are supported by police, judges, bailiffs, sheriffs, jailers, and, ultimately, the army. Willard Hurst has made the consequences of this proposition central to his jurisprudence.

> Law influences the decisions made by "private orders." . . .
> Every entrepreneur, in deciding how to invest his time, energy
> and money, calculates the profits expected from the course open
> to him. Every calculation includes an assessment of the law's
> impact on profits: subsidies make some investments more attrac-
> tive while laws that force the entrepreneur to absorb the "external"
> costs of an activity make that activity less attractive. To each
> entrepreneur, then, the law appears as a factor which affects
> his decisions but over which he has no control (41, pp. 116–17).

Warren Samuels (9), following Robert Lee Hale, makes a useful distinction between *volitional freedom* (the opportunity or capacity to choose between alternatives) and *voluntary freedom* (the opportunity or capacity to determine the alternatives themselves) (10). Since law structures the range of alternatives open to participants in any given market, the participants have only "volitional freedom." The state alone has "voluntary freedom."

Society conveniently can be defined in terms of its normative (or institutional) system. That is what distinguishes it from a hive of bees (17). Norms can be expressed only in terms of law or of custom. To state that all law and custom are externalities is to say that all society is external to the ideal type construct of the free market. At precisely the point at which the ideal type conceivably could exist, society disappears. To state that the market cannot exist without law, but that all law is an externality, is to state a paradox.

To the extent that the free market does not exist, its Invisible Hand does not limit the power of one party to an exchange over another. Since law and custom to a very great degree define the extent to which the ideal type free market does not exist, the power of one party over another must itself be a function of law and custom. Since law and custom are the indispensable components of organized society, this is to say no more than that the "free market" exists *in society*, and society itself determines the relative power of the participants.

The anticlassical understanding of facilitative law, therefore, focuses upon the framework of institutions within which bargains are struck and upon the power relationships of the parties. A bargain implies "freedom" only in that, *given the available alternatives*, both parties prefer the bargain struck. It is the framework which structures the alternatives available to each party which determines the extent of their volitional freedom.

It is further argued that the model of the value neutral state providing an impartial framework within which conflict can be resolved peaceably is not only empirically but also theoretically impossible. A decision-making structure—and the state is, par excellence, a decision-making structure—cannot be value neutral. The rules that define any decision-making process necessarily limit the range of potential inputs, conversion processes, and feedback functions. These rules, to that degree, predetermine the outputs, that is, the decisions. The state, perceived as a framework for the resolution of conflict, is a decision-making structure. No more than can any other decision-making structure can it be value neutral.

If the decision-making structure cannot be value neutral, its output cannot be value neutral. The laws of property and contract which are required by the ideal type model of the market economy therefore cannot be value neutral, for they are products of a decision-making structure.

The law of property, for example, contains a huge number of separate normative propositions: No other person may appropriate my desk unless certain conditions are met; I may dispose of it as I will; I may rent it, and so forth. The conventional definition of the word *property* is that it is a bundle of rights, duties, powers, and liabilities with respect to something. In most societies, *the content of that bundle buttresses the shape of the economy.* In an interdependent society, property is necessary to the livelihood of many more people than its owner. Ownership gives the proprietor the power to command others, through the exercise of contract (12). The precise scope of this power is determined by the details of property, tort, and contract law.

This normative character of property law is exemplified in the laws of land tenure. They define much more than who has the right to sell land or to exclude others. They limit who can obtain credit (if I do not own land, I cannot use it as security for a loan); who can hire labor (if I do not own land, I cannot hire anyone to work it); who can market crops (if I do not have an interest in land, I cannot farm and therefore have nothing to sell).

In short, the "free market" is not merely an ideal type which is approximated more or less closely by various societies. It is an impossibility. The market cannot exist without law, but law is an externality. The market cannot exist without a value neutral law and state; but the state and its principal output—law—cannot be value neutral. Behind the Invisible Hand there is a thumb on the scales. Gunnar Myrdal makes the same point: "Prices are manipulated. They are not the outcome only of the forces in the market; they are in a sense 'political prices,' depending also on the regulating activity of the state, of quasi-public and private organizations and of private businesses. The state interferences in the price system are, in a sense, the ultimate ones . . ." (13, p. 49).

The state must, willy-nilly, favor some and disadvantage others. For the state to stand by and permit the private activity of citizens to determine the configurations of the economy is as much state action as overt intervention.[1] *Cui bono?* is not simply a possible query: it is the most significant question of all.

We can summarize the anticlassical model in a set of propositions. (1) Facilitative law permits the parties to an interaction to determine their own norms of conduct. (2) Facilitative law ensures that the more powerful party to an interchange will impose his desires upon the weaker. Furthermore, the perfectly free market does not and cannot exist as a protection against the imposition of private power. (3) The state, by enforcing private agreements, lends its reserved monopoly of violence to enforce the norms agreed upon by the parties to the interchange. (4) Since every decision-making function is necessarily value laden, the state is not and cannot be a value neutral arbiter. (5) The enforcement of private bargains made under the guise of facilitative law is therefore as much a form of state intervention as more direct commands from the state to citizens. (6) Facilitative law therefore ensures that the state will delegate its power to the more powerful party to the exchange.

A Case Study: Colonial Anglophonic Africa, East and West

We are presented with alternative statements of expectations of consequences of the use of facilitative law as a surrogate for more explicit social engineering. The propositions involved are susceptible of empirical warrant. We explore, by way of example, one comparative case study: colonial Kenya and the Gold Coast (now Ghana).

Kenya was settler country. Its economy was dominated by whites, who took up land in the fertile White Highlands for commercial farming. The Gold Coast was nonsettler territory. Practically the only whites were officials. The British government paid vast sums in order to induce Englishmen to settle in Kenya. In the Gold Coast, by and large, whites were forbidden to purchase land. In Kenya, the government exercised wide compulsions to coerce Africans to work for white employers; no such compulsions were employed in the Gold Coast. In these and many other ways the government and economy of the two territories were as different as night from day. How are these differences to be explained? We examine each of these colonial territories in turn.

The Colonial Kenyan Economy

The highlands of Kenya were the locus of British colonialism in East Africa. During the long period of colonial control, political participation by Africans was effectively nil. The state systematically intervened into the economy with a series of overt steps to organize it in a way conformable to settler interests. (See, generally, 14, 15, 16, and 17.) First land, then labor, then the corporate organization of the economy were affected; the progression was toward ever-increasing direct intervention.

LAND. In 1895 the British government declared a protectorate over all the East African territory formerly administered by the British East Africa Company. Jurisdiction to legislate and administer a protectorate was granted by the Foreign Jurisdiction Act of 1843, as amended. In effect, that act gave the crown the same jurisdiction in a protectorate as if the country had been acquired by conquest.[2]

Beginning in 1902 the most beautiful and fertile lands in Kenya—some say the most beautiful in the world—were reserved systematically by the government for European settlers. After a period of indecision, by 1915 the complementary policy of herding Africans into reserves also was accomplished, under rules promulgated by the governor pursuant to power granted him by the Crown Lands Ordinance of 1915. By the early 1920s the pattern of colonial agrarian development had been firmly established: Whites lived on very large farms in the White Highlands, Africans lived in the native reserves. The result was not achieved by market forces but by state intervention resting ultimately on coercion.

LABOR. (See, generally, 18.) The great attraction of Kenya to white settlers was not only the abundant, rich, and beautiful land but also the availability of cheap black labor. Africans, however, in the earliest days were engaged in their own societies, based on subsistence agriculture or nomadic cattle herding. The problem posed was to transform them into a labor force for the white settlers. The standard colonialist myth the world over has ever been that the "natives" are not economically rational (19). As Frederick Lugard expressed it, "since . . . the wants of the African peasant are few and are not necessities, and since he can generally obtain sufficient cash to purchase them and pay his small tax . . . by the sale of a little produce, there is . . . but little incentive to earn wages, and it may often happen that as soon as the small sum he requires has been obtained he will cease to work. The higher the wages in such a case the less the work, as the Indian industrial report says is the case with the Indian coolie" (20, pp. 404–405).

In fact, the theory of the backward-sloping labor supply curve and the associated notion that Africans in the subsistence economy are not "economically rational" has been exploded over and over again (42, pp. 81, 82; 43). The remarkable transformation accomplished by Africans responding to the economic incentives of the Ghanaian economy through the development of cocoa and of Uganda and Tanzania through cotton and coffee; the complex and vigorous trading economies of West Africa; and the rapid development of African entrepreneurs in Nigeria, all these, and a host of other examples, are proof positive that the notion that the African is not economically rational is a thorough canard.

The theory of the backward-sloping labor supply curve was, nevertheless, the central ideology of the colonialists in Africa. The problem was to create a labor force without increasing wages. Slavery and forced labor, presumably, were not available. The British colonials were bound by the ideology embodied in what we have denoted as the classical viewpoint. L. S. Amery, Secretary of State for the Colonies, opening a conference in 1928 on forced and contract labor, stated: "We are all equally convinced that the only possible solution [for Africa] is a civilisation based on work, as all civilisation must be, but based on free work, based on the work of men who give their labour because they desire the fruits of their labour . . ." (21). At the same conference, E. S. B. Taggart, formerly Secretary for Native Affairs to the Government of Northern Rhodesia, stated the classical view even more explicitly:

> The first essential for the successful working of the labour contract is that its terms should be fair and reasonable and within the capacity of the parties to carry out; the second that there should subsist between the parties that *consensus ad idem*—to use the

legal phrase—that understanding and agreement to the same thing,
which is the basis of all contracts; and the third, that the agreement
should be faithfully carried out on both sides. That the agreement
should be voluntarily entered into goes without saying (21).

How to ensure a plentiful supply of labor without resorting to raising
wages and without violating the principle that the agreement should
be "voluntarily" entered into? The solution was found in the poll
or head tax, levied upon every male African. Sir Percy Girourard,
Governor of Kenya in the early twentieth century, said: "We consider
that taxation is the only possible method of compelling the native
to leave his Reserve for the purpose of seeking work. Only in this
way can the cost of living be increased for the native, and . . .
it is on this that the supply of labour and the price of labour depends.
To raise the rate of wages would not increase but would diminish
the supply of labour. A rise in the rate of wages would enable the
hut or poll tax of a family, sub-tribe or tribe to be earned by fewer
external workers" (22, p. 186). Sir Harry Johnstone spoke with feeling:
"A gentle insistence that the Native should contribute his fair share
to the revenue of the country by paying his tax is all that is necessary
on our part to ensure his taking a share in life's labour which no
human being should avoid" (23, p. 96).

Accordingly, poll tax laws were enacted, beginning in 1908. The
amount and the form were changed somewhat from time to time,
but the poll tax remained the principal device for engendering in
the African peasant that warm desire to earn wages which the settlers
so insistently wished. To each African the law appeared "as a factor
which affect[ed] his decisions but over which he ha[d] no control"
(9, p. 117).

The poll tax worked—as a labor recruitment device. Tanganyika,
also a British territory after 1920, had much the same sorts of laws.
Every District Office maintained a safari book, a diary kept by the
several district officials as they made their rounds of the villages.
The safari book for 1936 in Iringa records many such journeys. In
each case the official would trek during the morning to a new village,
stopping at any European farms on the way. The farmer would tell
him how many "boys" he needed. At the next village, the first task
would be to have the *jambe,* or village headman, arraign the tax
defaulters. The district official would order them sent to the European
farmer, or, if the African preferred, to work off his tax on road
work for the government. Viewed in gross, the tours of the villages
were hardly more than blackbirding trips. Most Africans, of course,
preferred to enter European employment voluntarily, thus exercising

some choice as to the individual employer and as to the period during which he would leave his own farm to work for European wages.

A variety of other laws tended in the same direction. The land areas in which Africans were forced to live were too small for the population imposed upon them. African soldiers in the army were fed 2,843 calories per day. On 1930 production, only 1,471 calories per day per person were available to Africans. To produce a diet of 2,873 calories per day, suggested by medical authorities (15, p. 42), would require 27.50 acres per family of five given the existing level of African food production. That would allow a density of 116 people per square mile. The population density in 1933 in Kavirondo Reserve was 145 per square mile; in the Kiambu, Fort Hall, and Nyeri Districts, Kikuyu density was 283 per square mile; in South Nyeri in 1944 it was 542 per square mile; at Buntore it was 1,200 per square mile. During this period the average density of the white population in the White Highlands was 16 per square mile. Land law structured the choices of Africans so that hunger drove them into white employment.

Despite the prevailing official ideology of "voluntary" labor, forced labor was not unknown. Compulsory labor by males for community projects was authorized for able-bodied adult males between the ages of 18 and 45. Male Africans employed by Europeans, or who had been employed for three months out of the preceding twelve, were exempted from compulsory labor. Unless so employed, they were subject to compulsory labor draft for sixty days out of the year. To avoid the effects of the Compulsory Labour Ordinance, many Africans preferred to work for Europeans, thus choosing their own time and place. During both world wars, direct compulsory labor for private employers was introduced and enforced (24).[3]

In order to ensure that employees continued to work for their employers, ordinary contract remedies were deemed insufficient. Master-servant ordinances were introduced at an early date. Leaving employment without permission of the employer was a crime punishable by fine or, in default of fine, imprisonment. The ordinances went even further. The Employment of Servants Ordinance of 1937 placed state power behind every employer. It was a crime if the servant became intoxicated during working hours; if the employee neglected "to perform any work which it was his duty to have performed or if he carelessly or improperly perform[ed] any work which from its nature it was his duty under his [employment] contract to have performed carefully and properly"; if he used abusive or insulting language to his employer; or if he refused "to obey any

command of his employer or of any person lawfully placed by his
employer in authority over him, which command it was his duty
to obey" (25, Para. 58).

Pass laws were enacted to keep track of the African population
(26). Every African was required by statute to carry with him a
registration certificate in which his present and past employment for
Europeans was entered. All endorsements in the pass were in English,
so that it usually was impossible for the servant to know the content
of the employer's endorsement.

Finally, Africans were excluded from the cash crop market by
a variety of devices. These will be examined in the following section.

The consequences of these various devices was to develop a wage
labor force for white settlers at very low wages. In 1944 the average
wage was 15 shillings per month (15, p. 112). The minimal charges
for support of a single man in 1944 were estimated by Sam Aaronovitch,
based upon *Report to Examine Labour Conditions in Mombassa
(Kenya)*, at 29.05 shillings per month. At about the same time a
government scientist estimated the cost for a married man and two
children residing in a town at 56.60 shillings per month.

The wages for the few whites who were working for wages were
much higher. In mining in 1938 the average European worker received
a monthly wage of 612.90 shillings per month; the average African
worker, 11.65 shillings per month (15). Average per capita income
for whites in Kenya in 1962 was £400 per year; for Africans, including
an estimate for subsistence crops, £14.9 per year (27). These differen-
tials can be explained not in terms of marginal utility theory, but
by the coercive mechanisms of the law.

ORGANIZATION OF THE ECONOMY. The Kenya government intervened
in the economy in a wide variety of ways. Direct government
expenditure subsidized the settler economy; £13 million were spent
to build a railway to the sea, with branch lines servicing most of
the White Highlands. Freight charges on the railway, set by the
government, favored the settlers. The better the growing year, the
higher the production of agricultural crops, and the greater the deficit
of the railways.

Other governmental infrastructural expenditures aided the settlers:
Roads, easy credit, and direct price support in some cases were all
made under the authority of statutes and subsidiary regulations. The
government established marketing boards in most cash crops which
guaranteed a minimum price to settlers that was usually above the
market price. Between 1931 and 1946 almost four times as much

was spent on these services for 2,000 white settler families as for several million African farmers.

Beginning with the Great Depression, government intervention was even more direct. Every branch of industry in which settlers were active was organized through an industry board, each supported by its own statute. The production of tea, coffee, sisal, pyrethrum, pigs, maize, cotton, and a variety of others was so organized. In most of these, effective control over the industry was given to the industry board. The Tea Ordinance of 1960 is a recent example of such statutes as amended in the period just prior to independence. The board was granted power *inter alia* to license tea growers and tea factories, to regulate, control, and improve the cultivation and processing of tea, and to control the export of tea (Para. 4(2)). It was made an offence for any person to grow tea other than in accordance with the terms of his licence (Para. 8(1)). The board was empowered "to issue a planting licence subject to such terms and conditions as it may think fit, or . . . [it] may refuse to issue a planting licence on any ground which may appear to the Board to be sufficient" (Para. 8). It was an offence to manufacture tea without permission of the board (Para. 13). The minister of agriculture might, with the approval of the board, make regulations governing every aspect of tea culture, even "empowering the Board or the Director to give directions to any planter as to the method of sowing, planting and cultivation of tea and the harvesting, collection, movement, processing and storage of tea leaf . . ." (Para. 25(2)).

The membership of the various industry boards were in the main elected by the white settler producers. The seven members of the Tea Board were, until the 1960 amendment, for example, appointed by the Kenya Tea Growers' Association, an organization of the white tea producers (28). As of 1960, the European growers elected or otherwise appointed all the members of the industry boards in coffee, tea, sisal, cereal, maize marketing, pigs, the Uplands Bacon Factory, and horticultural products. There was minority African representation, all appointed by the government, on the others.

These boards, as might be expected, manipulated the economy to suit the interests of their white constituencies. Africans effectively were barred from the major cash crop markets until the period just prior to independence.

SUMMARY. The government in Kenya was highly activist and interventionist. It created an East African version of the corporate state, differing in form but not in content from the organization of the economies of Fascist Italy and Nazi Germany. The African was manipulated by the state through law in the interests of the economically superior class.

The Gold Coast and the "Free Market"

The situation in the nonsettler territories of West Africa and of Uganda superficially was completely different. There, for reasons that need not detain us, indigenous African production of cash crops for export flourished: cocoa in the Gold Coast; oil palm, cocoa, and groundnuts in Nigeria; cotton in Uganda. There were few economic pressures to allocate land to settler agriculture or to generate a labor force for settlers (except for some relatively small mining enterprises). How did the government respond to this situation? We trace, first, the history of the cocoa industry in the Gold Coast, and, second, government response to the emergent problems of the industry.

THE COCOA INDUSTRY. (See, generally, 29, 30, 31, 32, 33, and 34.) Cocoa seedlings first were imported into the Gold Coast by the Basel missionaries in 1857, although legend dates the origins of the industry to an African laborer who smuggled some seeds out of Fernando Po in 1879. The industry grew at an amazing rate, entirely on the initiative of African growers, with very little overt government help (29). This growth is indicated below.

Years	Five-year average, tons
1891–1895	5
1896–1900	230
1901–1905	3,472
1906–1910	14,784
1911–1915	51,819
1916–1920	106,072
1921–1925	186,329
1926–1930	218,895

Marketing, however, was controlled by a handful of European factors. Almost the entire crop was purchased during the period after 1920 by only thirteen firms, of which four dominated the field: United Africa Company, a subsidiary of Unilever, one of England's greatest corporations; G. B. Ollivant, Ltd.; CFAO, a Swiss firm; and Cadbury and Frye, the great chocolate house. These giants either absorbed or drove out of the business their smaller competitors.

These firms also served as importers of manufactures for the Gold Coast. Their activities touched every aspect of life in the cocoa belt:

They financed crops, purchased and shipped the cocoa, and imported and sold manufactured goods to the farmers. A parliamentary Under-Secretary of State for Colonies wrote: "British West Africa, in contrast to East, is a country where large firms or combinations of firms have become established. As a result, there is a danger that in some places active competition which is the life blood of progressive commercial enterprise may be restricted. Rings and monopolies in regard to the purchase of native produce always tend to restrict development . . ." (quoted in 31).

These firms from time to time entered upon agreements concerning the price to be paid to the farmers and a division of the market (Nowell Commission report, 1938, quoted in 32, p. 652). The most important of these was made in 1937. This agreement divided the total purchases of cocoa by all members, allocated it in proportion to each firm's historical share of the market, and set a "limit" price for all members. The agreement thus removed the incentive to competition between the member firms.

The producers found themselves at the mercy of the factors. Cocoa can be stored only in costly, atmospherically controlled warehouses, none of which existed on the Gold Coast. There were few buyers, and, during the various periods when a price-fixing agreement was in effect, producers were faced, in effect, by a single buyer. The farmers had two choices: Sell to the factors or let their cocoa rot.

The farmers responded at various times by attempts at boycott, banding together to refuse to sell to the buyers except at a stipulated price. There was a serious strike in 1930, when the price offered to the farmers fell precipitously to about 10 shillings a headload (about 60 pounds), and the farmers demanded 25 shillings. In 1937 the buyers' agreement again precipitated a nation-wide strike by the producers. The advent of World War II radically changed the situation. We next discuss the governmental response to this history of economic development.

GOVERNMENT RESPONSE. The explicit, visible government response to all this economic activity was seemingly very little. Despite the serious difficulties engendered by the problem of land title, there was no legislation to solve the manifold problems. There were no programs for agricultural credit. Instead, the government simply permitted the large factors and local moneylenders to keep the peasant in their debt. There were only minuscule efforts at research or at agricultural extension. Serious cocoa tree diseases appeared, but nothing was done. In 1936 a colonial office expert reported that "the Gold Coast with the largest cocoa industry in the world is still contented with the present and is taking no steps to safeguard the future" (quoted in 29, p. 129). Two years later the first cocoa research station was created. Almost the only affirmative governmental activity was the construction of a railroad from Kumasi, in the center of the main cocoa producing area, to an artificial port constructed in Takoradi. The government did not build feeder roads, however, to help farmers bring their cocoa to a collecting point.

Beyond these slight efforts, the state in the Gold Coast until the outbreak of World War II followed the model of the noninterventionist state. In 1930, when the cocoa farmers held up deliveries to the companies, Governor Slater refused to interfere. "In the controversy as to what is, and what is not, a fair price for the cocoa farmer at this time, Government can take no position. . . . One thing is certain: Government cannot fix prices and compel buyers to pay those prices. However Government may deplore the present low prices, it is not practical politics to improve them by legislative or other means" (speech to the Legislative Council, 4 December 1930, quoted in 32, p. 626).

The government took the same position at the time of the 1937 cocoa agreement and the subsequent hold-up by the farmers. Governor Sir Arnold Hodson again declined to do anything, although he rather unhelpfully urged that the producers give the plan a one-year trial. The producers did not take up the offer. A parliamentary commission was appointed (the Nowell Commission) and negotiated a peace which lasted until World War II.

The government overtly did very little to help the producers in other ways. The majority of growers were hopelessly in debt to moneylenders, mainly brokers for the purchasing firms. The land tenure system was controlled by customary law and was functional to shifting agriculture, not to cash cropping from trees with a fifty-year productive life. Endless disputes over land titles ensued, and the utility of land for credit and its marketability were severely impaired. Over the years these rules gradually changed through the long, arduous process of common law adjudication (35). Little research and agricultural extension work was conducted, and technology remained on a low, very labor-intensive level.

Although the government seemingly did not intervene, its strong hand nevertheless shaped the Gold Coast economy. The common law, the doctrines of equity, and the so-called statutes of general application were received in the Gold Coast in 1874. Together they comprised the "general" law of the country. Africans retained certain rights arising under customary law, most important, land rights, but their relationships with non-Africans were controlled by English law. Supporting that law were the familiar coercive institutions of modern government: prisons (36), army, and police.

The law defined the property rights of the various economic actors and their consequent power. As a result of those rights, farmers had certain powers to grow cocoa on their land and to sell it. The factors were protected in their property rights to critical storage yards, transport facilities, docks, warehouses, and shipping. It was these rights of ownership, protected by property and criminal law and enforced ultimately by courts, police, army, and prisons, which clothed the factors with the power to structure the very limited freedom of the cocoa producers: Sell to us, or do not sell at all.

These laws and a host of others were necessarily perceived by the economic actors in the Gold Coast as relatively fixed constraints on their decisions. No doubt they were "free" to bargain within these limitations, but the constraints, in fact, determined the relative power of the participants and preformed the range of decisions. The principle of marginal utility operated *within* the framework imposed by the law.

CONSEQUENCES. The principal consequences of the way in which the market was constrained in West Africa can be defined in terms of power and price. Prior to the creation of the Cocoa Control Board during World War II, decision-making power about the cocoa industry was largely lodged with the great English firms. It was more or less equalized only momentarily when farmers organized their vast, disparate masses into unified action in 1937. The average per capita income in the Gold Coast, for all its "free market" form, was not significantly different from that of Kenya. In 1936-1937 the average per capita income for cocoa farmers was about £5/16 sh. *per year* (32, p. 653)—much less than a shilling per day. The profits of the cocoa industry, like the profits of Kenya industry, went not to the Africans who worked, but to the expatriate firms which bought and sold.[5]

Conclusion and Implications

The simplest and most general model of mankind "is one of an aggregate of people exercising *choice* while influenced by certain constraints and incentives. . . . Our central problem becomes what are the constraints and incentives that canalize choices" (37; see also 38). In East Africa the state directed various government officials and boards to act in ways which structured the choices open to Africans in a manner beneficial to the settler classes. In West Africa the same result was reached, but indirectly. There, officials were instructed to act in specified ways with respect to property ownership and contracts between private parties. The owners of property—for our purposes, the great factoring firms—then exercised the power delegated to them through property and contract law to structure economic choice.

The difference between the two techniques of structuring choice was no more than the difference between the two core myths of what Francis X. Sutton calls the American business creed:

> The classical strand centers upon the model of a decentralized, private, competitive capitalism in which the forces of supply and demand, operating through the price mechanism, regulate the economy in detail and in aggregate. The managerial strand differs chiefly in the emphasis it places on the role of professional managers in the large business firms who continuously direct economic forces for the common good (39, pp. 33-34).

Kenya operated in accordance with the managerial strand. The Gold Coast operated in accordance with the classical strand. In both cases, the law delegated power to the entrepreneurial class, which then exercised its power by structuring the choice of Africans. The imperial government was not schizophrenic; it merely used different legal means to lodge control with English entrepreneurs. Facilitative law as a solution to the question of authoritarianism, said to be inherent in social intervention, is a case of out of the frying pan, into the fire.

These propositions carry with them a variety of implications. We will discuss two: the question of state action and nonaction, and the broader question of conflict or consensus models of society.

State Action and Nonaction

It is obvious that the existence of positive law on a given subject raises legal questions. Does the *absence* of positive law on that subject, as appears to be the Gold Coast case, also raise a legal question?

The problem has arisen directly in the United States by the line of cases growing out of racially restrictive covenants. In *Shelley* v. *Kraemer* (40) a racially restrictive covenant prohibiting any "non-Caucasian" occupancy was denied enforcement by a court on the ground that to do so would require state action depriving the Shelleys, who were blacks, the contract purchasers of a parcel of land purportedly covered by the covenant, of the equal protection of the laws.

Carl Auerbach and others have asked: "Shall we say, then, that when the state chooses not to exercise its power to prohibit racial discrimination, it is sanctioning such discrimination and such inaction constitutes state action subject to constitutional commands'' (41, pp. 349-50)?

Questions of the same order can be asked about the problems of law in Africa. As the Kenya case shows, colonial governments had the power to intervene affirmatively in the economy on a massive scale. When the West African colonial governments chose not to intervene in the economy at a time when English merchants were exercising economic control of the market shall we say that these governments were exercising state power on behalf of the merchants?

If the answer is affirmative, the consequences for one's understanding of the interactions between the legal system and the social order seem far reaching. But for the particular application or nonapplication of state power at hand, the societal situation might be otherwise. The shape of institutions, whether formed overtly by legal rules or covertly by custom in the face of which the state has some power to effectuate change, is determined by the state. Society is not a mindless, accidental concatenation of roles and statuses. It is the existence of state power which makes possible rational, directed social change. Given that potential, the state must be charged with responsibility for whatever institutions exist if there are resources in the state sufficient to change them.

The perception that state nonaction and action are equally forms of state action requires the conclusion that there is no such thing as an economy without state intervention. The form of intervention may be relatively obvious, as in the Kenya case, or relatively concealed, as in the West African case. Both economies were shaped by state intervention through law.

So radical a perception is a necessary preliminary to any meaningful science of directed social change through law, that is, of a discipline of law and development. Unless one perceives a potential for change, it is fatuous to talk of inducing change. If there is a potential for change, then the state is responsible for permitting the existing situation to continue. Conversely, the fact that the state is responsible for maintaining the status quo demonstrates the potential for change through the use of state power, that is, through law as it was defined earlier.

Conflict or Consensus

Rather tentatively we propose one other consequential proposition which seems to flow from the analysis. We have asserted that however desirable it may be that the state constitute a value neutral framework within which struggle can take place, it is not only practically difficult but also theoretically impossible for it to fill that role. The pluralist conception, which rests upon the ideal of a value neutral state, is equally implausible.

If the state cannot be value neutral, then it is impossible to argue that it rests upon value consensus. The modern school supports the notion of value consensus upon the theory that the state exists to adjust conflict. Both classical and anticlassical perspectives agree that conflict is pervasive in society. The value consensus claimed by the structural-functional school is limited to the neutral, peacekeeping, society-preserving function of the state as arbiter of conflict. Once the impossibility of that function is demonstrated, then the minimum basis of societal consensus likewise is destroyed.

To say that there is no value consensus, of course, is not to deny that at particular stages in history there may not be particular sets of values, or paradigms of society, which are very widely shared. *Consensus,* as opposed to the values or interests of a shifting majority, however, can exist only upon the terms of survival. Survival of the polity, in the pluralist view, requires a value neutral state as the framework of struggle. That ideal is conceptually impossible.

That the state has a monopoly of legitimate violence in the polity is an axiomatic proposition. If its use of violence is not limited to a supposedly value free function which rests upon a value consensus as to its appropriate role, then, as Ralph Dahrendorf says of the conflict model, "every society rests on constraints of some of its members by others." In short, *it is the very existence of law and its enforcement institutions* which best demonstrates that the conflict model, rather than the value consensus model, best explains society.

Notes

1. The alternative to the value neutral state is not, as is sometimes argued, a conceptualization of the state as an evil cabal of a few powerful men. There is no evidence, for example, that the Colonial Office legal advisors who wrote the initial reception statute which imposed English law on Africa had anything in mind except to do what was "fair" and to devise a set of laws for Africa that would guide courts sufficiently in adjudication. The chief consideration was apparently the lack of manpower to write a new set of codes for the newly acquired African territories (44).
2. Full jurisdiction was asserted by the East African Order in Council, 1902 (S.R.O. 661, secs. 12(1) and 15(10)), by treaties of questionable validity (See, for example, the Masai Case, *Ole Njogo* v. *C.-G.- of the East African Protectorate,* 5 E.A.L.R. 70 [1914].), and by statute and rule (See, for example, the East African [Lands] Order in Council, 1901, S.R.O. 661.). By the Crown Lands Ordinance, 1902, the government

asserted power to sell land outright or, on 99 year leases (later extended to 999 years), to Europeans. As reinforced by the Crown Lands Ordinance, 1915, even land held by Africans in customary tenure had radical title in the crown.

3. The regulations even imposed hardships on Europeans. Male personal servants were limited, from three in the household of a single adult to five for two adults and two children. There was no limit on female servants. Defense (Limitation of Labour) Regulations, 1944 (Orders Applicable to Nairobi Municipality).

4. Regulations forbidding Africans to grow coffee ultimately were declared discriminatory and void under the Royal Instructions. *Koinage Mbui* v. *Rex*, 24(2) K.L.R. 130 (1950).

5. A gaggle of economists, following R. H. Coase's seminal article in 1960 (45), have argued that the allocation of resources is not affected by rules of law imposing or not imposing liability for damages by one producer upon another. They concede that they do, however, affect the return of the different producers. When the product is labor, they must affect the choice of technology, for the cheaper and more abundant the labor, the less incentive toward capital-intensive technologies.

References

[1] Stone, Julius. *Social Dimensions of Law and Justice* (Stanford: Stanford University Press, 1966).

[2] Maine, Sir Henry. *Ancient Law: Its Connection with the Early History of Society and Its Relation to Modern Ideas* (London: T. Murray, 1901).

[3] Nietzsche, Friedrich. *The Genealogy of Morals* (New York: Viking, 1967).

[4] Trubek, D. M. "Max Weber on Law and the Rise of Capitalism," *Wisconsin Law Review*, no. 3 (1972): 720.

[5] Cohen, M. R. *Law and the Social Order* (New York: Harcourt, Brace, 1933).

[6] Fuller, Lon. *The Morality of Law* (New Haven: Yale University Press, 1964).

[7] Trubek, D. M. "Toward a Social Theory of Law: An Essay on The Study of Law and Development," *Yale Law Review* 82, no. 1: 1.

[8] Tushnet, M. "Lumber and the Legal Process," *Wisconsin Law Review*, no. 1 (1972): 114.

[9] Hale, R. L. *Freedom Through Law* (New York: Columbia University Press, 1952); see W. J. Samuels, "The Economy as a System of Power and Its Legal Bases: The Legal Economics of Robert Lee Hale," unpubl. manuscript.

[10] Samuels, W. J. "Interrelations between Legal and Economic Processes," *Journal of Law and Economics* 14 (1971): 435.

[11] Blake, Judith, and Davis, Kingsley. "Norms, Values and Sanctions." In *Handbook of Modern Sociology*, Robert Paris, ed. (Chicago: Rand, McNally, 1964), p. 456.

[12] Renner, Karl. *Institutions of Private Law and Their Social Functions*, English translation, with Introduction by Otto Kahn-Freund (London: Routledge and Keegan Paul, 1949).

[13] Myrdal, Gunnar. *Economic Theory and Under-developed Regions* (London: Metliner, 1967).

[14] Ghai, Y. P., and McAuslan, J. P. W. B. *Public Law and Political Change in Kenya* (Nairobi: Oxford University Press, 1970).

[15] Aaronovitch, Sam, and Aaronovitch, Mary. *Crisis in Kenya* (London: Laurence and Wishart, 1947).

[16] Hailey, Lord. *African Survey: Revised, 1956* (London: Oxford University Press, 1957).

[17] Huxley, Elspeth, and Perham, Margery. *Race and Politics in Kenya* (London: Faber and Faber, 1944).

[18] Berg, Elliot. "The Development of a Labor Force in Sub-Saharan Africa," *Economic Development and Cultural Change* 18 (1965): 394.

[19] Boeke, J. H. *Economics and Economic Policy of Dual Societies* (New York: Institute of Pacific Relations, 1953).

[20] Lugard, Frederick. *The Dual Mandate in British Tropical Africa* (London: Frank Cass, 1st ed., 1922).

[21] The Conference on Forced and Contract Labour. *Journal of the African Society* 28 (1928-29):281.

[22] Leys, Norman. *Kenya* (London: Leonard and Virginia Woolf, 1924).

[23] Johnstone, Sir Harry. *Trade and General Conditions Report, Nyasaland 1895-96* (London: H. M. Stationers, 1897).

[24] The Defence Regulations, 1944 (Kenya).

[25] Employment of Servants Ordinance, 1937 (Kenya).

[26] The Native Registration Ordinance, 1919 (Kenya).

[27] Ghai, Dharam. "Some Aspects of Income Distribution in East Africa" (Makerere University, cyclosyle, 1962).

[28] *Report of the Committee on the Organization of Agriculture* (Colony and Protectorate of Kenya) (Nairobi: Government Printer, 1960).

[29] Bourret, F. M. *The Gold Coast: A Survey of the Gold Coast and British Togoland, 1919-1946* (Stanford: Stanford University Press, 1949).

[30] Bourret, F. M. *Ghana, The Road to Independence, 1919-1957* (London: Oxford University Press, 1963).

[31] Padmore, George. *The Gold Coast Revolution; The Struggle of an African People from Slavery to Freedom* (London: Dennis Dobson, 1953).

[32] Metcalfe, George. *Great Britain and Ghana: Documents of Ghana History 1807-1957* (Legon: The University of Ghana, 1964).

[33] Hill, Polly. *The Migrant Cocoa Farmers of Southern Ghana* (Cambridge: The University Press, 1963).

[34] Szereszewski, Richard. *Structural Changes in the Economy of Ghana, 1891-1911* (London: Weidenfeld and Nicolson, 1965).

[35] Asante, S. K. B. "Interests in Land in the Customary Law of Ghana: A New Appraisal," *Yale Law Journal* 74, no. 6 (1964): 848.

[36] Seidman, R. B. "The Ghana Prison System: An Historical Perspective." In *African Penal Systems*, Alan Milner, ed. (London: Routledge & Kegan Paul, 1969), p. 429.

[37] Barth, Fredrik. "Models of Social Organization." Royal Anthropological Institute Occasional Paper No. 23 (Glasgow: The University Press, 1966).

[38] Nadel, F. S. "Social Control and Self-Regulation," *Social Forces* 31, no. 2 (1953): 265.

[39] Sutton, F. X. et al. *The American Business Creed* (Cambridge, Mass.: Harvard University Press, 1956).

[40] *Shelley* v. *Kraemer,* 334 U.S. 1 (1948).

[41] Auerbach, Carl; Garrison, Lloyd; Hurst, Willard; and Mermin, Samuel. *The Legal Process: An Introduction to Decision-Making by Judicial, Legislative, Executive and Administrative Agencies* (San Francisco: Chandler Publishing Co., 1961).

[42] Hunter, Guy. *The New Societies of Tropical Africa* (London: Oxford University Press, 1962).

[43] Jones, W. O. "Economic Man in Africa," *Food Research Institute Studies* 1 (May 1960).

[44] Seidman, R. B. "A Note on the Gold Coast Reception Statute," *Journal of African Law* 13, no. 1: 67.

[45] Coase, R. H. "The Problem of Social Cost," *Journal of Law and Economics* 3, no. 1: 1.

2

Bargain and Contract Theory in Law and Economics

S. Todd Lowry

There has been expanded interest in recent years in the formal analysis of legal problems in economic terms. This work has been greatly influenced by R. H. Coase and the *Journal of Law and Economics,* published at the University of Chicago, which has provided a forum for investigations radiating out from Coase's classic article, "The Problem of Social Cost."[1]

It is the purpose of this study to examine the definitions and premises underlying the concept of bargain, upon which theories of transaction costs such as Coase's are predicated. It also will be necessary to examine the concept of contract, the economic implications of which deserve more specific attention. It is hoped that this approach will frame the diverse literature in the field in a clearer perspective.

Since so much of the current discussion has been provoked by the formulation that has come to be called the "Coase theorem," it will be desirable to use this specific formulation of the issues as a point of departure even though some of Coase's premises have not been conspicuous in subsequent literature purporting to be in the same tradition. In general terms, the Coase theorem states that individual bargaining will result in similar allocations of resources regardless of the presence or absence of legally enforced rights or liabilities if there are no transaction costs. Coase's classic illustration for this analysis is the confrontation between a farmer and a cattle rancher where the increase in the rancher's herd results in a higher income to the rancher but increased damage to the farmer's crop caused by straying cattle. The theorem holds that, in the absence of liability, optimum social efficiency will not be altered when a more remunerative economic activity is being damaged by a less remunerative activity because a rational decision maker will pay or bribe the operator of the less remunerative activity to have the activity discontinued. This illustration, as well as that of the railroad spark problem, has been used by Coase, and others,[2] to develop the thesis that, given rational individual behavior, the prime social concern in such situations *from the point of view of economics as the analysis of social cost and efficiency,* is whether or not there are transaction costs which must be countered by legal intervention to replicate a competitive market situation. In other words, it is socially desirable to favor whichever arrangement involves the lower transaction costs. A situation which involves tort liability with consequent legally assertable rights resulting in less than optimal allocation of resources, according to the Coasians, results in higher transaction costs since rights which are successfully asserted against another party can then be sold back as a property right. This arrangement is deemed to be socially inefficient compared to private bargaining.

Without becoming involved in the technical validity of this formulation,[3] it should be pointed out that the overriding result of the Coase theorem is to provide a base line or fundamental premise to the effect that there is a natural plateau of socially uniform, rational behavior generated by individual bargaining. Therefore, rational negotiations between competing economic interests will result in the same social costs and benefits, minus the costs of the transaction necessary to the adjustment. The prime economic objective thus becomes the elimination of unnecessary transaction costs. The legal burden, where transaction costs are unavoidable, is to replicate the ideal results of the rational bargain and to use this measure of social efficiency as the basis for conflict resolution and regulation. It seems pointless from the Coasian viewpoint to create legal rights simply to have them bought back, a procedure which introduces the costs of two transactions as a double hurdle in reaching economic efficiency.[4] The Coase theorem thus accepts the rational two-party bargain as the basic unit of social welfare and treats this plateau of two-party bargaining as the potential measure, or definition, of social cost. The two-party bargain is presumed to capture the same rational essence as more general social determination.[5]

It will be remembered that Adam Smith decried mercantilist policies which prohibited practices such as forestalling on the grounds that such regulations interfered with individual bargaining.[6] (Forestalling involved waylaying peasants on their way to the supervised public markets and buying their produce in an isolated bargain.) Smith's justification for permitting isolated bargains was that the greater flexibility thus made possible would result, in the long run, in a superior allocation of resources in the public interest. However, he placed little reliance on individual rationality in isolated exchange as a method of achieving economically equitable results. Instead, he looked to the workings of the natural market to ensure the furtherance of economic and social welfare and assumed that such a natural, competitive market would make unnecessary the cumbersome, governmentally structured market system through which mercantilist officials tried to keep private transactions consistent with the public interest.

Coase, unlike Smith, appears to be prepared to rely on subjective individual rationality as a means of minimizing social costs and to substitute unregulated bargaining for the legal system's use of tort liability to optimize resource allocation in unique or imperfect market situations. Gary Becker, however, retreats from reliance on the rationality of the individual bargain to a concept of the *average* of transactions as constituting an expression of optimum rationality.[7] He thus puts into question the usefulness of the assumption of rationality in individual bargaining by limiting the assumption to an aggregate market situation. It is important to make a clear distinction here between the derivation of socially or economically rational behavior from individual rationality, on the one hand, and the derivation of the rationality of individual transactions from general social or economic processes such as the market, on the other. The notion of a common optimality assumes the identity of individual values and purposes expressed in the bargain with those of society expressed in the market. Once it is conceded that the measure of optimality is derived from an organized, socially sponsored system drawing on the aggregate intelligence of the community, that is, the market or a political consensus, the individual bargain can no longer be defined as a generative unit but is seen in large part as a result of that process. This distinction also will be important in the discussion which follows of the theory of the social compact and of the bearing of contract on unique or specialized relationships.

As a first step in analyzing Coase's approach to the legal structure, it will be necessary to explore the assumptions implicit in the idea of a bargain between two rational individuals engaged in conflicting activities as being necessarily consistent with maximum social welfare where there are no transaction costs and in the absence of social prescriptions, entitlements, or rules of liability. Setting aside for the moment the question of individual rationality, let us examine the concept of bargain in Coase's system by pursuing the ramifications of his cattle and crop example. Suppose that Farmer A, who raises corn, suffers damage from Rancher B's growing herd of cattle. The Coasians argue that Farmer A, being a rational individual, will offer to pay B to curtail his herd if corn raising is sufficiently profitable. On the other hand, if cattle raising is more profitable, he will not be able to do so and will abandon corn farming where it conflicts with cattle raising and instead direct his efforts to some other more remunerative pursuit. In either case, the highest level of social production is assumed to be automatically forthcoming as a result of the bargaining process. There is no *causa* or reason for society to offer a remedy to either individual in furtherance of a social interest.

But let us examine another scenario equally plausible given the stated premises of the Coase theorem. Farmer A raises corn. Rancher B's expanding herd of cattle does x dollars damage on A's land and provides y dollars return to B. A then takes his 30-30 deer rifle, which constitutes an investment already written off to recreation, and communicates to B that he has invested 25 cents in a rifle cartridge with which he intends to shoot one of B's steers. This cost, z, where z is less than y, in the absence of liability, immediately sets up new criteria for bargaining. B stands to lose q dollars, where q is the capital value of the steer, while A stands to incur a cost of z, with z less than q. Social welfare will potentially be reduced by the cost of a dead steer spoiling in the field. Rancher B thus will be under bargaining pressure to pay A any sum up to the salvage value of the steer, minus z (25 cents), to avoid suffering an even greater loss. B will then fence his cattle on the assumption that A will not shoot them if they do not stray into A's field, or he will rationally be inclined to pay A nearly full value of any steer that does stray, minus A's cost of shooting it, plus salvage value.

But once A learns how vulnerable B's cattle are, he might threaten to shoot all of them unless B pays him the profit received from his ranching operation. If this bargain is struck, A will then recognize that, in the short run, if he wishes to liquidate this apparently captured ranching operation, all he need do is to threaten to shoot all of B's cattle unless B sells them and pays him the price for which the cattle can be sold, minus the transaction cost and potential cost of shooting them, plus some nominal recompence to B greater than zero. If B is rational, he will prefer to be left with any small amount of money in preference to the total loss of having his entire herd shot without recompence. However, B eventually may realize that shorter run pressures are even more remunerative and notify A that unless A liquidates his corn raising operation and pays the money to him, B, he will shoot A. If our premises include the absence of liability for breaches of legally defined rights, we need postulate no restraint on the exercise of rational self-interest by either party to a bargain.[8] That is to say, in the context of a relationship composed of only two parties, each of whom is guided *only* by self-interest, we may not define *any* action as antisocial behavior since a social reference has been excluded by our definition.[9] We leave A and B maneuvering in A's cornfield, each trying to shoot the other in self-defense in a modern version of Thomas Hobbes's "solitary, poor, nasty, brutish, and short" presocial compact state of nature.

The latter scenario demonstrates an unstated premise in the Coase theorem vitally important in the definition of bargain as a basis for social welfare: Only marginal or incremental transactions superimposed upon an established system of enforceable order are being considered. Moreover, the theorem takes for granted that only economically productive activities (and not willfully destructive ones) will be undertaken by a rational individual. Thus *rational* in terms of the Coase theorem actually means conformity with socially accepted and legally reenforced objectives, at least up to some unstated threshold. However, if individual rationality and the two-party bargain are to be the sole criteria for determining optimum social welfare, they would have to be deducible from a state of nature, that is, a condition prior to the existence of the social compact (the farmer and rancher stalking each other in the partially destroyed cornfield). This is nothing more than Hobbes's state of man as "a condition of war of everyone against everyone." We will leave aside for the present the premise of absolute rationality. It is the origin and nature of a social perspective which must be analyzed if bargain and contract are to be understood in the social context which is the *sine qua non* of their existence.

From Bargain to Contract and from Transaction to Relation

Since ancient times theorists have attempted to explain the social process in general and the economy in particular in terms of a self-generating system of atomic or individual relations based upon subjective rationality. Plato, in Book II of *The Republic*, presented two formulations of mutually advantageous bargains that have come to be known as the "social compact." The first is that society grew from two isolated individuals meeting in the forest and agreeing, out of rational, subjective self-interest, to enjoy the mutual advantages of peace by refraining from destroying each other's property since the gain to the destroyer was minor compared to the loss to the owner of the destroyed property. Based upon reciprocity, this essentially negative compact produced a great mutual advantage at a minor mutual cost.

After such a relationship has been established, the premise of subjective mutuality and rational self-interest may well serve to justify the continuation of such a relationship. But this begs the question of how, in the absence of the level of trust which would make such reasonable behavior automatic, the relation necessary to support the transaction began. Where did the level of trust or the threshold of good faith necessary for such a relation originate? In the absence of a perfect equilibrium of fear and immobilizing uncertainty, the first savage to catch another unaware and hit him on the head would most rationally serve his own self-interest and solve the whole problem without the stress of presuming on the other's good faith. This problem is not limited to ancient rationalizations of the origins of society. In our own time, when world community apparently must be re-rationalized with every generation of Department of Defense whiz kids, lack of a sense of mutual respect for world society leads directly to the rationality of the pre-emptive strike.

The second formulation of the social compact doctrine in Plato's *Republic* is based on the premise of affirmative benefit or mutual increment as a result of compact. This view suggests that the increased productivity resulting from cooperative activity and barter makes the crossing of the threshold of the social compact a nonzero sum game, where both parties stand to gain more than they lose or, more important, to gain more than they ever had before. This contrasts with the first statement of the social compact where both parties stand only to cease losing more than they gain from reciprocal, destructive activity. This recognition of a social welfare fund beyond the capacity of isolated individual efforts traditionally has been viewed as the binding force that holds a rationalistic society together.

The problem remains of the derivation of an established threshold of trust or enforcement—in short, society—for a relation cannot be logically derived from subjective individual rationality, but requires a comprehensive social rationality.[10] Once such a threshold of trust or presumption is established, there is no longer a surplus or relational benefit which can be attributed to the two-party transaction, and the bargain reverts to a zero sum game in which one party's gain is the other party's loss.[11] The general potential of relation therefore must be attributed to the relational fabric or setting which makes the bargain or transaction possible, and not to the bargain itself. Bargaining is essentially only a distributive or allocative process. The problem being explored here is the relationship of bargain or transaction to contract or relation.[12] Can bargains exist as atomized transactional units prior to the development of relation or contract, or must the requisite relations, rationalizations, and a threshold of social stability and trust provide a frame of reference before bargain or transaction can occur?

And how is the initial sense of relation developed? This brings us back to a basic anthropological questioning of the perspective of the social compact itself. The premise that two adults, presumably aggressive males, meet in the forest in a cultural vacuum to begin the formation of rational society seems to overlook the fact that human beings necessarily have a mother and father in whose care and under whose training they must subsist for a rather long period during their formative years. These simple facts of biology suggest a more plausible basis for a sense of society or community with its institutionalized sense of trust than bargaining based on natural rationality. At the very minimum, a sense of trust in human good faith is implicit in the mother-child relation. The extended family, with its institutional arrangements, is surely a better starting point for understanding social and economic relations than is the rationality of isolated individuals.

The basic relation in terms of which bargaining takes place is socially derived and involves limits and guidelines which keep it consistent with social goals. In this sense, bargaining can be viewed as taking place in a social or institutional arena rather than providing the natural base for society. Liability and entitlements are implicit in the fabric of relations which supports transactions.[13] The Coasian theorem, on the other hand, introduces an inversion of this perspective when it attempts to predicate social benefit on nominally independent, laissez-faire transactions. Its assumption of an implicit, socially desirable rationality distilled from individual bargaining provides a justification for minimizing transaction costs or liability rules for individual transactions, thus ignoring the role of transaction costs and liability rules as part of the necessary framework of the social structure in which transactions occur. The thesis of this article is that rules for transactions must be developed as values defined in terms of ongoing social relations, not as a problem of minimizing social costs where social welfare is deducible from an aggregation of individual bargains or transactions.

The Theory of Relation and Contract

Three facets of the problems being developed here may serve as organizing perspectives in terms of which the literature can be analyzed and kept in common focus. These are the concept of bargain, sale, or transaction versus contract or relation; the concept of a threshold between the presumptive or legally institutionalized aspects of social organization and the negotiative or individually arranged aspects; and the problem of individual rationality versus social rationality and the accompanying dilemmas of interpersonal utility comparisons.

As has been noted previously, the rationalistically defined bargain justified from the point of view of individual, subjective self-interest commonly regresses to a shorter and shorter calculation of advantage, with concomitantly more defensive and hostile gestures of self-interest unless the bargaining relation is crystallized in a setting of relational premises which define the boundaries of the arena of interaction for both parties. Entitlements and liability rules are the legal expressions of these institutional relations which confine the transaction. This set of relations is the social or economic threshold that is the necessary condition for the particular society or economy to function in its customary manner. Although the deduction of the basic social fabric has been attempted from the subjective mutuality of the isolated bargain under the social compact premise, the problem of deducing a relational setting as the necessary precondition for a bargain cannot be solved by postulating an initial bargain.

Several other approaches have been made to the problem of defining the foundations of this fundamental social or economic relation which has provided the stability necessary for constructive mutuality. Plato, as did later writers such as Hobbes and the nineteenth-century legal scholar John Austin, argued that stable social relations are an outgrowth of the assertion of authority or sovereignty by a king or head of state. There is in this tradition an echo of the authority implicit in the power focus of the Aryan patriarchal family. This view postulates the rationality of the sovereign imposed upon society in order to develop a framework of social benefits which secondarily may improve the lot of the individual in his role as a member of society. The guiding principle is the assertion of sovereign or administrative discretion as opposed to traditional institutions as a means of setting the threshold above which individual bargaining must operate.[14] The basic premise of the sovereign norm, whether an expression of the self-appointed ruler, philosopher-king, or legislative assembly, has produced the positivist approach to law which can be only vaguely paralleled with what Milton Friedman calls "positive economics."[15] The real parallel in both systems is the abiding faith in the consistent cogency of the rational individual.

Another view of the derivation of the relational threshold assumes an emergent institutional framework or body of custom which results from the steady crystallization of routine, habit, and ritual in a setting where large numbers of individuals follow consistent patterns of behavior or conduct unless interrupted. The emerging benefits of stable interaction tend to be reenforced by the stress brought to bear on deviant behavior in a conformist society. While this may not be a fair statement of the views of such diverse writers as John R. Commons, C. E. Ayres, Karl Polanyi, and even the game-oriented, multiple participant analyses of J. M. Buchanan, it summarizes a common thread which runs through all their theories, namely, the idea of a cumulative base line or threshold of relation which results from the crystallization of custom and working rules.

A last view is of interest because it specifically calls into question the premise of rationalism upon which most arguments are based which attempt to derive a social compact from bargaining among rational individuals. The social compact-oriented Greek Atomists, as represented by Epicurus, found it logically impossible to explain atomic interaction in terms of independent propensities by self-sufficient atomic particles and therefore developed a theory of sympathetic attraction or a cohesive force, the "swerving of the flow of particles."[16] The same dilemma was developed by Plato in the following terms. The purely subjective, self-interested individual requires only the effective *appearance* of social responsibility in order to benefit from society's protection. There is thus no necessary coincidence between individual rationality and social efficiency or between individual benefit and service to society. Adam Smith, who, like David Hume, found the social compact thesis unsatisfactory, developed a doctrine of human sympathy in *Theory of Moral Sentiments* in order to explain how rationally self-interested mankind could build a moral structure or cross the relational threshold that provides the infrastructure for individual bargaining.

The purpose here is merely to indicate that there historically has been considerable concern for the components of a relational threshold for constructive social arrangements. This threshold has been presumed to set social values or purposes and includes entitlements and liability rules. Our next step is to examine the conceptual framework in terms of which the details of social and economic interaction can be characterized as bargain, contract, or administrative decision.

By failing to recognize the relational threshold as a precondition for bargain, the distinction between bargain (transaction) and contract (relation) has been obscured in some discussions of legal and economic process. Many writers have followed a natural law approach, which assumes that the market emerges from an aggregation of individual bargains in the same way that some suppose the common law emerges from individual decisions. The common law, however, is the expression of a core of common judicial principles applied to an accretion of individual cases and not simply an averaging of unrelated, empirically derived opinions. So, too, the role of the legal system in setting up detailed rules defining property rights, enforcing transfers of title, and establishing liability suggests that the market in our society is a publicly structured, relational threshold defining the arena in which individual bargains, sales, or transactions take place. This structure serves the role of generating a consensus of economic opinion and current values (prices) which indicates the public's anticipation of others' needs and their potentiality for production. In the market relation built by the legal and customary framework, all that is needed is the simple sale. The average view, the average rationality, and the average anticipation of the future, all function to provide the social statement of aggregate intellectual judgment, and the ordinary buyer and seller can rely on the general safeguards of average price in this structured relation.[17]

The market, in other words, creates a forum for consensus economizing which requires for the exchange of goods only the legal device of the sale. The sale or individual bargain is supported by legal rules regarding the technicalities of the bargaining process, such as warranties of merchantable quality and valid title. In this setting, speculators may of course anticipate future market conditions different from the general consensus and make bargains for future delivery. Although this type of arrangement may involve the traditional form of contract, it is essentially a bargain or sale in a market context to take place at some time in the future. It is a future bargain relying on the socially structured market arena for its relational significance.

An increasingly detailed literature has directed attention in recent years to the difference between transactional arrangments and relational contract and to the difficulties created when relational contract is analyzed in transactional or exchange terms.[18] In this context, it is useful to examine the concept of contract from a specifically economic point of view. Suppose a shepherd with a flock of one hundred sheep is ready to sell them. The market is four days' drive from his pastureland. If the market is stable and effectively represents the willingness to buy and sell on the part of the buyers and sellers of sheep, the general set of economic relations between sheep raising and sheep buying exists as an established threshold which can be taken for granted. Where there is such a customarily or publicly structured relation, the shepherd would be content to drive his sheep to market and negotiate a bargain, transaction, or sale in the context of the established relational or market process. This would be a transaction within the relational structure provided by law, custom, or administrative fiat. If, however, the sheep herder believed the market price to be capricious and that he had superior quality sheep whose value would not be adequately protected by the market structure, he could go to individual buyers and discuss specialized terms for the sale and delivery of his specific sheep.

This system of building private specifications as the setting for bargain has elements of the structuring of relation which society provides through the market. This private negotiation has the potential of making special arrangements of mutual advantage to both parties and improving efficiency in terms of reduction in social costs, for example, by bypassing the trip to the market and thence to the buyer's processing facilities.[19] Moreover, the sheep may be more usefully delivered to a particular buyer in smaller lots at two-week intervals, and leeway for delivery dates may be allowed depending upon the weather. If there are mutual advantages in such arrangements, both parties will be influenced by the anticipation of future transactions of this type. With the increased complexity of the economy, the detailed structuring of individual relations would be expected to emerge as an even more desirable practice. The failure of the organized market to permit such unique arrangements is the type of problem Adam Smith was dealing with when he marshalled his natural market arguments in opposition to the unwieldy, publicly arranged market structures of the mercantilist period, which were partially designed to protect the peasantry from exploitation by foreign merchants.[20] In an economic sense, contract can be viewed as a form of individualized economic planning where voluntary initiative is permitted to organize its own relational structure supported by public recognition of the desirability of lending legal force to such arrangements. E. Allan Farnsworth summarized the legal history of contract by saying: "[Private] parties . . . were viewed as acting in a kind of legislative capacity, so that the enforcement of a contract by the state merely implemented a form of private law established by the parties."[21] This process is primarily premised upon economic voluntarism as a recognized source of public benefit.

Executory agreements to sell were not enforced in ancient Greek law, thus making all exchanges volitional up to the point of the actual transfer of goods or money by both parties.[22] That the economic significance of voluntarism was, however, appreciated in Hellenic times is evidenced by the importance accorded the concept in the following story from

Xenophon's *Cyropaedia*.[23] Cyrus the Great, while still a boy, was assigned the role of judge when quarrels broke out among his
schoolmates. A dispute was brought before him that arose out of the
following transaction. A tall boy with a short cloak spied a short boy
with a long cloak and, when the shorter boy refused the proffered rational trade, forcibly exchanged cloaks with him. Cyrus ruled that, since
both boys were better off as a result of the exchange, a case of reciprocal mutuality and higher social benefit, the forcible exchange was fair.
Similarly, under the Coase theorem, without liability and in the absence
of some defined threshold of accepted transaction costs, if the shorter
boy had no significant advantage from the longer cloak and was unwilling to pay a bribe or share such an advantage to keep his cloak, social
cost would be minimized by the exchange since the tall boy would not
have to get a longer cloak elsewhere. Cyrus's teachers, however, re-
buked him and told him that he had made an incorrect decision, since
the primary social value involved in the issue before him was whether
the exchange was voluntary. It should be noted that the Persian empire
was built upon a peasant agriculture and apparently recognized the superior productivity of voluntary efforts in contrast to the emerging
Greek and Roman reliance upon slave labor. The release of initiative
through voluntaristic exchange was also one of Adam Smith's concerns.
In modern times voluntarism is recognized as an indispensable measure
of justice and as a major element in evaluating fairness in individual
transactions. Reenforced with principles of disclosure and liability, it
has supported the private generation of arrangements which structure
future economic relations where the market does not provide the detailed specificity necessary for a complex commercial and industrial society.

The Legal Theory of Contract and the
Economic Theory of Exchange

In discussing the current literature in which attempts are made to
carry economic theory into law by superimposing bargain and exchange
analysis upon the legal formulation of commercial transactions, it will
be necessary to take cognizance of new developments in the legal theory
of contract. First, it should be reiterated that the traditional economic
analysis of exchange in a market setting properly corresponds to the legal concept of *sale* (rather than contract), since sale presumes arrangements in a market context and requires legal support primarily in enforcing transfers of title. Contract, on the other hand, evolved out of the
need of individuals for structuring unique patterns of commitment and

obligation over a period of time *in the absence of market alternatives.*

The concept of contractual commitment in the form of *obligatio* existed in Roman law, and various forms of long-term commitment were brought into the mainstream of English common law through the Law Merchant during the seventeenth and eighteenth centuries. However, the legal form for *enforcing* a promise to do something in the future in the English tradition grew out of the earlier action of assumpsit, which was essentially a tort action, a civil action available to the individual empowering him to seek redress for certain forms of malfeasance considered civil wrongs. This, in essence, meant that the state did not take the initiative in punishing this kind of misconduct in the general public interest as in the case of criminal law, but the injured individual was given the right to obtain redress in a public forum, thus punishing the culprit and alleviating the wrong simultaneously. This tradition involves the notion that a publicly desirable standard of behavior is to be enforced, but the penalty/award is assessed in light of the particular circumstances and injuries to the plaintiff. The enforcement of contract therefore provided a structure whereby individuals could design patterns of future relations upon which they could rely in the absence of readily available, dependable market alternatives. In other words, economic planning could then be developed at a complex level beyond the capacity of the individual enterprise because enforceable commitments permit the coordination of others' activities in specialized areas not supported by a general market.

Although these early planning contracts were mainly exchanges of commitments to make deliveries of goods in the future or to perform services in the future, it was tempting for the courts to deal with these agreements, designed to set relational patterns beyond the limits of individual ownership at a more detailed level than was possible in the open market, as simple sales of future commitments. Moreover, the emergence of Smithian and Ricardian economic theory seems to have contributed to a positivistic retreat from the broader and, in some respects, more advanced decisions made in some commercial law areas by Lord Mansfield in the latter half of the eighteenth century.[24] Mansfield, in an essentially pragmatic approach, tended to follow the customs of the merchants in providing legal reenforcement and support for the rapidly developing commercial economy of eighteenth-century England.

The quantitative *quid pro quo* analysis which deduced exchange commitments from sale seems to have dominated the thinking of nineteenth-century jurists in both England and the United States so that no broader legal formulation of what contract was about was able to develop. Morton Horwitz has argued that early nineteenth-century intellectual influence contributed to the formal rigidity and narrowing of the legal doctrines used in handling contract problems.[25] Grant Gilmore, in a detailed analysis of the strained emergence of a formal theory of contract in the United States under the influence of Langdell, Holmes, and Williston, contended that these legal scholars felt the need to reduce contract law to a consistent body of theory derivable from some common core of rational, internally consistent, transactional patterns occurring in the economy.[26] It would appear that this rational element being sought is the economic concept of exchange. The exchange of promises regarding future actions was treated in their writings as essentially exchanges or sales of commitments or rights. The title of Gilmore's book, *The Death of Contract,* indicates his contention that the notion of a logically coherent theory of contract deducible from some body of transactional principles is no longer a viable basis for handling modern economic problems. Piero Mini has suggested that this penchant for assuming the existence of an internally consistent, rational explanation for social phenomena in economic writings was derived from Locke and Descartes.[27] Rationalism, in general, of course, has much older roots.

The problem for the economist is to analyze the economic activities and relations comprehended by contract. Expectations and futurity are, of course, concepts with which economists have long been familiar, and they parallel the kinds of contract which some legal scholars have characterized as agreements which transfer anticipated risk.[28] In a smoothly working, competitive market context, the only reason for an individual to agree to deliver goods at a future time at a given price is because he anticipates the price will fall. The buyer of this promise, of course, anticipates that the price will rise. This partakes of both gambling and insurance, neither of which is relevant in a stable, perfectly competitive market where prices neither rise nor fall significantly, where both buyers and sellers have perfect knowledge, and where no individual can significantly affect supply or demand. Rationally anticipatable changes in price are systematically discounted by the competitive market so that only in the case of perishables is futures trading necessary. The view of contract as a transfer of anticipated risk therefore does not explain the building of economic relations characteristic of interactions in imperfectly competitive business. If economists are to make a contribution to the modern legal analysis of contract as relation, they will have to develop an analysis in terms of actual economic processes to which contract law applies.[29]

As a clarification of the traditional view of contract, the most provocative and imaginative formulation is Ian Macneil's concept of "presentiation."[30] In the flexible framework of modern jurisprudence, what is needed is a generalized picture of the economic impact of business relations so that judges may develop working principles of what social purposes are being achieved by the enforcement or nonenforcement of various types and levels of commitment dealing with future events. Macneil argues that traditional Willistonian contract theory approaches the planning of future business relations by creating rights which are bargained for in the present, thus assimilating planning into a current transaction. In other words, contracts "presentiate" the future, or bring the future into the present where it is arranged. At first glance it would appear that this formulation does nothing more than reduce contract to a special form of sale in a market context, but the future exchanges being presentiated are being formulated in terms of rights which can be legally accepted as *faits accomplis*. This approach to molding the future and structuring relations in terms of current transactions based on consent limits the ability of the law to deal properly with the dynamics of business relations by tying contract theory to the transaction or bargain.

In an institutionally stable, traditional society with limited market exchange, the future, the present, and the past are all structured by an established system of relations or institutions. This relational structure, although differing from society to society, provides the arena in which barter or sale takes place as exchange transactions. As economic life becomes more complex and the commercial phase of society dominates a larger and larger fraction of its activities, traditional stability is eroded, and social and technological change comes to be an expected phenomenon. In this context, it becomes apparent that the emerging future can be influenced or organized in better or worse ways through the exercise of human imagination and intelligence. Persons engaged in productive activities are thus not satisfied to count on future exchange on the open market when the relational context of the market is constantly changing. Those who can aggregate more control over the economic processes subject to being structured and manipulated are better able to plan their affairs, a form of planning by owning. As noted in Coase's 1937 article, the prime ownership institution for supplementary market planning in our day is the firm (corporation), which has largely replaced individually owned enterprise. The other form of economic planning in the private sector is one structured through commitments (contracts) which permit individuals and firms to create relational stability and achieve efficiency from planning in areas where there is no market or where the market is not a sufficient source of stability to foster planning of economic processes.

Where there is a perfected market, the going market price is not only an expression of the cumulative rationality and aggregated factual information available, but also a social consensus that can be self-validating.[31] Under such circumstances, the individual has little need to make private commitments regarding the future unless he doubts the stability of the market or has a penchant for gambling, of pitting his estimate of the future against those of professional forecasters. It is only when an individual or business is involved with an increasingly complex economic process with more and more unique and specialized problems that there arises a need to develop a private relational structure. It is in this context that contract can be thought of not simply as anticipating the future, but as actually organizing and planning future economic relations. What is going on is economic decision making which structures events in the scale of time similar to planning which structures relations in the scale of space and size. The market exchange system can thus become secondary or ancillary to the actual planning and organizing of the complicated and important processes that go on in a modern economy.

The Political Economy of Relational Contract

The concept of the competitive, two-party bargain as conceived by the Coase theorem falls short of providing an economic formulation to parallel the new legal analyses being developed in the modern theory of contract. Although the two-party bargain may superficially resemble the two-party contract, the burden of this article has been to show that bargain is a regressive, adversary transaction in which individualistic self-interest is paramount and that either party's gain is the other party's loss. On the other hand, the constructive process in which mutual advantage is structured through the building of relations with reciprocal content is an essentially social phenomenon and must be deduced from a primary commitment to social values in which the individual may find a threshold of stability. An increasing body of legal theory is taking cognizance of the empirical difference between contract and the adversary bargaining process (the isolated transaction or sale) in which parties take for granted the market or legally structured system of relations which they may individualistically exploit for their own advantage and to the disadvantage of opponents. Two-party contract in legal theory is being increasingly distinguished as a phenomenon where parties with long-term planning objectives are primarily concerned with structuring relational arrangements to provide a continuum of stability productive of reciprocal mutuality. There may be tactical bargaining eddies in the strategic stream of these relational arrangements, but increasingly businesses are so conscious of the triviality of these regressive bargaining issues in the context of long-term planning of relations that they frequently make their resolution secondary and are rather cavalier about detailing rights and duties on specific issues.[32]

This statement of economic relation as the essence of contract may suggest an economic version of the political theory of the social compact. In response to this suggestion, it should be pointed out that the threshold of trust and good faith which supports corporate relations is to be understood in the setting of generalized identification with the system of corporate property in our industrial economy in terms discussed by such writers as Charles Reich and John Kenneth Galbraith.

Reich dealt with elements of the influence of the relational structure on the planning process in his essay, "The New Property."[33] He argued that it was the legal protection of individual rights in property, in other words, the protection of private rights over the future, which historically has made it possible to extend the planning period of production. Reich concedes that the concentration of corporate power over property is a necessary structure for organizing and planning economic activity in a modern, complex society, but he points out that this concentration of power has meant that individuals no longer can rely on private property as the prime guarantee that the production process will serve their own interests as was the case, for example, in freehold subsistence farming. The separation of individual property rights from control over the productive process and the distribution of wealth in the modern corporate economy have resulted in the intervention of government to protect the public interest in the administration of property that was once guaranteed by a more dispersed, individualized control over production. However, even with representative government involved in controlling property through administrative procedures, similar problems of remoteness from individual rights still arise. Reich's recommendation is a new definition of the individual's primary claim on the fruits of social process within the necessary framework of organized and planned corporate and governmental processes.

Theories of entitlement and liability stated from the individualistic point of view may be expected to yield to theories of public interest which are the terms in which modern economic problems are being formulated. The concept of a free market where individual bargains take place in a structure which maximizes individual rights is more applicable in situations of semisubsistence agriculture, where individuals actually have a choice to buy and sell, or to boycott the exchange process. Where the production process is a pervasive structure controlling the economy, the argument that voters' choice and rational self-interest guarantee that the results of political and economic processes will be in the public interest has its shortcomings. It would appear that the political economy of a mixed system can best be correlated with the legal tenets of bargain and sale by considering them special instances of relation which must be structured by society through regulation when the market fails to provide a threshold for protecting individual rights. Relational contract is best seen as an expression of the specialized structuring of relations or private economic planning by participants in an economic continuum. Commitments between businesses are planning and organizing operations which should be viewed in terms of their contribution to social ends, which may include the protection of a zone of arbitrary choice and initiative. Where corporate purposes conflict with widely accepted social ends, the latter unquestionably will take precedence. In this sense, relational contract theory deals with the other end of the spectrum from antitrust law. It has a positive role of enforcing those arrangements found in the public interest, while antitrust regulations strike down and prosecute arrangements antithetical to the public interest.

The current literature takes cognizance of the constructive or planning aspects of economic interaction, on the one hand, and its competitive or zero sum aspects, on the other, in a variety of ways. It is this dichotomy which has been analyzed in terms of economic planning and relational contract versus sale, bargain, and exchange in this discussion. Whether these two aspects are viewed as superimposed layers in an ongoing process, or abutting, discontinuous processes, it is argued that the bargaining transaction is essentially divisive and zero sum, and that it must occur in a contained zone structured by a relational system. On the other hand, the relational structure necessary to an organized economy cannot be derived from an aggregation of bargains, but must be understood as a social construct developed in a setting of widely accepted social values and goals.

Notes

1. *Journal of Law and Economics* 3 (1969): 1–44.
2. Such as Richard A. Posner, *Economic Analysis of Law* (Boston and Toronto: Little, Brown and Company, 1972), pp. 16–21.
3. See H.H. Liebhafsky, " 'The Problem of Social Cost'—An Alternative Approach," *Natural Resources Journal* 13 (1973): 615–76.
4. This point of view is reminiscent of the Roman law doctrine of *causa*, which specified that the public force should not interfere with private transactions except to achieve a public purpose.

5. While Coase's position is somewhat equivocal in that he assumes that the measure of economic efficiency is a result of a total competitive equilibrium of efficiency considerations as well as an accumulation of individual bargains, he logically must derive the efficiency criteria of the market from either a comprehensive social force, individual subjective rationality, or some interaction between the two. He tends to take it for granted that the rational bargain will somehow coincide with a general market equilibrium reflecting total social efficiency. This is shown in his use of unique tort problems as illustrations. The premise that a socially efficient rationalization of tort and contract problems can be postulated in terms of open market criteria and applied as the basis for resolving conflicts, which is also followed by Posner, involves a certain amount of circularity since market relationships are apparently presumed to be expressions of pure bargain rather than some overriding social principle.

6. *The Wealth of Nations* (New York: Modern Library, 1937), pp. 500–501.

7. Gary Becker, "Irrational Behavior and Economic Theory," *Journal of Political Economy* 70 (1962): 1–13. But for opposing views see John F. Muth, "Rational Expectations and the Theory of Price Movements," *Econometrica* 29 (1961): 315–35; G. L. S. Shackle, *Epistemics and Economics* (Cambridge: the University Press, 1972), pp. 15–16, 132, 135–36; and Harold Wolozin, ed., *The Economics of Pollution* (Morristown, N.J.: General Learning Press, 1974), p. 12.

8. Coase does specify that "a system in which the rights of individuals were unlimited would be one in which there were no rights to acquire" ("The Problem of Social Cost," p. 44). He does not explain the apparent contradiction between this statement and his postulated bargain in the absence of liability, under which premise no rights would exist. His discussion of rational bargain is based on the unstated premise of a threshold of socially derived restraint. The problem seems to be, however, that he insists upon evaluating and deriving limitations on rights in terms of a pure theory of rational bargain as the building block of social efficiency expressed in the market. On the other hand, if he derives *limitations* on rights from some generally arrived at social standard, then the scope of bargaining and its results are a by-product of such a social standard, rather than vice versa.

9. If one is inclined to argue that only tortious and not criminal behavior is envisaged in the Coase theorem, it should be pointed out that the definition of torts encompasses acts which are also criminal and that both of these systems assess penalties for antisocial acts. There is an apparent presumption in the Coase theorem of a significant distinction between civil and criminal sanctions from the economic point of view. The only economic difference is that in the case of criminal sanctions, the public has the presumed burden to take the initiative in punishing what is deemed antisocial behavior. In the case of tort or other civil actions, the individual takes the initiative and must assert a claim as a prerequisite to punishment. In both cases, redress is available to the injured party since criminal prosecution does not bar a supplementary civil suit for damages. The real distinction important for the Coasian position is that criminal sanctions are generally publicly known, whereas civil ac-

tions may deal with emerging common law definitions of liability and are frequently debates over whether sanctions achieve a public purpose. In other words, novel issues in tort liability are often marginalist in nature.

10. For the classic eighteenth-century statement, see David Hume, "Of the Original Contract," in *Social Contract*, edited by Ernest Barker (New York: Oxford University Press, 1960).

11. The problem of a threshold which alters relationships was treated by J. M. Buchanan in a general way in "The Coase Theorem and the Theory of the State," *Natural Resources Journal* 13 (1973): 579–94. Ian R. Macneil ("The Many Futures of Contract," *Southern California Law Review* 47 [1974]: 778–79) recognized that allocative arrangements involve zero sum bargaining processes, whereas enterprise relations do not. The distinction between the mutuality implicit in relational arrangements and the zero sum aspect of bargaining has roots going as far back as Book V on justice in Aristotle's *Ethics*. See the author's "Aristotle's Mathematical Analysis of Exchange," *History of Political Economy* 1 (1969): 44–66.

12. The term *contract* is here being used to refer to economic relations which involve a planning function from the economic point of view and are characterized by the exchange of a promise for a promise. It should be pointed out that the legal definition of contract blurs into the definition of sale, which is characterized by instantaneous transactions involving the transfer of title. For a history of the early development of contract law, see E. Allan Farnsworth, "The Past of Promise: An Historical Introduction to Contract," *Columbia Law Review* 69 (1969): 576–607. Modern legal analysis has developed a distinction between transactional contract and relational contract. References to contract in this article should be associated with the theory of relational contract.

13. For a discussion of some of these problems in the modern context of pollution regulation, see Guido Calabresi and A. Douglas Melamed, "Property Rules, Liability Rules, and Inalienability: One View of the Cathedral," *Harvard Law Review* 85 (1972): 1089–1128.

14. This perspective can be applied to the material analyzed in Warren J. Samuels, "Interrelations Between Legal and Economic Processes," *Journal of Law and Economics* 14 (1971): 435–50.

15. See, generally, A. Coddington, "Positive Economics," *Canadian Journal of Economics* 5 (1972): 1–15; and Grant Gilmore, "Legal Realism: Its Cause and Cure," *Yale Law Journal* 70 (1961): 1037–48.

16. For a recent discussion of the influence of Atomist ideas on their contemporaries, see David J. Furley, *Two Studies in the Greek Atomists* (Princeton: Princeton University Press, 1967).

17. Coase recognized the significance of the individual's ability to rely on the market in routine situations in his 1937 article ("The Nature of the Firm," *Economica* 4 [n.s.] [1937]: 386–405) in which he developed the thesis that the firm is an administrative or organizational adjustment to specific efficiencies not available through the market. This view parallels the perspective on contract developed below and suggests an area of analysis in which the emergence of the corporation and the develop-

ment of contract law can both be viewed as supplements to the market structure.

18. For examples of this literature, in addition to that cited below, see E. Allan Farnsworth, "Legal Remedies for Breach of Contract," *Columbia Law Review* 70 (1970): 1145–1216; E. J. Mishan, "The Economics of Disamenity," *Natural Resources Journal* 14 (1974): 55–86; and Benjamin Ward, *What's Wrong With Economics?* (New York: Basic Books, Inc., 1972), pp. 199ff.

19. See Macneil, "Many Futures of Contract," pp. 718–19, for a somewhat parallel discussion of the relational role of contract. Macneil, however, lists exchange as one of the basic roots of contractual relations, characterizing it as the precondition of specialization and the division of labor. He thus assimilates some of the premises of the Coasian tradition. He ignores the overwhelming body of historical evidence from ancient societies which indicates that specialization and division of labor were developed in administrative societies at a stage when bargain and exchange were not significant elements in the allocation of goods, for example, in the centralized, aggregative and distributive Egyptian pharaohates.

20. Adam Smith's recognition that specialization is limited by the extent of the market addresses the problem of the necessity of large-scale economic relations as a prerequisite for mass produced, routinely merchandized goods. It was the need for growth of production on new terms outside the mercantilist market structure which seems to have motivated his analysis.

21. Farnsworth, "The Past of Promise," p. 599. The apparently contradictory statements by Farnsworth on page 604 regarding the intervention of the state in areas "in which the market mechanism was thought to be inadequate" can be explained by their reference to essentially transactional arrangements in the context of market failure rather than relational structures supplementing market limitations.

22. Fritz Pringsheim, *The Greek Law of Sale* (Weimar: Hermann Bohlaus Nachfolger, 1950), pp. 130, 137, 168.

23. *Cyropaedia* I.e. 16–17.

24. See, on Mansfield, S. Todd Lowry, "Lord Mansfield and the Law Merchant: Law and Economics in the Eighteenth Century," *Journal of Economic Issues* 7 (1973): 605–22.

25. Morton J. Horwitz, "The Historical Foundations of Modern Contract Law," *Harvard Law Review* 87 (1974): 917–56.

26. Grant Gilmore, *The Death of Contract* (Columbus: Ohio State University Press, 1974). Gilmore suggests that contract law is moving toward a more flexible system of rulings approximating the frame of reference in which tort decisions are made, an opposite view to the Coasian one that essentially tort problems should be decided in terms approximating traditional bargain theory.

27. Piero V. Mini, *Philosophy and Economics, The Origins and Development of Economic Theory* (Gainesville: University Presses of Florida, 1974).

28. Morris R. Cohen, *Law and the Social Order; Essays in Legal Philosophy* (Hamden, Conn.: Archon Books, 1967 [1933]).

29. See Lawrence M. Friedman and Stewart Macaulay, "Contact Law and Contract Teaching: Past, Present, and Future," *Wisconsin Law Review* 1967 (1967): 805–21.
30. Ian R. Macneil, "Restatement (Second) of Contracts and Presentiation," *Virginia Law Review* 60 (1974): 589–610.
31. The economist should take note of the fact that the measure of damages for breach of contract is generally in terms of the difference between the contractual claim and the currently available open market alternative. It therefore is irrelevant to use legal processes to enforce contractual claims where they parallel stable market conditions. Specific performance of contract is an exceptional remedy and is limited to unique situations.
32. See, for example, Stewart Macaulay, "Non-Contractual Relations in Business: A Preliminary Study," *American Sociological Review* 28 (1963): 55–67.
33. *Yale Law Journal* 73 (1964): 733–87.

3

Power, Contract, and the Economic Model

Ian R. Macneil

This article focuses on the often neglected subject of power in contract and economics.[1] *Power* is here defined as the ability to impose one's will on others irrespective of their wishes.[2] Two kinds of power may usefully be distinguished in analyzing contract and the economic model: unilateral and bilateral.

Unilateral power is the type a person can exercise to subject another to some particular effect without the other's consent. Members of any society have unilateral power arising from the existence of property and other rights (such as liberty) that confer on the holders the ability to impose sanctions on others interfering with those rights. In addition, participants in contracts can acquire unilateral power in a number of ways. Three of the most fundamental are by exercising bilateral power, thus giving rise to some kind of obligation, for example, a promise to repay money being lent; by external conferring of such power, for example, by giving an employee the power to recover damages for racially discriminatory practices; and by creating conditions of dependence, for example, the position of a car owner when his car is in pieces halfway through a repair job.

Bilateral power arises when the possibility of exchange exists by which two parties can release each other from some of the restraints imposed by their respective unilateral powers. For example, a potential employee may consider giving up some of his liberty in exchange for a potential employer's giving up some of his property rights in money. Bilateral power is thus held over different subjects (body and money) by different holders (potential employee and employer), but with an interparty nexus through potential or actual exchange. It is exercised through actual exchange.

Bilateral power is, of course, the foundation of the economic model and of classical contract law (and thinking).[3] Out of it, in pure form, come freedom of contract, maximization of efficiency (or wealth[4]), and much else. But bilateral power undergoes a transformation upon exercise, a transformation largely ignored in standard microeconomic analysis, but necessarily not ignored in contract law. As has been pointed out elsewhere, the microeconomic model collapses the future into the present; it presentiates.[5] Among the many consequences is avoidance of any need to examine this transformation which, in all *real* contracts, occurs when exchange, coupled with obligation, is projected into the future. When, for example, a seller agrees to sell 1,000 widgets and a buyer agrees to pay $10,000 within thirty days of their delivery, standard application of the microeconomic model simply assumes that the agreement will be performed. This assumption, except for time-value differentials, is identical to assuming that the agreement *is* performed when made.

In real contracts, something quite different emerges. When the agreement is made, that is, when the bilateral power is mutually exercised, each party acquires *new unilateral* power. The seller now has the power to impose on the buyer whatever sanctions, legal or nonlegal, society makes available for enforcing promises to buy goods, and the buyer has similar power respecting sanctions for enforcing promises to sell goods. All the pertinent bilateral power has disappeared into two pieces of new unilateral power.[6]

A further change occurs when the seller delivers the widgets according to the agreement. The seller's unilateral power—sanctions for failure to pay—stands by itself since the buyer's unilateral power—sanctions for failure to deliver—terminates when performance occurs. This is a typical contract pattern. Whenever there is agreement to future exchange, and the exchange is split so that one part occurs first, a period follows during which one party is subject to the unilateral power of the other and has no unilateral power of his own. Thus, even in the most paradigmatic of contracts, bilateral power is converted into unbalanced unilateral power.[7]

Unilateral Power

Of course, most modern contracts do not involve the paradigmatic and relatively simple exchanges illustrated by the forward sale of widgets on credit.[8] Quite the contrary, most are parts of contractual relations in which all exchange is relational.[9] In relational exchange, unilateral power arises not only from the kind of legal obligation described above, but also from many other sources. For example, the exercise of bilateral power may produce legal and nonlegal obligations such as those of a reputable businessman to fulfill promises to the extent normally expected in the trade, irrespective of their legal enforceability. Of equal or greater importance in relational exchange is the creation of unilateral power through the other two means mentioned earlier: external conferring of power on a party and creating conditions of dependence.[10] In modern contractual relations, a wide range of unilateral power arises from a variety of sources.

The importance of the foregoing for microeconomic analysis results from that model's complete dependence on *bi*lateral power as the only type with which it is designed to cope. That is, the microeconomic model can deal with power only bilaterally. As Warren Nutter said in his final article: "The economic approach is of virtually no use in analyzing behavior brought about through the use of force or the threat of its use, because the economic paradigm applies to voluntary choice, difficult as it may be to define accurately."[11] Voluntary choice, in this context, is the consequence of one party having bilateral power and exercising it; coercion is the consequence of one party having unilateral power and exercising or threatening to exercise it without the consent of another party.[12]

The difficulties posed for economic analysis by the existence of unilateral power *within* the exchange structure are manifold.[13] Four aspects will be discussed here: (1) the diffuseness and complexity of much unilateral power; (2) changes over time; (3) the interplay of unilateral and bilateral power; and (4) power and its restraint as an independent value.

Diffuseness and Complexity

The unilateral power created in the sale of widgets appeared to be quite specific and clear, namely, the legal right to enforce contractual obligations. But the legal system does not "enforce contracts." Rather, under certain circumstances it confers unilateral power on parties to enable them to follow expensive and complex processes. These *may* ultimately lead to the power to levy penalties on the property of another party, often in amounts difficult to predict, or possibly to have the party held in contempt of court for failure to obey a decree of specific performance. Even in very simple contracts the unilateral power is complex and diffused into risky channels, to say nothing of endless morasses. In relational exchange, unilateral power becomes infinitely more diffuse and complex, so much so that novelists can achieve fame and fortune in recounting its interplay, witness Arthur Hailey. An important reason for this complexity is the fact that much of the power originates in the dependence of the participants arising through development of the relation itself. This is not limited to "simple" or even complex economic dependence (such as that of an able older worker who might have great difficulty finding another job of equal quality, but still has marketable talents and might even be able to do better elsewhere). Psychological and social dependencies become important factors in creating unilateral power in others.[14] Such vaguely defined but nevertheless real and substantial dependence and the resulting power, also vaguely defined but real and substantial, are the core characteristics of relational exchange.

Diffuseness and complexity of unilateral power *within* exchange structures make economic analysis of relational exchange very difficult at *any* time. But the task becomes impossible if one attempts microeconomic analysis of future relational exchange at the start of the relation. The neoclassical route of ignoring unilateral power by collapsing all of it into *pacta sunt servanda*—agreements will be observed—becomes totally surrealistic when applied to highly diffuse and complex power.[15]

Changes over Time

Closely related to diffuseness and complexity is the fact that unilateral power is constantly changing in contractual relations, and in largely unpredictable ways. There is a story about a young Wall Street lawyer who walked into a partnership meeting, announced that he had just been retained in the Ford-Ferguson litigation,[16] and gave his colleagues fifteen minutes to decide whether to make him the senior partner or have him take the litigation (and a sizable part of the firm) with him. Whether or not the story is accurate is unimportant; nor is it important that such dramatic changes are relative—but only relative—rarities. What matters is that unpredictable changes of many kinds are a constant pattern in relational exchange, and they can never be entirely avoided by advance planning.[17] To the extent that such changes are unpredictable in any manageable sense, microeconomic analysis supplies no tools for dealing with unilateral power, for reasons similar to those pertaining to diffuseness and complexity.

Unilateral and Bilateral Power

The problems raised by the diffuseness, complexity, and changeability of unilateral power might not be so troublesome if unilateral power could be separated from *future* exercises of bilateral power. Of course, it cannot be. Every exercise of bilateral power is, by definition, exercise of unilateral power (with the consent of another holder of different unilateral power) through exchange. What the bilateral power *is*, therefore, depends upon what the respective unilateral powers are. Normal application of microeconomic analysis takes the status quo of bilateral power as a given. Although well-recognized problems arise, this works well enough for certain limited purposes (such as the sale of widgets mentioned earlier). But trying to apply this type of analysis to exchanges occurring in an ongoing relation requires some accounting for the fact that the status quo is constantly changing in diffuse and complex ways, thus becoming different at each application of the series. (As already noted, simply ignoring the changes and trying to analyze the situation as if everything happened at one time, by assuming a single and static status quo, is extremely unrealistic in relational exchange.) Without such accounting, each application is unconnected to the others, and what may appear to be a series of analyses dealing with a single continuing relation are, in fact, disconnected analyses of disconnected (discrete) events.

The consequences of the interplay of unilateral and bilateral power in the face of the diffuseness, complexity, and changeability in unilateral power may be seen by examining the innovative and excellent work of Oliver Williamson [1979], who analyzes how governance patterns in contractual relations vary with the presence or absence of these factors.[18]

Power and Its Restraint

Since I have elsewhere [Macneil 1981a; 1981b] raised questions concerning the impact on economic analysis of the human desire to acquire power as a utility in itself, the focus here is limited to *restraint* of power as an extremely important value. In terms of economic analysis, two questions emerge. First, is this value such an integral aspect of relational exchange that failure of economic analysis to take it into account necessarily deprives such analysis of empirical validity? Second, what is the relation between the restraint of power as an independent social value and economic analysis of law?

The answer to the first question is yes. I have argued elsewhere that the restraint of power is a norm common to all contracts, whether discrete (the paradigm of the economic model) or relational.[19] That is, what we view as contractual behavior does not and cannot occur without people behaving in accordance with the norm. Without repeating the arguments here, it may be noted that this norm is implicit in the microeconomic model itself. One of the model's assumptions is that *something* restrains theft (most users of the model would probably also include fraud), since without such restraint, exchange by the physically more powerful party usually would be irrational. But the question remains as to whether, beyond that point, some recognition of restraint of power as an essential element of contractual relations is so important that microeconomic analysis cannot proceed sensibly without such recognition. This is obviously a more difficult question; I believe that the answer is affirmative whenever the subject of analysis is other than quite discrete transactions. Some of the reasons for this are explored in Macneil [1981a; 1981b]. Another explanation is implicit, I believe, in the following discussion of the economic analysis of law and the restraint of power as an independent social value.

For some time, Richard Posner has been advancing the hypothesis that "common law rules and institutions tend to promote economic efficiency."[20] So stated, the hypothesis is unsurprising, and it is virtually certain to be proved correct upon empirical investigation, at least insofar as the law of contractual relations is concerned.[21] But Posner goes farther; implicit in his statement concerning what Frank Michelman calls the Shylock problem is a restatement of the hypothesis:[22] "The refusal [of the common law to enforce penalty clauses in contracts], which apparently promotes inefficiency, remains a major unexplained puzzle in the economic theory of the common law."[23] This refusal is a *"puzzle"* only if the hypothesis is restated as follows: Common law rules and institutions tend to promote economic efficiency *to the exclusion of contrary goals*. This, I take it, is what Posner means to say, at least insofar as the penalty rule is concerned.[24]

Michelman describes the Posner puzzle more fully in terms of *The Merchant of Venice*:

> I suppose [Posner] means that an economist would have to observe about the case that Shylock and Antonio must both have expected to improve their welfares by agreeing to the secured loan in the first place, and that if the law refuses to enforce in terrorem sanctions voluntarily agreed to by borrowers, thus destroying their credibility to lenders, the effect will be an inefficient syndrome of increased costs to borrowers, reduced demand for loans, and diminished profits to lenders. It thus looks as though the presumed unenforceability of Shylock's contract is significant evidence against the positive economic theory of law. . . .
>
> For [Posner], the Shylock case is really counterevidence to his theory—a "puzzle"—and will remain so until, if ever, he can figure out how to rationalize it in terms of an economic-efficiency calculus that counts only objectively appraisable commodities: goods, services, and states that can fairly be said to have prices or shadow prices.[25]

Let us take Posner at his word (the nonenforcement of penalties at common law is a puzzle for his hypothesis[26]) and accept Michelman's implication (that it is an insoluble one within that hypothesis); the question is then raised as to *why* it is insoluble. The answer must lie in the existence of some competing and inconsistent policy, one powerful enough to overcome the efficiency goal. While a special reverence for human life explains the actual Shylock problem, it hardly explains a case such as *Lee Oldsmobile, Inc.* v. *Kaiden*. The court refused to allow a car dealer to retain a deposit of $5,000 as liquidated damages; damages allowable under Uniform Commercial Code § 2-708 were around $3,000, and the dealer resold the car for about $5,000 less than the buyer had promised.[27] Kenneth Clarkson and others [1978] have also rejected, on the basis of their study of the law, explanations based on unconscionability, just compensation, and power of contract.[28] Without discussing whether these or other explanations are valid, I wish to offer a more encompassing and simple one. Before doing so, however, a brief review of the economic model and its relation to unilateral power is in order.

As already noted, the static, presentiating character of the economic model easily permits its users, including Posner, apparently to avoid the problem of existence of *uni*lateral power *within* the exchange structure.[29] But when a time factor is added (as it must be in actual contracts) between the time choice is exercised (bilateral power) and when the exchange(s) of goods takes place, unilateral power invariably comes into existence through one or more routes. While the economic model has no way to deal with that subject, other than by ignoring it,[30] the legal system must and does deal with it in virtually all contract matters actually or potentially in its realm.

Recognition of the existence of unilateral power *over a period of time within* contractual relations is essential to any valid analysis, whether economic or otherwise, of law, common law or otherwise. It is too important simply to ignore; *uni*lateral power may not be, and is not, what contract law is all about, but contract law is *always* about unilateral power.[31] I offer the following hypothesis: American legal rules and institutions, common law and others, tend toward limiting unilateral power in contractual relations of all kinds, whatever may be its source.

This hypothesis clearly takes care of the penalty problem, whether in its extreme form, exemplified by *The Merchant of Venice*, or its more common varieties in common or statutory American law. Moreover, it accounts equally well for the very limited nature of contract remedies, a pretty scrawny lot, particularly when one looks behind the rules and examines their practical effect.[32] The limited nature of contract remedies also means that the restraint of power hypothesis stands empirical testing even in the face of the most rigid formulations and applications of the freedom of contract doctrine. Even in classical contract law,[33] which includes such formulations, only as much unilateral power was created as was available through those limited contract remedies. This is not the place to elaborate, but I also believe that a systematic study of neoclassical (and certainly relational) contract legal doctrine will support the restraint of power hypothesis, beyond the subject of remedies into much of its substantive detail, for example, the doctrines of unconscionability and good faith. Moreover, it will be supported even more by examining contract law in action, and yet more by examining contract itself in action.[34]

It may be objected that the restraint of power hypothesis offers too imprecise a concept—limiting unilateral power—to be useful. But, certainly, unilateral power itself is not too imprecise to be subject to empirical exploration. Similarly, whether a legal system "limits" unilateral power is empirically observable, at least as much as whether that system "tends" to promote economic efficiency.

A more serious criticism is whether the restraint of power hypothesis as stated thus far is of any more interest than the uninteresting efficiency hypothesis as first stated. It, too, is unsurprising and virtually certain to be proved correct upon empirical investigation. Its only possible claim to slightly greater interest is that, during the past decade, power has been far more neglected in non-Marxist legal circles as a tool for analyzing the legal system than has economics.[35] But I would be the last to claim that that makes the hypothesis, as stated, of consummate interest.

One way to make the restraint of power hypothesis interesting would be to do as Posner impliedly does with the efficiency hypothesis: Restate it so that restraint of power becomes so exclusive that any failure to restrain power becomes evidence contrary to the hypothesis, just as penalty-clause law becomes a puzzle to Posner because it is (allegedly) inefficient. Indeed, I am willing to restate the hypothesis: American legal rules and institutions, common law and others, limit unilateral power in contractual relations of all kinds, whatever may be its source, overcoming all other policy considerations, including economic efficiency, when they are deemed to lead to excessive unilateral power.[36] Such a restatement remains empirically testable, although not as easily so as the relative truisms of the first statements of both the efficiency and restraint of power hypotheses. Moreover, it will find the same empirical support as the first statement of the restraint of power hypothesis in doctrines such as the limited nature of contract remedies, unconscionability, and good faith. Finally, if the hypothesis does test out empirically, it would seem to me of considerable interest that restraint of unilateral power is the dominating motif of the law relating to contractual relations.

Nevertheless, even as restated, the hypothesis may still be unsurprising and possibly even quite certain to be proved correct upon empirical investigation. After all, law itself may be viewed as consisting entirely of the creation *and restraint* of power, restraint both of power it creates and of power created otherwise. To add interest to the restraint of power hypothesis it then becomes necessary to add an element of circumstantial specificity. For example, one might advance the hypothesis that American courts in the 1970s tended to limit unilateral power in contractual relations to a greater extent than did those of the 1870s. Or one might advance the hypothesis that legislatures are more prone to restrain unilateral power in contractual relations than are courts. If this proved out, one might or might not be tempted to advance an efficiency hypothesis, as Posner evidently does, that courts are more prone to support doctrines promoting efficiency than are legislatures.[37] These seem to me interesting and relatively testable hypotheses, and many others of equal interest and testability could be advanced as outgrowths of the basic restraint of power hypothesis as restated above.

Several comments may be made summarizing the discussion of the restraint of power hypothesis and the Posner efficiency hypothesis. First, each hypothesis stated in its simplest form of "tends to" or "limiting" is almost certainly correct and equally certainly is of little interest, except for whatever interest the novelty of the restraint of power hypothesis may give it. Second, when restated so that an element of exclusivity or superiority over other goals is introduced, the restraint of power hypothesis describes far more accurately than does the efficiency hypothesis a much wider range of the law of contractual relations. It also deals successfully with the penalty clause doctrine, which the prime advocate of the efficiency hypothesis describes as a "puzzle" about that hypothesis. The restraint of power hypothesis is, in short, a better one, that is, more likely to test out as correct, than the efficiency hypothesis. Third, the restraint of power hypothesis is necessarily inconsistent with the efficiency hypothesis only if the latter is stated in exclusive or dominant terms, as Posner does by implication in his treatment of penalty clause doctrine as a "puzzle." If the efficiency hypothesis is limited to a "tends to" type of statement, it is probably entirely consistent with even a rigorous statement of the restraint of power hypothesis. Fourth, both hypotheses become of more interest when limited and restated in terms of comparison, institutions, time periods, doctrines, and so forth, than when stated in absolute terms.

Conclusion

The incapacity of the neoclassical model to deal with unilateral power, except for its bilateral aspects, leaves users of the model in great difficulty whenever unilateral power is diffuse, complex, or changeable *within* the structure of exchange. Unilateral power *is* diffuse, complex, and changeable in contractual relations of countless kinds. The shifting of the unilateral power status quo in continuing contractual relations also constantly affects the terms on which necessary exercises of future bilateral power will occur. This adds a further difficulty when, as is the case in continuing relations, further exchange, the terms of which are not yet agreed upon, is contemplated. Moreover, restraint of power is itself an independent value so integral to the maintenance of viable contractual relations—a fact recognized implicitly by the microeconomic model itself—that microeconomic analysis cannot proceed sensibly without such recognition. This becomes apparent when Posner's efficiency hypothesis of the common law is examined insofar as it concerns contractual relations. That hypothesis cannot explain a fundamental aspect of the common law—its refusal to enforce penalty clauses. This difficulty in the hypothesis parallels the difficulties for the neoclassical model generally in dealing with unilateral power in contractual relations. In contrast, a restraint of power hypothesis, even quite rigorously stated, solves the penalty doctrine "puzzle" and creates no puzzles of its own.

Notes

1. This article is a development of ideas introduced in Macneil [1981a; 1981b; and 1980]. It was not until the 1979 Rosenthal lectures [Macneil 1980] that I gave power its proper place in the analysis of discrete and modern relational contract, and I still have not done so respecting primitive contractual relations. Moreover, power is not among the primal roots of contract set out in my *The Many Futures of Contracts* [1974a]. It has only belatedly become clear to me that power, and the love of power, is an essential root of contract. This should have been clear from the start, since power is so evident not only in all human relations, but also among nonhominid social primates.
2. The definition accords with Max Weber's; variants of his are set out in Macneil [1980, p. 125, n. 50].
3. Classical, neoclassical, and relational contract law are explored at length in Macneil [1978]. In the American context, classical contract law is that of Samuel Williston, whose treatise was first published in 1920, and the first Restatement of Contracts, published in 1932. Neoclassical contract law is exemplified by Arthur Corbin, whose work overlapped Willis-

ton's, but whose treatise was not published until 1950, by Karl Llewellyn, and by the Uniform Commercial Code. Relational contract law is too widespread throughout the economy to personify it; it encompasses *all* contract law that has burst out of the constraint of the classical and neo-classical systems, or was never in them, as in the case of most domestic relations law.

4. For a discussion of the differences, and their importance to the thinking of Richard Posner (and many other law and economics analysts) see Frank Michelman [1979].

5. Macneil [1981a; 1981b; and 1974b]; Oliver Williamson [1979]; and Victor Goldberg [1976].

6. It remains bilateral only to the extent that mutual rescission is pertinent; in most analysis it is not.

7. This may also occur without a period when both parties have unilateral power, for example, in a loan.

8. See, for example, Goldberg [1980; 1976]; Macneil [1980; 1974a; and 1974b]; and Williamson [1979].

9. A term introduced (as far as I know) in Macneil [1974a] and adopted by Goldberg as a title [1980].

10. The conditions of dependence may or may not be accompanied by obligations resulting from the exercise of bilateral power.

11. Warren Nutter [1979, p. 268].

12. We need not get into the voluntariness of choice when bilateral power is exercised, the point to which Nutter alludes in his concluding clause. In any event, it is clear that responding to someone else's application or threatened application of *uni*lateral power would *not* be voluntary choice in Nutter's terms, or those of any microeconomic analysis of which I am aware. (This does not preclude analysis of responses to *uni*lateral power in trading or *bi*lateral power terms, for example, as in the economic analysis of the response of potential criminals to sanctions.)

13. See Macneil [1981a; 1981b].

14. Armen Alchian and Harold Demsetz's [1972] effort to maintain that the firm lacks power "to settle issues by fiat, by authority, or by disciplinary action superior to that available in the conventional market" falls flat precisely because they ignore the power that develops in relations, much of it created by dependence developing in the relation itself.

15. The consequences of this for economic analysis are explored in more detail in Macneil [1981a; 1981b].

16. Which involved, if I remember correctly, $300 million in pre-1950 dollars.

17. Some, but not all, may be sufficiently predictable to be calculated in terms of risk, but many will be altogether unpredictable, except in extremely general terms, such as "opportunism." See Williamson [1979]; Williamson's treatment of opportunism is discussed in Macneil [1981a; 1981b]. Macneil [1978] explores, inter alia, the limits of contractual planning.

18. See also Goldberg [1979], Macneil [1978].

19. Macneil [1980]. More accurately, it is part of a common norm. The entire norm is creation *and* restraint of power.

20. Posner [1979, p. 285].
21. Two of the norms running through all contractual relations are the im-
    plementation of planning and the effectuation of consent. See Macneil
    [1980, pp. 47–50]. These, constituting but two of a number of common
    contract norms, are the foundations out of which the concept of eco-
    nomic efficiency can arise. Since these norms *must* be reflected in the law
    governing *viable* contractual relations, it is inevitable that any such law
    will supply quantities of evidence for an efficiency hypothesis stated in
    this loose way. Moreover, as precision and single-minded focus become
    increasingly important in contractual relations, the intensity of these
    norms relative to other common contract norms increases correspond-
    ingly. (Indeed, they become so important as to be transformed into what
    is worth labeling and thinking about as a new norm: enhancing discrete-
    ness and presentation, see Macneil [1980, pp. 72–77]; this is the norm
    of the discrete transaction, the paradigm transaction of the microeco-
    nomic model [Goldberg 1976]. As so restated, this norm is almost a state-
    ment of the efficiency principle itself.) Needless to say, precision and
    single-minded focus do become of increasing importance the more con-
    tractual relations concern highly capitalized, technological economies
    demanding continuous decision making. Certainly, American common
    law of, say, the period 1875–1905 studied by Posner [1972] necessarily
    generated abundant evidence to support the efficiency hypothesis stated
    in this loose way; the economy simply could not have worked had it not.
        The foregoing is not to be taken as accepting the efficiency hypothesis
    so stated as making a great deal of sense. At the very least, there are
    Michelman's criticisms of it and the necessity to restate the hypothesis as
    follows: "The [common law] rules, taken as a whole, tend to look as
    though they were chosen with a view to maximizing social wealth (eco-
    nomic output as measured by price) by judges subscribing to a certain set
    of ("microeconomic") theoretical principles" [Michelman 1979, p. 308].
    I also have some basic problems with the concept of efficiency itself, even
    as redefined by Michelman, arising out of what seems to me to be con-
    fusion in the concept of rational maximization. But they are too com-
    plex to deal with here, and I mention them only so as to avoid appearing
    to accept as "scientific" a concept about which I have grave doubts.
22. Michelman [1979, p. 312].
23. Posner [1979, p. 290].
24. This restatement of the hypothesis, while clearly implicit in Posner's
    calling the penalty rules a "puzzle," appears to be inconsistent with some
    of the remainder of his discussion of the sweep of his hypothesis; see
    especially Posner [1979, pp. 291–95].
25. Michelman [1979, pp. 310–11]. Michelman sets out a possible "cheap-
    shot" maximization analysis "solving" the puzzle, but he gives Posner
    proper credit for not using it, and instead choosing to live with the
    "puzzle."
26. Posner [1979, p. 290] rejects out of hand any idea that Kenneth Clark-
    son and others [1978] have resolved the puzzle by supplying an adequate
    economic explanation.

27. 32 Md. App. 556, 363 A.2d 270 (1976). This differential was not available to the dealer to measure damages because he failed to give the buyer notification of intention to resell the car as required by UCC § 2-706.

28. The phrase is from the title of Macneil [1962]. Clarkson and others [1978] do me the honor of treating power of contract seriously before going on to reject it as an explanation of penalty law. In the course of doing this, however, they made at least one serious and basic analytical error, described in Macneil [1980, p. 125, n. 49]. Moreover, they ignored the difference between planning for performance and planning for remedies for nonperformance. I have not yet figured out what combination of their errors, their evident rejection of distinctions between the two kinds of planning (a rejection with which I strongly disagree), and my inadequacies of explanation may have led to their conclusions.

    There remains, of course, the possibility that their rejection of the power of contract argument is correct, that penalty doctrine cannot be explained in terms of the courts' refusal to do more than protect the restitution, reliance, and expectation interests. But I am not trembling in my boots for fear of destruction of the argument, partly because of the mistake mentioned above, and partly because other parts of their argument are fallacious on their face. For example, they object that part of my argument "does not explain the cases, however, since it fails to provide a basis for allowing the parties the right not to contract at all, while, at the same time, not giving them the right to contract for amounts greater than actual damages." The basis for the right *not* to contract is so obvious—and one would think especially to those trained in economics—that it hardly seemed necessary at the time to explain it or to explain that the basis was *not* to be found in the power of contract. It arises out of the basic property and liberty rights underlying the institution of contract. Property rights are rights not to have others interfere with possession, use, and so forth, and normally these include rights *not* to have to contract with others wishing to deprive the rights holder of those rights by agreement.

29. The origin of the static nature of the neoclassical model is to be found in the nature of choice, the exercise of which in the model is an instant event. This static nature and many of its consequences are explored further in Macneil [1981a; 1981b].

30. Or, as noted earlier, dealing with it bilaterally as a subject of trade. In *The Merchant of Venice* that would consist of analysis of how much Antonio would have to pay to avoid Shylock's knife. But the terms of such a trade are not the problem causing the Posner "puzzle." It concerns the unwillingness of the law to create such a penalty power (unilateral) in the first place, not how it might be used bilaterally after its creation.

31. Along with many other things.

32. When stated as rules they protect the restitution, reliance, and expectation interests; in operation they do far less. Although Clarkson and others [1978, p. 364] reject power of contract stated in terms of protecting those interests as an explanation of penalty law, they believe it "useful in un-

derstanding general principles of contract damages."
33. For definitions of classical, neoclassical, and relational contract law, see note 3.
34. See Hugh Beale and Tony Dugdale [1975]; and Stewart Macaulay [1963a; 1963b]. I include contract itself in action within the realm of law, as it is the foundation on which doctrines and formal legal processes are based, and from which they cannot be sensibly separated.
35. But see Goldberg [1979], Marshall Shapo [1977].
36. It is unnecessary to do so to achieve the goals of this article; indeed, it would muddy the waters to discuss the matter, but I would go farther and enlarge the hypothesis by striking the words "in contractual relations of all kinds." Nor, of course, would I limit it to the American scene.
37. "Scholars engaged in this branch of the positive economic analysis of law have advanced the hypothesis that the rules, procedures, and institutions of the common or judge-made law—in sharp contrast to much legislative and constitutional rulemaking—promote efficiency. The hypothesis is not that the common law does or could perfectly duplicate the results of competitive markets; it is that, within the limits of administrative feasibility, the law brings the economic system clos*er* to producing the results that effective competition—a free market operating without significant externality, monopoly, or information problems—would produce" [Posner 1979, pp. 288–89, emphasis added]. The sentence stating the hypothesis is without meaning unless "closer" means "closer than would *some*thing else." Clearly, Posner means closer than would legislative or constitutional rulemaking. This constitutes a fundamental change from Posner's other statements of his hypothesis, and the empirical evidence needed to prove it is quite different, since empirical evidence of *both* common law and legislative and constitutional rulemaking is necessary to make the comparison called for in the hypothesis.

References

Alchian, Armen A., and Harold Demsetz. 1972. "Production, Information Costs, and Economic Organization." *American Economic Review* 62 (December) : 777–95.

Beale, Hugh, and Tony Dugdale. 1975. "Contracts between Businessmen: Planning and the Use of Contractual Remedies." *British Journal of Law and Society* 2: 45–60.

Clarkson, Kenneth W.; Roger Leroy Miller; and Timothy J. Muris. 1978. *Wisconsin Law Review*, no. 2, pp. 351–90.

Goldberg, Victor P. 1980. "Relational Exchange." *American Behavioral Scientist* 23 (January-February) : 337–52.

Goldberg, Victor P. 1979. "The Law and Economics of Vertical Restrictions: A Relational Perspective." *Texas Law Review* 58 (December) : 91–129.

Goldberg, Victor P. 1976. "Toward an Expanded Economic Theory of Contract." *Journal of Economic Issues* 10 (March) : 45–61.

Macaulay, Stewart. 1963a. "Non-Contractual Relations in Business: A Preliminary Study." *American Sociological Review* 28 (February): 55–67.

Macaulay, Stewart. 1963b. "The Use and Non-use of Contracts in the Manufacturing Industry." *Practical Lawyer* 9 (November): 13–40.

Macneil, Ian R. 1981a. "Economic Analysis of Contractual Relations." *Northwestern University Law Review* (forthcoming).

Macneil, Ian R. 1981b. "Economic Analysis of Contractual Relations." In *Essays in Law and Economics*, edited by Paul Burrows and Čento Veljanovski. London: Butterworths.

Macneil, Ian R. 1980. *The New Social Contract: An Inquiry into Modern Contractual Relations*. New Haven: Yale University Press.

Macneil, Ian R. 1978. "Contracts: Adjustment of Long-Term Economic Relations under Classical, Neoclassical, and Relational Contract Law." *Northwestern University Law Review* 72 (January-February): 854–905.

Macneil, Ian R. 1974a. "The Many Features of Contracts." *Southern California Law Review* 47 (May): 691–816.

Macneil, Ian R. 1974b. "Restatement (Second) of Contracts and Presentiation." *Virginia Law Review* 60 (April): 589–610.

Michelman, Frank I. 1979. "A Comment on *Some Uses and Abuses of Economics in Law*." *University of Chicago Law Review* 46 (Winter): 307–15.

Nutter, Warren C. 1979. "On Economism." *Journal of Law and Economics* 22 (October): 263–68.

Posner, Richard A. 1979. "Some Uses and Abuses of Economics in Law." *University of Chicago Law Review* 46 (Winter): 281–306.

Posner, Richard A. 1972. "A Theory of Negligence." *Journal of Legal Studies* 1 (January): 29–96.

Shapo, Marshall S. 1977. *The Duty to Act: Tort Law, Power, and Public Policy*. Austin: University of Texas Press.

Williamson, Oliver E. 1979. "Transaction-Cost Economics: The Governance of Contractual Relations." *Journal of Law and Economics* 22 (October): 233–61.

4

Legal Foundations of the Corporate State

Arthur Selwyn Miller

It is with a certain wariness that I, an academic lawyer, stray into a den of economists. Not that law and economics are not closely allied; quite the contrary. As Justice Brandeis once said, a lawyer who knows no economics is a menace to his client. There are those, not all of whom are dead, who maintain that law, by and large, is a reflection of the economic interests of a given society. Perhaps I wish social and behavioral scientists recognized the need for knowing something about law, which, in my limited experience, they do not. Many economists, political scientists, and sociologists, to say nothing of newspaper columnists and assorted other pundits, habitually talk about law and legal institutions as if they were expert in the esoterica of and about law.

One need not, as William of Occam might have said, needlessly multiply examples of this phenomenon. As this is written, I have before me clippings of two brief *New York Times* pieces by Milton Friedman on morality and controls, in which that learned economist discourses not only on the morality of Phase II of the new Nixonomics, but also on its impact on the rule of law. One would be temerarious indeed to impugn the learning of such an outstanding exponent of that exact science called economics; but, although I find some of what Friedman says makes sense, there is much that verges on pure nonsense. My purpose here is neither to bury nor to praise Milton Friedman; his name is invoked only to show that we in the law are often prey to the intellectual incursions of others. Another example will suffice to show what I mean. We all remember John R. Commons's half-century-old classic, *Legal Foundations of Capitalism*. It is a classic not only because it is difficult to read — you will recall, I trust, the notion that in order to be profound one must be obscure (or to put it another way, if one writes racily he is put down as being journalistic or, what is worse, Galbraithian) — but also because Commons did have considerable insight into the constitutional order and the role of the Supreme Court *vis-à-vis* the economy.

To speak of John Kenneth Galbraith is to think of *The New Industrial State,* the book that first articulated a full-fledged conception of the corporate state, American style. That term, *the corporate state,* has become so current that it is now fashionable; people use it as if it had some accepted core of meaning, which, emphatically, it does not. Charles Reich of the Yale Law School, a law professor who thinks that wearing beads and bell-bottomed trousers is going to liberate all of us and bring us into some sort of terrestrial Nirvana, wrote in *The Greening of America* that this nation is indeed a corporate state. In so doing, he drew upon the existing literature, to the extent there was any, but with little attribution. He did not burden his exposition with the impedimenta of footnotes, which had the merit of making his book more readable. To some, perhaps it made him original.

Galbraith and Reich share one thing in common: In no place do they set out any workable definition of the corporate state that they perceive in the United States. They merely say that it exists, and we are left to glean from their prose what a corporate state is. A political scientist at the University of Wisconsin, H. L. Nieburg, suffers from the same malady — a failure to define terms or to construct a theoretical framework for thinking about a politico-economic situation. All three discuss the phenomenon and assume that their readers will agree with them. It would be easier if they helped us along with the elementary need of providing an adequate conceptual schema.

In this paper, I should like to essay a few tentative thoughts along that line. The subject matter is vast and complex, and there is much that is not known, or at least that can be validated empirically. If, as Ernest Nagel has told us, there is no simple and at the same time adequate explanation of any social phenomenon, so too there is no way to simplify the complexity of American corporativism. It seems to me that a proper definition of the American version of the corporate state, when developed, will have to encompass at least the following: (1) evidence that some sort of merger, actual or tacit, has taken place between political and economic power; (2) a legal nexus between the two; (3) a consequence of some type of corporate body that both encompasses the two and is greater than the arithmetical sum of the two; and (4) a diminution of the social and legal role of the individual *qua* individual. In short, the corporate state, to borrow a term from Otto von Gierke, is a type of *group-person*; perhaps it is the ultimate group-person in any given social order.

You will note, I am confident, that I have used the term *power* as if it, too, had some commonly accepted meaning. That it does not, or even if it does that it is exceedingly difficult to identify the actors and their various roles in the American polity, is one of the teachings of those few political scientists, such as Harold Lasswell and Robert Dahl, who have contributed to our understanding of that concept. As used here, *power* means the ability or capacity to make or influence decisions of national importance. That of course does not exhaust all there is in the concept, but for present purposes I find it sufficient.

The Context

It is well to begin with a page of history, which is worth, so Justice Holmes told us, "a volume of logic"; in this instance it is worth a peck of empirical data. One need not dwell upon the way in which corporations waxed in number and size from the beginnings of the Republic to the present time, so much so that we now have in existence an insitutation that is *sui generis*: the modern giant corporation. I do not mean to imply that corporate gigantism is the sole manifestation of the American version of the corporate state, although surely it is among the most important contributing causes to that development. Nor need one restate the many obvious subventions in favor of business enterprise that were the norm of the nineteenth century and that, as we all know, continue to the present day. Economic historians have traced that path and marked it clearly. What I should like to emphasize is that law and the legal system were employed by the business community during the nineteenth and early twentieth centuries to further its interests. The word *employ* is not used invidiously; there have been and are examples of venality and corruption in legislatures, courts, and administrators, but the situation is far more subtle and far more entrenched than instances of out-and-out criminality.

To put the point in other terms, there has always been a fairly close relationship between business and government, much more so than those who perpetuate myths, such as Supreme Court justices and corporate executives, have been willing to admit. As expressed by a lawyer, we may agree with Eugene V. Rostow that "the line between public and private action is blurred, and always has been blurred, in American law." Or, as economist William Letwin has said:

The path that economic policy follows in its historical development
is sinuous and obscure. To trace all its convolutions is an immensely
difficult task. Faced with it, historians fall back, as they must, on
simplifying notions. Instead of mapping all the meanderings of the
real path, scholars try to match it, however roughly, with
ready-made patterns. The professional tool-kit of economists and
historians contain a few basic patterns that are thought to be generally useful for dealing with economic policy. They bear such names as
laissez-faire, socialism, mercantilism, communism, and welfare state.

Letwin might well have added that quite often commentators use these
terms as if they had a commonly accepted meaning, which, most as-
suredly, they do not.

A basic pattern suggested here is this: The corporate state, if it exists,
did not spring full-grown like Aphrodite; it is the culmination of trends
that may be traced throughout American history. Trend analysis is
useful in our understanding. It does not unduly distort words to maintain
that some form of corporativism always has existed in this country, the
difference between the past and present being one of degree rather than
of type. Social phenomena are not to be understood as anything other
than a product of history—a truism, to be sure, but a fact not sufficiently
emphasized in the literature.

With that in mind, permit me to separate from the chaff of history a
few kernels for your consideration. The scrutiny is upon the law, both
private and public. I take as my text a notion of Franz Neumann's:

> The significance of political power should be squarely faced. No
> society in recorded history has ever been able to dispense with
> political power. This is as true of liberalism as of absolutism, as true
> of laissez faire as of an interventionist state. No greater disservice
> has been rendered to political science than the statement that the
> liberal state was a "weak" state. *It was precisely as strong as it
> needed to be in the circumstances.* [Emphasis added.]

Private Law

Private law, for example, in torts, was judge-made for the most part.
Rules of contributory negligence, assumption of risk, and the fellow-
servant doctrine all permitted the burgeoning corporations during
the nineteenth century to escape much of the human costs of industrial
development. In the area of contract law, which, as we will see, merges
into public law, the historical notion of Sir Henry Maine that the movement of progressive societies was from status to contract was written
into legal doctrine. This meant that the economic power of the corporation was said to be equal to, but no more than, the economic power of
the workingman, an obvious fiction, to be sure, but followed by the
courts and helpful to the corporations. Put another way, the lawmaking

capacity of public government was placed at the disposal of the private governments of American enterprise. That notion of contract, by the way, still is followed to this day in, for example, the books used for law school study of the subject.

Of even more importance were and are the contracts of adhesion, considered in law to be no different from a true arms-length transaction. Contracts of adhesion are *legislative* prescriptions by the private governments of industry and trade associations. Political power (mainly the courts, but at times the legislatures) was used to permit economic power (the corporations) to prescribe the terms and conditions of most of those transactions called contracts. We see, then, the beginnings of that merger between the two types of power that is the first criterion of my developing definition. The merger was articulated, and this is important, in terms of liberty or freedom of contract, the legal analogue of a laissez-faire economic system. (That is an early indication of the difference between the "law in books" and the "law in action"; or perhaps better, between myth and reality. We will return to this, for it is central to my theme.) The social basis for freedom of contract was never valid, although it surely was more so than at present. The law, in its magnificent majesty, told the rich as well as the poor that they were free to contract; no recognition was given to something known by, I believe, Alexander Hamilton: "Necessitous men are not free men." The law, furthermore, was quick to protect property rights of the business class, again through the courts, even though, to my knowledge, no court has ever held that there is a property right in a job. The result was that both common-law courts and courts of equity provided a means by which the new corporations that began to come into existence about 1850 received basic protection.

My final point about private law is taken from corporation law. Corporations were franchised by government for limited purposes and limited times; it is only within the last century that the notion of immortality has attached to them. Henry Carter Adams, in his presidential address to the American Economic Association in 1896, entitled "Economics and Jurisprudence," said:

> Corporations originally were regarded as agencies of the state. They were created for the purpose of enabling the public to realize some social or national end without involving the necessity of direct governmental administration. They were in reality arms of the state, and in order to secure efficient management, a local or private interest was created as a privilege or property of the corporation. A corporation, therefore, may be defined in the light of history as a body created by law for the purpose of attaining public ends through an appeal to private interests.

Adams, of course, merely called attention to an historical fact, but a fact that had been and has been clouded by a myth. That myth, in brief, was this: The corporation is merely a person, no more and no less than you or I; it exists, as do you and I, to maximize its economic interests (make profits for its owners); it is economic man writ large.

That bit of intellectual hocus-pocus, pandered by lawyers and economists, is on its way out. The businessman himself is coming to perceive that the *it* of a corporation is really a *they,* a collectivity rather than a monolithic entity, and that that form of private collectivism has responsibilities transcending the profit motive. Witness, for example, the recent statement of a so-called establishment business organization, the Committee for Economic Development.

> In relations with their constituencies and with the larger society, American corporations operate today in an intricate matrix of obligations and responsibilities that far exceed in scope and complexity those of most other institutions and are analogous in many respects to government itself. The great growth of corporations in size, market power, and impact on society has naturally brought with it a commensurate growth in responsibilities; in a democratic society, power sooner or later begets equivalent responsibility.

That seems to be a latter-day restatement of Adams, based, however, on the social fact that corporations having waxed large and strong now have to recognize that with power comes social responsibility. It is the corporations that say they serve the state, or, perhaps better in this age of egalitarianism, the people. Much of the committee's statement, in my judgment, cannot be faulted. I do have serious problems with the notion that America is a democratic society, either in the sense of widespread participation in decision making, or in Neumann's sense of "politically responsible decisions." We are elitist in our decision making, as Grant McConnell has pointed out. Furthermore, those who have power are not necessarily *responsible* or *accountable,* if I may use those two terms as being roughly synonymous.

So much for private law. I hope that what has been said is sufficient at least to suggest the need to look beyond the façade of law and the legal system to determine *who benefits,* and *how,* from that system. If politics, as Harold Lasswell has said, is a question of who gets what, where, when, and how, then judge-made private law—ostensibly normatively neutral and a product of a jurisprudential cosmology, attributed to Blackstone, that spoke in terms of eternal verities entirely divorced from the muck and mire of ordinary human affairs—historically helped to settle a number of those questions. In sum, it helped the corporations;

if we want to be charitable, we can say that it was for the achievement of some public end.

In any event, the corporations had the protection of the state, either for the purpose of furthering the ends of the state, or for merely furthering the ends of the companies (or perhaps an intermixture of both). If Henry Carter Adams was correct, and if the revisionist business historians, such as Allan Nevins, are correct, then the corporations indeed did exist in the nineteenth century for social ends. The legal nexus was effected, as I have said, by a protecting blanket of private law, and, perhaps of more importance, by a set of public law (that is, constitutional) doctrines created out of the whole cloth by the Supreme Court in the post-Civil War period, a period that lasted until 1937.

Public Law

Soon after the Fourteenth Amendment was added, the Court, in the *Slaughterhouse* case and in *Munn* v. *Illinois,* held that the amendment could not be used by corporations. Their remedy, said the Court in *Munn,* was to elect new legislators (a lesson, be it noted, that was filed but not forgotten). After the Supreme Court a few years later changed its mind and found that corporations were indeed persons within the meaning of the amendment, the businessman looked to Their Celestial Majesties on the Court as the ultimate protectors of his rights. As Commons said, this meant that the court occupied "the unique position of the first authoritative faculty of political economy in the world's history. They were a set of economic philosopher-kings, no less, and that even though William Howard Taft, when Solicitor General, called the justices a group of "mummies."

The justices not only discovered, in Jhering's "heaven of legal concepts," that corporations were persons, but also acted as a constitutional convention to revise the due process clauses to make them apply to the substance or content of legislation as well as to the procedure by which government dealt with life, liberty, and property. That remarkable invention enabled a majority of the Court to read, as Justice Holmes said in *Lochner* v. *New York,* Mr. Herbert Spencer's *Social Statics* into the Constitution. Holmes was quite right in maintaining that the *Lochner* decision was based on an economic theory that most of the nation repudiated, but that did not deter the Fumbling Five and Fallible Four. Reading their notions of good social policy into the Constitution, they did as much as any court could to insure that corporations would become large and strong, and much more than any court has in any other country.

If we consider the Supreme Court to be an instrument of governance, which it is, and that it renders decisions for reasons other than adherence to Blackstone's quaint jurisprudential notions, then we may perceive a corpus of public law that insulated the companies from the pressures of a rising trade-union movement, Populism, and Grangerism. Congress, to be sure, assisted by passing statutes that outwardly looked to be anti-business, for example, the Sherman Act and the Federal Trade Commission Act, and by standing still while the Court emasculated them in the name of sweet reasonableness. Some so-called radical historians, such as Gabriel Kolko, today maintain that such statutes were passed to help business. That period of judicial supremacy in economic policy matters lasted, as we all know, until the 1930s, at which time the economic system was shattered in the Great Depression.

At that point even the justices could see, however haltingly, that interests other than the entrepreneurs' desire for profit making had to be recognized. The trickle of cases that began with *Blaisdell* v. *Home Building and Loan Ass'n* (1934), crested in 1937 in *West Coast Hotel Co.* v. *Parrish* and the *Jones & Laughlin* case, and continued at flood stage through *United States* v. *Darby Lumber Co.* and *Wickard* v. *Filburn* in the forties, *Williamson* v. *Lee Optical Co.* in the fifties, and *Katzenbach* v. *McClung* and *Ferguson* v. *Skrupa* in the sixties. Economic policy had become thoroughly politicized—de-judicialized—and left to the political branches of government (more and more the executive) to control. The culmination of that we are seeing today in the New Economic Plan of the president, Phase II of which institutionalizes a type of corporativism on America.

The statutory corporate state, to be sure, is no newcomer to the American political economy. Something similar was tried in 1933 in the National Industrial Recovery Act, which permitted industry groups to establish codes of fair competition in return for the recognition of labor to organize. The NIRA, as we all know, was invalidated by the Supreme Court in 1935, thereby rescuing President Roosevelt from an increasingly chaotic, even embarrassing situation. Outlawing the NIRA did not mean that all of its manifestations died; many of them have continued in other forms, such as trade association activity and the like.

Since 1929 the United States has sped through a series of economic theories from laissez faire to Keynesianism (the Employment Act of 1946) to the present acceptance of Galbraithian notions—and the latter by a "conservative" president and the executives of the major corporations! This is said to be temporary, a short-run expedient preliminary to an attempted reversion to something else, with that something being so clouded in rhetoric that no one knows what it is. Presumably it might be Keynesianism, and possibly it may even be that ideal, never realized, of a free market economy. But the fog on Washington's Pennsylvania Avenue is thicker than the smog in Los Angeles. I am confident, although the thought is depressing, that no one in the higher reaches of government now knows what will happen after Phase II terminates. Maybe it will last forever, "somewhere short of infinity," as the *Wall Street Journal* put it.

I do not think it is possible to revert to any status quo ante. The government's hand will stay on the economic tiller, which means that management and labor will be asked, even forced, to further the ends of the state. The nation, the world is too small and too interdependent any longer to tolerate, even in theory, the idea of two governing structures — political and economic — purportedly separated from each other. Just as formal federalism in this country is now at least obsolescent and perhaps obsolete, even in the face of cries — touching cries, to be sure — for participatory democracy, so too the informal, functional federalism of government and the corporate giants will accent the positive of cooperation rather than the negative of autonomy. I should like to devote the remainder of this speculative paper to that notion.

The Government–Corporation Symbiosis

My thesis can be simply stated: There is a growing fusion of political and economic power into a new form of politico-economic structure, namely, a group-person, that at once transcends the arithmetical sum of its parts, which are the public group of government and the private group of the corporations (and other important social organizations). The shorthand term for this is the *corporate state*. How and why did it come about? What are its principal manifestations? What are the implications for the future?

Those are large questions, each of which would take a volume to answer. All I can hope to do now is to sketch in some of the outlines of the development. What has been said thus far, I hope, will serve to indicate that the corporate state, American style, is both the culmination of historical legal and economic situations and a milestone on the road to some other type of social order. If we use trend analysis, the beginnings of corporativism can be seen in the nineteenth century; it also is necessary to extrapolate into the future. What is said now relates, in the main, to a description of the present. Recall, if you will, the four segments of my proposed definition of corporativism: (a) the merger of political and economic power; (b) a legal nexus effecting that merger; (c) the creation of a transcendent group-person; and (d) the submergence of the individual into the group.

Rise of the Positive State

We should note the emergence of two characteristic institutions of the modern era: first, a government that has undertaken affirmative obligations toward the economy or the Positive State; and, second, the super-corporations, the few hundred corporate giants that dominate the economy and set its tone and direction. In point of historical time, the development has been simultaneous for all practical purposes, although, no doubt, the corporate juggernauts antedated the Positive State by a few decades. Each needs and complements the other; taken together, they are the United (Corporate) States of America.

In brief, the *Positive State* is a shorthand term for the express acceptance by the federal government—and thus by the American people—of an affirmative responsibility for the economic well-being of all. It involves a societal shouldering of a duty of constitutional dimensions, a duty to take action to create and maintain within the economy minimal conditions of employment opportunities and of the basic necessities of life. Exemplified in a broad range of programs, it is the American version of the welfare state. It received its "charter" in the Employment Act of 1946, which, although a statute, in its importance may be said to have made constitutional law.

According to that act, "the continuing policy and responsibility" of the federal government is "to use all practicable means consistent with its needs and obligations and other essential considerations of national policy, *with the assistance and cooperation of industry, agriculture, labor,* and state and local governments" to create and maintain conditions "under which there will be afforded useful employment opportunities . . . and to promote maximum employment, production and purchasing power." (Emphasis added.) In short, it is a commitment to promote economic growth as a Good Thing. As we all know, there are numerous programs by which the government seeks to carry out that commitment. And as we are beginning to realize, however slowly, the National Environmental Policy Act of 1969 is a commitment to further the "quality of life." The additional implication is that the government, by design or by inadvertence, has now enunciated two policies that are often basically inconsistent. But that is The American Way. I do not criticize it, but merely point out that at some future time some hard choices must be made between the quantitative goals of the Employment Act and the qualitative goals of the Environmental Act.

There are at least five characteristics of the Positive State that are worth mention.

The change from a Constitution of **limitations** *to one of* **powers.** No longer do we believe in the Jeffersonian idea that "that government is best that governs least"; the prevailing idea, in the words of Robert Hutchins, is that "that government is best that governs best." The turning point came in 1937 in Chief Justice Hughes's opinion in *West Coast Hotel Co.* v. *Parrish,* a minimum wage case in which a statute was attacked as a deprivation of freedom of contract. Said Hughes:

> The liberty safeguarded [by the Fourteenth Amendment] is liberty in a social organization which requires the protection of law against the evils which menace the health, safety, morals, and welfare of the people. Liberty under the Constitution is thus necessarily subject to the restraints of due process, and regulation which is reasonable in relation to its subject and is adopted in the interests of the community is due process.

Ponder that for a moment. The Supreme Court recognized that liberty could be infringed by forces other than government, and, even more important, those other forces may require the affirmative intervention of government to counteract them. Edward S. Corwin commented: "From being a limitation on legislative power, the due process clause becomes an actual instigation to legislative action of a levelling nature."

The advent of a system of **overt** *economic planning.* The open nature of the planning function of government is significant. A good case can be made, as George Soule has said, for the proposition that "the United States government has at all times followed plans of some sort that were directed toward the economic welfare of its citizens." However, with that infinite capacity of Americans for self-delusion, this was seldom, if ever, recognized. Planning was a bad word; governments were not supposed to do it, for that led down the path of creeping socialism; in our mythology only corporations and natural persons were allowed to plan. We are older now — I do not say wiser — and have a penchant for telling it like it is. No one blinks anymore when that bad four-letter word *plan* is used in connection with government and the economy. To the contrary, we have in recent months witnessed the extraordinary spectacle of corporate managers coming to Washington and telling government to regulate them; that is at least wryly amusing, and it might even be astonishing were we to believe that in so doing the corporate executives were acting contrary to their perception of the best interests of their companies. That quite obviously those hard-headed men do not so believe should make us all stop and wonder, at least a little, about the meaning of it all. My conclusion is that this is probative evidence that the president's economic planning by and large benefits the corporations. This is not a novel thought, to be sure, for more than a few have said the same thing.

The alteration of governmental framework. Federalism and the separation of powers are becoming obsolescent concepts. Economic planning, Karl Loewenstein once said, is the DDT of federalism, and so it seems to be. Planning by government generates a need for unified and probably uniform economic policies throughout the nation. That requirement runs counter to the diversity inherent in federalism, and it is also contrary to the fragmentation of power within the national government itself. The fifty states are anachronisms, on the way to becoming little more important than those vestigial remnants of an agricultural society, the county governments. Within the national government itself, power has flowed to the executive, aided by a more than willing Congress, members of which are quite happy to draw their paychecks and to act as ombudsmen for their constituents while letting effective control over national policies become presidential.

So, too, with the judiciary, which has quietly abdicated any significant role with respect to economic affairs, and which, for that matter, seems ever increasingly to want to exemplify the Hamiltonian label of "the least dangerous branch." I realize that in suggesting that the judiciary, including the Supreme Court, has more a ceremonial role than a position as an important actor in the political arena I am running counter to a large amount of the conventional wisdom. Those who dispute my view, however, must show—in this case, in economic matters—where the Court has wielded significant power recently. Surely it is fair to say that it no longer is an authoritative faculty of political economy, although it may be that it is trying (at least it did during the tenure of Earl Warren) to be an ultimate arbiter of social ethics.

The politicization of law and the legal process. Law, in the sense of interdiction, has little role to play in the higher reaches of the American bureaucracies, both public and private. With the advent of public law as the dominant force in our legal system, law has become purposive and instrumental. The net result, as Washington lawyer Charles Horsky said in 1952, is that ours is emphatically a "government of men, not of law." The guru of academic administrative law specialists, Kenneth Culp Davis, recently discovered this and let the world in on his secret in a book called *Discretionary Justice.* To me, a better book on the point is Theodore Lowi's *The End of Liberalism,* and its sequel, *The Politics of Disorder.* Power rests in the bureaucrats, whether they exist in Galbraith's "technostructures" or Meynaud's "technocracy." Despite the abundance of lawyers in Washington, it is lawyers as *apparatchiks* rather than as professionals that is the dominant theme of a government of lawyers, not of men.

Law has been politicized both in its making and its enforcement, in what might be called the inputs and the outputs; this is not entirely true, but enough so to indicate an emerging pattern. Bargaining among interest groups, as many observers have noted, tends to make public policy (that is, law) the resultant of a parallelogram of conflicting political forces. At the other end of the pipeline, a similar process of bargaining is evident in law enforcement. A number of examples may be mentioned. In criminal law administration, plea bargaining is now so widespread that we have the weighty testimony of the chief justice of the United States that it is necessary for the viability of the system. (Burger did not put it quite that way, to be sure; he said that if only 10 percent fewer suspects pleaded not guilty and demanded a jury trial, the process would break down.) For present purposes, law enforcement bargaining takes place in, for example, the consent decree practice in antitrust litigation. That is plea bargaining in the executive suites, in the area of white-collar crime. Trade offs are made and bargains are struck. Other examples include the guaranteed loan to Lockheed and rewriting its C5-A contract, and the way in which government caved in to the unions to allow retroactivity in previously negotiated wage contracts.

I do not wish to press this point too far, but do suggest that enforcement, which is outwardly the clearest instance of the separation of business and state, becomes merely an internal dialogue, a family squabble, to the extent that bargaining exists in the outputs of the system in business matters. Theodore Lowi, by the way, calls for something termed *juridical democracy,* which apparently means judicializing enforcement without the intervention of the human element, but that is hardly a happy, valid, or viable resolution of a perplexing legal situation.

The progressive blurring of the line between public and private government-business relationships. It is not only Lockheed and Penn Central that are systematically aided by government; so, too, are large segments of the economic order. As Robin Marris expressed it: "The industrial capital of western democracies is no longer divided into two classes, 'public' and 'private,' but rather into three, 'public,' 'private,' and 'corporate.' The corporate sector like to be described as 'private,' but this may represent no more than a desire to conceal." Marris, or any present-day observer, is not saying much that is new. As long ago as 1913 Woodrow Wilson called attention to the same phenomenon in *The New Freedom:*

> One of the most alarming phenomena of the time, or rather it would be alarming if the nation had not awakened to it and shown its determination to control it, one of the most significant signs of the new social era is the degree to which government has become associated with business. I speak, for the moment, of the control over the government exercised by Big Business. Behind the whole

subject, of course, is the truth that, in the new order, government
and business must be associated closely.

So they must be and so they are, then and more so now.

To some minor extent, it should be noted, the Supreme Court has
recognized the public nature of private business and has held that constitutional norms are applicable to corporations. There are only two
cases that do that directly, however, *Marsh* v. *Alabama* (1946) and the
Logan Valley Plaza decision in 1968. Two swallows do not a summer
make, nor do two cases a legal doctrine. Even so, we may well be in that
era that Alexander Pekelis predicted in the 1940s when he said that the
next generation of constitutional lawyers would have ever more to be
concerned with private governments. It is to be noted that the *White
Primary Cases* do recognize the private governing power of the Democratic Party, and that there are a clutch of other decisions in which the
Court has tended to blur the consitutional line between government and
private group. The technical doctrine revolves around the concept of
state action, for the Constitution runs against governments (the state)
only. The increasingly perplexing problem is this: What is a government?

The Supercorporations

The previous introduction into the nature of modern government is
too brief. What is emphasized is that, without amendment, a new form of
government has arrived in these United States. The other half of the
symbiotic relationship is the growth of the corporate giants, which needs
no documentation or restatement. Let me make four remarks only in
passing. First, there seems to be much in what Galbraith calls "the
principle of convergence." Industrial nations, wherever located, tend to
form similar institutions. That does not mean there is no difference
between, for example, General Motors and a Soviet organization. As
Raymond Aron, among others, has said, there is the great difference in
the matter of who owns and who controls. Second, Galbraith's "imperatives of technology" do not necessarily explain the growth of the supercorporations in the United States. Third, government and business, far
from being hostile to each other, exist in what may be called a system of
antagonistic cooperation. Quite possibly, or even probably, that antagon-
ism is more ostensible than real. Each needs the other, and perhaps
could not exist without the other. Finally, the supercorporations are here
to stay. Eighty years of antitrust enforcement should have taught us that
government is not going to do anything significant about their size. No
doubt a case can be made, and to me it is persuasive, that the large
enterprise is not as innovative as its apologists contend (the small busi-

ness and the individual inventor do things better), but it is there in disembodied immortality. The status quo ante of 1850 or 1890 or even 1920 simply is not going to reappear.

The Emerging Synthesis

There are those who suggest we are on the verge of a new renaissance. Just as the nation-state a few hundred years ago challenged the church for dominance in the Western world, so now the giant corporations are challenging the nation-states. Maybe so. However, it does not seem likely that the state will wither away, as these non-Marxists maintain, but rather that it will take on a new form. It already has, in my judgment. How it did this is the first question; what has been produced is the second.

A "Living Law" Analysis

The new form is the emerging corporate state, although we do not have a full-blown theory about it, nor even a theory about the giant corporations and their role in the American polity. As Andrew Hacker recently said, "neither our constitutional law nor our political theory is able to account for the corporate presence in the arena of social power. Indeed, it is not at all clear by what right the corporation is entitled to power at all." That, in sum, is the problem of legitimacy: How does the politico-economic power achieve legitimacy? As Dean Edward S. Mason has said: "Who selected these men, if not to rule over us, at least to exercise vast authority, and to whom are they responsible? The answer to the first question is quite clearly: they selected themselves. The answer to the second is, at best, nebulous. This, in a nutshell, constitutes the problem of legitimacy." It is a real problem, an ever growing one, but one that merely can be noted here.

The essential question at the moment is how it can be demonstrated that some type of legal nexus exists between the corporation and the state. The answer involves a "living law" analysis, which requires: (1) primary focus on the important societal decision and asking the question: *Who* makes those decisions, *how,* and with what *effects?* (2) a distinction between those who exercise formal authority to make such decisions and those who exercise effective control over them; (3) a knowledge of the factors that influence or control given decisions; and (4) an appeciation of what difference decisions make in the social structure.

Those are large and difficult questions; they cannot be answered briefly. The basic thought proffered is that important societal decisions tend more and more to be made by an amalgam of the interactions of public and private bureaucracies. Quite often these decisions—they are matters of important public policy—are put into official form through the formal authority of government officials. (This is not always so, for perhaps equally often corporate managers can do so, but only with express or tacit delegation of authority from the state.) The flow of decisions thus made, which often are administrative rather than legislative or judicial, constitute the living law.

The living law is principally associated with Eugen Ehrlich, a defunct Austrian jurisprude who wrote *The Fundamental Principles of the Sociology of Law* several decades ago. Ehrlich maintained that the living law is to be seen "in contrast to that which is in force merely in the courts and with the officials. The living law is that law which is not imprisoned in rules of law, but which dominates life itself. The sources of its knowledge are above all the modern documents, and also immediate study of life itself, of commerce, of customs and usage, and of all sorts of organizations, including those which are recognized by the law, and, indeed, those which are disapproved by the law." The living law, in other words, is the flow of decisions important to Americans; some are made by private officers, others by public officials. Many of those made privately are of national significance. Furthermore, many of those made by public officials are in fact influenced, not to say controlled, by outside forces, of which the giant corporation is the most important.

Law, then, is more than the "command of the sovereign" or a corpus of rules. It is what the important societal decision makers actually do; it is a flow of decisions, a process rather than a static system. The black-letter rules are important and necessary, but are only part of the picture. The myriad routine transactions between the two characteristic institutions of the day—big government and big business—make up a body of living law. At times it is formalized in statute, administrative rule, or even in judicial decision, but not always, or even mostly. This is particularly true of the "how" of decision making, the procedure by which decisions are made; it, too, is law in the sense used here.

What is suggested is that a system of law exists in the United States, which consists of the informal transactions between government and a pluralistic social group (in our case, the corporations). Although the system at times is formalized, it more often exists as a set of working rules which are understood by the participants, but which seldom receive formal cognizance. This system is not necessarily cohesive and consistent; it is a series of laws, rather than a logical whole. It is the means by which the various subgovernments within Washington operate.

In agricultural matters, to take one example, an obscure congressman from an obscure district in an obscure state, by the name of Jamie Whitten, exercises as much or more real power than does the secretary of agriculture. Another example are the many advisory committees that flourish in Washington which are made up of industry representatives. These committees have much to say about what is done in government, and their operations make up a body of procedural living law. The Business Council stoutly maintains that it is a private group that just happens to have a small office in the Department of Commerce; it also refuses to divulge what goes on within its meetings, save for an occasional article noting that some high governmental official has spoken to the council. Its actual power is unknown, at least to me, but it does seem to be considerable. Washington law firms tend to be brokers between the business community and government. The list is almost endless.

This complex web of informal interactions constitutes what I am calling, with Ehrlich, the living law of American corporativism. If the notion is valid, then it effects the legal nexus between the corporation and the state. It is law in that it enables power to be exercised, and it is invisible law in that it is not codified or otherwise entombed in the musty volumes of law libraries. I think that I can find some similar ideas in John R. Commons. For example, Commons speaks of the corporation's charter as a

> group of promises and commands which the state makes in the form
> of working rules indicating how the officials of the state shall act in
> the future in matters affecting the association, the members of the
> association, and the persons not members. It is these promises and
> commands, or working rules, of officials which constitute the charter
> and determine the status of the association. . . . This collective,
> intangible living process of individuals, the functionaries of the state
> find already in a trembling existence and then proceed "artificially"
> to guide the individuals concerned and give it a safer existence. The
> guidance is made through promising to them a certain line of behav-
> ior on the part of public officials, which sets forth the limits on their
> private behavior and the assistance they may expect on the part of
> officials.

This is not to say that Commons is openly embracing Ehrlichian jurisprudence, or that he would be in agreement with its application here, but as I read him, he comes close; his "working rules" seem to parallel Ehrlich's "living law."

To me it is persuasive that a legal connection can thus be shown between the corporation and the state, with the resulting synthesis a form of corporativism. There are, of course, other means by which the necessary nexus can be shown, principally the notion of contract. The arms industry provides the best illustration of the way in which large corporations are welded to the state; it is the "arsenalization" of a large segment of American business, a form of nationalization which, with Lockheed as an example, has few of the benefits of public ownership and many of the shortcomings. We have managed in the production of weapons to have the worst of two worlds. Perhaps the apt title for the product is Seymour Melman's, *Pentagon Capitalism*. In any event, the instrument of contract does provide the legal connection between state and enterprise, which is why Nieburg says arms production "at once resembles traditional private enterprise and the corporate state of fascism."

The Consequence

The consequence of a fast-moving development has been well stated by Allen Schick: "It is no longer possible to tell where private ends and the public begins as public and private funds and workers flow and work side by side in SST development, job training, and countless other programs. In the basic social accounts, the public–private distinction no longer is significant; more and more, the accounts concentrate on the aggregate social input and output, regardless of its public or private character." We have, in sum, a new social order, appropriately termed the corporate state, American style. Slowly emerging, its contours are becoming clearer with each passing year.

When President Nixon established a fifteen-person Pay Board in early November 1971, composed of management, labor, and public members, only one person—the chairman—was to be a full-time public employee. The others are private citizens. When the board acts, it has delegated power from the state—from Congress to Nixon to George Meany (and others)—that institutionalizes the corporate state. This was clearly seen by Judge Harold Leventhal when he ruled in October that Phase I was valid; Leventhal carefully excluded the question of delegation to private groups from his ruling, noting that "the President's plans . . . do present the very kind of delegation of government power to private groups" that was invalidated in 1935 by the Supreme Court. If that be so, then we need not rely on a living law analysis to show the necessary legal nexus. I am not predicting that the delegation to the Pay Board will be invalidated, when it is challenged in the courts. Since Congress has passed the Phase II statute essentially as drafted in the Treasury Department, that would take a more courageous Supreme Court than we now have, as well as one not so ready to constitutionalize what the politicians want.

A consequence of the development is the gradual emergence of the state as coordinator, as regulator, as the dominant member of the duo.

"The role of the state will rise and that of business shrink," Robert Heilbroner predicts; he bases his forecast on the deliberate application of intelligence to social problems. Heilbroner apparently agrees with Daniel Bell, who says that we are entering into a post-industrial society, and that the new men of power are the "scientists, the mathematicians, the economists, and the engineers of the new computer technology." They may be correct, although one should be careful about falling into the conceit of academics and unduly emphasizing the role of the men of ideas. Even so, Galbraith espouses similar views when he maintains that the locus of power is in our public and private bureaucracies, "the technostructure," or those who bring specialized knowledge to group or collective decision making. My own guess differs slightly: the state will become more and more important, but in the future, as in the past, those with the wealth will have the ultimate power. The United States, a timocracy today, is not likely to change in the future.

Government today, the Positive State or the corporate state, is a collectivity that is the hypostatization of the public interest, and the public interest is greater than the arithmetical sum of the private interests of the nation. Government has a momentum of its own, separate from and greater than individual interests. In a little noted statement a decade ago, President Kennedy expressed the same thought. In response to a question at a press conference about labor-management relations, Kennedy said: "These companies are free and the unions are free. All we [the executive] can try to do is to indicate to them the public interest which is there. After all, the public interest is the sum of the private interests, or perhaps it's even sometimes a little more. *In fact, it is a little more.*" The president thereby articulated a view of government basically different from that which existed historically (at least in theory).

A further implication was that the state is some sort of group-person, which, I believe, poses substantial constitutional questions. Suddenly, the age-old constitutional philosophy of limited government has been reversed; we now have a government of powers, rather than of limitations. That government has drives and interests of its own to further; since it has a monopoly on force and on the peaceful settlement of disputes, it does further them. Ernest Barker said in 1933:

> If we make groups real persons, we shall make the national State a real person. If we make the State a real person, with a real will, we make it indeed a Leviathan—a Leviathan which is not an automaton, like the Leviathan of Hobbes, but a living reality. When its will collides with other wills, it may claim that, being the greatest, it must and shall carry the day; and its supreme will may thus become a

supreme force. If and when that happens, not only may the State become the one real person and the one true group, which eliminates or assimilates others: it may also become a mere personal power which eliminates its own true nature as a specific purpose directed to Law or Right.

I submit to you that the state in the modern era has become an anthropomorphic superperson whose reality is as real as that of human beings; that this is being recognized in governmental policies from all branches of government; and that the Supreme Court, even when it has been making its rulings that appear to further individual rights and liberties, has really often been talking about individuals as members of groups.

That latter point is the final element in my definition of the corporate state—the submergence of the individual into the group. It is seen, for example, in the study of political science, where, since David Truman rediscovered Arthur Bentley, the prevailing ideology has been one of pluralism (although recent studies, such as those by Henry Kariel and Theodore Lowi, carefully note the shortcomings of the pluralistic group model of policy making). Economics, if I may venture to tread there, also is beginning, or has begun, to think in terms of the corporation as the basic unit of the economy, having developed somewhat since Andreas Papandreou's observation twenty years ago that "the economist has not evolved a theory of conscious cooperation."

Lawyers, as usual, have lagged; group theories of politics and of economics have not found a counterpart in a group theory of law. There has been a little—a very little—stirring by the lawyers in that direction, but not enough even to note. My suggestion is that the constitutional law produced by the Supreme Court in the past several decades can, in large part, be structured around a theme of group action, that the decisions usually said to protect individual rights and liberties have, rather, tended to create a constitutional law of associational activity. The cases include those involving racial segregation, urban voters (reapportionment of legislatures), and church and state (often the cases are brought by Jehovah's Witnesses or members of some other sect).

Of course, not all constitutional decisions fall into the law of associational activity category, but enough do to make the development worthy of note. Of possible interest also is the increasing use of class actions, a procedural device whereby one plaintiff is permitted to represent a large number (often neither identified nor readily identifiable) of others who are considered to be in the same situation. Finally, a constitutional right of association has, by judicial legerdemain, been found within the interstices of the First Amendment.

That the idea of human freedom is a sometime thing, quite possibly on its way out, is one implication of what I have just said. Freedom becomes that of choosing which group or groups with which one wishes to associate. Perhaps freedom is now Hegelian: the liberty to do what one should do. One need not be a disciple of B. F. Skinner to think that human freedom is a value limited in time and space, in time to the past two or three hundred years, in space to a portion of the Western world. I do not applaud that, but merely note it.

By way of conclusion, I should like to say what should have been said earlier: This paper is descriptive, not normative. There are no value judgments made or implied. A definition of the emerging politico-economic order has been attempted. Left dangling are a host of problems raised by that system of governance, which must await another time.

5

A New View on the Economic Theory of the State: A Case Study of France

Robert Delorme

The problem of the state has been challenging economists for a long time with respect to the questions of size, efficiency, and behavior. The apparently inexorable long-run growth of public expenditure remains a fascinating subject. It is always a matter of controversy between those who attribute the present economic difficulties to an excess of state intervention and those who denounce the insufficiency of state intervention and advocate more. A normative aspect linked to various conceptions of state efficiency comes in here. But is the underlying behavior—or role— of the state well enough known to explain and understand the problem?[1]

At the very time when economists usually postulate state behavior on the basis of given preconceptions, as do for instance the Public Choice or the Marxist approaches (which have much in common with normative views), we wish to show that it is possible to formulate this problem as an object of research, that statements on its main characteristics can be discovered through the systematic observation of state intervention and that there exists a relation between the questions of size and of behavior thus reformulated. Hence this article is concerned with an approach based on the observation of the genesis and evolution of state intervention in the economy. It does not deal with its effects, nor give advice on economic policy or efficiency matters.

We are thus led to formulate the problem in the following way: On

the one hand, explaining the genesis and evolution of long-run state intervention, including spending, requires knowledge of state behavior. On
the other hand, is it possible to make statements about the role of the
state on the basis of a systematic study of the origins and evolution of
public spending and other public interventions in the economy?

These two questions converge. They indeed raise several other questions. What are public interventions? What are their origins? What is their
evolution? What are the forces generating their development? What is
the importance of long-run tendencies and those of the medium term? On
this basis what is the emerging characterization of the present day role of
the state?

It is attempted here to show that it is possible to answer these questions
provided that we solve a major methodological problem. The method
does matter; it is examined in parts two to five. Results conclude the
article.

What is Observed? At the Start, the Evolution
of Public Expenditures

The present study began with research on the long-run growth of public
expenditure in France. The aim of the first phase was to build homogeneous and meaningful data series. It was done on a secular period basis,
ranging from 1872 to 1980, for the three public administration levels:
central and local governments and social security (created in 1945). The
common denominator of their outlays lies in the compulsory nature of
the public contribution to the main part of their resources (more than
90 percent), the remaining part coming from state property income and
from borrowing. The market public sector (notably the nationalized sector) is thus not included in the expenditure series.

The highest level of disaggregation is obtained for central government
and social security. It covers ten functions (general administration, defense, veterans, agriculture, industry and commerce, transportation,
housing and urbanism, education, social services, and public debt interest
charge) and six main economic categories (personnel, consumption, investment, capital transfers, current transfer, and interest of the public
debt).

Though this article does not aim to present an analysis of public expenditure as such, it seems necessary to mention some major points for
the sake of the clarity of the argument to come. They may be summarized
in the following way.

There are no surprises in the long-run global trend: its main characteristic is that of growth in spending (G), both in absolute and relative terms, measured by the ratio between G and a macroeconomic aggregate.

Table 1. *Ratio of Public Expenditure to Gross Domestic Production in Percent (Constant 1983 Prices)*[2]

Period	Minimum	Maximum	Average	Fiscal Resources (average)
1872-1912	11.0 (1872)	15.0 (1909)	13.9	9.3
1920-1938	18.8 (1929)	35.8 (1922)	26.1	15.4
1947-1974	38.3 (1949)	52.5 (1963)	48.5	36.1

Gross domestic product data go back to 1959. Two subperiods may be distinguished for the last two decades, 1959-1974 and 1975-1980.

Table 2. *Ratio of Public Expenditure to Gross Domestic Product in Percent (Data Deflated by the Implicit GDP Price Index)*

Period	Minimum	Maximum	Average	Fiscal Resources (average)
1959-1974	38.6 (1960)	42.0 (1963)	40.2	32.4
1975-1980	45.3 (1975)	48.3 (1980)	46.3	40.0

Though the overall tendency is clear, the pace of evolution is extremely irregular. A first kind of discontinuity is provoked by the two World Wars: they define the subperiods shown in the first table. But each subperiod contains contrasting movements. The last turning point in the evolution takes place in 1974-1975 with a jump in spending from 40.8 percent of GDP in 1974 to 45.3 percent in 1975, up to which time it had remained remarkably stable; between 1959 and 1974 it leveled out at a 40.2 percent plateau. The jump and the increase from 1974 to nowadays have been caused mainly by the slowdown in GDP growth on the one hand and the regular and sustained growth of social spending on the other.

The trend in fiscal resources goes in the same direction. The difference between fiscal resources and expenditure, which is different from the deficit since it excludes non-fiscal resources, fluctuates a lot.

This global tendency is highly heterogeneous. The share of central government has been diminishing for several decades: it amounts to less than half of public spending nowadays. This ratio is 17 percent for local governments and more than one-third for social security.

The growth of public social spending is a major contemporary phenomenon. It must be noted that in France, the social security system is separated from the central government budget. It is the largest part of social spending, which also includes social services financed directly by the central and local government budgets. More than 55 percent of public expenditures are now transfers, the major part of which consists of social transfers.[3] This is an ultra schematized view of a very complex phenomenon.

Another fact adds to this complexity. It is the non-independence between expenditure as a particular form of public intervention and the other forms of intervention: qualitative (regulation, market public sector, etcetera) and quantitative (action through resources and through monetary policy). Moreover, there are numerous instances of state intervention in a given sector taking changing forms, which makes it very hard to postulate that public spending may be studied independently from the other forms.

How to Explain? Four Available Approaches

Contributions on this question are numerous. It is natural in a first step to assess to what extent they help in explaining the evolution of public expenditure. The diversity of the proposed explanations parallels that of the main approaches or paradigms in economics. There exist some common points between all these approaches that lead to the fact that no thesis can be adopted as such as a satisfactory explanation. Let us be explicit.

Two postures may be distinguished. The first is essentially quantitative. It is based on establishing time series data for a single country or cross-section for several countries. It leads to a search for a confirmation of laws of evolution or to hypothesis testing. It is what we call the determinant approach.[4]

The second attitude is more deductive. It focuses on the theoretical specification and, precisely, on the theoretical conception of the state. The reasoning in this case is based on an explicit assumption of state behavior. But the options found within this approach are very diverse. Firstly, the student of state behavior may make an analogy to market categories and equilibrium and properties of optimality. The basis of the analogy is in traditional microeconomic theory—that of methodological individualism applied to political choices. It is illustrated nowadays by the Public Choice school. We call it the individualistic approach.[5] Secondly, the student may treat state behavior in a completely opposite way through specificity and rejecting the market analogy. Emphasis is then placed on a general notion of coercive power, as advanced through various theses such as an exogenous and arbitrating state or an explicit form of power over society (bureaucracy, technostructure, corporate state).[6] We call it the constraint approach.[7]

A special case is finally that of Marxist theories of the state. They all reduce to a conception of constraint, but with considerable differences. They range from a purely instrumental state manipulated by the capitalist class as represented by monopolistic or giant firms in the modern stage of capitalism, according to the view of state monopoly capitalism (SMC), on the one hand, to conceptions stemming from structuralism, on the other hand, which focus on the state's relative autonomy from the economic infrastructure.[8]

Only some of the explanations advanced by these four main approaches are schematized in Table 3. Are they satisfactory? We examine this question in the following parts of this article. We have tested some major determinant approaches for the French case. An example of the differential productivity approach is summarized in a technical appendix to this article available from the author.[9] It is difficult to answer the question directly. We are made uneasy by the very presence of numerous parallel contributions, dealing either with partial and local features (hospitalization spending, local government services, education costs in a given sector) or else belonging to global approaches, without any possibility of relating one contribution to another or of reaching a coherent overall vision other than by extrapolation and the researcher's own subjective feeling. A very deep difficulty arises at this stage.

A Special Difficulty: The One-Sidedness of the Existing Approaches

This difficulty is special insofar as it seems not to be commonly found to this degree in other areas of economics. It thus challenges one's very research attitude and is not merely a simple choice between assumptions to be tested or theses for interpretation. It may be called one-sidedness. It has three forms.

One-sidedness in the Research Object

The available approaches reveal a kind of general incapacity to account for the set of evolving interdependences through which the state is an economic actor. The word "interdependence" relates to numerous elements

Table 3.

Approaches	Examples	Explanatory Principle of Public Expenditure Growth	State Behavior
Determinant Models	Wagner's law Public goods as superior goods Fiscal barrier Displacement effect Productivity differential	Relation to industrialization Analogy to consumption theory Financing constraint Financing constraint and growth through a threshold effect Growing absorption of resources in sector with lagging productivity	No explicit theoretical conception
Individualistic Approach	Collective goods theory Public Choice	Market failure or no market due to the very high exclusion costs	Voluntary exchange The state as a benevolent device
		Institutional asymmetry, various biases (voting system, logrolling, etc.) Fiscal illusion Bureaucracy Property rights Politico-economic interactions	Political market Analogy to the market Pathological state, as a market degradation
Constraint	Exogenous state The industrial state, the corporate state	Arbitrating state State decisions oriented according to the interest of particular groups (ruling class, technostructure, etc.)	The state as a center of power radically different from the market Either benevolent state (public interest) or partisan state (particular and vested interests)
Marxist Approach	SMC (state monopoly capitalism)	Tendency of capitalism toward over accumulation, depressing the profit rate, with counteraction by the government through expenditure	Instrumental state

belonging to various fields (functions) appearing with different forms (ranging from the direct supply of services to transfers), being thus differentiated and at the same time being part of a whole, the state.[10] They are heterogeneous elements but are interrelated through their very belonging to a coherent set. What are these interrelations between the parts and the whole? How can we characterize this unity and differentiation? These relations are likely to evolve and change in the medium term and in the long run. The way they move may obey some regularities or laws of evolution, but also discontinuities, appearing as irregularities and singularities. Moreover, as was noted earlier, other forms than the quantitative exist. Their relations to the quantitative ones are unknown, and they are also likely to be unstable in the long run.

One-sidedness in the Method

The subject of our research may look strange according to common economic reasoning. It deals with an immense phenomenon, considered in the long run, highly heterogeneous and taking on irregularities and singularities. Notwithstanding these features, should it be reduced to *i*—its local dimensions (centered on given sectors, ignoring interdependences and the instability of the relation between categories in the medium term), *ii*—its logical contents (centered on the search for repetitive regularities, postulating given types of behavior, neglecting the historical dimension and singularities), or *iii*—its quantitative aspect (centered on public expenditure alone, independently of the other public intervention forms as substitute or complement to expenditure)?

It consequently does not seem exaggerated to emphasize a common feature of the available approaches. It is the often non-explicit choice according to which each method gives a priority to one term of three pairs of contrasting notions, respectively analytical-synthetic, logical-historical, and quantitative-qualitative. These couples contain notions usually considered as mutually exclusive in economics. It may not be troublesome in some cases but we have progressively discovered in the course of our research that these one-sided starting positions are a major obstacle here.

Analytical-Synthetic. The analytical standpoint aims at knowledge of reality through the study of parts of it. The synthetic view starts from the whole. These thought processes are maintained in opposition.

The explanations obtained with the analytical method do not much complement one another. Dividing reality and examining its fractioned parts is no doubt a necessary phase. But it is not enough here. One can hardly avoid putting them together in order to understand their articulation. On the other hand the synthetic approach gives a priority to the whole, thus erasing the unevenness of the parts and basing itself on a unified principle of explanation.

But, just as one may wonder whether it is possible to stay limited to an analysis of the parts without studying how they are related in a set going beyond each of them, is it possible to remain confined to an overall view—a holistic view—and neglect the parts or see them through a unique but reducing principle because it is imposed *a priori* on a subject of which every part is problematic? Our answer is negative.

What is needed is thus a conceptualization of the interlocking of the local and global dimensions and of the way they operate as a coherent totality. Neither a sum of partial analyses nor a unilateral global approach can satisfy this imperative. What is at stake is the articulation itself between the parts and the whole.

Logical-Historical. The conception according to which evolution boils down to discontinuities is as excessive as would be confining it to regularities, setting aside irregularities. The difficulty arises from their very unpredictability and uniqueness—in short from their historical nature. According to a still tenacious conception, science should be limited to repeatable events, having logic and some kind of universality. In this view the logical dimensions only would be explanatory. The latter would be incidental and descriptive.

Quantitative-Qualitative. Here too, one of these notions is still often considered as scientific, in the name of its quantitative dimension. Should we ignore what we cannot measure or what we do not know how to measure? The market analogy, where measurement is the least difficult, is dangerous if it leads to rejection of the qualitative features, all the more as they are frequent and important in our subject. Most studies confined to public expenditure data rely finally on this type of assumption by positing an independence between the various forms of public intervention. It is at best a working hypothesis. As such it must be justified on the basis of empirical evidence at some point in the demonstration. This requirement is even clearer for long-run series. Otherwise breaking points will be analyzed as mere quantitative facts when there may also be qualitative discontinuities through which numerical evolutions take on different meanings. These points are summarized in Table 4.

Two groups of paradigms may be distinguished, using as a criterion their dominating orientation with respect to the six notions. Thus dimensions (A,L,QT) appear six times out of six for the first two lines taken together, when (S,H,QL) appear twice out of six possibilities for the

Table 4. One-Sidedness in the Method

	Analytical (A)/ Synthetic (S)	Logical (L)/ Historical (H)	Quantitative (QT)/ Qualitative (QL)	Dominating Triplet
Determinants	A,S	L	QT	A,L,QT
Individualism	A	L	QT,QL	
Constraint	S	H,L	QL	S,H,QL
Marxism (SMC)	S	H,L	QL,QT	

same lines. The opposite occurs for the last two lines: (S,H,QL) appear six times out of six, against three times for (A,L,QT).

One-Sidedness in the Conception of the State

We obviously need a theoretical conception of the state. Otherwise how could we explain and understand the state's role in a general way? It does not mean that every question pertaining to public economics requires an explicit statement on it to the same degree appearing here. For current policy decisions, for small problems such as deciding on the optimal number of tollbooths on a given section of highway, an explicit theoretical conception of the state does not seem fundamental. It is not the same here.

Yet this question creates a specific problem in economics. With the exception of the Marxist approach, we are faced with an option. Either the state is viewed as a way other than the market to deal with allocation problems, in which case the market analogy follows, or else the state is treated as outside the market, the domain of conflicts solved by means of the public action in a way radically irreducible to the market.

It must be admitted that the state could hardly be treated right away as an economic agent, as are the consumer or the producer in market theory. For them there exists a clear and tight correspondence between their nature according to economic concepts and their reality as actors in economic life. They thus may be properly reduced to a single dimension. And the agreement between economists is by and large sufficient to allow them not to bother about the "role" of the consumer or of the producer. But the same is not true for the state, whose main characteristic lies in its multiple economic facets, as an economic actor within the existing legal framework and at the same time as exerting its capacity to modify the framework. These many facets of the state render it very difficult to reduce its behavior to a unique dimension.

As to the Marxist approach, a distinction must be made between doctrine and method. The application of the Marxist doctrine to public spending ends in viewing the concrete through pre-established and often fixed categories.

They become fixed abstractions used as reading devices when the very movement of the concrete may make them less and less relevant. That is what K. Kosik has described as the logic of abstract principle, which leads directly to dogmatism.[11] But is should be emphasized that there is no fatal dogmatism in the method illustrated by Marxian works. It is that of the search for an adaptation between the abstract and the concrete—what is called investigation-exposition—as distinct steps in the same knowledge process. The first step aims at the discovery of the common nature of singular facts, leading to some kind of abstraction. The second step consists of a return to the concrete on the basis of the abstractions previously achieved. Investigation is prior. On the whole it is an inductive-deductive method on a moving object, considered in a time dimension. It thus may be fruitful here. It is important not to confuse this particular method with other dogmatic drifts.[12]

The question raised about one-sided conceptions of the state is not minor. Since no multilateral conception readily applicable to public interventions seems available, we are left with a rather limited choice. It is a choice between alternatives that all exclude some features for which there exists no demonstration of their unimportance and of the possibility of rejecting them. Thus an arbitrary element is present in this conventional procedure.

At this stage it must be noted that there seems to exist no theory or study we could rely on to answer the questions previously asked. A common feature of the economic study of the state is the exclusive and one-sided character of the way the problem is dealt with. Dimensions whose irrelevance is not demonstrated are lacking. They are not the same from one method to another. Beyond their already mentioned limitations the available approaches offer no way to identify the possible presence of these dimensions and to assess their importance. The impression follows that the research object is something we cannot come to grips with.

We are at the heart of the problem. We are left with two alternatives. According to the first, the willingness to include these missing dimensions is irrelevant because it cannot be applied with the available methods to this question. Doing it would lead to mere description, little explanation, and to non-scientific or even non-economic research. This pretense should thus be abandoned. The status quo should be accepted.

A tension is thus created. It bears on the very legitimacy of the research object defined here. Why would it be illegitimate to hold to its nature of evolving interdependences? This second alternative leads us logically to examine carefully the reasons why the objections to what is suggested here would be right, thus inducing us to adhere to any one of the existing approaches. It leads in the end to the examination of their criteria for methodological validity.

What to Do? The Decision on the Method

We propose to assess the legitimacy of the research object on the basis of a comparison to the validity criteria of the individualistic and Marxist paradigms, whose claim to explaining and interpreting is the most active.

The Need for a Methodological Decision

Combined Instrumentalism and Conventionalism in the Individualistic Approach. The individualistic approach belongs to logical empiricism. This philosophy is based on three postulates: the conception of a methodological unity of science; the reference to natural sciences, manly physics, as a norm for the evaluation of the scientific level in other sciences, among which are social sciences; and deductive causality.

The hypothetico-deductive method proper to methodological individualism gives priority to the predictive contents of the results. The realism of assumptions is secondary or even not useful. The validity criterion bears on the results. The criticism directed at the unrealism of assumptions is indeed irrelevant. Instrumentalism is coherent. It contains in itself its own justification.

However, the instrumental method is never applied purely in economics. It is always accompanied by conventions, which, when they are permanently used, become a method: conventionalism.

Instances of usual conventions are the "as if" and "*ceteris paribus*" assumptions and the reference to a unique type of rational behavior. They guarantee that a theory will be "verified" in probabilistic terms and that it is always possible to reach a correspondence with reality. The neoclassical approach and especially the individualistic approach of the state tightly combine instrumentalism and conventionalism. Once again, let it be said that their coherence is unquestionable.

Any method must contain rules for the control of its validity. In the case of the individualistic approach, its very instrumentalism makes it capable of being applied as a computation rule and as a predictive tool to a lot of situations.[13] Its conventionalism renders the control of results innocuous. Its infallibility and its insensibility to refutation are its main weaknesses.

As for the Marxist approach let us recall the need to distinguish between the doctrine and the method. Within the latter, the abstract principle method ends in a doctrinal position, as in the SMC doctrine. On the other hand there is no such fatality in the investigation-exposition method.

A Common Feature: Insularity and Monism. These terms describe complex real situations through a conception based on a simple explanatory principle. The economic continent is viewed from the individualistic or from the Marxist islands. And there exist devices that protect the insular thinkers against the attacks on their positions, namely combined instrumentalism and conventionalism on the one hand, and the long-run tendencies ("à la longue," "en dernière instances") on the other.

The Public Choice approach extrapolates from a local starting point and extends to the whole. The SMC theory starts from a global standpoint and extrapolates from the whole to the parts, by reduction. Although there is no *a priori* reason to deny the possible relevance of these theories to some parts of reality, they give no clue as to their fields of validity. And an eclectic position here, combining various positive aspects, including also those of the determinant and constraint theories, would have a very strange methodological status!

The validity criteria of these approaches are thus not convincing. We are faced with a methodological problem that must be solved before we can find testable hypotheses.

Our refusal to become prisoner of a preestablished one-sided causality principle does not mean falling back to a pure description that, attempting to account for all events, would lack a guiding line for explanation. We are led to reflect on the way to reach a method adapted to the problem brought up here.

The Decision on the Method

The decision on method arises from the recognition that there exists no ultimate logical criterion demonstrating the superiority of one paradigm over others. It is consequently not compulsory to lock oneself up in one of them. But it is necessary to follow a method based on criteria rendered explicit.

In the face of the complexity of the present research object it seems proper not to exclude *a priori* any one of its main constitutive dimensions. A method must be found of avoiding one-sided views and of allowing consideration of the respective weights of these dimensions as results to establish in the research and not as truths taken for granted.

There thus exists a general and strong enough reason for studying this problem by way of a demarcation from the existing paradigms through a decision on method. It does not aim at solving a general question of "truth" at an epistemological level. It is pragmatic and applies only to the question raised in this article. Its criteria are thus related to reducing the arbitrariness of the existing approaches in order to reach a better adjustment to the research object. It leads to two sets of propositions, one of basic statements defining the method and one a general working hypothesis.

The Primacy of the Research Object. What is written above suggests that the problem may be summarized right away as a decision on which priority to attribute to one of the terms of the pair method-object. These terms are interrelated. Facts are not independent from theories. The existing paradigms are instances of the priority given the method. Taking the method as given, in a field in which there remain such large uncertainties, leads us to view real situations through preestablished categories and concepts, in a previously fixed language, which guarantees that we will obtain results or a confirmation. The absence or innocuousness of refutation and of experiment end in a circular process without any external controlling device.

The approach proposed here gives a priority to the research object. Adapting the method to the object is a starting point in apprehending questions excluded by the existing theories. Once again, method and object are not separate. Facts do not exist independently of a theoretical idea. Some degree of arbitrariness in the object cannot be avoided at the start. It must be diminished in the progressive adjustment of the object in the process of research. In our case, observation shows that the initial research object, public spending, is one form of public intervention and is related to other forms. Explaining expenditures thus require one to analyze it together with the other forms in order to identify and explain the moving border between them. To the author's knowledge no theory is readily available that would give the solution to this problem. Existing theories solve it in their own way by postulating this relation as given. It is manifestly untenable in the medium term and in the long run. Through its very permanence, this simple working assumption becomes an ad hoc hypothesis in a traditional conventionalism. The decision to reject this type of convention in auxiliary assumptions leads to submitting oneself to a strict discipline with respect to the research object.

The choice made here follows from the answer on the manner of augmenting the empirical bearing and diminishing the arbitrariness of the analysis, in comparison to the existing approaches. The answer is in the progressive construction of the object. It covers expenditure as such and its relation to other forms of public intervention. And the adaptation of the method rests on the recognition of the two major aspects: interdependences and their dynamic nature.

Instead of having an object adapted to a given method we end with a method adapted to a constructed object. Consequently the primacy of the object does not mean that the method is secondary or without importance. It simply means that no object is *a priori* illegitimate as soon as it is admitted that there is no overwhelming unitary model of science, which would select the "good" and the "bad" research objects.

The Methodological Rules Governing Statements. The methodological control bears on statements, be they on the explanatory procedure or on the results. It obviously must respect rules of coherence and objectivity. The experiment is their usual complement and most often the selecting device in empirical science. But it is practically ruled out in our domain. Observation alone remains. And it is known that in social science, more than in other fields, eliminating subjectivity is an impossible task. It must be admitted that it is inevitable. K. Popper has strongly emphasized the idea that scientific objectivity does not depend on the scientist's own objectivity but on the critical tradition within a discipline.[14] It opposes to T. Kuhn's normal science a kind of shared subjectivity in a system of rigidification. The Popperian notion of a reviewable and temporary inter-subjectivity is undoubtedly a utopia for a great part, but it is a mobilizing utopia. To admit the inescapable presence of subjectivity, to make it as explicit as possible and to try to minimize it, is the only way to avoid dogmatism in our field, in which, it must be repeated, experiment is out of hand and cannot help in the selection of acceptable theories.

A General Working Hypothesis: The State as an Evolving Relation. We tackle the theoretical conception of the state on a methodological level, as a relation in movement; we formulate the problem upstream, previous to the testable theories. The state is that through which public interventions take place. These reflect the relations between the state and the sectors to which they are directed. The notion of dynamic interdependences is a given substantive content here. It is that of the study of the evolution of public spending under the angle of the relation between the state and the main fields of intervention.

This assumption does not mean at all that we would put aside a theoretical conception of the state. It is only one step in a process of adapting the method to the object. The theoretical conception of the state is to be established in a subsequent phase.

Our assumption has two major consequences. The first leads to an inductive phase by way of a systematic study, for the entire period, of public interventions in major economic and social fields of activity: industry, agriculture, work force and social questions, education, and money and finance, together with the traditional fields of general administration and defense.

Secondly, study of these relations is required on the basis of three questions in the following order: (1) Why the public nature of intervention and not a private form, either individual or collective? (2) Next, once an answer to question 1 is established, why the expenditure nature of the intervention and not a qualitative form or a quantitative one other than spending? (3) Next, once question 2 is answered, what are the causes of the evolution of public expenditure for each function? We are thus led to study much more than mere public spending. This conception, and its difference from that of the existing approaches, is schematized in Figure 1.

In other words, we exclude any approach starting with a prior theory of the state. The reason comes from the complexity of the subject and the uncertainty following from it in our present state of knowledge. Either there exist analyses focusing on parts, on such and such category of expenditure, or else there are global theses. In the former case the manner according to which these parts make a whole remains unknown. In the latter case, the way the whole is differentiated into parts is also unknown. It is the articulation itself that is central to the problem studied here. An adjusted method must respect this many-sided nature of the object. The question of the conception of the state, which none can escape, is carried upstream, on methodology. Discovering the relative importance of the dimensions usually excluded by turns through one-sidedness is the first task, before one attempts to reach a theorization. It is thus by no means a study "without any theory." On the contrary, the theoretical step is part of the process. But this set of general statements and properties to be discovered is not fixed once and for all, which would give it the character of an abstract principle likely to exist as such autonomous from real situations. It stems from a process of reciprocal adaptation between the method and the object, between the abstract and the concrete. If the concrete, on which the object is always dependent in the end, is characterized by movement, by evolutionary phenomena, then the abstraction or theorization can be only temporarily established. The adaptation process is open. It is never ended. This is the reason for the dotted arrow at the bottom of Figure 1. That is not merely the condition of the desired correspondence with reality. It is also the main condition to prevent temporarily established results from becoming eternal and universal truths, that is, to avoid dogmatic drifts.

The Agenda: The Role of the State in the End

The previous portions of this article showed abundantly that public spending cannot be studied independently from its context, that is, the set of public interventions in the economic field in their various forms. For

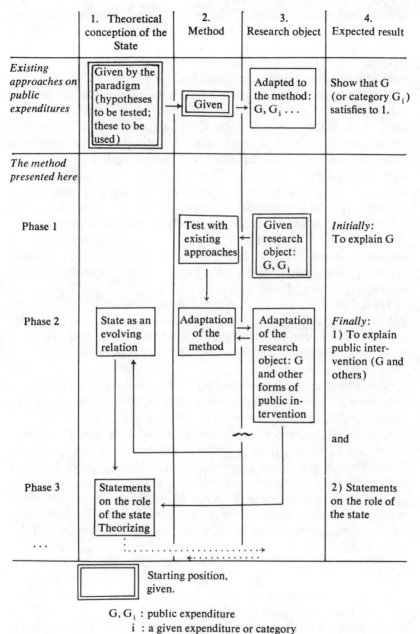

Figure 1.

it is the only way to apprehend the possible substitutability-complementarity relations with the spending form. No existing theory can give an answer on this. It is consequently necessary to systematically investigate this field without any exclusive assumptions other than working assumptions to which the research must return later.

Hence it begins with a systematic description of the relations between the state and the economy. It strives to discover meaningful configurations, to show how they stay stable or change and finally to characterize determinations. Instead of having a pre-established logic to which one gives afterwards a substance, which will be nothing but a concordance with the initial theory, we start here with a content, with problematic situations, and search afterwards for the possible underlying logic. But in this latter case, arrival at logic is not guaranteed. The aim is not to find determinations at any price, even artificially, in cases where there are indeterminacies. The method advocated here makes it possible to identify areas of indeterminacy. It leads us to consider indeterminacy as legitimate and as an integral part of the analysis. The goal is thus to reach statements on determinations and indeterminacy.

These statements are on an object modified from what it was initially. Public expenditure is considered in its appropriate or adjusted field, the one required for answers to the questions arising previously to the analysis of the expenditure itself: Why the public form? Why the expenditure form?

We are thus led to a systematic study of the genesis of public interventions in the economy in France in their unity and their diversity and their coherence-differentiation, expressions that should be clear by now.

What are the sources of public interventions? How and why do they evolve? Do they result from determinisms? What is the state capacity to initiate change? What are the constraints on it? What place do economic phenomena have in determinisms? What are the consequences for the present day economic policy? What remains of the unremitting daily economic policy activity when it is viewed from the medium-term observation post? It is indeed the economic role of the state that is at stake.

Results

The results are in the answers to the questions raised above and follow from the three steps presented in Figure 1 and from the agenda. It is clearly impossible to present a demonstration here, and we must stay limited to the general results. They are: the very possibility of the method, the determinations, the role of the state, and its theoretical bearing.

The Possibility of the Method

The very unfolding of the method presented above as it is put into practice is in itself a result. It shows that despite the immensity of the subject, it is possible to apprehend it from a progressively adjusted angle, in a way not arbitrary or erratic but following explicitly defined criteria.

It has led to the systematic elaboration of quantitative and qualitative data on the relation between the state and the economy for six large sectors: industry, agriculture, education, money, the workforce (social security, employment, housing), and the relation between central and local governments. Establishing homogeneous categories based on proper periodizations and specific logics of evolution has revealed the need to modify the initial expenditure functions. They are finally disaggregated into twelve fields (see Table 5). It has to be pointed out that our main concern is not with the state in itself nor with the history of economic policy. It is with the very relation between the state and the economy. And all forms of intervention are not scrutinized to the same degree. Thus the action through fiscal resources is a whole domain in itself. It is studied insofar as it influences public spending through a possible financing constraint. A total study of public intervention would be an immense task. We stay limited to what may be considered as enough to answer the questions raised above. It naturally leaves room for further extensions.

The Conception of Levels of Determination

The investigation has been based on expenditure first, then on the spending form and finally on the public form. The determinations are not the same though a hierarchy appears going down from the public form to expenditure. It gives a kind of cohesion to a set of determinations and indeterminacies divided into three levels.

The Public Form. Why the public form of intervention? To answer this question it is necessary to go back far beyond the beginning of the period (1870) for several domains (Table 5). The answers reveal the importance of three permanent phenomena. We call them the internal state, the external state, and economic evolution.

The first two can be associated with the fundamental feature of the territorial state: a principle of authority and organization. The state maintains this principle through the exercise of power over a population within a certain territory and conducts political as well as economic relations with other countries. State intervention is basically aimed at maintaining the state in the face of threats and tensions whose origins can be internal

Table 5.

Fields of State Intervention	Historical Origins	Source of Publicness
General administration	Birth of modern state Old regime	IS
Relations between central and local governments	Old regime	IS
Defense	d°	IS and ES
Money and financing	d°	IS, ES (wars), then EE
Debt	d°	d°
Transport infrastructure	d°	IS
Industry	Seventeenth and eighteenth centuries Mercantilism and protectionism	ES; EE
Agriculture	End of nineteenth century	IS, ES and EE
Education	Revolution: no consequences 1833: on local governments 1881: "nationalization" of primary education	IS. Then influence of EE
Labor force use conditions	1789 Revolution and 1st Empire	IS (public order). Then influence of EE
Housing and urbanism	Premises at the end of nineteenth century. Interwar and post W.W. II period	EE (industrialization, urbanization) and real estate right
Social security	Long period of gestation 1890 to 1928-1930: social insurance 1936: Popular Front 1945: Social security system	EE: effect of industrial workforce pressures and of the crisis of the thirties.

IS: Internal State
ES: External State
EE: Economic evolution.

(social unrest, political instability) or external (foreign relations, international economy). The third component includes industrialization and its consequences through the evolution of production, of the way of life, technical progress, urbanization, the growth of the wage-earning population, etcetera.

Several periods can be defined on the basis of a cohesion in the articulation between these three components. It leads us to characterize the relation between the state and the economy through configurations separated by periods of transition from one configuration to another.

The Expenditure Form. Three factors act as the origins of the expenditure nature of public interventions. The first one may be called the "legacy": it simply means that the expenditure form is given for several fields at the beginning of the period, in 1870. The second factor is the world wars. The third category is new. It is common to education and to social security. We call it the institutionalized compromise (IC).

The concept of IC is introduced to account for the articulation between the qualitative and the quantitative aspects in the two most important new public fields, education and social spending. We refer uniquely to the social security case.

As a compromise, social security is the result of profound tensions between socio-economic groups, extending over several decades. They result in institutions settling the nature of public intervention: expenditure through transfers to people when it could have been a direct provision of services through a nationalized service, as is the case in the United Kingdom. Later social groups adjust their strategies to this system. It rigidifies because any endeavor to modify it also attempts to modify a category of vested interests and is likely to fail. The institution has thus remained almost untouched. It acts as a permissive framework. It was well adapted to a rapidly growing economy, but the current slowdown has accelerated its financial crisis. With a growing demand on social services the only way left to the government has been to raise taxes. It appears as if only an enormous crisis, such as that which occurred in the past, notably the Second World War, could release so blocked a situation. The tension is financial. If no rapid and durable recovery occurs in the near future, it will intensify. Being an IC over a basic issue settled on a nationwide basis, it generates a kind of inertia against reforms.

The Evolution of Expenditures. We finally get to the purely quantitative aspect. Each domain requires specific analysis. It is obviously beyond the reach of this article. A global financing constraint played a role until the Second World War, but since this period its influence has diminished and greatly changed.

Among the supply-side growth factors, we find wages, technical conditions, a relative price effect and the institutional framework (regulations, administrative norms). Among the demand side variables are behavioral variables (health, education), demographic changes, urbanization, and economic variables (level of employment, subsidies to business and to agriculture).

In the medium-term range, the IC's shape to a large extent demand and supply for education and social security.

Three Levels of Determination. Many causal influences are present. There does not appear to be any simple determinism or unique causality for any of the fields of state intervention.

The answer to a question on the evolution of spending in the public health sector or in education, for instance, must assume that it is known why the public intervention in these fields is in the expenditure form, as direct supply or through transfers, rather than in another form. In turn, the explanation at this level must assume that the causes for public intervention are known at a higher level. In the upward direction, from level III to level I the permissive condition for a given level is the level immediately superior to it, as schematized below.

$$
\begin{array}{ll}
\text{Level I} & : \text{ public form} \\
\text{Level II} & : \text{ expenditure form} \\
\text{Level III} & : \text{ expenditure evolution}
\end{array}
$$

But it does not mean that there exists an overall determination from level I to level III. In the downward direction, there is no automatic passage from I to II, I to III, or II to III. There is no direct determination between, for instance, tensions in the labor force (level I) and the form of the IC resulting from them (level II), or between this latter one and the growth of expenditure (level III). In the same way ,the level of industrialization achieved in 1914 is not the direct cause for the war, but it is the condition that permitted an unprecedented amount of resources to be absorbed in the conflict. Hence there is an indeterminacy in the downward direction. The only exceptions are the "legacy" because of its very nature (public form and expenditure form as given in 1870 for several fields) and the two world wars. They are summarized in Table 6.

There thus exists no strict causality. The general influence of economic development or industrialization follows quite diversified and partially indeterminate ways. The sources of the dynamics of public expenditure are better explained through three levels of determination according to the conception developed here.

Table 6.

Determinations	Levels of Determination		
	I	*II*	*III*
Internal state	*		
External state	*		
Economic evolution	*		
Configurations of the relation between the state and the economy	*		
Legacy	*	*	
World wars	*	*	*
Institutionalized compromises		*	
Sources of the quantitative evolution of expenditures			*
. . .			

The Role of the State:
From the Circumscribed State to the Inserted State

A first way to identify state behavior follows from the determinations. The second is in the configurations of the relation between the state and the economy.

The Importance of Tensions and Institutions. The Overestimation of the State Capacity to Initiate. Our study shows a repetitive presence of tensions at the origins of the dynamics of public intervention. Every tension arises from the confrontation between forces pushing toward change and movement and counterforces resisting the movement. Tensions are not limited to economic crises. They are also social and political.

Public institutions, the IC in its modern form, are crystallized expressions of the tensions through which they originated. Not every tension ends in a new institution. One must distinguish between current tensions and major or structural ones, the solution of which cannot be implemented within the existing institutional framework. Being a transcription of a large tension, the new institution results in obligations and rights adapted to the context of the period in which it is created. Economic and social groups then adjust their strategies to it. It acquires a kind of very strong rigidity. The last major tension came to an end in the Liberation period (1944 to 1947). It enabled several reforms, notably in social security.

A paradox arises here. The absence of a strict economic determinism
and the role of tensions should logically leave room for an extended initiating capacity of the state. The stereotype of an interventionistic and
initiating French state is well known. It is misleading. The major medium-
term changes in public interventions are not a result of state initiatives.
There are three exceptions to this: the Second Empire, the case of primary
education in the 1880s, and the Liberation period. Major changes resulted
from large tensions that developed autonomously from state control. It is
a model of discontinuous evolution that imposes itself to the observer,
in which there are relatively stable periods separated by major phases
of change, public intervention most often simply accompanying them.

To summarize, state behavior is constrained but it is not instrumental.
The state is the place toward which tensions converge and through which
arrangements are institutionalized. It is a more complicated role than is
portrayed by the usual views. And the state-economy relation follows less
from a notion of causality than from configurations that must be explained
now.

The State and the Economy: The Configurations. We have progressed
to four basic propositions: (1) From their origins the state and the economy have been in a relation as exemplified in Table 5. (2) This relation
follows ultimately from three basic dimensions: internal state, external
state, and economic evolution. (3) These dimensions are interdependent.
It is possible to characterize their articulation according to the dominating
features giving it a cohesion over some period. (4) This relation is evolutionary. There are two types of periods: periods of stability in a given
configuration and periods of rupture of the cohesion and of transition to
a new configuration.

It can be summarized as a long sequence with three dominating configurations from the old regime to nowadays. *First configuration*: The
economy is mainly submissive to the state (old regime). Transition:
Eighteenth century, revolution, and first half of the nineteenth century.
Second configuration: Circumscribed State (from the mid-nineteenth century to the First World War). Transition: interwar period. *Present configuration*: Inserted State (since the Second World War). We naturally
emphasize the last configuration. It is easier to present it by first compar-
ing it to its preceding configuration (see Table 7).

The main features of the circumscribed state configuration lie in the
submission to the business cycle and to a monetary and financial constraint for the state, and in the implementation of a new system of rights
permissive to the development of the wage relation, implying state intervention in defense of the public order—not as a recognition of the specific

Table 7.

Configurations	Circumscribed State (Nineteenth century, until the 1st World War)	Transition	Inserted State (Since Second World War)
Internal state	Public order	Massification of economic and social problems. Birth of the social policy as distinct from the public order.	Growth of social policy. Growth of the indirect wage (social IC).
External state	Obedience to the monetary rule symbolized by the gold standard	Influences of the two world wars. International monetary crisis	Definitive forced currency. Public management of money, monetary constraint transferred to the Central Bank.
Economic evolution	Heterogeneous industrialization. Small farm production. Business cycle. Prices and wages dependent on the level of economic activity	Great Depression	Intensive accumulation centered on mass consumption. Loosening of the relation between prices, wages and the activity level.[15]

nature of social conflicts. The state is thus delimited with respect to so-called free economic activity. But it is controlling a lot of activities, it is protecting industry and agriculture, and it is an important and profitable opportunity for banks and savings because of its permanent indebtedness in a period of price stability. The state is thus far from being "non interventionistic." It is simply circumscribed.

World War I is the first modern instance of the massification of social life through the war economy and the huge scale of destruction permitted by the newly reached level of industrialization. A long process develops under pressure from the industrial wage-earning population to diminish social insecurity. It is reinforced after World War II and ends with the social security system.

In the new situation, domestic accumulation prevails, and money becomes dependent on it to a large extent. The monetary constraint no longer acts as a kind of universal rule on the banking system. It is borne by the central banks as the lender of last resort. It is coherent with the birth and the growth of the social wage, which implies a sufficiently regular growth of national income and hence a monetary management accompanying accumulation. In a country such as France, whose money is not an international currency, there exists an international monetary constraint. The United States is in a particular position with respect to this problem, once the international monetary nature of the dollar is recognized, since U.S. debts may be paid in dollars. For other countries it boils down to a foreign exchange constraint. It is not possible to go further on this point here. It does not look unreasonable, however, to point out the kind of complementarity between this type of social policy and this type of monetary policy.[16]

What is essential for our purpose is that these two phenomena are the main changes on the basis of which the state-economy configuration has itself changed and led to growth in the genuine economic and social responsibilities of the state—what we propose to call an insertion of the state. Whereas the amount of social allowances accounted for about 1 percent of total household disposable income in 1913 and 5 percent in 1938, it was more than 19 percent in 1960, 26.3 percent in 1970, and 34.5 percent in 1980.

Toward a Theory of State Insertion

A theory is a body of propositions derived as consequences of explicit antecedents, thus distinguished from mere practice and common knowledge and having some kind of general bearing. In a usual formal model the path from premises to conclusion follows from a linear chain of causal deductions. The reasoning developed here is many-sided. The antecedents are in the statements on the method. The aim is in the process itself and in statements that are abstract-concrete. The very movement of the concrete renders them temporarily satisfactory.

The theorizing (phase three, see Figure 1) is built on three main bases: the many-sidedness of the method, three levels of determinations, and configurations of the state-economy relation. The state-economy relation is conceptualized through the notion of configuration. This concept depicts the coherence in the articulation between fundamental elements.

The state-economy relation contains an unvarying component and contingent aspects. The permanent component is the presence of the three already analyzed dimensions, namely the internal state, the external state, and economic evolution. But the way they are interrelated is contingent, first, on time. The historical evolution shows alternative phases between those dominated by a given kind of coherence and those of transition in which the preceding coherence vanishes and is replaced by a new one, after some period of time that may be long. It is also contingent on space. It is in the essence of the territorial state to be defined in a given space. On the other hand, the economy, the law of the market, is a universalizing principle. The space of trade has always been global in the sense that it has always pierced through the territorial state boundaries. There is thus a permanent tension in the pair state-economy. But it is solved or managed very differently, between the polar situations in which the state would be entirely dominated by the market at one extreme or the converse at the other extreme. Every country solves it in its own way somewhere in the interval. The United States is certainly less far than France from the first limit. There thus exists an inescapable territorial nature of this relation. As it certainly varies from one country to another it is spatially contingent.

Its present form is the inserted state. The coherence it embodies is nowadays subjected to a heavy tension. This coherence relied on the permissive condition of sustained economic growth, beyond the already mentioned features of the intrinsically national nature of social policy and of monetary policy. The national and international slowdown of economic growth, added to the increasing dependence on world economic conditions (as measured by the growth of international trade relative to GDP), provoke a tension in the articulation of the three fundamental components in France. Until this last decade the tradition of a "virtuous growth circle" had settled. It was based on rapid growth associated with average inflation and periodic devaluations. Present day tensions are perceived through a financial crisis in the social security system in general. It is commonly referred to as "the crisis of the Welfare State." But unless one views it as the main or even as the sole cause of the present economic crisis, our analysis suggests that a set of interdependences is at stake. As a working assumption our conception would suggest that the very type of coherence intrinsic to the inserted state is subject to huge tensions: the one referred to as "the crisis of the Welfare State" as well as others. The notion of a crisis of the inserted state may better depict this situation. If the many-sided nature of the crisis is admitted then it would seem illogical not to analyze it by means of concepts accounting for this feature. A thorough-going theory of state insertion is needed at this point.

According to the conception reached here, if the logic of public intervention varies in time and in space, then there is room for a systematic study of the similarities and differences between countries in the present time. It would allow one to assess the possible degree of generality of a phenomena studied for a single country. It would also help in understand-

ing why there seems to be a high capacity of inflection of economic policies in some countries while the margins for maneuver seem to be very
narrow in other countries, especially in the present context of economic
crisis.

Conclusions

Most of the results, except for the methodological aspect, have been
presented without detailing the demonstration phases leading to them.
And the approach and the concepts are unusual. The results may thus
look somewhat disconcerting at first. But detailing the argumentation
more was impossible here. What can be said is simply that it is fully developed in the study inspiring this article.

It appeared very important to point out the need for a many-sided approach. If our view is considered acceptable, then is it logical to (1) go
on considering the state and the market as contradicting notions (with
the idea that once upon a time there was a market independent from the
state, that it was a sort of golden age and that a kind of reversibility of
history would permit us to go back to it); (2) go on considering that social
policy opposes to economic activity when they may be complementary;
(3) go on considering that public intervention is automatically in the
spending form? Is it also logical, then, to praise a sort of naive voluntarism for state intervention (in the neglect of constraints and of the weight
of long-run and medium-term tendencies that may oppose to short-run
policies) and to act as if the same model of the making of state intervention and of economic policy could be applied to all countries in the face
of a given problem?

Finally we hope to have shown, or at least to have suggested, that the
economic "role of the state" is a legitimate object of research. It is possible to come to grips with it. And considering the major uncertainties
developing nowadays its study may already be an urgent task.

Notes

1. This article is based on the results of several years of research in collaboration with Christine André, recently published in France: R. Delorme
   and C. André, *L'Etat et l'éonomie* (*The State and the Economy*) (Paris:
   Ed. du Seuil, 1983). This article is not a summary of this book. Only
   some of its results are presented here, together with an extended analysis
   of several aspects.
2. Gross domestic production differs from gross domestic product in that
   it excludes several services, mainly those rendered by administrations. A

long-run series of it was computed by J. J. Carré, P. Dubois, and E. Malinvaud, *La Croissance française* (Paris: Ed. du Seuil, 1970).

3. Tax expenditure is not included.

4. Instances of it are: A. T. Peacock and J. Wiseman, *The Growth of Public Expenditure in the United Kingdom* (London: George Allen and Unwin, 1967); S. P. Gupta, "Public Expenditure and Economic Growth: A Time Series Analysis," *Public Finance* 22 (1967): 423-61. See also R. M. Bird, *The Growth of Government Spending in Canada* (Canadian Tax Foundation, 1970).

5. See D. C. Mueller, *Public Choice* (Cambridge: Cambridge University Press, 1979).

6. In the sense that the state is a body acting in the name of a non-explicit kind of general interest and imposes solutions from outside the economic system.

7. Instances of it are, apart from J. K. Galbraith's *The New Industrial State*, D. R. Fusfeld, "The Rise of the Corporate State in America," *Journal of Economic Issues* 6 (March 1972): 1-22; W. C. Peterson, "The Corporate State, Economic Performance, and Social Policy," *Journal of Economic Issues* 8 (June 1974): 483-518. It must be noted that the individualistic approach refers also to a form of constraint, coming for instance from the bureaucracy and from the politicians. But its conception of state behavior is quite different from that of the "constraint approach."

8. See "Le Capitalisme monopoliste d'Etat," *Traité Marxiste d'économie politique*, (Paris: Ed. Sociales, 1971) for the SMC theory. Another Marxist presentation is S. de Brunhoff, *The State, Capital, and Economic Policy* (London: Pluto Press, 1978). See also R. Solo, "The Neo-Marxist Theory of the State," *Journal of Economic Issues* 12 (December 1978): 829-42.

9. Robert Delorme, CEPREMAP, 142, rue du Chevaleret, 75013, Paris, France.

10. There are numerous instances of this phenomenon. A given intervention may appear as spending when it is included in the budget. It may disappear from this category when it is transferred to a publicly controlled agency outside the state budget and belonging to the market sector. Public housing programs, highway construction, atomic energy, and telecommunications contain such instances. And the reverse also happens.

11. K. Kosik, *La Dialectique du concret* (Paris: Maspero, 1978), p. 40.

12. For a detailed analysis see Delorme and André, *L'Etat et l'économie*, especially chaps. 7 and 8.

13. K. Popper, *Conjectures and Refutations* (London: Routledge and Kegan Paul, 1974), p. 111.

14. K. Popper, "La Logique des sciences sociales (The Logic of Social Sciences)" in *La querelle allemande des sciences sociales*, ed. T. Adorno and K. Popper (Bruxelles: Ed. Complexe, 1979), p. 82 (translated from "Die Logik der Sozialwissenschaften," *Kölner Zeitschrift für Soziologie und Sozialpsychologie* [Köln und Opladen: Westedeutscher Verlag, 1962]), pp. 233-48.

15. The situation in which nominal prices and incomes are heavily affected

by fluctuations in production is also referred to as the "competitive" form of internal regulation, whereas the situation in which these variables are little affected by variations in production is designated as the "monopolistic" regulation. See M. Aglietta, *A Theory of Capitalist Regulation: The US Experience* (London: New Left Books, 1979); M. Aglietta, "World Capitalism in the Eeighties," *New Left Review* 36 (November-December 1982): 5-42; R. Boyer and J. Mistral, *Accumulation, Inflation, Crises* (Paris: PUF, 1983).

16. One of the first intuitions on this fundamental question is in J. R. Hicks, "Economic Foundations of Wage Policy," *The Economic Journal* 65 (September 1955): 389-404.

6

John R. Commons
and the Democratic State

John Dennis Chasse

John R. Commons supported his reformist activities with a conception of the state that remains largely unexamined. General surveys of his work have treated some aspects of it; a few authors have remarked on the similarity between his interests and those of the public choice theorists [Ostrom 1976, pp. 850,853; Rutherford 1983, pp. 735–36].[1] Others have stressed differences in methodology [Field 1979, pp. 53, 61; Atkinson 1983, pp. 1060–64]. No one, however, has shown how the different methods imply different conceptions of the state, nor has anyone isolated, for specific examination and appraisal, the conception that Commons developed, even though he devoted two of his earliest major works to the problems of the democratic state.

This article examines his conception of the state and suggests a preliminary appraisal. The examination and appraisal can be facilitated by a division of his conception into an evolutionary interaction of three related processes: first, a collective effort to control the use of violence as an incentive creates the state—a hierarchy of officials, each subject to some earthly authority; second, these officials control violence by enforcing rights and duties, necessarily "liberating and expanding" the powers of the citizen, and enforcing a particular distribution of liberty and property; third, an evolving public purpose determines the working rules that guide the officials, and hence the distribution of liberty and property. The first three sections of this article consider these three processes. A final section asks whether Commons made a contribution here, and concludes that, on this subject as on others, there are reasons to support his modest claim to having created a valid complement to standard economic analysis.

The Control of Violence

When he defined the state as the institution that controls violence, Commons appeared to be following a tradition that runs from Thomas Hobbes and David Hume to James Buchanan and Robert Nozick [Commons 1919, p. 38; 1934a, pp. 702–3; 1950, p. 74]. In accordance with that tradition, he found the root problem that the state must solve in the paradox of violence. Violence is necessary because the scarcity of resources engenders conflicts of interest which "Malthusian" men, biased by passion, tend to resolve by violence [Commons 1919, p. 38; 1934a, pp. 702–3]. But violence as an incentive is destructive because it strikes at the most fundamental of human desires, the desire for "security of expectations" [Commons 1934a, p. 703]. It breeds arrogance and capriciousness in the master and obsequiousness in the subject [Commons 1899–1900, p. 24]; it stunts innovation and creativity [Commons 1893, p. 73; 1899–1900, p. 42]. Persuasion, on the other hand, "educates the qualities of . . . eloquence, reasoning, politeness . . . devotion, love, heroism, ambition" [Commons 1899–1900, p. 25]. Violence, therefore, must be harnessed and made protective so that persuasion as an incentive may be encouraged. In this reasoning, focusing not on violence itself as an evil, but on its evil effects as an incentive, hints at a departure from tradition in this seemingly traditional conclusion.

Commons thought that traditional deductive methods falsified the relation between the customs of institutions and the habits of the "institutionalized personality" [Commons 1934a, p. 874]. He agreed that the only purpose for the state's activities must be the self-realization of the free person [Commons 1899–1900, p. 18; 1924, pp. 38,39; Gonce 1976, pp. 768–70]. But, following John Dewey, and later C.S. Peirce, he held that free rational behavior results largely from habits and that habits are learned largely from customs [Commons 1919, p. 38; 1934a, pp. 702–3; Harter 1965, p. 64; Dewey 1922, pp. 58–74]. Moreover, customs are constantly changing, making certain types of behavior unique to particular times and places [Commons 1934a, pp. 22, 74; Harter 1962, p. 232]. In his search for a structure that would control the threat of violence, Commons could not, therefore, deduce such a structure from a mental utopia like Buchanan's "methodological anarchy" or Nozick's "first position" [Buchanan 1975, pp. 2–6; Nozick 1974 pp. 150–53]. Such methods, by beginning with isolated rational and ethical individuals, leave out the institutions in which the individual becomes a reasonable and ethical person. His methodological convictions demanded that Commons look for a learning process in which "institutionalized personalities" and free institutions grow up together.

He defined two tasks that must be performed if the threat of violence is to be harnessed: first, the use of violence by one citizen against another must be controlled; second, violence against citizens by the officials of the state must be controlled. In British history, he found two processes corresponding to these two tasks.

In the first process, the state gradually deprives other institutions of the right to use violence, leaving to each a persuasive incentive appropriate to its nature and goals. For example, child labor, compulsory education, and child abuse laws deprive the family of the right to use undue violence against children, at the same time, leaving it the persuasive incentive of love. A similar process deprives the church of the right to use civil sanctions, while leaving it the powers of "preaching conversion and persuasion" [Commons 1899–1900, p. 74]. The firm is deprived of the right to use any incentive but the "love of work" or Adolph Wagner's love of activity [Commons 1899–1900, p. 86]. The state retains a monopoly on violence; this creates the second problem. How can the officials of the state be controlled so that they do not use this power in an arbitrary and capricious manner?

In the second process new groups force their way into the coalition controlling the state. Commons found this process continually repeated as England evolved from the despotism of William the Conqueror to the mass democracy of the late nineteenth century. First the nobles, then the townsmen, gained a voice in the decisions of the state. Commons specified three conditions for this process to work successfully. First, the group that gains a voice in the control of sovereignty must have organized voluntarily outside the structure of the state. This educates the group's members in the discipline needed to gain concessions from their collective strength and in the knowledge of governing to participate intelligently, once they have a voice in the affairs of the state [Commons 1899–1900, p. 50]. Second, there must be a shared set of values providing those in control some basis for considering as legitimate the demands of the interlopers and permitting cooperation with them once their demands have been met [Commons 1899–1900, p. 53]. Finally, the structure of government must change to accommodate the new groups. In England, for example, the legislative branch kept changing, with the addition first, of the House of Lords for the nobles, then of the House of Commons for the townsmen [Commons 1899–1900, p. 50].

The despotism ceases to be a perverse form, and the nation becomes a true state when all, even the highest, officials are made responsible to an earthly authority for their acts [Commons 1924, pp. 105–6]. But since new groups can always be formed, the process of controlling the power of the state never ends, and the democratic state at any time is never perfect. The state is "not an ideal superimposed on society, but is an accumulated series of compromises between social classes, each seeking to secure for itself control over the coercive elements which exist implicitly in society with the institution of private property" [Commons 1899–1900, p. 45]. This means that the power of violence is never perfectly controlled and can erupt at any time against groups that have not gained a voice in the control of the sovereign power. Commons, in his own time, was thinking of the working class when he wrote that "the state seems to be coercive because it does not represent all the people; . . . Many who are not truly anti-social are crushed by it" [Commons 1896, p. 228].

In his search for a way to reduce the violence unleashed against the working classes, Commons modified and changed many of his ideas, but he retained the fundamental vision outlined in *A Sociological View of Sovereignty* [Commons 1899–1900]. Thus, it is true, in a sense, that *A Sociological View of Sovereignty* contains in embryo much that Commons later wrote [Gonce 1976, p. 766; Rutherford 1983, p. 739]. But it is also true that a full understanding of his mature conception demands an exploration of the changes and modifications he made on the basis of his later studies and "experiments in collective action." The extent of the changes can be seen by examining how he abandoned or modified many of the positions he held when he wrote *Proportional Representation* [Commons 1896].

Commons felt that the government of his day failed to respond properly to working class needs because territorial representation favored bland candidates over real leaders [Commons 1896, pp. 29–31, 228; 1899, pp. 57–60; 1907, p. 358]. The candidate representing a territorial constituency is necessarily a compromise candidate with few enemies—a different sort of person from a leader chosen and trusted by the members of an identifiable interest group. The latter type of leader will more adequately represent the interests of his constituents because his own interests parallel theirs. The problem is that such a leader makes too many enemies to be elected by the heterogeneous population of a particular geographic area. To solve this problem, Commons first proposed electoral reform and an expanded role for the newly elected legislature. In *Proportional Representation*, he warned against judges usurping legislative functions and amassing power in an arrogant and dangerous manner [Commons 1896, pp. 6–8, 194], and he complained that the proliferation of commissions complicated the government and weakened the legislature [Commons 1896, pp. 4–5, 223–24]. At that time, he considered "log-rolling" an aberration to be replaced by statesmanlike compromise, with the advent of proportional representation [Commons 1899, p. 60]. This position stands in sharp contrast to his subsequent emphasis on collective bargaining by groups organized outside the formal structure of the state; and to his endorsement of the judiciary, of commissions, and of "log-rolling" [Commons 1934a, pp. 848–50, 685, 755].

This change in emphasis resulted both from his historical studies and from his life experiences. Significant among the life experiences was his presence in 1902 at the national conference of bituminous coal miners and their employees.

> I was struck by the resemblance to the origins of the British Parliament. On one side of the great hall were nearly a thousand delegates from local unions, an elected representative body. On the other side were about seventy employers appearing directly, as owners of the coal mines. It was evidently an industrial House of Commons and House of Lords but without a King. . . . I dropped much of what I had been arguing for in my book *Proportional Representation* as applied to legislatures and Congress; for here was, in actual operation, the main argument of my book, namely the Representation of Conflicting Interests instead of representation of artificial localities drawn on a map [Commons 1934b, p. 72].

In that same year, Commons went to work for the National Civic Federation, an organization that mediated between capital and labor, and that initiated reforms by presenting model bills to representatives who sponsored them either in Congress or in the State legislature. He was exposed there, for the first time, to the idea of a paid research staff that was responsible to an advisory board composed of representatives of business, labor, and consumers [Weinstein 1968, pp. 3–39]. While gaining experience as a mediator, he developed an admiration for Samuel Gompers and a sympathy for the latter's suspicion of direct government intervention in the affairs of labor [Commons 1935, pp. ix–x], and he learned how new groups that organize outside the state's formal structure can affect its operation without a massive reorganization of the legislative branch. In short, he learned the flexibility and value of the "device of collective bargaining." Because they are elected from a particular economic class whose concerns they share, the representatives fulfill Common's criteria for valid representation. They will not "sell out" their followers, and they will in turn be trusted [Commons 1934b, pp. 72–73; 1950, pp. 23–24]. Even before he reached the University of Wisconsin, therefore, Commons had begun to modify his conclusions about reforms needed in the structure of the state.

His research and experience at Wisconsin suggested further modifications. In "The American Shoemakers," the major theoretical result of his historical research, he showed how changing exogenous forces, like the extension of markets, could affect economic organization, the emergence of interest groups, and the nature of the threat to "security of expectations" [Commons 1909]. His later discussions of "banker capitalism" and its attendant cyclical instability underlined the changing nature of this threat [Commons 1934a, pp. 763–73; Harter 1962, pp. 176–82, 232–35]. In the changing nature and functions of the shoemakers' organization, Commons witnessed again the flexibility of the "device of collective bargaining." In his theory of economic evolution he established the need for a flexible government structure that could respond more readily to the challenges created by an evolving industrial society with its ever-new threats of violence and insecurity. Neither the legislature nor the judiciary possessed such flexibility, and this led Commons eventually to change his opinion of commissions.

He reversed his condemnation of them when he worked on the Wisconsin Industrial Commission. While he had expressed mistrust of the commission in *Proportional Representation*, he now praised. it as a "fourth branch of government" compensating for both legislative and judicial deficiencies [Commons 1913, p. 396]. In a rapidly changing technological society, the slow process of deliberation and debate is a deficiency that the legislature can remedy by passing a general rule and leaving particular applications to a commission able to respond more rapidly to changing circumstances. When technical questions are at issue, the knowledgeable litigant, usually the employer, has an unfair advantage in court because of deficiencies in the judge's background. The commission's technically trained staff can remedy this deficiency because the court takes up such questions only on appeal of the commission's decision, thus assuring that the judge receives a commission report that counterbalances the superior technical knowledge of some litigants. Consequently the commission renders both branches more adequate by its "constructive research . . . [which] reduces the coercive functions of government and increases the part played by persuasion" [Commons 1913, p. 12].

Commons, it is important to realize, advocated only a particular type of commission—with its staff insulated from politics by civil service status and its policies established by an advisory board composed of interest group representatives. It was essential in his view that the members of the board be appointed, not by the chief executive or any other politicians, but directly by the various outside interest groups, thus preventing direct control by the party in power [Commons 1934a, p. 848, 1950, pp. 256–57]. Commons wanted the commission controlled, not by politically acceptable leaders, but by "real leaders" who would make sure their constituents received a fair hearing. This would result, Commons hoped, in a decision based on all relevant facts and accepted as "reasonable" by all interested parties. The right to appeal the decision in the courts would act as a further brake on the arbitrary exercise of power.

His experience on the Wisconsin Industrial Commission also led Commons to reverse another early position—his mistrust of the judiciary. In order to write a workers' compensation law that would not be ruled unconstitutional, he had to study law and the concept of reasonable value. As a result of this study, he developed a respect for the common law process that reaches decisions based on customary principles of fairness. Such decisions, to gain acceptance, must be recognized by the parties to the dispute as resulting from some standards of reasonableness. A set of such standards, evolving over time, brings to bear the brake of custom on the arbitrary and capricious exercise of power. A system that stresses intellectual inquiry into these standards approaches "Plato's ideal" of a state governed by the idea of justice [Commons 1924, p. 360].

In his mature thought, Commons conceived of a society approaching this ideal with a set of "devices" [Commons 1924, pp. 104–5]. The device of "delegation of power" takes power from the hands of the sovereign and delegates it to agents who the sovereign cannot remove. The device of "official responsibility" subjects all officials to the possibility of removal. The device of "representation" means that citizens need not assemble in arms to exercise a veto on the actions of the officials of the state. Finally, there is the device of "collective bargaining" by which the exercise of the collective power of the concern is subject to the veto of any of the constituent groups.

Though he never abandoned his support for proportional representation as a solution to what he considered the unrepresentative nature of territorial representation, Commons did develop some misgivings about it [Commons 1934a, pp. 898–900]. In place of sweeping legislative reform, he turned to ingenious applications of the device of collective bargaining. Going far beyond the labor-management paradigm, he cited instances in which representatives of farmers and consumers set prices during World War I [Commons 1919, p. 39]; he used outside advisory boards to direct the work of his Industrial Commission of Wisconsin [Commons 1913, p. 408]; he suggested that farmer and consumer organizations appoint representatives to the Board of Governors of the Federal Reserve Bank [Commons 1950, pp. 256–57]. This flexible tool, to be developed by later "experiments in collective action," took precedence over reform of the bulky legislative process in Commons's agenda for social action.

That agenda, at the end of his career, as at the beginning, assumed a state in which every official is subject to some earthly authority and in which freedom of assembly is protected [Commons 1924, p. 106; 1934a, p. 901]. These he considered the necessary conditions for increasing control over the abuses of power by the officials of the state. In other aspects, however, his "experiments in collective action," and his research induced a change of emphasis. From sweeping legislative changes, he turned to more flexible devices—commissions with insulated staffs, the courts, and independent outside interest groups affecting the state through the "device of collective bargaining." He turned to these "devices" because of his conviction that the state needed the flexibility to respond to the rapid changes of an evolving industrial society in which coalitions shift and organizations change in response to continually changing threats to "security of expectations."

This results, at any time, in an organization of legislators, executives, judges, policemen, commission members and others—a "going concern," that exists before the citizens of the state are born and that will survive the death of any particular person. Behaviorally, the state is the actions of its officials [Commons 1924, pp. 112, 364]. As representatives of the sovereign power they can decide disputes between citizens and issue commands that citizens must obey. The citizens, on the other hand, can order state officials to protect their rights, even against other state officials. Commons was interested in two necessary results of this relationship: first, the state controls individual activity and simultaneously liberates and expands it; and second, in controlling the threat of violence, the state officials necessarily determine the distribution of income.

State Officials Enforce Rights and Duties

Following Bohm Bawerk, Commons defined a right as the power to command state officials to enforce one's will on others [Commons 1891, p. 62; 1924, p. 112]. This makes the state a party to every transaction, even the "bargaining" and "managerial" transactions conducted between citizens who are not officials. It is true that most transactions are conducted on an ethical level of mutual trust above the legal minimum [Commons 1924, p. 124]; but they must still be "authorized" by the state because the parties to an unauthorized transaction cannot call upon the officials of the state to enforce the terms of a contract. Consequently, although individuals can exchange commodities, only the state can transfer legal control [Commons 1934a, p. 60]. As a necessary consequence of its monopoly over violence, therefore, the state is a party to every transaction. This necessary consequence entails three further consequences: first, the state controls individual behavior; second, it liberates and expands the powers of the person; third, it determines the distribution of income.

Because it controls the incentive of violence, the state's typical transaction is what Commons termed the "authoritative" or "rationing" transaction. The term "authoritative" indicates that there is no bargaining that in this type of transaction, would be illegal. Rather all the instruments for the collective control of sovereignty come into play—negotiation, pleading, log-rolling, collective bargaining, judicial decision, and dictatorial decree [Commons 1934a, p. 754]. When the decision is made, the state official compels obedience from the citizen. Commons contested the "fiction" that citizens have given their consent to, say, compulsory education laws [Commons 1950, p. 5]. In fact, they have no choice in the matter. They must obey or face the police power of the state.

By enforcing the law, therefore, state officials control behavior. But paradoxically, they also "liberate" and "expand" the personality. They liberate the personality by enforcing "remedial rights," and they "expand" its effectiveness by enforcing "substantive rights." A "remedial" right corresponds to what Commons called "liberty," a relation between equals; it is the right to the "powers and means of self-expression, self-development, and self-realization" [Commons 1924, pp. 12, 38,

156]. Remedial rights include the power of a citizen to call upon the officials of a state to prevent another citizen from taking his or her property without due process of law. Without remedial rights, a human being is "not a person, but a thing that can be captured, bred, owned, and killed without violating any duty towards him" [Commons 1924, p. 143]. Thus, in a behavioral sense, the state creates all persons, both human and corporate [Commons 1924, pp. 143, 112, 145, 365; 1934a, p. 76]. Remedial rights thus liberate "individual action from coercion, duress, discrimination, or unfair competition by means of restraints placed on other individuals" [Commons 1934a, p. 73]. Substantive rights correspond to what Commons called "freedom," the sharing in the prerogatives of the sovereign. Substantive rights include the power to order officials to enforce one's last will and testament after one's death, to enter into contracts with foreigners, and to buy property in other countries [Commons 1924, pp. 50, 111, 118–119; 1934a, p. 695]. Substantive rights expand the effective range of the person's will over space and time.

By enforcing contracts, the officers of the state increase the probability that business will be conducted in the future as it is today [Commons 1924, pp. 1925–26]. This increased probability, in turn, enhances the present value of personal abilities and physical capital. [Commons 1924, pp. 23–24, 205–6; 1934a, pp. 645–46]. By universalizing the right of limited liability and incorporation, the state enables the creation and functioning of multinational corporations that organize individuals in productive enterprises of vast powers [Commons 1930, p. 13]. The officers of the state, by enforcing a wide array of remedial and substantive rights, make capitalism possible [Commons 1893, p. 60; 1924, pp. 100, 106; 1934a, pp. 412, 696].

Thus the anomaly—by enforcing duties that seemingly restrict action, the officers of the state "liberate" and "expand" the powers of the individual. In the first place, by enforcing duties, they automatically enforce rights that provide "security of expectations," satisfying the necessary condition for free rational activity, making contracts more secure, and increasing the expected return from enhanced personal abilities. In the second place, the protection of one man's liberty "exposes" others, denying them the right to use coercion, leaving only persuasion and bargaining—activities that exercise the freedom and rationality of the institutionalized personality. Finally, the state, through the grant of "substantive rights," puts its officials at the disposal of the citizens, extending their power of acting over space and time, protecting their corporations, increasing the range of choices available to the will of the individual, and, hence, expanding the consciousness of individual freedom. Thus, by controlling behavior, the state liberates and expands the personality.

But opportunities for such liberation and expansion are not equally available to all. The public officials, in providing the service of security, automatically enforce a distribution of property, liberty, and rights of association [Commons 1924, p. 367]. Commons coined the term, "rationing transaction," to emphasize this necessary distributional result of the enforcement of rights and liberties. One person's right is another person's duty; and one person's liberty, another's exposure. For instance, the slave has no right to share in what he or she produces [Commons 1893, p. 66]. The freeing of the slave "exposed" the employer to the worker's "liberty" to quit. When the state spends for "social needs" or levies taxes, it is "rationing" the national wealth [Commons 1934a, pp. 807, 831]. Commons did not say that the state is the only institution engaged in rationing transactions, but that anything a state official does, in some way, determines the distribution of wealth. There is no way to avoid it. The official who follows a laissez-faire policy is actually applying the police power of the state in the interests of those who currently own property, and against the interests of those who do not [Commons 1950, p. 82].

Every transaction of a state official, therefore, affects the distribution of wealth and liberty. The incompleteness of the democratic state implies that this distribution always falls short of any abstract notion of justice. At any particular time the state is an organization of short-sighted "Malthusian" personalities acting according to "persuasive, coercive, corrupt, misleading, deceptive and violent inducements. . . which the public and private participants deem to be, at the time, probably conducive to private, public or world benefit" [Commons 1924, p. 388]. The concept of public benefit, or public purpose, however twisted and perverted, always constrains, in some manner, the action of officials as they enforce a particular distribution of income. But the public purpose changes, and in the changing public purpose, Commons found hope that the democratic state might evolve in a progressive direction.

The Public Purpose

The public purpose, as Commons conceived of it, exists as an empirical reality in the justifications given by public officials for their decisions [Commons 1934a, pp. 761–62]. These justifications appeal to official working rules or customary notions of right and wrong. Official working rules include formally written laws and specific rules of procedure—like majority rule for legislators or the legal process for judges [Commons 1924, pp. 364–66]. Within the boundaries of these rules, the public officials may exercise discretion. Discretionary decisions will depend on the mental habits and habitual assumptions of the officials. But an official must justify even these decisions, either by the citizen's need for security from violence, or by customary notions of right and wrong; else the official risks the passive resistance of the citizens [Commons 1934a, p. 762]. For any time and place, therefore, the practices of the officials will appear "reasonable" in light of the ethical customs of that culture, though they may appear repulsive to later generations or to people from some other place [Commons 1934a, p. 763].

Working rules and habitual ethical beliefs result from the settlement of disputes. They change when new conflicts of interest result in new settlements that change the content of the public purpose. In these changes, Commons discerned the possibility for increasing reasonableness and humanity in the determination of the public purpose and hence in the conduct of the state's representatives.

The major characteristics of such settlements are: a mutual dependence between the parties in keeping the concern "agoing"; a conflict of interest over the distribution of rights and liberties; and order, a resolution which, if not perfect, avoids the chaos of continuing open conflict so that the parties can continue to act together in the "going concern" [Commons 1934a, p. 4]. These characteristics are all present in the disputes that determine the public purpose of the state.

Mutual dependence arises from the benefits that all parties to the dispute receive if the state continues to function. The fundamental benefit is "security of expectations," freedom from the arbitrary and capricious threat of physical violence, or material deprivation. In Commons's view of human nature, people prefer this to freedom from poverty or injustice [Commons 1924, p. 364; 1934a, p. 705]. Another common benefit is the growth of the commonwealth. Commons sometimes used the term as a synonym for the national product [Commons 1924, p. 361; 1934a, p. 819]. But, he also gave it a much larger meaning [Commons 1934a, pp. 807–8]. When, for example, he cited Sir Thomas Smith who wrote that England as a "commonwealth" was more than a "host of men," Commons was thinking broadly of a *kultur*, an organized unity that inspires loyalty and affection [Commons 1934a, p. 725; 1924, p. 222; 1913, p. 54]. The commonwealth is defined by the diverse hopes of the members born into and socialized by a "going concern" that will probably outlive them.

But the economy theory of the state is the theory of the going concern with its going business, having its roots in the past, its behavior in the present, held together by the hopes of peace, wealth, virtue and the fears of violence, poverty, vice, through control of which collective action proportions inducements to individuals to participate in the benefits and burdens of collective power [Commons 1924, p. 361].

The harmony of interests in the commonwealth inspires mutual dependence and social cohesion, and it creates an incentive for settling the disputes arising from conflicts of interest. Because of this pressure for settlement, Commons, following Hume, made scarcity and the resulting conflict of interests the source of ethics and justice [Commons 1924, p. 361; 1934a, pp. 141–42, 231]. The pattern of rights and duties imposed by an acceptable settlement must seem fair to the "institutionalized minds," of the parties, but it must also call for some altruism [Commons 1934a, pp. 698–99]. Once a settlement has been reached, it can guide future decisions the way habits guide the ordinary activities of the individual. When circumstances change, however, and new or different conflicts arise, habitual standards are found wanting, and the process of conflict resolution begins again.

In his search for a way to improve the process, Commons rejected Hume's skepticism for the fallibilism of Peirce [Commons 1934a, pp. 150–57]. Like Peirce, he defined the "real as that whose characters are independent of what anybody may think them to be" [Commons 1934a, p. 152]. Like Pierce, he also believed that scientific inquiry could only reduce uncertainty about propositions that can never be definitively proved. This occurs when a large number of experiments, separated in time and space, and disciplined by a common method, all converge to support a particular belief. The entire series becomes "a single collective experiment" [Peirce 1931–1935, vol. 5, p. 283]. Peirce's solution to the "metaphysical problem of the ultimate and fundamental reality, is, consequently, not individual bias but a social consensus of opinion" [Commons 1934a, p. 152]. Commons, like Peirce, thought that exactly the same type of inquiry could be applied to ethical questions [Commons 1934a, p. 743]. By following a method that controls individual bias, an inquiring community could expand its understanding of the ultimate aim that determines the legitimacy of any enterprise. "We can see ground for hope," wrote Peirce, "that debate will ultimately cause one party or both to modify their sentiments up to complete accord" [Peirce 1931–1935, vol. 2, p. 82].

Commons believed that the traditional procedures of the common law courts fulfilled the conditions laid down by Peirce for such an inquiry. Each case is an "experiment." The method demands that all the facts of the case be weighed and that the final decision be based on logic and historical precedent. As in the physical sciences, the criterion for belief is the agreement of all competent investigators—the legal profession and the community, including the historical community whose opinions exist in customs and precedent [Commons 1934a, pp. 224, 743]. Over time a set of decisions becomes an experiment in justice or fairness. Admitting the fallibility of any particular decision or series of decisions, the entire history constitutes the only inquiry of which a given community is capable into the nature of a just society [Commons 1934a, pp. 741–42].

This inquiry is related to the process by which new groups gain a voice in the affairs of the state. Different groups develop different assumptions and methods for settling disputes, and thus different perspectives on the nature of justice. Each group retains its traditions when it gains a share in the control of the state, and these traditions enter the body of common law precedents. Thus, in Britain, first the landlords, then the guilds, then the merchants, introduced their ideas of justice into the common law tradition [Commons 1924, pp. 220–30]. Commons thought that it was time to enrich this tradition further with working class conceptions of justice [Commons 1950, pp. 266–70].

The inquiry becomes part of a social evolution as conflicts arise, are settled and are reflected upon. Leaders, the "progressive minority," interact with the evolution of the law by showing concretely what is possible in a particular situation [Commons 1934a, pp. 844, 860–62, 874]. For example, the right of the state to limit hours of labor began with legislation based partially on the successful experience of humane employers, but it could not be accepted as constitutional until the Supreme Court reached the decision that workers needed protection for the same reason that women and children needed it—because of a weak bargaining position [Commons 1919, pp. 29–32].

Commons was under no delusions about the operations of the courts. He emphasized, in fact, that the biases of the "institutionalized mind" exist on the bench of the Supreme Court [Commons 1934a, pp. 699–701]. What impressed him was the common law method that places any particular decision into a historical process of examination and scrutiny on the basis of facts, circumstances and logic. In this way, a minority opinion of the court can, over a number of years become a majority opinion, as in the definition of property which Commons traced in the *Legal Foundations of Capitalism* [Commons 1924, pp. 6,

12, 16]. Since it was the method that impressed him, he applied it to other contexts, as in his method of "constructive research," or policy analysis [Commons 1913, pp. 7–14; 1934a, p. 707].

This view of ethical evolution had several unique elements. It is doubtful that Peirce would have agreed that the common law process satisfied his requirements for scientific inquiry—given his harsh comments about the legal process in general [Peirce, 1931–1935, vol. 2, p. 380]. Thorstein Veblen also considered training in law "alien . . . to the scientific spirit and subversive of it" [Veblen 1919, p. 20]. Commons, on the other hand, maintained that Veblen erred by eliminating purpose, including public purpose, from the scope of science [Commons 1934a, p. 654].[2] In addition, Commons's benign view of custom differed from that of Veblen and Clarence Ayres. They both seemed to look on custom as something that holds back progress and on technology as the source of social progress [Copeland 1936, p. 337; Ayres 1961, p. 29]. For Commons, on the other hand, the customary settlement of disputes was the origin of ethical growth and hence social progress.

Nor were his ideas totally without intellectual support; they rested on an honorable tradition of intellectual inquiry reaching back through Sir Edward Coke and Sir William Blackstone to Cicero's writings on the *Jus Gentium* [Lowry 1973, p. 610]. It may be that contact with this tradition through his legal studies accounted both for his benign view of custom and for his lifelong synthesis of legal method with Peirce's philosophy, though his lifelong identification with the common man probably affected his attitude toward the common man's customs.

In addition, his concept of the public purpose unified the elements he had first assembled in *A Sociological View of Sovereignty* [Commons 1899–1900]. Scarcity produces conflict and the threat of violence. Those who direct the state can use its monopoly on violence to exploit others. This abuse was controlled by new groups struggling to gain a voice in the direction of the state. A necessary condition for their success was a set of values shared by those who were already in control. Peirce's analysis of habits and customs, applied to the public purpose, explained the growth of these shared values. Fusing Peirce's principles of intellectual inquiry with the traditions of the common law, Commons conceived of a way to transform a "Malthusian" clash of opposed interests into an inquiry, however biased, into the nature of a just society. The resolution of such a conflict must produce, not only an end to exhausting conflict, but a new "working rule," an "experiment in collective action" to be examined, and then preserved, rejected or modified by later generations. This "working rule," in some way, incorporates the welfare of the previously disenfranchised class into the evolving public purpose.

Criticism from a Contemporary Perspective

Commons distinguished his position from that of the classical economists by asserting that he had started, not with "the ethical concept of the individual as a free man existing prior to the law," but with a historical autocracy imposing a despot's arbitrary and capricious will upon subjects without rights. When he looked at history, he saw in the expansion of the democratic state, not a threat to liberty, but a process by which, through the state, "liberty has been gradually taken away from the masters and bestowed on the subjects" [Commons 1924, p. 126].

Freedom for the individual was protected, not by curtailing the functions of the state, but by strengthening the checks upon the arbitrary and capricious use of power by the state's representatives; foremost among these checks was the right of free assembly. This right, like all rights, is a creation of the state [Commons 1934a, p. 901]. Commons, therefore, departing from the methodology of the classical economists, reached different conclusions. He rejected their minimalism, turning to "the device of collective bargaining" and the evolving public purpose as the source and criterion, respectively, of progressive change in the state. One way to appraise his contribution, then, is to examine, from a contemporary perspective, first, his methodology, then, his "device of collective bargaining," and finally, his concept of the public purpose.

By refusing to start with the assumption of "economic rationality," Commons separated himself, methodologically, not only from the classical economic tradition, but also from the modes of theorizing most acceptable in economic circles today. He did not draw refutable conclusions from spare assumptions, and consequently he failed to produce a theory by contemporary falsificationist standards. After his first book, he avoided microeconomics, and his consequent errors in tax incidence undoubtedly flaw his policy conclusions [Copeland 1936, pp. 338, 345–46]. His refusal to abstract from the complexity of the "institutionalized personality," dictated a historical beginning, and, as T.W. Hutchison has pointed out, an investigator who drops the simplifying assumption of "economic rationality," arrives not at a manageable "second approximation," but at "an almost unlimited variety of cases" "amenable only to historical examination" [Hutchison 1981, p. 292].

Commons proceeded, therefore, not with the tools of analytical economics, but with those of the historian, the participant observer, the grubber for facts. He produced, not a refutable theory, but a conceptual framework; although not explicitly falsifiable, it was not empirically irrelevant either [Commons 1934a, p. 722].

This makes Commons methodologically a fiscal sociologist in the tradition of E.R.A. Seligman and Joseph Schumpeter, and it places him today among the "Parsonian" theorists, as Brian Barry called them [Seligman 1926; Schumpeter 1954; Barry 1970, pp. 3–11, 165–80]. The argument by which Talcott Parsons supported his methods also validates, to some extent, Commons's claim to have developed a supplement to standard economic analysis. Parsons, like Commons, never denied the usefulness of assuming given wants and rational self-interested behavior. But he questioned policy prescriptions based only on standard economic assumptions that omit group influences like Vilfredo Pareto's residues or Max Weber's ultimate values [Parsons 1932, pp. 316–45; Commons 1934a, pp. 725–26]. Since people act differently in groups than when alone, other methods must complement those based on the unrealistic assumption of completely self-determined individuals. Commons accounted for Pareto's "residues" with his concept of the "institutionalized personality," and for Weber's values with his public purpose.[3] Any validity in the Parsonian position validates, therefore, Commons's claim, at least in the applied area of policy analysis, to have created a complement to standard economic methodology.[4]

Commons, following his methodology, came to emphasize the "device of collective bargaining." Today, it might be called interest group politics, and it would surely draw fire from public choice theorists and political scientists. Public choice theorists question any system that allows the organized few to exploit the unorganized many [Buchanan and Tullock 1967, pp. 283–95]. And a political system responsive to interest group pressure allows such exploitation because small groups can organize more easily than large ones [Downs 1957, pp. 260–76; Olson 1971, pp. 114–21]. Political scientists like Theodore Lowi claim that interest group theories rest on fallacious assumptions and result in undesirable consequences [Lowi 1979, pp. 50–63]. The fallacious assumptions are that competition between interest groups is self-correcting and that interest groups are necessarily good [Lowi 1979, pp. 59–58]. The undesirable consequences include the tendency for the triad—interest group, government agency and congressional committee—to shut out the public, create a position of privilege, and impose a conservative bias on government [Lowi 1979, pp. 59–61].

The "device of collective bargaining" would also draw fire from the left. The present alliance between monopoly capital and large unions, in the Marxist view, exploits the more competitive secondary sector, and this results, in large part, from the "device of collective bargaining" [O'Connor 1973, pp. 65–69]. Some radical historians consider the National Civic Federation nothing but a tool used by large corporations to prevent the growth of a socialist or labor party in the United States [Weinstein 1968, pp. 3–39; O'Connor 1973, pp. 67–69]. Commons, of course, worked for the National Civic Federation and shared its philosophy, and so he is indicted also—for basing his humanitarian concerns "on an elitist sense of corporate responsibility" [Isserman 1976, p. 311; Weinstein 1968, p. 202].

Commons would plead guilty to everything except the charge of elitism; he objected, not so much to the Marxist analysis of the problem, as to the Marxist solution. The Marxists, he objected, "fail to see that coercion is the basis of both private and government administration" [Commons 1899–1900, p. 84]. State ownership of the means of production would merely put the exploiting class in the government. Later he came to believe, with Gompers, that radical leaders tend to throw workers into unwinnable battles—with the workers paying the price for the utopianism of their leaders [Commons 1926; 1935, pp. ix, x].

There is a sense in which these criticisms reflect the perspective of the late twentieth-century, when minorities demand protection against white unions, when there is pressure to disband commissions that seem to have served mostly the interests of the regulated, and when interest group pressures hinder fiscal responsibility. As a result, the "device of collective bargaining" appears tarnished. These problems of a world that Commons never knew might support a *prime facie* case against some of his specific applications of the "device of collective bargaining."

When applied to his general conception, however, the objections seem overdrawn. The conclusion that large latent groups are impossible to organize without coercion or specialized incentives does not really invalidate his conception of the "device of collective bargaining." There is evidence, in the first place, that Commons understood the problem of organizing large latent groups; for this reason, he continued to support proportional representation in spite of his doubts about it [Commons 1900, pp. 362–63]. His support for the closed shop seems based on recognition of the free rider problem in large latent groups [Commons 1900, pp. 362–63]. His form of "interest group politics" does not rest on a rejection of the free rider principle. He was, in fact, searching for principles of organization that would overcome it, and he did not rule out "reasonable" coercion. Some of the strength of the objection to his position arises from a well-known weakness of contemporary public choice theory: its exclusion of any meaningful political leadership [Bluhm 1978, p. 279; Barry 1970, pp. 37–40; Colm 1962, pp. 121–22]. When Commons conceived of progressive social change, he gave a key role to leaders who are trusted because they will not "sell out" their constituents. Unlike the "political entrepreneur" of the public choice model, such leaders can articulate goals, create selective incentives, or appeal to motives omitted in a theory that sees only "economic rationality" in the forces of history. In addition, the static models of contemporary public choice theorists implicitly hark back to some golden age of "one man, one vote" when interest groups were presumably less influential [Buchanan and Tullock 1967, p. 83]. Commons's conception of the "rationing transaction" fits both the present clash of interest groups and the past, when aristocracies of landlords and businessmen used the state to exploit workers and enforce slavery [Commons 1896, pp. 28–31; Hutchison 1981, p. 24].

Finally, Commons never proposed any natural "balance of power." His point is better grasped in negative form. Unless a group organizes and struggles to share in the sovereign power, it will be exploited. Thus, he predicted, rather prophetically, that, in spite of three amendments to the constitution, American blacks would continue as second-class citizens until they organized under black leaders they could trust [Commons 1920, p. 50]. However difficult it may be for large groups to organize, it is hard to deny that protection of their right to do so is a necessary condition for the peaceful evolution of a free society, and that a concept of personal freedom grounded in the right of free assembly is a valuable supplement to one derived from the indeterminacy of abstract individuals in an impersonal market system.

The use of the public purpose in a combined normative-positive sense is a second result of Commons's methodology that differentiates his conception. The standard economic assumption is that only self-interest motivates people [Buchanan and Tullock 1967, p. 20]. Buchanan and Tullock argue that without an explicitly defined social welfare function, the concept of public purpose is ambiguous and perhaps meaningless [Buchanan and Tullock 1967, p. 284]. Commons would admit the ambiguity, but deny the meaninglessness, arguing that the public purpose, concretized in working rules, constrains state officials just as some common purpose controls the employees of any concern. It is hard to argue with this. In fact, some contemporary empirical evidence supports Commons [Kalt and Zupan 1984; Frohlich and Oppenheimer 1984]. His position is also consistent with a considerable body of evidence that the behavior of citizens during elections is at variance with the predictions of the simple "rational voter" model [Barry 1971, pp. 13–23].

One can go further, and argue with Colm that public choice theory, by denying the public interest, denies also the value of participation in government, implicitly prescribing a paternalistic "bread and circuses" government rather than a democracy and that an explicit concept of the public purpose is needed to explain merit goods and government activity in foreign affairs [Colm 1962, p. 123]. Like Colm, Commons conceived of the public purpose as ambiguous and changing because different groups with different values are continually hammering out "a common understanding of what is accepted as constituting the public interest" [Colm 1962, p. 121]. Commons was original, however, in the detail with which he described the evolution of the public purposes, specifying a role for customary methods of conflict resolution and judicial decisons, as well as legislative debate.

Commons may well have been ahead of his time when he refused to admit a hard and fast distinction between positive and normative statements [Commons 1924, pp. 349–53; 1925, p. 92]. Since there are so many facts and so many ways of treating them, an investigator must choose both facts and methods on the basis of some objective or purpose which is, by definition, a value. The "value-free" investigator is often marshalling facts to support some unadmitted normative purpose.[5] This objection is echoed in different ways by contemporary philosophers [Kaplan 1964]. For Commons, the only control to bias was confrontation with opposing points of view, both directly by hearing the arguments of the different interest groups and indirectly by consulting precedent.

When he criticized Commons for overlooking the role of a fixed constitution, V. Ostrom seems to have missed the point of the public purpose. The constitution of society, in the form of "working rules," was a dominant concern for Commons; but constitutions need not be written, and the meaning of constitutions can evolve because of changing historical circumstances or changing ethical convictions [Commons 1924, p. 298, 1934a, p. 654]. The correct distinction between Commons and the public choice theorists rests more properly on the difference between "strict" and "loose" interpretations of rigid univocal rules. Commons would trust more to the common law process of interpretation and evolving definitions of ideals like liberty and equality. Strict interpretation of a written constitution imposes the values of one generation on succeeding generations, without consideration for changing historical circumstances or new ethical insights. In Commons's "loose interpretation," past generations continue to influence policy through precedents that are, nevertheless, subject to inquiry and questioning.

His notion of a "rationing transaction" summarizes, to some extent, Commons's unique conceptualization of the democratic state. A method that treats such a transaction like a market exchange overlooks much that Commons understood. First, the outcome does not result from bargaining, but from the customs and working rules that affect the institutionalized personalities, of the citizen on one side, and of the state official on the other; second, these rules result from a history of log-rolling, interest group pressure, and legal debate, characterized by a uniqueness that defies deductive analysis; third, by coining the term, "rationing transaction," Commons emphasized that the working rules of the state necessarily affect the distribution of wealth and liberty; finally, the citizen, while helpless as a "single one" before the police power of the state, can, by organizing with others of like interests, affect the public purpose and hence the working rules that govern the behavior of the state's officials. Consequently, one is led back through the methodological presuppositions to the emphasis on the "device of collective bargaining," and the evolving public purpose. It is hard to deny the value of a conception that methodologically accounts for group influences in its explanation of human behavior, and that emphasizes freedom of assembly and disciplined intellectual inquiry as crucial to the evolution of the state in a progressive direction.

Conclusions

Commons, therefore, based his reformist activity on a reasoned conception of the state, not in minimalist terms as necessarily a threat to liberty, but as a potentially liberating force. Both the reasoning and the conception support his claim to have developed a useful complement to standard economic analysis. Like Peirce, who rejected Cartesian doubt as intellectually dishonest, Commons refused to support his conclusions with a hypothetical "first position" like Nozick, or an original anarchy like Buchanan [Thayer 1968, pp. 83–86; Nozick 1974, pp. 150–53; Buchanan 1975, pp. 2–6]. He insisted on studying the simultaneous development of free people and free institutions. His methods

produced "fallible" conclusions, but avoided the faults for which contemporary economic analysis of the state has been criticized. Com-
rions did not impose a normative concept of "economic rationality"
on citizens, bureaucrats and politicians. He allowed for the influence
of "real leaders," of Pareto's "residues" and of Weber's social norms.
His conception of the public purpose permitted him to explain phenomena that cannot be explained by economic models based on a denial of the public purpose. His method for dealing with values is more
philosophically robust than the feigned skepticism of "positive" investigator. In the shifting and uncertain terrain of policy science, his pragmatic insistence on consideration of all the facts and of all points of
view can only improve a process based solely on dogmatic minimalism.

His reasoning produced a conception of democracy as potentially liberating. By reducing the use of coercion, the state forces all parties to
use persuasive incentives that appeal to rationality, freedom, and dignity. Public officials, in controlling the threat of violence, cannot avoid
enforcing a pattern of rights to liberty and property. By increasing the
certainty that contracts will be honored, they permit people to cooper-
ate and increase the national wealth; wealth expands the range of
choice, hence, the liberty of the citizens. The distribution of rights to
that wealth will, at any particular time, reflect the ethical blindness, as
well as the ethical insights, of the citizens. It will reflect a fallible public
purpose. But Commons perceived, in the evolution of the democratic
state, a pattern by which former serfs and slaves rose to the dignity of
citizenship and enriched an evolving legal tradition with their unique
insights into the nature of a just society. On this basis, he developed a
conception of social evolution purged of Spencerian or Hegelian necessity. With proper discipline, citizens can, in time, transform a conflict
of interest from a clash of "Malthusian" bigots into a reasoned search
for a just society. Thus, the citizens, by dialogue, free themselves from
their own biases. The conception of human freedom implied here
differs from that based on the paradigm of the impersonal market. It
includes the right to freedom of assembly, to the means of self-
realization, and to freedom from "undue economic coercion." These
freedoms depend upon the protection of a well-ordered state.

Notes

1. There are a number of good introductions to Commons's theory of institutional economics. They include N.W. Chamberlain [1963], R.A. Gonce [1976], L.G. Harter [1962; 1965], K. Parsons [1950], M. Rutherford [1983], and one should not forget Commons [1931]. They all include aspects of Commons's view of government and the state (for example Harter [1962, pp. 236–37]). But their general focus is on other aspects of his thought.

2. I would tend to go further and claim that Commons thought in terms of "final cause," while Veblen thought in terms of "efficient cause." It is possible to disagree with this, however, as one reviewer did, on grounds that Commons's concept of the evolving public purpose is closer to Dewey's instrumentalism. Much that Commons wrote supports this conception, and so I hesitate to advance my interpretation as definitive. My reasons for sticking with the "final cause" interpretation are as follows: First, Commons made a point of following Peirce's philosophy of science rather than that of Dewey or William James. Peirce, coming from mathematics and chemistry, tended to hypostatize concepts. He was influenced by the medieval philosopher John Duns Scotus as well as by Immanuel Kant, and as a result he was more platonic than the other pragmastists, and his ethics included the concept of a *summum bonum*, incompletely comprehended, that legitimizes all activity. Dewey, coming from biology and medicine, and influenced more by G.W.F. Hegel, tended to look at things as more in flux and at ends themselves as continually evolving. My second reason is that this interpretation makes the most sense of the discussion of ethical ideal types in *Institutional Economics*, [Commons 1934a, pp. 741–43]. My third reason is that this is compatible with Commons's fundamentalist abolitionist background, which was probably always with him to some extent. In any case, what is important is that Commons was quite explicit about following Peirce's philosophy and about using the writings of Dewey and James to adapt it to the social sciences. He would not have been so careful to differentiate in such a manner if he did not follow Peirce where the latter diverged from Dewey and James. Attention to this could possibly improve interpretations of Commons. From an operational point of view, there is little difference between evolving goals and goals that are related to the true purpose as successive approximations are to the object of inquiry.

3. The argument here is similar to that advanced by A.M. Field [1979]. Field argued that the assumptions used in public choice theory do not yield predictions that are sufficiently restrictive. He also attributed the policy irrelevance of contemporary labor economics to its departure from institutionalist methodology. His first argument is considerably strengthened by R.A. Musgrave's demonstration that the assumptions of public choice theory can lead one to conclude either that government is too small or that it is too large [Musgrave 1981]. The only quibble with Field concerns his statement that "Commons . . . did not attempt to construct a general theory of institutions" [Field 1979, p. 53]. Rutherford has argued that he did [1983]. Such a theory is also implicit in the concept of evolution outlined by L.G. Harter [1965]. Of course, part of the quibble might arise

from the definition of theory. Commons did not develop a deductive theory, but he did develop a conceptual scheme.
4. G.W. Atkinson [1983] also notes the policy irrelevance of public choice theory. He implicitly brings in the public purpose when he criticizes public choice theorists for ignoring the influence of shared values, power, and uncertainty as elements in transactions.
5. In this context, Musgrave's objection to the Leviathan literature is interesting.

> While claiming to offer a positive approach, this literature reflects the consequences (derived neatly, and on occasion, gleefully) from a preconceived model of behavior designed so that it cannot but result in a demonstration of government failure [Musgrave 1981, p. 88].

References

Atkinson, G.W. 1983. "Political Economy: Public Choice and Collective Action." *Journal of Economic Issues* 17 (December): 1057–65.
Ayres, C.E. 1961. *Toward a Reasonable Society.* Austin and London: University of Texas Press.
Barbash, J. 1976. "The Legal Foundations of Capitalism and the Labor Problem." *Journal of Economic Issues* 10 (December): 799–810.
Barry, B. 1970. *Sociologists, Economists and Democracy.* London: Collier-Macmillan.
Bluhm, W.T. 1978. *Theories of the Political System.* Englewood Cliffs: Prentice-Hall.
Buchanan, J.M. and G. Tullock. 1967. *The Calculus of Consent.* Ann Arbor: University of Michigan.
Chamberlain, N.W. 1963. "The Institutional Economics of John R. Commons." In *Institutional Economics,* ed. Joseph Dorfman; pp. 63–94.
Colm, G. 1962. "The Public Interest: Essential Key to Public Policy." In *Nomos IV: The Public Interest,* ed. C.J. Friedrich. New York: Atherton Press.
Commons, J.R. 1893. 1963. *The Distribution of Wealth.* New York: A.M. Kelley.
_____.1896. *Proportional Representation.* Boston and New York: Thomas Crowell.
_____.1899."Economists and Class Partnership: Reply to President Hadley." In *Annual Meeting of the American Economic Association.* Reprinted in J.R. Commons. *Labor and Administration,* pp. 51–70.
_____.1899–1900, 1967. *A Sociological View of Sovereignty.* New York: Augustus M. Kelley.
_____.1907.1967. *Proportional Representation.* Second edition. New York: A.M. Kelley.
Commons, J.R. 1909. "American Shoemakers 1648–1895: A Sketch of Industrial Evolution." *Quarterly Journal of Economics.* 24 (November): 39–83.
_____.1913. *Labor and Administration.* New York: Macmillan.
_____.1919, 1969. *Industrial Goodwill.* New York: Arno Press.

_____.1920, 1967. *Races and Immigrants in America.* New York: Augustus M. Kelley.

_____.1924, 1959. *The Legal Foundations of Capitalism.* Madison: University of Wisconsin Press.

_____.1925. *Reasonable Value.* Madison: University of Wisconsin.

_____."Representation of Interests." *The Independent.* Reprinted in J.R. Commons, *Proportional Representation*, pp. 355–63.

_____.1926. "Karl Marx and Samuel Gompers." *Political Science Quarterly* 41 (June): 281–86.

_____.1930. "Evaluating Institutions as a Factor in Economic Change." *Special Lectures on Economics.* U.S. Department of Agriculture Graduate School. February–March.

_____.1931. "Institutional Economics." *American Economic Review.* 21 (December): 648–57.

_____.1934a, 1961. *Institutional Economics: Its Place in Political Economy.* Madison: University of Wisconsin Press.

_____.1934b. *Myself.* New York: Macmillan.

_____.1950, 1970. *The Economics of Collective Action* Madison: University of Wisconsin Press.

Commons, J.R. and Associates. 1935. *History of Labor in the United States,* Vol. 3. New York: Macmillan.

Copeland, M.A. 1936. "Commons' Institutionalism in Relation to the Problem of Social and Economic Planning." *Quaterly Journal of Economics.* 50 (February): 333–46.

Dewey, J. 1922, 1930. *Human Nature and Conduct.* New York: Random House.

Downs, A. 1957. *An Economic Theory of Democracy.* New York: Harper and Row.

Field, A.M. 1979. "On the Explanation of Rules Using Rational Choice Models." *Journal of Economic Issues* 13 (March): 49–72.

Frohilch, N. and J. Oppenheimer. 1984. "Altruism, Egalitarianism and Difference Maximizing." *Journal of Conflict Resolution.* 24 March: 3-24.

Gonce, R.A. 1976. "The New Property Rights Approach and Commons's Legal Foundations of Capitalism." *Journal of Economic Issues.* 10 (December): 765–97.

Harter, L.G. 1962. *John R. Commons: Assault on Laissez-Faire.* Corvallis: Oregon State University Press.

_____.1963. "John R. Commons: Conservative or Liberal." *Western Economic Journal.* 1 (Summer): 226–232.

_____.1967. "The Legacy of John R. Commons." *Journal of Economic Issues.* 1 (June): 63–73.

Hutchison, T.W. 1981. *The Politics and Philosophy of Economics.* New York: New York University Press.

Isserman, M.C. 1976. "God Bless Our American Institutions. The Labor History of John R. Commons." *Labor History* 17 (Summer): 312–28.

Kalt, J.P. and M.A. Zupan. 1984. "Capture and Ideology in the Economic Theory of Politics." American Economic Review 74 (June): 279-300.

Kaplan, A. 1964. *The Conduct of Inquiry.* San Francisco: Chandler.

Kennedy, W.F. "John R. Commons, Conservative Reformer." *Western Economic Journal.* 1 (Fall): 29–42.

Lowi, T. 1979. *The End of Liberalism*. New York: Norton.

Musgrave, R.A. 1981. "Leviathan Cometh—Or Does He?" In *Tax and Expenditure Limitations*, ed. H.F. Ladd and T.N. Tideman. Washington, D.C.: The Urban Institute.

Nozick, R. 1974. *Anarchy, State and Utopia*. New York: Basic Books.

O'Connor, J. 1973. *The Fiscal Crisis of the State*. New York: St. Martin's Press.

Olson, M. 1971. *The Logic of Collective Action*. 2d edition. Cambridge: Harvard University Press.

Ostrom, V. 1976. "John R. Commons's Foundations for Policy Analysis." *Journal of Economic Issues* 10 (December): 839–58.

Parsons, T. 1950. "John R. Commons' Point of View." J.R. Commons. *The Economics of Collective Action*, Appendix iii; pp. 341–75, In Parsons, T. "Economics and Sociology: Marshall in Relation to the Thought of His Time." *Quarterly Journal of Economics* 46 (February): 765–97.

Peirce, C.S. 1931–1935. *Collected Works* Cambridge, Mass.: Harvard University Press.

Rutherford, M. 1983. "J.R. Commons's Institutional Economics." *Journal of Economic Issues* 17 (September): 721–44.

Schumpeter, J.A. 1954. "The Crisis of the Tax State." In *International Economic Papers*, trans. W. Stolper. New York: Macmillan.

Seligman, E.R.A. 1926. "The Social Theory of Fiscal Science." *Political Science Quarterly* (June) 41: 193–218, 354–83.

Thayer, H.S. 1968. *Meaning and Action: A Critical History of Pragmatism*. New York: Bobbs-Merrill.

Veblen, T. 1919, 1961. *The Place of Science in the Modern World*. New York: Russell and Russell.

Weinstein, J., 1968. *The Corporate Ideal in the Liberal State: 1900–1910*. Boston: Beacon Press.

7

Legal Counsel, Power, and Institutional Hegemony

Steven R. Hickerson

Readers of the *JEI* are well aware that power, both as a fact of modern life and as an important concern in evolutionary economics, is central to a fully developed understanding of the corporate enterprise system. Indeed, a book of readings on this topic has evolved from past articles in the journal, and much of a recent issue was devoted to it as well.[1] Put simply, power is "a potential to influence,"[2] which in the economy centers on differential participation in decision making through effectual control or manipulation of property rights, income, or "other rights of economic significance."[3] Adolf Berle identifies several fundamental characteristics of power, three of which are relevant here: (1) Power is based on a system of ideas or a philosophy (ideology); (2) power is exercised through institutions (institutionalization); and (3) power is invariably confronted with, and acts in the presence of, a field of responsibility (forums of review).[4] This article is not intended to be a discussion of power in broad terms. Rather, the objective is to discuss the evolution of the institution of legal counsel in an historical perspective and its contemporary role in relation to power. Moreover, I intend to show that William Dugger's "institutional hegemony" is a useful frame of reference for analyzing this relationship.[5]

Legal Counsel as Social Institution:
Historical Perspective

The long tradition in institutional law and economics scholarship ante-
dates even John R. Commons's classic, *Legal Foundations of Capitalism.*
Adam Smith himself tilled this fertile ground in his ruminations concerning the English Navigation Acts.[6] This tradition has focused largely on the
incremental process of legal change in its effect on economic structure and
performance. It is not my intent to argue that this emphasis has been mis-
placed, for certainly law is an allocative mechanism which apportions
rights, duties, power, and liabilities. However, it is the legal system that
one turns to for a favorable interpretation of the rules; only that system,
not the rules themselves, provides a deliberative forum for such interpretation. "At the most general level, the function of the legal system is to
distribute and maintain an allocation of values that society feels to be
right."[7] Control of, or ready access to, this system denotes a unique and
favorable position with respect to Berle's attributes of power. In our
increasingly complex and technical society, legal counsel has become
"the chief mode through which the legal foundations of the system were
erected."[8]

In terms of Berle's attributes of power, then, we can view legal counsel
as one of the key institutions through which power is exercised. The underlying ideology is that of those who control, or at least routinely use, legal
services to achieve their specific aims. Finally, the institution of legal counsel stands at the forefront of the confrontation between power and its field
of responsibility. In short, the social and economic effects of alternative
legal arrangements that have traditionally interested economists are not
independent of the technique by which legal decisions are made. This is at
least in part a function of the institutional organization of the legal services
delivery system.

> Law and legal rules have their *distributive* side. "All rules have a *jurisdic-*
> *tional* aspect, or an aspect of *distribution of power*." . . . Critical to the
> performance of this distributive side is the provision of legal services. The
> significant question is: Who participates in this contest for the use of law
> in the struggle for power, privilege, and wealth? . . . Whose variables and
> values will govern the changing operation of the legal system and the
> transformation of law.[9]

The place of the institution of legal counsel in the modern world is best
understood in an evolutionary context of the historical legacy that has
molded the character of the profession. The cultural conditions in which
a distinct group of professional "law-men" emerged provide useful in-

sight into the place of this group in the structure of power. To specify these conditions requires a short digression on law as an anthropological phenomenon.

Law is to be regarded as "an integral part of a cultural whole."[10] Failure to grasp this fundamental point led some early students of the subject to an impasse, stemming from a culture-bound definition of their topic.[11] Definitions which held the presence of some specific legal decision maker (chief, witchdoctor, judge) or institution (court) as requisite to the existence of law excluded the benefits of a legal order from many non-western societies. Fortunately, this ethnocentricity was overcome in 1941 with the appearance of a classic work in the field, *The Cheyenne Way*.[12] The principal contribution of that work was its identification of four ubiquitous elements giving rise to law in all human societies: (1) the social group, (2) joined and continuing activity, (3) patterned behavior and the degree of its predictability, and (4) divergent motives of individuals and their occasional conflicting claims.[13] These elements "are all decidedly present in all human societies, forming the prerequisites for law and leading to its universal emergence."[14]

The point, of course, is that all human societies have law in this sense of the word. "The law-jobs are in their bare bones fundamental; they are eternal."[15] In order for a social group to remain a viable going concern, certain "law-jobs" must be performed to counteract abuses of the working rules of the group and maintain the integrity of its value structure. The performance of legal tasks, then, is an elementary and fundamental aspect of human survival. It is a functional category of activity which, as such, is pan-temporal, pan-cultural, continuous, and developmental.[16] This is illustrated in Figure 1.

The institutional structures that discretionary societies devise to perform these legal tasks, in contrast, are discontinuous and replacemental. They are, in other words, temporal, cultural, noneternal, and subject to change or adjustment.[17] Legal anthropologists report numerous cases wherein the institution of legal counsel, for example, is conspicuously absent from the legal processes of tribal societies.[18] Generally, such a professional group emerges only in complex societies characterized by the specialization of labor, a high level of literacy, urbanism, and industrialization.[19]

The role of the attorney in complex modern societies bears certain identifying characteristics which, according to Dietrich Rueschemeyer, include: (1) specialized knowledge of legal rules, (2) partisan advice to clients not related by kinship, and (3) representation of clients in relation both to other parties and to legal authorities.[20] But, as Roscoe Pound con-

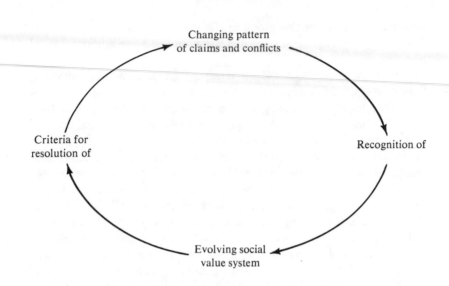

Changing pattern
of claims and conflicts

Criteria for
resolution of

Recognition of

Evolving social
value system

SOURCE: Adapted from H. Richard Hartzler, *Justice, Legal Systems, and Social Structure* (Port Washington, N.Y.: Kennikat Press, 1976), p. 85.

Figure 1. *Continuous and Developmental Function of a Legal System*

cluded, many of the functions of the lawyer have been performed in one way or another since ancient Greek, Roman, and Egyptian times.[21] The distinction between the role of modern attorneys and their ancient counterparts is put into focus when we consider their respective cultures and, more specifically, their "legal cultures."

It is not incorrect to think of culture as distinct from the more manifest web of actions and interrelations that constitute social, economic, political, or legal systems. In fact, the common culture shared by any particular group may well be outside the scope of their immediate cognizance.[22] Despite the current tendency to overextend the use and meaning of the term, the basic characteristics of culture were succinctly described more than a century ago by Edward B. Tylor: "Culture . . . is that complex whole which includes knowledge, belief, art, morals, law, custom, and any other capabilities and habits acquired by man as a member of society."[23] The upshot is that the association of human beings results in a culture, and that culture in turn tempers the character of this association; culture imposes a cost by mandating some degree of conformity. "It insists that members of the society assume definite obligations."[24] In some instances the obligations so imposed are quite general; incest, for example, is taboo in nearly every society. But many other kinds of obligations are peculiar to particular groups. Such specificity is the result of the differing experiences of each culture in solving its problems.[25] Specific cultural problem-solving styles are historical and cumulative. They account for both the successes and the failures of the past, thus guiding patterns of thought and action governing the social order into an established mold.

The legal postulates of a society derive their substance from other cultural postulates and form a matrix of symbols which transmit cultural values.[26] This legal culture can be described as "the values and attitudes which bind the system together and which determine the place of the legal system in the culture of the society as a whole."[27] In this sense, then, legal culture is organically related to culture as a whole, inextricably linking the network of values that people hold to discernible patterns in the use (or nonuse) of the legal system. Legal culture defines what does and does not constitute "legal problems."[28] It processes amorphous conflicts of interest into concrete demands on the legal system.

A part of the advocate's role is to articulate demands on the legal system in such a way that they become relevant to its workings.[29] Thus, the entire process of professional socialization through which lawyers develop their concept of "relevance" is critical in determining what types of claims are perceived as amenable to legal recourse, what types of clients are likely to secure representation, and for what purposes.[30] This in turn depends significantly on the dominant institutions of a particular place and time. The Greek, Roman, and Egyptian forebears of the modern legal profession, for example, emerged as part of a religious hierarchy. As such, the prevailing standard of relevance and the practice of law were largely the concern of the clergy; "law, theology and morals are intermingled and the corresponding offices are accordingly undifferentiated."[31]

The emergence of a secular institution of legal counsel, as identified by Rueschemeyer, closely paralleled the development of increasingly complex societies throughout medieval history.[32] As a society becomes more diffuse and heterogeneous, the task of settling disputes becomes more difficult. This requires "a group equipped to deal with the complex problems of law and administration under the wide variety of institutional set ups."[33] During this period, then, the clergy was gradually replaced in England and France by a professional class of lawyers. In the service of the state this group not only influenced the subsequent development of the law, but also helped consolidate the power of the monarchies in opposition to that of the church. "The lawyers played a most influential role in the vast process which led to the decline of the Roman Catholic church as a world wide state."[34]

Max Weber argued that bureaucratic rule and extensive market exchange were key developments leading to the emergence of secular legal counsel.[35] Brief consideration of the environment surrounding conflict resolution in "nonmodern" societies clarifies this proposition. Social value orientations in traditional societies typically link rights and obligations to membership in kin groups and political hierarchies which form a network of "multiplex relationships."[36] Here, legal relations are embedded in a complex infrastructure which is definitive of complete social personalities. Under these circumstances an individual litigant comes before a tribunal "not as a right and duty bearing *persona*, but in terms of his total social personality."[37] But where substantial elements of a given society become emancipated from these traditional orientations, there are ensuing problems of social integration, new interdependencies, and unprecedented conflicts that cannot be handled by traditional means of social control. Thus, the stage is set for bureaucratic regulation to step in.[38]

The consequences of a bureaucratic legal order have been the development and elaboration of legal norms and roles enhancing the centralization of political power, and the standardization of rules and procedures governing social relations and dispute resolution.[39] The effect of this process on society has depended on the extent to which various groups have been able successfully to rely on the coercive machinery of the state to further their own ends. "Law becomes a tool of the power interests of the groups that control the state."[40] At this juncture, then, market exchange enters the matrix of factors which have shaped secular legal counsel.

The transition from prototypical socioeconomic relations based on status to those based on contract, traced by Sir Henry Maine, supported the evolution of a market system and also was important in the subsequent development of secular legal counsel.[41] Contractual relations, in contrast to the "multiplex relations" mentioned above, are more vulnerable to problems of deviance and social control, due to their impersonal character and relatively short duration. As a result, legal guarantees of the fulfillment of promises are sought, leading contractual arrangements to become increasingly adapted to the expected reaction of the courts.[42] The role of advocate becomes transformed by a new set of dominant institutions. "The needs of the market place articulated by independent legal experts will create strong pressures for legal development and rationalization. Since these legal specialists are not immediately associated with religious, political, and judicial authorities and since control of their work is difficult to implement except indirectly, it is in the context of expanding market relations that partisanship of legal counsel develops most easily."[43]

Although this is probably correct as far as it goes, it gives a one-sided view. Undoubtedly the need for legal experts to articulate the needs of the marketplace contributed to the growth of secular legal counsel. But legal confrontations, after all, are adversarial in nature. Surely, the need for legal experts to articulate the needs of society under a market regime must have made an equally significant contribution. Consider, for example, the following observation by Karl Polanyi.

> The road to the free market was opened and kept open by an enormous increase in continuous, centrally organized and controlled interventionism. To make Adam Smith's "simple and natural liberty" compatible with the needs of a human society was a most complicated affair. Witness the complexity of the provisions in the innumerable enclosure laws; the amount of bureaucratic control involved in the administration of the Poor Laws . . . or the increase in governmental administration entailed in the meritorious task of municipal reform. And yet all these strongholds of governmental interference were erected with a view to the organizing of some simple freedom—such as that of land, labor, or municipal administration. Just as, contrary to expectation, the invention of labor saving machinery had not diminished but actually increased the uses of human labor, the introduction of free markets, far from doing away with the need for control, regulation, and intervention, enormously increased their range.[44]

Our brief overview of legal counsel as a social institution has established three things. First, the "law-job" is a functional category of activity which is, in Marc Tool's terminology, continuous and developmental. Social control and conflict resolution are requisite to the ongoing viability of societies as going concerns. Second, the institutional structures that societies create to perform these legal tasks are discontinuous and replacemental. Anthropologists tell us of legal institutions as varied and diverse as the economic institutions with which we are more familiar. Legal counsel is one such institutional arrangement that is, in its secular manifestation, unique to complex societies. Third, the role of legal counsel with respect to power is contextual. The lesson of history and anthropology is that the nature and scope of the legal expert's work are dependent upon the extant cultural milieu and the dominant institutions thereof. We turn, then, to a discussion of legal counsel in relation to power and institutional hegemony.

Legal Counsel and Power

As the foregoing discussion indicates, all social groups must make institutional provisions for the performance of legal tasks. In complex societies this requires the training and maintenance of legal experts. This group, like all trained professions, "demands a technique, a technical vocabulary and a common fund of technical information."[45] But from what source does this common fund derive? The answer, of course, is that the fund in question derives largely from the dominant institutions of a particular place and time. Thus, for example, "where the legal profession develops as part of a religious hierarchy, as it has in Egyptian, Mesopotamian, Hebrew, and Moslem and early Roman history, law, theology and morals are intermingled and the corresponding offices are accordingly undifferentiated. Under such conditions the legal profession is a part of the general theocratic system and possesses a distinct theological and moral cast."[46]

Viewed in this light, both the historical and the modern role of the legal profession in relation to power in the United States can be placed in clear relief. During the early colonial and post-Revolutionary period of American history, the legal profession commanded minimal respect.[47] This has been attributed to images and attitudes the colonists carried with them from Europe. The barrister, in their minds, was associated with the perceived system of oppression embodied in English common law, a system they sought to escape. Yet, despite this early history, the period between the Revolution and the Civil War witnessed what has been termed the "golden age" of American law.[48] "In seventy-five years at most, the English seventeenth century materials were made over into a common law for America. . . . This was the work of great judges and great lawyers practicing before them."[49] Largely as a result of this, there developed "a tradition that lawyers were fit for politics or statesmanship. They occupied a dominant ethical position analogous to that of clergymen and received a social recognition not given to the business classes. Their services . . . could and did mold the economic and political institutions of the country."[50]

Some of this tradition remains alive, even in the post-Watergate era. Americans continue to elect a greater proportion of lawyers to public office than do any other people on earth. But the dominant social position that the lawyer once held has been superseded by the financier and the directors of corporate enterprise. To paraphrase Thorstein Veblen, the nascent industrial order that reached fruition in the late nineteenth century engendered the businessman as one of the major institutions of modern life.[51] By the end of the nineteenth century, the legal profession was still very much a cottage industry; but the character of legal work was profoundly and permanently changed by the large-scale industrialization following the Civil War.[52]

In both England and the United States the dominance of commercial and industrial structures, the complexity of business organization and the position of world economic leadership steadily thrust upon the legal profession problem after problem which was not originally intended to form a part of legal practice. In both countries the legal profession in addition to exercising its historic monopoly over control of . . . the courts and over the giving of private counsel . . . became virtually an intellectual jobber and contractor in business matters.[53]

This does not mean that the role of the profession in relation to power atrophied in consequence of these changes. Quite to the contrary, the law "remained one of the careers through which a man could attain influence and wealth even without having capital at the start."[54] Industrialization, then, and the growing concentration of capital following the Civil War were closely mirrored by a parallel development in the structure and concentration of the legal profession which has become particularly acute in the last three decades. This trend was already in evidence by the beginning of the twentieth century, as the corporate law firm (largely as we know it today) rose to the very apex of the profession.

Modern sociological studies show that, as a result of this increased concentration, the profession has become a highly heterogeneous and stratified group, dominated by the elite large corporate practitioners.[55] "A paramount objective of this elite was to structure the legal profession—its education, admissions, ethics, discipline and services—to serve certain political preferences."[56] However, any conspiratorial overtones should be heavily discounted. The situation is a result of (1) institutional hegemony and (2) the ways that the adversarial process structures the possibility of using the legal system for redistributive change.[57] Consider the second point first.

Marc Galanter has argued that "legal contests do not ordinarily take place between rich guys and poor guys. They take place, for the most part, between individuals and large organizations."[58] For the individual, the legal confrontation is typically a one-shot affair. It is, if not an emergency, at least a disruption, and "the stakes represented by the tangible outcome of the case may be high relative to total worth."[59] For the organization, making or defending specific kinds of suits is likely to be a recurrent activity, and the tangible stakes are more probably small relative to total worth for any given case.[60] This implies certain strategic advantages for the recurrent litigant, not the least of which is the ability to play the odds; that is, to risk maximum tangible loss in the instant case in hopes of a favorable rule change that can be used to advantage in future cases. "Since they expect to litigate again RP's [repeat players] can select to adjudicate (or appeal) those cases which they regard as most likely to produce favorable rules. . . . Thus, we would expect the body of 'precedent' cases . . . to be relatively skewed toward those favorable to RP."[61]

This is not meant to suggest that rule development is determined, in some simplistic way, solely by this form of strategic advantage. On the contrary, the legal system has in the past ratified and sanctioned major systemic changes in the economic system.[62] Nonetheless, the organizational or repeat player does occupy a privileged position. He can initiate cases that are promising with respect to development of precedent with the "potential to influence" (power as defined here) future cases, and prevent (through settlement) the initiation of unpromising cases.[63] Furthermore, "those who occupy this position of advantage tend to enjoy other advantages as well."[64]

> Foremost among these are massive disparities in the quality and quantity of legal services utilized by individuals and by organizations. Indeed, legal professionals in the United States can be roughly dichotomized into those who provide a limited range of services to individuals on an episodic basis and those who provide a wider range of services to organizations on a more continuing basis. . . . There is a pattern of massive differences in education, skill and status between these groups. There is also a massive difference in the range and quality of services provided. The profession is organized to provide a wide range of services to organizations and a much narrower range to individuals.[65]

Thus, the institutional organization of legal counsel directly affects the rights determination process and, therefore, the structure of power in society. Power, as we began, is a "potential to influence" centering on the control or manipulation of rights of economic significance. The adversarial process itself structures opportunities to use the legal system for redistributive change; and the strategic advantage of recurrent litigants is accentuated by the institution of legal counsel (despite historical efforts to devise corrective delivery systems). The concept of institutional hegemony helps to explain this state of affairs.

Institutional Hegemony and Legal Counsel

Institutional hegemony is a process in which the ostensibly noneconomic institutions of society are "linked to the dominant economic institution, the corporation, in a kind of means-ends continuum. That is, the corporation uses other institutions as means for its own ends."[66] William Dugger argues that four social mechanisms function as instruments of hegemony: subreption, contamination, emulation, and mystification.[67] The intent in this section is to place the institution of legal counsel in a context of corporate hegemony.

Subreption, notes Dugger, "refers to the process whereby the function performed by one cluster of institutions becomes the means of another cluster of institutions."[68] The official functions and objectives of the legal profession are explicit. Ethical Consideration 1-1 of the lawyer's *Code of Professional Responsibility* specifies the objective "to provide ready access to the professional services of a lawyer of competence and integrity to every member of societey."[69] The ostensible goal, then, of the institution of legal counsel is to maintain a broadly based system of representation responsive to a diversity of claims and clients. But, as we have seen, this has been increasingly subrepted at least since the Civil War as the profession has become "an intellectual jobber and contractor" for corporate enterprise. Examine the course offerings in virtually any law school catalog. Note, beyond the freshman requirements, the preponderance of corporate, accounting, and tax law courses in the curriculum. These courses, although they may not be required for graduation, are essential if one expects to pass the bar exam. In a pecuniary civilization, pecuniary concerns matter most. Accordingly, the education and socialization of aspiring lawyers and, subsequently, the practice of law itself must necessarily conform to a pecuniary logic.[70] "Pressure on the lawyer to bend the letter and spirit of the law to accommodate the profit interest of his business client long has been recognized."[71]

In constructing and manipulating the legal foundations of the corporate enterprise system, influential upper echelon law firms became, in effect, an annex to said system. Their contribution has been in service to the evolving industrial scheme. The lawyers, then, have been the architects of an economic system founded upon the corporate entity, the seperation of ownership and control, and concentrated economic power.[72] Architecture is, of course, a technical occupation and, viewed in this way, the legal architects who toil in the dominant "institutions of representation" of our time have become technicians of corporate enterprise not unlike accountants, engineers, and managers.[73] Thus the "common fund of technical information" characteristic of the modern legal profession derives from the "business-like" ways of the corporate enterprise system in much the same fashion that the theocratic cast of the profession's ancient forebears was derived from its development as part of a religious hierarchy. The symbiosis is based on a common footing in technique.[74] "In Western societies, legal systems have grown to monstrous size. They constitute inbred, highly technical information systems."[75] Quite understandably, then, an attorney has come to conceive of himself "as a technician rather than an originator of policy."[76]

"Contamination," says Dugger, "occurs when the motives appropriate for the roles of one institution spread to the roles of others."[77] The evolution of the legal profession from ancient Rome onward shows a clear relationship between increased social differentiation and related problems of social integration, on the one hand, and changes in the nature and scope of legal work, on the other. These changes have forged the constellation of role partners that attorneys recognize, and of the groups and institutions directly interested in the administration of justice and the activities of the legal profession.[78] These factors, "in conjunction with the value orientations and historical traditions which may be common to the whole society or peculiar to the legal profession . . . influence the attitudes lawyers hold toward various groups and catagories."[79] This is reflected, in various ways, in the pattern of claims which actually become enmeshed in the legal process, and it is a result of contamination arising from the way in which legal counsel is institutionalized in a complex social structure.

Leon Mayhew suggests that the distinction between reactive and proactive law mobilization provides relevant insight into the channels of access linking clients to attorneys.[80] The traditional form of private practice for fees, which dominates the distribution of legal services, is a reactive strategy. The advocate waits passively for clients to bring their problems to him. Here, the pattern of contact between citizens and attorneys is founded in the private property–cash market nexus, which operates as a mechanism to provide financial resources to support legal representation and criteria (market criteria) for the distribution of services.[81] The proactive strategy is typical of the various alternatives to rationing by fees that have developed in recent years. Here, the advocate searches for clients either to serve some specific group more vigorously or to find a vehicle for pressing a strategic point of law.[82] Each strategy has its own biases; "the array of cases represented . . . is an organizationally selected subset of the rights and claims that might possibly be represented."[83] To the extent that the latter strategy exists, we witness contamination by bureaucratic constraint. But to the extent that the former strategy dominates, we witness contamination as an instrument of corporate hegemony.[84] "The legal ethic defines the lawyer and judge as social protectors of the system of law, but the primary mark of the successful lawyer in the market society is acquisition of wealth and power as employee or representative of the large corporation."[85]

Emulation, the third instrument of hegemony, is closely related to contamination and "occurs when one institution becomes *the* source of status.

Acquisition of status then comes from performing the top roles of the dominant institution."[86] Sociological studies indicate that there is a well-defined pecking order in the legal profession which is based on an intra-professional status hierarchy.[87] Low status is generally associated with a "personal practice" focusing on those areas of law involving personal legal problems (criminal, domestic relations, personal injury, debt collection, and so forth). In contrast, high status is conferred upon those who specialize in "corporate practice" (commercial law, labor relations [with a management orientation, of course] antitrust, banking, tax, patents, and so forth). Practitioners in this strata of the profession tend to be concentrated in large law firms, which pattern their internal organization and operations after the corporate model.[88] Not uncommonly, the senior partners in such firms divide their time between the law office and the board rooms of the corporations they represent.[89]

In roughly the past thirty years there has been considerable change in the structural organization of the legal profession. This has involved the gradual disappearance of the solo practitioner and the accretion of attorneys into larger law firms and the employ of private industry. This process has left in its wake a "lacunae of unrepresented interests" among the public.[90] Emulation as an instrument of corporate hegemony and status enhancement and the application of a pecuniary animus to the rationing of legal representation provide a plausible explanation of this unwelcome gap.

The final instrument of hegemony is mystification. "It occurs when one institution produces the most important or the most valued symbols of a society and other institutions attempt to emulate or support them."[91] The most valued symbols of U.S. society include "freedom of contract" and "private property"; they originate, as Dugger notes, in the corporate sphere, although the symbolic concepts are no longer coincident with their literal meanings. The institution of legal counsel, as subrepted by corporate enterprise, plays a key role in the support and distortion of these symbols. Law, as a process, procedes through the manipulation of symbols; it is "both a mechanism for sanctifying what is perceived or advocated as tradition and a resource for facilitating what is perceived or advocated as desirable change."[92] Legal principles and legal rules form conjunctive matrices which perform both instrumental and symbolic functions.[93] "A law is instrumental if it aims at concrete behavior; such a law has 'little effect' unless actually enforced. Symbolic laws 'do not depend on enforcement for their effect.' They take on meaning by symbolizing the public affirmation of social ideals and norms."[94] While these matrices are in a continual state of flux, their specific configuration at any one time is a product of power. Moreover, the matrices also define power and delimit its use as both dependent and independent variables in the manipulation of social structure and the distribution of opportunities, wealth, and income.[95] "Perhaps needles to say, there is much sophisticated power play exercised over the principles, the matrix, and the conceptions of society and interests for which, at any point in time, they are symbolic and functional."[96] Attorneys, then, as the manipulators of symbols *par excellence*, stand ready to support the most potent talismans of corporate enterprise and shroud them in a protective veneer of "legality."

Conclusion

Power is a "potential to influence," founded upon an ideology, exercised through institutions, and confronted with a field of responsibility. The institution of legal counsel plays a key role in relation to the exercise of power which is historically contextual. The nature and scope of the barrister's work is closely related to the dominant institutions of a particular place and time; where these have been religious in character, advocacy has taken on a theological cast; where they have been of a corporate character, the profession conforms to a pecuniary logic. In the latter case the underlying ideology that receives expression and support through the institution of legal counsel is that of the organizational (corporate) repeat players of the law game. The adversarial process is a significant part of the field of responsibility that power must confront and is itself structured to the strategic advantage of recurrent (mainly corporate) litigants. This advantage is accentuated by the institutional structure of the legal profession in its effect on the rights determination process.

The law continues to be a much maligned profession, unable completely to rid itself of the hired gun image. But there is nothing sinister or conspiratorial about the role of legal counsel in relation to power. It is simply a product of the mechanisms which function as instruments of corporate institutional hegemony. Through subreption the key "institutions of representation" have become a virtual annex of corporate enterprise. Lawyers perform in the capacity of technical advisers who develop strategies with which to confront the field of responsibility. Through contamination, the values and ideology of corporate institutions are transferred to the institution of legal counsel and are subsequently reflected in the pattern of claims which successfully secure representation. Through contamination in conjunction with emulation, the mark of success (prestige and status) in the practice of law comes to be closely associated with performing the key advisory roles required by corporate enterprise. As a result, the structure of the profession is gradually changing in favor of high status "corporate practice" and away from low status "personal practice." Through mystification the institution of legal counsel plays a key role in the manipulation, support, and distortion of symbolic legal principles which emanate from, and in turn help to legitimize, the corporate way of life. These remarks, it is hoped, underscore the conclusion that the problem of unbalanced access to the law is *not* a problem of "too many" or "too few" lawyers. It is, rather, a problem of institutional structure which stems from corporate hegemony.

Notes

1. Warren J. Samuels (ed.), *The Economy as a System of Power* (New Brunswick, N.J.: Transaction Books, 1979); and *Journal of Economic Issues* 14 (December 1980).
2. Leopold Pospisil, *Anthropology of Law: A Comparative Theory* (New York: Harper and Row, 1971), p. 60.
3. Samuels, *System of Power*, p. iii.
4. Adolf A. Berle, *Power* (New York: Harcourt, Brace, 1967), p. 37.
5. William M. Dugger, "Power: An Institutional Framework of Analysis," *Journal of Economic Issues* 14 (December 1980): 897–907.
6. Adam Smith, *The Wealth of Nations* (New York: Random House, 1937).
7. Lawrence M. Friedman, *The Legal System: A Social Science Perspective* (New York: Russell Sage, 1977), p. 17.
8. Warren J. Samuels, "The Evolving Institution of Legal Services," *Nebraska Journal of Economics and Business* 19 (Autumn 1980): 9.
9. Ibid., p. 6, citing Lawrence M. Friedman, "Legal Rules and the Process of Social Change," *Stanford Law Review* 19 (April 1967): 788, and "On Legal Development," *Rutgers Law Review* 24 (1969): 47–48.
10. Pospisil, *Anthropology of Law*, p. x.
11. Ibid.
12. Karl N. Llewellyn and E. Adamson Hobel, *The Cheyenne Way* (Norman: University of Oklahoma Press, 1941).
13. Pospisil, *Anthropology of Law*.
14. Ibid., p. ix.
15. Llewellyn and Hobel, *Cheyenne Way*, p. 290. The nature of the "law-job" is described by Paul Bohannan: "In carrying out the task of settling difficulties in the non-legal institutions, legal institutions face three kinds of tasks: (1) There must be specific ways in which difficulties can be disengaged from the institution in which they arose and which they now threaten and then be engaged within the processes of the legal institution. (2) There must be ways in which the trouble can now be handled within the framework of the legal institutions, and (3) be reengaged within the processes of the non-legal institutions from which they emerged. . . . There are, thus, at least two aspects of legal institutions that are not shared with other institutions of society. Legal institutions . . . must have some

regularized way to interfere in the malfunctioning . . . of the non-legal institutions in order to disengage the trouble case. There must, secondly,
be two rules . . . those that govern the activities of the legal institution itself (called . . . procedure by most modern lawyers), and those that are
substitutes or modifications or restatements of the rules of the non-legal
institutions that have been invaded (called 'substantive law')" (Paul Bohannan, "The Differing Realms of Law," *American Anthropologist* 67
[1965]: 35).

16. Marc R. Tool, *The Discretionary Economy* (Santa Monica: Goodyear,
    1979), p. 76.
17. Ibid.
18. See, for example, Max Gluckman, *The Judicial Process among the Bar-
    tose of Northern Rhodesia* (Oxford: Manchester University Press, 1955).
19. Richard D. Schwartz and James C. Miller, "Legal Evolution and Societal
    Complexity," *American Journal of Sociology* 70 (September 1964): 159.
20. Dietrich Rueschemeyer, *Lawyers and Their Society: A Comparative
    Study of the Legal Profession in Germany and the United States* (Cam-
    bridge, Mass.: Harvard University Press, 1973), p. 1.
21. Roscoe Pound, *The Lawyer from Antiquity to Modern Times* (St. Paul,
    Minn.: West, 1953).
22. Louis Schneider, "Some Disgruntled and Controversial Comments on the
    Idea of Culture in the Social Sciences," *Social Science Quarterly* 53 (Sep-
    tember 1972): 381.
23. Ibid., citing Edward B Taylor, *Primitive Culture* (New York: Henry
    Holt, 1871).
24. Henry W. Ehrmann, *Comparative Legal Cultures* (Englewood Cliffs,
    N.J.: Prentice-Hall, 1976), p. 7.
25. Ibid.
26. Ibid., p. 8.
27. Lawrence M. Friedman, "Legal Culture and Social Development," *Law
    and Society Review* 4 (Summer 1969): 29.
28. Ibid.
29. Ibid. See also Friedman, *Legal System*, chapters 8 and 9.
30. Leon Mayhew, "Institutions of Representation: Civil Justice and the Pub-
    lic," *Law and Society Review* 9 (Spring 1975): 401–29; and Jack Ladin-
    sky, "The Traffic in Legal Services: Lawyer Seeking Behavior and the
    Channeling of Clients," *Law and Society Review* 11 (Special issue 1976):
    207–24.
31. H. D. Hazeltine, Max Radin, and A. A. Berle, "Legal Profession and Le-
    gal Education," *Encyclopedia of the Social Sciences*, volume 9 (1938),
    pp. 324–45.
32. Ibid.; and Rueschemeyer, *Lawyers and Their Society*.
33. Ibid., p. 340.
34. Ibid., p. 330.
35. Max Weber, *Economy and Society*, edited by Guenther Roth and Claus
    Wittich (New York: Bedminister Press, 1968), pp. 775–802.
36. Gluckman, *The Bartose*.
37. Ibid., p. 23.

38. See Rueschemeyer, *Lawyers and Their Society*. See also Roberto Manga-berira Unger, *Law in Modern Society* (New York: The Free Press, 1976), especially pp. 58–66.
39. Ibid.
40. Unger, *Law in Modern Society*, p. 64. For an insightful analysis of how this takes place in a modern setting, see Marc Galanter, "Why the Haves Come Out Ahead: Speculations on the Limits of Legal Change," *Law and Society Review* 9 (Fall 1974): 95–151.
41. Sir Henry Sumner Maine, *Ancient Law* (London: J. M. Dent and Sons, 1917).
42. Rueschemeyer, *Lawyers and Their Society*.
43. Ibid., p. 5.
44. Karl Polanyi, *The Great Transformation* (Boston: Beacon Press, 1957), p. 140.
45. Hazeltine, "Legal Profession," pp. 339–40.
46. Ibid., pp. 324–25.
47. See Pound, *The Lawyer*; Hazeltine, "Legal Profession"; and Ruesche-meyer, *Lawyers and Their Society*. See also Charles Warren, *A History of the American Bar* (Boston: Little, Brown, 1913); Esther Lucile Brown, *Lawyers and the Promotion of Justice* (New York: Russell Sage, 1938); Erwin N. Griswold, *Law and Lawyers in the United States* (Cambridge, Mass.: Harvard University Press, 1965); Murray L. Schwartz, "Chang-ing Patterns of Legal Services," in *Law in a Changing America*, edited by Geoffrey C. Hazard, Jr. (Englewood Cliffs, N.J.: Prentice-Hall, 1968); and Jerold S. Auerbach, *Unequal Justice* (New York: Oxford University Press, 1976).
48. Pound, *The Lawyer*.
49. Ibid., p. 185.
50. Hazeltine, "Legal Profession," p. 334.
51. Thorstein Veblen, *Absentee Ownership and Business Enterprise in Recent Times: The Case of America* (Boston: Beacon Press, 1967), p. 101.
52. Auerbach, *Unequal Justice*. For basic data concerning structural trends in the legal profession, see American Bar Foundation, *The Lawyer Statis-tical Report* (Chicago: American Bar Foundation, selected years). For analysis and discussion of the trends, see Robert M. Segal and John Fei, "The Economics of the Legal Profession: An Analysis by States," *Ameri-can Bar Association Journal* 23 and 24 (February and March 1953): 110–16 and 216–63; John C. York and Rosemary D. Hale, "Too Many Lawyers? The Legal Services Industry: Its Structure and Outlook," *Jour-nal of Legal Education* 26 (Spring 1973): 1–31; Lillian Deitch and David Weinstein, *Prepaid Legal Services: Socioeconomic Impacts* (Lexington, Mass.: D. C. Heath, 1976); and Steven R. Hickerson, "The Nebraska Legal Services Delivery System: An Analysis of Structural Change and a Methodological Articulation for Program Evaluation," Ph.D. diss., Uni-versity of Nebraska–Lincoln, 1980.
53. Hazeltine, "Legal Profession," p. 340. There has been a long history of efforts to correct this situation through the invention of new institutional arrangements and delivery systems designed to expand access to legal care.

This began in 1876 with the establishment of the first legal aid office in New York City and has continued more recently with the establishment of the Legal Services Corporation (seriously threatened with proposed budget cuts at the time of this writing) under the Economic Opportunity Act of 1964. Other efforts to expand access have included lawyer referral services, public interest law, legal clinics, and a 1973 amendment to the Taft-Hartley Act allowing employer contributions to group and prepaid legal service plans. See Deitch and Weinstein, *Prepaid Legal Services*; The Council for Public Interest Law, *Balancing the Scales of Justice: Financing Public Interest Law in America* (The Council for Public Interest Law, 1976); Joel F. Handler, Ellen Jane Hollingsworth, and Howard S. Erlanger, *Lawyers and the Pursuit of Legal Rights* (New York: Academic Press, 1978); Earl Johnson, Jr., *Justice and Reform: The Formative Years of the OEO Legal Services Program* (New York: Russell Sage, 1974); Harry P. Stumpf, *Community Politics and Legal Services: The Other Side of Law* (Beverly Hills, Calif.: Sage Publications, 1975); Jane Lakes Frank, "Legal Services for Citizens of Moderate Means," in Schwartz, ed., *Law in a Changing America*; and Claude C. Lilly, *Legal Services for the Middle Market* (Chicago: National Underwriter Company, 1974). In addition, a series of court decisions during the 1960s established that "collective activity undertaken to obtain meaningful access to the courts is a fundamental right within the protection of the first amendment." See *United Transportation Union* v. *State Bar of Michigan*, 401 U.S. 577 (1971). Also see *NAACP* v. *Button*, 371 U.S. 415 (1963); *Brotherhood of Railroad Trainmen* v. *Virginia ex. rel. Virginia State Bar*, 377 U.S. 1 (1964); and *United Mine Workers of America* v. *Illinois State Bar*, 88 U.S. 353 (1967). Despite these developments, the delivery of legal services continues to be skewed in favor of business and property interests.

54. Ibid. Compare Thorstein Veblen, *The Theory of the Leisure Class* (New York: Mentor Books, 1953), p. 156.
55. See Auerbach, *Unequal Justice*; Jerome E. Carlin, *Lawyers on Their Own: A Study of Individual Practitioners in Chicago* (New Brunswick: Rutgers University Press, 1962); Joel Handler, *The Lawyer and His Community: The Practicing Bar in a Middle Sized City* (Madison: University of Wisconsin Press, 1967); and E. O. Smigel, *The Wall Street Lawyer* (New York: Macmillan, 1964).
56. Auerbach, *Unequal Justice*, pp. 3–4.
57. Galanter, "Why the Haves Come Out Ahead."
58. Marc Galanter, "Delivering Legality: Some Proposals for the Direction of Research," *Law and Society Review* 11 (Special issue 1976): 231.
59. Galanter, "Why the Haves Come Out Ahead," p. 98.
60. Ibid.
61. Ibid., pp. 101–102.
62. Warren J. Samuels and Nicholas Mercuro, "The Role of the Compensation Principle in Society," in *Law and Economics: An Institutional Perspective*, edited by Warren J. Samuels and A. Allan Schmid (Boston: Martinus Nijhoff, 1981), p. 220.
63. Galanter, "Why the Haves Come Out Ahead," p. 103.

64. Galanter, "Delivering Legality," p. 234.
65. Ibid. Various studies have shown, for example, that the distribution of attorneys is highly correlated with indicators of economic activity, such as the number or percentage of corporations, banks, manufacturing establishments, and so forth. See Segal and Fei, "Economics"; and Hickerson, "Nebraska." In addition, representative fields of practice, lawyer ability ratings, and representative clients bear a statistically significant relationship to the size of law firms and, to a lesser extent, the law school attended. See Hickerson, "Nebraska"; and Albert P. Melone and Loren J. Braud, *North Dakota Lawyers: Mapping the Socio-Political Dimensions,* Social Science Report, Second Series, Number 1 (Fargo: North Dakota Institute for Regional Studies, 1975).
66. Dugger, "Power," p. 898.
67. Ibid., p. 901.
68. Ibid.
69. *The Code of Professional Responsibility* (Chicago: American Bar Association, 1976), p. 3c.
70. Mayhew, "Institutions," p. 401; and Samuels, "Legal Services," p. 11.
71. Warren S. Gramm, "Industrial Capitalism and the Breakdown of the Liberal Rule of Law," *Journal of Economic Issues* 12 (December 1973): 594, citing Milton Mayer, *The Lawyers* (New York: Harper and Row, 1966); and Joseph C. Goulden, *The Superlawyers* (New York: Webright and Talley, 1971).
72. Hazeltine, "Legal Profession."
73. Mayhew, "Institutions."
74. Technique, that is, in the Ellulian sense. See Jacques Ellul, *The Technological Society* (New York: Alfred A. Knopf, 1964), especially pp. 291–300. In his use of the term *technique*, Ellul refers to the progressive adaptation of standardized complex means to carelessly examined ends. To the extent that modern societies have become enamored with the quest for the "one best means" in all endeavors, technique is extended to all spheres of life.
75. Friedman, "Legal Culture," p. 30.
76. Hazeltine, "Legal Profession," p. 341.
77. Dugger, "Power," p. 902.
78. Rueschemeyer, *Lawyers and Their Society,* p. 9.
79. Ibid.
80. Mayhew, "Institutions."
81. Ibid.
82. Ibid., p. 414.
83. Ibid., p. 419.
84. Ibid.
85. Gramm, "Industrial Capitalism," p. 594.
86. Dugger, "Power," p. 902.
87. See Auerbach, *Unequal Justice*; Carlin, *Lawyers*; Smigel, *Wall Street Lawyer*; and Handler, *Lawyer.*
88. See Hickerson, "Nebraska"; and Melone and Braud, *North Dakota.*
89. Smigel, *Wall Street Lawyer.*

90. Mayhew, "Institutions," p. 408.
91. Dugger, "Power," p. 903.
92. Samuels and Mercuro, "Compensation Principle," p. 219.
93. Ibid., pp. 224–27.
94. Friedman, *Legal System*, p. 50, citing Joseph Gusfield, "Moral Passage: The Symbolic Process in Public Designations of Deviance," *Social Problems* 15 (1967): 175.
95. Ibid., p. 169; and Samuels and Schmid, *Law and Economics*, p. 1.
96. Samuels and Mercuro, "Compensation Principle," p. 225.

8

On the Nature and Existence of Economic Coercion: The Correspondence of Robert Lee Hale and Thomas Nixon Carver

Warren J. Samuels

Economic activity in a market economy takes place within a framework of legal and moral institutions. One of the functions of these institutions of social control is to distinguish between permissible and impermissible coercion.[1] The conduct of economic analysis often is channeled, and its conclusions prefigured, by assumptions as to what is and is not coercion, or as to what is permissible and impermissible coercion, for example, in microeconomics, welfare economics, public choice theory, public finance, the economics of law and of property rights, labor economics, and so on. One of the fundamental differences between mainstream, neoclassical economics and varieties of heterodox economics, notably Marxian and institutional economics (although these latter are not fully in agreement as to the nature and existence of coercion, and there is a considerable variety of conceptualization within each school), arguably lies in the different conceptualizations given to coercion (and, of course, to such other terms as freedom, or liberty, and power). Indeed, there is a substantial history of discussion concerning the nature and existence of economic coercion and, therefore, the very definition of the term; modern discussions often are but echoes of past ones.

This article will report on the correspondence between Robert Lee Hale and Thomas Nixon Carver consequent to the publication by Hale of an article, "Coercion and Distribution in a Supposedly Non-coercive State," which used Carver's *Principles of National Economy* as a foil with which to present ideas and lines of reasoning that Hale eventually developed into a powerful and wide ranging, if controversial, analysis.[2] Carver was a leading orthodox, indeed highly conservative, economist at Harvard. Hale, who had a law degree as well as a B.A. and M.A. from Harvard and a Ph.D. from Columbia, taught at the Columbia University law school from 1919 into the mid-1950s. His analysis parallels that of John R. Commons; John Maurice Clark adopted it as a basic part of his *Social Control of Business.*[3]

As the reader of the correspondence presented below will discover, the exchange of views between Hale and Carver represents a straightforward juxtaposition of neoclassical and institutionalist conceptualizations of coercion in a market economy. Carver's neoclassical position generally maintains that coercion is either fundamentally absent from or severely constrained in a market economy, especially one that is competitive and exhibits relatively easy entry. Power, and therefore coercion, would comprise only command price, which competition prevents. In a market system there is voluntary exchange, consent, and individual(ist) choice within individual opportunity sets. Hale's institutionalist position generally argues that coercion is inevitable and ubiquitous in every economy, not excluding the market economy. There is generalized, systematic, and structural coercion. Coercion—both personal and, especially, impersonal—exists through the aggregate exercise of choice, through the control over resources and participation in the economy. Coercion is consequent to the exercise of choice based upon one's opportunity set and involves effects visited upon others; coercion is involved in the ongoing formation of the structure of opportunity sets. Voluntary exchange takes place only within the system of mutual coercion.

Whereas the neoclassical mind tends to see only the state (and perhaps, selectively, trade unions and cartels) as the repository of coercion, the institutionalist, and certainly Hale, sees both the market and the state as coercive. At stake, then, are quite different conceptions or definitions of "coercion," of the evidence of "coercion," and of the relation of "coercion" to "freedom" and "power," as well as different usages revealing a pejorative versus a neutral, analytic status of the concept. There obviously is at work a process of selective perception plus a general inability to comprehend the nature of rival thought systems, the neoclassicist being sensitive (or insensitive) to any model that seems to challenge the voluntary and consensual character of market exchange, and the institutionalist being sensitive (or insensitive) to any model that seems to rationalize the market as voluntary and consensual in a manner that supports certain power positions as noncoercive but others, arguably functionally equivalent, as coercive.

Hale argued that the economy *qua* economy is a system of mutual coercion, understood to comprise the impact of the behavior and choices of others (individually or in the aggregate). Such coercion limits one's freedom from the purely voluntary (meaning complete autonomy with the absence of constrained choice, in effect choice governing the range of alternatives among which one will choose)—to the purely volitional (the circumstantially limited exercise of choice among alternatives). Some of this coercion is seen by economic agents as freedom and some as coercion, with different perceptions among economic agents. Relative coercive capacity, furthermore, is ultimately founded in part on law but there would be coercion even with an equal distribution of property and other bases of power, even under a competitive market structure. There would be coercion with equality as well, inasmuch as in all cases there would be effects of aggregated individual choices upon the opportunity sets of others.

Hale begins his article on "Coercion and Distribution in a Supposedly Non-coercive State" by asserting that "the systems advocated by professed upholders of laissez-faire are in reality permeated with coercive restrictions of individual freedom, and with restrictions, moreover, out of conformity with any formula of 'equal opportunity' or of 'preserving the equal rights of others.' Some sort of coercive restriction of individuals, it is believed, is absolutely unavoidable, and cannot be made to conform to any Spencerian formula."[4] The individualist, market economy, says Hale, "has the appearance of exposing individuals to but little coercion at the hands of the government and to none at all at the hands of other individuals or groups. Yet it does in fact expose them to coercion at the hands of both, or at least to a kind of influence indistinguishable in its effects from coercion."[5]

Discussing the distribution of property and its effects, Hale says that "unless . . . the non-owner can produce his own food, the law compels him to starve if he has no wages, and compels him to go without wages unless he obeys the behests of some employer. It is the law that coerces him into wage-work under penalty of starvation—unless he can produce food. . . . In short, if he be not a property owner, the law which forbids him to produce with any of the existing equipment, and the law which forbids him to eat any of the existing food, will be lifted *only* in case he works for an employer. It is the law of property which coerces people into working for factor-owners—though . . . the workers can as a rule exert sufficient counter-coercion to limit materially the governing power of the owners."[6]

Apropos of income distribution, Hale argues that "the income of each person in the community depends on the relative strength of his power of coercion, offensive and defensive. In fact it appears that what Mr. Carver calls the 'productivity' of each factor means no more nor less than this coercive power. It is measured not by what one actually *is* producing, which could not be determined in the case of joint production, but by the extent to which production would fall off if one left and if the marginal laborer were put in his place—by the extent, that is, to which the execution of his threat of withdrawal would damage the employer. Not only does the distribution of income depend on this mutual coercion; so also does the distribution of that power to exert further compulsion which accompanies the management of an industry. . . . The distribution of income, to repeat, depends on the relative power of coercion which the different members of the community can exert against one another. Income is the price paid for not using one's coercive weapons."[7] Incomes are not the result of "voluntary" payments but payments "as the price of escape from damaging behavior of others."[8] He argues that "were it once recognized that nearly all incomes are the result of private coercion, some with the help of the state, some without it, it would then be plain that to admit the coercive nature of the process would not be to condemn it. Yet popular thought undoubtedly does require special justification for any conduct, private or governmental, which is labeled 'coercive,' while it does not require such special justification for conduct to which it does not apply that term. Popular judgment of social problems, therefore, is apt to be distorted by the popular recognition or non-recognition of 'coercion.' "[9]

Although Carver is recognized for his efforts to balance the effects of (what Hale calls) the coercive positions of workers and employers, Hale finds Carver's proposed legal remedies no different from coercion *qua* coercion than the remedies proposed by socialists and the I.W.W. This is a result, according to Hale, of Carver's "failure to see the coercive nature of the bargaining weapons, coupled with his keenness in scenting coercion in any legal arrangements which would alter the distribution of these weapons."[10] Furthermore, "the owner of every dollar has, by virtue of his law-created right of ownership, a certain amount of influence over the channels into which industry shall flow"[11]—and thus participates in the process of mutual coercion. "The channels into which industry shall flow, then, as well as the apportionment of the community's wealth, depend upon coercive arrangements. These arrangements are put in force by various groups, some of whom derive their coercive power from control over governmental machinery, some from their own physical power to abstain from working. The arrangements are susceptible of great alteration by government bodies, and governments are concerning themselves more and more with them,"[12] coercion being present under the existing system, the new system, and in the process of replacement. Contrary to the conventional defense (or understanding) of the market and of existing power positions, coercion (in the nonpejorative sense) is inexorable and ubiquitous.

Carver was, of course, a thorough-going individualist, or, as he put it, constructive liberalist. "A liberalist in economics," he wrote in the book Hale reviewed, "is one who believes in the freedom of the individual rather than in compulsion, either by the mass or by a despot. . . . There are only two ways of getting men to do what is necessary for their own maintenance and that of the public: one is to induce them by the offer of a reward, either of a material or of an immaterial kind; the other is to compel them by authority."[13] He opposed universal public ownership (socialism) and favored freedom of contract. But his was a "constructive liberalism" in which disadvantages of freedom of contract are recognized and "conditions can be created under which the average employer will find it as hard to get a man to work for him at liberal wages as the man will find it to get an employer to hire him at those wages," so that "the advantages in bargaining will be about even."[14]

It is possible that Hale did not fully appreciate that Carver advocated revising the power structure within which income was generated so as to result in a more equitable distribution of income. It also is possible that Hale did recognize this but saw that such an approach could not in a neutral, analytical fashion be distinguished from more radical approaches to reform. Certainly, as the letters make clear, they differed as to the nuances of coercion involved in distinguishing between cases.

While the tone and basic thrust of *Principles of National Economy*, as was the case with all Carver's writings, was clearly laissez faire, and while Carver certainly did not accept the idea of the economy as a generalized field of mutual coercion in the nonpejorative, analytical sense but did tend to see private voluntary activity as noncoercive and governmental action as coercive in the pejorative sense, he was not naively blind to phenomena perhaps more readily and more deeply analyzed with Hale's model rather than his own. Thus, in his *Distribution of Wealth*, Carver argues that profits are a result of advantages in bargaining power enjoyed by businessmen more than "the laborer, the landlord, or the capitalist." Businessmen are "in a better position to know what their factors are approximately worth than the other men are. The result is that the factors of production are more frequently employed at a price slightly under than slightly over their marginal productivity. . . . This means that the business men *as a class,* by reason of their superior advantages in bargaining, receive a share in addition to their net wages, rent, and interest." Moreover, "the share which results from the business man's superior bargaining power cannot be called the *product* of the business man, for superior bargaining produces nothing. . . . In the last analysis, the profits of the superior bargaining of business men, as a class, come out of the wages, rent, or interest, of the labor, land, or capital which they hire."[15] Superior knowledge is not the only source of coercive advantage; there is also "the deception which is frequently practised in order to out-bargain the consumer" and what Carver called "the method of terror" applied to other businessmen, as well as other sources.[16]

In his *Principles of Political Economy*, Carver recognized that workers are weaker than employers "in the process of individual bargaining," noting that they will, by virtue of their numbers, attempt to influence public opinion and elections. Indeed, he clearly uses a simple theory of public choice, or of power, to infer that inasmuch as "those who, because their numbers are few, are very strong in the process of peaceful and individual bargaining, must realize that politically they are very weak [sic], since they have very few votes,"[17] they will support nominally private, market solutions rather than political ones. However, he later recognizes that if "the system of free contract could be preserved and labor could be made independent and prosperous at the same time, . . . in all probability the demand for compulsion would again come from the employing classes. Finding themselves at a disadvantage in the bargaining process, they would seek government aid in the fixation of wages by compulsion."[18] Also, after noting the "universality of struggle" over resources and for "leadership and command" and after calling for government to "prohibit and prevent all the destructive and deceptive forms of conflict," so as to "transform the struggle for self-interest from the brutal struggle for existence, where the strong prey upon the weak and the ferocious upon the gentle, into a struggle wherein the persuasive and the productive triumph over the unpersuasive and the unproductive,"[19] Carver affirms his constructive liberalism in the very same words used later in *Principles of National Economy*.[20]

In his *Essays in Social Justice*, Carver combined coercion and voluntarism. "Power in exchange," he wrote, implies, among other things, "control over human conduct . . . to direct human enterprise, to influence human choices. Value is the *power* which an article or a service possesses of commanding other desirable things in peaceful and voluntary exchange."[21] Socialism he attributes to "a perfectly natural and almost inevitable" discontent resulting from the "very unequally distributed" strain of readjustment to economic change "throughout the social structure."[22]

As for that social structure, although his position is complicated, Carver argues that "the rich *are* largely responsible for the condition of the poor. . . . The poor may sometimes be poor because the rich are rich, but it is usually just the other way about. The rich are more frequently rich because the poor are poor. This does not mean that the rich rob the poor. . . . More frequently the rich are a help to the poor as individuals and yet, in spite of that, are responsible for the persistence of large masses of poverty. . . . Moreover, it can be shown that the rich are still, many of them, trying to keep the poor poor in order that they, the rich, may remain rich."[23] He refers, for example, to "the concern which certain well-to-do persons have lest the poor should cease to be poor, that is, cease having to sell their services cheap, and begin selling them at a high price," which reduces "the opportunity for profitable exploitation. The rich cannot get so very rich because there are none so very poor."[24] If there were abundant capital, the structure of (what Hale called) mutual coercion would be reversed; in Carver's words, "labor would then be independent, capital dependent."[25]

The purpose in presenting the correspondence that follows is not to assert the correctness or accuracy of either position versus the other, nor is it to argue that Carver's position can or ought to be restated by way of Hale's model (or, for that matter, vice versa). That I have my own views in these matters, developed in articles in which I have used Hale's analysis (see note 4), is irrelevant at present. The purpose is rather to make available for the first time correspondence that represents a classic example of the two interpretive positions directly confronting each other. Although neither correspondent may have thoroughly and effectively developed his position, their interaction, including their talking past each other, is instructive. Whatever one's personal views, the careful reader must distinguish between the pejorative and analytical uses of the term "coercion"; between personal and impersonal, systemic or general coercion; between conditional and unconditional coercion; between various selective perceptions of freedom, or liberty, and coercion, including particular actions of government and of others as coercive; and between the fact of and choice within an array of alternatives and the formation of the array. What is ultimately involved, of course, is a conflict of paradigms, semantics, or discursive systems.

The correspondence dates from 9 November 1923 through 15 December 1923, encompassing six letters in all.[26] Unfortunately, Carver's initial response to Hale's article and letter of transmittal is missing. I have been unable to locate it; it is not in the Carver Papers at the University of California, Los Angeles.[27] Happily, however, Hale's reply (and, indeed, the remaining correspondence) enables us to perceive Carver's initial reactions.

R. L. Hale to T. N. Carver, 9 November 1923

"My dear Mr. Carver:

"I am taking the liberty of sending you, under separate cover, a copy of my review article on your 'National Economics.' My analysis of 'liberty' and 'coercion' differs so radically not only from yours, but from that of most people, that I cannot help suspecting there may be some error in my contentions. I cannot honestly find a flaw in my reasoning, but if there is one, I should like to be set right. I have no right to take up your time, but if you *should* have leisure to read my article, and, being convinced, to point out what you consider my fallacies, I should regard it as a great favor.

"A part of my reasoning on 'liberty' is set forth more fully in a short address to the Academy of Political Science, which I also enclose.[29]

"Sincerely yours,

R. L. H."

R. L. Hale to T. N. Carver, 22 November 1923

"My dear Mr. Carver:

"Your letter astounds me. You attack me for omitting what I did not omit. It looks to me as if you [had] read my attempted demonstration of the coerciveness of ownership, assumed that I was making a 'socialistic' attack on owners because I called the owner's bargaining power 'coercive,' and then failed to read that part of my article wherein I undertook to show that owners were themselves subject to coercion practised by laborers [and] that part wherein I tried to show that the fact of coerciveness was not necessarily a condemnation, and that part wherein I defended so much of the 'coercive' income of ownership as functions as incentive and even some portions of it which do not. Indeed I suggest in several places that there are arguments against reduction of property-incomes to which you seem to give too little weight.

"With most of your letter I am in complete accord, except for its application to me. To choose an extreme case and assume it to be representative is undoubtedly, as you say, grotesquely unfair. I never meant to make or to imply any such assumption. The extreme case illustrates a principle, but I fail to see how you read into the article any assumption that it was typical. It is true that I cite cases where laborers must starve if not employed, but only to illustrate the owner's coercive power *when not counteracted by the coercive power of labor*. I then go on (pp. 474-77) to point out the existence of the latter. Moreover, if you had read more carefully, you would have seen that my illustration on pp. 472-73 was not, as you assert, one where the laborers would starve unless the *particular employer with whom they are dickering* gives them jobs. On page 472 I say that failure to comply with an owner's terms would [lead] either in absence of wages *'or obedience to the terms of some other employer.'* I add that the threat of a particular employer to withhold money would be effective 'in proportion to the difficulty with which other employers can be induced to furnish a 'job.' '

"In your second paragraph you [say] we might just as well show that the laborer is coercing the farmer as that the farmer is coercing the laborer. Of course. I say that myself in the article. Again you ask, 'If you choose to call an appeal to the interest of the individual coercion, why do you not treat the matter fairly, and recognize that that kind of coercion is just as great on one side as the other.' The only answer I can make is that I do. Is not that an adequate answer? I wonder what you thought was the point of the entire discussion from the top of 474 to the middle of 477. I really must ask you to read those words again, taken from p. 474, to read them carefully, and then to see whether your objection is not met. '. . . the owner's coercive power is weakened by the fact that both his customers and his laborers have the power to make matters more or less unpleasant for him—the customers through their law-given power to withhold access to their cash' (this negatives your implication on p. 3 that I fail to recognize that the seller is as much under coercion as the buyer), 'the laborers through their *actual* power (neither created nor destroyed by the law) to withhold their services. Even without this power, it is true, he would have to give his laborers enough to sustain them. . . . But whatever they get beyond this minimum is obtained either by reason of the employer's generosity and sense of moral obligation, or by his fear that they will exercise the threat to work elsewhere or not at all. If obtained through this fear, it

is a case where he submits by so much to their wills. It is not a "voluntary" payment, but a payment as the price of escape from damaging behavior of others. . . . But for their will, he has no reason for paying them.
Yet he does. What else is "coercion"?' And you attack me for not recognizing that a laborer exerts coercion against the owner as well as the reverse!

"Let me give a few other scattered examples of my recognition of the
laborer's coercive power. 'It seems to follow that the income of each person in the community' (that includes laborers) 'depends on the relative
strength of his power of coercion, offensive and defensive' (477). 'Productivity' of each factor 'is measured not by what one actually *is* producing, . . . but by the extent to which production would fall off if one left
and if the marginal laborer were put in his place—by the extent, that is,
to which the execution of his threat of withdrawal would damage the employer' (477). Again, 'Income is the price paid for not using one's coercive weapons. One of these weapons consists of the power to withhold
one's labor' (478). Yet I present a one-sided case, 'lashing myself into a
fury over the plight of one of the parties and trying to make out that he is
under coercion' (although I carefully point out that to call an income
coercive is not to condemn it), and 'failing to point out that the other is
equally under coercion.' If that were true you would be perfectly just in
calling me 'rather unscientific to say the least.'

"How it escaped your notice that I pointed out exactly what you say I
failed to point out is very difficult to understand. My very analysis showing (or attempting to show) that threatening to withhold labor is coercion,
you cite (bottom p. 5) as another example of 'the same general mistake'
—namely, presenting a one-sided case in favor of labor. I do not see the
illustration of the rope and the drowning man in the article, but it is an
illustration I use frequently in my classes. I use it as an extreme illustration (but not a typical one) of the power of *labor*. In the exact case, you
and I would agree in doing something to the man, but my reason is that
there is no social ground for letting him be enriched for doing a trivial act
(or trivial sacrifice, I mean), but I should not go so far as to say that *evey*
refusal to do a positive good without payment deserves punishment. The
payment obtained by such refusal is, in my opinion, coercive, and the
amount of it should be considered and disturbed *only* if it exceeds what
we think the man *ought* to be paid. If it does exceed it, and if there is any
practical way of cutting it down (taxation or the like), I should have no
more hesitation in reducing it because it is a labor-income than I should
if it were a property-income which exceeded what I thought desirable.

"Again on p. 5 you misinterpret my statement that 'Not only does the

law of property secure for the owners of factories their labor; it also se-
cures for them the revenue derived from the customers.' I meant the *gross*
revenue, and thought that would be clear enough. As I point out elsewhere
the [laborer's] 'personal liberty' (absence of a legal duty to work for the
particular employer) forces the employer to part with some of this gross
income to his laborers, and the law of property in its other aspects forces
him to pay money to those who furnish raw materials etc. My statement
is one-sided, however, only if one ignores, as you do, the very next paragraph, which presents the other side.

"If you have the patience to read this letter, I think you must admit,
as an honest-minded man, that your criticisms are irrelevant to my article.
I wonder if the cause of your overlooking the passages for the alleged
omission of which you take me to task, was not because you jumped to
the conclusion that I was a 'socialist' (I gather this implication near the
bottom of p. 2), and that all socialists try to make out on *a priori* grounds
that all laborers are at the mercy of all property owners. You may not
believe it, but I assure you that I am not trying to 'make out a case,' that
I am quite as ready to admit that labor-incomes are at times excessive as
that property-incomes are at times, and that the only sense of the word
in which I am conscious of being a 'socialist' is in the sense of not being
an 'individualist.' In that sense of the word I try to show that the things
you or any other 'individualist' advocates are 'socialistic' too. In short the
antithesis between 'socialism' and 'individualism' appears to me meaningless. When it comes to justifying particular inequalities in income, one
could accept my analysis of 'coercion' and still stand for the most extreme
inequalities; only one would have to defend them on other grounds than
that they are the result of voluntary arrangements. That there are such
other grounds (though they do not seem conclusive to me in all cases) I
not only admit in writing to you, but I tried to bring out in the latter part
of the article. And as I have said before, in one or two places I point out
where your equalization program seems to me to be unduly 'radical'—
i.e., to give too little weight to certain arguments that can be advanced for
inequality. Examples are the danger of temporary dislocations (482),
the 'non-prospective stimulus' argument (485) (an argument that frankly
puzzles me—i.e., I do not see my way to any clear conclusion one way or
the other), and the argument of the rich man's habits (488).

"I see there is one point in your letter I have not answered. On p. 5
you say 'the law of property will not secure any revenue whatsoever for
the owners of the factory unless the owners are unusually capable men
etc.' In the first place it seems to me you are ignoring your own economic
analysis which differentiates the income attributable to 'the plant' from

that attributable to the entrepreneur. Certainly I myself get income from the ownership of property with the management of which I have nothing whatever to do. But more fundamental, as an attack on my analysis, your criticism is not valid even if true. If my analysis is sound, the income imputable to 'ability' is a kind of coercive labor-income—the *weapon* by which it is secured is the power to withhold one's able workmanship. When the entrepreneur's income is in the *form* of profits from the sale of goods, the weapon of calling on the government to forbid the taking of the goods is an essential weapon to the realization of the income. Similarly a patent right may be an essential weapon to the realization of an income for inventing. In both cases the *weapon* is essential, though it is not in itself sufficient. One must have the ability to use it as well—as is true concerning the effectiveness of all weapons. If ability is essential, that does not disprove the coercive mechanism of the process. In calling it coercive, I made no implication (this you find hard to believe, but it is so) that it was necessarily unjustifiable. In fact on the bottom of p. 478 you may observe that I point out that 'by threatening to use these various weapons, one gets (with or without sacrifice) an income in the form etc.' In justifying a particular income, if it comes only from a socially desirable sacrifice, even though coercive in process, the fact of sacrifice would seem to me to have a bearing. If you think ability should be rewarded, such a position is entirely consistent with an assertion that the income of the able man is secured by a coercive weapon.

"Very sincerely yours,
R. L. H."

T. N. Carver to R. L. Hale, 24 November 1923

"My dear Mr. Hale:

"If we agree so nearly as your letter of November 22 seems to imply, I wonder why you wrote such an antagonistic review of my book. As a matter of fact, I do not think we agree at all; though I must have failed to make my position clear in my letter.

"My purpose in contrasting the different phases of what you have chosen to call coercion was to show the utter absurdity of using the word coercion at all in connection with ordinary business and contractual relations. The use of that word in describing the ordinary wages contract or the ordinary contract of purchase and sale seems to me perfectly designed to obscure the real questions and confuse the minds of readers. Except in the extreme cases which are not at all representative, there is no coercion in any sense or form whatsoever, and it is either stupid or disingenuous to suggest that there is. The opponents of liberalism have been deliberately trying to confuse the issue in this way in order to make it appear that the extension of government authority does not involve an increase of coercion, but at most it involves a change in the form of coercion. Any one who is capable of believing that is also capable of believing that to win a lady's affection by the offer of love, loyalty, and devotion until she wants to marry you does not differ in kind from hitting her over the head with a club and dragging her to your cave, but they are merely different forms of coercion. In one sense you coerce by physical force; in the other by creating an emotional interest. All such subterfuges are mere twaddle. I am interested in getting people back to sanity and commonsense in their discussion of ordinary economic relations. This cannot be done until the word coercion is reserved for cases of real coercion and not made to cover cases of persuasion and of rational appeal to economic interests.

"I find myself in equally strong disagreement with your general position as to the law of property. I disagree with you even on your restatement that you mean gross revenue. The law of property does not secure for the owners of factories even a gross revenue, any more than light, air, and sunshine secure it for him. Of course in one sense if the sun were blotted out, he would get no more income either gross or net. If you want to use words in this way, you can say that it is the sun that gives the owner of property his income. If violence were not repressed, there is very little likelihood that the possessor (he would not be an owner) of property would be able to get any income from it unless he could defend it and exact an income by his own physical prowess. But so long as the sun shines equally on all, one would not be justified in singling out the property owner as the recipient of the benefits of the sun. Neither would one be justified in singling out the property owner as the recipient of the benefits of the repression of violence which transforms possession into property.

"Finally, I do not know just why you call me an individualist unless that is a name that applies to any one who desires to put fairly definite limits upon the coercive powers of government. I have not called myself an individualist as far as I remember. Instead of calling me an individualist and then finding that some of my positions are inconsistent with what you choose to define as individualism, it would be better, I think, for you to study to find out what [my position really is and then decide whether] the term individualism properly applies [or not].

"Very sincerely yours,
T. N. C."

R .L. Hale to T. N. Carver, 3 December 1923

"My dear Mr. Carver:

"Thank you for the frankness of your letter. The language of your second paragraph leaves no doubt whatsoever that you dissent from what you take to be my position. What is lacking is a statement of the precise grounds of your dissent; and your illustration in that paragraph leaves me in some doubt as to whether you know just what I would and what I would not include under 'coercion.' *Dragging* the woman to my cave would not be coercing, any more than killing a man would be. To coerce, as I understand it, involves at least getting the other person to do something which he does not wish to do. Inducing the lady to marry me by *threatening* to kill her would be the example which you and I would agree in calling coercion. On the other hand, arousing in her a desire to marry me, if not as a mere means of getting me to do or not to do something, I should not label 'coercion' any more than you would. Where we should disagree is in the case where I tell her that *unless* she marries me I will *not* pay off her father's debts (or *if* she will marry me, I *will* pay off her father's debts). If she marries me as a result, the marriage would be coercive according to my definition, but not (I take it) according to yours. Likewise my payment of her father's debts would be coerced according to my, but not according to your, definition. Notice I do not say my act is ethically like threatening to kill her, nor do I say it is so strong a form of coercion as that. I do not assert that the two things are alike in any respect whatever except that they both involve coercion. Even this similarity I understand that you deny. You may be right, and if so I want to know the reason. You seem to question my sincerity, but the fact remains that I have no desire to hold any opinion the untenability of which I can see. If you would only make it clear to me where you draw the line between coercion and non-coercion, I might be convinced; much more so than by being told that my position is either stupid or disingenuous, a subterfuge and mere twaddle.

"In the case above, I do not now see how any valid line can be drawn between the two inducements to the lady to marry—by threatening to kill her if she does not, and by offering to pay her father's debts if she does. Any line, I mean, by which one can be said to be coercive and the other not. Again I repeat I have no reference to ethical distinctions between them. In the article I have set out at length my reasoning for not thinking the distinctions generally made to be valid. You have said nothing to tell me by what test *you* distinguish the coercive from the non-coercive. You have mentioned a few instances which you place on the one side of the line or the other, and the best I can do is to infer from these instances where you draw the line. But to me the instances seem confusing. Let me explain why. Where the penalty for failure to comply with the will of the inducer is death, by starvation or otherwise, you seem to agree that the conduct so induced is 'coerced.' And I gather you do not think it essential that the penalty be death, provided that the person induced has no practical choice but to obey whatever the other person commands. But if absence of choice is essential, why is the tobacco tax coercive? and if it is not essential, why do you rule out the ordinary business contracts? (I am asking in order to elicit a distinction, not because I think the question 'puts you in a hole.') The tobacco tax is avoidable, of course, by abstaining from smoking. Sometimes you seem to suggest that if the person who (according to me) is 'coerced,' can exert pressure against the other party, then it is not 'real coercion.' He does not have to accept whatever terms the other party lays down, but can make the other party modify his terms. If that is your distinction, apply it to the tobacco tax. The treasury wants the citizen's money, the citizen wants to smoke (if he does not, the law does not succeed in coercing *him* to pay). If the tax is fixed above a certain limit, he will withhold his cash from the treasury even if he has to go without smoking. He does not have to accept whatever terms the government lays down; the government has to modify its terms by reason of his counter-pressure. Yet you agree with me in calling the tobacco tax compulsory—at least you call it 'compulsory only conditionally' (620),[29] and I take it you do not mean by that phrase to deny coerciveness to it. The penalty for non-incurrence of the duty to pay is not sufficiently heavy to secure the payment of more than a limited tax. A tax of $1,000 a pound would not induce many people to bring themselves under the obligation. They would incur the penalty of abstaining from tobacco first. So the lightness of the penalty, or the fact that it will only suffice to secure compliance with *moderate* commands, do not seem to prevent you from using the term 'coercive.' What is your test then?

"Please do not take it amiss if I wonder whether you have thought the matter through to a definition consistent with all the concrete cases to which you apply it. I am not at all sure that I have myself, and my suspicion that you have not may be groundless. If you have thought it out, I wish you would set down your definitions. If you have not, and should proceed to do so now, you may reach a point where you can show me inconsistencies or inadequacies in my definition, or you may be led to revise your own. That you may the more clearly point out the shortcomings of my definition, let me remind you what it is. I should apply the word 'coercion' to every case where one person induces another to comply with

his wishes, [provided] the second person complies for the purposes of
avoiding the disadvantages of adverse behaviour or adverse inactivity
which the first person will otherwise practice. By this definition it makes
no difference whether the disadvantage avoided is light or heavy, whether
the conduct induced is important or trivial, whether the results are desirable or undesirable, provided only that the sole motive for the conduct
of the other party is to avoid the detriment which the inducer's conduct
would otherwise cause. When I say it makes no difference, I mean, of
course, only that it makes no differences in the term ('coercive' or 'non-
coercive') applied to it.

"In your next to last paragraph you argue that 'the law of property
does not secure for the owners of factories even a gross revenue, any
more than light, air, and sunshine secure it for him.' Granted. But property is the last link in a chain of causes. The legal obligation to go without
the producer's products except on payment, taken together with the previous situation, is the pressure by which the owner enforces payment. This
is not saying that he ought not to do it. It is not denying that he has incurred sacrifices or displayed ability in order to be in a position where he
can exercise this pressure. In many cases he *has*. It is not "singling out
[the] property owner" as receiving the benefits of the entire legal system,
unless he gets more in proportion to sacrifice than do others. And if he
does, my statement does not deny that there is justification for it. You
would not object to the statement, I hope, that a rainy summer benefits
the umbrella makers more than it does the makers of straw hats, although
the rain falls on all alike. Nor do I think that you would, on reflection, put
your objection to my statement on the ground that the pressure of the
property-law is but the last step in a process which involved many previous steps. For instance, you would not object, I suppose, to a statement
that the presentation of my ticket secured for me my access to the performance of Hamlet. That statement contains no implied denial that the
work of Shakespeare was also essential to give me access to that particular play.

"You reiterate, I see, that the repression of violence transforms possession into property. In your first letter you intimated that by 'extending
the concept of possession' you can account for ownership of things not
actually in one's hands. But this extension of the concept of possession
stretches [it so that it covers much besides] repression of violence—unless
you extend the concept of violence too.[30] I leave my car in the street. You
walk up and drive away in it without asking my consent. That is the sort
of thing which the law of property represses. The physical acts you per-

form are no different from the physical acts I should perform if I drove away in it myself. If you extend the concept of violence, you would have to say that the same physical acts when performed by you are violence, when performed by me, not. The law not only represses violence, it is also the law which has to choose to *whose* acts it shall apply that term, to whose it shall not. In the particular case it discriminates in my favor. It may (*or it may not*) make an equivalent discrimination in favor of you as against me, respecting some other car or some other object. If it does not, still the discrimination in my favor may be defended on grounds of sacrifice, ability, incentive, or what not.

"The lawyers do not use terminology which necessitates this extension of the concept of violence, for they do not extend the word possession to cover all cases of ownership. In the case supposed, the car was owned by me, but not in my possession. When you took it, *you* would be recognized by the law as the possessor, though a wrongful one. Far from transforming what it calls possession into property, the law will use violence if necessary to take possession away from the possessor and give it to the owner.

"You object to my calling you an individualist. I gladly withdraw the term. I thought in your first letter you meant to imply that you were one, but I was evidently mistaken. You will note in the article that I was very careful not to say more than that the view of the so-called individualist would seem to be your general view, and that your final conclusions 'do not differ materially from those of the more orthodox' of the so-called individualists. I also stated that your 'individualism' (I used quotation marks) was 'not entirely orthodox' (pp. 470-71).

"Let me add a personal word about your first paragraph. My review was not intended to be 'antagonistic,' though it *was* critical. I pointed out what seemed to me to be errors, but most of us can think a man guilty of errors without feeling antagonistic to him and without thinking that he is 'deliberately confusing issues' with some [word indecipherable] sinister purpose—for most of us realize that there must be errors in our own work. I also deplored the fact that your errors (if such they are) prevented you from taking an interest in certain problems which to me seemed important, and on which a mind like yours could shed much light. I also expressed appreciation of much of your book. I believe you were wrong (in your first letter) in saying that I failed entirely to grasp the point of your balancing program. You will find it summarized at the top of p. 479 and on 480-81. If you should ever read the whole article again and see what I really said, you will find that I am in sympathy with much of your program. You will see also that I think your voting program commits the government to a greater degree of what you yourself would term compulsory interference with economic matters than you seem elsewhere in the book to welcome. Let me add that if ever I write a book as important as yours, I shall be entirely content to see it reviewed in the same spirit as that in which I reviewed yours.

"You are mistaken in the first paragraph in reading into my letter of Nov. 22 an implication that we are pretty nearly in agreement. What I said was, not that I agreed with your *book*, but that I agreed with the point made in your *letter* that it would be one-sided to assert that the factory owner exercises coercion against his customers and his workmen, without at the same time asserting that they both exercise coercion against *him*. I agreed with that statement and proved that I had not been guilty of that particular offence.

"Pardon the length of this letter. Though you may not believe it, it is due to a genuince desire to be set right if my view of the matter is erroneous.

"Very sincerely yours,
R. L. H."

T. N. Carver to R. L. Hale, 14 December 1923

"Dr. Mr. Hale:

"If you mean the typical case of melodrama where the heroine's weak-minded father is in debt and likely to go to jail unless he can raise some money, and the rich villain offers to come to her father's rescue and keep him out of jail or some other calamity if she will marry him; and she sees no alternative except to marry the villain or see her father overtaken by disgrace and calamity, I should certainly say that the heroine was under coercion. I wonder what made you imagine that I would say otherwise.

"If, however, you mean to infer that this is a representative case, I do not care to argue the question but will submit it to any jury without argument. I wonder if I am right in inferring that you think that coercion would exist in the following case. The girl's father is not in any sort of a trap; neither is the girl. There are plenty of other places where he can borrow money and he is not likely to suffer any serious hardship even if he never borrows a cent. Some rich suitor presents her father with an automobile and offers a good house, servants, fine clothes, jewelry, and various other material advantages to the lady if she will marry him. My own inclination would be to call it a commercial marriage or possibly some worse name. I certainly would not call it coercion. Would you? If so, again I would not waste time arguing the question, but will permit you to present the full argument and will leave it to any sensible jury without argument on my side.

"I believe that my position here is perfectly consistent with the one I took with respect to coercion in ordinary business affairs. The laborer who is facing hunger or who sees his family in danger of calamity, and finds only one possible employer and therefore has to accept a job on such terms as this one employer is willing to offer as the only alternative to seeing his family suffer calamity is, as I submitted before, under coercion. But this, as I argued before, is not a representative case and is becoming more and more rare, as we progress in the direction in which I am trying to promote progress. The representative case in the economic system which we are developing is that of a laborer who has a good job and several others, perhaps not quite so good, but fairly good, waiting for him. He chooses the one that offers the largest number of positive advantages. The question of calamity does not enter in. His own behavior seems to me to show that he does not feel under any degree of coercion whatsoever. He behaves in a very independent, sometimes in an almost over-bearing way. Am I right in inferring that you think he is under coercion? If so, to repeat what I have said before, I am willing to submit the case without further argument; you may have all the time you want to present it to the jury.

"You will note that up to this paragraph I have refrained from using the word, absurd, with respect to the contention that such a man is under coercion or that the woman who makes a commercial marriage of the typical case, is under coercion.

"Very sincerely yours,
T. N. C."

R. L. Hale to T. N. Carver, 15 December 1923

"My dear Mr. Carver:

"In the melodrama case, I never imagined you would call it anything but coercion. I do not regard the case as typical. There is no dispute between us on that point.

"In the case in the second paragraph, I would call it coercion. You would not. I have said why I would. You will not tell me where I am wrong.

"You will note, however, I do not call it *irresistable* coercion; you will also note that I hold there is coercion on both sides, the lady getting the riches by 'threatening' not to marry. I pass no judgment on which has the greater power of coercion.

"My entire argument has nothing to do with what was typical and what not. That is an important inquiry, but a quite distinct one. In what you call the typical cases, the coercion is not so strong as in the extreme ones, nor so one-sided. This, I admit, distinguishes them in *degree*, but I fail to see how it does in kind.

"Take your overbearing laborer. Perhaps he exerts more coercion than that exerted against him. My sole point is that *some* is exerted against him. After all, he does *some* work not solely because he loves it. But because he himself coerces and acts independently, you deny that he *is* in any way coerced. That is a possible definition to give to a term—in [this] last letter you seem to call an influence coercion *only* if it is irresistable. The trouble is, that other definitions than this particular one are very common. And you yourself do not stick to this.

"If you doubt my last statement, can you explain why you call the tobacco tax coercive? Or am I wrong in thinking you do? If you do—can one not say that many a man who pays that tax 'behaves in an independent, sometimes in an almost overbearing way'?

"As for leaving it to a jury, I very much question whether popular judgment is an infallible test of scientific correctness in the use of terminology.

"Very sincerely yours,
R. L. H."

Notes

1. Inasmuch as the definition of "coercion" is often, and in the correspondence herein reported on, the fundamental issue, it will be best to let it remain a primitive, undefined term.
2. Robert Lee Hale, "Coercion and Distribution in a Supposedly Non-Coercive State," *Political Science Quarterly* 38 (September 1923); Thomas Nixon Carver, *Principles of National Economy* (New York: Ginn and Company, 1921). Other articles by Hale include "Force and the State: A Comparison of 'Political' and 'Economic' Compulsion," *Columbia Law Review* 35 (February 1935): 149-201, and "Bargaining, Duress, and Economic Liberty," *Columbia Law Review* 43 (July 1943): 603-28. The final and most complete exposition of Hale's analysis is to be found in *Freedom through Law* (New York: Columbia University Press, 1952). For a summary and interpretation of Hale's ideas, see Warren J. Samuels, "The Economy as a System of Power and its Legal Bases: The Legal Economics of Robert Lee Hale," *University of Miami Law Review* 27 (Spring/Summer 1973): 261-371. See also Joseph Dorfman, *The Eco-*

nomic Mind in American Civilization, vol. 4 (New York: Viking, 1959), pp. 160-63. Hale's analysis is used in Warren J. Samuels, "Interrelations Between Legal and Economic Processes," *Journal of Law and Economics* 14 (October 1971): 435-50; "An Economic Perspective on the Compensation Problem," *Wayne Law Review* 21 (March 1974): 113-34; and "Welfare Economics, Power, and Property," in *Perspectives of Property*, ed. G. Wunderlich and W. L. Gibson, Jr. (University Park: Institute for Research on Land and Water Resources, Pennsylvania State University, 1972), pp. 61-148.

3. John R. Commons, *Legal Foundations of Capitalism* (New York: Macmillan, 1924), e.g., pp. 59, 82 and *passim*; John Maurice Clark, *Social Control of Business* (New York: McGraw-Hill, 1926 [2d ed., 1939]), pp. 111-19 and *passim*. Clark also cites Commons's *Legal Foundations of Capitalism*, p. 112n.1).
4. Hale, "Coercion," p. 470.
5. Ibid., p. 471.
6. Ibid., p. 473.
7. Ibid., pp. 477-78.
8. Ibid., p. 474.
9. Ibid., pp. 474-75.
10. Ibid., p. 481. Apropos of Carver and Harry Gunnison Brown, on the same point applied to land taxation *vis-a-vis* manpower retraining, see Samuels, "An Economic Perspective on the Compensation Problem," pp. 115-16, concerning which also see Hale, "Coercion," pp. 482-83.
11. Hale, "Coercion," p. 490.
12. Ibid., p. 493.
13. Carver, *Principles of National Economy*, p. 750.
14. Ibid., p. 756.
15. Thomas Nixon Carver, *The Distribution of Wealth* (New York: Macmillan, 1918), p. 261.
16. Ibid., pp. 266-86.
17. Ibid., p. 407.
18. Ibid., p. 553.
19. Ibid., pp. 41, 42.
20. Ibid., pp. 51, 578. See text, *supra*, at note 18.
21. Thomas Nixon Carver, *Essays in Social Justice* (Cambridge: Harvard University Press, 1915), p. 35.
22. Ibid., p. 233.
23. Ibid., p. 376.
24. Ibid., pp. 377-78, 379.
25. Ibid., p. 381.
26. The correspondence is in Folder 1, Hale Papers, Law Library, Columbia University. Copies are in the possession of the author. Insertions in pen (but not typographical corrections) are indicated by brackets. The letters from Carver to Hale are the originals, and from Hale to Carver, carbons. Minor punctuation changes have been made.
27. Letter from Anne Caiger, Historical Manuscripts Librarian, University Library, UCLA, to Warren J. Samuels, 17 January 1983. Other possible sources also were pursued, to no avail.

28. Robert L. Hale, "Economic Considerations in the Restatement and Clarification of the Law," *Proceedings of the Academy of Political Science* 10 (1923): 50-54.

29. This reference is to *Principles of National Economy*.

30. Inserted words replace "beyond possibility of covering only."

9

Judicial Regulation of the Environment Under Posner's Economic Model of the Law

Margaret S. Hrezo and William E. Hrezo

Risk assessment (cost-benefit analysis) is becoming the dominant evaluatory standard for U.S. public policy. Fifteen major laws require it as the basis for agency or judicial decision making, and several academic institutions such as the Law and Economics Center of Emory University are working to expand judicial acceptance of cost-benefit analysis through lectures, workshops for judges, fellowships, and publications. Further, several scholars closely identified with the economic model formulated by cost-benefit analysis recently have received federal appellate court appointments. Among them is Richard A. Posner (8th Circuit), whose work provides the foundation of the economic model of the common law.

If the economic model is correct, legal scholars can simplify their models of judicial decision making immensely. The political scientist's search for explanations of judicial behavior based on values, socialization, interest group behavior, and attitudes toward judicial activism and self-restraint may be forgotten. Instead, researchers will need to learn merely how judges consciously or intuitively calculate economic costs and benefits. Those interested in jurisprudence will be able to give up efforts to illuminate law as a pattern of social order reflecting a variety of competing values and concentrate on the prime mover—wealth maximization. Finally, political and legal philosophers will need no longer concern themselves with the problems of justice or political obligation. These questions have been decided by default. Justice is economic efficiency and citizens are obligated by economic self-interest.

This article will outline Richard A. Posner's economic model of the common law, assess its implications for judicial decision making and the U.S. conception of justice, and attempt to apply the model to an area of the law for which it should be particularly relevant (policies affecting the environment and workplace health and safety). It will argue that while Posner's model represents an effort to implement possessive individualism through the legal system,[1] there is little evidence supporting his claim that analysis of economic factors determines judicial decisions in the cases considered here.

Economic Theory as the Heart of the Common Law

Posner claims that the economic theory of the common law is both a descriptive and a normative approach. In the positive sense, it provides a tool for understanding why courts reach certain decisions. Economic analysis also offers a normative standard for evaluating the adequacy and reasonableness of judicial decisions and, hence, is a tool of "criticism and reform."[2]

Economics, writes Posner, is the "science of human choice" in a world where scarcity circumscribes human action and desire.[3] Through this definition he seeks to make clear that economics is about resource use, not merely monetary transactions.[4] Noninterference with the three fundamental concepts of economics (the inverse relationship between price charged and quantity demanded, the existence of opportunity costs, and the tendency of resources to gravitate toward their highest valued use) results, under a system of voluntary exchange, in the shift of resources "to those uses in which the value to the consumer, as measured by the consumer's willingness to pay, is the highest."[5] At that point society has utilized its resources where "their value is greatest" and has achieved efficiency. Moreover, since value and efficiency allocate resources to their most highly valued use based on willingness to pay, they maximize wealth.

Thus efficiency and value are the primary objectives of any society populated by individuals who rationally seek to maximize their self-interest. Through reliance on those two concepts, individuals maximize personal and social satisfaction by maximizing wealth. This is the only rational way, Posner argues, that a free society can fairly allocate scarce resources and still take individual differences seriously.

Legal decisions, because they allocate resources, can have important consequences for the individual's ability to maximize wealth, for "the typical common law case involves a dispute between two parties over which one should bear a loss."[6] The question presented judges is whether that loss was caused by "wasteful, uneconomical resource use."[7] Posner believes that answering this question is essential in any economic system based on scarcity. Economists can aid judges in finding the answer by "predicting the effect of legal rules and arrangements on value and efficiency in their strict technical senses and the existing distribution of income and wealth."[8] Even without the help of formal economic theory, judges intuitively decide cases on the basis of the most efficient allocation of scarce resources—on the basis of economic costs and benefits.

Neither the economist or the judge are primarily interested in the impact of particular legal disputes on the parties immediately involved. Rather, they are concerned with the "probable impact of alternative rulings on the future behavior of people" engaged in similar activities.[9] Once the issue becomes "what is a just and fair result for a *class* of activities," the case cannot be resolved without some consideration of the "impact of alternative rulings" on the most efficient distribution of the particular type of resource.[10] In addition, the law is impersonal, competitive, and "relies for its administration primarily on private individuals motivated by economic self-interest rather than on altruists or officials."[11] These, too, are characteristics of the free market. The law is less efficient than the market because in the market individuals must "back up their value assertions with money."[12] It is thus easier to fix the relative weight of personal preferences in a market situation. Still, in exchanges characterized by high transaction costs, judges will simulate the market by utilizing the criterion of efficiency.

It is not only fortuitous that judges consider value and efficiency in reaching their decisions; it is also essential. Resources will not be utilized efficiently, Posner maintains, unless property rights are universal, exclusive, and transferable. These conditions are not sufficient for the efficient use of resources, but without them the allocation of resources to their "highest valued, most productive uses" is not possible.[13] Through the legal protection of property rights, the judicial system creates "incentives to use resources efficiently."[14] If courts did not encourage efficient resource use where transaction costs are high it would be difficult to achieve the economic system's second criterion—exclusivity of property rights.[15] Any decline in exclusivity reduces the efficiency of the entire propery rights system.[16] As a matter of common sense, then, judges will weigh the effects of each alternative decision's benefits and costs on achieving the goal of wealth maximization.

If judges do intuitively utilize the economic model, then when faced with conflicts over resource or property rights, courts will assign the right

> to the party whose use is the more valuable—the party, stated otherwise, for whom discontinuance of the interference would be most costly. By assigning rights in accordance with this principle the law can anticipate and thus obviate the necessity for a market transaction. Transaction costs are minimized *when the law* (1) *assigns the right to the party who would buy it* from the other party instead and if transaction costs were zero, or (2) alternatively place liability on the party who, if he had the right and transaction costs were zero, would sell it to the other party.[17]

This assignment principle allows the legal system to mirror the market by using opportunity costs to reward efficient resources use and the maximization of wealth. In effect, compensatory damages perform the same function for the legal system that opportunity costs do for the market. In such instances the impact of liability "is not to compel compliance with the law but to compel the violator to pay a price equal to the opportunity costs of the violation. . . . The legal system, like the market, confronts the individual with the costs of his act but leaves the decision whether to incur those costs to him."[18] If the liability costs are less than the satisfaction the individual derives from the action, then efficiency will be maximized by his violation of the law. On the other hand, if damage costs are higher than the activity's value to the individual, he or she will refrain from the prohibited conduct because violation will be inefficient.

Economic Theory and the Possessive Market Model

Critics have attacked Posner's methodological (see [Baker; Whiting; Rosen; Ingram; Williams; Berger and Riskin; Freeman; and Coleman]), economic (see [Coleman; Baker]), and philosophical (see [Baker; Dworkin; Goodman; North; Chapman; Minda; and Baram]) assumptions. A central concern of all three groups of critics is that the utilitarianism exhibited by Posner's work ignores the normative and ethical basis of economic issues.

Posner himself seems to acknowledge this in his *Economic Analysis of the Law* by specifically citing Jeremy Bentham as an important philosophical influence. In a later article, however, he contends that his work is not based on utilitarian values.[19] Instead he contends that his work represents the value tradition of Adam Smith (as outlined by Donald Devine).[20] The authors of this article believe that while Posner's work reflects more influence by Bentham and J. S. Mill than he probably would like to acknowledge, his theoretical roots are grounded firmly in the work of the classical liberals—Thomas Hobbes, John Locke, David Hume, and Adam Smith.

The real problem with the economic analysis of the common law is that the concept of justice inherent in classical liberalism conflicts with a more expansive idea of justice found in judicial decisions since 1936. These two conflicting conceptualizations of justice and their implications for the legal system can best be seen by closely examining how Posner views individual worth and political obligation.

Individual Worth. It has been well documented by Louis Hartz and others that classical liberalism provides the historical foundation for the union of values and practical policies in the United States. The values of classical liberalism are those of a possessive market society where individuals have property interests in both resources and their labor. They structure the use of their labor and resources according to their interests, without outside (governmental) interference. Since talents, possessions, and aggressiveness in the pursuit of self-interest are not equally distributed, there exists an unequal, but fair, distribution of wealth. The distribution will be fair because each individual has the opportunity and sufficient, although not equal, capabilities to maximize his or her personal goals. Personal merit does not depend on what an individual is internally, but on whether he or she possesses qualities useful or agreeable to the person himself or to others.[21] Individual worth is price, "that is to say so much as would be given for the use of his power."[22]

This possessive market society is the foundation upon which Bentham and Mill built utilitarianism. It also appears to be the basis of Posner's economic model of the law. Both reflect Adam Smith's conception of justice. To Smith, justice is concerned with "protection against positive acts of injury, while beneficence, mercy, charity, and gratitude are to be left to the prudence of the individual."[23] Government cannot impose beneficence. Instead, its function is to protect citizens from injury to life, liberty, and property—from "real hurt to particular persons."[24]

In a possessive market society, "real hurt by particular persons" is hurt to production and possession. All social and individual qualities are derivatives of possession. Justice, worth, honor, power, rights, rationality, hurt, purpose, and self-interest receive their operationalizations from economics.[25] This is the legacy of the classical liberals, and despite Posner's utilitarian vocabulary, it is the theoretical system most closely attuned to the economic model of the law.

Under Posner's model rights are not inherent; they are a function of the proper productive use of one's initial resources. One's body, even one's sexual behavior, are economic units under Posner's assignment principle. For, as the earlier discussion of the assignment principle demonstrated, "the wealth maximization principle requires the initial vest-ing of rights in those who are likely to value them most. This is the economic reason for giving the worker the right to sell his labor and a woman the right to determine her sexual partners." Thus it makes no difference whether rights were assigned correctly in the first instance. Once assigned their only function is to incrase production as measured by monetary wealth. This normative approach has implications for individual rights and political obligation that affect the U.S. judicial system.

Posner believes that in order to "take the differences between persons seriously" society cannot treat "the inventor and the idiot equally so far as their moral claim to valuable resources is concerned."[26] Since the inventor is more productive, his share must be greater and law will reflect the need to reward the productive. Unfortunately, the other side of this reasoning is that the "idiot" has no legitimate claim at all to society's resources. This reasoning could be used to justify the legality of certain types of abortions and to prohibit others. For example, Posner suggests that the proper standard for determining the goodness or badness of an increase in population is "whether the social product of the additional population exceeds its social cost."[27] Since "productive people put more into society than they take out of it . . . so long as the additional population is productive, the existing population will benefit."[28]

Moreover, his grounding of rights in productivity is not much comfort to socially unpopular groups. Posner agrees that instances exist where segregation would maximize social wealth. It is, however, "rare that the ostracism, expulsion, or segregation of a *productive* group will maximize the wealth of society."[29] Since society often bases its discrimination against religious, ethnic, or racial groups on their perceived lack of productivity (laziness, stupidity, etcetera), Posner's analysis could easily be used to justify segregation.

Political Obligation and an Alternative Notion of Justice. For Posner individuals remain instrumentalities. They are economic commodities whose purpose is to foster wealth maximization. The individual who is not economically productive has no claim to social resources. Non-economic uniqueness is derogated. And the wealth to be maximized is social wealth.[30] There is no appeal from this fact to justice or the law. For justice is the remedy of economic damage, and in a system whose goal is to maximize the society's wealth, the "distribution of wealth that results from paying people in (rough) proportion to their contribution to that good is not arbitrary. . . . A just distribution of wealth need not be posited."[31]

However, the traditional power of a nation's law has been its ability to generate consent and a sense of political obligation in its citizens. The ability of the law to accomplish these tasks has been intimately connected to some perception that the law is just. Whatever one may think of the adequacy of the work of John Rawls, William Galston, Lawrence Kaplan, and others, they are asking questions essential for any society based on citizen consent. This does not mean efficiency should not be considered. Yet, as Rawls demonstrates, most curves will exhibit several efficient ponts. A choice among them must still be made. It is here that questions of social values and choice, and questions of justice, occupy the stage. Posner considers justice an adjunct to the initial distribution of rights. Once that distribution has taken place, he believes, inquiry should shift from justce to human capacities, rationality, energy, and luck. The distribution of wealth depends on these individual characteristics, not on the justice or injustice of the system. In a society where individuals are viewed strictly as economic commodities, Posner may be right. The developmental capacity of an economic unit is somewhat limited and questions of justice easily may be relegated to determinations of restitution for past economic harm.

But what about a society where this initial assumption does not hold? How compatible are the theory and consequences of a legal system based on efficiency and wealth maximization with the U.S. idea of justice?[32] Influences other than classical liberalism also have affected the U.S. conception of justice. The Greek notion of justice as general societal fairness reached western thought through the work of St. Augustine. More recently, John Kenneth Galbraith, among others, argues that scarcity no longer dominates U.S. social and economic life as it did in a less affluent era. And a wide variety of writers now recognize opportunities for human development as an essential characteristic of a just political system. Some agree with Du Bois that human nature is infinite. Others (such as Galston, C. Edwin Baker, and Rawls) see definite limits within which change may occur. These strains, which seem to represent developments of the Greek and Patristic conception of justice, also appear in recent judicial decisions. Since 1936, for example, the United States Supreme Court has shown great deference to congressional regulation of the economy under the commerce clause.

A shift in U.S. values from the possessive market model to an expanded notion of justice also could have consequences for the operative conceptualization of political obligation. Under Posner's model the individual obeys because he or she realizes that the wealth maximization principle furthers his or her economic self-interest and that in any given situation no better trade can be made. Once again that view is based on the assumption that individuals are "fully formed" economic commodities with little knowledge of or interest in others. More recent conceptions, based on the Greek and Patristic idea of justice, suggest that without at least some sense of community it is very difficult to envision a sense of political obligation.[33] In effect, the individual dwelling in Posnerian society is obliged only to himself, especially if one rejects (as Posner seems to do) contract theories. If the goal is maximization of economic self-interest defined as societal wealth, there are two options available: (1) almost no state action, and (2) state coercion. The economic analysis of the law leaves society no middle ground.

Further, despite its intent, it seems to tip the balance toward state coercion. Everything in society is geared toward wealth maximization. That is definitely a coercive process for those who accept different social goals. Beneficence is supposed to enable the deficient to survive. Yet the individual cannot count on beneficence; all the individual can count on is himself or state coercion. Should a sufficient number of "deficients" inhabit Posner's market society, the outcome could be authoritarian because there is no reason for the deficient to obey. These two conceptions of justice, individual worth, and political obligation force U.S. society to face an important question: What is the better social cement, efficiency or justice? An examination of actual judicial decisions should help determine which cement the U.S. legal system currently emphasizes.

The Economic Model and Regulating the Environment and Workplace Health and Safety

Since 1936 the federal courts have upheld a gradual extension of Congressional power under the commerce clause. Congress has used this clause to outlaw racial discrimination, to protect consumers, to justify the extension of wage and price controls to the states, and to impose additional regulations on the conduct of commerce and industry.[34] Until recently, only *National League of Cities* v. *Usery* appeared to limit Congress's regulatory authority under the commerce clause.[35] In short, Congress seemed to have found the grounds for a national police power in the commerce clause. This police power rests on the notion of justice as general societal fairness—even if the realization of that goal limits wealth maximization.[36]

Judicial adoption of an economic model of the law as the evaluative criterion for reaching decisions would have serious consequences for this national police power. Whiting, Grove, and others believe that judicial use of Posner's model could severely limit the authority of regulatory agencies and the power of Congress under the commerce clause. Such scholars are especially concerned about the application of cost-benefit procedures to the fields of environmental policy and the enforcement of workplace health and safety. Yet, if Posner's model is correct, congressional action in these areas seems susceptible to judicial veto for several reasons.

First, these subject areas represent relatively recent extensions of congressional authority and, thus, are not supported by the force of tradition. Second, they mark a definite expansion of congressional power over the conduct of private commerce and industry. Third, they demonstrate a congressional determination that certain community values should take precedence over the goal of wealth maximization and the model of success and failure based on individual capacity. In effect, congressional enactment of laws governing environmental quality and workplace health and safety are examples of the Greek view of justice as general societal fairness rather than avoidance of Smith's "real hurt to particular persons." Finally, Posner argues that the economic function of the law is smaller in areas where transaction costs are low.[37] Thus, one could expect more judicial concern with economic criteria as transaction costs rise. Cases involving the environment and workplace health and safety are viewed as imposing high transaction costs. Under Posner's model, then, one would expect a large amount of judicial concern for the economic factors involved.

There are cases reflecting acceptance of Posner's contention that the common law allocates responsibilities so as to "maximize joint value" and "minimize the joint cost of activities."[38] On October 27, 1980, the Fifth Circuit Court of Appeals in *South Louisiana Environmental Council, Inc.* v. *Sand* denied a petition to protect some coastal Louisiana wetlands by ruling that although 42 percent of the project's economic justification was invalid,[39] "and its continued inclusion 'arbitrary and capricious,' the deletion of these benefits did 'not change the cost-benefit ratio to such a degree that it actually distorted the context in which the environmental analysis occurred.' "[40] The court based this decision on its interpretation of the National Environmental Policy Act of 1969's (NEPA) mandate to assess costs and benefits. In addition, the Supreme Court's interpretation of the Occupational Health and Safety Act in *Industrial Union Department, AFL-CIO* v. *American Petroleum Institute* (decided July 2, 1980) also relied on risk assessment. While the court did not rule on whether "there must be a reasonable correlation between costs and benefits" in the formulation of worker health and safety regulations, Justice Stevens did give implicit recognition to cost-benefit tradeoffs: "As presently formulated, the benzene standard is an expensive way of providing some additional protection for a relatively smaller number of employees."[41] Throughout his opinion, Stevens makes reference to economic considerations even though the act does not define the disputed words (feasible and reasonably necessary) in economic terms, and a number of lower court cases have held that feasibility could mean "technology forcing,"[42] even if forcing adoption of new technologies meant the collapse of individual companies.

On the other hand, during the summer of 1981 Justice Brennan wrote that section 6(b)(5) of the Occupational Safety and Health Act (which regulates exposure to toxic substances) does *not* require utilization of cost-benefit analysis. Because Congress specifically based this section on feasibility, "agreement with petitioners' argument that section 3(8) imposes an additional and overriding requirement of cost-benefit analysis on the issuance of section 6(b)(5) standards would eviscerate the 'to the extent feasible requirement.' Standards would inevitably be set at the level indicated by cost-benefit analysis and not at the level specified by section 6(b)(5)."[43] In his opinion Brennan relied on Thurgood Marshall's dissent in *American Petroleum Institute*, not on the majority opinion written by Stevens. Yet this time Stevens joined Brennan's opinion as did another member of the benzene case majority, Justice Powell.[44]

It thus appears important to elucidate where and in what types of situations the federal courts are utilizing Posner's model of cost-benefit analysis. This is particularly true because, according to Posner, one of the tests of his theory is its use by the judicial system. The authors analyzed disputes brought to the U.S. Supreme Court and the federal Circuit Courts of Appeals under several environmental and worker health and safety acts from 1978 to May 1983.[45] Legislation studied includes the National Environmental Policy Act of 1969, Clean Air Act of 1970, Occupational Safety and Health Act of 1970, Water Pollution Control Act of 1972, Resource Conservation and Recovery Act of 1976, Clean Water Act of 1977, Surface Mining Control and Reclamation Act of 1977, and Toxic Substances Act of 1977. Decisions based on these acts were examined in an attempt to (1) distinguish among those based on agency procedures, those based on the merits of the regulation or action, and those based on narrow procedural grounds and (2) determine whether the decision rested on cost-benefit analysis or some other grounds. The method for analyzing the data was content analysis. Ole Holsti defines content analysis as "any technique for making inferences by systematically and objectively identifying specified characteristics of messages."[46] The implications here are those necessary for any good data collection and analysis—that all relevant material is treated in the same unbiased manner and that the means for gathering information are precise enough to allow replication.

To accomplish these goals and generate acceptable data through content analysis, one must meet certain criteria. One must describe the population and unit of analysis, select the sample, develop categories, and code the data.[47] The judicial decisions that constitute the population for this analysis are described above, and since all cases were included sampling is not a problem. There were 415 cases discussing 518 decisional issues. In this study the unit of analysis is theme, defined here as the specific legal grounds for each decision. Some cases included both substantive and procedural questions and thus the analysis focuses on the decisions, not the number of cases. Coding was based on reading the judicial opinion for each case and the coded data were classified by the categorization described in Table 1. Tables 2-5 present the findings.

Whatever one may think of the merits of Posner's theoretical argument, this analysis demonstrates that, at least in the area of environmental and workplace health and safety policy, the federal appellate courts do not rely heavily on cost-benefit analysis in reaching their decisions. Only 14 (8.40 percent) of the 166 substantive decisions studied reflected a strict economic approach (Table 2). Moreover, genuine cost-sensitivity was evident in only 29 (17.5 percent) of the decisions. The plurality of these decisions demonstrates a reluctance to second-guess administrative agency decisions and a commitment to ranking health and safety factors ahead of cost considerations.[50]

Those few decisions that did cite cost-benefit analysis factors appear to arise in the District of Columbia Circuit and the Fifth Circuit. Eight of the fourteen decisions utilizing strict cost-benefit analysis are based on the National Environmental Policy Act (NEPA), which does require consideration of the costs and benefits of proposed projects (Table 3).

The great bulk of decisions based on agency procedures also rested on grounds other than Posner's model might predict. For the most part, they were decided on representational grounds and seem to reflect judicial deference rather than judicial activism.[51] On the other hand, only one procedural decision rested upon cost-benefit analysis (Table 4).

Finally, judges disposed of 137 decisions on very narrow legal grounds (Table 5). Of these 137, 53 (31.3 percent) were dismissed for lack of either jurisdiction or standing to sue. The 69 decisions categorized as "other" addressed such issues as ripeness, mootness, and liability for attorney's fees.

Table 1.

Decisions Based on Agency Procedures

1. Cost-Benefit	Does the administrative record adequately reflect the project's costs?
2. Representational Concerns	Does the procedure utilized provide for formal representation of major interests affected and does the record discuss relevant impacts on these groups?
3. Agency Authority	Was the action (1) within the agency's jurisdiction or (2) an abuse of its discretion?
4. EIS	Was the environmental impact statement (1) needed and/or (2) sufficient?
5. Due Process	Did the administrative action violate the fourth, fifth, or sixth amendments?
6. Other	

Decisions Based on the Merits of the Regulation

1. Cost-Benefit	On the basis of strict cost-benefit analysis, do the merits outweigh the costs?
2. Cost-Sensitive	Was the administrative decision the best practicable, most economically feasible, or most efficient way to achieve the goal?
3. Cost-Oblivious	Costs were not considered as important as was achievement of the goal.
4. Political Process	Court seeks to determine whether the action was broad enough "in character and affects a sufficiently large group of individuals" that the imposition of the burden is "fair and just, and that the interests of the burdened parties were protected adequately in the political process."[48]
5. Statutory Interpretation	The court's interpretation of concepts such as "point source" or "person."
6. Arbitrary and Capricious	The court deems the substantive action unreasonable. Such a finding is usually accompanied by reference to the procedural issue of representation.
7. Other	

Decisions Based on Questions of Law

1. Standing to Sue	Do appellants have sufficient interest in the action or regulation to grant them standing?
2. Jurisdiction	Does the particular court have jurisdiction in this case?
3. Liability	Should the rules of limited or strict liability be applied in the particular case? In cases where penalties could be assessed under two acts, which one takes precedence?
4. Other[49]	

Table 2 (N = 215). Decisions Based on the Merits of the Regulation.

Cost-Benefit	Cost-Sensitive	Cost-Oblivious	Political Process	Statutory Interpretation	Arbitrary/Capricious	Other
14	29	28	7	35	39	13
0.084	0.175	0.169	0.042	0.210	0.235	0.078

Table 3. *Decisions Reflecting Cost-Benefit Assessments*

Circuit	Law	Number
DCC	FWPCA	1
DCC	NEPA	4
3	CAA	1
4	FWPCA	1
5	FWPCA	2
5	NEPA	2
5	OSHA	1
6	NEPA	1
9	NEPA	1

Overall, while cases utilizing economic reasoning garner the publicity, economic analysis appears to have only limited support in the decisions of most federal appellate courts. Cost-benefit and cost-sensitive concerns dominate only 44 (8.5 percent) of the 518 total decisions studied. At the same time, 5.6 percent of the decisions were categorized as cost-oblivious. The common law view of justice governing the regulation of the environment and of workplace health and safety does not appear to be "real hurt to particular persons" in its narrow Smithian sense. Instead the federal appelate courts seem still to rely on the notion that justice defines a totality of social relationships and is compatible with a relatively active governmental authority. However, the use of cost-benefit analysis by the judicial system requires additional study. Approximately 27 percent of the decisions in Category 2 (Table 2) demonstrated economic concerns although some of them are less a function of judicial interpretation than of statutory requirement. In particular, work needs to be done on the adoption of Posner's model by state courts, where adherence to substantive due process traditionally has been stronger than in the federal courts.

Conclusion

Professor Posner bases his argument for an economic analysis of the law on both normative and descriptive grounds. The common law mirrors the market (although not perfectly) because the wealth maximization standard is ethically appealing to any society that values individual differences, and accords with U.S. beliefs—especially the U.S. conceptualization of justice. Not only should the common law embody this model, he argues, but also judges intuitively do base decisions on its components.

Table 4. (N=166). *Decisions Based on Agency Procedures.*

Cost-Benefit	Representational Concerns	Agency Authority	Environmental Impact Statement	Due Process	Other
1	90	43	54	15	12
0.004	0.418	0.200	0.251	0.069	0.056

Table 5. (N = 137). *Decisions Based on Questions of Law.*

Standing	Jurisdiction	Liability	Other
18	35	15	69
0.131	0.255	0.109	0.503

This article has questioned both of these assumptions. U.S. values may not strictly be those of a pure possessive market society. In addition, his analytical framework does not appear to fit one of the areas (regulation of the environment and of workplace health and safety) where he believes it should and does govern. Available evidence suggests that despite Posner's contentions, U.S. law currently exhibits concern for a more expansive idea of justice.

Whether the economic analysis of the law will remain outside the judicial mainstream is, however, a matter of conjecture. As long as the Supreme Court refuses to rule on the merits of cost-benefit analysis, federal courts will remain free to experiment with or reject it as they see fit. This freedom is reinforced by the Court's somewhat inconsistent approaches in the benzene and cotton dust cases. The decision in *American Textile Manufacturers*, while not excluding cost considerations completely, is less cost-sensitive than that in *American Petroleum Institute* and relies heavily on the reasoning of benzene case dissenters. At the moment the Court appears undecided about the viability of a doctrine that has important implications for the future work both of administrative agencies and of Congress under the commerce clause. As a result the lower federal courts are without coherent guidance.

Notes

1. C. B. MacPherson, *The Political Theory of Possessive Individualism* (Oxford: Clarendon Press, 1962).
2. Richard R. Posner, *Economic Analysis of the Law* (Boston: Little-Brown, 1973), p. 6.
3. Ibid., p. 1.
4. Ibid., p. 3.
5. Ibid., p. 4.
6. Ibid., p. 99.
7. Ibid.
8. Ibid., p. 5.
9. Ibid., p. 7.
10. Ibid., pp. 7-8.
11. Ibid., p. 321.

12. Ibid., p. 323.
13. Ibid., p. 11.
14. Ibid., p. 10.
15. Ibid., p. 13.
16. Ibid.
17. Ibid., p. 18, emphasis in the original.
18. Ibid., p. 320.
19. Richard A. Posner, "Utilitarianism, Economics, and Legal Theory," *Journal of Legal Studies* 8 (January 1979): 103-40.
20. Donald Devine, "Adam Smith and the Problem of Justice in Capitalist Society," *Journal of Legal Studies* 6 (June 1977): 399-409.
21. David Hume, *An Enquiry Concerning the Principles of Morals* (LaSalle, Ill.: Open Court Press, 1966), p. 78.
22. Thomas Hobbes, *Leviathan*, ed. Michael Oakeshott (New York: Collier Books, 1971), p. 73.
23. Ibid., p. 403.
24. Adam Smith, *Lectures on Justice, Police, Revenue, and Arms*, in *Adam Smith's Moral and Political Philosophy*, ed. Herbert Schneider (New York: Harper and Row, 1970), p. 288.
25. Hume, *An Enquiry*, pp. 27, 54, 66.
26. Posner, "Utilitarianism . . .", p. 128.
27. Ibid.
28. Ibid., p. 129.
29. Ibid., p. 134, emphasis added.
30. Ibid., pp. 123, 135.
31. Ibid., p. 135.
32. Posner asserts that compatibility with intuitive ethical notions is one of the standards by which the adequacy of an ethical theory should be judged.
33. See William A. Galston, *Justice and Human Good* (Chicago: University of Chicago Press, 1980) and Morton A. Kaplan, *Justice, Human Nature, and Political Obligation* (New York: The Free Press, 1976).
34. See *Fry* v. *United States* 421 U.S. 542 (1975); *Heart of Atlanta Motel* v. *United States* 379 U.S. 241 (1964); and *Perez* v. *United States* 402 U.S. 146 (1971).
35. 426 U.S. 833 (1976).
36. See Joel B. Grossman and Richard S. Wells, *Constitutional Law and Judicial Policy-Making* (New York: John Wiley and Sons, 1980) and William W. Van Alstyne, "The Recrudescence of Property Rights as the Foremost Principle of Civil Liberties," *Law and Contemporary Problems* 43 (Summer 1980).
37. Posner, *Economic Analysis*, p. 13.
38. Ibid., p. 98.
39. 629 F.2d. 1005.
40. *National Wetlands Newsletter* (January-February 1981), p. 15.
41. 10 Environmental Law Reporter (ELR) 20494.
42. "Cost-Benefit Analysis of Standards Regulating Toxic Substances Under the Occupational Health and Safety Act: *American Petroleum Institute* v. *OSHA*," *Boston University Law Review* 60 (January 1980). See also

AFL-CIO v. *Marshall* (D.C. Cir. Oct. 24, 1979); *American Iron and Steel Institute* v. *OSHA* 577 F.2d. 825 (1978); *Republic Steel Corp.* v. *OSHA* 48 U.S.L.W. 3092 (1979); and *Industrial Union Department, AFL-CIO* v. *Hodgson* 499 F.2d. 467 (1974).

43. *American Textile Manufacturers Association* v. *Donovan*, 11 ELR 20494.

44. This decision seems more closely aligned with that in *Vermont Yankee Nuclear Power Corp.* v. *Natural Resources Defense Council* 435 U.S. 519 (1978) than does the opinion in *American Petroleum Institute*.

45. Case sources volumes 8-11 (1978-1981) of the *Environmental Law Reporter*, the *Federal Reporter*, and volumes 16-18 (ending May 1983) of *Environment Reporter Cases*.

46. Ole Holsti, "Content Analysis," in *The Handbook of Social Psychology*, ed. Gardner Lindsey and Elliot Anderson (Reading, Mass.: Addison-Wesley, 1968), p. 601.

47. E. Terrence Jones, *Conducting Political Research* (New York: Harper and Row, 1971), p. 77.

48. Kenneth E. Pringle, "Regulation Without Just Compensation: A Political Process-Based Taking Analysis of the Surface Mining Act," *Georgetown University Law Journal* 69 (1981).

49. This typology is based in part on the work of Pringle, "Regulation Without Just Compensation"; W. H. Rodgers, "Benefits, Costs, and Risks: Oversight of Health and Environmental Decision Making," *Harvard Law Review* 4 (1980): 191-226; and Steven O. Rosen, "Cost-Benefit Analysis, Judicial Review, and the National Environmental Policy Act," *Environmental Law* 7 (Winter 1977): 363-81.

50. See, for instance, *Citizens to Save Spencer County* v. *Environmental Protection Agency* 8 ELR 20194 (July 17, 1979); *Illinois* v. *City of Milwaukee* 9 ELR 20347 (April 26, 1979); *In Re Surface Mining Regulation Limitation* 10 ELR 20465 (May 2, 1980); *Mississippi Commission on Natural Resources* v. *Costle* 10 ELR 20931 (September 18, 1980); *Cleveland Electric Illuminating Company* v. *Environmental Protection Agency* 8 ELR 20312 9 (February 13, 1978); *Natural Resources Defense Council* v. *Costle* 11 ELR 20361 (April 22, 1981); *Missouri* v. *Department of the Army* 17 ERC 1001 (March 9, 1982); *Kennecott Copper Corp.* v. *EPA* 17 ERC 1921 (December 10, 1979); *National Steel Corp.* v. *Gorsuch* 18 ERC 1794 (February 14, 1983); and *PPG Industries, Inc.* v. *Costle* 16 ERC 1329 (July 30, 1981).

51. See *Sierra Club* v. *Hassell* 11 ELR 20227 (February 1980); *Sierra Pacific Power Company* v. *Environmental Protection Agency* 11 ELR 20670 (June 5, 1981); *Virginia Electric Power Company* v. *Costle* 8 ELR 20049 (November 1977); *Kennecott Copper Corporation* v. *Costle* 8 ELR 20373 (April 5, 1978); *Shell Oil* v. *Train* 9 ELR 2003 (November 3, 1978); *Crown Simpson Pulp Company* v. *Costle* 9 ELR 20603 (June 29, 1979); *Adler* v. *Lewis* 19 ERC (April 30, 1982); *Providence Road Community Association* v. *EPA* 18 ERC 1742 (July 1, 1982); and *Connecticut Fund for the Environment, Inc.* v. *EPA* 18 ERC 1436 (December 1, 1982).

References

Baker, C. Edwin. 1975. "The Ideology of the Economic Analysis of the Law." *Philosophy and Public Affairs* 5 (Fall): 3-48.

Baram, M. S. 1980. "Cost-Benefit Analysis: An Adequate Basis for Health, Safety, and Environmental Decisionmaking." *Ecology Law Quarterly* 8: 473-531.

Barkdoll, G. L. 1979. "Perils and Promise of Economic Analysis for Regulatory Decision Making." *Food, Drug, Cosmetics Law Journal* 34 (December).

Baumol, William J., and Wallace E. Oates. 1979. *Economics, Environmental Policy, and the Quality of Life*. Englewood Cliffs, N.J.: Prentice-Hall.

Berger, J. L., and S. D. Riskin. 1978. "Economic and Technological Feasibility in Regulating Toxic Substances Under the Occupational Health and Safety Act." *Ecology Law Quarterly* 7: 285-358.

Chapman, B. 1979. "Law, Morality, and the Logic of Choice." *University of Toronto Law Journal* 29 (Spring): 114-37.

Coleman, J. L. 1980. "Efficiency, Exchange, and Auction: Philosophic Aspects of the Economic Approach to Law." *University of California Law Review* 68 (March): 221-49.

"Cost-Benefit Analysis for Standards Regulating Toxic Substances Under the Occupational Health and Safety Act: *American Petroleum Institute* v. *OSHA* (581 F.2d. 493)." *Boston University Law Review* 60 (January 1980): 115-43.

Cranston, R. 1977. "Creeping Economism: Some Thoughts on Law and Economics." *British Journal of Law and Society* 4 (Summer): 103-15.

Delli-Priscoli, Jerry. 1981. "People and Water: Social Impact Assessments Research." *Water Spectrum* 13 (Summer) 8-17.

Deutsch, J. G. 1976. "Law, Capitalism, and the Future." *University of Florida Law Review* 28 (Winter): 309-50.

Devine, Donald. 1972. *The Political Culture of the United States*. Boston: Little-Brown.

Devine, Donald. 1977. "Adam Smith and the Problem of Justice in Capitalist Society." *Journal of Legal Studies* 6 (June): 399-409.

Freeman, D. M. 1976. "Social Well-Being Framework for Assessing Resource Management Alternatives." *Denver Journal of International Law & Politics* 6 (Spring): 377-93.

Fried, Charles. 1980. "The Laws of Change: The Cunning of Reason in Moral and Legal History." *Journal of Legal Studies* 9 (March): 335-54.

Galbraith, John Kenneth. 1976. *The Affluent Society*. Boston: Houghton Mifflin.

Galston, William A. 1980. *Justice and the Human Good*. Chicago: University of Chicago Press.

Goodman, J. C. 1978. "Economic Theory of the Evolution of the Common Law." *Journal of Legal Studies* 7 (June): 393-406.

Grossman, Joel B., and Richard S. Wells. 1980. *Constitutional Law and Judicial Policy Making*. New York: John Wiley and Sons.

Hartz, Louis. 1955. *The Liberal Tradition in America*. New York: Harcourt, Brace and World.

Hobbes, Thomas. 1971. *Leviathan*, edited by Michael Oakeshott. New York: Collier Books.

Hrezo, Margaret. 1978. "The Reinforcement of Social Cohesion: Humeian Philosophy, the Therapeutic State and the Exclusion Ritual." *The Journal of Psychiatry and the Law* (Fall): 377-402.

Hume, David. 1966. *An Enquiry Concerning the Principles of Morals*. La-Salle, Ill.: Open Court Press.

Ingram, Ginna. 1980. "Economic Feasibility of Occupational Safety and Health Standards Under OSHA." *University of California at Davis Law Review* 14 (Fall): 155-73.

Kaplan, Lawrence S. 1981. "Tenth Amendment Challenges to the Surface Mining Control and Reclamation Act of 1977: The Implication of *National League of Cities* on Indirect Regulation of the States." *Fordham Law Review* 49.

Kaplan, Morton A. 1976. *Justice, Human Nature, and Political Obligation*. New York: The Free Press.

Koelling, Thomas W. 1981. "The Burden of Proof in Environmental and Public Health Litigation." *University of Missouri—Kansas City Law Review* 49.

Landes, William M., and Richard A. Posner. 1975. "The Independent Judicial in an Interest-Group Perspective." *Journal of Law and Economics* 18: 875-911.

Lee, D. R. 1977. "Discrimination and Efficiency in the Pricing of Public Goods." *Journal of Law and Economy* 20 (October): 403-20.

MacPherson, C. B. 1962. *The Political Theory of Possessive Individualism*. Oxford: Clarendon Press.

Magat, W. A. 1979. "Effects of Environmental Regulation on Innovation." *Journal of Law and Contemporary Problems* 43 (Winter-Spring): 4-25.

Minda, G. 1978. "Lawyer-Economist at Chicago: Richard A. Posner and the Economic Analysis of the Law." *Ohio State Law Journal* 39: 439-75.

Monaghan, Henry P. 1983. "The Burger Court and 'Our Federalism.'" *Journal of Law and Contemporary Problems* 43 (Summer): 29-38.

North, D. C. 1977. "Political Economy and Environmental Policies." *Environmental Law* 7 (Spring): 449-62.

"OSHA and the Work Environment." *Labor Law Journal* 30 (August 1979): 514-31.

Pagoulatos, A., and A. Randall. 1975-76. "Surface Mining and Environmental Quality." *Kentucky Law Journal* 64: 549-71.

Posner, Richard A. 1979. "Utilitarianism, Economics, and Legal Theory." *Journal of Legal Studies* 8 (January): 103-40.

Posner, Richard A. 1973. *Economic Analysis of the Law*. Boston: Little, Brown.

Pringle, Kenneth E. 1981. "Regulation Without Just Compensation: A Political Process-Based Taking Analysis of the Surface Mining Act." *Georgetown Law Journal* 69.

Rawls, John. 1971. *A Theory of Justice*. Cambridge: Harvard University Press.

Rodgers, W. H. 1980. "Benefits, Costs, and Risks: Oversight of Health and

Environmental Decision Making." *Harvard Environmental Law Review* 4: 191-226.

Rosen, Steven O. 1977. "Cost-Benefit Analysis, Judicial Review, and the National Environmental Policy Act." *Environmental Law* 7 (Winter): 363-81.

Rubin, P. H. 1977. "Why Is the Common Law Efficient." *Journal of Legal Studies* 6 (January): 51-63.

Russell, Clifford S., ed. 1979. *Collective Decision Making.* Baltimore: The Johns Hopkins University Press.

Sandalow, Terrance. 1980. "Federalism and Social Change." *Law and Contemporary Problems* 43 (Summer): 29-38.

Scherer, F. M. 1977. "Posnerian Harvest: Separating Wheat From Chaff." *Yale Law Journal* 86 (April): 974-1002.

Scorcia, Maria. 1980. "Section (6)(b)(5) of the Occupational Safety and Health Act: Is Cost-Benefit Analysis Required." *Fordham Law Review* 49 (December).

Shuman, Samuel I. 1963. *Legal Positivism.* Detroit: Wayne State University Press.

Smith, Adam. 1937. *The Wealth of Nations,* ed. Edward Cannan. New York: Modern Library.

Smith, Adam. 1970. *Lectures on Justice, Police, Revenue, and Arms.* In *Adam Smith's Moral and Political Philosophy,* ed. Herbert Schneider. New York: Harper and Row, 1970.

Stewart, Richard B. 1979. "The Resource Allocation Rule of Reviewing Courts." In *Collective Decision-Making,* ed. Clifford Russell. Baltimore: The Johns Hopkins University Press.

"The Billion Dollar Benzene Blunder: Supreme Court Scrutinizes OSHA Standards." *Tulsa Law Journal* 16 (1980): 252.

Tullock, Gordon, and James M. Buchanan. 1965. *The Calculus of Consent.* Ann Arbor: University of Michigan Press.

Tullock, Gordon. 1971. *The Logic of the Law.* New York: Basic Books.

Van Alstyne, William W. 1980. "The Recrudescence of Principle of Civil Liberties: The First Decade of the Burger Court." *Law and Contemporary Problems* 43 (Summer): 66-82.

Whitney, S. C. 1979. "Economically Responsible Environmental Control." *William and Mary Law Review* 20 (Spring): 441-61.

Wildavsky, Aaron. 1976. "Economy and the Environment: Rationality and Ritual." *Stanford Law Review* 29 (November): 183-204.

Wildavsky, Aaron. 1979. *Speaking Truth to Power.* Boston: Little, Brown and Company.

Williams, D. L. 1979. "Benefit-Cost Analysis in Natural Resources Decision Making: An Economic and Legal Overview." *Natural Resources Lawyer* 11: 761-96.

10

Property Rights and Human Rights: Efficiency and Democracy as Criteria for Regulatory Reform

Stephen E. Barton

In recent years there has been a stream of proposals to reform the regulatory process. Particularly in vogue are proposals to increase the role of private property rights, either by eliminating regulations or by changing them so that property owners can more closely approximate market behavior. Proposals for effluent charges to replace specific emission standards as a means of reducing pollution are an example of this approach. Other critics of the regulatory process have called for extending the scope of regulation and increasing public participation to counteract the influence of private power. Following this approach, several states have increased their supervision of local land use controls, often including elaborate systems for public comment. In the following pages, I will review and criticize the theoretical basis of the privatization approach to regulatory reform, using the example of zoning. I will then discuss how certain weaknesses in regulatory processes can be overcome through extending the scope of human rights, rights entirely removed from the domain of the market.

Neo-Classical Property Rights Theories

The dominant tradition in U.S. political and economic thought is Lockean liberalism.[1] This tradition holds that private property is essential to individual freedom and to democratic government, and that government interference with private property rights is suspect as a step toward despotism. With private property so understood as the basis of freedom, the market can then be understood as an expression of that freedom and market efficiency as the embodiment of the free choices of sovereign consumers and producers. This is the foundation of neo-classical economics.

Externalities, which once appeared to be a minor anomaly in neo-classical economic analysis, have emerged as a challenge to the discipline. It followed from the assumption of free exchange in the market that "the owner benefits from all services rendered by his property and suffers for all the damages caused to others by its use," or at least that any deviation from this is voluntary.[2] Economics then faced the problem of accounting for instances where this was clearly not the case, where such things as "the smoke and noise of factories" created what was described as a divergence between private and social cost. The term "externalities" was used to indicate costs or benefits not compensated through the market, and over the years the term became, as E. J. Mishan put it, "a convenient peg on which to hang a variety of economic phenomena which might be used to justify (government) intervention in the private enterprise sector of the economy."[3]

A critique of externality justifications for government intervention was developed by writers who claimed that, as a practical matter, the market is sufficiently flexible to handle the situations frequently used as examples of the need for government intervention, and that the theoretical justification for intervention was incorrect, that only an economic system based on capitalism and private property rights could operate efficiently.

Bernard Siegan presented the practical critique of zoning: that it is at best unnecessary and at worst harmful, that it is either too rigid to deal with the actual harms and benefits of different land uses or too vulnerable to corruption where it is flexible, and that it is used to exclude moderate-cost housing, thus harming lower-income people for the benefit of the well-to-do.[4] The vehicle for this critique of zoning was a detailed description of land use patterns in Houston, which did not have zoning until 1982. His description of Houston showed that a city with subdivision, building, and traffic regulations, pollution control and nuisance laws, and a Federal Housing Administration that makes mortgage financing available only to developers who protect their neighborhoods with restrictive covenants, was not very different from cities with zoning. Siegan felt that this demonstrated the superiority of private agreements such as restrictive covenants over government regulation.

The theoretical basis for a critique of regulation was provided by the

Coase Rule, after R. H. Coase, which states that the assignment of property rights and their attendant liability rules will not affect the outcome of economic activity unless there are transaction costs that inhibit market exchange.[5] Thus there is no need for government to modify private property rights because the owner whose use of the land is the most valuable will be able to compensate other owners, through private agreements (transactions), for any costs his most efficient use may cause them. In this view, social costs result from transaction costs: search and information costs in setting up a possible transaction, bargaining and decision costs in making the transaction, and policing and enforcement costs in making sure the transaction is carried out.

Coase dealt with interactions among producers only, and critics pointed out that consumers' effective demand for any good is determined not only by their subjective inclinations but by their wealth, the extent of their property ownership.[6] Assignment of property rights has an income effect that alters the allocation of resources efficient for a given set of subjective demands. Coase used the example of a rancher and a farmer, each of whom could compensate the other to reduce or change their operations so as not to interfere with a use that was more profitable. In dealing with a factory that pollutes the air of a nearby city, however, if residents have the initial right, then they will probably demand cleaner air than they would if they had to sacrifice part of their current standard of living in order to provide compensation to the factory. The amended Coase rule, then, is that assignment of property rights does not affect the efficiency of resource allocation in the absence of either transaction costs or income effects. The conclusion that the "Coasians" draw from this is that while government is necessary to establish and protect private property rights, there is no justification for any further government action.[7]

Robert Ellickson made the first use of transaction cost minimization as a guide to land use regulation in his article "Alternatives to Zoning."[8] Ellickson describes regulation as a continuum of legal mechanisms distinguished by their degree of direct government control versus delegation of control to private parties (centralized - decentralized), and by whether nuisance costs are restrained by liability rules (liability-laissez faire). He argues that the debate on regulation has been about centralized government regulation versus decentralized laissez faire, ignoring the possibility of a decentralized system using expanded liability rules. Such a system would replace zoning with revised private property rights, and the revisions would be guided by the goal of minimizing transaction costs.

According to Ellickson, "Efficient resource allocation is accomplished through the minimization of the sum of nuisance costs, prevention costs, and administration costs arising from land use conflicts."[9] Following the Coase rule, Ellickson disregards nuisance costs since, like any externality, they are two-sided. The prevention of a nuisance imposes costs just as the nuisance does and, assuming zero transaction costs and no income effects, the most profitable use will be implemented through bargaining and payment of compensation among the affected parties. Ellickson sees prevention costs as mostly determined by technology, and thus not directly affected by legal rules. What the law can affect, then, are the administrative costs, which Ellickson equates with transaction costs. He then suggests that administrative costs will be minimized if the liability for nuisance costs is placed on the party who has the most knowledge, is best organized, and controls the property where preventive action can best be taken. This should lead to the maximum preventive action at the least administrative cost.[10]

Following this line of reasoning, air rights should be held by local residents rather than by a nearby factory that emits pollutants, and thus the factory should compensate the local residents, because the factory has the knowledge of what pollutants it emits and the ability to modify its production facilities and engage in research of new technologies. Nearby residents, on the other hand, have little knowledge, are loosely organized, if at all, and can control pollution only in their own homes, if at all. Ellickson makes a similar argument concerning a convenience store locating in a residential neighborhood. This application of the transaction cost argument seems to support the anti-corporate approach of the consumer and environmental movements.

I would argue that this approach is mistaken, however. If local residents are really so lacking in information and organization, then they will be unable to make the best possible agreement, and they will be unable to monitor the agreement once it is made. On the other hand, if they organize themselves and employ experts who know about pollution problems, then there is no reason to assume they are in greater need of help than the factory.[11] This is also the case for conflict between neighbors and a convenience store. Indeed, middle-class residents may well have higher incomes and more education than the shopkeeper to start with. Control over a transaction is based on a combination of information and power. Changing the ownership of air rights or development rights does not change the costliness of the transaction, it only changes who has more power.

Other writers claim that private property rights inherently minimize transaction costs, a claim based on the concept of "attenuation."[12] They start with the point that property rights must exist if transactions are to take place, and make the claim that the difficulty of making transactions increases the farther the structure of rights moves away from private property in the direction of common property. At its mildest, the attenuation of property rights may simply be the result of organizational problems such as the difficulty absentee owners may have in controlling the management of a business. Utilities regulation provides an example of moderate attenuation. Since the state regulates the utility's profit level, the managers have an incentive to conceal profits above the legal limit in such forms as better offices and shorter working hours.[13] The extreme case of attenuation is the "tragedy of the commons," in which the uncontrolled public use of a scarce natural resource leads to its complete destruction.[14]

I would argue, however, that the concept of attenuation confuses public or common property rights with the lack of rights and with lawlessness. The tragedy of the commons results from the lack of any regulatory structure at all, whether based on private or public ownership. Common property rights are individual rights of access to scarce resources that belong to every member of a group. People have an interest in protecting such rights, and the value of the resource, just as they do with private property rights. If the value of each individual right is small, then it is true that each individual will have less interest in overseeing the management of the scarce resource than would a single owner. This is a problem of organization that the corporation can solve for shared private property and that democracy can solve for common property. In either case managers compete for management positions on the basis of offers of improved management made to the shareholders or citizens, and in either case management has an incentive to weaken voter control once in office.

The public/private ownership distinction is not adequate to explain the attenuation of social control. Publicly owned utilities, for example, apparently have lower management costs than regulated private utilities.[15] Even when management costs are higher, as is apparently the case in mutual insurance companies, we need to consider whether the member-shareholders think the additional costs of a one-member, one-vote system have compensating benefits.[16] Consumer democracy protects small shareholders and consumers against the self-interested control over management that a large private stockholder can exercise in an entirely capitalist private firm.

The attenuation theory is the implicit basis for work on zoning reform by Robert Nelson and William Fischel.[17] Their insight is that, through zoning, neighborhoods and local governments have established collective, but incomplete, ownership of development rights. Since the vast majority of homeowners seem to favor zoning protections, it is not realistic to try to eliminate zoning and replace it with private covenants, as Siegan suggests, but it should be possible to make the rights established by zoning more closely resemble private property rights. This will ensure that gains from trade can take place and smooth out problems of neighborhood transition. Where the benefits of a change in zoning are reaped entirely by the owner, who is able to develop, while the costs are borne by the entire neighborhood, it is understandable that residents oppose development. At its most flexible, zoning may require nuisance prevention measures and compensating amenities, but cash payments are ruled out. For this reason, residents are more resistant to change than they would be if they were, in effect, shareholders in a neighborhood land development corporation and could receive cash payments for the right to develop.

One can easily make the case, particularly in suburbs, which are in effect independent neighborhood governments, that zoning is sold already. New development is generally scrutinized for its net fiscal impact, and towns naturally favor development that will bring in more in taxes than it will cost in services. In addition, developers are often required to make contributions to parks, roads, schools, etcetera. Measures that lower the taxes on old residents are equivalent to a cash payment for zoning. But more important than saleability may be the question of allocation of property rights, saleable or not.

Neither Fischel or Nelson deal with how neighborhood boundaries are to be drawn and how payments will be distributed within them. Clearly, inclusion in one neighborhood rather than another under a saleable zoning plan will be as important as inclusion in one zone or another is today, as would decisions to allocate funds based on the value of the property one owns, the fact of ownership within the neighborhood, or the fact of residence within the neighborhood, whether or not one is an owner. All the political conflict involved in today's non-saleable zoning is recreated in the process of establishing the rules for a zoning market, because the new property rights, like all property rights, must be established politically. Saleability allows gains from trade, but if the initial entitlements are fundamentally unsatisfactory, then trading will not make them much better.

Fischel notes that the non-saleability of zoning protects third parties from the effects of potential transactions, but considers this a minor point.[18] It is not. Sale of zoning would take place through a political process rather than by the unanimous consent of all residents. A minority who oppose the sale of their zoning are, in this case, a third party to the transaction. And, unlike the investor who can easily sell shares of stock and move on to another investment when dissatisfied, these people have their homes at stake. The police-power basis of zoning limits bargaining to infrastructure and services that mitigate the harms caused by a proposed change in the pattern of land use. This weights the transaction in favor of those residents most strongly attached to the area they live in and the quality of life it allows, and against those who are more transient or oriented toward homeownership as an investment. This is neither "inefficient" nor "an incomplete assignment of property rights." Rather, it is a structure of rights that protects one set of values rather than another. Not all rights are property rights, and full or partial protection from inclusion in the market is a valuable form of right.

Oliver Williamson calls transaction cost analysis "the new institutional economics," but so far its practitioners have ignored the central insight of the old institutional economics, that economic relationships reflect the underlying balance of power.[19] For John R. Commons, for example, liberty and coercion go hand in hand, because one person's liberty requires the exposure of others to the consequences of that liberty.[20] This is not to say that society is inherently a zero-sum game in which the total amount of freedom is always the same. Freedom and coercion are weighted by values, and it is possible for people to arrange a society in ways that allow them more freedom, according to their values, than would other societies. Unless the values are held unanimously, however, they are necessarily imposed on some members of society. There is no such thing as "social cost." There are individual costs and benefits that lead people to come in conflict with each other, as each person or group of people tries to realize her own values. The problem of social cost, of externalities, of transaction costs, is really the problem of social conflict. The Coase rule, ironically, describes a communist utopia in which people are in perfect harmony and in which property rights, like the state, have withered away. Neo-classical economic analysis cannot determine the appropriate structure of rights because efficiency, the central value for neo-classical analysis, is determined through the market, and the market can exist only if property rights already exist.

Property Rights and Human Rights

The analysis of economic institutions should clarify the values implicit in the different forms of rights embodied by those institutions, and the effect that those values have on the political process by which rights are established. The attraction of the free market model is that it proposes a consensual decision-making process.[21] But a market cannot exist without property rights, and rights can only be established politically. The problem then is to find a political procedure that people can agree is fair, and this inevitably raises the question of equality. Private property rights are a form of power created by government but insulated from democratic control by their private status. Instead of dispersing power and limiting the Leviathan State, private property can serve to harness the power of government to create great accumulations of wealth and power. People with little wealth or income have little market power, and to the extent that market power is convertable into political power they are in an inferior position in the political arena as well. People with little power can simply be brushed aside, rather than treated with the respect due to someone whose views, while they may not be accepted now, may prevail in the near future.

Inequality is a corrosive force in any democratic process, yet as conservatives never tire of pointing out, the creation of a government apparatus capable of redistributing income, and the creation of regulatory agencies that intervene in the market in the name of the public interest, could themselves create a tremendous source of inequality of power. The public interest, unlike market efficiency, rests on the outcome of political processes in which goals are not set in advance but rather may change in the course of discussion. Both left and right point out that the rich and powerful can often bend these procedures to their own advantage. Zoning, for example, is legally based on the police power to prevent harm, yet it frequently serves as a harmful exclusionary barrier by which suburban towns and city neighborhoods prevent construction of apparatus, rental housing, and even single-family homes affordable by people with modest incomes.

Human rights play an essential role in resolving this dilemma by equalizing power and by insulating the political domain from the effects of market power. By human rights I mean rights that are universal, so that everyone has them, and inalienable, so that they cannot be permanently sold or given away. (In today's world of nations, they are universal only among citizens, members of the nation-state.) Their universality ensures initial equality, while their inalienability ensures that they cannot be transferred to and accumulated by a small number of people. Votes, for example, cannot be legally sold. The lack of enforceable voting contracts and the use of the secret ballot, which makes private enforcement activity difficult, make it more difficult to convert permanent accumulations of market power (property) into permanent accumulations of political power. This is not a restriction on people's freedom to sell their votes, as economists enamored of the "freedom of contract" seem to believe.[22] Rather, it is a refusal to enforce an agreement to give up some freedom in the future. Anyone who buys votes must rely entirely on the good faith of the seller and cannot come running to the government to enforce the agreement. This may be harmful to an individual who would like to be able to make such an enforceable sale contract because he or she could get more money that way, but it protects both that person and the other members of society from the consequences of great political inequality.

Human rights extend far beyond voting and free speech. They can be instituted wherever property rights create disparities of power that prevent equal participation in a bargaining process. In California, for example, despite provisions to the contrary in the standard rental agreement most tenants sign, tenants have an inalienable right to sue their landlord for negligence leading to an injury to persons or property, a right to a court order prior to any eviction, a right to use rent money to make emergency repairs if the landlord does not act, and many others. If these rights could be signed away, if they were not inalienable, then they would rapidly lose their universality as well in the face of the landlord's greater market power.

Human rights can make regulatory processes more effective. For example, rent control serves as a means of protecting tenants from eviction, except for causes set down in the law, such as non-payment of rent or damage to the building. Without such protection, tenants who exercise other rights, such as demanding repairs or putting political posters in their windows, are subject to retaliatory eviction by their landlord. With such protection, tenants can act openly rather than relying on sending complaints to a government agency and trying to remain anonymous. Often they will be able to deal directly with their landlord, rather than bringing regulatory agencies or courts into the process, because their power is made relatively equal through the rights established by rent control.[23]

In effect, rent control creates a human right to remain in one's home, even if one does not have a property right over it. This reflects the belief held by many, renter and homeowner alike, that their homes should not be treated simply as commodities. Most people would be horrified if the town they lived in were controlled in the same way as the corporation they work for. Residents' rights and residents' control have won acceptance, while so far, workers' rights and workers' control have not. Similar provisions for residents' rights are necessary for tenants of publicly owned or subsidized housing if they are to be protected from similar abuse by government administrators. Rights that are universal and inalienable are removed from both the domain of the market and private property and from the domain of administrative discretion that characterizes state property.

Human rights are essential to the functioning of a democratic system, but they are not easy to establish or maintain. The ideal of private property is so firmly rooted in American culture and institutions that it tends to reassimilate non-conforming institutions. As dramatic a break with established institutions as the utopian communist Oneida Community eventually became the Oneida Corporation, and privatization is a typical pattern for successful communes and workers' cooperatives.[24] Sometimes the reassimilation is the result of repression ordered or condoned by the authorities, sometimes it is the result of a lack of needed supporting institutions, and sometimes it simply results from a failure of will in a society in which collective action is not prized.

The same pattern of reassimilation affects government programs. Some, such as the Federal National Mortgage Association, have been turned into private corporations. Others, such as the Tennessee Valley Authority, have been led to act in the same manner as private corporations.[25] And rights can be privatized as well. Rent control in Hong Kong, for example, has been made saleable as a way of smoothing its gradual elimination.[26] Concepts such as "fair market value" effectively subordinate the rights potentially established by regulation to the value structure established by private property rights. It is not the least of the defects of Ellickson's proposal that if society allows nuisances to be created as long as their creator pays compensation based on fair market value, then the same nuisance will cost less when inflicted on the poor than on the rich.

Local government in the United States has, almost from its inception, mirrored the characteristics of the private corporation in the market. Local government has often served as an arm of private land development schemes competing for population and industry with other landowners and their local governments, and this form of competition continues unabated. The creation of autonomous suburban towns that could avoid annexation by the central city created a new element, the exclusive private development with its own government. It allowed the successful intraregional competitor to exclude less desirable residents and land uses and to avoid all responsibility for them, financial or otherwise. The proposals by Fischel and Nelson are logical extensions of this pattern by which government is assimilated into the market.

Local governments, like cooperatives, are mixtures of types of rights, occupying an intermediate position on the continuum from property rights to human rights. They carry rights that are "universal" only within a limited group, such as residents of a town, and that are only partially inalienable. There are continual efforts to bring such mixed institutions closer to one or the other pole. That is why it is missing an important distinction to simply label all rights as a form of property, as Charles Reich does with his concept of "new property."[27] In my concluding pages I will discuss the rights involved in land use regulation, but it should be understood that, in my view, only a broad extension of human rights in many areas will reduce the inequalities of power built into our economic system sufficiently to prevent the reassimilation of any extension of human rights in a single area such as land use.

Land Use Regulation in a Democracy

Land use regulation is rooted in the police power to prevent harm, but defining harm is not easy. There is the problem of trade-offs, since preventing harm to one person will often cause some other harm to another person, and there is the problem of uncertainty and defining acceptable risks. The risk of harm is pervasive in human action, so that the police power leads not to the limited "nightwatchman state" postulated by Robert Nozick, among others, but to the imposition of a set of basic values that govern. The reach and scope of the police power are particularly evident in land use regulation, because every action must *take place* in some location, and thus involves neighbors or future occupants of the site who may be affected. And the situation is complicated by the fact that the importance of different harms and benefits changes with changing circumstances and changing values. The doctrine of ancient lights, for example, was a part of English common law that forbade neighbors from depriving each other of the sunlight through construction of tall buildings or fences. It was abandoned in the early years of the nineteenth century as an impediment to economic growth, but has recently been revived by some state courts in cases involving protection of solar energy systems.

In this spirit, Michael Goetz and Larry Wofford propose that in order to understand zoning we must shift our attention "from gains-from-trade (situation) to a system of rules to deal with change (process)."[28] The main problem Goetz and Wofford see for a process perspective is "an apparently irreconcilable conflict between the need for stable and continuous expectations, and modification of established rules or procedures dictated by either changing circumstances and/or some sort of societal consensus."[29] This is a problem, but it is not impossible to deal with. Social regulation does not usually change wildly and randomly, but rather gradually, with the support of large sections of the population to whom such changes appeal.[30] Newly emerging community standards may prevent someone from profiting from the use of her land as much as she might have under a previous standard, but in a democratic and decentralized society, such changes will emerge sufficiently slowly, and with sufficient warning, that people can plan for possible changes well in advance of their occurance.[31] The U.S. pattern of multiple levels of government provides a means of experimenting with small variations in rights at the local level with the necessary level of political support increasing as larger changes require the consent of higher levels of government.

The issue of particular concern in any decentralized system is that the local units will internalize benefits and externalize costs without regard for the effect on surrounding units. This is just as true for local government's use of land use regulation as it is for private landowners' use of their land. Both homeowners and renters, in effect, buy into a neighborhood as well as a home. When the neighborhood is a self-governing suburban town the problem is to extend rights to residents of the region as a whole without eliminating decentralized government. Thus it is quite appropriate that the main thrust of regulatory reform in the area of land use has been toward creation of a framework of state regulation of local land use controls, as well as requirements that various potential impacts of these controls be investigated and compensated for in local plans.[32]

California, for example, has adopted a "fair share" plan that requires all towns to accept a share of regional housing needs for each income level as long as there is available land. In a related area the California State Supreme Court ruled that the quality of a child's education should not be limited by the amount of taxable property per child located in the child's town. As a result the state government has had to allocate funds to equalize educational opportunities. This is an important, though insufficient, step toward tax sharing plans that eliminate intra-regional competition to gain tax revenues and avoid causes of expenditures.

Regulation suffers from enforcement problems precisely because, as a means of allowing a measure of decentralization of control, it leaves the initiative in the hands of those being regulated. Thus it is important that those on whose behalf the regulations exist are given the right to take independent action. An essential step toward this is the gradual recognition by the courts that non-residents and non-landowners are entitled to standing to challenge in court local measures that affect them. There are also a number of examples of zoning based on performance standards, which more clearly specify the harms to be prevented and the benefits to be encouraged, and allow flexibility in meeting these goals.

Useful and important as these reforms are, they need to be accompanied by efforts to change the cultural patterns maintained by exclusionary land use regulations. Zoning is shaped by Americans' desire for tranquility at home and in their neighborhoods, and by their fear that people different from themselves will create conflicts. Homeowners in particular fear increased density housing, whether for renters or condominium owners, because it carries with it the image of the city, with its crime, deviance, and contact with other ways of life, and is often associated with racial minorities. Constance Perrin investigated the roots of homeowners' fear of increased densities and found that it reflects the view "that unwanted social contact and the possibility of social conflict are best dealt with by the single-family detached house in a socially homogeneous block."[33] She concluded that "lacking objective, qualitative, systematic, and credible information about how people negotiate their differences, social frights are perpetuated, and segregation by race and income is the social tranquilizer."[34]

This tradition of exclusion as a means of avoiding conflict is a cultural heritage of our private property system. The basis of private property is the right to exclude others, and our identification of freedom with private property encourages us to employ exclusion as the solution to any potential conflict. The tradition of citizenship and democracy, which provides resources for dealing with and resolving conflicts, seems to be regarded as a fall-back, an unfortunate necessity, rather than as a social process of great value in daily life.

The homogeneous residential neighborhood is no longer as homogeneous as it once was, as a result of the changing demographic structure of the United States. Where, at the peak of the baby boom, the majority of U.S. households contained two parents with children in the home, this is now only one pattern among many. Neighborhoods of detached single-family homes now house single individuals, single parents, couples without children, couples whose children have left, and families where both husband and wife are working, and very few housewives who keep an eye on the neighborhood during the day, watch children, and maintain social contact between neighboring families. Homogeneity and exclusion are even less suited to their task than they once were, while democratic conflict resolution is needed now more than ever.

Conflict resolution is not an area in which Americans have a great deal of experience. Our legal system encourages an adversarial approach rather than trying to reach agreements that both sides can live with and that would enable them to work together in the future. Experiments with environmental conflict mediation and with community dispute resolution boards outside of the legal system are steps in the right direction.

Privatization of zoning restrictions will not make it easier to resolve land use conflicts. The extension of the form of rights embodied in private property will only strengthen people's belief in exclusion as the solution to social problems. It is certainly true that land use regulation can be used by the more powerful to strengthen their own position at the expense of the less powerful, but so can the lack of regulation. The solution lies in extending a wider range of both human rights and material resources to those with less power and property.

Notes

1. Louis Hartz, *The Liberal Tradition in America* (New York: Harcourt, Brace and World, 1955).
2. F. A. Hayek, *The Road to Serfdom* (London: Routledge & Sons, 1944), p. 28.
3. E. J. Mishan, "The Post-War Literature on Externalities: An Interpretive Essay," *Journal of Economic Literature* 9 (March 1971): 1–28, parentheses added.
4. Bernard H. Siegan, *Land Use Without Zoning* (Lexington, Mass.: Lexington Books, 1972).
5. R. H. Coase, "The Problem of Social Cost," *Journal of Law and Economics* 3 (October 1960): 1–44.
6. Mishan, "The Post-War Literature," pp. 18–21.
7. E. Edwin Baker, "The Ideology of the Economic Analysis of the Law," *Philosophy and Public Affairs* 5 (Fall 1975): 3–48.
8. Robedt C. Ellickson, "Alternatives to Zoning: Covenants, Nuisance Rules, and Fines as Land Use Controls," *University of Chicago Law Review* 40 (1973): 681–781.
9. Ellickson, "Alternatives to Zoning," section V.B.1.
10. Here Ellickson follows the analysis made by Guido Calabresi and A. Douglas Melamed in "Property Rules, Liability Rules, and Inalienability: One View of the Cathedral," *Harvard Law Review* 85 (1972): 1089–1128.
11. A somewhat similar point is made by A. Allan Schmid and Ronald C. Faas in "Medical Cost Containment: An Empirical Application of Neo-Institutional Economic Theory," in *Law and Economics: An Institutional Perspective*, eds. Warren J. Samuels and A. Allan Schmid (Boston: Martinus Nijhoff, 1981), pp. 183–84.
12. Eirik G. Furubotn and Svetozar Pejovich, "Two Essential Concepts: Transaction Costs and Attenuation," in *The Economics of Property Rights, eds. Furubotn and Pejovich* (Cambridge: Ballinger, 1974), pp. 45–48.
13. Armen A. Alchian, "Corporate Management and Property Rights," in Furubotn and Pejovich, *The Economics of Property Rights*, p. 147.
14. Garrett Hardin, "The Tragedy of the Commons," in *Managing the Commons*, eds. Garrett Hardin and John Baden (San Francisco: W. H. Freeman, 1977).
15. Thomas Brom and Edward Kirshner, "Buying Power: Community-

Owned Electric Systems," *Working Papers for a New Society* 2 (Summer 1974) : 46–55.

16. Alchian, "Corporate Management," pp. 149–50.

17. William A. Fischel, "Equity and Efficiency Aspects of Zoning Reform," *Public Policy* 27 (Summer 1979) : 301–31; William A. Fischel, "A Property Rights Approach to Municipal Zoning," *Land Economics* 54 (February 1978) : 64–81; Robert H. Nelson, *Zoning and Property Rights* (Cambridge, Mass.: MIT Press, 1977).

18. Fischel, "A Property Rights Approach," p. 72.

19. Oliver E. Williamson, "Transaction Cost Economics: The Governance of Contractual Relations," *Journal of Law and Economics* 22 (October 1979) : 233–61.

20. John R. Commons, *The Legal Foundations of Capitalism* (Madison: University of Wisconsin Press, 1968 [1924]).

21. Indeed, under conditions of perfect competition the market even insulates participants from some of the effects of inequality, since competition can force people to make their best possible offer even if they have greater resources than the person they are dealing with. A. Allan Schmid, *Property, Power, and Public Choice: An Inquiry into Law and Economics* (New York: Praeger Publishers), p. 207.

22. James Tobin, "On Limiting the Domain of Inequality," *Journal of Law and Economics* 13 (October 1970) : pp. 267–77; Arthur M. Okun, *Equality and Efficiency: The Big Tradeoff* (Washington, D.C.: Brookings Institution), p. 9.

23. This point is made for the workplace by Matt Witt and Steve Early, "The Worker as Safety Inspector," *Working Papers for a New Society* (September 1980) : 21–29.

24. Martin Buber, *Paths in Utopia* (Boston: Beacon Press, 1958), pp. 41–42, 66–67, 77–79; Maren Lockwood Carden, *Oneida: Utopian Community to Modern Corporation* (New York: Harper & Row, 1971); Stuart Perry, *San Francisco Scavengers: Dirty Work and the Pride of Ownership* (Berkeley: University of California Press, 1978), provides a recent example.

25. Peter Barnes, "Backdoor Socialism: Reflections on TVA," *Working Papers for a New Society* (Fall 1974) : 26–35.

26. Steven N. S. Cheung, "Rent Control and Housing Reconstruction: The Postwar Experience of Prewar Premises in Hong Kong," *Journal of Law and Economics* (April 1979) : 27–53.

27. Charles Reich, "The New Property," *The Yale Law Journal* 73 (April 1964) : 733–87. A similar usage, involving the modes of election of local judges, can be found in Josef M. Broder, "Citizen Participation in Michigan District Courts," in *Law and Economics: An Institutional Perspective*, eds. Warren J. Samuels and A. Allen Schmid (Boston: Martinus Nijhoff, 1981), p. 178.

28. Michael L. Goetz and Larry Wofford, "The Motivation for Zoning: Efficiency or Wealth Redistribution," *Land Economics* 55 (November 1979): 472–85.

29. Ibid., p. 482.

30. A point made by Commons, *Legal Foundations of Capitalism.*
31. Daniel Mandelker, "The Taking Issue in Land Use Regulation," in *The Land Use Policy Debate*, ed. Judith I. deNeufville (New York: Plenum, 1982), especially Chap. 6.
32. Frank J. Popper, *The Politics of Land-Use Reform* (Madison: University of Wisconsin Press, 1981).
33. Constance Perrin, *Everything In Its Place: Social Order and Land Use in America* (Princeton: Princeton University Press, 1977), p. 85.
34. Ibid., p. 179.

11

Institutionally Determined Property Claims

R. Larry Reynolds

The nature of property ownership and what have come to be known as property rights has long been both a practical and a theoretical issue. Every society must have a system that defines and enforces property rights. This system is dynamic and may be the result of planned or unplanned behavior patterns. The structure of the rule system that defines these property rights and the institutions that enforce them play a large role in determining the relationships and activities in the society. In turn the rule system is shaped by the values and activities of the members of the society.

Theorists and philosophers, from the utopians to the pragmatists, suggest variations in property rights to create "better" societies. Policy choices invariably involve restructuring the system of property rights. One of the crucial differences between the various schools of thought is the way in which they justify and structure property rights. There are different approaches ranging from various forms of anarchism to strict state ownership, from property rights held in common to private property rights. The crucial point is that every society must have a system of property rights. The nature of this system of property rights influences the relationships between individuals and between individuals and social groups. Changes in the specification of property rights will alter the relationships and behavior of social units. Further, the perspective that the members of a society have toward property rights reflects the values of that society.

The purpose of this article is to bring into focus the role of property rights from an institutionalist perspective, and to offer an explanation of how these property rights are specified and how they can be altered to resolve economic problems.

Property Claims and Property Rights

The term "property rights" suffers from the problem of being emotionally charged. The term is associated with private property rights held by individuals; it implies that these individuals have "natural rights." For that reason, the term "property claims" is preferred here and is used to suggest that these claims to property are granted by society and are not "natural rights." However, to correlate the concept to the conventional literature, the term property claims is roughly the same as property rights and the two are used interchangeably.

The conventional definition of property rights in neoclassical literature is best stated by E. Furuboton and S. Pejovich:

> Property rights are understood as sanctioned behavioral relations among men [sic] that arise from the existence of goods and pertain to their use. These relations specify the norms of behavior with respect to goods that each and every person must observe in his daily interactions with other persons, or bear the cost of non-observance. The term "good" is used here for anything that yields utility or satisfaction to a person. Thus, and this point is important, the concept of property rights in the context of the new approach applies to all scarce goods. The concept encompasses both the rights over material things (to sell my typewriter) as well as 'human' rights (the right to vote, to publish, etcetera). The prevailing system of property rights in the community is, then, the sum of economic and social relations with respect to scarce resources in which individual members stand to each other.[1]

Their definition is interesting from an institutionalist perspective. First, the definition is broad. It implies that an individual has a bundle of "rights" or claims empowering him/her to control the outcome of specific events. Secondly, it recognizes that these claims are "sanctioned behavioral relations" among individuals. Presumably, society is the sanctioning body and these property claims are seen as "economic and social relations." This definition serves as a springboard for the "New Institutionalists" like Lance Davis and Douglass North.[2] (The "New Institutionalists" should not be confused with institutionalists or neoinstitutionalists.) Davis and North attempt to use neoclassical economic theory to explain how society defines and changes property rights. Their approach considers efficiency the sole criterion by which society selects the rules that define property rights. Notions about equity, habits, institutions, and power are not included in their analysis. Further, the Furuboton and Pejovich definition focuses on the "individual" as the unit of analysis. A broader view that considers property claims of individuals and groupings of individuals (society, the state, by socio-economic class, sex, legal creations, etcetera) can provide valuable insight into the nature of relationships that exist in society.

A third observation about Furuboton and Pejovich's definition is that its utilitarian foundation, as is the case with all neoclassical economics, has a value theory that gives a weak criteria by which society can judge "better": if individuals prefer to choose to pay more for heroin than milk, then the "best" solution is to have a system that produces heroin. This utility value theory serves as a justification for a "free market" approach to property rights.

When property rights are not clearly defined or are "incorrectly" specified, externalities, collective goods, and common property resources create allocation problems for a market system. Alan Randall observes that R. H. Coase's treatment of externalities, which typifies the Chicago Property Rights-Public Choice (PR-PC) approach, was an attack on Pigovian externality theory, which was the last arena that justified government intervention in the market.[3] Stephen Barton restates this notion: "The Coase Rule . . . states that the assignment of property rights and their attendant liability rules will not affect the outcome of economic activity. . . . The conclusion that the 'Coasians' draw from this is that while government is necessary to establish and protect private property rights there is no justification for any further government action."[4]

An instrumental theory of value allows normative judgements to contribute to the formation of a system of property claims "which provides for the continuity of human life and the noninvidious re-creation of community through the instrumental use of knowledge."[5] Neoclassical economics provides a paradigm to evaluate the efficiency aspects *within* a system, given values, rules, and preferences, but does not provide a means of evaluating the efficiency and equity aspects *of different systems* when values, rules, and preferences are not constant. A simple analogy is that neoclassical economics is useful to analyze the strategies used in a game of football but does not provide the criteria to determine whether football is the "best" game or whether it should be played at all.

The notion of property claims is central to any analysis of societal relations, and institutionalists should not abdicate the field to neoclassical analysis. In fact, institutionalists have long seen property claims as an important concept. Richard T. Ely uses the notion of property rights as an important aspect of understanding societal relations. In *Studies in the Evolution of Industrial Society*, Ely implies that the "idea" of property is dynamic and includes both private and public property.[6] Ely also ties the notion of property ownership to justice and the distribution of wealth.[7] In his book *Property and Contract in their Relation to the Distribution of Wealth*, Ely establishes the ideas of property as a right and as "qualified property."[8] Ely clearly identifies the notion of property as a right; "but it must be borne in mind that, strictly speaking, property refers to rights only. Property is an exclusive right. Speaking accurately, then, property is not a thing but the rights which extend over a thing. A less strict use of the word property makes property include the things over which the right extends."[9]

Another of Ely's important insights is that even in the case of "private property" there are two sides, the individual and the social. The social side must be regarded as essential: "The two necessarily go together, so that if one perishes the other must perish. The social side limits the individual side, and as it is always present there is no such thing as absolute private property."[10]

J. R. Commons also places great emphasis on the role of property and property rights. The first few pages of the *Legal Foundations of Capitalism* make the tie between working rules, property, and behavior (particularly in regard to transactions). Commons argues that property is a relationship between a person and his or her environment. Property and property rights become interrelated: "Hence property is inseparable from the *right* of property. The term 'rights,' as we have seen, cannot be defined except as reciprocal rights, duties, liberties and exposures. Every so-called right implies all of these dimensions."[11] In *Institutional Economics* Commons continues: "The term 'property' cannot be defined except by defining all the activities which individuals and the community are at liberty or required to do or not to do, with reference to the object claimed as property."[12] The above quotations are only an illustration of Commons's views on property and property rights.

The concept of property plays an important role in C. E. Ayres's analysis of the "modern economy":

> The institution upon which by general agreement the institutional weight of the modern economy chiefly rests is that of property. Property is sometimes described as a modern innovation, but this is true only in a very limited and special sense. The institutional structures of all societies have a property aspect, although it is nowhere else as fully separated from family, state, and church as in modern Western civilization. That is, the behavior-system of every community contains a cluster of mores which

define the fashion in which certain articles and instruments are thought to be imbued with the personality of their 'owner,' as we would call him, specifying the powers he exercises with respect to them and the limits to be observed by others by which they are sometimes forbidden even to touch or see specified articles.[13]

While there are variations in how property claims are viewed, the common element is that each society must specify property claims, and the structure of those claims influences the behavioral relations. Further, the property claims are evolutionary and must be sanctioned by society.

Property claims are defined here as the privilege, granted and sanctioned by society, to control activities and their effects. These property claims may be granted to individuals or groups of individuals. They are never absolute and are subject to change in response to other conditions. Society grants and sanctions these privileges through either implicit or explicit rules.[14]

Evolution of Property Claims

The implicit rules are the customs, traditions, and mores that specify behavior (activities that the individuals or groups in a society may or may not do). The explicit rules are those consciously created rules that organizations or governments enforce to control the activities of their members. Society must choose a mix of the implicit and explicit rules that balance the efficiency and equity concerns of the society with the physical rules or technology. Physical rules or technological knowledge are simply society's understanding of the physical relationships in nature. This understanding may or may not be correct but it can be used to solve some problems. Other problems that cannot be explained with an "incorrect" understanding of the physical rules require a change in knowledge. As the understanding of physical rules changes (technological change), the matrix of implicit and explicit rules that define the property claims must also change.

The neoclassical approach seems to argue that the property rules are determined only by human nature and by values that remain constant. Therefore, once the correct rules are established by government there is no need to allow government or any institution to modify them. In reality it seems that the rules defining property rights must reflect human nature and values (which change), technology, and the institutions. Obviously, there is a great deal of circular causation: institutions reflect and shape human values, technology shapes institutions and is directed by them. Each interrelates with the other. In summary, as technology, human values, and institutions change, the rules by which property rights are specified must also change. If ceremonial behavior regarding "private" property rights prevents society from accepting these changes in rules, it creates problems, rather than solving them.

The members of society and the institutions must be capable of creating and adapting to rules systems that take into account changes in technology, values, and institutions. It must be noted that these rules systems need not be explicit rules created by formal institutions. They may be implicit rules. In either case they are embedded in the institutions. A denial of the existence of property claims can be as ceremonial as the belief that only the existence of "private" property rights is correct.

The issue then is, How are these property claims modified over time to reflect the needs of society? Marie Leigh Livingston uses the work of Ely, Fagg Foster, Warren Samuels, Marc Tool, and others to offer an explanation. Her model of change is

> both sequential and recursive. To summarize, any particular sequence begins with a change in circumstance (A). If circumstantial change impedes goal achievement by one or more groups (B), there is stress on the system (1). Stress causes concerned groups to organize, propose change in formal policy and seek influence in policymaking (2). Given political action by interest groups, along with myriad other poltical influences, a set of policymakers will decide which, if any, policy (C) to implement. Any policy change will necessarily change the choices and behavior of some economic agents (3), which will in turn have an impact on circumstance (A).[15]

"Compensating escapements," as described by Adolph Lowe, seem to suggest that the linkage between stress (or pressure) and responses may have slack and can be used to extend Livingston's analysis.[16] These compensating escapements are based on expectations about such things as mobility, resource availability, technological change, and social adaptability. If the members of society believe that changes alleviating problems will occur, stress is reduced and responses to the pressures will be altered. Marie Leigh Livingston's model addresses explicit rules and the activities of interest groups that lobby to achieve their goals. Livingston also recognizes the role of power in shaping the property rights that result.[17]

Livingston's model of changes in explicit rules can also be applied to implicit rule structures. Depending on compensating escapements and the relative power of individuals and groups, either the implicit or explicit rules that define property claims may be altered. Examples might include the rules specifying the property claims of the members of a family. As technology and values change, the property claims of the members of the family change. This takes place explicitly through contracts and the law but also implicitly through changes in mores, customs, expectations, and the like. These property claims may explicitly specify the claims to property of the members of a family, like a child's right to medical care, or it may implicitly give property claims to a child for an education, summer camp, or car.

Another interesting case is in medicine. With changes occurring in medical technology, values, and institutions, property claims are in a state of flux. Values and technology are changing so dramatically that those concerned with the rule system and institutions are struggling to redefine the property claims: What claims do individuals have to medical care? To sell or purchase organs for transplant? Who should be the recipient of organ transplants when only one organ is available? Should resources be devoted to transplants rather than to better health care and prevention? In short, what are the property claims of various patients, society, medical researchers, physicians, pharmaceutical companies, and other interested groups? These property claims will be resolved by changes in implicit and explicit rules.

Similar, but less dramatic, problems exist in the property claims of writers and publishers, which are altered by copying technology. Property claims in TV and movies are also in a state of change resulting from changes in video technology. Property claims to jobs have long been an issue. Are these claims based on seniority, discrimination, antidiscrimination laws, or some other set of rules? Case studies of these property claims offer great opportunity for institutional lists.

Property Claims and Policy

Property claims are specified by the "working rules" of society. These rules may be explicit or implicit and are embedded in institutions. The rules that define property claims must be consistent with the values of the society as well as with the physical rules (technology). If they are inappropriately specified there will be socioeconomic problems. Stress in the system is the stimulus to encourage change.

The institutions not only define the property claims but also sanction them. The property claims can be exercised only if society recognizes them as legitimate. These property claims may be transferred by exchange, reciprocity, or redistribution.[18]

Ceremonial values that prevent the evolution of the property rules are the source of many socioeconomic problems. A society's ceremonial attachment to "private property" prevents inquiry into many potential property rules that might prove useful. Similarly, for purposes of analysis a reaction against "property rights" may also prove to be ceremonial.

Another ceremonial aspect of property claims is the notion of "human rights" as discussed by Barton or "personal rights" as defined by David Ellerman.[19] Barton defines human rights as those that "are universal, so that everyone has them, and inalienable so they cannot be permanently sold or given away." Ellerman says of personal rights: "In particular, personal rights are nontransferable and nonmarketable." In fact, these human or personal rights exist at the discretion of society and may be granted or withdrawn by a system of rules. Many societies have practiced complete or partial slavery of specific groups. In short, these property claims can be taken away and transferred if society sanctions the other property claim. Discrimination against particular groups also defines property claims in a particular way, and may be sanctioned by society without explicit rules. This does not mean that slavery or discrimination is advocated, it simply recognizes that even so-called human rights are a function of the rules that society accepts. Further, these human rights may be structured so as to be transferable by exchange, reciprocity, or redistribution. Coercion may be used to accomplish redistribution (if society accepts the rules structure). The crucial task is to revise rule structures that define property claims in a manner that allows the adoption of behavior patterns consistent with instrumental values and technology. Either ceremonial adherence to a myth of "private property" or abdication of the analysis of property claims to the neoclassical economists ensures that society will not allow the evolution of new forms of property claims that coordinate values and technology.

Notes

1. Eirik Furuboton and Svetozar Pejovich, *The Economics of Property Rights* (Cambridge, Mass.: Ballinger, 1974), p. 3.
2. Lance Davis and Douglass North, *Institutional Changes and American Economic Growth* (Cambridge: Cambridge University Press, 1971).
3. Alan Randall, "Property, Institutions, and Economic Behavior," *Journal of Economic Issues* 12 (March 1978): 1-21.
4. Stephen E. Barton, "Property Rights and Human Rights," *Journal of Economic Issues* 17 (December 1983): 915-30.
5. Marc Tool, *The Discretionary Economy* (Santa Monica: Goodyear, 1979), p. 293.
6. Richard T. Ely, *Studies in the Evolution of Industrial Society* (New York: Macmillan, 1903), p. 87.
7. Ibid., p. 271. Emphasis in this argument is on inheritance.

8. Richard T. Ely, *Property and Contract in Their Relations to the Distribution of Wealth* (New York: Macmillan, 1914), pp. 101-102.
9. Ibid., pp. 107-108.
10. Ibid., pp. 136-37.
11. J. R. Commons, *Legal Foundations of Capitalism* (Madison: University of Wisconsin Press, 1924, 1957), pp. 6-7.
12. J. R. Commons, *Institutional Economics* (Madison: University of Wisconsin Press, 1934, 1961), p. 74.
13. C. E. Ayres, *The Theory of Economic Progress*, 2d ed. (New York: Schocken Books, 1944, 1969), pp. 194-95.
14. R. Larry Reynolds, "Foundations of an Institutional Theory of Regulation," *Journal of Economic Issues* 15 (September 1981): 641-56.
15. Marie Leigh Livingston, "A Conceptual Model of Institutional Change and Its Application to Natural Resource Policy" (Paper presented to the Association of Institutional Thought Annual Meeting, San Diego, California, 23 April 1984), pp. 5-6.
16. Adolph Lowe, *On Economic Knowledge* (New York: Harper Torchbook, 1965/1970), pp. 65-66.
17. Livingston, "A Conceptual Model," pp. 4-5.
18. F. Gregory Hayden, "Social Fabric Matrix," *Journal of Economic Issues* 16 (September 1982): 637-62.
19. Barton, "Property Rights and Human Rights," p. 922; David P. Ellerman, "Theory of Legal Structure: Worker Cooperatives," *Journal of Economic Issues* 18 (September 1984): 861-92.

12

Dangers in Using the Idea of Property Rights: Modern Property Rights Theory and the Neo-Classical Trap

Anne Mayhew

Two apparently contradictory opinions about the usefulness of the idea of property rights seem to have merit. The first is that the recent literature on property rights represents a foolish and illegitimate extension of concepts of microeconomic theory to social organization and institutional change.[1] The second and apparently contradictory view is that, in the writings of economists such as John R. Commons and Richard T. Ely, and of those, such as Larry Reynolds, who follow in their tradition, the concept of property rights is a useful tool for exploration of social processes.[2] My attempts to deal with this contradiction have led to three conclusions.

First, the task of discovering and accounting for changes in property rights is important and can be revealing about wider social processes. One task of the economist as ethnographer is to learn the ways in which the natives in any system use terms that describe rights over things and over others, and to show how those rights integrate into a working system. The tasks of the economic historian include understanding how such systems and their component parts—"property rights" among them—change over time.

Second, it may be revealing and powerful to use the concept of property rights in ways that the natives do not, in order to draw useful analogies. This is particularly important in a system such as ours, where "property" is a strong *organizing* concept and its use is likely to help those desiring to effect changes.[3]

Third, where the purpose is to understand social processes rather than to change them, the use of the term "property rights" in ways not used by natives is dangerous precisely because, in our own language, it is such a strong concept and so deeply a part of a system of thought about human relationships. I shall proceed by dealing with each of these arguments in turn.

In *Legal Foundations of Capitalism* Commons illustrated the importance of understanding the changing meaning of the term property in our own economy. What Commons did, of course, was to show how, in the last third of the nineteenth century, courts in the United States changed the meaning of property in a way that was crucially important to the evolution of industrial capitalism. Although institutionalists have often been more interested in Commons's conception of the evolutionary process, it is also true that he gave us a powerful explanation of the difference between the U.S. economy in 1872, when the Slaughter House Cases were decided, and in 1897, when the Allgeyer Case was decided. What Commons argued was that the courts extended the meaning of property so as to include not simply "the use value of physical things" but also the "exchange values of anything."[4] Along the way expectations of returns from property also became, to use Karl Polanyi's phrase, "fictitious commodities" with exchange value. The courts changed the meaning of property as part of the process of enlarging the scope of the market in the organization of the U.S. economy—as part of the process in which the "anythings" of Commons were turned into commodities to be bought, sold, and treated as property.

A major reason why Commons's treatment of the legal evolution of the idea of property is not a narrow treatise, of interest only to legal scholars, is that the idea of property is so important in our system that changing definitions of what constitutes property must entail changes in the social, economic, and political systems. Where, as in our own system, rights over property are important powers, changes in the nature of those rights and changes in the range of things that can be treated as property must be described by the good social analyst. Thus my first conclusion amounts to little more than saying that changes in important features of a system must be described if the system is to be described accurately.

This conclusion can be extended to encompass comparative work such as that by Walter Neale in his paper in this issue of the *JEI*.[5] Although our idea of property may not be found in other social systems, using it as a focus for comparison with other systems of organizing people and nature may serve us well as we seek to understand those systems *and* to understand our own. Such comparisons would thus fall within the descriptive uses that are useful and legitimate.

The second conclusion is slightly less obvious. It is sometimes legitimate for social scientists or reformers to use the idea of property rights in ways that are not descriptive. A quotation from William Gomberg illustrates this use:

> Many . . . work rules define an emerging property right . . . . For example, a jurisdictional claim of a yard worker that he and he alone can handle a train in the yard and the corresponding claim of a road worker that he and he alone can handle a train on the road stems from a property right . . . in the particular job area . . . . It would be silly and pointless to deny that work in many cases could be performed more cheaply if these property rights . . . did not exist . . . . Many automobile public roads and expressways wind a serpentine path between two points. The road is much longer than if a surveyor and engineer were permitted to lay out the most effective path. . . . It is true that society has invented the concept of eminent domain. Its purpose is to prevent the holder of private property from imposing too absolute a restraint on public purpose and public efficiency. However, the exercise of this right of eminent domain is reserved to the government and its specified agents; then the government can only take over after due process and fair competition.[6]

Gomberg is here using the analogy between property in land and property in jobs in order to defend a social change. His analogy makes his defense of the right of labor unions to deny managerial perogatives in altering jobs far stronger than it would otherwise be.

The use of the idea of property rights in jobs as a way of extending the laborers' control is, of course, not new. Warren Gramm traces the use of the idea back to the 1890s.[7] More recently would-be reformers have used a similar technique to advocate a variety of reforms. For example, proposals have been made for offering well-defined and transferable ownership rights over shares of aquifers in order to encourage conservation of water.[8] This idea is similar to the range of proposals that we have heard for internalizing externalities—proposals for assigning both the rights and costs of ownership of things that were not previously property. These proposals come from the right (sell the Ogallala Aquifer) and from the left (recognize tenure in a job as a property right) and they derive their power from the power of the idea of property in our society. Whether one agrees or disagrees with this or that particular goal, it is a legitimate way to argue for reform in our society.[9]

What is not legitimate is to pretend—wittingly or unwittingly—that some things are property when they are not, and that some kinds of property are the same as other kinds of property when they are different. When—as in recent uses of the concept of property rights—this is done, a number of problems arise.

First, there is the problem of the moral element. When economists describe some things as property and some rights as property rights, this serves, in our society, to imply a moral element. This is precisely what makes the strategy of calling a job a "property right" so effective. But when analysts, as opposed to reformers, do this, then an element of morality enters even though it is not recognized as such. In his article on jobs as property, Warren Gramm appears as both analyst *and* reformer and alternately argues that jobs *are* property rights and that jobs are not but *should be* property rights. He is aware of introducing a moral element, but when the concept is used in the guise of a simple analytic concept, then our morality inherent in the idea of property is not always acknowledged. Most economists may not be prepared to say boldly, as the Austrian economists do, that "the right of property does not mean merely that a person has a legal title to something, but that a person has a moral claim to something,"[10] but most economists, as do most of us in Western society, feel something close to this as an emotional reaction. When a hope or expectation is defined as a property right, then that hope or expectation gains a superiority over other hopes and expectations.

A second problem arises because, when we combine our basic Western notions about the sanctity of property with the widely compelling notion that exclusive property will be managed more efficiently than that which is not privately owned, we have some powerful word magic at our disposal. If, as Harold Demsetz says, "a primary function of property rights is that of guiding incentives to achieve a greater internalization of externalities,"[11] and if individuals can be trusted to manage their own properties efficiently, then world-wide efficiency and goodness can be accomplished by redefining property rights. Inefficiencies or problems become a consequence of inadequately specified property rights. All manner of things can be explained and all sorts of problems solved. No additional analysis is needed if the problem is always that property rights have been inadequately specified or wrongly assigned.[12]

Thirdly, there is the danger that the analogy to what is regarded as property within our society may carry with it the temptation to extend the analogy to motives in the manipulation of the relationships or things that are described as property. How easy it is to move from a description of the way in which any sensible and conscientious person will manage a portfolio of stocks to a like description of how that person will manage a piece of Nebraska farmland to how a person will manage herself as a piece of human capital to how a person will make decisions about a child's schooling. And—put in the right frame of mind—one can even write in all seriousness:

> When the rule of willing consent applies, the transfer (exchange) of property is expected to benefit both parties. In contrast, when the coercive power of government is employed to transfer property from one party to another, neither equity nor efficiency can be assumed. It was these politically determined transfers that disturbed Sitting Bull—with serious consequences for Custer and his party.[13]

I certainly do not deny that Sitting Bull was disturbed, but I do think that the view of his motives and reasoning may be a trifle misleading. Of course there is a sense in which Sitting Bull was objecting to a transfer of property and a sense in which his decision to fight can be stated as a consequence of the expected benefits outweighing the expected costs. However, to explain Sitting Bull's actions that way is to miss most of what is important in an explanation of how he and General Custer came to do battle. The greatest problem may be that the adoption of the idea of property rights in things and in human relations makes it more difficult for an analyst to ask the important questions.

What we need to understand as analysts are the habitual patterns of action and of thought and how these patterns are affected by and changed by emotion and reasoning. When we ask questions about property we are led to ask questions about *management* and about *rights*. Even if we could expunge the moral element, we would still be asking the wrong questions.

What we ought to be discovering as social analysts is how people modify and transform their habitual behavior through the ongoing processes of instrumental valuing. These questions are made harder to ask if we begin by asking ourselves questions about the handling of property. The danger that the right questions will not be asked is perhaps less obvious but is in fact greater when a suggested property right has come to seem close to traditional property rights. It does not *now* seem so terribly far-fetched to think of trading some cleanliness of water or breathability of air for a monetary return. As we find it increasingly easy to think of clean water or breathable air as property, we find it increasingly difficult to ask other, often more important questions. Property is something that you "manage" and the goals of that management are usually pecuniary—or, by logical if unwarranted extension, utilitarian. But the prominence of property rights tends to obscure the questions about the roles and consequences of the long-term health of a stream for the long-term ecology or the enjoyment that neighbors or as yet unborn grandchildren may get from it. Building in a term for tastes and preferences or choosing an appropriate discount rate does not allow us to escape the pecuniary and managerial bias, just as it does not allow us to deal adequately with complex and changing goals. Even the most committed of neoclassical economists will probably think to themselves that Sitting Bull and Custer had reached their big moment as a consequence of a process of learning about each other, but will they remember that today's attitude toward the stream is a consequence of an ongoing process of instrumental reasoning that is going to continue to produce *varying* sets of values and decisions?

When Ely wrote, "The essence of property is in the relations among men arising out of their relations to things,"[14] he was trying to broaden the view of the consequences of property. Modern property rights theorists seek to make all "relations among men" the consequence of the same kind of reasoning that they think we use in managing a piece of physical property. All decisions—whether to fight because of a "political transfer," whether to marry, whether to buy a TV set, whether to sell a bond—become the same. Even—or perhaps especially—group action becomes a matter of the aggregation of individual decision making.

There is also danger for the analyst because of the impossibility of separating ideas of morality from the word "right." If I have a "right" to do something, you must offer a superior moral claim to justify your denial of my right. It is clear that the desire to turn Proudhon upside down and say that "Politics is theft" is what has attracted many economists to the extension of the idea of property rights. If institutionalists do not share the mission of these economists, they may nevertheless fall into the trap of enshrining social patterns in a moralistic terminology. If we ask ourselves whether some group has a "right" to a particular "property" or course of action, then our answer, even if offered as analysis, serves to justify that which we describe.

I return to the conclusions with which I began. Institutionalists as good social analysts should describe systems of property rights and, as reformers, will find it effective to use analogies to recognized property rights. But when we use a concept as powerful as property is in our own society to try to understand social processes not organized by that concept, we create unnecessary dangers for ourselves and the risk of falling into a neo-classical trap.

Notes

1. I have been most interested in the applications of "property rights theory" to economic history as illustrated by Douglass C. North and Robert Paul Thomas, "The First Economic Revolution," *Economic History Review* 30 (2d ser.) (1977): 229-41; and Douglass C. North, *Structure and Change in Economic History* (New York: W. W. Norton, 1981). I discussed this literature in a paper entitled "Rational Man in Economic History," read at the 23rd Annual Meeting of the Western Social Science Association and later published as " 'The First Economic Revolution' as Fiction," *Economic History Review* 35 (2d ser.) (1982): 568-71. The property rights literature is, of course, extensive and well-known. Those seeking an introduction to it might consult Erik Furubotn and Svetozar Pejovich, "Property Rights and Economic Theory: A Survey of Recent Literature," *Journal of Economic Literature* 10 (1972): 1137-62; or Harold Demsetz, "Toward A Theory of Property Rights," *American Economic Review* 57 (1967): 347-73. For a somewhat different approach see A. Allan Schmid, *Property, Power, and Public Choice* (New York: Praeger, 1978).
2. Richard T. Ely, *Property and Contract* (New York: Macmillan, 1914); and John R. Commons, *Legal Foundations of Capitalism* (Madison: University of Wisconsin Press, 1957 [c1924]).
3. By "organizing concept" I mean a concept that is used by the native participants themselves to organize their lives. An "analytical" concept—one used by an analyst—need not be an "organizing" concept. I borrow this distinction from Paul Bohannan, *Social Anthropology* (New York: Holt, Rinehart, and Winston, 1963), p. 11. See also Walter C. Neale, "Property in Land as Cultural Imperialism," *Journal of Economic Issues* 19 (December 1985):
4. Commons, *Legal Foundations of Capitalism*, p. 21.
5. Neale, "Property in Land," pp. 951-58.
6. Neil W. Chamberlain and Donald E. Cullen, *The Labor Sector*, 2d ed. (New York: McGraw-Hill, 1971), p. 244.
7. Warren S. Gramm, "Property Rights in Work," *The Journal of Economic Issues* 15 (June 1981): 363-75.
8. Richard L. Stroup and John A. Baden, *Natural Resources: Bureaucratic Myths and Environmental Management* (San Francisco: Pacific Institute for Public Policy, 1983), esp. chap. 6.
9. F. Gregory Hayden questioned whether I was arguing that the idea of property rights was like liquor or sex—effective in political persuasion but not legitimate. That is not the argument. Rather, I am saying that it is proper to argue that my claim to a job or breathable air is as legitimate

as your claim to a property right and to make this point by analogy. This
is an open intellectual process and not bribery.

10. Jack High, "The Case for Austrian Economics," *The Intercollegiate Review* 20 (1984): 41.
11. Demsetz, "Toward A Theory of Property Rights," p. 348.
12. Demsetz and Stroup and Baden provide good examples of this type of reasoning.
13. Stroup and Baden, *Natural Resources*, p. 13.
14. Ely, *Property and Contract*, p. 96.

13

Property in Land As Cultural Imperialism:
or,
Why Ethnocentric Ideas Won't Work
in India and Africa

Walter C. Neale

The idea of property in land is not one idea but a great many ideas. It is not about property but about a great many relationships of people to the surface of the earth *and* to other people. And it is not about parcels of land, but about the ways in which people exploit the earth.[1] These statements clearly follow in the spirit of the works of Richard T. Ely, John R. Commons, and others.[2] However, evidence from Asia and Africa shows that the ideas about property current in economic literature may be fatally ethnocentric and positively wrong-headed.

Property is an English word and derives the meanings that we attribute to it from the history of English-speaking peoples. Because the histories of the ideas, laws, and other institutional arrangements of French- and German-speaking peoples have been sufficiently like those of the English-speaking peoples, there are closely parallel (but not semantically identical) words in German and French. But the histories of peoples in India and Africa (and elsewhere) have been very different from ours, and so one must doubt that the word *property* should be used when discussing arrangements in respect to land or cattle over the course of Indian or African history (and probably the histories of many other places).

Property is certainly a possible focus of interest—*if* the word is taken as a rubric for investigations into how different peoples and groups use and dispose of things and parts of nature and other people. That there is such a focus of interest is incontrovertibly established by the participation in this symposium of Anne Mayhew, Larry Reynolds, and myself. What is not established by our participation—nor by the interest in property rights—is that there is such a thing as property in general or a universal institution of property. Property in comparative and historical studies should merely be the word we use to identify our focus of interest upon those aspects of any institutions that we have reason to believe can be analyzed, in part *and only in part*, by asking under what conditions or circumstances one person can say what some other person may do with something—what Karl Polanyi called "the appropriational movement of goods."[3]

For the student in comparative or historical studies there are two ways to organize and present material. One is the folkview of the people and period being described and analyzed. This is the *organization for action* used by those people to direct their own activities. The other is the *organization for analysis* that the scholar uses to analyze, draw conclusions, and make comparisons *for his audience*. The two should never be confused.[4] There is also a third way to organize and present material: to use the *organization for action* that the scholar uses to direct his own actions in his own society, or that he uses to describe his own society. Although the greatest danger is that the scholar will confuse his own *organization for action* with either or both of the other two, that is exactly what seems to have been happening in much recent "property rights" theorizing and analysis.

In *organizing* information *for action* there are ideas that significantly affect the ways that people in a society perceive the world around them. These ideas differ from society to society.[5] In this article and in Mayhew's article we use the term "strong organizing ideas" to express their impact upon the ways that information is *organized for action* in our own and in other societies.

Property is a very strong organizing idea in our society. There is therefore a strong tendency to think of property as having a universal core that is given expression in the Germanic allodial tenures or the Roman slogan, *"Usus, usufructus, abusus et vindicatio."* Or, in more familiar terms, "It's mine, all mine, and I can do what I like with it. So there!"

Differences from these models may be treated as superficial variants whose non-essential aspects can be stripped away to expose the core. Fee simple becomes an allodial tenure from which the sovereign has expropriated for his own the right of eminent domain. An estate in fee tail is an estate in fee simple except one can alienate it only to an eldest son. However, to view "complexities of property" as "mere variations" on a clear and universal core evades the problems raised by the role of social organization and by perceptions of the possible, of right and wrong, and of power by substituting logical speculation for fact. A quotation from Sir Henry Maine's *Ancient Law* seems apposite here:

> What mankind did in the primitive state may not be a hopeless subject of inquiry, but of their motives for doing it it is impossible to know anything. . . . Sketches of the plight of human beings in the first ages of the world are affected by first supposing mankind to be divested of a great part of the circumstances by which they are now surrounded, and then by assuming that, in the condition thus imagined, they would preserve the same sentiments and prejudices by which they are now actuated—although, in fact, these sentiments may have been created and engendered by those very circumstances of which, by the hypothesis, they are to be stripped.[6]

The idea of property makes it easy to oversimplify complex situations by creating a homogeneous whole made up of substantively different but logically fungible parts. Thus we speak of property as a bundle of rights: each right is different in substance but each can be treated like any other one. It is also easy to assume that the rights that constitute the bundle are always the same—to farm or to leave fallow, to let, to sell, or so on—so that the "total mass" of each bundle is the same as the "mass" of any other bundle. This would mean, for instance, that the right to sell was always at least implicitly present, or the right to let, and so on. At this point it is as easy as it is tempting to think that, if all the right holders could get together and agree, then the whole of this "body corporate" could do as it pleased with the bundle—a step in reasoning that creates "bodies corporate" out of logic by ignoring the fallacy of composition.

It makes more sense to view the power and privileges of people and groups of people as deriving from the relationships among people and groups and the roles of people and groups in societies, and not from an anterior or superior idea of property, whether that idea be one that is universally immanent or one that is out there waiting to be discovered (like Australia or like the steam engine—it is not clear like which).

I now turn to topics under the rubric "Indian land tenures." In the late eighteenth and early nineteenth centuries the administrators of the East

India Company set out to determine who owned the land, believing that if the king had owned the land, then the Company now owned the land and could rent it at a competitive Ricardian rent; but if someone else owned the land, then the Company could only tax. How strong a hold one's concepts can have upon one's ethics! Within a few decades British administrators were arguing that Indian tenures could not be sensibly discussed within the confines of British thought and that they had misunderstood what was going on in the countryside.[7]

It is curious, but more significant than curious, that wherever one finds discussion of property in land in India, there one finds the *land revenue* at the center of the discussion. The land revenue was a tax, a tribute, or a share derived from the harvest of a village or cluster of villages, a part of a village, or a plot. Which was it—tax? Tribute? Share? After two hundred years we still cannot say which, but we do know that the land revenue was the *jamabandi* in the *khasra* (assessment in the village record). The curiosity is this: in the European tradition we levy a tax payable by the owner of the land; in India the "owner" of the land, if such there be, was—and still is—the person or group responsible for paying the tax. B. H. Baden-Powell, whose three-volume study of British land tenures has not been superceded since its publication in 1891, points out that one of the more ancient Indian codes—the Institutes of Manu—"has nothing to tell us of how individual (family) holdings were apportioned," and goes on to remark, "It is not easy to explain why Manu tells us nothing of the original possession of cultivating holdings. He is, however, chiefly concerned with the Raja of high or military caste and his learned Brahman counsellors, and how these allotted the country for rule or overlordship."[8] But we have the clues needed to make it easier to explain. *Land revenue*—and thus rule and overlordship—was the strong organizing idea. *Property* was *not*. "All we can assert as undeniable," says Baden-Powell, "is, that both Hindu and Muhammadan authorities have always recognized a strong right in land of *some* kind"—*"some"* in Baden-Powell's italics.[9] Then he goes on, "From very early times a *right* was asserted *in favor of* the person who *first cleared the land*."[10] That the clearer had some claim against the non-clearer appears to be property so far as Manu was concerned. Other early documents inconsistently speak of both rulers and peasants as owners.[11]

There were also, said Baden-Powell, "the strong claims put forward by the high-caste families and descendents of conquering or colonizing chiefs."[12] After citing James Tod's *Annals of Rajasthan* to the effect that Rajput claims to land were based upon clearing, Baden-Powell then goes on to "doubt whether the Rajputs (as landlords) laid so much stress upon the *first clearing*, as upon another equally widespread idea, that land *conquered and inherited* by the next generation, is a very firm possession."[13]

In Baden-Powell's view, "the productive power of the soil" is "the real subject of ownership" in India, and "the possibility of the land bearing a series of concurrent interests, depends on the fact that the several parties *only determine* how the *produce* is to be divided, *and leave every other question in abeyance*."[14] Obviously one cannot leave the question of who owns the land "in abeyance" if it is a real question. But, if it is a nonquestion to the members of that society, then "in abeyance" is the only sensible place to leave the question.

In most Indian villages before British rule—and in many during British rule and in some since—dominant castes managed the affairs of the village. The members of the dominant castes certainly enjoyed a disproportionate share of the usufruct. Actually, they "held" the village rather than the "land"—and it would be more accurate to say that they "ruled" the village and the land rather than that they "held" them.[15] If one asks, "Wherefrom did their original rights or powers come?" the answer appears to be "from original settlement by clearing" or "by conquest."[16] If "by conquest," the concepts of "spear" and "shield" might be more appropriate than "property." If "by clearing," the continuation of a dominant tenure implies a recognized capacity to call upon spear and shield. To whom, then, could the dominant castes alienate? To whomever managed to dominate them in turn, or to drive them out. Since the village and its lands were where the dominant group lived, questions about disposition or alienation are empty.

Large "subordinate" populations in the villages filled such roles as artisans (carpenters, blacksmiths, potters, and so on), public servants (watchmen, barbers, washermen, and so on), and agricultural laborers. I have said, "and so on," because upwards of a dozen roles may appear on a list. Some laborers have been called virtual slaves,[17] and others have been called permanent servants. W. H. Moreland, perhaps still although posthumously the leading economic historian of Muslim India, doubted that any laborers were free to choose for whom they worked in Mughal India.[18] Sometimes the Brahman priest, while prestigious, could be called "subordinate" if he lacked membership in the dominant caste group. All these people shared in the harvest—according to their role (which certainly included a large element of ascribed status) and *not* according to the amount of work actually performed during a season and *not* according to a contract. Could we not call these roles *property rights*? They were certainly *expectations*, but if the expectations were unfulfilled, to what authority could the deprived artisan or servant appeal? He could appeal to the council of the dominant caste group, and if an aberrant cultivator had refused to include the deprived in the division of the harvest, the council could insist that he be given his share. But if the cultivator or landholder were powerful, perhaps the chairman of the council, it would be recognized that he could do as he pleased. A summary of an inquiry into the rights of tenants in the Kingdom of Oudh (north-central India) in the mid-nineteenth century is illustrative: "There was also no standard of law and right; and though the ryots [peasants] said that a Talookdar [local lord] ought not to turn them out, when asked whether he formerly had the power to do so, they said 'of course he had—the man in power could do anything.' "[19] Here also the ideas of "law and right" are British—the peasants obviously had another idea, of an "ought" that was morally but not politically or administratively binding.

Conversely, peasants, artisans, and servants often had the option of leaving a village and settling elsewhere, so long as there were vacant lands. This did tend to alleviate the conditions under which "subordinate" people lived. But threat and fear of desertion are not a contract—leastwise not an enforceable one—and an "option to desert" is not a right, especially if it is an option contingent upon "being able to get away with it."

Power or politics and produce were strong organizing ideas in India. Property was not. When we, as analysts, focus on property—our concept for our interest—we examine "appropriational powers," and the appropriate terms for India are probably village, revenue, rank, role, power, and share, *not* right.

From this review of "appropriational powers" in India it appears that we should use property as a descriptive term only where there is a superior authority able to enforce rights and redress wrongs according to some law recognized as binding by and upon the people concerned.

In order to make the point that the issues are not somehow peculiarly Indian, I would like to introduce one case from sub-Saharan Africa.[20] A map of the land, as perceived by the Tiv of central Nigeria, can be thought of as a rubber sheet. Instead of longitudes and latitudes defining a point, two points a compass direction, and three points an area, place and distance are expressed in terms of agnatic consanguinity. Thus the position of a group is expressed in relation to those surrounding it; and the closer is the relationship, the closer is the group, no matter how many English miles away. A group moves away from more distantly related groups that are expanding and powerful. It moves toward distantly related groups that are less powerful. In systems of segmental opposition such as this one— and such systems are quite frequent in Africa—security depends not only upon the power of a group but also on the power of the groups upon which it can call in any particular dispute. As the groups move over the surface of the earth, they always stay in the same place, so far as they are concerned. Paul Bohannan calls it a rubber sheet because, if one of our Mercator projections were to be fitted over the African perception, our projection would have to be made of rubber to stretch and contract to fit the positioning views of the Tiv. In a slash-and-burn system of shifting agriculture, a particular, latitudinal/longitudinal piece of land is not nearly so important as the group's relations with others. *Place* is here *derived* from *kinship*, or from the nature of relationships with other tribes when a group is on a tribal border.

The consequence is that Tiv have no property in land. A Tiv does have the right to farm—on soil not being farmed by near relatives. Is this a property? It is no more property than a group's position within the Tiv kinship system. If property includes place in a tribal kinship system, and by extension therefore prospects of marriage and alliances in war, then one is coming close to saying that all Tiv life is property—and that which explains everything explains nothing.

The illustrations could go on. There is no shortage of evidence. Land in Africa would provide other cases,[21] and all sorts of "complexities" can be found in the various systems of cattle holding and use in Africa.[22] In Thailand before "The King and I" the organizing idea in agriculture was mobilizing people, not land,[23] as may also have been true in the Philippines at an even later date.[24]

Comparatively and historically, *property* as "appropriational powers and movements" is a perfectly legitimate focus of interest. But once one moves beyond naming the focus of interest, once one moves into description and analysis, then all the cultural encumbrances of *our* use of *our* strong organizing concept—not only connotative, but also quite specifically denotative—are all too likely to distort and mislead.

Notes

1. Anyone who reads Paul Bohannan, " 'Land,' 'Tenure' and Land-Tenure," chapter 3 in *African Agrarian Systems*, ed. Daniel Biebuyck (London: Oxford University Press, for the International African Institute, 1963, pp. 101-15), will realize how great is my debt to him for the ideas and phrasings used here.
2. See the citations in Anne Mayhew, "Dangers in Using the Idea of Property Rights: Modern Property Rights Theory and the Neo-Classical Trap," immediately following in this issue.
3. Karl Polanyi, *The Livelihood of Man*, ed. Harry W. Pearson (New York: Academic Press, 1977), pp. 31-32, where Polanyi attributes the phrase to Max Weber.

4. Paul Bohannan, *Social Anthropology* (New York: Holt, Rinehart and Winston, 1963), pp. 8-11.

5. The importance of this point is made by Benjamin Lee Whorf, *Language, Thought, and Reality* (New York: John Wiley & Sons, 1956), *passim*, but see especially pp. 207-70. The anthropologist F. G. Bailey has called this "how people word the world" (oral communication).

6. Sir Henry Sumner Maine, *Ancient Law*, 10th ed. (Gloucester, Mass.: Peter Smith, 1970, [c1861]), pp. 246-47.

7. Holt Mackenzie, "Memorandum by the Secretary Regarding the Settlements of the Ceded and Conquered Provinces, with Suggestions for the Permanent Settlement of those Provinces, dated 1st July 1819," in *Selections from the Revenue Records of the North-West Provinces, 1818-1820* (Calcutta: Military Orphan Press, 1886).

8. B. H. Baden-Powell, *The Land Systems of British India*, 3 vols. (Oxford: Clarendon Press, 1892, reprinted Delhi/Columbia, Missouri: Oriental Publishers/South Asia Books, n.d. [c1892]), vol. 1, p. 127.

9. Ibid., p. 221.

10. Ibid. Italics of *right* and *in favor of* are mine. The other italics are Baden-Powell's.

11. A. L. Basham, *The Wonder That Was India* (New York: Grove Press, 1959 [c1954]), pp. 109-10.

12. Baden-Powell, *Land Systems*, vol. 1, p. 221.

13. Ibid., p. 222. Italics are Baden-Powell's.

14. Ibid., p. 221. All italics mine except *produce*.

15. Walter C. Neale, "Land Is To Rule," in *Land Control and Social Structure in Indian History*, ed. R. E. Frykenberg (Madison: University of Wisconsin Press, 1969), pp. 3-15, presents the case for this position.

16. See above, notes 10, 12, 13.

17. P. J. Thomas and K. C. Ramakishnan, *Some South Indian Villages: A Resurvey* (Madras: University of Madras Press, 1940), p. 350.

18. W. H. Moreland, *India at the Death of Akbar: An Economic Study* (London: Macmillan, 1920), p. 115.

19. Sir George Campbell, "Tenure of Land in India," in *Systems of Land Tenure in Various Countries*, ed. Cobden Club (London: MacMillan, 1870), pp. 218-19.

20. Bohannan, " 'Land,' 'Tenure' and Land-Tenure," pp. 105-106. Also Paul and Laura Bohannan, *Tiv Economy* (London: Longmans, Green, 1968), pp. 77-92.

21. Bohannan, " 'Land,' 'Tenure' and Land-Tenure," pp. 107-10, also provides brief descriptions of the systems of the Plateau Tonga of Northern Rhodesia and of the Kikuyu of Kenya. There are a number of other excellent essays in Biebuyck.

22. The literature is enormous. The curious reader will find a rather large number of works on Africa cited in Walter C. Neale, *Monies in Societies* (San Francisco: Chandler & Sharp, 1976), pp. 101-104. Most have something to say about cattle.

23. George Rosen, *Peasant Society in a Changing Economy* (Urbana/Chicago/London: University of Illinois Press, 1975), pp. 131-34.

24. Ibid., pp. 35-50.

14

In Defense of Government Regulation

Barry Price and Roslyn Simowitz

For nearly a decade, major American policymakers have successfully promoted "deregulation" as a cure for this nation's economic ills. In March of 1977, for example, President Carter declared that "one of my administration's major goals is to free the American people from the burden of overregulation."[1] Within a year, President Carter signed into law a bill to deregulate the nation's air passenger service industry. By 1980, his administration had also secured passage of major bills that would deregulate both the trucking and railroad industries.[2] President Reagan took office in 1980 even more committed to deregulation than his predecessor. Soon after taking office, he proposed major funding cuts in the annual budgets of a wide range of existing regulatory agencies. Some of these cuts were so severe that the Occupational Safety and Health Administration (OSHA), the Federal Trade Commission (FTC), and the Federal Communications Commission (FCC) had to reduce personnel significantly, close field offices, and sharply cut back investigative efforts.[3] Wearing these deregulatory achievements on his political coat sleeve, President Reagan was reelected by a landslide vote in 1984. In his Budget message to Congress in 1985, the president proudly noted that "we have reduced the number of new regulations in every year of my first term;" and made it clear that he was more determined than ever to press on with economic deregulation.[4]

What accounts for the success of these anti-regulatory policymakers in contemporary American politics? The major argument of this article is that much of it stems from the ideological edge they hold over defenders of government regulation.[5] This ideological edge is rooted ultimately in the fact that the American public continues to accept in some vague form the Libertarian view of property, and government's role vis-à-vis this institution. This does not mean that the average American is able to articulate in any detail the role of property rights in the Libertarian perspective. But the apparent success of such catchy political phrases as "Government has no right to tell an employer who he can hire!"; or "Government has no right to tell a farmer what he can grow!" strongly suggests that many Americans continue to react to government regulation within the mental images of Libertarian values and beliefs. Continued public acceptance of these beliefs makes it easy for defenders of private property rights to portray even necessary government regulations as unfairly confiscatory, or, at the very least, highly suspect.[6]

The remainder of this article provides a more in-depth look at the ideology behind efforts to deregulate the American political economy. It also argues for a more political view of property as a necessary armor in defense of legitimate government regulation.

When government regulates it redefines existing property rights. Property rights guarantee an individual that he or she can use an item largely independent of the will or interference of others. When government policymakers establish regulations prohibiting property holders from using their property as freely as they have in the past, these policymakers are, in essence, reducing existing property rights. When officials of the Environmental Protection Agency, for example, notify factory owners that they can no longer release certain pollutants into the air, they are eliminating the previously existing right of property holders to use the air above their property without interference from others. By eliminating this particular practice, government regulators are reformulating the bundle of rights that attaches to a piece of property. The public's perception of the legitimacy of this regulatory activity therefore depends heavily upon its view regarding the sanctity of property rights. That view is drawn largely from the Libertarian perspective on property and property rights.

Libertarians maintain that a person has a natural right to property.[7] He or she appropriates this property originally by carving it out of the state of nature,[8] and subsequently alters this pattern of original acquisition through inheritance and voluntary exchange.[9] In the words of Murray Rothbard, a well known proponent of this perspective: "The origin of all property is ultimately traceable to the appropriation of an unused nature-given factor by a man and his 'mixing' his labor with this natural factor to produce a capital good or a consumer good."[10]

From the Libertarian perspective, an individual's right to property is one held apart from the collectivity or its agent, the state.[11] Libertarians claim that people first acquired property in a state of nature *prior* to the establishment of any political community.[12] They then established the state primarily to protect property *already acquired*.[13] Since the individual acquired property independent of the state, the argument goes, this right cannot justly be taken from him by government. Or, as Rothbard has put it: "Once the mixture [of man's labor with the land] takes place, the man and his heirs have appropriated the nature-given factor, *and for anyone else to seize it would be an invasive act*."[14] Of course, "anyone else" for Rothbard includes government as well as other individuals.

Transported to the United States in the Liberal political philosophy of John Locke, Libertarian beliefs about the sanctity of property have become a cornerstone of U.S. political culture. According to Louis Hartz, who has written extensively on this issue, the persistence of the liberal tradition in the United States can be traced ultimately to the fact that the nation "grew up with Locke."[15] According to Hartz, even the Great Depression of the 1930s was unable to undermine the liberal faith in this country.

> If the Great Depression of the 'thirties suggested anything, it was that the failure of socialism in America stemmed from the ideologic power of ... liberalism rather than from economic circumstance. For however "objective" the conditions for the Marxian apocalypse now became, what emerged to deal with the economic problem was a movement within the framework of the liberal faith, or, in other words, a movement which belonged to the genre of Western Liberal Reform.[16]

Evidence that the "liberal faith" observed by Hartz in the 1950s is still an important part of the American political culture was recently offered by Lorand Szalay and Rita Mae Kelly. Using a research strategy based on inferences drawn from thousands of free-word associations, Szalay and Kelly compared the political ideologies of fifty American and Slovenian college students. With regard to the American students, they concluded that

> the weight and consistency with which the American group refers to civil rights—the rights of the individual to be free in movement, choice, and expression—reflect the American philosophy of individualism and freedom. The most popular American ideals are individualistic.[17]

In contrast, for the Slovenian students they concluded that

> the weight and consistency of Slovenian references to social rights, group ideals, equality, and brotherhood reflect a collectivistic orientation; these concepts have their roots in the collectivism of Marxist-Leninist theory as well as in the agricultural ethnic traditions.[18]

The work of Kelly and Szalay, as well as other contemporary research efforts, suggests that the basic principles of the liberal faith remain an integral part of the American political culture. None of these principles is more basic than the Libertarian perspective on property and property rights.

Because many Americans continue to view property rights from the Libertarian perspective, government regulations designed to alter these rights are easily portrayed by political opponents as unfair—as a case of one player changing the rules in mid-game. For most of us this conflicts with a sense of "fair play." At the very least we expect proponents of these rule changes to bear the burden of persuasion. It is precisely this expectation, however, that prevents proponents of government regulation from receiving an impartial hearing. An impartial hearing requires that interests seeking to protect an existing private property claim bear the same burden of persuasion as interests pressing a public property claim. But, for those who subscribe to the Libertarian view of property, "the presumption is always against government intervention, and of things being allowed to run their own course."[19] In American society this presumption against government intervention is even written into the law itself. The Administrative Procedures Act of 1946, for example—a major statutory basis for government regulatory activity in this country—clearly states that "except as otherwise provided by statute, the proponent of a rule or order has the burden of proof."[20]

A first step in defense of the legitimacy of government regulation is to increase public awareness of an alternate, more explicitly political view of property rights. This alternative view stresses the fact that property is inevitably a social, legal, and political institution.[21] Many Americans think of property as physical entities such as land, houses, and cars. A smaller number of people would also include more intangible items such as inventions, creative ideas, or a company's trade name. The political perspective, however, stresses that it is not the intrinsic qualities of these items that define them as property. Rather, it is the choice by society to allow individuals to use and dispose of these items without interference from others that identifies them as property. Unless the community sanctions and enforces the individual's right to property, it remains nothing more than a subjective claim that he must defend against the equally subjective claims of others. Carl Sandburg's poem on "Private Property" illustrates this point nicely.

> "Get off this estate."
> "What for?"
> "Because it's mine."
> "Where did you get it?"
> "From my father."
> "And where did he get it?"
> "He fought for it."
> "Well, I'll fight you for it."[22]

Because social choice creates property, social choice also eliminates property. Until about a hundred years ago, for example, American society allowed individuals to hold property rights in other human beings. Yet, today, Americans no longer think of slaves when they think of property. This is not because slaves or their descendants have changed their intrinsic characteristics, but rather because American society has changed its collective mind about permitting any individual to hold property rights in another human being.

A political alternative to the Libertarian view of property must do more than stress the fact that property rights (and, therefore, property) do not exist unless they are sanctioned by the state. It also must stress the critical role that conflict and coercion play in determining property rights in any society. Political decisions about how to allocate property rights inevitably specify who must pay whom to use society's scarce resources.[23] Imagine, for example, a society in which ruling interests define the property rights of a landowner to include oil under his land. In this society someone who wants oil must pay the landowner for its use. If he attempts to take oil without paying, government will enforce the landowner's property right. Now imagine a society where government allocates property rights differently. In this society ruling interests define a landholder's property rights to exclude oil under his land. Here it is the landowner who must pay someone else to use the oil in question. In either case, the decision about how to allocate property rights dictates who must pay whom and, therefore, who gains and who loses. For this reason decisions about property rights are inevitably the product of intense political conflict.

Winners in the struggle over property rights generally define these rights in a way that is most compatible with their own objectives. Losers in this struggle often must accept a definition of property rights that is detrimental to their interests. In the words of Margaret Levi and Douglas North:

> The distribution of property rights that the state specifies will reflect the interests of those with coercive power, whether they be the personnel of the state or powerful subjects. In this sense, the state is predatory: the ruler designs property rights and policies intended to maximize the power and wealth of those individuals or coalitions who already possess power.[24]

A clear example of the predatory use of property rights in American society is the way ruling interests have traditionally defined property rights so as to exclude workers having property rights in their jobs. Since at least the early 1800s, owners and managers of capital have attempted to increase profits by substituting large-scale capital innovations for more labor-intensive technologies. This has frequently displaced large numbers of workers. Yet, ruling interests have resisted strenuously workers' claims to "property rights" in jobs lost to technological change.[25] They have done so for obvious reasons. If displaced workers were granted property rights in their jobs, managers of capital would have to pay job holders to adopt labor-saving technology. This definition of property rights would, of course, be incompatible with capitalist interests.

The political view of property and property rights as primarily the product of struggle, conflict, and coercion is in stark contrast to that typically offered by Libertarians. Locke, Rothbard, and Robert Nozick, for example, have all written extensively on the issue of property rights. Yet, their combined work lacks a description of the way individuals in Western society have actually acquired property.[26] This is not surprising since each of these authors has approached the issue of property rights largely as a logical exercise, rather than as an empirical or historical investigation. In *Man, Economy and the State*, for example, Rothbard does not attempt to ascertain how contemporary definitions of property rights actually developed. Instead, he provides an explanation of how they *might* logically have come about. Like other prominent Libertarians, Rothbard begins his explanation by postulating a "Crusoe Economy," where man is portrayed as acquiring property by laboring upon an "unused nature-given factor."[27] In this imaginary setting it is at least conceivable that man might acquire possessions without engaging in intense interpersonal or intergroup conflict. After all, on Rothbard's hypothetical deserted island, who is there for Crusoe to struggle with over property? As one moves chronologically and conceptually away from a "state of nature," however, an individual's attempt to carve property out of nature inevitably brings him into conflict with others intent on resisting such efforts, or on pursuing their own interests.

Consider the potential for conflict and coercion in even the simplest process of acquiring property by "mixing" one's labor with an unused nature-given factor. First there is conflict over the issue of what constitutes an "unused" part of nature. Lumber companies in the United States regularly petition the government for access to publicly owned forest lands, which they see as not being fully "used." Environmentalists contest this view. They claim that such lands are already being "used" as natural wilderness preserves. Which definition of "used" are we to accept? Closely related to the question of what qualifies as an unused factor of nature is the question of what counts as labor. In a discussion of the "admixture" version of property acquisition offered by many Libertarians, Walter Horn points out that

> Rothbard does not require that a piece of land actually be tilled to be labored upon. He [Rothbard] includes clearing for a house or pasture and caring for some plots of land among the sorts of "cultivation" that create property rights for first appropriators. But if "care" of timberland counts as labor, what about keeping an eye on a particular waterfront property or admiring a mountain range? Are these not uses of a sort?[28]

According to Horn, the admixture theory of appropriation not only leaves open to question what counts as labor, but also, what qualifies as "labored-upon object": "How far does the labored-upon object stretch? . . . Does the farmer own only those plowed strips? If it is only the outermost strips that count, with everything between them counting as labored upon property, what would prevent one from simply plowing around the perimeter of a huge tract?"[29] There are no obvious answers to these questions. The answers emerge only as a result of intense political struggle.

A political view of property rights does more than focus attention on the role of conflict and coercion in what Nozick calls man's "original acquisition of holdings." It also focuses attention on the conflict inherent in the subsequnt "transfer of holdings." The Libertarian perspective strongly suggests that individuals who have increased their holdings have done so primarily by some combination of diligent saving, clever invention, and skillful involvement in voluntary exchanges.[30] Nozick, in particular, emphasizes the role voluntary exchange plays in generating "new holdings": "What each person gets, he gets from others who give to him in exchange for something, or as a gift. In a free society, diverse persons control different resources and new holdings arise out of the voluntary exchanges and actions of persons."[31]

The political view does not deny the importance of exchange as a means of amassing new holdings. But it focuses one's attention on the conflict that inevitably determines what constitutes a "voluntary" exchange. What qualifies as a "voluntary" exchange, as opposed to a coerced exchange, depends in large part on judgments about how people are entitled to behave toward others.[32] Steven Kelman recently illustrated this point with the case of an exchange between a drowning man and a passerby with access to a life jacket. In response to cries from the drowning man, the passerby offers to throw a life jacket, but only if the drowning man agrees to pay $10,000. Is this a voluntary or a coerced exchange? As Kelman points out, the answer to this question depends largely on whether those in authority believe the passerby has a duty to throw the drowning man a life jacket. Likewise, the classification of an exchange of labor for pay between a starving worker and a factory owner as voluntary or coerced depends on whether those in authority believe that society has an obligation to assure all workers a minimum standard of living. The point is that what constitutes a "voluntary exchange" is invariably a source of political conflict. We can expect those who win such conflicts to define "voluntary" exchanges in a way that is most compatible with their own interests.

A political view of property must stress one final point. It must emphasize that political decisions about property rights, while extremely important, are only one of many political choices that infuse property with much of its market value. Local governments install sewers, roads, and street lights, which increase a land owner's investment tenfold in a matter of weeks. State governments invest millions of dollars annually in agricultural research, which continually increases the productivity and profitability of private farm and ranch properties. The federal government spends billions of dollars annually to keep employment high enough to assure sufficient levels of consumption and business activity.[33] These and hundreds of other government programs generate massive amounts of income for various property holders in U.S. society. In some cases, these government programs are responsible for nearly all the profit generated by a property. A federal water project in the Westlands water district of California, for example, accounts for more than 90 percent of the profits generated by agricultural property in this district.[34] These few examples illustrate that government decisions contribute greatly to the value of property in American society. They also call into question the Libertarian suggestion that it is primarily the "mixing of man's labor with nature" that makes property valuable.

The political view of property sketched out above is, of course, not something we have created from scratch. The history of political theory is rich with works reflecting this perspective. Even political philosophers sympathetic to Locke's view of property commented on its overly apolitical character. William Godwin, for example, argued in *Political Justice* that although certain kinds of property may be highly beneficial, the right to their use clearly requires the consent of the community.[35] In the *Social Contract*, Rousseau provides a broad scale attack on Natural Rights Theory. In doing so he also provides a positive statement on the political origin of property rights. According to Rousseau, the individual has no absolute right of property or anything else. All rights are ultimately a creation of the state. Or in his own words, "The State, with regards to its members, is the owner of all of their property, by the social contract, which in the State, serves as the basis for all rights."[36] One of the most explicit accounts of the state's role in the creation of property is provided by Karl Marx in *Capital*. In part VIII of that work the author characterizes the claim that men acquired property by diligence, intelligence, and frugality as "the intellectual food of the infant."[37] He argues instead that "in actual history it is notorious that conquest, enslavement, robbery, murder—briefly, force—play the great part."[38] He then proceeds to spell out in great detail the historical creation of bourgeois private property in England. For Marx, this entailed "nothing else than the historical process of divorcing the producer from the means of production."[39]

While a political view of property and property rights is not new, its potential contribution to a defense of legitimate government regulation should now be more apparent. This view of property necessarily casts the government regulation issue in a wholly different light than the more apolitical view of property offered by most Libertarians. So long as one sees property as something individuals create on their own, independent of and prior to entry into a political community, one can easily concede that limitation or restriction of property rights through government regulation is inherently suspect. If, on the other hand, one understands the state's role in creating property and investing it with much of its value, one is likely to see government redefinition of existing property rights through regulation as perfectly legitimate. Once one understands the key role of the state in creating and enhancing property rights, the Libertarian assertion that government "has no right" to tell an individual what to do with his property takes on a hollow ring.

The political view of property described above rarely surfaces in any systematic public debate over government regulation. Yet, this debate has raged almost continuously for more than a decade in the United States; and "excess government regulation" has served as a whipping boy for at least the last three administrations in this country. The answer to this puzzle, we believe, is found in the fact that acceptance of a political view of property rights has disturbing implications for many Americans. For some, acceptance of this view is seen as a crack in the wall of Natural Rights Theory. For those who see natural rights arguments as a necessary defense against totalitarianism, any perceived crack in this wall is disturbing. For others, acceptance of a political view of property is disturbing simply because it shatters the weighty natural rights defense of private property. After all, if one accepts the argument that an individual has no natural right to property, one is inevitably led to conclude that individuals are entitled only to such property rights as society, or its collective agent, government, may decide to grant them. Widespread public acceptance of this conclusion is disturbing to those who enjoy a privileged economic position largely because of their expansive property rights. At the very least, widespread acceptance of the political view of property forces defenders of private property to fall back on a utilitarian defense of this institution. The utilitarian defense of private property recognizes that property rights are ultimately a grant from the state, but holds that such rights are desirable because they serve to benefit society as a whole. For those who wish to preserve the most expansive property rights possible, however, this argument is less appealing than the natural rights position. The utilitarian defense of property ultimately forces private property holders to justify their rights by demonstrating that their property rights advance the public interest. This is an unpleasant prospect to property owners who have become accustomed to a society that traditionally has put the burden of persuasion on the propertyless.

In *Social Justice in the Liberal State*, Bruce Ackerman postulates an imaginary world in which powerholders must respond to those who question their justification of privilege. In the real world, however, those who hold power often attempt to suppress questions concerning justifications for property holding. Ackerman explains that the reason for this is obvious. "As soon as I begin to play the game of justification, I run the risk of defeat. I may not find it so easy to justify the powers I so thoughtlessly command. . . . And if this is so, is it not better to suppress the conversation before it begins?"[40] And, as Ackerman goes on to point out:

> It [suppressing the discussion of justification] is a tempting prospect which becomes more seductive as my effective power increases. Power corrupts: the more power I have, the more I can lose by trying to answer the question of legitimacy; the more power I have, the greater the chance that my effort at suppression will succeed—at least for the time that remains before I die.[41]

In American society those who hold power do not suppress the discussion of justification for property by use of physical coercion. Instead, they rely on the much more subtle mechanism of "mobilization of bias."[42] The mobilization of bias entails the regular and repeated promotion of the belief that the individual has a natural right to property and that he acquired this property "on his own" independent of government. To the extent that those who hold power in American society fill people's heads with this belief, they shift the need for justification to those who wish to limit or restrict property rights.

The conclusion that emerges from this analysis is a simple one. If proponents of a robust public sector expect to hold their ground in future struggles with private property interests, they must labor hard to impart an alternative ideology to the traditional Libertarian perspective on which these interests draw. Using whatever forums are at their disposal, they must work hard to impart to the American public a more accurate and more political view of property and property rights. They must continually teach about the role that the state plays in creating property, and in enhancing much of its value. Because it is only when the public understands that government creates property and property rights initially that it will see government's efforts to subsequently alter these rights as the "natural order of things." It is only when the public understands government's role as a creator of property values that it will view subsequent public claims on existing property rights as "fair play."

Notes

1. Martha V. Grottron, ed., *Regulation: Process and Politics* (Washington: Congressional Quarterly 1982), p. 89.
2. Ibid., pp. 89-93.
3. "The Budget Weapon Hits Regulations," *Business Week*, February 22, 1982; "Regulation and the 1983 Budget," *Regulation* (March/April 1982): 9-11.
4. *New York Times*, February 4, 1985.
5. For an interesting discussion of the ideological character of the Reagan Administration, see Irving Howe's "Reagan and the Left," *Dissent* 31 (Fall 1984): 389-91.
6. For an analysis of changing public opinion regarding the role of government in society, see Seymour M. Lipset and William Schneider, "The Public View of Regulation," *Public Opinion* 2 (January/February 1979): 6-13; also see "Opinion Roundup," *Public Opinion* 5 (February/March 1982): 27-29.
7. Libertarianism includes a wide range of sometimes very diverse thought. Some Libertarians are anarchists. Some accept the need for a minimal state, so long as this state is not a coercive one. According to John Hospers, however, the common thread that connects these diverse thinkers

is "that every person is the owner of his own life, and that no one is the owner of anyone else's life." For a look at other fundamental principles of this creed, see Hosper's "What Libertarianism Is" in *The Libertarian Alternative*, ed. Tibor Machan (Chicago: Nelson-Hall Company, 1974), pp. 3-20. This same volume contains writings from a wide range of Libertarian philosophers for those who are interested in seeing the diversity of thought within this general perspective. In this article we address ourselves only to those Libertarians who accept the need for at least a minimal state.

8. The clearest statement of this argument in a more traditional version of the Libertarian creed is found in the liberal philosophy of John Locke. See especially Locke's "Of Property" in *Concerning Civil Government, Second Essay. Great Books of the Western World* 35 (Chicago: Encyclopedia Britannica, 1952), pp. 30-36; A slightly different version of this Libertarian argument in its more contemporary form is found in Robert Nozick's *Anarchy, State and Utopia* (New York: Basic Books, 1974), p. 175. While rejecting the "admixture" theory of property appropriation offered by Rothbard and Locke, Nozick also claims that "laboring on something improves it and makes it more valuable; and anyone is entitled to own a thing whose value he has created."

9. Murray Rothbard. *Man, Economy and the State* (Princeton: D. Van Nostrand, 1962), pp. 67-159.

10. Ibid., p. 147.

11. Hospers, "What Libertarianism Is," p. 6.

12. The importance of the sequence of events in the Libertarian perspective (first people create property; then they create government) is emphasized by Thomas J. Lewis in "An Environmental Case Against Equality of Right" *Canadian Journal of Political Science* 8 (June 1975): 263, 264.

13. Nozick, *Anarchy, State and Utopia*, pp. 12-25.

14. Rothbard, *Man, Economy and the State*, p. 148.

15. Louis Hartz. *The Liberal Tradition in America* (New York: Harcourt, Brace & World, 1955), p. 6.

16. Ibid., p. 259.

17. Lorand B. Szalay and Rita Mae Kelly, "Political Ideology and Subjective Culture: Conceptualization and Empirical Assessment," *American Political Science Review* 76 (September 1982): 593.

18. Ibid.

19. Nicholas Rescher, "On the Rationale of Governmental Regulation," in *Rights and Regulation: Ethical, Political and Economic Issues*, ed. Tibor Machan and Bruce Johnson (San Francisco: Pacific Institute for Public Policy Research, 1983), p. 255.

20. Grottron, *Regulation: Process and Politics*, p. 155.

21. For an excellent discussion of the social and political character of property, see David Spitz's thorough review of Nozick's *Anarchy, State and Utopia*, "Justice for Sale," *Dissent* 23 (Winter 1976): 72-89.

22. From Carl Sandburg, *The People, Yes* (New York: Harcourt, Brace and Company, Inc. 1936), reprinted in *Readings in Economics and Politics*, ed. H. C. Harlan (New York: Oxford University Press, 1961), p. 257.

23. Harold Demsetz, "Toward a Theory of Property Rights," *American Economic Review* 57 (May 1967): 347-50.

24. Margaret Levi and Douglas North, "Toward a Property Rights Theory of Exploitation," *Politics and Society* 11 (Summer 1982): 319.

25. For a discussion of early Supreme Court decisions interpreting the meaning of property, see John R. Commons, *Legal Foundations of Capitalism*, (Madison: University of Wisconsin Press, 1950, pp. 11-21. For more recent decisions about what qualifies as property, see Charles Reich, "The New Property," *Yale Law Journal* 73 (April 1964): 778-80. Also, for a thorough discussion of 1980 Supreme Court decisions regarding the patentability of laboratory-modified micro-organisms, see "Proprietary Rights and Public Interests," *Environment* (Special Issue) 24 (July/August 1982).

26. Spitz, "Justice for Sale"; Edward S. Greenberg, "In Defense of Avarice," *Social Policy* 6 (January/February 1976): 59-63.

27. Rothbard, *Man, Economy and the State*.

28. Walter Horn, "Libertarianism and Private Property in Land: The Positions of Rothbard and Nozick, Critically Examined, Are Disputed," *The American Journal of Economics and Sociology* 43 (July 1984): 345.

29. Horn, "Libertarianism and Private Property," p. 345.

30. Rothbard, *Man, Economy and the State*, pp. 67-159.

31. Nozick, *Anarchy, State and Utopia*, pp. 149-50.

32. Steven Kelman, "Limited Government: An Incoherent Concept," *Journal of Policy Analysis and Management* 3 (Fall 1983): 31-44.

33. For comprehensive discussions of the positive role of the state in contemporary American society, see Edward Greenburg, *Serving the Few: Corporate Capitalism and the Bias of Government Policy* (New York: John Wiley and Sons, 1974), pp. 1-32; Norman Furniss and Timothy Tilton, *The Case for the Welfare State* (Bloomington: Indiana University Press, 1977), pp. 15-21; Edward R. Tufte, *Political Control of the Economy* (Princeton: Princeton University Press, 1978), pp. 71-154.

34. See "Battle over the Westlands," a documentary film produced and directed by Carol Mon Pere and Sandra Nichols, written by Carol Mon Pere, 1980.

35. Paschal Larkin, *Property in the Eighteenth Century* (New York: Howard Fertig, 1969), pp. 126-30.

36. Ibid., p. 191.

37. Karl Marx, *Capital*, ed. Friedrich Engels in *Great Books of the Western World* 50 (Chicago: Encyclopedia Britannica, 1952), p. 354.

38. Ibid.

39. Ibid., p. 355.

40. Bruce Ackerman, *Social Justice in the Liberal State* (New Haven: Yale University Press, 1980), p. 3.

41. Ibid., p. 4.

42. For a detailed discussion of how the powerful in society mobilize bias by the constant promotion of one concept that automatically discourages a competing concept, see Mathew Crenson's *The Unpolitics of Air Pollution: A Study of Non-decision Making in the City* (Baltimore, Md.: Johns Hopkins University Press, 1971).

PART II

PROBLEMS OF THE SOCIAL CONTROL OF CORPORATE POWER

Introduction to Part II: Problems of the Social Control of Corporate Power

The previous section addressed and assessed the form, extent and use of economic power, and in particular, the variety of law and economics defenses or apologia for such use through recourse to common law traditions, free market ideology, deference to property rights, and so on. This section is concerned with finding ways and means of holding achieved economic power accountable to the larger community. Here, analyses of the relevance and vitality of antitrust laws, the effectiveness of regulation, and other social control options are critically considered. Finally of concern is the recognition that unrestrained or unregluated power cannot be presumed to reflect the public's interest in expanding growth in real income, in more equitable income distribution, and in the provision of meaningful and effectual participation in the decision structure that determines the character and problem-solving capabilities of the economy.

Chapter 15 by Willard F. Mueller opens this section with an historical assessment of the effort to control corporate power through antitrust legislation and implementation. Acknowledging that many skeptics regard this whole effort as no longer viable, Mueller insists that "the wake for antitrust is premature. Although its vital life signs are weak and its critics are many, not only can its health be restored, but also it can lead a long life in which it contributes immensely to the social control of corporate power." He addresses this ailing control instrument "by surveying briefly the intellectual and institutional history of the antitrust movement in the United States, by examining some recent successes and failures, and finally by reflecting on its role in restraining the development and use of market power in our modern mixed economy." It should be noted that antitrust control leans rather more to an orthodox, rather than to an institutionalist, response to corporate power. Its goal is to break up large corporate enterprise, conglomerates, or holdings sufficiently to permit or require conventional competitive market forces to appear and resume or assume their alleged role to control or reduce market power.

The historical evolution of the antitrust approach through legislation and enforcement, beginning with the Sherman Act in 1890, continued in spite of its critics well into the 1930s when Thurman Arnold succeeded in institutionalizing the effort in the Department of Justice. Long after the reformistic efforts of the antitrust movement had passed, the institutionalized enforcement and prosecution efforts continued when and as funding, manpower, and executive branch initiative permitted. Mueller acknowledges that enforcement in the last twenty-five years has not really disturbed "major aggregations of corporate power," but it has had significant bearing on the merger movement. "Contemporary antitrust enforcement . . . has not been a consistent record of victories or defeats . . . it has been a holding action against those forces in our economy that otherwise would have concentrated power in even fewer hands." Currently, "the antitrust agencies are outnumbered, outgunned, and are forced to fight on the defendants' terms." Mueller's agenda for reform includes: "More enforcement officials more publically accountable for their actions;" strengthening antitrust laws "to expedite industrial restructuring by shifting the burden of proof to the defendents;" and greatly increasing "the resources of the antitrust agencies." For such to happen, antitrust supporters must develop a vigorous, supportive, and broadly based political constituency. But Mueller does not presume that even these reforms would be sufficient to control corporate power. Some direct controls and economic planning will also be required.

In the following chapter, Harry M. Trebing explores the comparable century-long effort to generate and sustain social control of large scale enterprise through commission regulation of public utilities. Early on, public utility regulation "occupied a place of major importance in the work of . . . institutional economists and was incorporated within the programs of progressive reformers. . . . The corporation was the villain, regulation was the hero, and control of monopoly profits was the objective." But after World War II regulation "lost much of its legitimacy." It was "accused of being a captive of the regulated, of having a perverse effect on efficiency, of failing to protect the consumer, and of contributing to crises in energy and transportation." To its critics, "regulation now has become the villain, and the regulated firm often appears as simply a passive participant reacting to faulty signals."

The early institutionalists, Trebing observes, "perceived regulation as a means of protecting the public against the adverse effects of monopoly." It would constrain corporate power while assuring that "the public would receive the scale and load-factor economies associated with monopoly supply." In practice the regulatory commission agenda concentrated primarily on "the limitation of monopoly profits via rate base regulation, a search for cost-of-service pricing standards, and continuing concern over matters of equity and fairness." Largely fixed by the late 1920s, this agenda has not been adequately updated, adapted, and modified with changing problems and circumstances.

Trebing reviews and critiques the orthodox economists' attack on, and proposed revisions in, commission regulation in the areas of marginal cost pricing, the theory of the regulated firm, and the "adequacy of and alternatives to commission control." With minor exceptions, Trebing does not find much that is constructive in the orthodox contributions to the theory and practice of regulation. Instead he argues for a program of regulatory reform that retains the goals and some of the techniques of the early institutionalists, but would give much greater attention to the changed market structure of public utility industries. These industries do "possess very distinctive characteristics or structural features that will affect conduct and performance, *with or without reglation.*" "What is needed," he concludes, "is a revised concept of social control that places proper emphasis on industry structure while recognizing the implications for corporate behavior and the need to devise new methods to promote performance in the public interest." Basic reform in four distinct but related areas are recommended.

In the decade after the previous paper was written policy did not follow Trebing. Those leading the conservative counterrevolution of the late 1970s and the 1980s implemented a program of deregulation. This followup report by Trebing assesses this deregulation effort with special reference to the energy and telecommunications industries. By the mid 1980s, "more and more consumers, regulators, and industry" were speaking "of the market as the ultimate arbiter, and deregulation as the obvious step toward improving efficiency. Regrettably, much of the debate over deregulation has compared the worst features of traditional rate base regulation with the performance of idealized markets or market behavior similar to what would be expected to prevail under perfect competition." Trebing's main purpose is to "examine a number of the significant problems that will emerge under conditions of phased deregulation."

Those pushing the deregulation agenda contend that "promoting efficiency is superior to promoting equity as a goal for public policy," that "regulation cannot induce levels of efficiency superior to those attained in unregulated markets," and that "opportunities for competition abound." In the energy and telecommunications industries, Trebing finds that much of the support for deregulation rests on mere anecdotal information. For this deregulation agenda to succeed, Trebing argues,

> four conditions must be met: new markets must be capable of producing a competitive outcome sufficiently pervasive to eliminate all opportunities for price discrimination and predation; strategies of incumbent firms must be inconsequential in their impact on the viability of competition; markets must be able to clear in a fashion that minimizes costs of production over time; and agencies must be able to set prices that neutralize monopoly focal points and constrain cross-subsidization in residual monopoly markets.

In an incisive critique, Trebing finds none of these conditions are likely to be met. In sum, "the combined effect of high levels of concentration, differentiated markets, retaliatory power of incumbent firms, demand/supply imbalances, and the difficulty of setting neutral pricing guidelines indicates clearly that accelerated deregulation will not result in high levels of competition in the energy and telecommunications industries. Rather, oligopolistic market structures will emerge that are conducive to significant inefficiencies and adverse distributional effects." Since "flawed markets will not perform significantly better than flawed regulation . . . a more promising course of action for public policy involves incorporating existing and potential market forces within the framework of a broader program of regulatory reform designed to promote industry performance and the general welfare. A sketch of such reforms concludes Trebing's work.

The chapters that close this section invite consideration of "the social control of corporate power" in a much wider context than that of the historic approaches of antitrust and regulation. Warren S. Gramm's article explores implications of emergent oligarchic market structures, the concentration of economic power associated therewith and their probable accompaniment by oligarchic politics—"by *de facto* political and social control by the few." This exploratory and speculative work argues that "there exists an historical and prospectively causal connection between advanced industrial capitalism and authoritarian politics." After some initial terminological clarifications, Gramm describes elements of the power structure of the United States to include "market concentration and functional ties between financial and production ownership units and between big business and the federal government." The concentration of economic power is traced through consideration of concentration ratios, the conglomerate merger process, external controls involving banks and interlocking directorates, internal control by owners or managers, superfirm units or trade associations, and the *Zaibatsu* syndrome (close working relationships between private producers, financial firms and the central government). Concentrations of private power are then joined with the political process through elaborate lobbying organizations and activities, the development of political action committees (PACs), and the capacity of the rich to fund and shape campaigns to serve their own agendas.

Given these interlocking economic and political interests, "it does not seem simplistic to envisage the possibility . . . that a small Millsian [C. Wright] power elite could exercise effective political control." Is it also conceivable, then, that "oligarchic capitalism—some variant of fascism—is a likely prospect for the twenty-first century?" According to Gramm, this would occur only if the power concentrations described were to "promote specifically fascist norms and behavior." Among the latter are deliberate appeals to nonrationality, belief in human inequality, recourse to lies and violence, culminating in "a breakdown of the rule of (liberal) law." To the extent, then, that our "capitalist" political economy tolerates or promotes wide inequality of income and wealth, economic and racial discrimination, hyperindividualism reflected in secrecy, commercial lying, reinforced conflict over cooperation, "systematic avoidance, evasion and outright disobedience of government regulations of private market actions," the risks of movement toward a "friendly fascism" increase.

In the final chapter in this section, William M. Dugger argues the case for democratic economic planning, aided and abetted by greater worker participation in decision making, as an appropriate and effective response in the quest for social control of corporate power. At the outset, Dugger's concern is to distinguish between "progressive" views of planning held by institutional economists and those that would be labeled "corporatist." Dugger contends,

> Corporatism is a fundamentally elitist approach to the social problems of industrial civilization that relies very heavily on trained experts to supply technical fixes to social problems and then relies on the existing, centralized corporate power structure to implement the technical fixes. Corporatism strengthens the inequality of the status quo by softening it, and by touching up a few of its racist and sexist features, while keeping the vested interests firmly vested. Corporatism is capitalism with a human face, planned by a centralized structure of corporate power. Corporatism is not what institutionalists have in mind when they call for economic planning.

In contrast, Institutionalists turn "away from assumed market automaticity to some form of conscious democratic planning as the principal form of social control in the industrialized economy." Institutionalists, as Dugger quotes K.P. Cochran, conceive the economic system "as a social or human phenomenon rather than a congeries of natural laws and natural forces which are not to be tampered with." They deny the "most important tenet of orthodox theory—the efficacy of the market mechanism as the organizing force in the modern industrial economy." Dugger further asserts that "the industrial system is a product of collective action and inaction. The exchange arena—the market—reflects the results of the underlying power plays and technological changes that drive the industrial economy. The parameters within which exchange takes place are set by forces outside the exchange arena." The giant corporations guide markets, set most prices, and have achieved sufficient size to "outgrow the bounds of the nation state."

While no detailed democratic planning structure or function is developed here, it is clear that basic discretion over economic policy must be relocated in a body or bodies that will in fact serve the public interest and not the corporatist interest. Its goals must be to further "equality, efficiency, and social responsibility." This quest must be accompanied by internal corporate reform, and will be materially enhanced by institutional changes that enfranchise workers through participatory prerogatives, ownership options, and the "unbundling" of corporate and managerial prerogatives. But Dugger acknowledges that "a fundamental democratization and reconstitution of the political system is needed . . . before public planning can be either effective or democratic."

15

Antitrust in a Planned Economy: Anachronism or an Essential Complement?

Willard F. Mueller

The conventional wisdom among many popular commentators, historians, political scientists, and economists is that, for all practical purposes, the antitrust laws are dead, ineffective or, worse, still pernicious.[1] Feeble antitrust enforcement has become, in John Kenneth Galbraith's view, a "charade" acted out "not to prevent exploitation of the public" but "to persuade people in general and . . . liberals in particular, that the market is still extant."[2]

But the wake for antitrust is premature. Although its vital life signs are weak and its critics are many, not only can its health be restored, but also it can lead a long life in which it contributes immensely to the social control of corporate power.

This is not to argue, however, that current programs for the social control of industry cannot be improved. Indeed, although the "charade" view of antitrust easily can be exaggerated, I must confess—which is painful for one having devoted much of his life to antitrust enforcement—that I have become increasingly sympathetic to the Galbraithian view.[3] Much antitrust action, including some current talk about strengthening enforcement, is little more than a charade. By promising more than they can deliver, antitrusters inadvertently mislead the public into the belief that entrenched economic power is being policed successfully, thereby legitimizing such power and abetting it in escaping effective social control.

To correct this problem, antitrust officials and the public they serve must come to a better understanding of the proper role of antitrust in a modern industrial economy, one already subject to large doses of government planning and subject to even more in the future. In this address I want to move toward such an understanding by surveying briefly the intellectual and institutional history of the antitrust movement in the United States, by examining some recent successes and failures, and finally by reflecting on its role in restraining the development and use of market power in our modern mixed economy.

Orthodoxy, Institutionalism, and the Antitrust Laws

Most orthodox and institutionalist economists viewed the great turn-of-the-century trust movement as the inevitable product of economic imperatives, with few economists of either school strongly supporting the Sherman Act of 1890. Prominent orthodox economists generally viewed the trusts as natural and inevitable, more to be embraced than condemned.[4] Evolving as they did from an earlier stage of laissez-faire capitalism, the trusts "came because they must,"[5] and the antitrust laws were seen as anachronisms prescribing "things simply impossible."[6]

With the benefit of half a century of hindsight, George Stigler in 1950 leveled a serious indictment on the leading orthodox economists of the early 1900s:

> Economists as wise as Taussig, as incisive as Fisher, as fond of competition as Clark and Fetter, insisted upon discussing the [merger movement around 1900] largely or exclusively in terms of industrial evolution and the economies of scale. They found no difficulty in treating the unregulated corporation as a natural phenomenon. . . . Ida Tarbell and Henry Demarest Lloyd did more than the American Economic Association to foster the policy of competition.[7]

Some institutionalists shared the early orthodox economists' diagnosis of events, if not their prognosis. Thorstein Veblen, one of the fathers of institutionalism, accepted the conventional economic wisdom of the day. Veblen believed competitive markets were incompatible with the technical requirements of the new machine age which he saw all about him.[8] Much as does his modern disciple, Galbraith, he emphasized that the tendency toward combination was overpowering and that antitrust was a futile effort. He urged that the private property of the avaricious businessman be expropriated and the industrial system be given over to the exclusive management of the engineers, who, having constituted themselves the "General Staff of Industry," a "Soviet of Technicians," could bring the machinery to full efficiency, eliminate unemployment, increase output by 300 to 1,200 percent, and bring about a more equitable distribution of income.[9]

Veblen's legacy is Galbraith's New Industrial State,[10] where technological imperatives dictate the fall of competitive markets and the rise of private/state planning presided over by technocrats reminiscent of Veblen's heroes. In this view, as in Veblen's, antitrust policies aimed at preserving or developing effectively competitive markets are futile. Veblen predicted the death of the market; Galbraith would bury it.

But Veblen did not speak for all institutionalists of his era. Most of the two generations of institutionalists who Harry Trebing identified as making major contributions in developing institutions to exercise social control over "natural monopolies" did not believe monopoly was inevitable elsewhere in the economy.[11] Time permits only the briefest review of other institutionalists' ideas of industrial organization and the use of antitrust as an instrument of social control.

Richard T. Ely, an early reformer and the mentor of John R. Commons, rejected the notion that monopoly and high industrial concentration were inevitable outside the areas of "natural monopolies." Denying the "claim that competition in industry is self-annihilating and invariably makes way for monopoly," he believed the trusts were products of artificial restraints, special privileges, and predatory practices subject to legal reform.[12] Changes in the patent laws, increased inheritance taxes, and "some kind of federal bureau to exercise general supervision over private corporations" would, Ely believed, help to undermine the power of the trusts.[13] "The sole purpose of this control," however, "should be honesty and individual responsibility; and to secure this, complete publicity is necessary."[14] But there was no place in Ely's reform program for antitrust, which he viewed as a "faulty and indeed deplorable" policy subversion of free enterprise capitalism.[15] Ely was reluctant to support steps disrupting private institutions; for example, he did not "see how" mergers restraining competition could be prevented "if private property, as we now understand it, is to be maintained."[16]

The views of John R. Commons differed from those of his teacher. Commons apparently made his first public comments on the trust problem in 1900 at the National Antitrust Conference in Chicago. The conference, sponsored by the American Antitrust League, had issued invitations to "citizens of public spirit, sincerely opposed to monopolies and special privilege, including what are commonly known as 'Trusts.' "[17] Commons not only was one of the two academic economists to address the conference, but also had joined those who called for convening it.[18] It is hardly surprising that Commons did not say a great deal about the trust problem, since he was not working in the field at the time. However, in his address he urged that "instead of attacking the trusts directly . . . we should attack their causes," which he saw as the New York bank monopoly, "which controlled credit, freight discrimination by which trusts destroyed their competitors, and protective tariffs."

Commons's views were always heavily influenced by his personal experience in a field. It was not until the 1920s that, in his words, he first "piled up experience" in the antitrust field.[19] In 1923 Wisconsin and three other states directed their attorneys general to proceed against U.S. Steel before the Federal Trade Commission because of the discriminatory delivered price system, later to become the famous *Pittsburgh Plus* case. Commons was asked to take charge in developing the economic case with the aid of two prominent economists, Frank A. Fetter of Princeton and William Z. Ripley of Harvard. In his autobiography Commons credited this experience in working with Federal Trade Commission lawyers as rounding out "remarkably my efforts to coordinate the theories of law and economics."[20] He later inserted, "almost verbatim,"[21] much of his brief for the FTC in his *Institutional Economics* and also wrote an account of the case in the *American Economic Review* for September 1924.

This experience evidently led Commons to view the antitrust laws as a viable means of collective action to control corporate power. In 1932 he was one of the first economists to sign a statement condemning the efforts of the American Bar Asssociation to repeal or amend the Sherman Act.[22] The statement had been prepared by Frank A. Fetter, his old friend, and was later signed by about 100 economists, including such other prominent institutionalists as Leo Sharfman, James C. Bonbright, and George W. Stocking. The economists urged that the antitrust laws be preserved and that competition be maintained outside the regulated areas. They asked both political parties to adopt in their platform an antitrust plank embodying, among other things:

> Opposition to the amendment of the existing antitrust laws in any manner that would weaken them as agencies for preserving the policy of free markets.

> Reaffirmation of the essential principle of fair competition in all
> lines of industry not given over to the public price control through
> commissions; recognition that unless there be such public protec-
> tion the policy of free markets is essential to the interests of the
> great mass of people—the consumers, workers, and multitudes of
> independent businessmen.[23]

The statement apparently had some effect: the 1932 Republican platform contained no plank on antitrust, positive or negative, despite the
fact that the chairman of the Resolutions Committee favored one, and
the Democratic party platform included a brief statement embodying the
main features of the "Economists' Statement." The economists' satisfaction at their apparent success was short lived, however, as the National
Industrial Recovery Act of 1933 repudiated the Democratic antitrust
plank.

John R. Commons's interest in the antitrust laws was not surprising,
since he viewed them as potential instruments for developing working
rules to control private power. This is particularly so because antitrust
enforcement always has involved the interaction of legal and economic
concepts. And as already noted, Commons's experience with Fetter and
Ripley at the Federal Trade Commission in the *Pittsburgh Plus* case was
the crucible in which he combined the disciplines of economics and law
in formulating social rules.

Although Commons and Veblen agreed on many counts, "unlike
Veblen," Allan Gruchy has written, "Commons was an optimist who believed that the American economic system could be reconstructed with
the aim of improving its operations without changing the essentials of
private business enterprise."[24] This contrasted with Veblen's view that
"the system of private business enterprise would pass away in the course
of time [and that] the demise of capitalism would be followed by the
establishment of a military dictatorship or a socialist state."[25] Time
seems to have dated both views, to a degree.

Outside the Veblen tradition, there is no single consistent strand of institutionalist thought toward antitrust as an instrument of social control.
While Commons directly or indirectly influenced the thinking and methodology of many later economists, others in the mainstream and eddies
of institutionalist thought had a more direct effect. America's most famous father and son economist team, John Bates Clark and John Maurice Clark, influenced industrial organization and public policy thought
over a span of seven decades. Although the elder Clark, whose favorite
student was Thorstein Veblen,[26] initially was very reluctant to attack the
trusts, shortly after 1900 he waged an active campaign against "predatory big business," even allying himself with the populist critic Ida Tar-

bell.[27] After his friend Woodrow Wilson became President, the elder Clark's views were invited as to the efficacy of early versions of the Clayton Act of 1914.[28]

Although John Maurice Clark shared with his famous (and more orthodox economist) father an initial distrust of the antitrust laws, events led him first to tolerate and finally to embrace them. William Lee Baldwin succinctly characterized this conversion of the pragmatic J. M. Clark: "Thus he was opposed to the antitrust laws until they proved effective, and then supported them on the grounds that they worked."[29]

In addition to the institutionalists already mentioned, others also have played a central role in marrying the disciplines of antitrust law and economics. George W. Stocking, my mentor, Edwin S. Mason, Corwin Edwards, and Paul T. Homan all used an interdisciplinary approach embracing law and economics in formulating legal rules to control economic power. A later generation of similar persuasion and approach includes, among others, Walter Adams, John Blair, Joel B. Dirlam, Alfred E. Kahn, Samuel M. Loescher, David D. Martin, and Wallace C. Peterson. Although not sharing a common heritage, nearly all were exposed to institutionalist ideas in their early years and have become active members of this Association. Once into the field of industrial organization, they have all embraced, consciously or unconsciously, Commons's multidisciplinary approach involving the complex relationship between law and economics.

It is possible to overstate, in the pursuit of historical continuity, the tie between contemporary institutionalists and their intellectual forebears. Many entering the institutionalist camp did not do so because of an early exposure to institutionalist thought; rather, in their own pursuit of better understanding of our modern industrial society, they discovered a vast gulf between reality and the postulates of orthodox theory. They did not reject all orthodox theory, they simply found much of it irrelevant to many important problems of the day. In the field of industrial organization, for example, the great contributions made by Joan Robinson and Edward H. Chamberlain have proven largely useless in examining the conglomerate enterprise, which increasingly is the rule rather than the exception among large modern corporations. Indeed, preoccupation with orthodox oligopoly theory has led many industrial organization economists to focus on narrow problems, ignoring such pressing issues as industrial conglomeration, multinational corporations, and administered inflation. Unfortunately, industrial organization economists generally, as well as most of his own students, have ignored the observation of Edward S. Mason in 1939: "The theory of oligopoly has been aptly described as a ticket of admission to institutional economics. It is to be regretted that more theorists have not availed themselves of this privilege."[30]

I suspect that Gardiner C. Means, in explaining how he entered the institutionalist camp, describes a route familiar to many of us. In accepting the Association's Veblen-Commons award this year Means explains:

> In my search as a scientist for the appropriate postulates to under-
> lie a macrotheory for the modern economy, I found myself in the
> camp of the institutionalists. Certainly my studies of the modern
> corporation, of price behavior, and of the structure of the Ameri-
> can economy were studies of institutions. But my drive throughout
> was to obtain the essential postulates for a new and realistic mac-
> rotheory, a new paradigm to displace the orthodox.[31]

In tracing the various roads leading to modern institutionalism, I have tried to explain why there is a strong institutional legacy in the field of industrial organization and public policy, and why this legacy differs from that of Veblen and Galbraith. But as I contend below, in my view there is no inherent contradiction between the necessity of planning as argued by Veblen, Galbraith, and others and the use of antitrust as a complementary means to control market power. Before turning to this, however, I shall review briefly the institutionalization of antitrust policy and examine some of its successes and failures.

The Institutionalization of Antitrust Enforcement

The initial antitrust movement lasted about three decades, commencing in the 1880s and culminating with the enactment of the Clayton and Federal Trade Commission Acts in 1914. As with other populist reform movements of the period, it was choked off by World War I.

Anti-antitrust sentiments prevailed during the 1920s, as enforcement efforts dwindled and a laissez-faire revival carried the day. The coming of the New Deal, although it brought fundamental political change and reforms, seemed for a time to be tolling antitrust's last hours.

The National Industrial Recovery Act (NRA) of 1933 replaced competition with a system of government and business directed "cooperation" and essentially suspended the antitrust laws to accommodate NRA codes. Antitrust faced its darkest moments. But at the eleventh hour, a new antitrust movement was born.

The year was 1938. President Franklin D. Roosevelt's NRA, already sick, had been given a death sentence by the Supreme Court in the *Schechter* decision. Moreover, Roosevelt was deeply disturbed when, in 1937, the economy went into a decline, demonstrating that past policies had failed to revive it. This situation gave Brandeis liberals, who had been pushed outside the inner circle by the brain trust, an opportunity to gain the President's ear. Their advice to the worried Roosevelt was to abandon the system of planned cartelization implicit in the NRA and to turn instead to the renewal of market competition through vigorous antitrust efforts. Their arguments rested partly on the "administrative price" thesis developed by Gardiner C. Means in the early 1930s, which held that the market power of big business was frustrating monetary and fiscal policies designed to cure the depression.[32] Secretary of Interior Harold Ickes and Assistant Attorney General for Antitrust Robert Jackson warned Roosevelt that big business was frustrating the New Deal through a "strike of capital."[33] They called for a direct assault on the holders of vast corporate power.

This was the stuff from which the antitrust revival was born. Seldom one to be encumbered by the requirements of ideological consistency, Roosevelt was receptive to new approaches. The result was a sharp turn away from a system of planning whose central tenet had been government-sponsored cartelization of business and toward a policy of renewed attention to making market competition more effective.

In 1938 Roosevelt called for the creation of a Temporary National Economic Commission (TNEC) to be composed of members of both legislative chambers and the executive branch, including the chairmen of the FTC and SEC and the Assistant Attorney General for Antitrust. The TNEC was attacked from the left as well as the right. Many on the left felt betrayed because, as Thurmond Arnold later recalled, "there was a belief among liberals at the time that the age of competition had gone and the age of planning had come."[34] Critics on the right charged Roosevelt with launching a hostile attack on the capitalistic system itself. Actually, TNEC's chief goal was to learn how twentieth-century capitalism worked and how it could be improved.[35] The numerous TNEC hearings and monographs not only drew attention to the dangers of concentrated corporate power but also provided incentive for further studies of the structure and performance of contemporary corporate capitalism. Because the committtee drew heavily upon the expertise of the professional staffs of the antitrust agencies, it elevated their status in the mind of the Congress and the public.

In his message urging the creation of the TNEC, Roosevelt also called for a strengthening of antitrust enforcement.[36] To lead the new antitrust movement, Roosevelt appointed Thurmond Arnold head of the Antitrust Division. Arnold came into his new job with many proposals for reform; only a year earlier he had written a scathing indictment of past antitrust enforcement.[37] During the next five years, a period regarded by many as the golden age of antitrust, he put new life into the division, expanding its manpower by 500 percent. In the peak year, 1941, more Sherman Act cases were filed than during the first 20 years of the act's history. But the main legacy of Arnold's reign was not his big cases and the growth of the division, but the demonstration that antitrust still had a meaningful role in the modern U.S. economy. As a result, even though antitrust enforcement was partially demobilized during World War II, the agencies rebounded strongly at the war's end, and the big cases went forward.[38]

Although considerably diminished in the eyes of the general public, an antitrust movement still stalked Washington in the immediate post-war years. Politicians and government officials schooled by Thurmond Arnold and the TNEC pushed for stronger antitrust laws, particularly for a new antimerger statute. It was this environment that made possible the enactment of the Celler-Kefauver Act of 1950, which greatly strengthened Section 7 of the Clayton Act. The passage of this act might well be viewed as the capstone of the antitrust revival initiated over a decade before; it also roughly coincided with the close of the antitrust "movement." The movement itself, however, left in its wake an essentially bipartisan consensus that antitrust enforcement was an indispensable, if not popular, instrument of public policy in the mid-twentieth century.

While antitrust as an active "movement" was dormant during the fifties and sixties, the enforcement effort did not wither away as it had just prior to World War I. The reason for the difference, as Richard Hofstadter persuasively argued, was that Arnold's regime had resulted in the "institutionalization" of the antitrust process: "Despite the collapse of antitrust feeling both in the public at large and among the intellectuals, antitrust as legal-administrative enterprise has been solidly institutionalized in the past quarter of a century."[39]

Hofstadter viewed the transformation of the antitrust movement into an accepted institution as "an excellent illustration of how a public idea, vaguely formulated and often hopelessly at odds with stubborn realities can become embodied in institutions with elaborate, self-preserving rules and procedures, a defensible function, and an equally stubborn capacity for survival."[40] The result was that whereas "once the United States had an antitrust movement without prosecutions; in our time there have been antitrust prosecutions without an antitrust movement."[41] This explains why, in a sense, it was an historical imperative that the antitrust agencies respond as they did when the current merger movement first began accelerating in 1954–1955. In 1950, Congress gave the agencies a mandate to prevent potentially anticompetitive mergers. The institutionalization process identified by Hofstadter provided the agencies with the authority to carry out the mandate to a degree eclipsing the enforcement effort following enactment of the original antimerger statute in 1914.[42] More on this shortly.

Contemporary Antitrust Enforcement: Victories and Failures

Antitrust enforcement over the past 25 years defies neat labels. What has been to some a noble crusade to control corporate market power has been to others a vain pretense full of sound and fury and signifying nothing. In fact, neither interpretation is wanting in empirical support. Candor requires admission that Section 2 of the Sherman Act has fallen into a kind of dignified desuetude, leaving undisturbed major aggregations of corporate power. But it is also true that aggressive enforcement of the Celler-Kefauver Act has stopped numerous potentially horizontal and vertical combinations that otherwise would have increased concentration to a dangerous point in many industries.

Contemporary antitrust enforcement, then, has not involved a consistent record of victories or defeats. It has not been a mere Fourth of July parade of tired, flag-waving legionnaires, but neither has it been a populist holy war. Most correctly, it has been a holding action against those forces in our economy that otherwise would have concentrated power in even fewer hands.

The response of the antitrust agencies in merger enforcement perhaps best illustrates how the institutionalization process described by Hofstadter permits antitrust to be an effective weapon. It also illustrates some of its shortcomings.

Beginning with the district court decision in the *Bethlehem-Youngstown* case in 1958, the courts have given the antitrust agencies a clear mandate to prevent horizontal and vertical mergers threatening competition. Since January 1951 the agencies have issued about 400 complaints challenging over 1,000 acquisitions with combined assets exceeding $20 billion.[43] Nor has this effort been a charade, as Galbraith implies, an assault largely on mergers among small companies.[44] Over 90 percent of all challenged acquisitions (measured by assets of manufacturing corporations) involved acquiring companies with assets in excess of $100 million. Most industrial corporations with assets exceeding $1 billion have had one or more merger complaints filed against them since 1950.

But even more important than the actual relief achieved through these actions has been the deterrent effect on others contemplating such mergers. During 1951–1958, about 75 percent (measured in assets) of all acquisitions by corporations with $1 billion in assets involved horizontal mergers. In subsequent years this percentage dwindled—to below 10 percent by the late 1960s. This comparatively massive enforcement effort must be seen as a victory for antitrust, as it prevented further concentration in many industries and opened up opportunities for deconcentration in others.

But this is not to say it was an unqualified victory. Indeed, the belated assault on conglomerate mergers in 1969 led by antitrust chief Richard W. McLaren foundered, as Hency C. Simons might have said, on "the orderly process of democratic corruption." The ITT merger cases ended in consent settlements that prevented the Supreme Court from rendering judgment and, worse still, were negotiated under a cloud of political intrigue.[45] Sordid as these events are, they do not represent the greatest failure of contemporary antitrust. That lies elsewhere.

Galbraith is correct that the trust-busters have not laid siege to the many existing citadels of market power, have not indeed even kept their siege engines free from rust. The cost of this neglect has been high. While academic economists may quibble endlessly about the precise degree and trends of market power in the United States, it is clear that in many industries market concentration already is very high and will not be eroded significantly by natural economic forces.[46] It is also clear that in many industries product differentiation created by advertising is raising barriers to entry and conferring ever greater measures of pricing independence on dominant firms. As an ever increasing share of U.S. industry falls under the domination of huge conglomerate enterprises straddling numerous industries, corporate decision making becomes more centralized.

Aside from merger policy, antitrust has had little influence on these trends toward growing centralization of economic power. Virtually nothing has been done to break up those industries where concentration already is too high to permit effective competition. Fewer big Sherman Act Section 2 monopoly cases have been initiated and carried to conclusion in the last two decades than in the first two decades of this century. This dismal record occurred despite an enormous growth in the Justice Department since the days of Theodore Roosevelt, when the antitrusters "sallied out against the combined might of the great corporations with a staff of five lawyers and four stenographers."[47] The simple truth is that the existing holders of substantial market power have enjoyed for years *de facto* immunity from the antitrust laws. Nor should anyone become overly optimistic about recent promises to step up antitrust enforcement, especially the promise to attack more price conspiracies in battling inflation. I suspect this promise is primarily an effort to distract public attention from the heavy costs of the administration's current contractionary policies, which rely solely on monetary and fiscal policy and ignore the role market power plays in the inflationary process. But even if more conspiracy complaints are issued, the long-run benefits of many such cases are questionable. For let there be no mistake: White-collar crime in the business suite pays well even when the criminals are found guilty and sentenced.[48] It is doubtful, for example, that the recent conspiracy case brought against steel companies, or the seven brought in the 1960s, will have any lasting impact on the competitive behavior of the steel industry.

Some may accept this judgment and yet point with hope to the filing of several substantial Sherman Act complaints, beginning with the IBM suit launched in the last hours of the Johnson administration. But do the new FTC monopoly cases against the big four breakfast cereal makers and the big eight petroleum corporations and the Antitrust Division's similar cases against IBM and AT&T portend a new broad-scale attack on the market power problem in the United States? Certainly these actions are evidence that some changes are in the wind. A decade ago the environment was too hostile to tolerate such cases. But hard realities compel the conclusion that these actions represent only a small beginning. In antitrust litigation the launching is infinitely easier than the voyage, and I therefore fear that the outlook for government victory in these cases is bleak. The two FTC cases appear to be hopelessly bogged down. Fifteen months after bringing the petroleum case, the FTC staff admits that the case "has ground to a virtual halt."[49] The Justice Department's IBM suit, begun in January 1969, has yet to come to trial. In some respects this is not too surprising, for vast resources are required to prosecute enormous corporations under the existing law. In a private suit between IBM and Control Data Corporation, for example, the settlement included an item of $15 million merely to pay for legal and other expenses, an amount greater than the annual budget of the entire Antitrust Division. AT&T is expected to spend $60 million defending itself, and a Justice Department official acknowledged the litigation ."will strain" the Antitrust Division to the limit, resulting in fewer antitrust cases in the years to come.

Simply put, under existing circumstances the antitrust agencies are outnumbered, outgunned, and are forced to fight on the defendants' terms. Today an antitrust confrontation more closely resembles Custer's last stand than a shoot-out at the OK Corral.

Unless we can do better than this, the antitrust laws merely will perpetuate the myth, as Thurmond Arnold observed in 1937, that by performing "an occasional legal ceremony" we are forcing great corporations to behave competitively.[50] What, then, must we do to be saved? Galbraith preaches salvation through *direct* control of corporate power and renunciation of the temptations of relying on antitrust. He is a good and noble spirit, and in my darkest hours his sermon almost leads me to the confessional. But there is another way. The antitrust laws need not be abandoned to permit effective planning of economic activity where it is necessary. And even where direct price, profit, and wage controls may be necessary—as I will argue they are in some industries—there is still an important place for a reformed antitrust program and for other policies to make market competition more effective. But what is required for success?

The first essential is the creation of a constituency that will support a new antitrust *movement*. Many may reject this notion as politically naïve. Perhaps it is. But I detect breezes of reform blowing across the land, many in the direction of industrial restructuring. The Watergate scandals linking corporate economic and political power, and the political machinations of ITT at home and abroad have taught a new generation of Americans, and refreshed the memories of others, that economic and political power are fellow travelers. Consumer groups, Ralph Nader, and many other social reformers include antitrust reform among their top priorities. These and other events explain why in 1974 more politicians have been discussing the problems of corporate market power than at any other time in recent history.

My own agenda for reforming antitrust would, in broad terms, include the following:[51] (1) Make enforcement officials more publicly accountable for their actions;[52] (2) strengthen the antitrust laws so as to expedite industrial restructuring by shifting partially the burden of proof to the defendants;[53] and (3) greatly increase the resources of the antitrust agencies. Important initiatives already have been taken or are being given serious consideration in each of these areas.

It would be a mistake, however, to rely exclusively on the antitrust laws to bring about public control over excessive corporate power. History suggests the advantages of direct legislative action to bring about selective industrial restructuring. The massive divestitures required by the Public Utilities Holding Company Act of 1935 are well known. Less well appreciated are the achievements of the Banking Act of 1933, which divorced investment from commercial banking, and the McKellar-Black Air Mail Act of 1934, which forced General Motors to relinquish its interests in various airlines and aircraft manufacturers. The latter acts, alone, accomplished more divestitures than the total achieved in over 80 years under the Sherman Act.

For example, similar legislative action might be pursued to divorce

Western Electric from AT&T and large petroleum corporations from their interests in coal and other areas. Without such legislation, the anti-trust agencies may well become hopelessly mired down in a few big cases.

But industrial restructuring, however achieved, will not be enough to ensure all powerful corporations will perform in the public interest. They therefore must be treated as quasi-public institutions. Federal chartering can be an appropriate first step in recognizing that the large corporation is an essentially public, not private, enterprise, that most of what it does is very much the public's business, and that, consequently, more of its business should be conducted in public.[54] In a free society no institution vital to the public interest can maintain a claim to legitimacy if its affairs are shrouded in secrecy. Yet, as corporations become larger and more conglomerated, more and more of their actions are kept secret from the public. Much has been accomplished in opening to public view many government affairs. Similarly, federal chartering could be used to make public the actions of large corporations, premised on what Justice Louis Brandeis emphasized as "the essential difference between corporations and natural persons."

Antitrust and Planning

The Employment Act of 1946 was the culmination of over a decade of experimentation to achieve full employment and economic stabilization. Some economists viewed the act as a vehicle for comprehensive state planning that made the antitrust laws obsolete. This is neither a correct interpretation of legislative history nor of experience under the act. The Employment Act mandated that the federal government, in the words of Edwin G. Nourse, first chairman of the Council of Economic Advisors (CEA), accept responsibility "to make systematic study of its several policies and programs to see that they move consistently toward maintaining the health of the economy and continuous high-level utilization of the nation's resources."[55] Included in the act's "declaration of policy" was the charge that it be carried out "in a manner calculated to foster and promote free competitive enterprise and the general welfare." Nor was this mere laissez-faire rhetoric designed to protect vested corporate interests. Although those implementing the act were expected to employ a broad mix of government policies to achieve economic stabilization and growth, particularly fiscal and monetary policies, they were not expected to resort to direct controls over price and other business decisions so long as the private sector was effectively competitive. This meant, of course, that the act emphasized the duty of promoting competition through antitrust and other means.

From the outset, the Joint Economic Committee (JEC) of the Congress, also created by the Employment Act of 1946, was more faithful to this responsibility than was the Council of Economic Advisors. The JEC generally has argued that the objectives of the Employment Act should include vigorous antitrust programs. Joseph O'Mahoney, the first JEC chairman, also had chaired the TNEC (1938–1941) investigation of concentrated economic power. Edwin G. Nourse, first chairman of the Council of Economic Advisors, recalled that O'Mahoney conceived "the Joint Committee set up under the Employment Act as a permanent national economic committee, taking up about where the TNEC left off." Except for two brief interludes, 1947–1949 and 1953–1955,[56] the committee has been headed by strong proponents of antitrust: Senator Joseph O'Mahoney, 1947–1948 and 1951–1953; Congressman Wright Patman, 1955–1974; Senator Paul H. Douglas, 1955–1965; and Senator William Proxmire, 1965–1974 (the chairmanship alternates between the Senate and the House every two years).

Procompetition policies initially received scant attention from the CEA, and in a 1956 symposium on the act Senator Douglas expressed displeasure that the country had not yet solved "the problems of preserving the free enterprise system against the encroachment of monopoly and bigness." Under Douglas's chairmanship, the JEC held a series of comprehensive hearings examining the manner in which market power frustrated efforts to attain full employment by relying solely on monetary and fiscal policy. These hearings dispelled the belief that "economic planning" required only simple Keynesian measures whereby the economy could be stabilized at levels of high employment by manipulating aggregate demand. Douglas's hearings made a persuasive case for including market power in the complex equations explaining the trade-off between full employment and inflation.

The JEC consistently, usually with bipartisan support, has argued for procompetition policies. Recently, under the direction of Senator William Proxmire, a committee report prepared at the request of President Gerald Ford once again emphasized the relation between market power and inflation: "In the private sector, industrial concentration, collusive practices, administered profits and anti-competitive behavior must bear a large part of the responsibility for the current inflation."[57]

To cope with these problems the JEC recommended new legislation to promote competition through such actions as "divestiture and reorganization, improved antitrust laws and administration and removal of artificial barriers to employment."[58]

What then is the place of antitrust in a planned economy? In Galbraith's New Industrial State the government engages in extensive economic planning in areas where the market cannot adequately serve the public interest. The state strives to stabilize aggregate demand, promote economic growth, and control inflation; underwrites most basic and applied research; educates our technical and scientific manpower; attempts to redistribute income, aid the elderly, and assist the less fortunate; protects the environment; guards the consumer; and preserves our natural resources. I agree totally with Galbraith that such state intervention indicates that the public is unwilling—and properly so—to accept the verdict of the marketplace on these and other affairs. For these are matters that the market, whether competitively or monopolistically structured, cannnot be relied upon to handle in the public interest. But to acknowledge this is not to say the market should be abandoned in other areas. Indeed, it argues the opposite. Whenever the state assumes additional responsibilities, the more important it is that wherever possible the market "regulate" economic activity, thereby minimizing the burden on government planning, a lesson that even some socialist states have learned. Nowhere is this more evident than in the state's efforts to maintain full employment without excessive inflation.

The evidence seems irrefutable that excessive market power creates an inflationary bias in modern capitalistic economies, that it is therefore no longer possible to rely solely on monetary and fiscal policy to achieve full employment without excessive inflation. Although there are still unbelievers—especially in that bastion of nineteenth-century laissez-faire economics, the University of Chicago—events have forced economists to discard theoretical models fashioned for a system of competitive markets.

Credit for much of the public's education about this phenomenon must go to President Richard M. Nixon, who conducted an historic experiment. In January 1969 he announced a "game plan" that promised to bring about price stability without any government intervention in key price and wage decisions. For many months he steadfastly pursued this laissez-faire policy. But instead of abating, inflation rose, and unemployment swelled from 3.3 percent to 6 percent, and the GNP gap widened to over $100 billion. On 15 September 1971 President Nixon admitted defeat and decreed a 90-day wage-price freeze, followed by a series of ill-conceived and poorly administered "phases" of controls.

The fatal flaw in this game plan, of course, was the assumption that market forces were sufficiently powerful to discipline key price and wage decision makers. If market forces had been truly competitive in all industry, the overall price level would have begun moderating shortly after fiscal and monetary policy had contracted aggregate demand. That they did not is hardly surprising. As Gardiner C. Means has taught for forty years, market power enables corporations to practice "administrative" pricing, the ability to maintain or even increase prices despite falling demand.[59]

The failures of Nixon's game plan are now history. But, incredibly, President Ford's advisors persuaded him to replay the same game plan, which has led to even more disastrous consequences. Anyone who argues that the Ford plan will succeed must explain why it will work today when the Nixon game plan failed so miserably in 1969–1970. The conditions conducive to success were much better in 1969 than in 1974, which explains why the results are even worse this time.

Nixon's and Ford's experiments have laid bare the terrible waste of human and economic resources that follow from a laissez-faire approach toward market power. The problem points to its own solution. Galbraith is correct. Not only must action be taken to manage aggregate demand, but also direct controls must be imposed on the holders of market power. Because the need for such controls stems from the possession of market power, ordinarily it will be necessary to apply them only to those with such power.

It cannot be emphasized too strongly that the extent of government involvement in price and wage decisions is directly related to the *amount* of market power in the economy. We therefore have a choice: Enlarge the area of competitive markets, or enlarge the area of government involvement in business pricing decisions.

Moreover, the extent of market power in business bears directly upon the extent and use of market power by labor. The former often begets the latter, as well as encourages labor to make maximum use of its power. But perhaps even more important, when firms enjoy persistently exorbitant profits, as in the drug industry, such excess profits must be eliminated if we are to expect labor unions not to exercise their full power. It is not convincing to argue, as have some economists, that eliminating monopoly profits in a particular industry is not really very important because it will affect only slightly the allocation of resources or the distribution of income. The critical point missed by this argument is that antitrust may play an indispensable role in an equitable incomes policy by *minimizing* the struggle over income distribution, the rock upon which incomes policies of other nations so often have foundered.

There is growing sentiment for such a policy. Although antitrust received scant support, and even some scorn, from the "new economists" in the early 1960s, attitudes changed over the decade. The last will and testament of President Johnson's Cabinet Committee on Price Stability included antitrust among the essential ingredients of a comprehensive incomes policy.[60] An increasing number of public officials, including Federal Reserve chairman Arthur F. Burns, responsible for implementing the objectives of the Employment Act of 1946, have come to share the view that antitrust is an important long-run tool in coping with market-power induced inflation.[61] Antitrust is not, of course, a short-run solution to the inflationary bias created by excess market power. But as Gardiner Means has said, although the current inflation requires mandatory price controls over corporations with great power, "in the long run antitrust can perform an important role."[62]

So ends my Epistle for the day. Some fellow antitrusters, and certainly others, may interpret this as a confession that antitrust has failed and that I have sold my soul to the devil of state intervention and planning. Not so. For antitrust is an essential complement to planning, not an alternative.

Notes

1. Murray Edelman, *The Symbolic Uses of Politics* (Urbana: University of Illinois Press, 1964), especially chapter 2; Richard Posner, "A Statistical Study of Antitrust Enforcement," *Journal of Law and Economics* (13 October 1970): 365; Abram Chayes, "The Modern Corporation and the Rule of Law," in *The Corporation in Modern Society*, E.S. Mason, ed. (Cambridge, Mass.: Harvard University Press, 1959), p. 37; and Gordon Bjork, *Private Enterprise and Public Interest* (Englewood Cliff, N. J.: Prentice Hall, 1969).
2. John Kenneth Galbraith, in "The Third Reich Lecture, Control of Prices and People," *The Listener,* 1 December 1966, p. 794. See also Galbraith, *The New Industrial State* (Boston: Houghton Mifflin Co., 1967), especially pp. 184–97.
3. See my criticism of John Kenneth Galbraith in W.F. Mueller, "Comment on the New Industrial State," *Antitrust Law & Economics* 1 (Winter 1967): 29–44.
4. For a comprehensive review of this literature see William Lee Baldwin, *Antitrust and the Changing Corporation* (Durham: Duke University Press, 1965).
5. Ernst von Halle, *Trusts or Industrial Combinations and Coalitions in the United States*, 1895, p. 143.
6. Ibid., p. 147.
7. George Stigler, "Monopoly and Oligopoly by Merger," *American Economic Review* 40 (May 1950): 30–31.
8. Thorstein Veblen, *The Theory of Business Enterprise,* p. 266.
9. Thorstein Veblen, *The Engineers and the Price System*, 2d ed. (New York: Harcourt, Brace & World, 1963).
10. Galbraith, *New Industrial State*.
11. Trebing includes, among others, Richard T. Ely, John R. Commons,

and William Ripley in the first generation, and Martin Glaeser, James Bonbright, J.M. Clark, and Leo Sharfman in the second generation. Harry M. Trebing, "Realism and Relevance in Public Utility Regulation," *Journal of Economic Issues* 8 (June 1974): 210–11.

12. Richard T. Ely, *Monopolies and Trusts* (New York: MacMillan Co., 1912), p. 179.
13. Ibid., p. 217 ff.
14. Ibid., pp. 268–69.
15. Ibid., p. 234.
16. Ibid., p. 345. Of course, Ely was writing before the first trusts had been dismembered.
17. *Official Report of the Antitrust Conference* (Chicago: 1900), p. 7. The only other economist to speak at the conference was E.W. Bemis.
18. Ibid., p. 24.
19. John R. Commons, *Myself* (Madison: The University of Wisconsin Press, 1964), p. 195.
20. Ibid., p. 197.
21. Ibid.
22. "The Economists Committee on Antitrust Policy," *American Economic Review* 22 (September 1932): 464.
23. Ibid., p. 467.
24. Allan G. Gruchy, *Contemporary Economic Thought* (Clifton: Augustus M. Kelley, 1972), p. 36.
25. Ibid., p. 23.
26. Joseph Dorfman, in his introduction to John Bates Clark and John Maurice Clark, *The Control of the Trusts* (1912) (New York: Augustus M. Kelley, 1971), p. 17.
27. Ibid., p. 9. Tarbell stirred up sentiment against the trusts in her popular book, *The History of the Standard Oil Company* (1904).
28. Ibid., pp. 10–12.
29. Baldwin, *Antitrust*, p. 65.
30. Edward S. Mason, "Price and Production Policies of Large-Scale Enterprises," *American Economic Review* 29 (March 1939): 64–66.
31. Gardiner C. Means, "Remarks upon Receipt of the Veblen-Commons Award," *Journal of Economic Issues* 9 (June 1975): 149–57.
32. Means, an advisor to the Secretary of Agriculture at the time, originally presented his thesis in a memorandum to the secretary. It was later published as a Senate Document, *Industrial Prices and Their Relative Inflexibility*, Senate Document No. 13, 74th Cong., 1st sess. (1935).
33. Richard Hofstadter, "What Happened to the Antitrust Movement?" in *The Business Establishment*, Early F. Cheit, ed. (New York: John Wiley & Sons, 1966), p. 116.
34. Thurmond Arnold, *Fair Fights and Foul* (1965), p. 138.
35. In his message to the Congress calling for the creation of the committee, President Roosevelt declared: "[G]enerally over the field of industry and finance we must revive and strengthen competition if we wish to preserve and make workable our traditional system of free private enterprise. In outlining "the choice before us," he concluded, "the enforcement of free competition is the least regulation business can expect."

36. Roosevelt's message also recommended a deficiency appropriation of $200,000 for the Department of Justice. Appropriations grew from $414,000 in 1938 to $2,325,000 in 1942. Thereafter they declined for several years as the nation fought World War II instead of the trusts. *Congress and the Monopoly Problem, History of Congressional Action in the Antitrust Field, 1890–1966, Seventy-Five Years*, Select Committee on Small Business, House of Representatives, 89th Cong., 2d sess., Committee Print (1966).

37. Thurmond W. Arnold, *The Folklore of Capitalism* (New Haven: Yale University Press, 1937).

38. The wartime revelations of the Kilgore, Truman, and Bone Senate Committees regarding the prewar operations of international cartels also kept alive the need for effective antitrust. These revelations kindled concern over the relationship between decentralized economic power and preservation of democratic political institutions, which ultimately became a part of the legislative history of the Celler-Kefauver Act of 1950. See, particularly, Wendell Berge, *Cartels: Challenge to a Free World* (Washington, D.C.: Public Affairs Press, 1944).

39. Hofstadter, "Antitrust Movement," p. 116.

40. Ibid., p. 114.

41. Ibid., p. 145.

42. This would not have been possible had not the Supreme Court rendered a series of decisions sustaining the FTC and Justice Department efforts, beginning with its important *Brown Shoe* decision in 1962 (*Brown Shoe v. United States*, 370 U.S. 294). This was in sharp contrast to the Supreme Court's treatment of the initial cases brought under the original Section 7. In a series of decisions during 1926–1934 the Court rendered the act almost totally ineffective. David D. Martin, *Mergers and the Clayton Act* (1959), pp. 104–147. In a report to the TNEC the FTC stated that "the effectiveness of this section has been completely emasculated as a result of court decisions." *FTC Report on Monopolistic Practices in Industry,* 1939.

43. For a discussion of enforcement during 1951–1967, see Willard F. Mueller, *The Celler-Kefauver Act: Sixteen Years of Enforcement*, Staff Report to the Antitrust Subcommittee on the Judiciary, House of Representatives, 16 October 1967. Data for enforcement since 1967 based on unpublished study by the author.

44. Galbraith, *New Industrial State*, p. 187.

45. Willard F. Mueller, "The ITT Settlement: A Deal with Justice?" *Industrial Organization Review* 1 (1973): 69–86.

46. Willard F. Mueller and Larry Hamm, "Trends in Industrial Market Concentration: 1947–70," *Review of Economics and Statistics* 56 (November 1974).

47. Hofstadter, "Antitrust Movement," p. 114.

48. Walter B. Erickson, "The Profitability of Violating the Antitrust Laws: Dissolution and Treble Damages in Private Antitrust," *Antitrust Law and Economics Review* 2 (Spring 1969): 101–18; and Alfred L. Parker, "Treble Damage Action—A Financial Deterrent to Antitrust Violations?" *Antitrust Bulletin* 15 (Summer 1971): 483–505.

49. "FTC Seeks to Get 'Big Oil' Case Moving," *Antitrust and Trade Regulation Report*, Bureau of National Affairs, 22 October 1974, p. A-1.

50. Arnold, *Folklore*, p. 221.

51. For a more detailed discussion of possible reforms see Willard F. Mueller, "Current Policy Issues in Antitrust," in *The Antitrust Dilemma*, J.A. Dalton and S. Levin, eds. Lexington: Lexington Books, 1974), pp. 117–35.

52. See "The ITT Case: Reform of Department of Justice Consent Decree Procedures," *Columbia Law Review* 73 (1973): 594–634.

53. See Senator Philip Hart's "Industrial Reorganization Act," S.1167, 1973.

54. For a discussion of the case for federal chartering see Willard F. Mueller, "Corporate Disclosure: The Public's Right to Know," in *Corporate Financial Reporting*, A. Rappaport and L. Revsine, eds. (Evanston: Northwestern University Press, 1972), pp. 67–94.

55. Edwin G. Nourse, *Economics in the Public Interest* (New York: Harcourt, Brace & Company, 1953), p. 67.

56. Senator Robert A. Taft was chairman during 1947–1949 and Congressman Jesse P. Wolcott was chairman during 1953–1955.

57. *An Action Program to Reduce Inflation and Restore Economic Growth, Interim Report of the Joint Economic Committee*, 92nd Cong. 2d sess., 21 September 1974, p. 29.

58. Ibid., pp. 30–31.

59. For a survey of this empirical literature see Willard F. Mueller, "Industrial Concentration: An Important Inflationary Force?" in *Industrial Concentration: The New Learning*, H.J. Goldschmid, H.M. Mann, and J.F. Weston, eds. (Boston: Little, Brown & Co., 1975), pp. 280–306.

60. *Report of Cabinet Committee on Price Stability, in Market Efficiency and Inflation* (New York: Arno Press and the *New York Times* 1969), p. h.

61. Arthur Burns told Senator Hart that he wished him well in his effort to enact the industrial reorganization bill. In a letter to Hart (Hearings on the Industrial Reorganization Act, Senate Subcommittee on Antitrust and Monopoly, U.S. Senate, 27 March 1973, pp. 43–44), Burns wrote, in part: "Currently we are enjoying a brisk recovery. But we are plagued with continuing inflation, and stabilization policies that rely on management of aggregate demand do not offer assurance, of themselves, of success in restoring stable prices. Selective controls on wages and prices for a limited period will be helpful, but they are no substitute for vigorous competition."

62. Letter to Willard F. Mueller from Gardiner C. Means, 11 June 1974.

16

Realism and Relevance in Public Utility Regulation

Harry M. Trebing

Public utility regulation was one of the pioneering areas of study in the social control of industry. It occupied a place of major importance in the work of the institutional economists and was incorporated within the programs of the progressive reformers.[1] Principal concern focused on the exploitative power of the corporation, and equity and the distribution of income were important themes in the writings of the period. It is not an exaggeration to say that the corporation was the villain, regulation was the hero, and control of monopoly profits was the objective.

But in the years since World War II, regulation has lost much of its legitimacy.[2] Criticism has come from a number of sources, including political scientists, practitioners, popular reformers, consumer advocates, administrative lawyers, former regulators, and economists. Regulation is accused of being a captive of the regulated, of having a perverse effect on efficiency, of failing to protect the consumer, and of contributing to crises in energy and transportation. From the standpoint of its critics, regulation now has become the villain, and the regulated firm often appears as simply a passive participant reacting to faulty signals.

Regulation stands at the crossroads. Major decisions must be made regarding the future of the commission system. However, there are a variety of conflicting recommendations, each with its own persuasive advocates of how best to promote the public interest.

At the risk of painting too large a canvas, this article will attempt to place the problem in a somewhat different perspective by contrasting the position of the early institutionalists, as champions of regulation, with the more recent critical evaluations put forth by orthodox or positive economists. A comparative assessment of these schools of thought will serve as a point of reference for a survey of purposeful future reforms in the commission system. Optimistically, this type of social experimentation should provide the type of challenge for which neoinstitutionalism is uniquely qualified.

Institutional Economics and the Development of Regulation

Background

Institutionalist involvement in the development of regulation had its roots in the late-nineteenth and early twentieth century. Among the earliest contributors were Richard T. Ely, John R. Commons, Henry C. Adams, B. H. Meyer, William Z. Ripley, and A. T. Hadley. The thinking of these men in the area of public utilities and transportation reflected a common frame of reference which was distinguished by the following characteristics.

First, there was a disenchantment with the adequacy of competition and its applicability or relevance to the newly emergent utility and transportation industries. The commonly held view was that the high fixed costs associated with these capital-intensive industries were conducive to "ruinous" competition.[3] If unchecked, such rivalry would force rates below the cost of service, resulting in discriminatory practices, restrictive efforts to divide markets, and monopolistic combinations. The preferable alternative was government intervention.

Second, there was serious doubt whether the interplay of market forces, reflecting the motive of self-interest, could reconcile conflicting pressures stemming from the transition to an industrialized and urbanized society. Greater social control was viewed by many institutionalists and progressives as a means for assuring orderly change. Social control was not envisioned by E. A. Ross and others as performing a static, stabilizing, or restorative function. Rather, it was oriented to change, to the future, and to progress.[4]

Third, there was a growing interest in the interrelationship between law and economics. It followed, therefore, that concern over property rights and the criteria used by the courts to resolve conflicts of interest would lead to a study of public utility regulation. From this point it was only a short step to a consideration of regulation within a larger context of collective action as a means for liberating individual action.

The work of these early institutionalists subsequently was carried forward by a second generation which included Martin Glaeser, James Bonbright, Philip Locklin, J. M. Clark, John Bauer, Max Lorenz, Leo Sharfman, C. F. McNeill, and others. Their efforts played a prominent role in refining and polishing the techniques of regulation, and by the late 1920s and early 1930s the concept and mechanics of the social control of public utilities had been formalized in a fashion that would not change significantly over the next forty years.

The Institutionalists' Concept

A majority of the institutionalists perceived regulation as a means of protecting the public against the adverse effects of monopoly.[5] It would serve as a constraint on corporate power, on the one hand, while assuring that the public would receive the scale and load-factor economies associated with monopoly supply, on the other. In practice, three distinctive operational features came to characterize this concept of regulation: the limitation of monopoly profits via rate base regulation; a search for cost-of-service pricing standards; and a continuing concern over matters of equity and fairness.

The rate base approach to the control of the level of earnings required a determination of allowable operating expenses and depreciation charges, the proper valuation of assets, and the calculation of a rate of return. In order to prevent these components from becoming mere "empty boxes," Henry C. Adams developed the uniform system of accounts to monitor most of the expense and rate base items. The result was a pioneering application of accounting methods for purposes of social control. This system, developed shortly after the establishment of the Interstate Commerce Commission, became the prototype for all subsequent state and federal accounting and reporting systems.[6]

The search for cost-of-service standards is less well known. However, there was a continuing effort to find a cost basis for setting prices and determining the revenue contributions by class of service. The work of J. M. Clark in the area of overhead costs figures prominently, as do the efforts of Morris L. Cooke and others.[7] Some of the work, possibly excluding that of Clark, seems somewhat naïve in retrospect, but it was the objective which was important. These

institutionalists sought to relate price to cost and thereby prevent
the flagrant forms of price discrimination embodied in value-of-service
ratemaking.

Finally, great weight always has been placed on considerations of
fairness and equity. This concern is evident during the period spanned
by the writings of Thomas M. Cooley (as first chairman of the ICC)
in 1888 through the recent defense of regulation given by Joseph
Swidler (as chairman of the New York Public Service Commission)
in 1970.[8] Equity and fairness have involved not only questions of
income distribution (between utility shareholders and consumers and
between classes of consumers), but also a deeper sense of what is
ethically and philosophically correct from the standpoint of society.

Deficiencies in the Institutionalists' Vision

The major deficiency in the institutionalists' concept of regulation,
in actual practice, has been its failure to evolve, or, more correctly,
in its failure to accommodate change.[9] The form and content of
commission regulation was essentially fixed by the late 1920s, and
it has changed relatively little in the intervening years. Some institutionalists, such as Horace M. Gray and Leland Olds, called for radical
reforms. Gray's "Passing of the Public Utility Concept" in 1940
represented a landmark indictment.[10] Others, like Glaeser, shifted
their attention to new concepts such as the Tennessee Valley Authority.
Indeed, Glaeser went far beyond the regulation of monopolies, to
envision the provision of utility services through a diversity of
institutional forms ranging from TVA to regional power authorities
and municipal power systems. For these forms of social experimentation, planning and coordination were more important issues than
the control of the level of earnings.[11]

The inability to accommodate change meant a widening gap between
what the commissions perceived as socially relevant and the problems
that confronted society in the real world. For their part, the commissions devoted more and more attention to the mechanics of regulation
and the procedural rights of litigants. From the 1920s to 1944, the
great debate was waged over fair value versus original cost. From
1945 to the present, the debate shifted to estimates of the allowable
rate of return, introducing mountains of wearisome testimony on topics
such as the relative merits of earnings-price ratios versus discounted
cash flow as a measure of the cost of equity capital. Procedural
reforms seemed to aggravate the passive posture of regulation and
to magnify the infirmities of its quasi-judicial case-by-case approach
to problems.

During the same period real problems and crises arose which either were handled partially within the context of regulation or simply resolved elsewhere. As evidence, one need only recall the holding company scandals during the Great Depression; the creation of REA to extend electricity and telephone service to rural areas; the establishment of public power projects; the dissatisfaction with rate regulation during World War II; the postwar decline of the railroads, highlighted by the bankruptcy of the Penn Central; and, more recently, the emergence of an energy crisis. Each case has revealed the inability of the commission system to come to grips with broader social problems or to anticipate the future. Furthermore, the growing number of successful interventions by the Department of Justice before commissions in recent years has served to indicate regulation's woeful indifference to matters pertaining to market structure and new technology. The principal exception has been the effort of the Federal Communications Commission to utilize selective competitive pressures in portions of the communications industry.

The withdrawal of the commissions from reality also was accompanied by other somewhat more ominous implications. For example, there is growing discomfiture that regulatory independence may be largely illusory. Indeed, as Warren Samuels has argued, regulation not only is a means to curb power but also is subject to capture and hence becomes a means for establishing, concentrating, and maintaining economic power.[12] The basis for concern need not be drawn from illustrations out of the dim past, however. One only need look at the American Telephone and Telegraph's vigorous insistence in the fall of 1973 that commissions declare a moratorium on competition in the field of telecommunications.[13]

There can be little doubt that regulation in practice not only diverged from reality with the passage of time, but also diverged sharply from the optimistic expectations of the institutionalists.

Orthodox Economics' Assault on Regulation

Background

In the past twenty years, orthodox economists have come to take an increasing interest in public utility economics. In contrast with the institutionalists, they generally have been critical of regulation and have advocated major changes in regulatory policies and techniques. Moreover, their position is exerting an increasing influence on the entire economics profession to the point where scarcely any economist currently would advocate expanding regulation.[14] Indeed, insofar as regulation is concerned, we have been admonished to "think small." Any examination of public utility regulation or any study of proposals for reform must give recognition to the orthodox position.

In order to place the orthodox contribution in perspective, it is necessary to enumerate the differences between it and the earlier work of the institutionalists. For the most part, the orthodox economists have been general economists whose involvement in public utility regulation is more in the nature of a sortie than a life-long campaign. Furthermore, they often have been attracted by unique operational features of the industry, such as the peak-load pricing problem, rather than by any sense of commitment to social reform.

Their precursors also differ from those of the institutionalists. The orthodox economist examining a specific problem in the public utility field today is a legatee of the tradition established by Dupuit, Knut Wicksell, F. Y. Edgeworth, W. S. Jevons, Frank Taussig, A. C. Pigou, and Hotelling. He is clearly not a product of the German historical school or of U.S. political reformist movements.

But perhaps the most substantive difference between the orthodox and institutional economist lies in the frame of reference within which each perceives the regulatory problem. For the former, the Pareto optimum and the pursuit of allocative efficiency are cardinal tenets. It is logical, therefore, to expect that efficiency would serve as both the rationale for regulation and the principal test of its success or failure. It also follows that the impact of price on resource allocation rather than revenue requirements would be the center of attention, and it is reasonable to expect that the orthodox economist would be uneasy when considering the goals of regulation which are not compatible with the efficiency criterion.

The nature of both the contributions and the shortcomings of orthodox economics in this field can best be ascertained by examining the three areas of its principal involvement. These are marginal cost pricing, the theory of the regulated firm, and the adequacy of and alternatives to commission control.

Marginal Cost Pricing

There is a vast literature on marginal cost pricing for public utilities. This is not the place to review it in detail, except to note that the marginal cost principle has been examined from the standpoint of the short run, the long run, combinations of the short and long run, revenue deficiencies under increasing returns to scale, and peak-off peak efficiency pricing.

Yet after more than thirty years, controversy continues. To some,

$P = MC$ is a pillar of welfare economics and the foundation for rational public policy; to others it is largely irrelevant. At the base of the controversy remain a number of important conditions that have to be satisfied before the concept can be convincingly shown to produce an optimal outcome.

Acceptance at the theoretical level requires an admission that the following conditions have been satisfied. First, all externalities pertaining to the service must be reflected in $P = MC$; second, the current distribution of income must be acceptable; and, third, deviations from $P = MC$ elsewhere in the economy must not require compensating adjustments in the utility sector (that is, there must be no second-best problem).

Acceptance at the applied level requires general agreement that a host of operational problems have been overcome to everyone's reasonable satisfaction. These include the difficulty of calculating marginal cost as envisioned by the economist on the basis of available data; acceptance of the allocation process used for distributing residual or uncompensated costs in excess of marginal costs; and a satisfactory resolution of McKie's so-called sequence problem. [15]

In addition, there are even broader problems relating to the structure of the economy which require some consensus or agreement. For example, $P = MC$ says nothing about industry structure or the distribution of power in the setting in which marginal cost pricing is being applied. In such circumstances, the proposal may be a powerful force for maintaining the status quo, and this outcome may be politically or economically unacceptable.

But if there are considerable grounds for debate at an essentially academic level, marginal cost pricing's transition into the regulatory realm has been an agonizing adventure for all parties involved (except for highly paid consultants). AT&T's surrogate for marginal cost pricing, known variously as full additional cost, LRIC (long-run incremental cost), the relative benefit principle, or the burden test, has been hotly contested in FCC Dockets 16258 and 18128. Orthodox economists may wish to attribute this resistance to regulatory illiteracy, yet the real reason probably rests on a deeper distrust based on a belief that the concept is arbitrary, indeterminate as to output, and shot through with value judgments. In short, regulatory reluctance may simply mean that the proposal has no greater claim to theoretical validity than the cruder cost-of-service measures of the earlier institutionalists. [16]

On balance, the best contribution of marginal cost pricing would seem to relate to improvements in rate design. In this use it provides a basis for curbing peak expansion and promoting off-peak usage; in fact, this is where the concept has achieved its greatest acceptance, as demonstrated by the French Green Tariff. A second use could be as a test of the validity of block rate structures when unit costs rise with increased output. But if these are the areas of greatest contribution, then Maurice Dobb's observation on marginal cost pricing seems particularly appropriate: "One need hardly add that all this flows (or should . . .) from simple commonsense. A reader might be justified in saying that, since it does so, a sophisticated journey through the tortuous byways of the marginal cost discussion was scarcely necessary to reach so plain and easy a destination."[17]

Theory of the Regulated Firm

Orthodox analysis has made an important contribution toward a better understanding of the behavior of the regulated firm. This is the familiar Averch-Johnson model which states that when the allowable rate of return is greater than the cost of capital, the firm will substitute capital for labor and serve markets at less than long-run marginal cost. These distortions are shown to be perfectly consistent with the objective of the firm, which is to maximize profits subject to regulatory constraint.[18]

This analysis marked a significant advance over the earlier work of the institutionalists. It always had been assumed, of course, that revenue requirements could be increased by padding expenses and the rate base. But the institutionalist analysis did little to relate this phenomenon explicitly to either pricing strategies or to a deliberate distortion of resource allocation.

The A-J model also shows that there are serious infirmities in relying too heavily on a casual review of the overall level of earnings. For this test is not only subverted by A-J, but its very existence serves as an inducement to reinforce the A-J effect.

At the present time, much of the work on the A-J effect consists of theoretical refinements. Anticipated advances since the publication of the original article in 1962 have been disappointing, and this suggests an ironic prognosis: Any real improvement in the theory of the regulated firm will depend upon successful studies of actual corporate behavior of public utilities. In other words, the initiative for further advance rests with sophisticated institutional analysis. By the same token, a better understanding of the interaction between the A-J effect and regulatory reform also rests on an institutional examination of potential inconsistencies involved in reconciling the A-J effect with a system of incentives and penalties seeking to motivate utility management.

Theory of Regulation and Evaluation
of Commission Performance

Orthodox analysis has been less successful in developing a theory of regulation than it was in developing the theory of the regulated firm. Much of the work on the theory of regulation has been done by G. J. Stigler and various proponents of the Chicago School.[19] Stigler believes that every industry can perceive government regulation either as a potential resource or as a potential threat. By employing regulation to its advantage, an industry can achieve control over entry, control over substitute goods and services, and control over prices. However, utilizing government in this fashion involves potential hazards in the form of some loss of control by the dominant firms, procedural delays in effecting changes, and the possible intrusion of outside forces into the decision-making process. Accordingly, an industry is confronted with a trade-off, and it will endeavor to select that degree of regulation which it believes to be optimal for its purposes.

As one might expect, this trade-off theory of regulation provides an ideal framework for the work of the historical revisionists. It is completely consistent with the arguments of those historians who claim that regulation was promoted in order to enforce cartelization or to legitimize monopoly.[20]

There can be little doubt that utility management gives some consideration to the possible gains from regulation as well as to the attendant burdens. The 1973 AT&T policy statement on competition, noted earlier, would seem implicitly to reflect such a weighing process. However, the trade-off theory is very far from a general one. Instead, it is essentially a partial explanation of management's position *vis-à-vis* regulation and government.

Many other factors shape the nature and objectives of the regulatory process as well as the rights, actions, and objectives of the major participants in that process. An orthodox theory of regulation, hoping to provide a generalized insight, would have to be able to integrate all of these considerations. That the orthodox economists have been unable to do so again reinforces the previous conclusion, notably that a significant advance will await a comprehensive recognition of the relevant institutional phenomena.

Several other deficiencies of the trade-off theory of regulation should be mentioned. First, it gives little recognition to the fact that utility management can employ a wide range of strategies other than regulation to achieve its objectives. Hence, we are given little appreciation or insight into the priorities involved in structuring trade-offs or choosing among alternative courses of action. Second, the theory provides very little assistance to those who might be seeking constructive ways in which to improve regulation, except to suggest that the attractiveness of prospective gains be diminished by making the burden of regulation far more onerous to management!

There have been parallel efforts to assess commission performance through the use of a benefit-cost calculus. Two caveats are appropriate insofar as these studies are concerned. First, a review of benefit-cost studies made to date contributes relatively little to an understanding of the differences between the orthodox and institutionalist positions on regulation. Second, generalizations about the studies are hazardous because the degree of rigor and emphasis varies significantly among them. Accepting this lack of uniformity, one can conclude that a review of the Gerwig, MacAvoy, Friedlaender, and Posner studies indicates that the costs of regulation outweigh the benefits.[21] Rather than scrutinizing each study, it would be preferable to accept these conclusions as an expression of the sentiment of a large part of the profession that the net gains of commission regulation are highly dubious. The next logical step is to consider what the critics of regulation offer as an alternative.

It should be noted, however, that not all such studies are in agreement that costs exceed benefits. Nelson and Reschenthaler argue to the contrary.[22] Also, to be realistically effective, a benefit-cost estimate must be able to evaluate the net gains associated with the major options for public policy on an *ex ante* basis. The options include total deregulation, partial deregulation, and significant improvements in the character of regulation. We are a long way from achieving this degree of proficiency.

Alternatives to Commission Regulation

If regulation is thought to be inefficient and wasteful, then the orthodox economist is confronted with the task of prescribing an alternative course of action for public policy. The work of Posner (as an attorney in the Chicago tradition[23]) and Demsetz deserves particular attention.[24]

Posner argues that the evils of unregulated monopoly are largely exaggerated, but he believes that political reality forecloses complete deregulation, so that a qualified course of action is necessary. For industries that are not natural monopolies (gas production, aviation, and trucking), he advocates deregulation. For industries that are natural monopolies he advocates removal of restrictions on entry, removal of controls over specific rates, and the substitution of an excess profits tax for a regulatory limitation on overall earnings or profits. This tax would be moderate in order to assure that the firm would retain those incentives necessary to motivate performance.

Demsetz concentrates exclusively on those industries where pervasive economies of scale exist. Under these conditions, he grants that a single supplier will seek to set price and output at monopoly levels, but he argues that this alone does not justify regulation as the appropriate corrective measure. As an alternative he suggests competition between bidders for the activity characterized by production scale economies. Increasing quantities would be supplied at lower prices, so the bidder with the lowest bid price for the entire operation would get the contract. Thus there would be competition for the field and not within the field. Government would not need to regulate prices and output; rather, it could confine itself to selecting the lowest bidder. The principal conditions for success, Demsetz believes, are that inputs be readily available to all bidders at competitive prices and that the cost of collusion among bidders be prohibitively high.

Posner's attempts to minimize the impact of unregulated monopoly, on the one hand, and introduce a moderate excess profits tax, on the other, are less than convincing. The total weight of orthodox analysis is against unregulated monopoly, and it will take more than an *a priori* survey of potential problem areas to dissuade most economists. Furthermore, Posner does not consider how these problem areas might grow or change in importance when viewed as an interrelated whole, particularly as the monopolist devises a range of strategies to maintain his position. The case for a moderate excess profits tax is hardly more persuasive. If the excess profits tax is set too high, it will produce all of the waste and inefficiency attributed to cost-plus regulation; if it is set too low, it will have only salutary effects. In practice it is reasonable to assume that such a tax ultimately would be shifted forward to the consumer and that the rate would be either too low to be bothersome or high enough to be the subject of continuous adjudication and revision.

Demsetz moves one step closer to a competitive optimum by seeking to negate monopolistic behavior in the form of high prices and restricted output through competitive bidding. Bidding would seem to hold promise in certain areas, such as the awarding of local CATV franchises, but it also would suffer from many of the same infirmities which brought about the demise of franchise regulation sixty-five years ago.

Bidding can increase uncertainty, especially when future events cannot be adequately forecast and discounted. As a result, capital costs may increase significantly. Various parties to the bidding process may seek to employ strategies to reduce this uncertainty, but the prospects for success are not encouraging. If the participants turn to long-term contracts, then the risk of totally unforeseen changes increases, and with it the prospect of a desire on the part of at least one of the parties to renegotiate the contract. This, in turn, will require either a structure of penalties for reopening contracts or administrative machinery to allow arbitration. If the participants turn to short-term contracts, then there is the prospect both of excessive transaction costs as properties are sold and resold between successive bidders and of increased risk for the successful bidder if the service is potentially lucrative. In either case, there will be the persistent problem of monitoring the quality of service regardless of the terms of the contract or franchise.

There are also other problems pertaining to bidding. For example, the bargaining agents for the public may lack competence or adequate information, or such bargainers may be too diffused, fragmented, or decentralized to perceive all of the issues involved. The selection of the appropriate public bargaining agent or agents for message toll telephone service is a case in point. In addition, there is the problem of matching the bid to the socially optimal scale of enterprise. Bidders may be quite willing to isolate the most financially attractive segments of the enterprise, leaving less desirable portions or segments. While this might be consistent with the private market criterion of efficiency, it may not coincide with the desired level of social development and consequently could require some form of subsidization.

More important, however, is the fact that successful bidders may be unwilling to undertake long-term experimentation involving new services, new pricing concepts, or new technologies if the results threaten to jeopardize the permissible level of earnings anticipated under the contract. This would apply whether innovation yields deficits or excessive earnings. The effect of the former is obvious; the effect of the latter could be to force a renegotiation of the contract. In short, the bidding process gives no promise of overcoming the lack of resilience attributed to traditional commission regulation.

Finally, bidding does not take place in a setting devoid of economic power. Given a prior distribution of power and concentration, bidding could permit the dominant firm to strengthen its position in the overall market. Such a firm could use limit-entry pricing via low bids to capture markets or service areas as well as functions or resources necessary to assure its dominance. Perhaps the best illustration would involve the radio frequency spectrum. It is not unreasonable to assume that the Bell System would pay a bounty (or charge a negative price) to acquire control of this resource if the result were to foreclose the entry of private microwave carriers.

On balance, bidding may have relevance for certain localized utility services, but it by no means would remove or eliminate the need for government intervention and surveillance. Monitoring would continue in a variety of areas, including quality of service, performance, earnings levels, and adherence to contract. Procedures for renegotiation would have to be established, and public facilities or goods used in providing the service would have to be priced (or at least shadow priced) in order to reflect the full economic cost of service. There also would have to be extensive safeguards to assure neutralization of economic power.

In summary, neither taxation nor competitive bidding appears to hold a great deal of promise as a general alternative to direct regulation in the public utility field.

A Critique of the Critics

Orthodox economists' writings in the areas previously reviewed have had relatively little impact at applied levels or in public policy formulation.

One might argue, of course, that many of the recent changes in electric rate design represent the direct application of formal economic analysis. However, it would be very difficult to sustain this claim. Pricing innovations in electricity supply, such as the British Bulk Supply Tariff, the French Green Tariff, and selected U.S. wholesale-pooling tariffs, are at best tenuously related to the economic literature on marginal cost pricing. Similarly, recent proposals for the abandonment of promotional rates in favor of inverted block rates or other pricing structures designed to discourage consumption stem from concern over conservation and the environment rather than from an awakening to the logic of marginal cost pricing. In virtually all of these cases, the new pricing proposals appear to owe much more to the pragmatic solutions posed by ecologists, public-interest groups, operating engineers, practitioners, and a small band of institutional economists working in the field than to an adherence to formal economic theory.

Much the same conclusion can be drawn from recent efforts at regulatory reform. Growing concern over consumer representation owes much more to the populist efforts of Senator Metcalf than to the systematic implementation of the orthodox theory of regulation or the theory of the regulated firm.[25]

To some, this lack of receptivity might be attributed to political inertia, ignorance, pressure group action, or a lassitude in the absence of crises. But there is reason to suspect more profound limitations which hinder general acceptance of much of orthodox economic analysis. At least three possible factors deserve mention.

First, it has been difficult to make the transition from formal theory to applied problem solving in a fashion that leaves the objectivity of theory unimpaired. This already has been noted in the case of efforts at applied marginal cost pricing, particularly in the debate over LRIC.

Second, much of the orthodox analysis of public utility problems has been hampered by an adherence to modern welfare economics. In practical application, this means that the analysis tends to define issues too narrowly and to obscure or omit essential value judgments. Expressed somewhat differently, orthodox analysis has been handicapped by what T. W. Hutchison has called "welfarist monism," with the result that it fails "to bring out the possibilities and actualities of competing objectives, and of conflicts that have to be faced."[26]

Third, much of the formal analysis displays a lack of appreciation of the major institutional and structural determinants of behavior and performance. Too often there is little or no explicit recognition of the role of market structure, technology, established institutional arrangements, the distribution of power and income, social values, or externalities. This can be illustrated by reference to public utility pricing, which is viewed almost exclusively in terms of allocative criteria. Matters of cross-subsidization and income distribution usually are subordinated within this context, and virtually no weight is given to price as a strategic factor in the contest between established firms and potential entrants in shaping market structure. In other words, the strengths of the institutionalists are the weaknesses of the orthodox economists.

When guidelines are ambiguous or arbitrary, objectives too narrowly construed, and major structural and institutional elements neglected, it is not surprising to find that much of formal analysis is ignored at applied and policy levels. However, this does not mean that orthodox economics has made no contribution. On the contrary, it has fulfilled a very valuable function as a critic. It has focused attention on the greater need to relate price and control of earnings to efficiency; it has emphasized the persistent danger of ignoring the ramifications of regulatory actions which can result in impairment of the market mechanism through cartelization; and it has pointed to the need for a periodic reassessment of regulation to determine whether it merits continuance. What is somewhat intriguing about such a role is that it is exactly the same type of role often assigned to institutional economics by its detractors, namely, that of a critic.

Market Structure and Regulatory Reform

Toward Greater Relevance

What course of action holds the greatest promise for the future? Unfortunately, it is difficult to make judgments if one confines the frame of reference exclusively to the present commission system and the criticisms of orthodox economists. A more promising alternative involves exploring the requisites for effective economic regulation and the type of overhaul that must be carried out to accomplish this task.

As a point of departure it is appropriate to accept the premises of the early institutionalists, notably that government intervention may be preferable to a reliance on highly imperfect market structures; social control can play a purposeful role in promoting the public interest; and legal and economic institutions are inexorably involved in the solution. But at the same time it is necessary to recognize that the present commission system displays obvious signs of atrophy and that the operational tools of the institutionalists, such as rate base regulation and the search for cost-of-service criteria, may require drastic modification, especially in the light of new research, whether by institutional or orthodox economists.

The evolving market structure of the public utility industries provides an excellent illustration of the need for regulatory reform as well as the magnitude and complexity of the issues involved in effective social control.

Most of the institutionalists gave relatively little attention to market structure, believing that utilities were natural monopolies and that regulation should proceed accordingly.[27] Transportation also was viewed as inherently anticompetitive, or at least as an industry where unchecked rivalry would result in ruinous competition. Orthodox economics typically accepted natural monopoly as a special case and assumed that all other industries were inherently competitive—except for distortions and forms of cartelization induced by government intervention.

However, these views of market structure are far too simplistic, with the result that attendant analyses and public policy prescriptions tend to be deficient. The natural monopoly concept may have an intuitive appeal in the utility industries, but it is not supported by sophisticated empirical research or by corporate behavior.

Econometric research dealing with economies of scale in the energy and communications utilities has been confined almost exclusively to particular phases or stages of the productive process, such as power generation. There have been no successful efforts which demonstrate that economies of scale are pervasive on either a firm or an industry-wide basis. Allegations that such industries are characterized by scale economies usually appear in introductory texts, testimony, or self-servicing declarations, and they are supported, if at all, by general assertions, references to quasi-engineering studies, or imprecise statements about falling unit costs. This type of proof is hardly sufficient to justify a disregard of market structure and structure-related alternatives for improving industry performance such as arm's-length bargaining and structural diversity.

Corporate behavior also raises serious doubts about the pervasiveness of the natural monopoly concepts. If industry-wide scale economies were overwhelming and were passed on to the consumer in the form of lower prices, then entry by new firms would be irrational. Yet, once the legal barriers to entry were relaxed by the FCC, the interconnect and private-line markets in telecommunications became extremely attractive to new entrants.[28] Furthermore, the persistent objections raised by public-owned utilities and rural cooperatives that they either are excluded from power pooling arrangements or admitted only under disadvantageous terms suggest that the simple logic of expanding output to exhaust all scale economies is subordinated to corporate policies of a higher priority.

Nevertheless, it is abundantly clear that the public utility industries do possess very distinctive characteristics or structural features that will affect conduct and performance, *with or without regulation.* These include: (1) a high degree of concentration in specific phases or stages of the supply function due to decreasing costs relative to the size of the market. These costs fall on a per unit basis because of the interaction of technology and increasing returns to scale; (2) a high threshold investment stemming from the need to establish and maintain comprehensive networks to serve all customers; (3) a high degree of interdependence in corporate decision making because of (a) the interdependence of technical operations and (b) the division of revenues or settlements stemming from the joint provision of services; (4) technical and other conditions which limit options in certain strategic phases or stages of supply, thereby creating potential focal points for monopoly control; (5) elements of necessity in demand and low cross-elasticities of demand between particular markets; and (6) important externalities or spillover effects.

Industries with such features are not candidates for the naïve across-the-board application of antitrust laws. Conversely, much of rate base regulation is simply irrelevant for either detecting or handling the special problems stemming from these structural conditions. What is needed is a revised concept of social control that places proper emphasis on industry structure while recognizing the implications for corporate behavior and the need to devise new methods to promote performance in the public interest.

The magnitude of this task can be demonstrated by considering three specific factors as they are influenced by or relate to the market structure of the public utility industries. These are: oligopolistic coordination as a feature of corporate behavior, system optimization, and the structure of consumer wants.

Tacit Oligopolistic Coordination

Public utility firms will endeavor to follow patterns of behavior that will minimize the uncertainty and vulnerability which they perceive in the politicoeconomic setting within which they operate. One effective means to achieve this objective is to stabilize the industry through oligopolistic coordination. This, in turn, involves the maintenance of behavior patterns that promote the common interest of the industry. Although each firm typically operates in a discrete market, at the industry level it will seek to stabilize innovation, develop a common response to pressures for change, and collectively resist hostile forces such as the threat of public ownership.

The market structures of the utility industries are well suited to support such oligopolistic coordination.[29] The high degree of interdependence in corporate planning provides an ideal basis for coordination and communications to reduce potential conflict. At the same time, the structure permits each member a large degree of discretion in adjusting to local conditions. Furthermore, the degree of interdependence provides a means for disciplining mavericks or dissident members of the industry. There are the crucial focal points, noted earlier, where common usage via pooling, interchange, or interconnection give those in control considerable power to dictate conditions for access. In addition, there remains the power inherent in the distribution of revenues from jointly supplied services.

Oligopolistic coordination also enhances the position of the dominant firm in maintaining price leadership, and where no price leader exists, it facilitates conscious parallelism in price decisions.

Furthermore, there are strong forces working to perpetuate oligopolistic coordination. The usual pressures that erode oligopolistic collusion are absent: Product heterogeneity is minimal, and prices and earnings are easily monitored. In addition, new entrants who are successful will find it to their advantage to accommodate such collaboration. Entry in these industries is not a self-reinforcing force, and there is a great temptation for the second generation entrant to carve out a secure share of the market and vigorously resist third generation entrants.[30] This best can be accomplished by participating in the process.

On the basis of current information it is difficult to ascertain the effects of such coordination on industry performance. It certainly encourages a homogeneity of action on major regional and national problems, and it tends to penalize or discourage independent innovative action. But it also may serve to maintain excess capacity, obsolete plant, and inflated rate bases. As new entrants and supposed rivals come to terms with the establishment, there could be an implicit umbrella effect which shields all incumbents as well as plant and facilities of differing vintages against exogenous changes. Those excluded from participation, such as rural power cooperatives, will turn to other alternatives, such as publicly financed grids and networks, thereby yielding a different form of redundancy.

Effective social control will face a major challenge in evaluating the effects of oligopolistic coordination as well as prescribing appropriate corrective measures. An important step in the solution will involve stimulating independent action on the part of firms functioning in such a setting. Perhaps the early institutionalist B. H. Meyer perceived this in 1906 when he observed that competition alone was inadequate, but that successful regulation required a number of companies acting independently.[31]

*System Optimization and
Structure of Consumer Wants*

Other structure-related variables also require investigation. These include the social benefits and costs of a policy of liberalized entry, the boundary problem (that is, the demarcation between regulated and nonregulated activities), and the interrelationship between pricing practices and market structure.

However, an imperfectly competitive market structure also poses problems which are less directly related to corporate strategy and behavior. One of these is the need to assure system optimization. This involves the integrated planning and development of separate segments of a network in a fashion that will avoid denigrating performance and wasteful redundancy. The concept of optimization applies to electric power grids, pipeline complexes, and common carrier communications networks. System optimization, in the absence of perfect competition, cannot be achieved without some form of controlling force that provides a degree of nationwide and regional planning. A number of alternatives are feasible, including oligopolistic coordination, oligopolistic coordination under regulatory surveillance, and direct government planning. The infirmities of the first alternative are evident; the second and third alternatives present social control with heroic policy choices and new dimensions of involvement in industry structure and performance.

The structure of consumer wants is another area closely related to market structure. Public convenience and necessity requires more than an uncritical acceptance of consumer wants as given. In some cases, demand functions for individual services may be interdependent and subject to manipulation by a monopolistic firm serving a range of markets. Under such circumstances, the pattern of service desired by the public can diverge significantly from the pattern actually supplied because of the existence of market imperfections. In other cases, the potential demand for services may be more akin to the demand for public or collective goods and services and may require an entirely new perspective for evaluation. Unless such factors are considered, it will not be possible to speak with authority about the presence or absence of unsatisfied public wants.

Format for Improved Social Control

The existing commission system is ill equipped to meet the types of problems posed by these market-structure considerations. But the task of reformed regulation is even broader, for it must integrate structure and structure-related variables within a conceptual and decision-making framework that also includes matters of motivation (incentives and penalties), equity and fairness in the treatment of parties, the prevention of monopolist earnings, the establishment of pricing guidelines, and the forecasting of future requirements and available resources. At present the commissions assume an essentially passive posture, emphasizing a review audit rather than a forward planning perspective. This role is hardly conducive to an exploration of this range of issues, whether in a rulemaking or in an adjudicatory proceeding.

There have been numerous efforts at regulatory reform, but virtually all either have failed or been dismissed. Often this has been due to the scope of the administrative reorganization proposed or to the belief that they were only partial solutions of dubious effectiveness.

The following four recommendations are offered as a possible way to resolve the impasse, while at the same time retaining the place of the commission as an arm of the legislative branch of the government. These recommendations also seek to give expression to the need to bring improved social control into alignment with current problems and needs.

First, the thrust of regulation should be changed to recast it in an affirmative role. The regulatory agency should be charged with the responsibility for assuring that the performance of the industries under its jurisdiction is consistent with the public interest. This means that the agency would be required to delineate public interest objectives and set forth what it perceives as the appropriate steps for achieving these.

Plans would be reviewed on an annual basis by an appropriate legislative committee. As part of this review, the agency would be required to report its progress in attaining such objectives, together with a detailed analysis of whether regulation should be continued and, if so, in what form. Needless to say, the agency's appearance would permit an excellent public forum to reassess what constitutes the public interest and how best to attain it.

Second, agencies should reform their administrative procedures and regulatory techniques in light of this new responsibility. Policy formulation and planning would assume much more significance relative to adjudication, and examiners and administrative law judges would be expected to implement such policies in their decisions.

New regulatory concepts and tools would have to be developed, giving particular attention to the interrelationship between market structure, price regulation, and control of earnings. Most agencies have broad, although inadequately appreciated, controls over these variables. The task will be to expand our knowledge of how they can be employed, selectively and in combination, to maximize public interest objectives. Traditional regulatory practices would be largely irrelevant for this type of problem.

New concepts and techniques, in turn, will have to be matched by new reporting requirements and a modernized data collection system. Regulators will have to assume the independent responsibility for determining the data and information needed. It is both unreasonable and unfair to believe that management should volunteer information that may serve to jeopardize its posture in a regulatory setting. Furthermore, the information and data which might be appropriate for the management of an enterprise will not necessarily be adequate for the social control of that enterprise. A recognition of this fact is certainly in the Henry C. Adams tradition.

Third, there should be a concerted effort to avoid establishing an authoritarian system of super regulation in the sense that utility management is displaced by regulatory management. Each group should have its areas of comparative advantage. Regulators should be concerned with establishing goals and guidelines, monitoring performance, and applying various inducements and constraints. Management should be concerned with efficient operation within these parameters. Acceptance of this division of responsibility should serve to rechannel some of management's energies away from political and adjudicatory involvement and into the search for more efficient methods to produce utility services—encouraged, hopefully, by a system of incentives and penalties.

Fourth, regulation will need to maintain a continuing program of research and education. The importance of research is obvious, particularly in the development of new concepts and techniques as well as an improved appreciation of how to employ structural diversity and selective competitive pressures to maximize industry performance. Such research is also crucial if planning is to remain dynamic and flexible. Given the limited resources of most commissions, this type of research probably can be achieved only on a centralized basis.[32] Maintenance of a formal educational program is equally vital. The administrators and senior staff members of such agencies simply must have a high level of professional competence. The day when commissions can serve as a repository for defeated politicians has long since passed.

These recommendations could be refined in greater detail, but hopefully the thrust of the argument is clear. Social control can be formed into a purposeful concept capable of promoting the public interest. Moreover, the opportunities for the application of sophisticated institutional analysis as part of the process of reform are virtually unlimited.

Notes

1. The continuing collaboration between Robert M. LaFollette and John R. Commons in Wisconsin in the early 1900s provides an excellent blending of institutional economics and public policy in all facets of government intervention, including public utility regulation. For a contemporary note on the latter, see J. R. Commons, "How Wisconsin Regulates Her Public Utilities," *American Review of Reviews* (August 1910): 215–17.
2. The magnitude of the shift in sentiment may be illustrated by contrasting

current proposals for abolishing economic regulation by the Interstate Commerce Commission with the eulogies contained in the commemorative papers presented at the agency's 75th birthday. See *Exercises in Observance of the 75th Anniversary of the Interstate Commerce Commission, 1887–1962*, especially remarks by Justice Felix Frankfurter (Washington, D.C.: U.S. Government Printing Office, 1962).

3. The logic of ruinous competition in the railroad industry is set forth in A. T. Hadley, *Railroad Transportation, Its History and Its Laws* (New York: Putnam, 1892), pp. 63–99.

4. The most sophisticated early work on social control usually is credited to Edward A. Ross. See E. A. Ross, *Social Control, A Survey of the Foundations of Order* (New York: Macmillan, 1901). The influence of Ross on Roscoe Pound, Theodore Roosevelt, Oliver Wendell Holmes, John R. Commons, and later on J. M. Clark is discussed in the Introduction to the reprint of this work in 1969 by the Press of Case Western Reserve University.

5. This view is evident in the writings of the institutionalists over the period extending from Henry C. Adams's *Relation of the State to Industrial Action* (1887) to James C. Bonbright's *Principles of Public Utility Rates* (1961). See *Relation of the State to Industrial Action and Economics of Jurisprudence*, two essays edited by Joseph Dorfman (New York: Columbia University Press, 1954), especially p. 110; and J. C. Bonbright, *Principles of Public Utility Rates* (New York: Columbia University Press, 1961), especially pp. 19–23. Of the earlier writers, A. T. Hadley was probably the least sanguine regarding the prospects for mandatory regulation. See Hadley, *Railroad Transportation*, pp. 144–45. The evolution of regulation and the independent agency concept was surveyed at length in Martin G. Glaeser's *Public Utilities in American Capitalism* (New York: Macmillan, 1957), pp. 31–154.

6. After an impressive academic career Henry C. Adams became the first statistician of the ICC in 1888. He served there for 24 years and was successful in persuading Congress to allow the ICC to compel the railroads to file the uniform accounts on an annual basis. Also, see note 5 above.

7. See J. M. Clark, *Studies in the Economics of Overhead Costs* (Chicago: University of Chicago Press, 1923), pp. 318–34. See also J. M. Clark, "The General Problem of Cost Allocation," in *What Electricity Costs*, Morris L. Cooke, ed. (New York: New Republic, 1933), pp. 13–23. Other essays in the Cooke collection illustrate the use of cost-of-service criteria to determine distribution costs for electricity.

8. Swidler argues: "We have found that uncontrolled business forces, operating in an economic environment far from the pure model of theoretical economics, may work great hardships upon individuals and classes and may give rise to grave political consequences. We value the vision of a just society, and it may be that without that vision, supported by steps toward its attainment, our society would lose its most important cohesive force." J. C. Swidler, "Comments on the Case for Deregulation," *Stanford Law Review* 22 (February 1970): 521.

9. For a further discussion of this problem, see H. M. Trebing, "A Critique of Regulatory Accommodation to Change," in *Experiments in Regulation*, W. G. Shepherd and T. G. Gies, eds., forthcoming.

10. See Horace M. Gray, "The Passing of the Public Utility Concept," *Journal of Land and Public Utility Economics* 16 (February 1940): 8–20. See also Leland Olds, "The Economic Planning Function under Public Regulation," *American Economic Review, Proceedings* 48 (May 1958): 553–61.
11. See Glaeser, *Public Utilities,* pp. 436–573.
12. See Warren J. Samuels, "Public Utilities and the Theory of Power," in *Perspective in Public Regulation,* Milton Russell, ed. (Carbondale: Southern Illinois University Press, 1973), pp. 1–27.
13. "An Unusual Obligation," speech by J. D. deButts before the Annual Convention of the National Association of Regulatory Utility Commissioners, Seattle, Washington, 20 September 1973.
14. Where a major expansion of regulation has taken place, as in the establishment of the Postal Rate Commission in 1970, the action appears to have been premised largely on political grounds and legal reasoning.
15. McKie's sequence problem focuses on the need to juxtapose the static conditions underlying marginal analysis with the requirement that decisions, in practice, be made serially on a real time basis. His critique of marginal-cost pricing in a market structure context also deserves special attention. See James W. McKie, "Public Utility Regulation: Structure and Performance," in *Perspectives in Public Regulation,* Russell, ed., pp. 85–105.
16. The debate over LRIC has focused primarily on the problem of determining the appropriate revenue contribution for individual classes of service. For a sympathetic view of LRIC, see W. J. Baumol and A. G. Walton, "Full Costing, Competition and Regulatory Practice," *Yale Law Journal* 82 (March 1973): 639–55. See also W. J. Baumol, "Rate Making; Incremental Costing and Equity Considerations," and A. M. Froggatt, "Incremental Costing in Practice," in *Essays on Public Utility Pricing and Regulation,* H. M. Trebing, ed. (East Lansing: Division of Research, Michigan State University, 1971). For a critical assessment of LRIC, see W. H. Melody, "Interservice Subsidy: Regulatory Standards and Applied Economics," in the same collection. Also note R. R. Braeutigam, *An Examination of the Burden Test,* Staff Research Paper OTP-SP-13 (Washington, D.C.: Office of Telecommunications Policy, 1973).
17. Maurice Dobb, *Welfare Economics and the Economics of Socialism* (Cambridge: the University Press, 1969), p. 249.
18. See Harvey Averch and Leland L. Johnson, "Behavior of the Firm under Regulatory Constraint," *American Economic Review* 52 (December 1962): 1053–69. For a tenth anniversary reappraisal by Johnson, see his, "Behavior of the Firm under Regulatory Constraint: A Reassessment," *American Economic Review, Proceedings* 63 (May 1973): 90–97.
19. See George J. Stigler, "The Theory of Economic Regulation," *Bell Journal of Economics and Management Science* 2 (Spring 1971): 3–21.
20. For example, see Gabriel Kolko, *Railroads and Regulation, 1877–1916* (Princeton: Princeton University Press, 1965); and George W. Hilton, "The Consistency of the Interstate Commerce Act," *Journal of Law and Economics* 9 (October 1966): 87–113. Harbeson's rejoinder and authoritative statement rejecting the Kolko hypothesis also should be noted: R. W. Harbeson, "Railroads and Regulation, 1877–1916: Conspiracy or Public Interest?" *Journal of Economic History* 27 (June 1967): 230–42.

21. See R. G. Gerwig, "Natural Gas Production: A Study of Costs of Regula-
tion," *Journal of Law and Economics* 5 (October 1962): 69–92; Ann F.
Friedlaender, *The Dilemma of Freight Transport Regulation* (Washington,
D.C.: The Brookings Institution, 1969); P. W. MacAvoy, "The Effective-
ness of the Federal Power Commission," *Bell Journal of Economics and
Management Science* 1 (Autumn 1970): 271–303; and Richard A. Posner,
"Natural Monopoly and Its Regulation," *Stanford Law Review* 21 (Feb-
ruary 1969): 548–643.

22. See Boyd L. Nelson, "Costs and Benefits of Regulating Communications,"
American Economic Review, Proceedings 61 (May 1971): 218–25. Also
note F. M. Westfield, "Methodology of Evaluating Economic
Regulation,"ibid., 211–17; and G. B. Reschenthaler, "The Impact of State
Commission Regulation: Electric Utilities in Texas," unpublished manu-
script, University of Alberta, Edmonton, 181 pp.

23. See Posner, "Natural Monopoly," pp. 635–43.

24. See Harold Demsetz, "Why Regulate Utilities?" *Journal of Law and
Economics* 11 (April 1968).

25. See *Utility Consumers' Counsel and Information Act of 1971*. Hearings
before the Subcommittee on Intergovernmental Relations of the Committee
on Government Operations on S. 607, U. S. Senate. 92nd Cong., 2d sess.,
28–29, October 1971.

26. T. W. Hutchison, *"Positive" Economics and Policy Objectives*
(Cambridge, Mass.: Harvard University Press, 1964), p. 173.

27. The institutionalists were concerned with matters of public ownership, river
basin development, and the holding company. But the natural monopoly
concept seems to have been accepted in such cases. To illustrate, Bonbright
and Means examined the public utility holding companies in detail in 1932,
but their emphasis was on financial abuses and the capacity to evade
regulation *per se* through this form of corporate organization. There was
little attention to matters of market structure and future industry performance. See James C. Bonbright and Gardiner C. Means, *The Holding Company* (New York: McGraw-Hill Book Co., 1932), chap. 7.

28. Traditional regulatory policy has placed the burden of proof on the potential
entrant to demonstrate that existing service is deficient and that new entry is
the appropriate remedy. In the "Above 890" megacycles case (1959), the
Carterfone case (1968), the MCI case (1969), and the Policy Statement
endorsing free entry by specialized carriers (1971), the FCC departed
dramatically from this tradition. The commission's liberalized attachment
and entry policies have elicited considerable interest on the part of new
entrants in the interconnect and private-line markets. There also has been a
vigorous reaction on the part of AT&T, particularly in the area of pricing
(for example, proposals to depart from system-wide averaging, selective
price reductions for bulk offerings and terminal equipment, and the
broadened application of the LRIC concept to both inter- and intrastate
competitive services). It is still too early to discern long-run shifts in market
shares in these areas, and available data are limited. For a survey of FCC
policies, interconnect companies, specialized carriers, and attendant problems, see *The Industrial Reorganization Act*. Hearings before the Subcommittee on Antitrust and Monopoly of the Committee on the Judiciary on
S. 1167. U. S. Senate, 93rd Cong., 1st sess. Statement of Manley R. Irwin, 2
August 1973.

29. This form of tacit oligopolistic coordination should be distinguished from cartelization or collusive arrangements in which the participants seek to establish a joint output that maximizes profits. Rather, the objective in this case is to stabilize the industry, minimize uncertainty, and assure the firms an opportunity to achieve a satisficing level of earnings.

30. Once established, new entrants will resist third generation entrants with vigor, employing both commission regulation and other strategies to block entry. United Parcel Service's tactics to foreclose American Delivery Systems from the small parcel market provide an illustration of this practice. See Motion of U. S. Department of Justice for Leave to Intervene and Petition for Reconsideration, *American Delivery Systems, Inc., Freight Forwarder Application*, ICC Docket No. FF-376, 16 May 1972.

31. See Balthasar H. Meyer, *A History of the Northern Securities Case*, Bulletin of the University of Wisconsin (Madison: 1906).

32. A modest step has been taken in this direction as a result of the recent recommendation for the creation of a national research institute to assist federal and state commissions. See "Report of the Ad Hoc Committee on the Institute for Regulatory Research," National Association of Regulatory Utility Commissioners, 1973 (mimeographed).

17

Apologetics of Deregulation in Energy and Telecommunications: An Institutionalist Assessment

Harry M. Trebing

The proponents of deregulation appear to have scored substantial gains on all fronts in the energy and telecommunications industries. More and more, consumers, regulators, and industry speak of the market as the ultimate arbiter, and deregulation as the obvious step toward improving efficiency. Regrettably, much of the debate over deregulation has compared the worst features of traditional rate base regulation with the performance of idealized markets or market behavior similar to what would be expected to prevail under perfect competition. This article will examine a number of the significant problems that will emerge under conditions of phased deregulation. In essence, the article concludes that a program of deregulation that culminates in reliance on highly imperfect markets will not improve efficiency, nor will it achieve equity goals. Furthermore, since flawed markets will not perform significantly better than flawed regulation, the article suggests that a more promising course of action for public policy involves incorporating existing and potential market forces within the framework of a broader program of regulatory reform designed to promote industry performance and the general welfare.

The Rationale for Deregulation

The modern case for deregulation rests on three points.[1] First, promoting efficiency is superior to promoting equity as a goal for public policy in the energy and telecommunications industries. Proponents of deregulation argue that an increase in allocative and X-efficiency that lowers prices will do more to enhance consumer welfare than targeted equity or welfare programs. Furthermore, attempts to use regulation to redress the inequitable treatment of particular groups will not achieve the equity objectives sought, but will serve only to depress efficiency by recourse to protectionism.

Second, regulation cannot induce levels of efficiency superior to those attained in unregulated markets. Market forces will compel the selection of least-cost methods of supply, control market power, and set rates of capital recovery in a far better fashion than any regulatory agency. Critics argue that the regulated firm has been able to capture consumer surplus and convert it into producer surplus, which, in turn, has taken the form of goldplating, high wages, and excessive investment. As evidence they point to American Telephone and Telegraph's write-offs of plant and the Bell operating companies' (BOCs) reduction in wage costs and accelerated plant retirements following divestiture. At best, they argue that regulation can only bring about a pattern of income distribution different from that which would have prevailed in a free market.

Third, opportunities for competition abound. Removal of legal restrictions on entry, exit, diversification, prices, and earnings will create new markets and new services, and will lead to the employment of new technology to the maximum advantage of society.

In effect, the case for deregulation is premised on efficiency and the emergence of competitive or contestable markets in virtually every phase of the energy and telecommunications industries. Proponents argue that historic measures of concentration are meaningless, and that support for deregulation must be future-oriented. E. E. Bailey and W. J. Baumol are particularly sanguine about the role of potential entry (theory of contestable markets), noting that "the theory of contestability calls for a major reorientation of both the charters and operating programs of regulatory authorities . . . by and large the new directions of public policy (deregulation) have been remarkably consistent with what contestability theory would suggest."[2]

Much of the support for deregulation is anecdotal. In telecommunications, advocates of deregulation point to competition in the interexchange market, where AT&T, other common carriers (OCCs), carriers' carriers, and more than 100 resellers compete to provide various switched and private line services, as well as capacity between exchanges. They note that competition flourishes because of freedom of entry and the absence of restrictions on interconnection with the local exchange, and because of AT&T's vertical divestiture. At the local exchange level, proponents of deregulation point to current and potential competition confronting the local telephone company in the form of shared tenant services, teleports, and cellular radio. This potential for bypass is cited as evidence of the lack of market power of the BOCs.[3]

In the natural gas industry, proponents of deregulation argue that producer markets are competitive and that pipelines have relatively little market power.[4] More modest proponents of reliance on market forces argue that Federal Energy Regulatory Commission (FERC) Order No. 436 (October 9, 1985),[5] will neutralize much of the inherent market power of the natural gas pipelines by giving producers and consumers an opportunity to negotiate directly, in effect using the pipeline only to transport gas. This would supposedly make it difficult for pipelines to shift risk forward to the consumer, and at the same time present the pipelines with a form of direct competition for pipeline-owned gas. Local distribution companies (LDCs) would have new options to secure gas under Order 436, but they would also face interfuel rivalry from oil and gas-on-gas competition at the retail level. For LDCs that cannot lower costs, the threat of bypass again emerges because large retail customers will choose to deal directly with the pipeline. Proponents of competition also point to the emergence of new markets, such as the spot market for gas where prices are currently below the weighted average cost of pipeline gas. Indeed, it is argued that the spot market has become so attractive that many buyers are turning to this market to meet their needs whenever possible. Augmenting the spot market are the new brokers, such as Yankee Exchange Service, that will resell gas from any source to any purchaser.

In electricity, two areas of actual or potential competition are emphasized. These include the threat of cogeneration, self-generation, and conservation at the retail level, and competition at the bulk power or at the wholesale level. Critics of regulation point out that commissions have been unable to prevent the rapid rise of costs for central station service, and, as a consequence, bypass has again emerged in the form of cogeneration, self-generation, and conservation. This bypass is price-driven, with the result that an average retail rate of 8–10 cents per kilowatt-hour will induce the rapid growth of cogeneration (that is, using independent heat sources to produce non-utility electricity). Proponents of cogeneration are optimistic. They point out that 7 to 10 percent of all power in California currently comes from cogenerators, and that if all contracted amounts come on line, this will increase to 25 percent.

In Maine, cogeneration may increase to 33 percent of total kilowatt-hour sales in three to four years. It is argued that this form of bypass will be much more pervasive than that occurring in telecommunications or natural gas, where large-volume users are involved. Cogeneration will have appeal not only to large paper mills, chemical companies, et cetera, but also to hospitals, schools, and fast-food establishments that can readily install prepackaged, pad-mounted, gas-fired cogeneration units.

Supporters of deregulation argue that the appropriate course of action for public policy involves the rapid deregulation of traditional controls with little more than the interim retention of ceiling prices in residual monopoly markets and the setting of economically neutral prices for bottleneck services such as pipeline transmission, power transmission, or access to the local telephone exchange.[6]

Conditions for the Emergence of Sustainable Efficient Markets

To replace regulation with deregulated markets, four conditions must be met: (1) new markets must be capable of producing a competitive outcome sufficiently pervasive to eliminate all opportunities for price discrimination and predation; (2) strategies of incumbent firms must be inconsequential in their impact on the viability of competition; (3) markets must be able to clear in a fashion that minimizes costs of production over time; and (4) agencies must be able to set prices that neutralize monopoly focal points and constrain cross-subsidization in residual monopoly markets.

Applicability of Contestable Market Theory

The first condition might be satisfied if it could be shown that energy and telecommunications were susceptible to potential entry along the lines of the theory of contestable markets. W. G. Shepherd notes that contestability requires three conditions for success: (1) entry must be free and without limit; (2) an entrant must be able to establish itself before the incumbent can make a major retaliatory pricing response; and (3) entry must be perfectly reversible (sunk costs must be minimal).[7]

With respect to natural gas and electricity, the prospects for potential entry as a disciplining force are minimal. FERC Order 436 does not facilitate free, unlimited entry. Pipeline carriage for buyers and sellers is not mandatory, nor is it mandatory that the pipeline expand capacity to meet demand. As a result, the opportunities for pipeline foreclosure are immense—especially during crucial peak periods. It is also problematical whether many customers will have access to any form of direct dealing with producers. This is particularly true in the case of residential and commercial consumers and small LDCs. It can be argued that these groups can form buying cooperatives to deal directly with producers, but the transaction costs of facilitating such a market will be very large. As a consequence, many "captive" or "core" customers will be off limits to new entry. A question can also be raised whether the brokers will be able to function equally well during periods of over- and undersupply. If the broker is considered a new entrant, it is doubtful that he will be able to outbid pipelines serving a range of different markets during a period of shortage or curtailment. If this type of entrant can only function during a period of oversupply, then the viability of such a competitor is extremely limited. Rather than contestability, much of the natural gas industry will probably continue to be characterized by bilateral oligopoly.

In the electric utility industry, it would initially appear that cogeneration is ideally susceptible to potential entry. The initial investment is low, many cogenerating units have better heat rates than the utility's plant, and commercial/industrial sales of electricity are widely diffused. However, cogeneration depends upon (1) high retail electric rates, (2) low gas prices, and (3) an ability to sell excess capacity. Each of these areas is vulnerable to a major retaliatory pricing response. If electric utilities introduce promotional rates, if gas prices increase, if utilities refuse to buy cogeneration output at prices that reflect avoided capital costs (because of excess utility capacity), and if utility standby or back-up prices are high, then the cogenerator must face the prospect of absorbing substantial losses or continuing to use a source of supply that has lost its comparative advantage. Self-generation, on the other hand, involves a more substantial investment. This option has appeal only to large industrial customers, but, again, it is vulnerable to retaliatory actions on the part of the utility.

Insofar as the gas and electric utilities are concerned, potential entry will not be pervasive. Exit costs will undoubtedly be modest for brokers and small-scale cogenerators, but for self-generation, exit costs could be substantial as long as these producers are denied access to retail markets. In the absence of direct regulation, such barriers to the transmission network are apt to remain in place as a matter of utility self-interest.

Initially, the theory of contestable markets would seem to be applicable to telecommunications—especially the interexchange market. To challenge AT&T, the OCCs (or any new entrant) must be able to expand rapidly and capture an important share of the interexchange market to provide a service comparable to that of AT&T. This requires (1) adequate earnings to support a large-scale capital investment, (2) substantial advertising expenditures (since AT&T has effectively shifted message toll telephone service (MTS) from a homogeneous service to a differentiated product), (3) an ability to lease lines from AT&T to get comprehensive coverage, and (4) a price spread between AT&T and OCC rates sufficient to attract customers to the latter.

While AT&T has complained that earnings are poor in some intrastate, inter-local access transport area (LATA) jurisdictions because of state commission actions, there is no question that AT&T enjoys good earnings in the interstate markets.[8] In contrast, OCC earnings are in poor shape. Western Union has reported continuous losses for 1983, 1984, and 1985. Satellite Business Systems (SBS) incurred significant losses before it was sold to Microwave Communications Inc. by International Business Machines in 1985,[9] and General Telephone and Electronics-Sprint continues to report losses.[10] For MCI, 1983, 1984, and 1985 demonstrate a period of rising revenues and declining earnings. To illustrate, for the 12 months ending September 30, 1984, total revenue was $1.9 billion and net operating income was $217 million. For the 12-month period ending September 30, 1985, total revenue increased to $2.4 billion while net operating income declined to $177 million. For the same period, net income was squeezed by substantial increases in access charges ($412 million to $743 million), depreciation expenses ($237 million to $327 million), and internal operating expenses (which includes advertising), ($650 million to $795 million).[11] As a consequence, MCI reports declining earnings, and the other OCCs report negative earnings at a time when they must raise an estimated $6 billion in new capital by 1989 to invest in new capacity. Barring a dramatic reversal, one might anticipate a scenario for the OCCs in which the cost of equal access, promotion, and depreciation will depress earnings so that new financing is either foreclosed or is very costly. With new capital expansion limited, market share will be lost and future earnings, in turn, will be further depressed.

To secure market share, the OCCs must also maintain a price spread between themselves and AT&T. While the OCCs will find access charges increasing because of equal access, AT&T will gain relief to the extent that access charges imposed on the carrier decline, or BOC-redesigned access charges reflect volume usage. Once again, the prospect for the OCCs is not encouraging. For 1984, the price spread between AT&T and the OCCs for MTS was approximately 13.3 percent; for 1985 it had dropped to 12 percent; for 1989 it is forecast to be 4.7 percent.[12]

Contestability also requires zero exit costs. The history of the interexchange and terminal equipment markets is scattered with the names of major firms that unsuccessfully challenged AT&T—including General Electric (1973), Litton (1974), Datran (1976), and Xerox Xten (1981). Considering that the OCCs' investment currently exceeds $4.5 billion, it is clear that the cost of disinvestment is great—especially when the emergence of excess capacity (as noted later) will diminish the opportunities for disposing of assets as part of the disinvestment process. The cost of exit is far from zero, as IBM's experience with SBS indicates.[13]

Contestability also requires that all interexchange markets be vulnerable to entry. This is not the case for 800 WATS service, where AT&T will retain a monopoly for at least several more years.

At best, contestability appears to operate in a few limited submarkets, such as reselling, but even here hit-and-run resellers are vulnerable to retaliatory actions by the dominant firm. It is interesting to note that ALLNET, the largest reseller, has moved to establish itself as a facilities-based carrier, while at the same time strengthening its market position by merging with Lexitel.

Market Concentration

If contestability is largely irrelevant as a constraining force, then the analysis of markets must turn to traditional industrial organization criteria. The roles of market dominance and market concentration become immediately evident.

In the natural gas industry, concentration at the wellhead level has been a subject of continuing controversy. Concentration among producers should be measured in uncommitted reserves by major producing fields. However, the Energy Information Agency used only eight broad geographic producing areas (for example, Appalachia-Illinois) to measure such concentration. In this context, EIA found low levels of market concentration as measured by the Herfindahl-Hirschman Index (HHI).[14] However, these geographic regions are too large to allow any definitive conclusions. In addition, HHI ignores the role of joint ventures, interlocking directorates, and the joint operation of fields, which tend to greatly enhance the market power of the producers.

The concentration of buyers at the field level (that is, pipelines) has also been estimated by EIA using Federal Energy Regulatory Commission-Purchased Gas Adjustment data. On the basis of sales, the data show much greater concentration among pipelines as buyers than among producers. Furthermore, the recent wave of pipeline mergers has served to reduce the number of pipeline buyers even more.[15]

In the wholesale market, where pipelines sell to the LDCs, concentration is still greater. The 80–20 rule suggests that 80 percent of the LDCs have only one pipeline supplier, while 20 percent have two or more. However, in the large wholesale markets, where there may be five or more pipelines, the effective number of sellers is fewer than two, due to high concentration among the largest pipeline suppliers. Once again attention must be given to the recent wave of pipeline mergers, which has further concentrated the number of suppliers in the wholesale market.[16]

At the LDC level concentration remains extremely high, and a sample survey by the author of large midwestern LDCs suggests that only a small portion of the retail market may be vulnerable to intense inter-energy competition in the form of fuel switching. For these LDCs, approximately 55–60 percent of sales revenues are residential, 20 percent are commercial, 20–25 percent are large commercial or industrial. Only 20 percent of the latter 25 percent currently have alternate fuel capability. This means that approximately 5 percent of total retail sales can readily switch between No. 6 fuel oil and natural gas on the basis of price.

In electricity, the market most susceptible to intra-industry competition is the wholesale bulk power market. At present, pooling and wheeling arrangements limit competition in this market. Furthermore, as the recent Southwest Power experiment has shown, even liberalized interchanges do little to increase the number of third party participants. In any event, it is important to note the magnitude of the bulk power market. A sample survey by the author of large midwestern electrics (excluding American Electric Power Co.) revealed that 95–97 percent of the revenue comes from retail sales and only 3–5 percent from wholesale/bulk power sales. Potential entry by cogenerators into the retail market has already been discussed.

In telecommunications, market share data again reveal high levels of concentration, despite the alleged prevalence of competition at the interexchange and exchange levels. For example, AT&T had 88 percent of the domestic interstate telecommunications market for 1984 (measured in operating revenues). MCI had 5 percent; Sprint, 3 percent; Western Union, 1.3 percent; International Telephone and Telegraph, .4 percent; SBS, .4 percent; and all resellers, 1.1 percent.[17] Interestingly, one analyst suggests that a threshold market share of 10 percent is needed to assure long-run viability in the interexchange markets.[18] The international market reveals similar high levels of concentration with Intelsat controlling approximately 95 percent of satellite transmission in the Atlantic basin, and AT&T moving into a position of dominance *vis à vis* the international record carriers at the retail level. In 1966, AT&T's overseas revenues were slightly less (approximately 12 percent) than those of the international record carrier. By 1983, AT&T's overseas revenues were 2.4 times greater than those of the IRCs.[19]

The only potential change that might dramatically upset these concentration figures in the domestic inter-LATA market would be the removal of Judge Harold H. Greene's restrictions on the BOCs.[20] But it is by no means clear that the BOCs would be willing to challenge AT&T by establishing a rival nationwide MTS/WATS network. Rather, the BOCs would be more inclined to offer specialized service to large customers on a regional or national basis.

On balance, if one accepts that market share is positively correlated with rate of return, retaliatory power, and ability to create entry barriers, it is clear that existing levels of concentration in energy and telecommunications will constitute a mammoth obstacle to the establishment of competition—in the absence of massive government intervention.

The Emergence of Differentiated Markets

Complementing the existence of high levels of concentration in selected markets is the existence of differentiated markets, in which some customers have access to alternatives while others have no meaningful alternatives. The former would include high-volume MTS users, industrial firms with dual-fuel capability, and large industrial firms capable of self-generation. The latter would include most residential electric, gas, and telephone service.

Market differentiation is further complicated by the concentration of high-volume users. This is particularly true in telecommunications, where 8 percent of business customers account for 75 percent of MTS business revenues and 10 percent of residential customers account for 50 percent of MTS residential revenues.

If such markets can be effectively segmented, the potential for price discrimination is evident.

Strategies of the Incumbent Firm

With high concentration, the incumbent firm will have both the incentive and the means to employ prices to exploit differentiated markets to maximum advantage. To maintain hegemony in principal markets through rate structure design, the firm will seek to promote high minimum bills, incremental volume discounts, and high standby or back-up charges. For natural gas pipelines, the high minimum bill-selective volume discount strategy was severely weakened by FERC Order No. 380 and by the Maryland People's Counsel case—but this strategy could be reinstated under conditions of tight supply and deregulation.[21] For the electrics, there has been renewed interest in raising minimum bills and introducing promotional rates to utilize excess capacity. For telecommunications, AT&T has introduced a broad range of promotional rates designed to exploit all segments of the telecommunications market. For the small user there is the standard MTS tariff; for the larger residential customer, "Reach Out America"; for the small business user, "Pro America"; and for the large business user, "Megacom" and "Software Defined Networks." These optional calling plans (OCPs) fully exploit the demand curve. Similar pricing patterns can be expected to appear at the local level as BOCs gain greater rate flexibility through state deregulation legislation.

The incumbent firm may also seek to employ varying forms of limit-entry pricing to foreclose or circumscribe a potential entrant. AT&T's TELPAK rate was a classic example. More recently, the natural gas industry developed a series of flexible pricing arrangements and special marketing programs designed to yield gas prices that would foreclose the loss of large-volume customers to suppliers of alternative fuels. As a consequence, for the period 1982–1984, natural gas prices at the retail level rose more rapidly in markets where demand was inelastic, and fell more rapidly in markets where demand was more elastic.[22]

For electricity, pricing strategies appear to be emerging with respect to cogeneration and self-generation. These include not only a return to promotional rates, but also an argument (not without merit) that marginal capacity costs are zero when the utility has excess capacity, so the avoided-cost criterion used to determine payments for cogenerators' output should reflect only marginal energy costs.[23] Utilities also argue that standards must be imposed on cogenerators to maintain reliability and protect the ratepayer. These standards could take the form of requirements for standby capacity and the establishment of cash escrow accounts by cogenerators when the utility makes levelizing capacity payments to the cogenerators. All of these efforts have the net effect of diminishing the attractiveness of cogeneration. An alternative strategy by Arkansas Power and Light deserves particular attention. This involves setting low industrial rates for customers susceptible to cogeneration, with the option that the utility can enter into a joint-venture arrangement with these customers to produce power if cogeneration becomes the low-cost option in the future.

Other strategies available to the incumbent firm include foreclosing the potential entrant from pooling arrangements and shifting risk forward to the consumer in the face of growing uncertainty. Risk shifting can be accomplished by (1) charging high minimum bills, (2) shifting overhead costs to inelastic markets, (3) accelerating the rate of depreciation, and (4) phasing-in high-cost capacity with the guarantee of full recovery of all costs at a future date.[24]

Demand/Supply Imbalances

When growth was stable over long periods of time and capacity additions reflected falling average unit costs, demand and supply in the utility industries tended to track each other closely and real prices fell. However, with the emergence of diminished rates of growth, rising energy prices, long gestation periods for base load plant, removal of legal barriers to entry in telecommunications, and new methods of supply, chronic demand/supply imbalances occurred with greater frequency. To the extent that these imbalances reoccur with some pattern of regularity, the viability of competition will be jeopardized (excess capacity will foreclose entry and cause price instability), the cost of service will increase, risk will increase, a greater distributional burden may be placed on residual monopoly markets, and the incentive to merge will increase.

The natural gas industry went through a period of undersupply in the 1970s and oversupply in the 1980s. The cause of the undersupply has been vigorously debated. Producers attributed it to Federal Power Commission ceiling prices that held the price of gas below an alleged competitive equilibrium. Proponents of regulation argued that the prospect of speculative profits and monopoly power led producers to hold gas off the market. The oversupply of the 1980s was essentially price-driven. The rapid price increases of the 1970s (when the wellhead price of new gas increased over 900 percent) induced conservation on the one hand (which depressed demand), and increased supply of high-cost gas on the other. Rolling in low-cost gas and high-cost gas produced an average retail rate that was sufficient to stimulate the production of high-cost gas. When worldwide oil prices softened, there was considerable fuel switching in the industrial sector—especially for boiler fuel sales—leading to oversupply. This demand/supply imbalance was aggravated further when the price of gas continued to be pushed upward because of contract provisions with the producers in the form of take-or-pay, most favored nation (MFN), and indefinite escalator clauses. As a result, a gas bubble emerged of 3–7 trillion cubic feet per year, depressing current prices and inducing various forms of discriminatory marketing programs on the part of pipelines. A casualty of this oversupply was the synfuels program.

A question can be raised whether these periods of under- and over-supply were unique to the 1970s and 1980s, or whether they can be repeated in the future. With the deregulation of new gas, it is doubtful that regulation can be accused of holding the price below equilibrium levels in the future. On the other hand, a scenario in which a worldwide energy crisis drives up oil prices, which in turn leads to a fly-up in gas prices, is quite possible. To the extent that gas prices have become demand-oriented and are determined largely by the price of fuel oil, one can anticipate rapid fly-ups during periods of scarcity that will stimulate overproduction and strengthen the market power of the producers. This, in turn, will lead to the reimposition of take-or-pay, MFN, and escalator provisions—in the absence of direct government intervention—and will terminate in overproduction, depressed demand, and excess supply.

A second question can be raised: will the emergent spot, futures, and long-term markets be adequate to constrain this type of scenario? Despite FERC Order 436, the pipelines do not constitute an interconnected network linking a large number of buyers and suppliers. Furthermore, it is highly doubtful that such an interconnected network will emerge without direct regulation. It is irrational for pipelines to invest in interconnection facilities that will erode their ability to exploit market differentiation in retail sales and diminish any monopsony power that they might have in producer markets. What can be anticipated is the continued existence of spot markets and some arbitrage pressure during periods of oversupply, with brokers contributing to the allocation of surpluses. But much of the negotiation in this industry will continue to take the form of bilateral oligopoly, with the market power of the participants depending on whether there is over- or undersupply.

Excess capacity in the electric utility industry is a function of (1) rising prices, (2) declining rates of growth in demand, and (3) the introduction of large increments of base load capacity. The rapid increase in electric utility prices initially reflected higher fuel charges and general price inflation, but at the present time the major factors forcing rates higher are the cost overruns associated with new nuclear and coal-fired units. New nuclear units range in cost from $900 to $5000 per kilowatt of installed capacity, and this translates into costs of 20 cents and more per kilowatt-hour. With forecasted average annual growth rates of 2.7 to 3.2 percent through 1990, and reserve margins of 35 percent or more for the nation, it is clear that the 28 nuclear plants coming on line by 1989–1990 will aggravate the redundancy problem and at the same time serve to raise prices even more.

A substantial increase in retail electric rates will serve as a stimulus to cogeneration and self-generation—thereby aggravating the excess capacity problem still further. This gives rise to a number of intriguing questions: first, is the cogeneration capacity more economical than a modern efficient coal-fired steam plant? If not, then the new mix of plants will not only add to excess capacity, but it will also raise the average cost of power to the consumer. Second, is the cogeneration reliable? Third, is it economically efficient to compel the utilities to modify existing plants to meet peaks while the cogeneration is being employed to meet base load? Fourth, is the stimulus to cogeneration largely a function of artificially inflated accounting costs for new utility plants that would not pass the strict application of the prudence or the used-and-useful tests? Deregulation would not provide answers to these questions. The cogenerator would have no incentive to curtail expansion as long as retail electric prices increase. On the other hand, the electric utility would have every incentive to recover its cost through price discrimination rather than write off the costs of redundant plants.[25] If there were any curtailment of cogeneration it would come about because the utility engaged in restrictive interconnection practices and employed its monopsony power in setting rates for purchases from the cogenerator.

The problems of demand/supply imbalances and excess capacity in the electric utility industry will not be resolved in the coming decade by deregulation. New and imaginative public policy solutions are needed to assure the selection of the lowest cost additions to capacity.[26]

Demand/supply imbalances in telecommunications appear to arise because of the desire of carriers and new entrants to participate in rapidly developing markets by employing new technology. In the domestic market, unrestricted entry plus new supply options, such as fiber optic capacity, will greatly increase the number of circuit miles. It is estimated that U.S. circuit miles will increase from 1.4 billion in 1984 to 7.2 billion in 1988. Even with growth rates of 14 percent per year for services such as MTS, it is doubtful that demand can match capacity over this period.[27]

In the international market, the demand/supply imbalances threaten to be even more out of line. At a time when Intelsat is operating at about 47 percent of capacity, the FCC has authorized five new satellite systems and two new fiber optic cable entrants in the international market.[28] If these new entrants are successful in attracting capital, excess capacity may reach a point where only one circuit in ten is actually used.

If excess capacity materializes, a short-run scenario built around price wars, shifts in market share, and falling earnings can be anticipated. The long-term effect will be write-offs, possible bankruptcies, and mergers until capacity is brought into line with demand. The resulting mergers will increase concentration, enhance market power, and raise prices. The alternative of handling massive excess capacity through resale, brokers, or sharing seems remote in a setting where excess capacity is widespread and prices and profits are depressed. Furthermore, the transaction cost of fashioning this excess capacity into a rival network would be great, and the prospects for financial success would be dim.

Agency Pricing Guidelines

The emergence of competition will depend on the ability of state and federal agencies to set prices for bottleneck facilities that are economically neutral and, at least for an interim period, to set ceiling prices in residual monopoly markets. The short experience of FERC and the relatively long experience of the FCC in attempting to come to grips with these problems indicate that no clear-cut solutions are at hand. FERC has treated price squeezes and exclusion from pools on a case-by-case basis. It has attempted to mitigate the effect of percentage adders on power transmission and, as part of Order 436, it has sought to allocate pipeline costs for new transmission services using the volumetric method, in the belief that this would not burden monopoly markets. At this point, it is by no means clear that such steps are adequate to achieve these objectives.

The FCC has struggled with the problem of constraining price discrimination and cross-subsidization for more than 25 years. It has examined and rejected various forms of fully distributed cost, marginal cost, and Ramsey pricing. It has also adopted separate subsidiaries as a check on cross-subsidization, but even separate subsidiaries appear to be on the verge of being dismissed as part of Computer III. The only constraint on cross-subsidy would then be the Interim Cost Allocation Manual (ICAM). This is a highly flawed, superficial full-cost allocation which is hardly adequate to the task.[29]

Perhaps the best example of the difficulty of setting economically neutral prices is in the development of access charges. Cost causation has not played a crucial role in the design of access charges for interexchange carriers or for end users. The design of access charges has been based on a definition of non-traffic sensitive (NTS) and traffic sensitive (TS) costs, which is more a reflection of the strategy of pressure groups than of "pure" economic analysis. If NTS costs vary with the number of customers and are not customer specific, then they are part of a distribution system and should be priced accordingly. Exchange carriers, on the other hand, argue that such costs should be assigned to the ultimate user to prevent bypass. It should also be noted that access charges have not been designed to reflect the burden each type of service places on the local exchange, and historically, access charges were promulgated before the costs of equal access were fully known.

As new pricing concepts emerge in telecommunications, it is reasonable to assume that FCC guidelines will become more and more lax. This can be seen in the decision on optional calling plans (Docket No. 84–1235, October 4, 1985).[30] In effect, the Commission will permit OCPs if it can be shown that anticipated increases in revenue over a 36-month period will cover current and projected costs associated with the plan. Given the agency's move toward deregulation, it is doubtful that any significant losses associated with unsuccessful OCPs will fall exclusively on the shareholder.

Conclusion

The combined effect of high levels of concentration, differentiated markets, retaliatory power of incumbent firms, demand/supply imbalances, and the difficulty of setting neutral pricing guidelines indicates clearly that accelerated deregulation will not result in high levels of competition in the energy and telecommunications industries. Rather, oligopolistic market structures will emerge that are conducive to significant inefficiencies and adverse distributional effects. A more reasoned solution calls for reforming regulation to come to grips with the current problems in these industries.

The task for regulatory agencies in the coming decade will be (1) to monitor the adequacy and availability of service supplied by the energy and telecommunications industries; (2) to assure that service is supplied in a least-cost fashion; (3) to control the exercise of market power; and (4) to constrain the shifting of risk to consumers and of social costs to third parties.

To achieve these objectives, regulatory reform will have to take four important steps. The first involves improved regulatory planning which, in turn, requires a greatly improved capability to forecast demand and establish criteria for determining when to terminate projects, when to carry excess capacity, when to modernize, and when to promote alternatives to traditional sources of supply. The objective will be to monitor adequate service, determine least-cost options, and send the proper signals to incumbent firms, new entrants, and consumers. An introductory appreciation of the potential gains to be made in this area can be seen by contrasting the actions of the Wisconsin and Michigan commissions in monitoring capital expansion programs in electricity supply. The Wisconsin Commission took the initiative of curtailing the expansion of new construction programs for which there was no apparent demand, with the result that projects were terminated with minimum burden on the ratepayer. In contrast, the Michigan Commission took no comparable action with respect to the Midland nuclear plant, with the result that amortization of the unfinished plant will place a long-term burden of more than $7 billion on state ratepayers and utility shareholders.

A second step involves consideration of equity and distributional issues in a planning context. These issues include the obvious problems of assuring service to low-income consumers and thin markets, but they also include more sophisticated issues, such as the secondary effects of deaveraging, the impact of telecommunications modernization plans on the average cost of service to all classes of customers, and the intergenerational impact of phase-in plans and accelerated cost recovery.

A third step involves renewed efforts to isolate the cost of providing service to residual monopoly markets in a fashion that permits customers in these markets to participate in the economies of joint production. The time is past for relying on simple propositions such as the stand-alone test and Ramsey pricing.

A fourth step involves the recognition that industry structure issues have become a permanent, integral part of any overall regulatory framework designed to improve industry performance. Agencies will have to seek new opportunities to remove barriers to potentially competitive markets (such as bulk power), and at the same time monitor potential restrictive practices in traditional markets. In effect, competitive markets can be used as an important complement to the task of improving industry performance.

If regulatory reforms along these lines can be achieved, then higher levels of economic efficiency can be attained and social values enhanced. If reforms cannot be achieved, then deregulation will not point to greater efficiency, but rather to greater reliance on the corporate conscience.

Notes

1. For a representative sampling of the current deregulation literature, see: E. Subissati, "Subsidized Entry, Regulated Competition and Public Policy in Telecommunications in Canada"; and S. L. Levin and J. P. Gillan, "Regulatory Considerations in the Introduction of Competition into the Telecommunications Industry"; and for a rejoinder see: H. M. Trebing, "Challenging Some Policy Assumptions: A Response to Levin and Gillan and Subissati," all in *Telecommunications and Equity: Policy Research Issues,* ed. James Miller (Amsterdam and New York: Elsevier/North Holland, in press). Also, see R. J. Pierce, "Reconsidering the Roles of Regulation and Competition in the Natural Gas Industry," *Harvard Law Review,* 97 (December 1983): 345–85.
2. E. E. Bailey and W. J. Baumol, "Deregulation and the Theory of Contestable Markets," *Yale Journal on Regulation* 1 (1984): 111–37, at p. 112. Proponents of contestability argue that potential entry will constrain monopoly profits, price discrimination, and predation, even though markets may be highly concentrated.
3. Citing a Touche Ross study, J. S. Kramer argues that one in four large customers is engaging in some form of bypass of the local exchange, and that an increase in exchange prices of 10 percent will lead to a massive loss of traffic. J. S. Kramer, "An Analysis of Local Exchange Bypass," in *The Impact of Deregulation and Market Forces on Public Utilities: The Future Role of Regulation,* ed. P. C. Mann and H. M. Trebing (East Lansing: Michigan State University, 1985), pp. 59–64. For a critical response see H. Schwartz, "A Critical Assessment of the Bypass Argument as a Justification for the Access Charge," ibid., pp. 78–102.
4. See Pierce, "Reconsidering the Roles," pp. 376–82.
5. Federal Energy Regulatory Commission, *Regulation of Natural Gas Pipelines after Partial Wellhead Decontrol,* Docket No. RM85-1-000 (Parts A–D), Order No. 436, Issued: 9 October 1985.
6. Between 1 January 1983 and 1 January 1986, fourteen state legislatures enacted general statutes involving some form of selective deregulation in telecommunications. For the most part, these statutes provide for selective or comprehensive deregulation of the company if there is a demonstration that competition or alternative suppliers exist. In some cases, the authority to deregulate individual services is given to the state commission.
7. See: W. G. Shepherd, " 'Contestability' vs. Competition," *American Economic Review,* 74 (September 1984): 572–87.
8. AT&T's total earnings for 1985 rose 14 percent. Moody's Investors Service did cut AT&T's ratings on nearly $9 billion of its debt and preferred shares in 1986; however, this was not because of the long distance business (which was characterized as a "highly profitable line"), but because profit margins on computers, workstations, and other office equipment were lower than

originally anticipated. Moody's also felt that sales of switching equipment to the BOCs would come under increased competitive pressure. See: Janet Guyon, "Moody's Lowers Ratings on AT&T Debt, Preferred on Failure to Meet Profit Goal," *Wall Street Journal,* 10 February 1986, p. 4.

9. On June 25, 1985, IBM reached an agreement with MCI and Aetna Life and Casualty under which IBM acquired Aetna's ownership interest in SBS and transferred the ownership of SBS to MCI in exchange for 45 million shares of MCI and an option to purchase 7 million more at $15 per share. This provided IBM with a 16 percent interest in MCI (which could increase to 18 percent). IBM agreed to pay off SBS's $400 million in outstanding debts. MCI is acquiring SBS debt-free. It is estimated that SBS had been losing at least $100 million per year. See "IBM, SBS, and MCI: Mixed Signals for Intercity Service Competition," 10 *Trends in Communications Regulation,* (July 1985): 7.

10. On January 17, 1986, GTE Corp. and United Telecommunications announced that they would each have a 50 percent interest in a new company called U. S. Sprint Communications. The new enterprise would acquire the long distance operations of GTE-Sprint and United. GTE had apparently invested $2.8 billion in Sprint trying to make the operation profitable, but the unit had been "sustaining operating losses of close to $100 million a quarter." GTE would take a charge against earnings of $1.3 billion. United would take a charge against earnings of $170 million. Janet Guyon, "GTE Will Shed Sprint and Take Big Write-Off," *Wall Street Journal,* 17 January 1986, p. 3.

11. Data supplied by MCI to the author.

12. The OCCs originally paid a lower access charge to the BOCs because of lower quality interconnection. This charge was approximately 55 percent below that paid by AT&T for access. With the establishment of equal access for AT&T and the OCCs, all interexchange carriers will pay the same access fee. This increase in access payments for the OCCs is a principal cause of the narrowing gap between AT&T and OCC rates. Some analysts believe that MCI's rates will be only 5 percent less that AT&T's by 1987. See John Wilke and Mark Maremont, "The Long-Distance Warrior," *Business Week,* 17 February 1986, pp. 86–94. At the same time, AT&T's initial access charge payments will decline as an increasing portion of BOC access costs are assessed against end users instead of carriers.

13. See Footnote 9, above.

14. The Herfindahl-Hirschman Index, as a measure of market concentration, is obtained by expressing the market shares of the firms in decimal form, squaring these shares, then summing them up. The number of effective sellers is $\frac{1}{HHI}$. An HHI of 1.0 equals monopoly control. A post-merger HHI of .18 appears to be a threshold of concern for the U. S. Department of Justice. R. P. O'Neill found HHIs of .02 to .06 among producers. See R. P. O'Neill, "Pipeline Mergers and Their Potential Impact on Natural Gas Markets," paper presented at the Seventeenth Annual Conference of the Institute of Public Utilities, 9–11 December 1985, Mimeographed, p. 16. Paper to be published in 1986.

15. O'Neill estimates HHIs for interstate pipelines (as buyers) to range from .13 to 1.0, with 17 out of 26 producing areas at or above the .18 concentration level. O'Neill, "Pipeline Mergers," p. 17.

16. O'Neill, "Pipeline Mergers," p. 21. Significant natural gas pipeline mergers and acquisitions began in 1982, when Burlington Northern acquired El Paso Natural Gas Pipeline. In 1983, CSX Corporation acquired Texas Gas Transmission, MidCon Corporation acquired Mississippi River Transmission, Williams acquired Northwest Pipeline. In 1984, Houston Natural Gas acquired Transwestern and Florida Gas Transmission. In 1985, Coastal Corporation acquired American Natural Resources, InterNorth acquired Houston Natural Gas, Tenneco acquired Mid-Louisiana Gas, and MidCon acquired United Gas Pipeline. In 1986, Occidental acquired MidCon but was required to divest Mississippi River Transmission.

17. By using interstate revenues, it is possible to exclude intrastate MTS provided by the BOCs, which is largely not competitive with AT&T. Source of data: *Telecom Marketing Newsletter,* No. 250, 14 January 1985, *Telefocus* 2 (January 1985), and tabulations by Bethesda Research Institute, Ltd.

18. Comments of Glenn Pafumi, Analyst at Dean Witter Reynolds, as reported in *USA Today,* 17 January 1986, p. 8A. In the long run, Pafumi anticipates that consumers will have two long-distance choices: MCI or AT&T.

19. See: H. M. Trebing, "A Critique of Structure Regulation in Common Carrier Telecommunications," *Telecommunications Regulation Today and Tomorrow,* ed. E. M. Noam (New York: Harcourt Brace Jovanovich, 1983), p. 141. Updated calculations by the author.

20. In issuing the modified final judgment in the AT&T divestiture case, Judge Harold H. Greene limited the BOCs to intra-LATA services and required special permission from the court for any diversification activities by the Bell regional holding companies, which serve as the parent holding companies for the BOCs. He has steadfastly maintained this position. See: *U.S. v. AT&T, et al.,* Civil Action, No. 82–0192, Opinion, 13 January 1986.

21. Federal Energy Regulatory Commission, *Elimination of Variable Costs from Certain Natural Gas Pipeline Minimum Commodity Bill Provisions,* Docket No. RM 83–71–000, Order No. 380, 25 May 1984. Also, Order No. 380A, 30 July 1984. U. S. Court of Appeals for District of Columbia, *Maryland People's Counsel v. FERC et al.,* No. 84–1090, 10 May 1985. Also, USCA, *Maryland People's Counsel v. FERC, et al.,* No. 84-1019, 10 May 1985.

22. See: H. M. Trebing, "Reforming Gas Regulation in the Face of Rising Costs and Increased Uncertainty," *Journal of Petroleum Accounting* 4 (Summer 1985): 119–38, at pp. 136–37.

23. The utility can argue that flexibility is needed in estimating the avoided energy cost payment to a cogenerator during a period of falling fuel prices. Such a price could be based on spot market fuel costs or the cost of economy power from the next most efficient source of supply. Either option, when combined with the absence of a long-term fixed price for sales to the utility, would make it difficult for the cogenerator to get adequate financing. Typically, the cogenerator must sell to the utility and to another retail customer over the utility's transmission network.

24. Examples of these strategies are readily observable in subscriber line charges, the shift to equal life group depreciation, and the introduction of elaborate phase-ins for nuclear plants.

25. For a utility confronted by high depreciation and capital costs, on the one hand, and falling fuel costs on the other, the preferred solution to maximize

revenue growth and minimum risk is to raise prices in inelastic markets and lower prices in elastic markets. Both pricing strategies will raise revenues while assessing capital costs against those with few options, giving the customer with alternative sources of supply the benefits of lower fuel costs. These actions would clearly be enhanced by deregulation.

26. On 3 February 1986, the Massachusetts Commission issued proposed regulations that would constitute a new policy toward cogeneration and small power producers by permitting them to bid competitively for given amounts of power. The utility would be required to sign contracts of up to 20 years' duration with the winning bidders in each solicitation. Utilities would be required to wheel power for small power producers for sale to other utilities. Cogenerators and small power producers not wishing to enter into long-term contracts would be permitted to sell power to utilities at an "as-available" avoided cost rate that reflects the cost of fuel used by utilities. This rate would change on a monthly basis. See Massachusetts Department of Public Utilities, Order and Notice of Proposed Regulations, 84–276–A, 3 February 1986.

27. At an average annual growth rate of 14 percent, demand would increase 69 percent over this period, but capacity would increase by 414 percent (assuming that all capital plans are carried out).

28. Federal Communications Commission, *In The Matter of Tel-Optik Limited and Submarine Lightwave Cable Company,* FCC Docket 85–99, Memorandum, Opinion, and Order, 1 March 1985. Also, Federal Communications Commission, *In the Matter of Establishment of Satellite Systems Providing International Communications,* CC Docket No. 84–1299, Report and Order, 3 September 1985.

29. For a more detailed discussion of ICAM, see K. B. Levitz, "Separate Subsidiaries, the Interim Cost Manual, and AT&T Divestiture," in *The Impact of Deregulation and Markets Forces on Public Utilities,* pp. 209–28.

30. FCC, *Guidelines for Dominant Carriers' MTS Rates and Rate Structure Plans,* CC Docket No. 84–1235, Memorandum Opinion and Order, 4 October 1985.

18

Oligarchic Capitalism:
Arguable Reality, Thinkable Future?

Warren S. Gramm

Oligarchic market structure and the associated concentration of economic power have been the natural drift of advanced industrial capitalist economies. Given the functional connection between economics and politics, such economic concentration is likely to be accompanied by oligarchic politics—by *de facto* political and social control by the few. For the United States this would mean oligarchic rule within republican forms. Since the 1940s, in the setting of the cold war, these relationships largely have been ignored [38, p. 3].[1] Democracy has been the assumed accompaniment of capitalism, a "given" ingredient in the "free world" of the private market system. Neofascism has been seen as microcosmic, as successfully resolved episodes (for example, McCarthyism) rather than as an ongoing process. Consequently, the possible recurrence of authoritarian capitalism has been generally ignored. Milton Friedman has recognized that "history *suggests* only that capitalism is a necessary condition for political freedom. Clearly it is not a sufficient condition. Fascist Italy and Fascist Spain, Germany . . . Japan, and tzarist Russia . . . —are all societies that cannot conceivably be described as politically free. Yet, in each, private enterprise was the dominant form of economic organization" [17, p. 10, emphasis added].

Since concentrated power is the hallmark of authoritarianism, the major focus in the next section is on contemporary economic and political power relationships in the United States. The linkages between contemporary

353

capitalism and neofascism are discussed in the general context of William Ebenstein's seven "elements of fascist doctrine and policy," which include "denial of basic human equality, code of behavior based on lies and violence, government by elite, and racialism" [15, pp. 104–105]. This is the setting for the thesis developed in the last section of the article: There exists an historical and prospectively causal connection between advanced industrial capitalism and authoritarian politics.

Authoritarian, Oligarchic Capitalism: Concepts, Method, Terminology

It is necessary at the outset to deal with several semantic and conceptual problems involving the so-called isms approach and the several competing theoretical approaches to fascism. The current anti-isms position is based on two major propositions.[2] First, variations within the several capitalistic and socialistic nations are so great that there is no longer a basis for such categories. Similarly, the terms *communism* and *fascism* are judged to have little useful analytic content. The second and related proposition is that capitalism will continue indefinitely to make successful institutional responses to new problems and circumstances. Representative of this position is a statement by Robert Heilbroner: "I believe that capitalism will again evidence its extraordinary institutional and ideological flexibility and will accept the necessary next 'socialistic' steps as the only means by which it can extend its nervous, expansionary life" [27, p. 141]. Capitalism survives by becoming more socialistic!

The increased role of government in Western market economies, especially since the Great Depression, is beyond dispute. The process has been characterized, somewhat paradoxically, as welfare capitalism, state capitalism, or Tory socialism. At the same time, for polemical political purposes, these economies have characterized themselves as the "free world," as democratic capitalism. A way out of this semantic and ideological morass is to establish a normative base that identifies the criteria for *viability* for any given institution or social system.[3] On such grounds judgment may be made concerning constructive and socially desirable adaptations and the relative degree of health or senescence of a given system.

Two useful conceptual grounds in this regard are the polar opposite relationship and the biological life-cycle metaphor. Polar opposites involve the analytic relevance of metaphysical relationships—of ideal types in a particular context. The most common case in economic analysis involves the polar opposites of pure competition and pure monopoly. Thus, Friedman observes: "Of course, competition is an ideal type, like a

Euclidean line or point. No one has ever seen a Euclidean line" [17, p. 120] or a purely competitive market. Yet, the latter stands as the normative base, the ideal type, for judgment concerning the viability of the capitalist market economy.[4] Other criteria must be applied to capitalism as a social system, particularly its behavioral and psychological grounds and related function. The biological life-cycle metaphor appears in the Physiocrat's *Tableau Economique* and among post-Darwinian economists as diverse as Alfred Marshall and Thorstein Veblen. Simply stated it views human institutions and social systems as having a birth (initial genesis), an acceptance and application (maturity), and a decline and senescence (a "withering away" into "imbecilic" disfunction and *de facto* "death").

In general, the anti-isms school does not make use of the polar opposite perspective and overtly rejects the life-cycle paradigm, at least as it applies to capitalism. It accepts the historical reality of the rise and fall of Western European feudalism, but the ensuing market system will survive in perpetuity. Kenneth Arrow argues that "capitalism has survived long enough in advanced countries to show that the Marxian contradictions can hardly be fatal, though they may have been avoided only by the development of new institutions, such as *labor unions and government intervention*" [1, p. 107, emphasis added]. This position is, in effect, reactionary. There is a dangerous complacency in accepting one's culture as "modern," in the sense of final or definitive [21, p. 32]. The survival of capitalism in any socially and historically relevant sense is to be judged not on the continued formal existence of its key institution, private ownership of the means of production, but on its continuing successful performance in meeting its problems—equitable economic progress.

The analysis here builds on the proposition "that there is an intimate connection between economics and politics" [17, p. 8]. The classification system employed identifies four major institutional combinations, four ideal types which can be approached but which, as abstract extremes, cannot literally be realized. These are liberal and authoritarian capitalism, and liberal and authoritarian socialism. In historical terms, liberal capitalism is associated with Great Britain, France, and the United States in the nineteenth and twentieth century. Authoritarian socialism is associated with the Soviet Union (Stalinism), and authoritarian capitalism with Italy and Germany after World War I. Liberal (democratic) socialism has been approximated in Scandinavia in recent decades, but its future remains an open question.

Liberal republican polity and liberal capitalist economy evolved together after about 1700. That there were important elements of mutual support seems beyond dispute; a liberal economy—private property, reinforced by and reinforcing the broader legal protection of individual rights —was the historically "logical" and necessary accompaniment of the new liberal society. But given the fundamental differences between the worlds of the eighteenth and late twentieth century as well as the history of capitalist performance since the 1920s, there is no general basis for simple extrapolation of the historical association of private property rights and individual freedom.

Whatever the set of arrangements that eventually displaces capitalism, it likely will not be characterized and labelled a system until long established. There is no teleological drift to one resolution or another. "The capitalist or any other order of things may evidently break down—or economic and social evolution outgrow it—and yet the socialist phoenix may fail to rise from the ashes. There may be chaos and, unless we define as socialism any non-chaotic alternative to capitalism, there are other possibilities" [49, pp. 56–57]. Some despotic variant is as likely an end for industrial man as the conceptual and ideological opposite, Marx's communism. The basic question is whether creeping statism will evolve into an authoritarian or liberal variant.

The second conceptual problem mentioned at the beginning of this section concerns the terms *fascism* and *neofascism*. A common or uniformly accepted meaning must be established. Writing in 1936, Ernst Basch (under the pseudonym E. B. Ashton) observed: "Today it is no rare occurrence to hear two intelligent and well-informed Americans give exactly contradictory definitions of Fascism" [5, p. xi]. By the 1960s, *fascism* had come to be a generic pejorative for almost any radical dissenting person or group. *Totalitarian* became a synonym for fascism and a substitute for the more descriptive term *authoritarian*.[5] The red fascism of Stalin became the Communist counterpart of the black fascism of Hitler. Renzo De Felice has argued strongly for "the need to put an end to this indiscriminate and distorted use of the adjective 'Fascist' "[13, p. 9].[6] "After 1945, the rightwing as a political idea, hence as a practicable alternative to democratic-liberalism, was defeated and swept aside. The term 'fascism' no longer describes the sequel adequately, [and] political science well-nigh refuses to discuss the issue in depth" [38, p. 4].

There is minimal disagreement concerning the fundamental nature of fascism. It is antidemocratic (elitist) and violent. Out of the continuing dispute concerning its historical grounds and causes, the argument here builds on approaches that emphasize the interrelationships among economic problems, economic power, and fascism.[7] Those who have associated concentrated monopolistic capitalism with the rise of fascism include not only Marxists and socialists, but also U.S. institutionalist economists such as Robert A. Brady [10], sociologists [12, 37], and many German writers.[8] Very generally, the economic argument is summarized in Karl Polanyi's 1944 statement: "Fascism, like socialism was rooted in a market society that refused to function. Hence, it was world-wide, catholic in scope, universal in application" [46, p. 239]. The possibility of non-liberal extension of existing state or welfare capitalism is a recurring theme in contemporary "futures" literature [such as 16 and 21] as well as in the writings of Marxists and other "pessimistic" observers. Most likely such a development, neofascist in substance, would come under another and more amiable name,[9] perhaps corporatism (fascism with a "human face") [45, p. 30]. The essence of Western liberalism is the diffusion of both economic and political power. Hence, a necessary condition for liberal polity has been institutionalization of the separation of power. Its demise would involve loss of such separation.

Concentration of Private and Public Power: The Antithesis of Democracy

The focus here is on the power structure of the United States as an industrial capitalist society.[10] The major elements are market concentration and functional ties between financial and production ownership units and between big business and the federal government. In earlier analytic treatments of this broad subject area, terminology was developed by, among others, J. K. Galbraith ("countervailing power" and "new industrial state") and C. Wright Mills ("power elite," the "military-industrial" and similar complexes, "Tory socialism," and "government-business symbiosis").

The related power perspective is that the business community has a natural interest in controlling the "state" (government as an instrument of power). Within competitive capitalism this control was strongly tempered by competing internal power centers, but by the early twentieth century the power position of big business became less constrained. This situation is directly opposed to the liberal, pluralist view that in contemporary capitalist societies power is dispersed both within and among diverse social groups.[11]

Concentration of Economic Power: Market Structure

Concentration of economic power is based on limited numbers of firms in particular industries, compounded and reinforced by a complex web of overlapping interpersonal and ownership ties. Market concentration is most easily identified in the dual economy frame of reference. A few large corporations have come to dominate basic industries and finance in the past half century.

Concentration ratios have not increased significantly since World War II. Based on market share of the top four corporations, concentration in manufacturing in recent decades has been declining in industrial goods and rising in consumer goods, with the latter outweighing the former.[12] Concentration in agriculture has risen steadily since World War II. Between 1964 and 1974, the number of farm units accounting for one-half of all farm product sales decreased from 205,000 to 100,000.

The critical issue is whether or not the market system is "naturally competitive" in the sense of atomization of economic power conducive to the social end of harmony as premised in the "invisible hand" concept. There are strong historical and empirical, as well as intuitive and analytical, grounds for arguing that advanced industrial capitalism is naturally monopolistic. The functional connection between self-interest and conspiracy and collusion was noted in several contexts by Adam Smith. In 1974, Donald J. Dewey observed that when "the legal framework . . . is a close approximation to laissez-faire, that is, to the legal framework of the United States before 1890 or Great Britain before 1956. . . . in the manufacturing sector of mature capitalist economy . . . production will ultimately be concentrated in a relatively small number of firms" [14, p. 1].

Concentration in communications is particularly significant for a workable democracy. There has been a dramatic decline in competition in newspapers. "In 1973 only 5.4 percent of newspaper firms had direct competition in the same city," contrasted with 60 percent in 1923 [44, p. 49]. The conglomerate merger process has resulted in overlapping ownership of operating firms in several media. By the early 1970s, about 30 percent of all television stations were owned by newspapers in the same city.

More important than market concentration ratios is aggregate and "super" concentration. One aspect of the former is the proportion of economic activity, by industry groups, accounted for by the 200 largest manufacturing corporations. The share of value-added by manufacture by the top 200 rose from 30 to 42 percent between 1947 and 1966 [6, p. 69]. In terms of employment, "in some three-fifths of all industries, comprising more than half of all manufacturing employment, the 200 largest firms employed, on the average, nearly half of the workers" [6, p. 74].

A second aspect of aggregate concentration is the conglomerate merger process. The significance of this activity for overall economic concentration is indicated, for the period 1947–1968, by the 18.5 percent increase in share of manufacturing assets of the 200 largest manufacturing firms, of which it is estimated 15.6 percent came from mergers [6, p. 307]. The record for corporate takeovers occurred in 1969, when the total dollar value of acquisitions was $4 billion. Despite some indications of increased resistance by 1978, the high takeover rate in the first half portends a new record in 1979.

Superconcentration

Several dimensions of ownership and control of producing firms will be considered here: external controls involving banks and interlocking directorates, and internal control by owners and/or managers. These are the several overlapping components of a pyramid of private economic power. The major issues were addressed in a recent U.S. Senate study examining voting rights in 122 large U.S. corporations (total stock was valued at $373 billion, which is 41 percent of all outstanding U.S. common stock at the end of 1976). Of the 610 top five "stockvoters," 600 were identified. In this group, voting rights are held by only 21 institutions. These include eleven banks, five investment company combines, four insurance companies, and one family group (the Kirby family controls the largest U.S. investment company combine).

How extensive is bank control of operating companies? David M. Kotz [29] argues that it has increased significantly in recent decades. Based on his study of 200 of the largest nonfinancial corporations (in terms of assets), he concludes that by the late 1960s 34.5 percent (69 firms) were under financial control, which involved 25.4 percent of these companies' assets. The degree of financial control varied. Of the 69 firms, 13 were fully controlled by financial institutions, 38 were partially controlled by only one financial corporation, and 18 were partially controlled by a combination of two or more financial institutions and individuals [29, pp. 97–98].

Edward S. Herman has argued that Kotz's study is seriously flawed, that his questionable conclusion on direct financial control seriously obscures the very important symbiotic ties between the largest financial and nonfinancial corporations. Rather, "bank power and leverage with customers is almost always based on the lending function rather than on stock ownership. The typical situation as regards major firms is one of reciprocity and community of interest and influence" [28, p. 55].

A major controversy concerns the internal control of the corporation;

in general, the problem of separation of ownership and management [35, pp. ix–xv] or the "managerial revolution" [11]. Kotz identifies three major schools: the managerial, owner control, and financial control proponents [29, pp. 2–9]. John Blair lumps the last two under " 'financial control' investment houses, owning families, and, more recently, institutional investors and commercial banks" [6, p. 76]. There may be, however, a strong community of interest between the managers and other major owners of large corporations [13, pp. 34–35].

Kotz's data do not directly reject the managerial thesis. About 51 percent of the 200 firms sampled were judged subject to either financial or owner control. This means that more than 45 percent "are left having no confirmed or suspected center of control" [29, p. 98]. This residual leaves open the possibility that the relevance of managerial elements may be significant. The several power dimensions are joined in Kenneth Nowotny's observation that "if . . . the owners of the modern corporation are viewed in the context of their economic *class*, rather than as individuals, there exists the strong possibility of an intersection between the [separation of ownership and management and the wealthy stockholders—the power elite thesis]. It is quite likely that the 'ruling elite' as defined by Mills and Domhoff, controls the major U.S. corporations, perhaps 95 percent or more of the largest 1,300" [42, p. 497].

Short-run, profit-oriented competition continues as a functional component of industrial capitalism. However, it exists within a larger frame of symbiotic common interests,[13] reflected in suprafirm units such as industry trade associations and "peak" organizations. The latter include the now relatively moribund National Association of Manufacturers (NAM) and its *de facto* successors, the Business Council and the Business Roundtable.

The implications of these trends in economic and financial concentration may be characterized broadly as the *Zaibatsu* syndrome. *Zaibatsu* is the identifying term for Japanese business organizations since the onset of Japan's industrial era about a century ago. "Derived from the Japanese terms for wealth (*zai*) and a clique or estate (*batsu*), the term has been used to designate a few huge, family-based combines" [6, p. 82].[14] Its major functional elements are close working relationships between the private producing (industrial) and financial sectors and the public sector (central government). The functional ties between industry and finance in the United States, described above, reflect the larger historical experience of industrial and finance capitalism. Accelerated pressure for U.S. business to move toward the *Zaibatsu* "solution" stems from the internal (domestic) desire for profitable finance and market control and from outside pressure of foreign competition. For example, it appears that the lower price of some Japanese manufactures is based partially on the industrial firm's functional coordination with the financial sector and government.[15]

Economic and Political Power

A necessary condition for oligarchic capitalism is the effective joining of concentrated economic power with the political process. Such a functional interconnection has been assumed in the Marxist analysis of capitalism since 1848. As Friedman has observed, "if economic power is joined to political power, concentration seems almost inevitable" [17, p. 16]. In the past, the United States and Japan have been contrasted in terms of individualism versus feudalism. But, discussing the contemporary *Zaibatsu*, Morton S. Baratz observes: "The prospect is, in short, that by the year 2000, give or take a decade or so, the United States will find itself possessed of an indigenous *Zaibatsu*. . . . Should the American enterprise system attain this [*Zaibatsu*-like] stage of development—and it well might —it would fully merit Ghent's [1902] label . . . 'our new Feudalism' " [4, p. 80].

In representative government, especially in the United States [58, p. 11], the lobby has developed as the functional link between economic and political power—between economic interests and political action. Lobbying has become a primary function of trade associations, which became legalized in the late nineteenth century. By 1940, some 8,000 such associations had been organized, of which 2,000 were nationwide. Most important for the present context was the "peak" coordinating unit, the National Association of Manufacturers, organized in 1903 [10, p. 192]. Between the late 1950s and the 1970s, the new strategic peak business organization has been the low-profile Business Council. Composed of some 200 executives of the largest corporations, it holds biannual meetings. Top federal officials—members of the cabinet and heads of major agencies, such as the Federal Reserve Board—communicate with the group concerning mutual problems and interests. In 1975 a parallel organization, the Business Roundtable, was established. This group also consists of almost 200 chief executives of the largest corporations. It serves as a direct lobbying contact with Congress and the executive branch on specific issues.

Prior to 1974 it was illegal for companies selling to the government to establish a corporate political action committee (PAC).[16] By 1976, following changes in the law, over 400 PACs had been formed; by 1978 the number had risen to 711, which included 134 formed by *Fortune* magazine's top 500 corporations. The funds are based primarily on "voluntary" contributions from corporate executives (estimated at $40 million in 1977). Between the 1974 and 1978 elections, the amount of money devoted to congressional and gubernatorial campaigns almost doubled, from $110 to $200 million. The bulk of the increase came from these business sources. The bipartisan nature of such support represents a drift toward a "one-party" probusiness politics.

These recent changes in the locus of political action have been characterized as a movement from party to group politics. Leftists—pessimists and social critics—infer that this indicates the evolution of a one-party system. Centrists—optimists and meliorists—maintain their pluralist view by regarding the shift of political action from parties to interest groups, or lobbyists, as a new form of democracy. However, given the direct relationship between money and power, the issue of concentration of wealth remains crucial; political groups who control highly concentrated wealth militate toward plutocracy, not democracy.

A major alternative for maintenance of liberal polity is development of a private corporate conscience which values "not just profits but . . . a broader and deeper conception of the public good" [53, p. 238]. But it seems, as Friedman has argued, that this is to ask the leopard to change its spots: "Few trends could so thoroughly undermine the very foundation of our free society as the acceptance by corporate officials of a social responsibility other than to make as much money for their stockholders as possible. This is a fundamentally subversive doctrine" [17, p. 133].

Considering the three major overlapping elements of concentrated economic power (ownership of wealth, market concentration, and a managerial elite), is it possible that *Fortune* magazine's top 500 corporations have their political counterpart in a top 500 individuals or families who effectively dominate major national policy? In 1959 a similar question was posed by Edward S. Mason. Noting that the management, the control, of the 500 largest corporations "is in the hands of, at most, a few thousand men," he asks: "Who selected these men, if not to rule over us, at least to exercise vast authority, and to whom are they responsible?" The answer to the first question is "themselves"; to the second question the answer is nebulous, at best [35, p. 5]. As Wolfgang Friedmann has observed, "the corporate organizations of business have long ceased to be private phenomena" [40, p. 17]. It does not seem simplistic to envisage the possibility—given the interlocking interests described above—that a small Millsian power elite could exercise effective political control.

Capitalism and Fascism:
Contemporary Linkages and Trends

Is oligarchic capitalism—some variant of fascism—a likely prospect for the twenty-first century? The problem is trivialized in equating a contemporary authoritarian threat with such residual fascistic forms as local Nazi party cells. Rather, its essence will be seen in deterioration of the Bill of Rights and the rule of law, in general. The manifestations of power concentration cited above will be elements of an authoritarian trend only if they promote specifically fascist norms and behavior.

Major noneconomic aspects of fascism, and neofascism, are: (1) policy and actions based on nonrational grounds; (2) belief in the desirability and/or inevitability of basic human inequality, which leads to racism and other types of discrimination against selected scapegoats; (3) behavior based on lies and violence; all of which, in significant respects, culminate in (4) breakdown of the rule of (liberal) law [15, p. 105]. Fascism is associated both philosophically and historically with irrationality, with reliance on nonrational argument and behavior. For example, with respect to Germany, Nazism found philosophical support in the nineteenth-century German Romantics Johann Fichte, Friedrich Gentz, and Adam Müller. Their basic position was antidemocratic, anti-individualistic, and nonrational.

But the role of rationalism here presents an interesting and important paradox. Alongside its nonrational philosophical base, fascism is characterized in particular respects by the polar opposite—"ultra-rationality."[17] This is seen in the eulogistic cliché that under Mussolini and Hitler, at least the trains ran on time. The serious relevance of this "efficiency appeal" of fascism has been detailed by Herbert Lionel Matthews [see 13, p. 193]. The pathological nature of fascistic ultra-efficiency is symbolized by gruesome details of the death camps.

This paradoxical element of fascism is resolved when one recognizes that human beings are endowed with both mind and heart, with intelligence and emotions;[18] human behavior involves various combinations of both in response to different problems. Fascism, as monstrosity, dichotomizes these elements and bifurcates human beings in its political process. That is, both intellect and emotions become tools of the state rather than elements of balanced human development. The nonrationality of the specific attributes of fascism outlined below (and their reflections in capitalism) is historically and culturally relative. They run counter to the Western liberal ethos. Rational behavior is a function of values and problems and the interdependence of ends and means.

Consonant Economic and Social Elements of
Capitalism and Fascism

In what ways and to what extent does capitalism reinforce, even ramify and compound, inequality, lying and violence, and the breakdown of the rule of law? Wide inequality in distribution of income and wealth is a functional aspect of capitalist society. The general nature of inequality in distribution of wealth has been indicated above. Annual money incomes range from a minimum subsistence level of about $2500 to millions of dollars; over 25 percent of family units live in poverty, while perhaps one percent live in great wealth. Some decrease in inequality began during World War II, perhaps continuing into the 1950s, but that trend has reversed during the 1970s. Recent inflation and tax policy portend decreased real income of the middle income groups that had experienced significant improvement after the war.

Economic discrimination tends to reflect the larger social setting. The business community plays an influential role, given the general interactions of profit maximization, job discrimination, treatment of minorities, and social control. Most simply, wage and salary discrimination *vis-à-vis* "minorities" works to lower costs.

As in the case of income inequality, post–World War II reductions in some aspects of racial and other types of discrimination in the United States have ceased, and the process has perhaps been reversed. Greater access to education has not led to a proportional increase in job opportunities. Genuinely open, rather than limited or "token," entry of blacks, women, and other "minorities" into the labor force has yet to be realized.

To what extent may the expanding clouds of lies and violence be attributed to capitalism? In some respects such behavior stems directly from the market system, particularly from the hyperindividualism stimulated by the capitalist ethic. Individualism *per se* is a natural extension of ego; hyperindividualism involves its extension into antisocial behavior (see note 21). For example, self-interest often requires secrecy; secrecy readily evolves into necessary lies, and these become the habitual lies of expediency [7, pp. 10–11]. The content of much commercial advertising may be characterized as half-truths, fiction, or lies, depending on individual information or tastes. In the public sector, the basis for systematic lying historically has been alleged protection of national security (as in the case of Watergate); more recently, in the era of environmental controversy, lies also have been told about atomic energy costs and risks.

Capitalistic emphasis on self-interest and behavioral competition [17, p. 119] reinforces conflict rather than cooperation among individuals.

There is conflict between the Christian and the capitalist ethic [57]. In important respects, the "acquisitive bent" or ethic runs counter to the golden rule. Cut-throat competition, dog eat dog, and the law of the jungle are terms used to describe market competition. The compatibility of violence with the capitalist ethos is seen in the history of industrial warfare (1870–1940) and in recent responses to consumerism. Most noteworthy are the attempted character assassination of Ralph Nader [51, pp. 373–98] and the willingness of business firms knowingly to market dangerous— even lethal—products, such as the Corvair, the Pinto, International Harvester's Farmall tractor, and Beech aircraft (see, for example [7, pp. 11–12]).

Kenneth Boulding's distinction between positive and negative payoffs helps explain how the means for social control within societies change over time. When the society—economy—is viable, it can rely primarily on positive payoffs (provision of real goods and services) for popular support. When the society weakens, it becomes necessary to rely increasingly on negative payoffs (punishment) as a means of social control [8, pp. 300–301]. Still, "monied oligarchies prefer democratic to authoritarian rule. The stability of the system is enhanced by periodic popular ratifications of oligarchic rule" [3, p. 156]. When such "bourgeois democracy" breaks down, capitalists accept the need to resort to authoritarian control. Societal breakdown stems from undue reliance on force and violence. The recent revolutionary changes in Iran and Guatemala are contemporary historical examples of this phenomenon. "One way to understand history, is to trace the rise, the maintenance, change in, and toppling of legal systems with their annexed instruments of violence" [55, p. xv]. The status, the tendency, of the rule of law under capitalism is perhaps the most strategic factor in judging the question of a shift from liberal to nonliberal capitalism.

The major points presented here have been spelled out elsewhere [23]. They are that the social roots of acceptance of the liberal rule of law in the United States are relatively shallow, and that the private corporation's response to public restraints (regulation) in the past century has taken on the dimension of "civil disobedience," or recourse to a higher law. Bases for the first proposition lie in two major grounds of hyperindividualism: these are habits and behavior best characterized as "frontier anarchy," and transformation of Adam Smith's invisible hand into the rationalization of self-interest as the sufficient means for improved social welfare under capitalism.

The major manifestation of the higher law of private property has been systematic avoidance, evasion, and outright disobedience of government regulations of private market actions, which necessarily involve restraints on use of private property. A Joint Economic Committee study has estimated that such crime and related "antisocial" behavior amounted to about $44 billion in 1976 (consumer fraud, illegal competition, and deceptive practices by business, $27 billion; loss from embezzlement and pilferage, $8.7 billion; and loss from bribery, kick-backs, and payoffs, $3.8 billion). It well may be that getting caught remains the greatest crime. With *nolo contendere* pleas, virtually no imprisonment, and minimal fines so prevalent, Secretary of Labor Ray Marshall has observed: "Employers have found it cheaper to disobey the law than to obey it, because the penalties are so weak." The result is a dual system of justice with special privileges for the rich and influential which erodes respect and compliance by others.

Breakdown of the liberal rule of law is a necessary and probably sufficient condition for the evolution of neofascism. The possibility of such a breakdown becomes credible when we recollect relevant historical episodes; for example, in response to "threats" to private property or "national security," corporations repressed worker organizations and executed "anarchists" following the Haymarket Massacre. More recently, and of most significance for the present context, were the examples of internment of Japanese citizens during World War II and of opponents of the Viet Nam "police action" in the 1960s [23, pp. 594–96].

The Drift Toward "Friendly Fascism"

In 1961, William Ebenstein concluded his discussion of fascism with this question: "Is fascism still a threat in the leading democratic nations?" His answer was that it continued to be a "serious menace," fed by continued anti-intellectualism, racism, and the "unnatural" alliance of democrats and fascists against their common fear, communism [15, pp. 119–21]. Given the recent drift toward "friendly democratic" fascism, it seems thinkable that a *de facto* authoritarian politics may evolve in the Western democracies, with continuing high material payoffs for the bulk of the population and minimal overt repression. Such a development would be "unfriendly" only for those—likely a small minority—who actively oppose the system. Radical dissent can be contained with numerically minimal (yet individually harsh) carefully rationed persecution,[19] and poverty or urban ghettos become, in effect, nonproblems as long as they involve a politically impotent minority.

When *It Can't Happen Here* appeared in 1935, the proto-fascist microcosm described by Sinclair Lewis was in actual operation under Governor

Huey Long of Louisiana. The phrase "it is happening here" has recurred since World War II, stimulated by recognized parallels to propositions or episodes in works such as Aldous Huxley's *Brave New World* and George Orwell's *1984*. Of particular note are developments in electronics, with their potential for invasion of privacy, and the rapid shift in political alliances. Thus, reflecting an Orwellian scenario [43, p. 137], in 1946–1947 our German and Japanese enemies become our allies, bastions of the new "free world."

In 1972, David Goodman judged that of 137 specific predictions found in *1984*, 80 had been realized; five years later, it appeared that over 100 had come true [22].[20] More relevant to the prospect for oligarchic capitalism, Stahrl Edmunds has sketched "Six Scenarios for the Future of the United States" [16]. Of two based on direct extrapolation of recent economic, social, and political trends, he finds that "The Sovietization of American Capitalism" seems much more likely than "The Industrial Democracy Model." The remaining four scenarios are those that could occur with appropriate new policies. Of these, the two with oligarchic overtones, "The Roman Replay" and "The Medieval Replay," seem most likely. The historical liberal scenario, "The Greek Replay," is ruled out on the ground that "in most respects Americans are very unlike the Greeks, since they were highly individualistic and Americans are highly institutionalistic" [16, p. 9].[21] Edmunds sees some possibility for his sixth scenario, an "Original American Replay," which would involve rebirth of small-scale capitalism.

Facts versus Illusion in
Understanding and Social Control

While rational decisions must be based on facts, on reality, effective organizations depend on successful management of strategic myths. The operating myths are maintained by various forms of information that may be called education or indoctrination. A system on the wane loses contact with its myths, comes to believe its own propaganda. A useful operational concept here is the willful suspension of disbelief. Our political myth is democracy; our economic myths are individualism and free enterprise. People know they do not literally exist, yet they serve and have served as vital norms and goals. We suspend our disbelief as a basis for their attainment. If these myths become transformed into belief, nirvana has been achieved—and social stagnation and retrogression set in [21, p. 102].

Insofar as such beliefs are illusions, they become elements of non-rational thought, symptoms of and vehicles for drift toward friendly fascism. The problem is not that people find these myths useful; rather, our leaders—those who generate and control information—have come to believe them. Belief in the truth of one's own propaganda is a characteristic of despotism and the path to rule based on "unreason," on *de facto* madness.[22] Evaluation of contemporary relevance of the issue of unreason would require assessment of programs in terms of a pervasive and socially oriented benefit-cost analysis.

Perhaps the single common ingredient in Western fascist developments has been the existence of a frightened, alienated middle class [13, pp. 91–92]. Within capitalism the petite bourgeoisie are readily disposed to "an odd theory of conspiracy . . . [that] the very top and very bottom of society are in collusion to destroy those in the middle" [50, p. 277–78]. In this light, the growing economic and related social pressures on the U.S. middle class in the 1970s and 1980s—inflation and taxes that impinge most heavily on middle incomes[23]—will tend to compound other neofascist tendencies and passive, perhaps unconscious, acceptance of *de facto* oligarchy.

Notes

1. There is a direct relationship between anticommunism (and socialism) and empathy for fascism. This association is one of the major threads in historical fascism of the 1920s and 1930s and of fascist tendencies since then. Formal overt statements of this position are found in the works of such fascist writers as Oswald Mosley, where fascism is accepted as the only alternative to communism, as the necessary stage or step to a society that will "reach beyond both Fascism and Democracy" [39, p. 80].

   Thus, a major operational aspect of international politics since 1946 has been U.S. opposition to moderate "socialistic" governments and support of capitalist regimes, despite their "authoritarian" politics.

2. Marc Tool has presented a strong clear-cut statement of this position: "We attempt to dispel interest in the query of whether or not we are headed 'down the road' to one or another ism" [56, p. 19]. The opposite position taken here is illustrated by Daniel R. Fusfeld's statement that "the object of inquiry [is to concentrate] on how a particular type of economy such as modern industrial capitalism changes over the course of time. . . . for example, the transition from feudalism to capitalism or capitalism to socialism" [19, p. 743].

3. In broadest terms, the historical viability of social systems can be judged only after the fact, that is, by applying some "golden age" [21, pp. 29–32, 182–83] perspective. The society's success in response to a particular problem-set then can be seen to have peaked and then diminished, for example, capitalism's response to the problem of scarcity.

4. Also see Joan Robinson's discussion of the interrelationships between metaphysical and scientific propositions. Thus, both extremes of a polar

opposite relationship are "a *point* ... which has position but no magnitude" [47, p. 2]. Such metaphysical elements are important (even though not scientific). They "provide a quarry from which hypotheses can be drawn. . . . Without them we would not know what it is we want to know" [47, p. 3]. A key element in Tool's anti-isms approach is his specification of "ism-ideologies" (that is, capitalism, socialism, communism, and fascism as economic systems). These ism-ideology institutional sets are relegated to the analytically irrelevant status of "pure" systems. Actually, all systems are mixed, as Tool indicates in stating that fascism "appears to offer something of a mixed economy" [56, p. 69].

5. The terms *authoritarian* and *totalitarian* have been used almost interchangeably in discussions of fascism since the 1930s. *Totalitarian* was introduced to emphasize certain new, perhaps unique, aspects of the dictatorial police states that evolved in Italy, Germany, and the Soviet Union during that period. It was argued that this new authoritarianism differed from the earlier versions (such as monarchy) in both its desire and capability for control over all aspects of its subjects' lives, "from the cradle to the grave" [13, pp. 60–76; 19, pp. 213–37]. James Burnham observed in "Totalitarianism and Managerical Society": It is "necessary to separate from the problem of totalitarianism the question of *what kind of society* is being totalitarianized: for whose benefit and against whom . . . . When we hear, merely, that Russia or Germany is 'totalitarian,' there is not much that we have learned about them" [11, p. 153].

6. Fascist variants have been found in a wide range of national settings, in addition to the etymologically proper Italian base. In recent decades, the term has been used as a synonym for almost any intensive, exclusionary, or in some sense exploitative activity.

7. The major interpretations of the fascist phenomenon have been summarized by Renzo De Felice: (1) the classic interpretations (fascism as Europe's moral disease, a result of historical development of certain countries, a product of capitalist society, and an antiproletarian reaction); (2) other interpretations, 1930s–1960s (Catholic, totalitarian phenomenon, metaphysical phenomenon); and (3) interpretations by social scientists (psychological, sociological, socioeconomic) [13, p. xv]. James A. Gregor has presented a more detailed treatment of the third category in his "survey of social science attempts to 'explain' the fascist phenomenon [attempts which leave us still] without a compelling account of the entire complex sequence" [24, p. iii].

8. See, for example, Alan S. Milward, "Fascism and the Economy" [37]. Included are the works of W. G. Welk, M. Clemenz, J. Kucyznski, and R. Kühnl. De Felice observes that "no comprehensive scientific study of the Fascist phenomenon has been made from this perspective to date" [13, p. 39].

9. For the United States, it will incorporate national patriotism: "Huey Long, who as Governor of Louisiana in the early 1930s set up the nearest thing to a fascist dictatorship in the United States, once jokingly said that if fascism ever came to the United States it would be under the slogan of 100 percent Americanism" [15, p. 120]. It is on such grounds that the terms *friendly fascism* [26] and (an ultimate contradiction in terms)

democratic fascism [18] and *authoritarian democracy* have appeared in the 1970s.

10. Major points apply in general to other industrial capitalist states. Particularly important are parallels with Great Britian, the "cradle of liberty." The argument of R. E. Pahl and J. T. Winkler is based upon trends in Great Britain, where they see the emergence not of socialism but of "a form of state control with private ownership," a corporatism that "is fascism with a human face" [45, pp. 28, 30].

11. The function and status of the pluralist argument since World War II is a key element in analysis of contemporary power relationships. In reviewing Charles Lindblom [32], Robert Lekachman judged that, "among other achievements, Lindblom has laid to rest the myths of pluralism [and has] propounded a most convincing explanation of the reasons why the desires of large corporations on issues of importance prevail over consumer, labor union and government opposition" (*New Republic*, 17 December 1977, pp. 32–34). Also see Gramm [23, p. 596] for a critical comment on the pluralist position and Joseph Bower [9, p. 183] for its continued support.

12. "For the full sample of 212 [four-digit SIC manufacturing] industries, concentration rose by 0.83 percentage points between 1963 and 1972. This embraces, however, a more substantial increase in consumer goods concentration . . . accompanied by virtual stability in producer goods (and a noticeable *decline* in producer durables)" [2, p. 291]. "Although it is not possible to equate concentration directly with oligopoly, the fact that increases in concentration have outnumbered decreases is still not without significance" [6, p. 24].

13. The most tangible manifestation of the symbiotic working relationship between government and business is in the military-industrial (and related) complexes. A covering term, and one that makes direct contact with "corporatism," is the "contract state," analyzed by H. L. Neiburg. With respect to military production he observes: The "prime contractors are becoming brokers of the managerial elites that control American industry, their power limited only by self-restraint and political necessity" [41, p. 191].

14. Historically, these "family units" have been the key organizations of Japanese monopoly capitalism. Brady observed in 1943 that "generically the term *Zaibatsu* means 'money cliques,' and 'of these, four are outstanding—namely, Mitsui, Mitsubishi, Sumitomo, and Yasuda.' More loosely the term is applied to large-scale business combination in general" [10, p. 89]. "Thus, business enterprise in Japan has, from the earliest days, unfolded its activities in an atmosphere . . . coherent with what we in the Western world have come more recently to identify as *Fascism*" [10, pp. 84, 86].

15. In December 1977, it was observed that "the Carter administration is on trial before a jury of steel companies, their workers and the 177 members of a newly formed congressional steel caucus" (*Los Angeles Times*, 18 December 1977). In early January 1978, a new "trigger" price was established to protect steel produced in the United States from lower priced foreign steel, particularly Japanese. This protective action was justified on the ground that a significant amount of imported steel was being

"dumped." Japanese steel is low cost because of greater productive efficiency and favorable financial advantage based on special relationships with Japanese banks and the government.

16. In 1974 the Supreme Court reversed its position that had prohibited private corporations from engaging in funding direct political action, on the ground that this would allow an equitable balance with labor union PAC activity.

17. The fascist philosophical base of nonrationalism—association of behavior with emotion and nonreason—is the opposite of the rational humanism of socialism and Marxism. This perspective is directly opposed to the position represented by James Gregor, who has characterized any attempted contrast between fascism and socialism as "transparently silly" [25, p. x].

    Ultra-rationalism is a counterpart of monopoly capitalism. Rationalist domination of capitalist society is seen by Jurgen Habermas as a natural extension of capitalism as a growth engine. In Tom Burns's words, "as such, [modern capitalism] is a mechanism that ensures the continuous expansion of rationality in all forms of social activity [and] the expansion of rationality can only take place at the expense of institutions grounded in tradition" [12, p. 134]. This position may be regarded as an extension of Polanyi's seminal argument concerning market (capitalist) domination of society. "Nineteenth century civilization alone was economic in a . . . distinctive sense, for it chose to base itself on a motive only rarely acknowledged as valid in the history of economic societies . . . namely, gain" [46, pp. 29–30].

18. This duality is embodied in the physiology of the brain: The left cerebral hemisphere is the center of logic and "linearity," the right hemisphere is the locus of "holism and . . . cyclical thought," of imagery and intuition—the one leads to rational and the other to nonrational "metaphorical" thought [48, pp. 41–44]. Only in the past two centuries, and only in the industrial capitalist West, has the former become dominant. See, for example [21, pp. 87, 118].

19. Here the "Good German" and "Nuremberg" syndromes become operative. The viability of Hitler's regime depended on the passive acquiesence of the German population. The fact that most Germans initially disapproved of the dispossession and persecution of the Jews became irrelevant as they "looked the other way." In the "active mode," civilized behavior requires that action be constrained by principle, as opposed to blind obedience to orders. The generality of the phenomenon is seen in Jose Ortega y Gasset's characterization of centuries of Spanish behavior: Their "degradation is nothing less than the acceptance, as a normal, constituted condition, of an irregularity, of something, which though accepted, is still regarded as not right . . . [thereby] making [themselves] a part of the crime or irregularity" [21, p. 140].

20. In April 1979 the *Futurist* (vol. 13, no. 2, pp. 110–17) published four responses to Goodman's article, two in favor (Ralph Hamil and Joseph Maloney) and two against (Burnham Beckwith and Frederik Pohl).

21. The "incentive individualism" (for example, as expressed in Adam Smith's support of economic self-interest) of earlier capitalism has been supplanted in large degree by "commercial individualism." Thus, a major

side effect in mass production–mass consumption commercial capitalism
has been transmutation of a Calvinistic individualism, oriented toward
work, into a narcissistic, sybaritic preoccupation with one's own satisfac-
tions and pleasure. It is manifested in the behavioral appeals of advertising, on the one hand, and the decline of public concern or social conscience, on the other hand. See [50] and "The Self-Satisfied Age," chapter
11 in [21, pp. 97–106].

22. Irrationality or madness necessarily applies, literally, only to individuals.
     However, in the context of psychohistory it is useful to extend the relation-
     ships to social entities, to nations: "The menace of madness in a nation is
     a greater threat than the menace of a deranged man achieving power. It is
     high time that the essential insanity of much of our [military and eco-
     nomic] policy be recognized" [31, p. 18]. See, for example [34, p. 144].

23. "A state of perennial inflationary pressure will have, qualitatively, all the
     effects of weakening the social framework of society . . . that every com-
     petent economist is in the habit of attributing to more spectacular infla-
     tions" [49, p. 422]. This statement is from Joseph Schumpeter's 1949
     paper, "The March into Socialism," delivered to the American Economic
     Association (he made it clear that he was neither predicting nor advocat-
     ing socialism).

References

[1] Arrow, Kenneth J. "Capitalism, for Better or Worse." In *Capitalism, the Moving Target*, edited by Leonard Silk. New York: Praeger, 1974. Pp. 105–13.

[2] Asch, Peter. "The Role of Advertising in Changing Concentration, 1963–1971." *Southern Economic Journal* 46 (July 1979): 288–97.

[3] Baran, Paul A., and Paul M. Sweezy. *Monopoly Capital*. New York: Monthly Review Press, 1966.

[4] Baratz, Morton S. *The American Business System in Transition*. New York: Thomas Y. Crowell, 1970.

[5] Basch, Ernst. *The Fascist: His State and His Mind*. New York: E. B. Ashton, 1937.

[6] Blair, John. *Economic Concentration*. New York: Harcourt Brace Jovanovich, 1972.

[7] Bosquet, Michel. *Capitalism in Crisis and Everyday Life*. Sussex, Eng.: Harvester Press, 1977.

[8] Boulding, Kenneth E. "The Legitimacy of Economics." *Western Economic Journal* 5 (September 1967): 299–307.

[9] Bower, Joseph L. "On the Amoral Organization." In *The Corporate Society*, edited by Robin Marris. New York: John Wiley & Sons, 1974. Pp. 178–213.

[10] Brady, Robert A. *Business as a System of Power*. New York: Columbia University Press, 1943.

[11] Burnham, James. *The Managerial Revolution*. New York: John Day, 1941.

[12] Burns, Tom. "On the Rationale of the Corporate System." In *The Cor-*

porate Society, edited by Robin Marris. New York: John Wiley & Sons, 1974. Pp. 121–77.

[13] De Felice, Renzo. *Interpretations of Fascism*. Cambridge, Mass.: Harvard University Press, 1977.

[14] Dewey, Donald J. "The New Learning: One Man's View." In *Industrial Concentration: The New Learning*, edited by Harvey J. Goldschmidt, H. Michael Mann, and J. Fred Weston. Boston: Little, Brown, 1974. Pp. 1–14.

[15] Ebenstein, William. *Today's Isms*. 3d ed. New York: Prentice-Hall, 1961.

[16] Edmunds, Stahrl. "Which Way America?" *Futurist* 13 (February 1979): 5–12.

[17] Friedman, Milton. *Capitalism and Freedom*. Chicago: University of Chicago Press, 1962.

[18] Fusfeld, Daniel R. "Fascist Democracy in the United States." *Conference Papers* (of the Union for Radical Political Economics). Ann Arbor, Mi.: December 1968. Pp. 3–35.

[19] Fusfeld, Daniel R. "The Development of Economic Institutions." *Journal of Economic Issues* 11 (December 1977): 743–84.

[20] Gappert, Gary. *Post-Affluent America, the Social Economy of the Future*. New York: Franklin Watts, 1979.

[21] Gasset, Jose Ortega y. *The Revolt of the Masses*. New York: W. W. Norton, 1932.

[22] Goodman, David. "Countdown to 1984: Big Brother May Be Right on Schedule." *Futurist* 12 (December 1978): 345–55.

[23] Gramm, Warren S. "Industrial Capitalism and the Breakdown of the Liberal Rule of Law." *Journal of Economic Issues* 7 (December 1973): 588–603.

[24] Gregor, James A. *Interpretations of Fascism*. Morristown, N.J.: General Learning Press, 1974.

[25] Gregor, James A. *The Fascist Persuasion in Radical Politics*. Princeton, N.J.: Princeton University Press, 1974.

[26] Gross, Bertram M. "Friendly Fascism, A Model for America." *Social Policy* 1 (November-December 1970): 44–52.

[27] Heilbroner, Robert L. "Reflections: Inflationary Capitalism." *New Yorker*, 8 October 1979, pp. 121–41.

[28] Herman, Edward S. "Kotz on Banker Control." *Monthly Review* 31 (September 1979): 46–57.

[29] Kotz, David M. *Bank Control of Large Corporations in the United States*. Berkeley: University of California Press, 1978.

[30] Laquer, Walter, ed. *Fascism A Reader's Guide*. Berkeley: University of California Press, 1976.

[31] Lee, Russel V. *The Menace of Madness in High Places*. Corte Madera, Calif.: Omega Books, 1977

[32] Lindblom, Charles L. *Politics and Markets: The World's Political Economic Systems*. New York: Basic Books, 1977.

[33] Lipset, Seymour Martin, and Earl Raab. *The Politics of Unreason, Right-Wing Extremism in America, 1790–1970*. New York: Harper & Row, 1970.

[34] McNamara, Robert S. *The Essence of Security.* New York: Harper & Row, 1968.

[35] Mason, Edward S., ed. *The Corporation in Modern Society.* Cambridge, Mass.: Harvard University Press, 1959.

[36] Mills, C. Wright. *The Power Elite.* New York: Oxford University Press, 1959.

[37] Milward, Alan S. "Fascism and the Economy." In [30]. Pp. 379–412.

[38] Molnar, Thomas. "Political & Literary Fascism: A Conservative Perspective." *Intercollegiate Review* 15 (Fall 1979): 3–17.

[39] Mosley, Sir Oswald E. *The Alternative.* Ramsbury, Wilts.: Mosley Publications, 1947.

[40] Nader, Ralph; Mark Green; and Joel Seligman. *Taming the Giant Corporation.* New York: W. W. Norton, 1976.

[41] Nieburg, H. L. *In the Name of Science.* Chicago: Quadrangle Books, 1966.

[42] Nowotny, Kenneth. "Private Property: With or Without Power." *Journal of Economic Issues* 13 (June 1979): 498–503.

[43] Orwell, George. *1984.* New York: Harcourt, Brace, 1949.

[44] Owen, Bruce M. *Economics and Freedom of Expression, Media Structures and the First Amendment.* Cambridge, Mass.: Ballinger, 1975.

[45] Pahl, R. E., and J. T. Winkler. "The Coming Corporatism." *Challenge* 18 (March-April 1975): 28–35.

[46] Polanyi, Karl. *The Great Transformation.* Boston: Beacon Press, 1944.

[47] Robinson, Joan. *Economic Philosophy.* Chicago, Ill.: Aldine, 1962.

[48] Samples, Bob. *The Metaphoric Mind.* Reading, Mass.: Addison-Wesley, 1976.

[49] Schumpeter, Joseph A. *Capitalism, Socialism and Democracy.* 3d ed. New York: Harper & Row, 1950.

[50] Sennett, Richard. *The Fall of Public Man.* New York: Alfred A. Knopf, 1974.

[51] Sethi, S. Prakash, ed. *Up Against the Corporate Wall: Modern Corporations and Social Issues of the Seventies.* 2d ed. Englewood Cliffs, N.J.: Prentice-Hall, 1974.

[52] Silberman, Charles E. *Criminal Violence, Criminal Justice.* New York: Random House, 1978.

[53] Silk, Leonard, and David Vogel. *Ethics and Profits: The Crisis of Confidence in American Business.* New York: Simon and Schuster, 1976.

[54] Smith, Adam. *The Wealth of Nations.* New York: Modern Library, 1937.

[55] Tigar, Michael E., and Madeleine R. Levy. *Law and the Rise of Capitalism.* New York: Monthly Review Press, 1977.

[56] Tool, Marc R. *The Discretionary Economy.* Santa Monica, Calif.: Goodyear, 1979.

[57] Veblen, Thorstein. "Christian Morals and the Competitive System." In *The Portable Veblen,* edited by Max Lerner. New York: Viking, 1948. Pp. 480–98.

[58] Vogel, David. *Lobbying the Corporation: Citizen Challenges to Business Authority.* New York: Basic Books, 1978.

19

Democratic Economic Planning and Worker Ownership

William M. Dugger

Contemporary progressives in the United States call for democratic economic planning and for worker ownership/participation as alternatives to retrenchment and Reaganomics.[1] Institutionalism has long been a reform-oriented school of thought, and institutionalists have long been noted for their progressive and pragmatic approach to social problems. In spite of the difficulty encountered in formally studying institutionalism in U.S. universities, this proud tradition attracts a number of new institutionalists every year. Nevertheless, institutionalism is often viewed with some suspicion by progressive reformers who fear it as a new form of "corporatism."[2]

Corporatism is a fundamentally elitist approach to the social problems of industrial civilization that relies very heavily on trained experts to supply technical fixes to social problems and then relies on the existing, centralized corporate power structure to implement the technical fixes. Corporatism strengthens the inequality of the status quo by softening it, and by touching up a few of its racist and sexist features, while keeping the vested interests firmly vested. Corporatism is capitalism with a human face, planned by a centralized structure of corporate power. Corporatism is not what institutionalists have in mind when we call for economic planning, so it is very important to differentiate institutionalism from corporatism, lest institutionalism lose its standing as a progressive school of thought. Since economic planning and worker ownership/participation are central issues in contemporary progressivism, exploring economic planning and worker ownership/participation from an institutionalist perspective will help clarify the relation of institutionalism to progressive thought in general.

Planning and Institutionalism

Institutionalists reject ism-ideologies and shy away from utopian thinking. Although socialism is not necessarily ideologically rigid, nor is it unrealistically utopian, most institutionalists are not advocates of socialism. But since institutionalists lack the orthodox economist's faith in the market, support for economic planning is inherent to institutional economics. Being fully aware of the overwhelming role played by power in the shaping of the "market mechanism," institutionalists look with jaundiced eye at competitive models and at the so-called "laws" of supply and demand. Warren J. Samuels, former editor of this journal, collected a whole set of institutionalist articles on the role of power in the modern economy.[3] Furthermore, being philosophically anchored by instrumentalism, institutionalist thought realistically turns away from assumed market automaticity to some form of conscious democratic planning as the principal form of social control in the industrialized economy. Allan G. Gruchy, the chronicler of the last fifty years of institutionalist thought, has emphasized repeatedly the planning implications of institutionalism.[4] And Kendall P. Cochran, a founding member of the Association for Institutional Thought, stated the institutionalist position very clearly over thirty years ago: "Thus, with the economic system conceived as a social or human phenomenon rather than a congeries of natural laws and natural forces which are not to be tampered with, the institutionalist denies what is perhaps the most important tenet of orthodox theory—the efficacy of the market mechanism as the organizing force in the modern industrial economy."[5]

Following the lead of C.E. Ayres, institutionalists can see that the U.S. economy is not really an automatic market system. So institutionalists know that the "natural" laws of the market will not automatically clothe, feed, educate, and cure us. The automatic operation of benign natural laws has not been the characterizing feature of the exchange arena. Instead of a market system, the U.S. economy is an industrial system.[6] And, if society does not plan for the continuing reform and revitalization of its industrial system, no natural laws will come to its rescue. The natural laws of the market do not provision society in the first place. The industrial system does. Furthermore, the industrial system is not a natural growth. It is not automatic. The industrial system is a product of collective action and inaction. The exchange arena—the "market"—reflects the results of the underlying power plays and technological changes that drive the industrial economy. The parameters within which exchange takes place are set by forces outside the exchange arena. At the close of the twentieth century, the U.S. industrial system is falling far below its potential, and despite the deregulation and supply-side nostrums of the market advocates, no automatic market rejuvenation is in sight.[7] The "market" is not causal. The "market" merely facilitates exchange. The exchange arena does not cause major change; it reflects major change.

Institutionalists have come to realize that the "market" is not the most powerful institution in the economy. A number of realistic studies have concluded that the mature corporation is often more powerful than the "market." The mature corporation often administers the markets it serves. Markets do not so much guide such corporations as such corporations guide markets. As explained by John R. Munkirs, corporate power has coalesced into centralized private sector planning.[8] As explained by John M. Blair, in good times or in bad, the giant corporation, not the market, sets most prices.[9] Through successive waves of horizontal integration, vertical integration, and now conglomorate integration, the mature corporation has become so large and so powerful that it has outgrown the bounds of the nation state. As explained by Richard J. Barnett and Ronald E. Muller, the large corporation is now more powerful than many of the smaller nation states.[10] As explained by Charles E. Lindblom, the giant corporation can insist that government meet its demands in most cases, even when its demands run counter to social needs.[11] Paying close attention to all these realistic explanations, institutionalists generally conclude that the U.S. industrial economy is planned by powerful corporations. It is not the result of automatic market forces. And with the corporate planned economy in the United States performing very poorly, institutionalists also have come to realize that a new form of planning is needed to boost industrial performance.[12]

In particular, the planned scarcity and inequality of corporate power must be replaced by a process of democratic economic planning. Since neither corporate power nor market automaticity will generate industrial abundance and social progress, this replacement is an institutional imperative.[13] Progressives everywhere call for something better, for something more democratic. Charles Lindblom is representative when he states, "The large private corporation fits oddly into democratic theory and vision. Indeed, it does not fit."[14] Most progressives in the United States have long called for some kind of worker ownership/participation and for some kind of democratic planning, both of which are seen as processes for enlarging the individual's active role in making decisions and in evaluating outcomes with respect to all matters that affect the individual's life prospects.[15] A century ago, the Knights of Labor strongly supported worker-owned and worker-managed enterprises. The idea fell out of favor in most labor circles, however, with the decline of the Knights. But then, a quarter of a century ago, even before the passion and repression of the Vietnam War, the Students for a Democratic Society, in their famous Port Huron Statement, exclaimed: "We see little reason why men cannot meet with increasing skill the complexities and responsibilities of their situation, if society is organized not for minority participation but for majority participation in decision-making."[16]

Tom Hayden, an early leader of the Students for a Democratic Society, has spent the last quarter of a century as a social activist in the United States. In his recent book, *The American Future,* he continues to call for democratizing both the giant corporation and the economy the corporation has molded to serve its own interests.[17]

Worker Ownership and Institutionalism

Support for the process of democratic economic planning has become a major characteristic of institutionalism. But institutionalists, in their strong distaste for ism-ideologies and their disavowal of all panaceas, are mixed about worker ownership. Nevertheless, Peter Lichtenstein and others have held well-attended and lively sessions on worker ownership and participation at the Association for Institutional Thought's annual meetings, almost since its inception. Thorstein Veblen, as evidenced by his support of the Industrial Workers of the World and by his ruminations about the likelihood of a soviet of engineers coming together in the United States, supported worker control of industry, if not worker ownership. However, his call for a disavowal of *absentee* ownership is not quite the same as a call for *worker* ownership.[18] Furthermore, Veblen was strongly influenced by Edward Bellamy, who was not an advocate of decentralized worker ownership of individual workplaces. Bellamy leaned toward the centralized control of the industrial economy by a trained elite. Veblen was a close student of Bellamy, with considerable sympathy for Bellamy's cooperative commonwealth.[19] Nevertheless, Veblen was a supporter of the workers' soviets in revolutionary Russia, and they were at least a form of worker ownership. Furthermore, Veblen was almost certainly an admirer of Peter Kropotkin, the anarchist Prince, for the two of them had quite similar views of biological and social evolution.[20] So maybe Veblen supported worker ownership. He certainly supported worker participation.

As far as I can tell, Clarence Ayres neither supported nor opposed worker ownership. Apparently, he was silent on the subject. Ayres, however, did retreat from Veblen's firebrand radicalism, which leads me to believe that Ayres would not have been much of a supporter of worker ownership. Further, to the best of my knowledge, none of Ayres's numerous students have been active in any of the worker ownership/ participation movements. The *Journal of Economic Issues,* the journal for institutional economics, has contained very few articles on worker ownership. The June 1976 issue, made up of papers presented at the 1975 meetings arranged by then-President of the Association for Evolutionary Economics, Seymour Melman, did contain several such articles. All of them concluded that increased worker participation in decision making and democratization of the workplace resulted in significant improvements in performance. However, in that very issue, Paul Bernstein stated, "Analysis of empirical cases indicates that transfer of ownership to workers is not absolutely necessary for significant democratization to occur in some firms. There are also firms which are entirely worker owned yet lack any degree of democratization (for example, the Chicago-Northwestern Railroad; Kansas City *Star;* Milwaukee *Journal*). Such findings force one to question the common assumption that to increase workers' power one must first abolish private ownership."[21]

In his typically institutionalist resistance to the clarion call to abolish private ownership of the means of production, Bernstein was following the long institutionalist tradition of disavowing any ism-ideology. Nevertheless, institutionalists are not opposed to worker ownership; such opposition would cut deeply against our experimental and egalitarian grain. Furthermore, opposing new ways of organizing production would violate the spirit of institutional thought's two major dichotomies: the J. Fagg Foster and the Thorstein Veblen dichotomies. The Fosterian dichotomy states that structure is replacemental, while function is developmental.[22] So particular structures of production can easily be replaced in order to improve the function of production. To be specific, corporate structures of hierarchical control can be replaced with structures of worker control, because any structure designed to exercise social control over the industrial system is a social tool, and better tools should be used to replace outmoded ones. The existing structures of production are merely means for provisioning society. They are not ultimate ends, but tools for pursuing ends in view. When their functioning deteriorates, institutionalists would urge their replacement with better tools. Structures of worker ownership and worker participation may be such better tools. They may provision society better than existing corporate structures. And, of course, institutionalists would expect those with a vested interest in the existing structure of corporate control to resist the use of new structures of worker control. Such resistance is inherent in the cultural lags that occur during periods of institutional adjustment. Vested interests cannot be expected to give up their usufruct gladly.

Supporting extant corporate structures against the advocates of worker ownership/participation would also violate the spirit of the Veblenian dichotomy of industrial versus pecuniary. Industrial activities and proclivities, Veblen argued, aimed at social serviceability. Pecuniary activities and proclivities aimed at getting something for nothing. The industrial bent is acquired by those who work closely with the machine process; while the pecuniary bent is acquired by those who work closely with property ownership. So, according to Veblen, the industrial workers will acquire an industrial animus, a desire to be serviceable, a desire to keep the machines going, to keep the power flowing, the food growing. The property owners, on the other hand, will want something for nothing: higher prices for coal and oil, higher rents, more dividends. Veblen would have supported more industrial worker participation in decisions regarding the industrial process, particularly since he counted on them to have a more industrial animus than the absentee owners. But for the same reasons, he may have understood "worker ownership" to be an oxymoron. A Veblenian industrial worker does not "own" property. She produces goods. To Veblen, the two were very different.[23]

Contemporary institutionalists are not sold on worker ownership either. Our reticence is because of the way we understand the industrial economy as a complex, highly interrelated and interdependent system in dire need of overall coordination and planning. Separate worker ownership of the individual production facilities making up the interdependent and interrelated industrial system will not provide the needed overall coordination and planning. Some form of integration at a higher level is needed to insure that the activities of each worker group mesh with the activities of the other worker groups. And, unlike market socialists, institutionalists place little faith in the "market" as being able to provide the needed integration and coordination. So if worker ownership/participation at the micro level, so to speak, were combined with some kind of democratically integrating and coordinat-, ing process at a higher level, institutionalists might be more supportive.

What Kind of Planning?

Existing U.S. Planning

Institutionalist economics is the economics of planning and reform. But, lest it be confused with the economics of the vested interests, the nature of existing planning in the United States must be made very clear. From John Kenneth Galbraith through John R. Munkirs, contemporary institutionalists agree that corporate planning has replaced the market in a significant portion of the U.S. economy.[24] We also agree that corporate planning does not necessarily serve the public purpose. Here we part company with those who call themselves "new institutionalists." The self-styled "new institutionalists," particularly Oliver E. Williamson, argue that corporate power and corporate planning are in the public's best interests; and they argue that this is still the best of all possible worlds, even if corporate planning has replaced the market. For, according to the "new institutionalists," corporate mergers, managerial hierarchies, and joint ventures all further economic efficiency rather than economic power.[25] The self-styled "new institutionalists" are clearly old-styled corporatists.

But when serious institutionalists call for economic planning, they are not suggesting a reinforcement of the existing system of corporate planning. They are not supporting corporatism. Quite the contrary. We are calling for a replacement of the inequality, inefficiency, and irresponsibility of corporate planning with a democratic planning process that furthers equality, efficiency, and social responsibility. Such a process of democratic economic planning does not now take place in the United States. Instead, the central planning core of the U.S. economy, as Munkirs calls it, is a system of entrenched corporate power and privilege. Entrenched corporations plan for their own benefit, for their own profit at the expense of whoever bears the cost.[26] They do not plan for social efficiency. Their profits are not related to social efficiency, but to raw power. That is, they earn profits because they exercise power, profits because they can avoid the social responsibility of their actions. They can pay wages too low to support a reasonable level of life. They can treat labor as a variable cost of production. They can pollute the air, the water, and the soil with their effluent. They can even pollute the culture with their managerial propaganda.[27] And, most importantly, entrenched corporations can plan how to do all of these things. Helping them do so is not the objective of institutionalist planning. Instead, institutionalist planning is aimed at reinforcing the serviceable aspects of corporate performance. Institutionalist planning is aimed at strengthening the industrial over the pecuniary drives of corporate structures.

Significant amounts of the kind of planning institutionalism is all about already take place in the governmental sector. At all three levels of fragmented government in the United States, public officials try to overcome social problems through planning and reform. Examples of public planning at all three levels abound. At the local level, school officials, for example, try to deal with the educational problems of a modern, mobile population. But with several thousand different independent school districts, parochial schools, and private academies, plus thousands of public junior colleges, regular colleges, and universities, all of which go their own ways, education problems remain recalcitrant. At the state level, welfare officials try to address the problems of the 30 to 35 million people living below the poverty level. But with the inadequate staffing and funding inherent at the state level, progress is too slow. And then at the federal level, Environmental Protection Agency officials try to deal with the rising pollution problems of our socially irresponsible form of industrialism. But they are out-planned, out-lawyered, and out-expert-witnessed by the entrenched corporations at every turn. So, although governmental planning exists, it is largely a series of uncoordinated, knee-jerk responses to public problems.

Reforming Planning in the United States

Democratic government planning must go hand-in-hand with internal corporate reform. Without corporate reform, democratic planning will inevitably be coopted and turned to corporate account. This is the major fear raised in the minds of democratic and Marxian socialists when they hear about institutionalism with its planning and reform: Will the institutionalist planners be coopted by the corporate planners? Will institutionalist planning be turned to corporate account in a new form of corporatism? Will institutionalist planning be of the authoritarian, top-down variety?

Institutionalists have long argued that corporate planning for the private purpose must be redirected by governmental planning for the public purpose, and governmental planning itself must be strengthened and improved. However, institutionalists also must emphasize that planning initiatives in the United States run a very grave danger of further institutionalizing corporate power unless fundamental realignments in power relations are made in the political system and in the corporate system. What the needed democratization and reconstitution of government will entail must be the subject of other discourses. Suffice it for this article to say that a fundamental democratization and reconstitution of the political system is needed in the United States before public planning can be either effective or democratic. At the very least, a vibrant labor party must be constructed, and proportional voting instituted. We also must install democratic and participatory processes inside U.S. corporations to weaken the pecuniary and strenthen the industrial interests of corporate America. This is where worker ownership/participation may play a crucial role.

What Kind of Worker Role?

ESOPs, Coops, or Unbundling?

ESOPs (Employee Stock Ownership Plans) are not the way to establish worker ownership in the United States.[28] Such plans work out to be massive tax subsidies for the banks that finance them, not tentative steps toward economic democracy. Furthermore, ESOPs have been more a way for family-owned enterprises to finance lucrative buyout deals than a way for workers to acquire ownership and democracy in the workplace. ESOPs generally do not vest voting or managing power with the workers themselves. Instead, the workers' shares of stock are usually held in some kind of trust where the trustees vote the stock and where the trustees are usually chosen by or beholden to management rather than the workers. ESOPs are owner-initiated more than worker-initiated. Those that are worker-initiated are often the products of worker desperation. Workers often sacrifice their pension rights, their workplace rules, and their union-scale wages to establish an ESOP as a last-ditch attempt to save their jobs. Were ESOPs structured to give workers majority voting rights and to preserve their pensions, work rules, and wages, perhaps they could evolve into progressive institutions. But such is not the case with contemporary ESOPs in the United States.

ESOPs begin with a privately-owned firm. But the worker coop movement generally starts out with a totally new, worker-owned firm.[29]

The worker coop movement, therefore, offers much greater opportunity for establishing all worker ownership and worker management. A coop production facility is based on the initiative of the workers themselves, the power and influence of entrenched bankers, owners, and managerial elites is not there to distort the coop, at least not at first. Nevertheless, the coop movement in the United States has had a very difficult time of it. The coop movement has lacked adequate access to finance and to technical assistance throughout its existence. Institutionalists should support providing both to the still-struggling coop movement. Nevertheless, the coop movement is not going to penetrate into the heart of corporate power any time soon, no matter how well financed and technically financed it becomes. Something else is needed.

An unbundling of the property rights of private corporations might be more in keeping with the general thrust of institutionalism than a reliance on worker ownership through ESOPs and coops. By "unbundling" is meant a separation and reallocation of specific rights. Institutionalists have long been aware that developments along these lines have already taken place to some extent, at least, in the form of the separation of ownership from control in the mature corporation.[30] Furthermore, institutionalists recognize that property is not a natural right; it is not god-given; it is not an indivisible whole. Property is a bundle of diverse rights created and defended by collective action.[31] To democratize the heart of corporate America, we can unbundle those rights and reallocate them to workers and to the public, one at a time if necessary. Just like splitting the atom, property can be split too. The owners of corporations now have the right to elect a corporate board of directors. A part of that right can be split off and vested in the public. Public directors could form a majority on the boards of very large corporations or on the boards of utilities, defense contractors, and other similar corporations. Worker directors could also be placed on corporate boards in a U.S. adaptation of codetermination. Then owner or manager directors might be phased out entirely. The boards of corporations now have the right to select the top managers of that corporation. Their right to do so can be separated from their rights and given to someone else. Management has already done so in most large, mature corporations. That is, the right to select top managers has already been unbundled, by management itself. The right could easily be reallocated from the management to the workers themselves. The owners of a corporation have the right—and often the power to back up the right—to administer the prices charged by the corporation. During times of wage-price control programs, the public reallocates that right to its own representatives. That right could easily be kept permanently where it belongs—in the hands of democratic planners and industrial workers. The owners of a corporation have the right to open new plants and close existing ones. That right also could be unbundled and reallocated to the workers or to the democratic planners. The owners of a corporation have the right to acquire other corporations. That right could be rescinded. The owners of U.S. corporations have the right to invest in South Africa. That right could be unbundled or rescinded too. And so on, with every single right contained in the bundle of corporate property rights. Every single one of them can be unbundled and reallocated or rescinded entirely. Unbundling can penetrate into the very heart of corporate capitalism and reallocate rights to workers and to democratic planners in an orderly fashion. Unbundling is a better way of democratizing the corporate organizations that now dominate the industrial economies of the West. It is better than ESOPs because ESOPs are not democratic in the first place. It is better than coops because coops show little promise of being able to penetrate the industrial bastions of entrenched corporate power.

Conclusion

The enlargement of worker participation is a step toward greater economic democracy and toward more equality. As such, it passes the instrumentalist test of social value.[32] When examined in light of the Fosterian and Veblenian dichotomies, increased worker ownership/participation warrants institutionalist support. So support for worker participation is clearly in the institutionalist tradition. But, from the institutionalist point of view, worker ownership in the form of ESOPs or coops is not necessarily the best way to promote worker participation in the industrial economy. In the form of unbundling, increased worker participation would drive the democracy principle deep inside the heart of corporate power. It would insure that the democratic planning urged by institutional economists would remain democratic. By itself, worker participation will not provide for the smooth, coordinated working of our industrial system. For that, we also need a process of national, democratic economic planning.[33] Not even the most beautiful of worker coops will naturally coordinate their activities with the activities of other coops. Coordination requires national planning. But, at the same time, not even the most progressive of planning officials will naturally remain democratic. They must be kept on the straight and narrow by a powerful, grassroots economic democracy—by a continually larger role for workers in the decision making and evaluating processes of the industrial economy. The two must develop together. And, among the progressive movements working for reform in the United States, the institutionalist movement need take a back seat to none.

Notes

1. Three recent examples include Christopher Eaton Gunn, *Workers' Self-Management in the United States* (Ithaca: Cornell University Press, 1984); Martin Carnoy and Derek Shearer, *Economic Democracy* (Armonk, N.Y.: M.E. Sharpe, 1980); and Samuel Bowles, David M. Gordon, and Thomas E. Weisskopf, *Beyond the Waste Land* (Garden City, N.Y.: Anchor Press/Doubleday, 1983).
2. Two critical views are Donald Stabile, *Prophets of Order* (Boston: South End Press, 1984) and Bertram Gross, *Friendly Fascism* (Boston: South End Press, 1980). Neither address institutionalism by name, but Stabile criticizes Veblen and Veblenians while Gross criticizes many of the general reforms and institutional adjustments suggested by institutionalists. Both Gross and Stabile are critics of "corporatism."
3. For a collection of institutionalist essays on power, see *The Economy as a System of Power* ed. Warren J. Samuels (New Brunswick: Transaction Books, 1979).
4. See the following by Allan G. Grunchy, "The Concept of National Planning in Institutional Economics," *Southern Economic Journal* 6 (October 1939): 121–44; *Contemporary Economic Thought* (Clifton, N.J.: Augustus M. Kelley, 1972), pp. 287–339; and "Uncertainty, Indicative Planning, and Industrial Policy," in *An Institutionalist Guide to Economics and Public Policy*, ed. Marc R. Tool (New York: M.E. Sharpe, 1984), pp. 177–98.
5. Kendall P. Cochran, *The Concept of Economic Planning in Institutional Economics* (Ph.D. diss., Ohio State University, 1955), p. 15.
6. Further discussion of the industrial nature of the modern economy is in C. E. Ayres, *The Industrial Economy: Its Technological Basis and Institutional Destiny* (Boston: Houghton Mifflin, 1952). Further discussion of power in the evolution of the U.S. economy is in Douglas F. Dowd, *Twisted Dream;* 2d ed. (Cambridge: Winthrop, 1977).
7. Further discussion of the deterioration of the U.S. industrial economy is in Seymour Melman, *Profits Without Production* (New York: Alfred A. Knopf, 1983) and in William M. Dugger, *An Alternative to Economic Retrenchment* (Princeton: Petrocelli, 1984).
8. See John R. Munkirs, *The Transformation of American Capitalism* (Armonk, N.Y.: M.E. Sharpe, 1985).
9. See John M. Blair, "Market Power and Inflation: A Short-Run Target Return Model," *Journal of Economic Issues* 8 (June 1974): 453–78.
10. See Richard J. Barnet and Ronald E. Muller, *Global Reach* (New York: Simon and Schuster, 1974).
11. Charles E. Lindblom, *Politics and Markets* (New York: Basic Books, 1977).
12. See Walter Adams and James W. Brock, "Corporate Power and Economic Sabotage," *Journal of Economic Issues* 20 (December 1986): 919–40.
13. See J. Ron Stanfield, *Economic Thought and Social Change* (Carbondale: Southern Illinois University Press, 1979).

14. Lindblom, *Politics and Markets,* p. 356.
15. See the essays in *Alternatives,* ed. Irving Howe (New York: Pantheon, 1984).
16. Students for a Democratic Society, "Port Huron Statement," in *Individualism: Man in Modern Society,* ed. Ronald Gross and Paul Osterman (New York: Dell, 1971), pp. 233–40.
17. Tom Hayden, *The American Future* (Boston: South End Press, 1980).
18. See Thorstein Veblen, *The Engineers and the Price System* (New York: Augustus M. Kelley, [1921] 1965).
19. The best recent discussion of the Bellamy-Veblen connection is Rick Tilman, "The Utopian Vision of Edward Bellamy and Thornstein Veblen," *Journal of Economic Issues* 19 (December 1985): 879–98.
20. For a comparison of the evolutionary theories of Veblen and Kropotkin see William M. Dugger, "Veblen and Kropotkin on Human Evolution," *Journal of Economic Issues* 18 (December 1984): 971–85.
21. Paul Bernstein, "Necessary Elements for Effective Worker Participation in Decision Making," *Journal of Economic Issues* 10 (June 1976): 490–522.
22. Further discussion is in J. Fagg Foster, "The Effect of Technology on Institutions," *Journal of Economic Issues* 15 (December 1981): 907–13.
23. Thorstein Veblen, "Industrial and Pecuniary Employments," in *The Place of Science in Modern Civilization and Other Essays* (New York: B.W. Huebsch, 1919), pp. 279–323; and *Absentee Ownership and Business Enterprise in Recent Times* (New York: Augustus M. Kelley, [1923] 1964).
24. John Kenneth Galbraith, *Economics and the Public Purpose* (Boston: Houghton Mifflin, 1973) and John R. Munkirs, *The Transformation of American Capitalism* (Armonk, N.Y.: M. E. Sharpe, 1985).
25. For the latest in this line of ersatz institutionalism, see Oliver E. Williamson, *The Economic Institutions of Capitalism* (New York: Free Press, 1985).
26. K. William Kapp, *The Social Costs of Private Enterprise* (New York: Schocken Books, [1950] 1971).
27. William M. Dugger, "The Continued Evolution of Corporate Power," *Review of Social Economy* 43 (April 1985): 1–13.
28. The following draws heavily on discussions with Charles Craypo of Notre Dame University and on his seminar at Roosevelt University in March of 1986.
29. See Peter M. Lichtenstein, "The U.S. Experience with Worker Cooperation," *Social Science Journal* 23 (Spring 1986): 1–15; Joseph Edward Miltimore, *Why the American Movement for Worker Ownership and Management of Enterprises Failed* (Master's Thesis, DePaul University, 1985); and David P. Ellerman, "Theory of Legal Structure: Worker Cooperatives," *Journal of Economic Issues* 18 (September 1984): 861–91.
30. Adolf A. Berle and Gardiner C. Means, *The Modern Corporation and Private Property,* revised ed. (New York: Harcourt, Brace and World, 1968).
31. Much of my understanding of property rights comes from John R. Commons, *Legal Foundations of Capitalism* (Madison: University of Wisconsin Press, [1924] 1968).
32. See Tool, *Discretionary Economy,* pp. 292–314.
33. Further discussion is in Dugger, *Alternative to Retrenchment,* pp. 155–259.

PART III

THE INTERNATIONAL CORPORATE AND NATION-STATE SYSTEMS OF POWER

Introduction to Part III:
The International Corporate and
Nation-State Systems of Power

In this final section, the focus broadens to include considerations of economic and political power at the global level. In different ways, all of the chapters in this section acknowledge the fact, extent, and importance of international interdependence and of the interplay of economic and political power in that context. Demonstrated in particular is the relevance of the institutionalist approach to the analysis of this array of complex inter-relationships, issues, and problems. Where does and should discretion over the flow of real income lie? Through which institutions are economic and political power exercised? What roles do multinational corporations play? What ends are served? Whose interests matter? What mechanisms exist, if any, for the adjustment of structure (national and international) to enhance the flow of real income? These are the concerns addressed by chapters in this section. Although the individual chapters are quite comprehensive treatments of topics considered, in the aggregate they should be regarded as indicative and illustrative. No claims to definitive treatment of the questions posed above can be made.

The lead chapter by Karl de Schweinitz, Jr., addresses the theory and practice of economic imperialism. Whereas some writers in the nineteenth century (especially British) viewed imperialism favorably as an opportunity to extend national hegemony "to sparsely populated locations on the globe or as a system of governance well designed for performing the trustee responsibilities of a beneficent and improving culture for less fortunate non-European peoples," later writers rejected this "noble vision." As the behavior of Western imperialists was assessed, a pejorative meaning developed, the Western commitment to democracy and national rights evolved and was communicated abroad, and resistence to foreign rule increased in colonies.

According to de Schweinitz, "Imperialism relates to coercion and the restriction of freedom. It may be defined as a system in which A dominates, controls, or coerces B, preventing B from acting in its own interests or compelling it to act in the interests of A." After demonstrating that even in a closed economy in which markets organize exchange there is and must be coercion from laws that define the nature and extent of choice (recall papers by Seidman and Samuels in Part I), de Schweinitz sees international interrelationships as also coercive but much more complex. Here "A and B are collective entities differentiated from one another by various parameters, language, religion, ethnicity, cultural values, political organizations" and the like. Central is the contention that the differences in A and B sytematically generate inequality. Such inequality may be rooted in "wealth, military power, knowledge, organizational capacity, and ideology." The remainder of the chapter considers the importance of these differing sources of inequality by examining "the history of imperialism, largely, although not exclusively, [with regard to] the effect of Great Britain in India." In the course of this compelling historical canvass of the evolution of institutions of control, de Schweinitz considers, among other issues, land settlement constraints, access to reliable knowledge, intercultural transfer of institutions, imposition of law and order, creation of social overhead capital, and public administrative organization. He concludes by considering the extent to which, in the post World War II era, the imperial control devices that reflected economic and political coercion have been in fact abandoned. While the political imperial devices are formally gone, for a variety of reasons substantial economic inequality still exists between the metropolitan countries and the former colonial, now independent, countries.

The chapter by Walter C. Neale, also addresses aspects of the imperial relationships between metropolitan powers and their colonies. In particular, it is Neale's position that colonial institutions tend to evolve in complex and unanticipated interactions of metropolitan power and colony. Such institutions are not laid down as a template on the colony with full awareness of the consequences that will result. Consequences of action taken are simply not that predictable and there is "no single mind considering and then deciding how to act" in the metropolitan country; many persons, interests and groups contribute to policy making.

> The metropolitan countries, as the governing powers in the colonies, must bear moral responsibility for many institutions associated with modern colonial rule, but it would not be correct [to] say that the metropolitan countries *intended* from the start to impose these institutions upon the colonies, that they planned to make these institutions permanent features of colonial rule,

or that they anticipated the results of their actions. Rather, these institutions *emerged* in the processes of an unequal but nevertheless *mutual* adaptation of the metropolitan and the colonial cultures to each other."

The case study undergirding Neale's contention involves British Central Africa (now Zimbabwe, Zambia, and Malawi)—an area that was unusual in the "presence of a large immigrant European population and the starkly pervasive, racist, and dominant way in which they exercised power." In this unlikely setting, Neale argues that three "peculiarly colonial institutions"—native reserve areas (land allotted for native use), compounds (dormitory accomodations), and locations (townships for migrant native families)—were not aprioristically designed and imposed; they evolved or emerged. Neale describes how the British colonizers entered Central Africa believing the "land and movables were the property of someone; that any normal person would use his land, movables, and ability to work to achieve as high a material standard of living as he could; and that any normal person lacking a property income would be glad to work for wages." Efforts to make these assumptions the basis for control and economic exploitation of the natives failed. The emergence of the above named institutions resulted from an on-site revision of beliefs and behaviors and an adjustment to the realities confronted. So one should view "the development of colonial institutions as a series of adaptations, by groups with varying interests and perceptions, to problems that arose from the conflicts of cultures in contact."

The next chapter addresses another important area of international economic interdependence in which economic power is present and exercised. Ronald Müller presents a structural analysis of the United States economy, and of the global economy generally, that diagnoses "the *systemic* impacts arising out of contemporary worldwide conglomerate competition between global corporations" to be of such significance and magnitude that the development of "explicit public sector social planning in the United States" is now required. "The globalization of the world's largest private enterprises, industrial and financial alike, represents a structural transformation in the location of their activities and the manner in which they behave as institutions." Behavioral assumptions of orthodox economics no longer apply. "Because these corporations account for the dominant share of economic transactions within and between nation-states, it is hypothesized that their own transformation has brought about a structural transformation of the national and international economy." Two general characteristics of this transformation are the historic increase in the foreign dependency of the U.S. economy, and "the historic upsurge in the industrial and financial concentration of the domestic private sector."

Müller summarizes the "institutional characteristics of actual corporate behavior" that empirically confirm the above-mentioned transformation as follows: "the basic change in goals [of national corporations] is that of maximizing the long-run profits of the parent's total global system" without particular regard for national welfare. International firms are now conglomerates that "compete as oligopolies, not as perfectly competitive firms." Given the foregoing, "more and more of the private sector's total domestic and international transactions are between subsidiaries of the same parent corporation. ... The global corporation is largely a *post-market* enterprise." The pace and magnitude of expansion "has necessitated that global enterprises shift significantly their basis of financing from internal to external sources" thus eroding "the autonomy or sovereignty of a nation's money supply." Finally, the global corporation, as a social institution, has "heightened structural mobility" and increased its "capacity to change rapidly where and what it produces." This structural transformation is so extensive and dominating that no one nation can generate adequate national stabilization policies. Domestic "public sector social planning" is required to restore some measure of national control over the nation's economic destiny. Although no details or components of such a planning process are provided, the chapter does close with suggestions about appropriate goals, targets, and the implementation of such a planning process.

Milton D. Lower's chapter addresses international interdependence of yet another kind—the causal consequences for the U.S. industrial economy of "international price shocks," and later "industrial import shocks," in the recent past. As a basic institutionalist analytical tool, Lower incorporates the Veblenian-Ayres dichotomy between pecuniary and technological judgments. It is his contention through recourse to this dichotomy, but without claiming exclusive causal generality, that these two somewhat sequential "shock" phenomena have precipitated industrial derangement and decline for the U.S. economy—that pecuniary concerns, by design or inadvertently, have prevailed over technological-industrial concerns.

The fact of international price shocks in the 1970s, particularly the "price fixing by an international oil cartel," came as no surprise to institutionalists. They have "from Veblen on ... identified specific power centers and instituted decision-making processes in modern economics by which prices have been set, manipulated, negotiated, or administered." Consequences for the U.S. of these price increases included: derangement of industries dependent on oil, the forcing of many industries "to utilize existing [energy-intensive] capital equipment . . . at a suboptimal rate and to make ad hoc substitution of labor for both energy and equipment." Both productivity and growth were adversely affected. Sectoral derangement occurred. Both an internal and external transfer of purchasing power resulted. Energy price increases were the major cause of inflationary pressures in the late 1970s. Macroeconomic policies were held hostage to inflated energy prices and rising inflation. Deliberately induced recessions by restrictive monetary policy occurred in both the mid-1970s and the early 1980s.

Finally, Lower explains how price shocks of the 1970s led to "industrial import shocks" of the 1980s. He traces the emergence of the latter "from the Reagan option in 1981 for 'pecuniary' policies—in the Veblenian sense—to address 'industrial' problems." A circular causation phenomenon of "structural deficits, high interest rates, an overvalued dollar, trade deficits, and debt—though seemingly a self-sustaining demand-side engine of recovery—was in fact an engine of deindustrialization." At issue, then, "is not whether, but how the industrial economy is to be internationalized."

This section and volume conclude with a chapter by William H. Melody on the implications of the information technology revolution for the character and control of economies. "Technologically advanced economies," Melody observes, "are in the process of moving beyond industrial capitalism to information-based economies that will bring profound changes in the form and structure of the economic system." Melody explores these "changes" in three areas: technical efficiency and market extension, the role of national governments, and the role of market theory. Still another area of de facto international interdependence (and dependence?) will be evident in these changes.

The expansion of available information and improved telecommunication "should permit more efficient decision making and the extension of markets across transnational boundaries." But in fact, "the benefits of these technologies will not be distributed uniformly across markets. . . . Certain segments of society will be made poorer both in absolute as well as relative terms." It seems already clear that "only the largest national and transnational corporations (TNCs) and governmental agencies have the need for, and the ability to, take full advantage of these new opportunities." Smaller firms will face new entry barriers. "The new competition is simply intensified oligopolistic rivalry among TNCs on a world wide basis."

Government's role changes as well: national governments show "greater tolerance for increased domestic monopoly power because it enhances the power of their resident TNCs in international markets." TNCs receive research and development funding, tax breaks, investment guarantees, protective tariffs, and other forms of governmental support. Governmental aid shifts from support of markets to support of individual firms. There is a much closer identification of the national and public interests with the corporate interest of the dominant home-based TNCs.

Traditional orthodox market theory provides a new apologia for "this expansion of TNC market power." If one assumes that "technology is autonomous . . . that oligopolistic rivalry . . . is competition . . . and that maximizing short run profit will yield optimal resource allocation" the "power positions of the dominant firms" are validated. But of course this is a misuse of market theory; given the elasticity of meanings exhibited, "neoclassical market theory can justify equally well virtually any result." It provides a convenient blanket to cover an otherwise exposed reality.

In sum, this chapter intends to "bring to the foreground and accentuate . . . the oligopolistic character of most national and global markets. In making the reality more visible, the problems may be addressed more directly." Melody concludes with a fresh research agenda for "the analysis of real markets."

20

What Is Economic Imperialism?

Karl de Schweinitz, Jr.

It may seem late in the day to ask what economic imperialism is. For a century, a literature has flourished on what at various times has been called imperialism, the new imperialism, or neoimperialism. Much of this literature, however, has concerned its causes, the phenomenon itself being taken for granted or perceived through the theories and ideologies thus generated. When the word itself, as distinct from empire or imperial, first appeared in English usage in the nineteenth century, it evoked a sense of pride in Western achievement.[1] British writers, such as Charles W. Dilke, John R. Seeley, and J. A. Froude, and proconsuls, such as Lord Cromer and Lord Curzon, viewed imperialism either as an opportunity to extend "Greater Britain" in sparsely populated locations on the globe or as a system of governance well designed for performing the trustee responsibilities of a beneficent and improving culture for less fortunate non-European peoples.[2]

The noble vision of imperialism soon had competition from a less flattering view. Doubts were raised about its morality through greater knowledge of the behavior of Western imperialists in the non-Western world, the increasing commitment in the West to democracy and national rights, the growing resistance to foreign rule in colonial countries, and a literature of economic imperialism which sought its explanation in the geriatric ailments of capitalism. By the end of World War I, most people concerned with these matters surely thought imperialism was a "bad," or at least not a "good." The pejorative meaning that it has today was rapidly displacing the exalted meaning.

If imperialism is now seen as a bad, it is because it is associated with one group of people being pushed around or prevented from doing something by another group of people. In short, it relates to coercion and the restriction of freedom. It may be defined as a system in which A dominates, controls, or coerces B, preventing B from acting in its own interests or compelling it to act in the interests of A. This definition is hardly free of ambiguities. While it may not be difficult to identify A and B as groups, states, communities, or collectivities of some sort, the matter of interests, both substantively and as they may or may not be expressed, is complex, as the expanding industry of welfare economics and social choice attests. Putting those issues aside, there is a question that comes to mind in the very rationale of economics. If there are not enough resources to go around, some people, who receive less than they need, want, or think they deserve, may feel coerced by whatever system is used to allocate resources and distribute output. Is economic imperialism, then, merely a special manifestation of the institutional constraints associated with the scarcity of resources?

We may lay the groundwork for answering this question by looking briefly at a closed economy in which markets organize exchanges of goods, capital, and labor between A and B. In neoclassical economics, it is held that so long as these exchanges are bilaterally voluntary and informed, they maximize freedom of choice. No one is compelled to exchange goods or labor for money or wages; therefore, transactors must think they are better off by engaging than not engaging in markets. Thus it is possible to conceive of the market system, with its pari-mutuel of relative prices, as accomplishing a social function without relying on the coercive powers of a central political authority. Nonetheless, the system cannot work without a set of rules that define legitimate economic behavior. Property entitlements, with their rights and obligations; contracts and torts; statutes and administrative rulings as they express a public interest in private economic behavior; and criminal law all constrain behavior and are necessary complements to the budget limitations on individual choice. The distribution of freedom in a competitive economy, then, has an inverse counterpart in the distribution of coercion; the laws validating economic constraints bear more heavily on people with less than with more income.[3]

The matter is not that simple, however. The laws affecting the distribution of assets may be accorded legitimacy that is not wholly related to one's possession of property, their acceptance depending on the process by which they were enacted or adjudicated as well as on ethical values about how one should regard other people's property. Furthermore, the economic restraints on choice are not fixed in the long run and may be diminished by working inside the law. A person with a low time preference at any level of income will save now and thus expand future income more than will a person with a high time preference. Or, another aspect of the same behavior, he may incur greater costs now in education and training so that his future marginal product will be higher.

These considerations mitigate, but do not obviate, the coercive effect of the market. Even when the marginal conditions are fully satisfied and there are no external diseconomies impinging on households and firms, the unequal distribution of the assets with which people pursue their various purposes imparts to them varying perceptions of the normative worth of market outcomes. These assets include wealth, knowledge, and skills, the accumulation of which depends on some combination of factors inside and outside the economic system. Whatever their relative importance, these factors prevent individuals from having full choice or control of their value or strength. As the old saying goes, children do not choose their parents. Especially when transactions are technically or legally complex, involving highly durable commodities or intricate services, or are critically important as determinants of wage income, inequality in these assets influences the attitudes of transactors who in every respect observe the rules of the game. The slum dweller is not likely to be as pleased with his rental contract as is his landlord. Nor is an unskilled worker as likely as his employer to feel that he is using market exchanges purposely to achieve his objectives.

It scarcely needs to be pointed out that frustrations with their market performance have led individuals to compensate for their weakness by joining with other similarly frustrated individuals. Trade unions are but the more recent in a long lineage of collective organizations seeking to do in combination what individuals cannot do singly. The business corporation, indeed, appeared earlier on the economic scene than did trade unions because managers had less difficulty than did workers persuading the state of the legitimacy of their collective efforts. In capitalist countries this was because corporations were less of an affront to private property than were unions.

Turning now to economic imperialism, it is clear that the relationship involves something different from the A and B of a closed market economy. Rather than being firms and households, both of which are constrained by some set of authoritative rules or laws, A and B are collective entities differentiated from one another by various parameters, language, religion, ethnicity, cultural values, political organizations, and so on.

Closed economies harbor some of these differences, but they are subordinated to a dominant set of institutions that are defined by those
authoritative laws.

In both cases, however, the differences in A and B systematically generate inequality. The inequalities of collective A's and B's may be conceptualized by a modification and extension of the assets of individual
A's and B's and identified as wealth, military power, knowledge, organizational capacity, and ideology. The importance of some of these
assets is more apparent than others, and I shall clarify their role in economic imperialism by considering a series of relationships between collective A's and B's suggested by the history of imperialism, largely, although not exclusively, the effect of Great Britain in India.

States versus Tribes

In the modern era, from the rise of the European states and their expansion out of the Eurasian peninsula around the turn of the sixteenth
century, the initial encounters of Europeans and non-Europeans brought
together people of widely disparate capabilities and motivations. The fact
that Spaniards and Englishmen, for example, came to the Indians in South
and North America, rather than vice versa, tells us a lot about their relative strength. Isabella and Ferdinand had the wealth and interest to spon-
sor the voyages of Christopher Columbus after he had failed to persuade
the Portuguese of the merits of his plans for reaching the Far East. If
knowledge is embodied in human beings, technology, and data about the
social and physical worlds, then Portugal, Castile, and England applied
it more comprehensively in problem solving than did the Indians. The
Portuguese, for example, turned down Columbus because of their investment in the opening up of the all-water route around Africa to the Indies.
As early as 1416, Prince Henry the Navigator founded an academy at
Sagres where cartographers, navigators, astronomers, shipbuilders, and
others sought to solve the many problems that prevented ships from sail-
ing out of sight of land. The knowledge thus acquired furthered the immediate purposes of the Portuguese but had external benefits for other
societies similarly interested in trade and exploration. However much
the Portuguese veiled their ocean navigation research, they could not contain the pool of knowledge they did so much to expand.[4]

The Portuguese research was only one manifestation of the spirit of
experimentation then stirring in Europe. Prince Henry was a contemporary of Johann Gutenberg (1397–1468), considered the first European
to print with movable type, an invention with incalculable consequences

for the spread of knowledge. In the next century, the Copernican revolution made irrevocable inroads on the geocentric cosmology of Christianity. By the seventeenth century, the scientific outlook had become sufficiently rooted in Europe that it received institutional status in the establishment, for example, in 1662 of the Royal Society of London and in 1666 of the Académie Royale des Sciences in France, both of which grew out of "informal gatherings of friends interested in the new science."[5] If now we look at Mexico when Cortés conquered it in the early sixteenth century, we do not observe a disorganized society. On the contrary, given the Aztecs' fears of the powerful and vengeful gods that dominated their lives, they devised a system of human sacrifice for propitiating them that required an extraordinary investment in fixed capital and a continuing supply of variable capital, that is, human beings. The rulers and priests, at least, must have been persuaded that they were using available means effectively to achieve fundamental ends. The external benefits, however, of knowledge acquired in the perfection of sacrificial skills presumably were limited or nonexistent, and their external diseconomies made it a good deal less difficult for Cortés to overthrow Montezuma and replace him as the ruling deity.[6]

The point is not that the Aztecs wantonly destroyed human life, whereas the emissaries of "modern" Europe viewed it as sacred and inviolable. The high priests of the Inquisition surely rivaled the Aztec priests in the body count. Rather, the interaction of knowledge and organizational effectiveness in Europe imparted to navigators, warriors, merchants, and colonists a wider outlook and a broader understanding of world forces than informed the people with whom they came in contact in the non-European world. In other words, they had more control over the environment than did the local population when the encounters took place, if not initially, then at some later date.

In these circumstances, economic imperialism assumed a number of forms. If tribal divisions were pronounced and the population-land ratio relatively high, the imperialists could enslave tribes (for example, to mine gold and silver) at minimized costs because local enmities prevented the unenslaved from perceiving the enslavement of others as a threat to their own freedom and security. This parochialism reflected the absence of overarching beliefs and values among local populations which might have diminished the force of their individual tribal commitments. For their part, the imperialists perceived slaves as nonpersons apart from their own community and not privy to the equitable considerations, if any, appropriate for themselves. The enslaved received maintenance, just as fixed assets are depreciated, the magnitude of which depended on the availability of replacements and the cost of training them. In any event, the imperialists—the *conquistadores*—received a surplus that was the difference between the value of gross output and the maintenance of slaves in mining and complementary activity.

From this surplus the *conquistadores* would have deducted some amount for their own consumption and for further investment in mining or other assets, the balance being shipped to Spain in regular convoys. The annual value of these shipments constituted an export balance on current account for which there was no equivalent return to the local populations; it was a drain or an expropriation of goods from them to Spain. The organizational capabilities of the Spanish in conjunction with their general knowledge, particularly of military assets and shipping technology, allowed them to plunder resources in the New World.

Another type of economic imperialism depended less on enslavement than on controlling land and restricting the customary usage to which it had been put. This occurred from the opening of the New World in the sixteenth century to the occupation of Bantu lands by the Boers and the British, the colonization of Australia and New Zealand, the opening up of the American West, and the movement of white settlers into the East African highlands in the late nineteenth century. In these cases, different technologies confronted one another with their conflicting requirements in the management of land. These conflicts may not have been immediately apparent to either the local populations or the colonists, and in the early years of European expansion their resolution was often in doubt. The Jamestown, Virginia, settlers, for example, were not as efficient as the Indians in raising subsistence crops, the former bartering for or seizing corn from the latter as they struggled to adapt a European social order in an unfamiliar physical environment. Inexorably, however, the land was settled and ownership confirmed in law derived from the charter originally granted by James I. Property law and the courts and magistrates, which adjudicated conflicts over property entitlements, and the House of Burgesses, which originated in the instruction to the first governor of the Virginia Company to call annual assemblies, all evolved outside the rudimentary but viable institutions of Indian life and in time destroyed them.[7] The Indians were dispossessed by the emergence of plantation Virginia as surely as black Africans were enslaved within it.

A third kind of imperialism in the state-tribe encounter involved neither enslavement nor pre-emption of land, but inadequate compensation for the use of the land, which may not have been apparent to indigenous populations at the outset. The imperialists' representatives negotiated with headmen or tribal rulers for contracts specifying where and for how long the former could develop the resources of the latter. One can imagine that the neoclassical conditions for free exchange were fully satisfied, yet the unequal knowledge of the contracting parties left a legacy of a deep and rankling sense of having been robbed. Consider a nineteenth-century setting in which an industrial society, no longer able to satisfy its raw material needs locally, explored with increasing energy and zeal the natural environment of nonindustrial societies. On discovering in location X coal in abundance which hitherto had no domestic use because its properties were not known, representatives of country Y negotiated with local headmen a treaty or contract granting an industrial firm from Y the right to mine coal in return for delivery to the headmen of X a specified quantity of smooth, round stones; these were highly regarded in X as a medium of exchange and as a store of value, but were in short supply. The inhabitants of X were pleased to receive the stones and, indeed, viewed the transactions as a windfall, since they could not understand why anyone wanted coal. For their part, the industrialists, although equally perplexed, had no difficulty finding the stones in places inaccessible to X. By neoclassical criteria, exchange reallocated resources so that both parties were better off, at least in the short run.

In the long run, however, the inequality of knowledge relating to the understanding of markets as they were at the time of the contract and as they were likely to be in the future undermined the satisfaction of the local populations. While both transactors were pleased by their good luck, they were asymmetrically informed about exchange. The imperialists viewed X as a small corner of world markets that were becoming increasingly interconnected by the expansive input and output needs and capabilities of industrial systems. X viewed itself as a more or less self-contained world whose external links with amorphous and unknown societies were adventitious and unimportant. The industrialists were more informed than the headmen because the probability was high that the understanding of the latter would move in the direction of the former, rather than vice versa. In consequence, the preferences of the headmen would change; they would come to value coal as it was priced in world markets, and thus the value of smooth, round stones in X would depreciate sharply.

If this story is a parody of the economic contracts of East and West in the nineteenth century, it nonetheless points up the dynamic effect of trade on preferences. It also suggests that, unlike the inferences one might draw from neoclassical economics, exchanges consummated in one period are not then expunged from memory in all subsequent periods. If preferences change, these may be projected into the past and lead to a reassessment of an exchange initially thought to be eminently satisfactory. Subsequent generations in X might well feel that their forebears' ignorance was unconscionably exploited and that, in consequence, their economic patrimony had been diminished. Presumably, they would have preferred that their forebears had declined to trade (assuming, of course, that the imperialists conducted themselves as exemplars of the normative neoclassical model and did not, when their exchange overtures were rebuffed, enslave the headmen and their tribes or seize their lands).

But the expanding West was not trying to demonstrate the admirable ethical virtues of exchange; its economic interests were grounded in its resource needs and market opportunities. In 1888, Cecil Rhodes's agents negotiated with King Lobengula of the Matabele and Mashone tribes, in what subsequently became Rhodesia and then Zimbabwe, a contract that makes our story seem not implausible. For the "complete and exclusive charge over all metals and minerals situated and contained in [his] kingdom, principalities and dominions," with the right to "exclude from [his] kingdom all persons seeking land, metals, minerals, or mining rights therein," Lobengula received 1,000 rifles, 100,000 ball cartridges, 1,200 pounds sterling annually for life, and a second-hand river steamer.[8] This exchange, of course, was not wholly to be accounted for by unequal knowledge. Inequality in armaments and military strength inevitably affected the ambience of exchange. In 1876, King Leopold II of Belgium established the International Association for the Exploration and Civilization of the Congo, and with the considerable assistance of Henry Stanley by force of arms he turned it into a private investment preserve that acquired European legitimacy when the Conference of Berlin in 1884–1885 approved the Congo Free State. As D. K. Fieldhouse put it, Leopold was "the conceptual economic imperialist of the late nineteenth century whose acquisitive instincts were uncomplicated by humanitarianism, the pressure of domestic public opinion or diplomatic or strategic considerations."[9]

Ten years after Lobengula signed away his economic kingdom, Lord Kitchener demonstrated in the River War on the Upper Nile the carnage that the West could inflict on natives who resisted Western aggression more persistently than the tribal peoples in the Congo. Systematically laying down rail transportation behind his advancing troops, who were equipped with breech-loading rifles and Maxim machine guns, and copiously supported by artillery and naval gun boats, he had little difficulty in subduing the dervishes. The latter, although armed only with spears and inferior firearms obtained in secondary markets, under the Mahdi had laid seige to Khartoum and taken it in early 1885.[10] In the bloodiest action of the Khartoum campaign, the Battle of Omdurman, about 13,000 dervishes were killed at the cost of 48 lives and 434 wounded in the Anglo-Egyptian army.[11] Even if the execution at Omdurman, as one war correspondent referred to it,[12] had a less direct economic rationale than the egregious behavior of Leopold's men in the Congo, both symbolized the raw military power of the West that always lurked in the background of exchange negotiations. Lobengula was hardly as innocent as our coal-rich tribal headmen.

State versus Impaired Ancient States

Thus far we have been concerned with encounters between states and tribes when the one had command of superior assets, enabling it to enslave local populations, seize land, or enforce unequal treaties or contracts affecting the development of local resources. These encounters led to direct governance; the dominant state often exported its own population as colonists, with varying consequences depending on the demographic characteristics of the areas being settled. The history of the West in the New World and Africa was, of course, a by-product of its search for an all-water route to Asia that would by-pass the interior trade routes of the Eurasian continent. For centuries, the European imagination had been excited by a fragmentary knowledge of the great societies of the East and its commercial appetite whetted by the pepper, spices, silks, fine cotton fabrics, and porcelains abounding in Asian markets. When Westerners, in the years following Vasco da Gamma's successful voyages to India, established direct water routes to these markets, they entered into a highly developed international trading system that for centuries had been exchanging and carrying highly valued commodities throughout the vast reaches of Asia and to the terminuses of the European trade routes in the eastern Mediterranean.[13] This was an extraordinarily varied world whose great imperial system had flourished long before the modern states of Europe had emerged from their feudal origins. There was little reason to believe, when the latter began to take shape in the sixteenth century, that they threatened the fabled splendor of India or China.

When, for example, William Hawkins landed at Surat in the Bay of Cambay in 1608, the power of the Mogul empire was at its peak in north India. Jahangir had recently succeeded Akbar, whose reign exceeded Queen Elizabeth's in magnificence. In the eyes of Indian rulers, Hawkins came as a suppliant, not as an ambassador fully entitled to the respect and honors symbolic of the sovereign state he represented. Far from being an imperialist, Hawkins, pursuant to British East India Company policy, merely was trying to make a treaty that would entitle it to rent or build a factory—a warehouse—in which commodities acquired in exchange could be stored pending transhipment to other ports in Asia or Europe. He had few assets, none of which were threatening to India's rulers.[14]

In the next century and a half, the British East India Company established and strengthened its trading posts along coastal India, its primary locations being at Calcutta, Madras, and Bombay. These were small foreign enclaves (in the late seventeenth century there were about 114 European civilians in Madras and less than 300 soldiers); movement in India was restricted, and contact with home was intermittent (it took at least eight months to reach Madras from Plymouth by way of the Cape of Good Hope).[15] In the century after 1750 the British East India Company became the pre-eminent European imperial power in Asia. We are not concerned with the history of England's conquest of the subcontinent, beyond noting that it was facilitated by the long-run decline of the Mogul empire. Weakened central authority exacerbated the struggle for control of north India among local rulers, including the Company. Simultaneously, the Industrial Revolution increased the asset strength of the West, particularly England, relative to the East and changed the structure of world trade. Initially, the West sought the natural commodities of the East, such as the spices that made the European diet more palatable. In the nineteenth century, the input demands and market opportunities of the industrializing West led it into deeper involvement with Asian production and markets.

If the century before World War I may be termed the epoch of high Western imperialism, how was it experienced by the imperialized? In a society such as India's, already bound by subsistence, what difference did it make to the vast peasant majority that the Company ruled directly in Bengal rather than a Mogul viceroy acting for an emperor in Delhi? In its long history, India had survived a succession of conquerors, and it is not unreasonable to conjecture that its highly complex, differentiated social structure served the purpose of insulating village life from the power struggles and conquests at the state level. How many Indians had heard of, let alone seen, Englishmen or Europeans? And if they did have contact with them, how did the conduct of the latter make villagers' lives more restricted or coerced than they had been under previous rulers? Or is it conceivable that their lives were less restricted?

The answers to these questions, although hardly easy to come by, may be suggested by the differences between British imperialists and their predecessors. The earlier invaders came by land from the steppes of Asia or the Middle East, through the Hindu Kush mountains in the northwest to the plains of the Indus and Ganges, the economic resources of which were both the strength of India and the lure for aggressors. Unlike the British, who came by sea, the economic motivation of these peoples of Mongol, Turk, Irani, or Afghan origin tended to be secondary to their desire to conquer. Akbar, for example, was a descendant of Genghis Khan and Tamerlane and, while he was "domesticated" by the problems of governance in India, he never lost his warrior outlook. The Company, as already noted, was first and foremost a commercial venture, however much its merchant fleet and presidencies—the trading centers at Calcutta, Madras, and Bombay—were armed against known and unknown enemies. With the establishment of direct rule in Bengal in 1765, the Company formally assumed dual roles: responsibility as before for commercial affairs according to the policies of the directors in London, and for the collection of the land revenue (*diwani*) in Bengal on behalf of the Mogul emperor. In the periodic renewals of the Company's charter, its governing function came under increasing scrutiny, reflecting both the expanded territory it acquired through conquests in the nineteenth century and the insistence of the English government that it have more control over the Company in India.[16] In 1833, the Company was relieved of its commercial responsibilities, and in 1858, in the aftermath of the Sepoy Rebellion, its rule was abolished and replaced by direct Crown rule. The Governor-General of India, who had been responsible to the Court of Directors and indirectly to the Board of Control of the British government, now became Viceroy and Governor-General, directly responsible to the Secretary of State for India.

There was an explicit intention in Britain's Indian policy to develop institutions that would serve its economic purposes and, as some proconsuls thought, those of the Indians as well. The Mogul emperors were largely uninterested in trade and technology; they depreciated the attenuated Indian commercial classes, looking rather to the seizing and holding of land as the source of military power. In contrast, the British were persuaded that the adaptation in India of English methods of governance and land management would increase the productivity of Indian agriculture, thus swelling the land revenue while creating a class of agrarianists loyal to them. What this meant for governance was that the British imposed a rule of law in territories they governed directly, in contrast to indirect rule in the hundreds of princely states, where they governed through residents attached to the courts. The British brought their own administrative standards to the collection of land revenue, adjudication of disputes with respect to tax liabilities and landholdings, and maintenance of order. These standards existed alongside ancient systems of Hindu and Muslim law and traditional justice in village India, and there was gradually introduced a Western system with greater emphasis on a written, universal, substantive law and formal procedural law, sufficiently complex to stimulate the growth of an Indian bar.[17]

This extraordinary venture in the transmission of political-legal institutions from a society in which they had evolved to one with institutions of profoundly different moral, social, and political roots was sustained by an ideological self-assurance reinforced by the prodigies wrought by the Industrial Revolution. The tolerance, if not approval, of Indian customs and values that had once characterized the Company's representatives gave way in the nineteenth century to the improving ethic, the belief that with political order and proper education Indians could transform uncivilized customs—suttee, infanticide, slavery, thuggery, the caste system—and attain a Western state of grace. In fact, the governments of India moved more circumspectly in matters of personal and familial law than they did in areas that had a more direct bearing on economic performance. Suttee was approached gingerly, the government fearing the alienation of the Brahmins, among whom the practice was most widespread; land settlements, in comparison, were made with verve and little understanding of the underlying structure of landholding they were affecting.[18]

Land settlement during the years of British rule in India was an extraordinarily complex process on which there is an extensive literature.[19] We enter into the subject, if only briefly, because it so aptly illustrates the effect of economic ideology on local populations when combined with strong British civil administration and military command. Before the establishment of *Pax Britannica*, land in India had been held in a bewildering variety of traditional tenures; property rights that identified the owners of land were not defined in law.[20] In Mogul India, neither the emperor, nor his ennobled retainers (the superior holders of revenue-raising privileges), nor the cultivating peasants owned the land. The emperor had first claim on its output, taking from one-third to one-half the gross product; the balance was apportioned among the remaining claimants according to their status and community customs. In the eighteenth century, during the decline of Mogul rule, there was increasing resort to open coercion in the collection of land revenue; tax farming privileges were sold and subdivided, the holders frequently claiming their share with the assistance of armed retainers. The harsh system did have the virtue of traditional accommodation to the inevitable calamities that beset subsistence societies in a monsoon environment. Tax liabilities in villages could be deferred, and patrons with a surplus stock of grain might provision their clients to retain their loyalty and prevent them from fleeing the land. The foreclosure and sale of land for failure to meet tax or interest payments was unknown.

While the British were establishing direct rule in India, technical and institutional transformations in the agrarian sector were both cause and effect of the Industrial Revolution. Among the causes was the continuing evolution of the law of property through enclosures and the individuation of landholdings. And, of course, the economics of it all bore fruit in the classical tradition that, among other things, addressed the matters of landownership and management as they bore on the growth of net product. Ricardian theory of rent in particular had various implications for the organization of agriculture, and it served as ideological inspiration for the proconsuls in India who attempted to settle the land in order to make clearer and more certain the obligations and benefits in its use; thus would the productivity experienced in English agriculture be transmitted to Indian agriculture.

There were various kinds of land settlements. In Bengal in the late eighteenth century, Charles Cornwallis, the governor-general of the Company in India (and the same who surrendered at Yorktown), made a permanent settlement with a small number of *zamindars,* a class of landlords with extensive holdings; he guaranteed that the tax liability, once assessed by the collectors, would remain fixed in perpetuity. In south India, the settlements were with the *ryots,* or cultivating peasants, for long but not permanent terms. Similarly, in the Northwest Provinces, long-term settlements were made with cultivating villages. None of these arrangements fully satisfied Ricardian criteria, if only because the determination of the "original and indestructible powers" of the soil for tax purposes was pretty well beyond the capabilities of the most assiduous land assessor. The settlements in Bengal were especially galling to James Mill (whose monumentally prolix *History of British India* epitomized the strength and arrogance of utilitarian doctrine) because they granted legal entitlements to *zamindars,* legitimizing landlordism and rack-renting and inhibiting the interest of cultivators in raising agricultural productivity.[21]

Whatever their specific form, the land settlements were backed by the force of British law. Tax liabilities were enforced in the courts, and nonpayment could result in the alienation of land through forced market sales. The courts became the focus of endless litigation, particularly in Bengal, where the settlements were particularly incongruent with the customary holdings system. The skirmishes of armed retainers of various claimants to the output of the land gave way to court battles.

On the face of it, such uses of the law would appear to have mitigated arbitrary and coercive means for resolving economic conflicts between private parties and between the state and landholders. Yet, the British courts apparently were detested by Indians and were partially responsible for turning many civilians in North India in favor of the rebelling sepoys in 1857.[22] This unpopularity may be accounted for by the abruptness with which the British introduced these institutions in India and the imperial presumption that there need be little consultation with the people who would be affected by them. That the British acted in this manner, however, was as much a consequence of the Indians' inability to express their opposition effectively as it was of the ability of the British to pursue their purposes, well advised or not, through the strength of their military, administrative, and ideological resources.

Similar to the land settlements in India, the enclosures in England had a coercive effect on holders of customary tenures who had no deed or other legal document to support their claim to a share of the common land. But the enclosures were brought about by the economic motivation of English landed interests. They had been occurring at least since the sixteenth century, sometimes through voluntary exchanges of widely scattered land, but more often through the application of the common law of property and the enactment of parliamentary statutes. By the late eighteenth century, the procedures for carrying out enclosures were well established. Commissions set up by Parliament heard the claims of those who had access to the common land and assessed their validity, awarding proprietary rights or not according to the commissioners' assessment of the legal evidence. If the literate and wealthy landowners had a distinct advantage over the illiterate peasant in making claims for the unenclosed land, there at least was a procedure for allowing the latter to be heard. And if their claims were disallowed for lack of legal documentation, or if they received too small a share for survival, they could work as farm laborers, the demand for which increased among improving landowners who acquired larger farms and estates to manage. They were coerced by the change in the institutional arrangements in the countryside, but the incidence of coercion was in part assuaged by the employment opportunities afforded them in the structural changes in output, industrial as well as agricultural, occasioned by economic development.

The land settlements in nineteenth-century India, in contrast, were neither a consequence nor a cause of economic development. They did accelerate the intrusion of markets in the traditional economy, inducing a selective growth of output that served English interests but that had weak spread effects on local Indian economies. This outcome, oddly enough, may have been facilitated by the success of British rulers in preserving law and order as well as by the construction of economic overhead capital initially undertaken in earnest during the governor-general-ship of Lord Dalhousie in the decade before the Sepoy Rebellion.

The elimination of internal wars and banditry with the imposition of political order and, after the turn of the century, the more effective control of famine caused the rate of population growth to increase. The first Indian census, taken by the British in 1871, recorded a figure of 255 million. Pre-Rebellion population in 1855 has been variously estimated between 175 and 225 million. In 1911, the census enumerated 303 million Indians. If one takes the higher 1855 estimate as the more likely size, by 1911 it had grown by 78 million or 35 percent, an average annual increase of about one-half of one percent.[23] Low by the standards of nineteenth-century industrializing societies, this rate was nonetheless higher than the rate of growth of population in pre-British India in the eighteenth century. In any case, the addition of more than 75 million people during the half-century before 1911, superimposed on a traditional order already disrupted by the land settlements, made landlord-tenant relationships more embittered and increased rural indebtedness. The numbers of poor cultivating owners, poor undertenants, and rural proletariat grew, even as there was a concentration of larger property holdings among a small Indian elite. The moneylender in village India increasingly became an opprobrious figure, bound less by the constraints of traditional obligations than by the legal contractual commitments of a money economy. Indeed, ironically, he often became the parasitical landlord that the British thought they were exorcising in the land settlements before the Rebellion.

The construction of railroads and the improvements of harbor facilities brought the Indian agrarian hinterlands into closer contact with world markets and spurred growth in primary output and exports. Indigo (until the mid-nineteenth century), cotton, opium, and jute production for overseas sales expanded at the expense, it was contended by Indian nationalists, of food grains for domestic consumption. In an extreme variant of this argument, the British emphasis on railroad as opposed to canal and irrigation investment, to satisfy British steel interests, prevented the development of more arable land, which affected subsistence agriculture and exacerbated famines in the late nineteenth century.[24]

One gets a sense of the local effect of these broad economic and legal changes in India in the story of the indigo industry prior to its decline in the second half of the nineteenth century. A plant whose properties were known in both ancient Egypt and India, indigo produced a highly durable blue dye used in the finishing of textiles. Early in the eighteenth century, the Company tried to expand indigo production in India, but it had not been able to compete successfully with plantation output in the West Indies. With the expansion of the cotton textile industry in England during the Industrial Revolution, the demand for dyes increased. As Company rule extended in Bengal, Europeans entered directly into the management and supervision of indigo production, the technical characteristics of which required continuous attention to cultivation and exacting care for the timing of the harvest. The interest in producing indigo was further heightened by its suitability, as pressed cakes or molds, for the remittance trade, a market by which Europeans resident in India transmitted funds to Europe. In 1833, the Charter Act separated the Company from its commercial functions, and British territory in India was opened to settlement by Europeans; indigo production, already a major agricultural enterprise, increased in lower Bengal. In the thirty years before the Sepoy Rebellion, the exports of indigo expanded to become second only to opium.

The European indigo planters either leased land from *zamindars* or bought land, which the Government of India had ruled was legal in British territory. While there was sometimes friction between the foreigners and the *zamindars*, who may have felt that their leaseholders were not properly appreciative of the social and behavioral obligations of the agrarian order, the more enduring and serious conflict was with the *ryots* on whose labor indigo production depended. The sources of conflict inhered in the monopsonistic relationship between planter and cultivator, an exploitative setting familiar to any student of labor movements. The peasant was confronted by a landowner or leaseholder with specific production interests that differed from his. The relative prices of rice and indigo made the cultivation of the former the more profitable for the peasant. With rice, he met his subsistence needs directly and was not subject to the adverse terms of trade between rice and indigo; these terms were made all the more unattractive by the monopsonistic purchase by the planter of the cultivator's services. The latter were spelled out in some detail in contracts. The peasant was required to plant, cultivate, and harvest indigo in a specified area of the land he worked. The planter supplied seed at a contracted price, bought the harvested indigo at a contracted price, and kept the financial records. It was an arrangement not dissimilar to sharecropping or the advancement of wages in kind through a company store in an isolated mining community. Like the sharecroppers or the miners, the indigo *ryot* seldom knew what his financial position was and might find after the harvest that he had little more than the rupees needed to cover the cost of seed. Moreover, the contract was enforced by the police or the planters' own retainers, and toward the end of the period the planters were bringing pressure to bear on the government to enact a criminally enforceable contract law. They thus anticipated that the rule of law could be used to discipline disaffected indigo cultivators.[25]

The discontent of the Bengali peasants producing indigo became sufficiently acute that in the aftermath of the Sepoy Rebellion there were disturbances in lower Bengal that became known as the Blue Mutiny. Eventually, the peasants' specific grievances faded with the long-run decline of the indigo industry, initiated by the synthesizing of the first aneline dye in 1856 and hastened by the prodigious growth of the German dyestuff industry. The story we have related, then, was an ephemeral occurrence in the history of economic imperialism in India, yet it left its mark. The European planters imposed costs on the peasants, although these were not unequivocally a net increase over the costs the *ryots* bore prior to the expansion of indigo production. Even as producers of rice, the peasants raised little more than subsistence, and, if they were not held in financial bondage to a European planter, they may have been similarly indebted to a local moneylender. Poverty prevailed, regardless of what was produced. Nonetheless, the history of the indigo peasants endured in the Indian consciousness and played a part in the formation of an anti-imperial outlook. In the minds of a developing Bengali and Indian intelligentsia, the very fact that the planters were a foreign presence made them culpable for conduct that was more easily excused or ignored when the principals were Indian.

The land settlements, the construction of railroads, and the plight of the indigo peasants were only a few of the economic consequences of the British presence. Others included the indenturing of peasants to labor in the sugar plantations of Mauritius and the West Indies and in the tea plantations of Assam, the relative decline of the Indian handloom weavers, and the fiscal burden of the Indian Army and the administration of British India. In isolation, each did not constitute a compelling economic imperialism. Each of them may not have represented a substantial net increase in the burden of subsistence; in their absence, the life of the Indian peasant very likely would have been constrained by the actions and policies of a different set of overlords, but ones whose interests presumably would have been no less self-serving than those of the British. It is of first importance, however, that there needed to be some theory, model, or ideology at hand that related what otherwise appeared to be discrete happenings and so dismayed or angered people who had no direct contact with them. If economic imperialism was to become a bad distinguishable from the everyday trials of living, it had to be possible, for example, for a *kshatriya* in Gujarat to empathize with the plight of the indigo peasant in Bengal. This required that there be some common identity—a sense of Indianness, for example—as well as a feeling that the adverse treatment of the one was offensive to the other.

In India, an economics of imperialism that served some of these purposes began to take shape with the development of the Indian nationalist movement. In 1867, Dadabhai Naoroji put forward the idea of the economic drain in a speech in London before the East India Association, "England's Debt to India."[26] A Parsi born in Bombay in 1825, Naoroji took a college degree in mathematics and went to England in 1855 to open up an Indian commercial house; through quantitative evidence about the Indian economy, he attempted to persuade British authorities that their rule was a cause of Indian poverty. Generally, he charged that British policies, subordinate to the industrial interests of the home economy, aborted the development of the industrial sectors of the Indian economy, encouraged the growth of industrial raw materials and food grains for export, and imposed revenue demands on India for imperial, non-Indian purposes, all of which impoverished the economy and exacerbated the chronic famine problem, even while it led to a drain of goods and resources from India to England.[27] The drain, alternatively called trade with no equivalent returns, remittance of surplus, the annual tribute, or unrequited exports, was the charge to which the British were most sensitive. They thought their rule was just in the sense that India benefited from the high standards of administration and the maintenance of order they brought to the subcontinent. As Sir John Strachey, an eminent Anglo-Indian proconsul, wrote: "It is an inevitable consequence of the subjection of India that a portion of the cost of her government should be paid in England. The maintenance of our dominion is essential in the interests of India herself, and, provided that she is not compelled to pay more than is really necessary to give her a thoroughly efficient Government, and in return for services actually rendered her, she has no reason for complaint."[28]

This assertion hardly moved Naoroji and other Indians of his persuasion, who argued that there was no exchange of benefits in the relationship. Rather, England was doing in the guise of superior administration what the Company had done so openly after assuming the *diwani* in 1765: appropriating India's surplus output. The concept of the drain helped them to perceive British policies throughout the subcontinent as interrelated activities that were diminishing, or at least holding back the increase in, India's economic well-being. An economics of imperialism, which first saw the light of day a generation in advance of the literature of imperialism in the Western world, thus heightened the sense of Indian grievance against external agents for the burdens of poverty that traditionally had been submerged in the complex social order of Hindu society. Whether or not this economics of imperialism was well founded, it had ideological power.[29] At the outset, when Naoroji argued his case in London, he was making a plea for the British to govern India with Indian interests as their primary goal; subsequently, the force of his argument led him to be the first of the Indian National Congress leaders to call for the withdrawal of the British from India. Their continuing rule no longer seemed compatible with Indian interests.

States versus Newly Independent States

In 1947, India attained independence within the British Commonwealth; the next year, Burma declared independence outside it. In Africa, the rush of British colonies to independence started with Ghana in 1957. Elsewhere, the other Western colonial systems also declined, the events differing from one empire to another as the inevitable emergence of the Third World was resisted with varying energy, will, and bitterness. In the event, the world has become reticulated by political jurisdictions whose number, as represented in the United Nations in the mid-1980s, has reached 152. There are now a plethora of spokesmen for interests long repressed or at best only indirectly articulated in the colonial relationship. The organizational and ideological inequality between East and West has been diminished if for no other reason than that Western nationalism, socialism, or democracy has penetrated the richly diverse and particularistic values of traditional societies.

While the old imperial systems were being transmogrified, the metropolitan states that had originally widened international economic inequality in accelerated economic growth and industrialization continued to maintain their lead and in many instances increase it. The unevenness of world economic development, however, has become an issue on which the leaders of newly independent states sharpen their polemical skills while they cope with the immensely difficult problems of organizing their societies to increase economic growth and overcome poverty. The terms neocolonialism and neoimperialism have gained currency in the decrying of the continued dominance in the international order of the advanced economies.

These catchwords encompass a variety of relationships the intent of which, it is held, is to perpetuate the dependence of the former colonies on their old imperial masters. The multinational corporations based in Europe, North America, and Japan, more often than not generating gross revenues in excess of the gross national products of the typical less developed countries, control the transfers of resources and technologies whose characteristics are determined more by the profit demands of the multinationals than by the development needs of their several hosts. If the technology is capital intensive, it minimizes the employment effect in local labor markets and requires skilled personnel who either are imported from the West, thus enlarging a foreign enclave, or are drawn from an indigenous elite who become clients of the multinational, a comprador class with interests centered less in its own country than in the metropolitan opportunities offered by its employers. If the multinational develops natural resources, it may be tying the developing economy into the needs of the industrialized West without stimulating the growth of those backward, forward, and lateral linkages that are critical for self-sustained growth. In any case, the multinational repatriates profits to the metropolis that otherwise might be applied to its development or social needs.

In the absence of direct investment by the multinationals, the developing country in need of capital may turn to public sources for loans on advantageous terms or grants. Even here, it is argued by the believers in neoimperialism, the scope for maximizing the country's interests is severely constrained. Bilateral aid may depend on a patron-client relationship subordinating the economic aspirations of the latter to the international power politics of the former. And if these objectives are muted, it nonetheless may require that the less developed country spend aid funds in the markets of the donor country. While multilateral aid may place political considerations at several removes from the deliberations and negotiations of the international personnel who work, for example, for the World Bank, their disinterestedness still may be constrained by the policy preferences of the dominant contributors of capital to the bank.

Moreover, the long-term indebtedness of the less developed countries, even when assuaged by interest rates below market and by moratoriums on repayment provisions, is rendered more burdensome by the adverse terms of trade against primary output as well as trade discrimination in the advanced economies against their manufactured products. The sluggish growth of foreign exchange earnings may exacerbate the debt service problem, leading them to turn for short-run financial assistance to the large international commercial banks or to the International Monetary Fund—and the oversight and supervision which may be a condition for financial assistance.

In what respects can it be said that this scenario of growing international involvement of great and small states constitutes a continuation in new guise of the coercive relationships outlined in the previous sections? There are a number of observations that this question prompts. First, if formerly colonial countries possess oil and other natural resources desperately needed by the industrial economies, they may be able to join forces, as has been so dramatically demonstrated by OPEC, and through cartelization secure a larger share of the surplus generated in production and marketing. It is hardly an exaggeration to assert that after so many years of prodigally low petroleum prices, Western (as well as many Third World) consumers feel coerced by the exuberant pricing policies of OPEC; are we in the West now being imperialized?

Second, and this obviously bears on the first point, political independence has reduced an inequality that hitherto prevented the articulation of the interests of colonial peoples. That new states and newly independent old states express their views in national and international forums has had a hand in shaping a *Weltanschauung* in the Third World that makes it extremely sensitive to the persistence of economic inequality and injustice and to the seemingly ineluctable problems of governance. So long as nationalist leaders were struggling for independence, they often were able to subordinate their local differences in common hostility to the foreign intruders. When the latter withdrew or were forced out, these differences —ethnic, tribal, religious, or linguistic—became the responsibility of national leaders and became more compelling as the link between political power and the distribution of domestic economic benefits became more direct. A civil persona coinciding with the territories and labels of the newly independent states—India, Uganda, Cambodia, Ghana, Sri Lanka —was not yet strongly enough internalized to moderate the antagonisms of more personal, ancient, and local identities. The Third World has become a breeding ground for military juntas, revolutionary regimes of the left, and dictatorial rulers of the right; all of these, with rhetorical or ideological claims to being the custodian of the national welfare, struggle to impose order on their fractious subjects. Even India, the most democratically committed of the newly independent states, has not been immune to the lure of authoritarian methods in the quest for order.

Nonetheless, what is done in the Third World now is the work of indigenous rulers. Indira Gandhi turned to authoritarian rule in India in her campaign to eradicate poverty. She did not declare the emergency at the insistence of foreign powers whose interests were threatened by the dilatory behavior of Indian politicians. Rather, it was the threat to Indian interests that induced her to repress opposition. She may have miscalculated these interests, or even felt more comfortable with authoritarian governance, but she was not being a proxy for more powerful foreign

states. The same applies to Idi Amin in Uganda, however grim the consequences of his brutal rule.

By the same token, Third World governments negotiate with multinationals as to the conditions on which the latter may invest in their countries. The negotiations may not be fully informed, but they are not likely
to be as unequal as those of the late nineteenth century between Lobengula and the representatives of Rhodes. Moreover, if the agreements lead
to direct investment, the advantages the multinational may have before
contracts are signed may diminish as real assets are constructed and become a physical presence in the host economy. If the multinational has an
interest in the maximization of net income throughout its international
operations that conflicts with the development interests of the host, these
assets cannot be removed to escape the conflict. Prudence may induce
accommodation. While we may be aware of the surreptitious means by
which governments in the metropolis have subverted developing country
governments—the role of the United States in Chile comes readily to
mind—it is implausible to predict such conduct as the modal response
of metropolitan governments when the interests of their nations are not
dominant in the periphery. The machinations of the CIA and the Secretary of State are perforce an imperfect substitute for the gunboat diplom-
acy of the era of high imperialism. And if the less developed countries
learn by doing, they may be expected to become more adept in developing
organizational strength that not only will render such egregious behavior
by foreign states more difficult but also will raise their capability in negotiating the terms on which the latter legitimately do business in their
countries.

Third, the charge that a pattern of asymmetrical relationships is emerging from the growing interdependence of the international economy—
that former colonial countries on the periphery have become more dependent on dominant economies in the metropolis at the cost of their own
economic welfare—is far too general to explain how the incidence of
coercion is affected. Consider, for example, the profit repatriated by
multinationals from operations in the Third World. It arises from direct
investment, and whether it constitutes a drain depends upon the performance of the host economy. If productivity growth and increases in the
rate of economic growth are high enough, export expansion can facilitate
the transfer of profits, with greater output for domestic use still accruing
to the host country. This certainly has happened historically, as in the
United States during the nineteenth century. Whether it is as likely to occur
in Asia, Africa, and Latin America is problematical. But to approximate
an answer one needs to know, at a minimum, the kind of enterprise (re-

source developing, manufacturing, or service) in which the multinational has invested, the extent to which it undermines or stimulates the growth of local firms, its effect on labor allocation and the development of labor skills, and the contractual conditions it enters into with the host country that bear on the distribution of net income. Apparently, more often than not, officials in the Third World believe that, on balance, the relevant considerations are positive. Multinationals do not force their services on them behind the gunboats of their own countries; they typically are sought after by the host societies, whose governors, of course, are not immune to personal financial considerations.

Withal, even under the most optimistic assumptions about the relative performance of the less developed countries, international economic inequality is not likely to be reduced dramatically in the near future. Furthermore, notwithstanding modest progress in some countries in the control of population growth, the Malthusian specter has not yet been exorcised and the world released from those positive checks, notably famine, that Malthus thought essential for the maintenance of a subsistence equilibrium. Scarcity still stalks the international economy in its grimmest manifestation. Just as an impoverished worker may not appreciate the mutual benefits of market exchanges, so international economic inequality may not lend credibility to the arguments presented above. Indeed, it may render plausible the belief that rich countries continue to hold poor countries in bondage to subsistence.

Scarcity, poverty, and economic inequality cannot be denied. I do deny that in and of themselves they constitute imperialism, a power relationship in which there is no doubt about what country is dominant and what country determines the interests to be maximized. It is, moreover, a relationship in which the dominant party is perceived as a foreign and unwanted presence. Imperialism thus depends as much on the formation of the relevant values in the imperialized country as on the aggressive conduct of the imperialist. If a foreign presence is welcomed, or if residents in colonial territories serve their colonial masters without a sense of incongruity or guilt, imperialism is the less pernicious. Western imperialism did not reach the peak of its coercive effect until the eve of its decline, when nationalist and independence movements had precipitated or shaped values hostile to the foreign presence. Great Britain, in this sense, was more imperialist in its second century in India, when it had perfected the system of colonial rule, than in its first century, when it acquired the territory of the subcontinent by military conquest.

By the same token, when nationalist forces succeeded to their political patrimony and assumed the responsibilities of governance, imperialism receded as the state system, which first emerged in the West, expanded. In their newly found independence, Third World countries are vigorously repeating the history of the West as they quarrel among themselves in the expression and protection of their interests. What makes their conflicts different from those of the Western states after 1500 is that today they cannot be projected into world space that is empty or occupied by societies with relatively weak assets. Instead, they are part of a highly interdependent international economy whose markets have made all peoples more dependent on one another and of an institutionally prolix international political community bound only by the uncertain consequences of the maximization of state interests. England, Holland, Spain, France, and Portugal competed for and came to control Asian markets and societies; those they once controlled now reach out for the world in the corridors of the United Nations. If international institutions have not been successful in reducing international economic inequality, they are of a piece with domestic economies in which inequality is singularly intractable. And inequality, domestic or international, inevitably has coercive consequences for those with relatively weak assets. But this is to say that scarcity is still very much part of the human condition, not that economic imperialism is the force that it was during the two centuries prior to World War II. Imperialism does survive, of course, as the Russian presence in Afghanistan and Eastern Europe or the ill-fated efforts of the United States to impose its will on Vietnam remind us. The trauma associated with these histories, however, may be a measure of the weakness in the contemporary world of imperialism in general and of economic imperialism in particular.

Notes

1. Richard Koebner, *Empire* (New York: Grosset & Dunlop, 1965), pp. 85–104.
2. Charles W. Dilke, *Greater Britain* (New York: Harper, 1869); J. A. Froude, *Oceana* (London: Longmans, Green, 1883); and John R. Seeley, *The Expansion of England* (London: Macmillan, 1883). Lord Curzon stated the imperial mission with unembarrassed clarity: "In Empire we have found not merely the key to glory and wealth, but the call to duty, and the means of service to mankind." Quoted by A. P. Thornton, *The Imperial Idea and Its Enemies—a Study in British Power* (London: Macmillan, 1959), p. 72.
3. For a discussion of these issues, see Karl de Schweinitz, "The Question of Freedom in Economics and Economic Organization," *Ethics* 89 (July 1979): 336–53.
4. Christopher Bell, *Portugal and the Quest for the Indies* (London: Con-

stable, 1974); and Henry M. Hart, *Sea Road to India* (New York: Macmillan, 1950).

5. J. D. Bernal, *Science in History* (Cambridge, Mass.: M.I.T. Press, 1971), vol. 2, p. 451.

6. Maurice Collis, *Cortés and Montezuma* (New York: Avon Books, 1978).

7. Edmund S. Morgan, *American Slavery, American Freedom—The Ordeal of Colonial Virginia* (New York: W. W. Norton, 1975), pp. 44–107.

8. Parker T. Moon, *Imperialism and World Politics* (New York: Macmillan, 1926), p. 169.

9. D. K. Fieldhouse, *Economics and Empire, 1830–1914* (Ithaca: Cornell University Press, 1973), p. 343.

10. It was at the end of the siege, when the dervishes burst through the defenses of Khartoum, that the Victorian hero, General Charles Gordon, was killed. On Gordon, Lytton Strachey is still worth reading: *Eminent Victorians* (New York: Capricorn Books, 1963), pp. 233–338.

11. Daniel R. Headrick, "The Tools of Imperialism: Technology and the Expansion of European Colonial Empires in the Nineteenth Century," *Journal of Modern History* 51 (June 1979): 231–63; Philip Magnus, *Kitchener—The Portrait of an Imperialist* (London: John Murray, 1958), pp. 126–32; and Bernard Porter, *The Lion's Share* (London: Longmans, 1975), pp. 163–65.

12. "No white troops would have faced the torrent of death for five minutes. It was not a battle but an execution." G. W. Steevens, quoted by Alan Moorehead, *The White Nile* (New York: Dell, 1962), p. 360.

13. M. A. P. Meilink-Roelofsz, *Asian Trade and European Influence in the Indonesian Archipelago between 1500 and 1630* (The Hague: Martinus Nijhoff, 1962).

14. Brian Gardner, *The East India Company* (New York: McCall, 1972), pp. 17–53.

15. Percival Spear, *The Nabobs—a Study of the Social Life of the English in Eighteenth Century India* (London: Oxford University Press, 1963), p. 11.

16. Holden Furber, *John Company at Work—A Study of European Expansion in India in the Late Eighteenth Century* (Cambridge, Mass.: Harvard University Press, 1948); P. J. Marshall, *Problems of Empire, Britain and India, 1757–1813* (London: George Allen and Unwin, 1968); and C. H. Philips, *The East India Company, 1784–1834* (Manchester: Manchester University Press, 1940).

17. Marc Galanter, "The Displacement of Traditional Law in Modern India," *Journal of Social Issues* 214 (October 1968): 65–91.

18. Percival Griffiths, *The British Impact on India* (New York: Archon Books, 1965), pp. 216–25.

19. See especially Robert E. Frykenberg, ed., *Land Control and Social Structure in Indian Society* (Madison: University of Wisconsin Press, 1969); Walter Neale, *Economic Change in Rural India: Land Tenure and Reform in Uttar Pradesh, 1800–1955* (New Haven: Yale University Press, 1961); and Eric Stokes, *The English Utilitarians and India* (Oxford: The Clarendon Press, 1955), and *The Peasant and the Raj: Studies in*

Agrarian Society and Peasant Rebellion (London: Cambridge University Press, 1978).

20. M. Athar Ali, *The Mughal Nobility under Aurangzeb* (Bombay: Asia Publishing House, 1968); Irfan Habib, *The Agrarian System of Mughal India, 1556–1707* (Bombay: Asia Publishing House, 1963); and W. H. Moreland, *India at the Death of Akbar—an Economic History* (London: Macmillan, 1920).

21. *The History of British India* (London: J. Madden, 1818) initially appeared in six volumes and made a sufficient impression in England to bring Mill to the attention of the East India Company and an offer in 1819 of a position as assistant to the Examiner of Correspondence. Mill soon had influence enough to place his son John Stuart in the same office in 1823, the latter's qualifications perhaps being that at the age of eleven he helped his father correct the page proofs of the book. Mill became Chief Examiner in 1836, and in 1856 John Stuart became the last Chief Examiner of the Company. This office was crucial, for its staff drafted the letters sent out by the India Office to the proconsuls in India that embodied its economic, political, and social policies. It also received dispatches from India. The staff in the office of the Examiner of Correspondence was thus a kind of civil service that strengthened the Company's administrative continuity.

22. According to Thomas R. Metcalf, the agricultural classes "neither understood nor benefitted from the vaunted British legal system. Although it was designed for his protection, its extreme complexity only repelled the simple villager. To him the courts were instruments of oppression in the hands of the rich and crafty." *The Aftermath of Revolt: India, 1857–1870* (Princeton: Princeton University Press, 1964), p. 62.

23. Kingsley Davis, *The Population of India and Pakistan* (Princeton: Princeton University Press, 1951), pp. 25–27.

24. B. M. Bhatia, *Famines in India: a Study in Some Aspects of the Economic History, 1860–1946* (Bombay: Asia Publishing House, 1963).

25. Blair B. Kling, *The Blue Mutiny—The Indigo Disturbances in Bengal. 1857–1862* (Philadelphia: University of Pennsylvania Press, 1966).

26. This speech influenced H. M. Hyndman, who already was viewing England's economic relationship with India as imperialistic before he had become familiar with and committed to the economics of Karl Marx. See H. M. Hyndman, "The Bankruptcy of India," *Nineteenth Century* 4 (October 1878): 585–608. A collection of Naoroji's articles, speeches, and letters was published in *Poverty and Un-British Rule in India* (Delhi: Publications Division, Government of India, 1962).

27. On the issue of the drain, see Pramathanath Banerjea, *Indian Finance in the Days of the Company* (London: Macmillan, 1928); Bipan Chandra, *The Rise and Growth of Economic Nationalism in India* (New Delhi: People's Publishing House, 1966); B. N. Ganguli, *Dadabhai Naoroji and the Drain Theory* (London: Asia Publishing House, 1965); John McLane, "The Drain of Wealth and Indian Nationalism at the Turn of the Century," *Contribution to Indian Economic History*, edited by T. Raychaudhuri (Calcutta: Firma K. L. Mukhopadhyary, 1963), vol. 2, pp. 21–40;

Tapan Mukerjee, "Theory of Economic Drain: Impact of British Rule on the Indian Economy, 1840–1900," in *Economic Imperialism*, edited by K. E. Boulding and Tapan Mukerjee (Ann Arbor: University of Michigan Press, 1972), pp. 195–212; and John Strachey, *The End of Empire* (London: Victor Gollancz, 1959).

28. Sir John Strachey, *India—Its Administration and Progress*, 3d ed. (London: Macmillan, 1903), pp. 192–93.

29. The subject of the drain cannot be separated from the question of India's potential for economic development in the nineteenth century. In the view of Morris D. Morris, "the British did not take over a society that was 'ripe' for an industrial revolution and then frustrate that development. They imposed themselves on a society for which every index of performance suggests the level of technical, economic, and administrative performance of Europe five hundred years earlier." *Journal of Economic History* 23 (December 1963): 611. This strong position, not surprisingly, called forth counterarguments; these, along with a rebuttal by Morris, were published in *India Economy in the Nineteenth Century: a Symposium* (Delhi: Indian Economic and Social History Association, 1969).

21

The Evolution of Colonial Institutions:
An Argument Illustrated from the Economic
History of British Central Africa

Walter C. Neale

It is a commonplace legal axiom that a person is to be held responsible for the consequences of actions when a "reasonable man" would expect those consequences. Too often has the history of the colonial empires in Africa and Asia been treated as if the metropolitan powers were the "reasonable men" of legal tradition. First, even the most reasonable of men could not have anticipated the consequences of the actions taken by the metropolitan countries or by their nationals in the colonies. Secondly, it is an anthropomorphic fallacy to think of an imperial power as if it were a person making decisions. Rather, the different experiences, interests, and points of view of different groups affected the social and political processes from which imperial policies *emerged*. There was no single mind considering and then deciding how to act. The metropolitan countries, as the governing powers in the colonies, must bear moral responsibility for many institutions associated with modern colonial rule, but it would not be correct say that the metropolitan countries *intended* from the start to impose these institutions upon the colonies, that they planned to make these institutions permanent features of colonial rule, or that they anticipaed the results of their actions. Rather, these institutions *emerged* in the processes of an unequal but nevertheless *mutual* adaptation of the metropolitan and the colonial cultures to each other.

Each adaptive act was, of course, intended—sometimes by the government of the metropolitan power; but also often by its nationals in the colonies, in the absence of instructions from, and even in defiiance of, the metropolitan country's avowed policy to the contrary. But it does not follow that the longer-term cnsequences of the acts were foreseen, nor that the colonial powers set out to create peculiarly colonial institutions. In fact, quite the opposite was true.

I take as my example British Central Africa (now Zimbabwe, Zambia, and Malawi).[1] It was an unusual case in a number of respects, not the least of which was the presence of a large immigrant European population and the starkly pervasive, racist, and dominant way in which they exercised power. But these are the very traits that have made it easy to argue that metropolitan countries "knew what they were doing." If it can be shown in such a case that colonial institutions evolved in unexpected ways, then, is it not likely that colonial institutions elsewhere were not intended but evolved or emerged?

To argue the point I discuss three peculiarly colonial institutions that emerged in British Central Africa: Native Reserved Areas, Compounds, and Locations. None of them had precursors in Bantu institutions, and none of them existed in British culture. Rather, they were unique to colonial Africa, products of the conflict of cultures.

Native Reserved Areas were large sections of land allotted to the Bantu tribes, in which the Bantu were expected to manage their own affairs, bar raiding and warfare, according to the customs of the tribes. Native Commissioners (British civil servants) oversaw the administration of the Areas. The idea was to allow the Bantu to live as they had until they were assimilated into a "civilized, European style of life." It was a version of "indirect rule," designed to disrupt Bantu life as little as possible.

Compounds were dormitory accommodations (barracks), providing room and board for the migrant Bantu laborers who worked in the mines.

Locations were "townships" for Bantu families who migrated to the new European settlements and stayed to work for extended periods of time, or even for their lifetimes.

How did these institutions arise? It is easy to attribute them to straightforward exploitation. Reserved Areas were the poor lands not wanted by the Pioneers (the name the British settlers gave themselves), and so were left to those Bantu not yet needed as farm workers or miners. Migrant labor was the cheapest kind of labor. Compounds were the cheapest way to manage and to provide for migrant labor. Locations were a cheap way to provide for and to control more permanent labor. These explanations are plausible. The only trouble is that they are half truths. The more accurate story is more complex.

The British entered Central Africa with three propositions about society and about people that they regarded as obviously true: (1) that land and movables were the property of someone; (2) that any normal person would use his land, movables, and ability to work to achieve as high a material standard of living as he could; and (3) that any normal person lacking a property income would be glad to work for wages.

From the first proposition it followed, in British logic, that land that was not clearly the property of particular people (those cultivating it at the moment, for instance) was the property of the "king" as "sovereign" (both European concepts). The British South Africa Company had succeeded to the position of sovereign.[2] There is no question that the original invasion of Southern Rhodesia (Zimbabwe) by Cecil Rhodes, S. L. Jameson, and the Pioneers under cover of the Company was a grand "land and cattle grab." In the eastern area not much harm was done thereby to the Shona tribes since the lands the Pioneers wanted was not the land the Shona wanted. But in the west, "virtually the whole of Ndebele land and by far the greater part of Ndebele cattle passed into white hands" during the conquest.[3] If the partial restitution made after the suppression of the Ndebele rebellion hardly made up for the original seizures, it does indicate the imperial policy was not designed to "grab all the land."[4] It is also important to note that exhuberant, violent seizure of land and cattle occurred only in Southern Rhodesia. Northern Rhodesia (Zambia) and Nyasaland (Malawi) did not suffer these outrages and the distribution of land in those colonies approximated to London's intentions. If the insufficiency of the land left to the Ndebele in the west of southern Rhodesia is to be cited as evidence of exploitative intent, then one should also account for the sufficiency of land left to the Mashona tribes in the east. In fact, the lighter, sandy soils, which the Bantu used for slash-and-burn agriculture, were left to the Bantu—*reserved* for the Bantu, and Native Commissioners were appointed to protect and guide them.

From the second proposition—that normal people try to achieve a higher material standard of living—it followed that the land should be improved. If the Bantu were not improving the land—and they were not —then they should be taught and induced to do so. The areas assigned to the Bantu, and the *de facto* permission for Bantu to use other lands not yet granted to Pioneers or assigned to other uses, were thus regarded as temporary expedients to allow for the Bantu to larn to manage their land more productively or to learn all those other skills and roles that a progressive society needs. Thus were the Reserved Areas created; and, in fact and as late as 1915, only some of the migratory Bantu cattle herders were deprived of land that they were using, or that they particularly wanted to use.

The railways were built to transport the output of the mines and the saleable produce of the land. Since the Bantu did not want to sell, this meant the railways were built through the areas occupied by the Pioneers, and to the mines. It was only later, certainly after the First World War, that the Bantu began to want to farm for sale. By 1928 Bantu in Nyasaland (Malawi) were leasing European-owned land for cash or a share of the crop.[5] Bantu in the Central Province of Nyasaland were growing tobacco for export between the World Wars. In Northern Rhodesia the Tonga began cash-cropping in the mid-twenties.[6] Sales of "surplus" output above family needs increased with each good season.[7] Beginning in the period between the wars the population/land ratio in the Reserved Areas became so large that the Bantu system of slash-and-burn agriculture and extensive grazing threatened to destroy the productivity of the land reserved for the Bantu (although William G. Barber says that it was not acute in Northern Rhodesia as late as the 1950s).[8] Thus the original division of land had not been so very inequitable—given, of course, that the Pioneers were in the position of conquerors and were going to take a considerable amount of land away. Only later did the division of the land become an inequitable deprivation of the Bantu's means of livelihood.

From the third proposition—that normal people would work for wages —the British derived the expectation that Bantu would come to work on the European farms; and, shortly thereafter, in the mines. After all, everyone "knew" that the offer of a wage that would enable a person to buy more would call forth a supply of willing workers.

The Bantu also had propositions about society and about people. The surface of the earth was there to be used so long as it was useful—the Bantu practiced a shifting, slash-and-burn, digging-stick agriculture—and left to nature when it lost its carrying capacity. There was always vacant land. If two clans tried to occupy the same area, one or both would move off; or, where there was a powerful kingdom, the powerful would drive the weak off, very likely killing the men and carrying off the women and children.

Bantu did not have a right to land. What they had was a right to farm, which they exercised by moving onto unused land.[9] Where, as among the

Ndebele, there was a strong king, the king told his people where to farm, but it never occurred to any Bantu that the king would not assign sufficient areas to cultivate and to support the cattle. The Bantu said, "The king is the land and the cattle," meaning that the king's command, his assignment of land, and his giving and taking away of cattle were the laws of the land, ignored at the peril of one's life. The British translated the statement into their own cultural norms as "The land belongs to the king," which has quite different connotations, not only of rights to sell or to lease, but also of rights to evict and to *withhold* from use.

As to whether the Bantu worked hard, their answer would have been, "Of course." Bantu men cut the brush and burned it. They hunted. They danced. They went on raiding parties, or served in the *impis* of the army of the king. They herded the cattle of *kraal* or clan, or the cattle that the king had assigned to them—in daily life it did not make much difference which. The women prepared the soil with digging sticks. They planted, tended, and harvested the grain. They made beer. And very largely, they did as they were told.

The result was that Bantu did not come forward to earn wages. They knew that *women, not men,* cultivated the fields. They knew what goods any reasonable person would want, and they knew that hunting and dancing were more rewarding activities then digging in a pit. "Why on earth," they might have asked, "would anyone choose to be transsexual or a mole in order to buy a skillet?"

Consider the situation from the point of view of the Pioneers. A man who will not work for wages for himself or his family, but rather hunts and dances, must be lazy or irresponsible, or both. Only ignorance or stupidity could account for the failure of Bantu to take advantage of wages and what wages would buy. No Bantu was asked, but he could have told the Pioneers that he knew how to recognize the faces of two hundred different cows, that he could outrun most Europeans, and that he was as careful in his own affairs as the European was in his. However, that would have been beside the point: Pioneers and mining companies did not want cowherds who could run a marathon in phalanx. Civilized people work hard. Chasing an antelope is not hard work—it is an exhausting sport, but it is not hard work.

At this point in the argument one must recognize that there were differences between the British at home and the British in the colonies.[10] The Pioneers were British, but they were not the sort that one found in the Colonial Office or the House of Commons. People who grab a rifle to carve out a family fortune in a strange land are acutely sensitive to immediate cultural differences, but less sensitive to humane imperatives, and the Pioneers needed labor badly and were willing to use compulsion if they had to. If labor, not civilizing, was first on the Pioneers' list of priorities, the Pioneers did think that hard, responsible work was a necessary characteristic of civilized societies. Self-interest and duty thus coincided.

The British at home looked forward to a long civilizing mission.[11] They hoped, in the end, to assimilate the Bantu into a society British in every respect except the color of the skin. These British were decent people. One of this sort, of a later generation, a member of a Methodist men's club, once asked me, "Don't you agree that, next to Christianity, the British Empire has been the greatest civilizing influence in history?" He thought that his country had been "doing good." When his forefathers sent Native Commissioners to the Rhodesias, it was to protect and to civilize the Bantu, not to exploit them. The British at home were strongly opposed to forced labor—they abhorred anything that smacked of slavery.

J. S. Furnivall, perhaps the most percipient historian of modern colonial systems, has pointed out that

> colonial policy is only one aspect of national policy; each generation evolves its own social philosophy with no direct reference to colonial affairs, and inevitably colonial policy is framed in terms of the broad general conceptions which dominate the national outlook. . . . When we came to accept the principle of freedom of person, property, and trade, consistency required that it be extended to colonial relations. Similarly the idea of social justice that took shape in Europe during the nineteenth century permeated colonial policy. . . . Liberty, Social Justice, Democracy, if approved as sauce for the domestic goose, are served up later with the colonial gander.[12]

However, between the London goose and the Rhodesian gander stood the Pioneers.

A compromise emerged. London forbade forced labor but allowed a head tax payable only in money. Young Bantu men came to the farms in order to earn the money to pay their tribe's head tax—because they had to—but they did not try hard and they went home after a few months. In this manner the compromise created a labor force that was transient and uncommitted and thus unwilling to learn the skills and habits of work needed to make it more productive.

The mining companies thus faced a problem: how were they to use such a workforce? To solve the problem the companies organized the productive processes so that they could use large numbers of these unskilled workers and a small number of skilled workers (and some not so skilled) drawn from Britain. The companies paid the Bantu workers what they were worth to the companies—and what each Bantu was worth to a company was a wage too low to support a family, basic food rations, and housing in a compound.[13] It makes no difference here whether one subscribes to a marginal productivity theory of wages or to some other view. An appreciable increase in wages—one large enough to allow workers to live in houses with their families—could not have been paid out of profits. A different way of organizing production would have been necessary, and this would not have been possible without a different kind of labor force. The Bantu, living in compounds without families or others toward whom they felt responsible, and without prospects of advancement, did what any sane person would do: the minimum necessary, moving from job to job. This behavior only confirmed European prejudices about the Bantu and so discouraged efforts to change the system.

The pattern was set before one or two generations' experience of working for wages and enjoying the things wages would buy began to change Bantu attitudes. Too late they became increasingly desirous of money incomes. At the same time, the men became less and less enamored of sharing their earnings with an extended kinship network back in the Reserved Areas, and wanted to settle with their families, at least more or less permanently, at their place of work.[14] The companies, meanwhile, had discovered that Bantu who settled with their families provided a more responsible workforce and began to establish *locations* where families could live and farm small subsistence plots nearby. It might have seemed —as it did to Godfrey Wilson[15]—that a policy of slow assimilation had become possible.

The system had, however, created a constituency of highly paid and privileged European workers who had much to lose—their high pay and privileged position—and nothing to gain by any policy that would have upgraded the Bantu workforce. They lived in the Rhodesias and so could make their desires effective on the spot. They voted in the elections for the colonial legislatures, which enjoyed semi-autonomous powers over the internal affairs of the colonies, and they were organized in unions that could bring mining to a halt if they struck. Thus the organization of production and the institutions of racial segregation reinforced each other.

Actually Rhodesian Selection Trust, one of the two large copper mining companies in Northern Rhodesia, wanted to start up-grading its Bantu labor in the early 1940s and was willing to ride out a strike to do so, but was persuaded to make no changes in the interests of maintaining production during the war and, because of the dollar earnings, in the years immediately after the war.[16] Here we have a case where metropolitan interests did retard Bantu development (under, one might note, a socialist as well as an earlier wartime coalition government).

While the mining companies and their directors had no great long-run interest in maintaining the *status quo*, neither did they have strong reasons for wanting it changed. Since the skilled Europeans could quickly close down the operations of the companies, and as voters could influence local law and administration, the companies, quite naturally, chose commercial discretion over moral valor. This choice was almost certainly made more compelling by the thought that to change would be to give up a known, workable system in order to engage in a difficult, time-consuming experiment with an unknown system.[17] So long as Europeans were powerful in Central Africa and the existing productive system continued to supply minerals, the companies were in a situation where the only sensible thing to do was to continue to hire many unskilled, migrant Bantu and a few skilled Europeans.

There should be no difficulty with the ideas that the companies were sensible, the British workers were sensible, and the Bantu migrant laborers were sensible. Nor should there be problems with the ideas that the Bantus were simultaneously exploited and paid all that they were worth, or that the system was self-defeating. But it was not planned that way.

The anthropomorphic assumption that a metropolitan country acted as if it were a person, with a control over its nationals in the colonies analogous to the control that a person exercises over his limbs, leads to the unhistorical view that a nation, like a "reasonable man," could have anticipated the long-term consequences of its actions or the actions of its nationals in the colonies. Instead of interpreting colonial histories as conscious efforts to use power to exploit at the cost of humane values, one would do better to view the development of colonial institutions as a series of adaptations, by groups with varying interests and perceptions, to problems that arose from the conflicts of cultures in contact.

Notes

1. For the early history of the British in Central Africa (1890-1920ish), see Phillip Mason, *The Birth of a Dilemma: The Conquest and Settlement of Rhodesia* (London: Oxford University Press, 1958). For the situation during the last decade of British rule (1950s), see William J. Barber, *The Economy of British Central Africa* (Stanford, Calif.: Stanford University Press, 1961). In this essay I follow Mason's account for the early years. Barber's account of "The Character of the Indigenous Economy" (chapter 3) tells much the same tale. T. O. Ranger, *Revolt in Southern*

Rhodesia, 1896-97: A Study in African Resistance (Evanston, Ill.: North-western University Press, 1967), presents a picture of shameless greed on the part of Cecil Rhodes, S. L. Jameson, the Pioneers, and the British South Africa Company during the conquest, but it is not inconsistent with the argument in this essay, and he refers (p. 90) to Mason's as a "fine book." See notes 6 and 8.

2. Or "as agents [of the sovereign], and if agents, either for the crown or for the people of Rhodesia, who again might be variously defined." Only "a few eccentrics [said] that [the land] had never been alienated from the original inhabitants" (Mason, p. 258). It is a curiosity that the same issues of title and sovereignty were debated in India during the late eighteenth and early nineteenth centuries, and that the British rulers there had, by the 1840s, decided that they had completely misconceived the issues. The literature on British India that deals with these matters is now enormous, but still perhaps one of the finest short statements is George Campbell, "Tenure of Land in India," in *Systems of Land Tenure in Various Countries*, ed. Cobden Club (London: Macmillan, 1870). More easily located would be B. H. Baden-Powell, *The Land Systems of British India*, 3 vols. (Delhi: Oriental Publishers, and Columbia, Mo.: South Asia Books, reprint, n.d., c1892), vol. 1, pp. 216-40; Walter C. Neale, *Economic Change in Rural India: Land Tenure and Reform in Uttar Pradesh, 1800-1955* (Port Washington, N.Y./London: Kennikat Press, 1973, c1962), pp. 18-47; and Walter C. Neale, "Reciprocity and Redistribution in the Indian Village: A Sequel to Some Notable Discussions," chapter 11 in *Trade and Market in the Early Empires*, ed. Karl Polanyi, Conrad M. Arensberg, and Harry W. Pearson (Glencoe, Ill.: Free Press, 1957), pp. 218-36.

3. Ranger, *Revolt in Southern Rhodesia*, pp. 90, 101 for details.

4. Ibid., pp. 318-20, 340-42.

5. Barber, *The Economy of British Central Africa*, p. 65.

6. Elizabeth Colson, *Marriage and the Family Among the Plateau Tonga of Northern Rhodesia* (Manchester: Manchester University Press, 1958), pp. 66, 70.

7. Barber, *The Economy of British Central Africa*, pp. 67, 95.

8. Ibid., p. 66.

9. Paul Bohannan, " 'Land,' 'Tenure' and Land-Tenure," in *African Agrarian Systems*, ed. Daniel Biebuyck (London/N.Y.: Oxford University Press, 1963), pp. 101-11 is a fascinating account of cultural differences in perceptions of geography, rights, and tenures.

10. Throughout *Revolt in Southern Rhodesia* Ranger contrasts the attitudes and behavior of the white settlers with the orders from London and with the attitudes of civil servants and many other British in Southern Rhodesia and South Africa. It is important to realize that there was not one "British position" but at least two quite opposed "British positons."

11. The assertion that the long-term objective was to civilize the Bantu is not an assertion that the British in Southern Rhodesia, including colonial civil servants, began by liking or respecting the people whom they had come to civilize. On the contrary, "The reaction of settlers, missionaries

and administrators alike ... was one of contempt and dislike" (Ranger, p. 3; the following instances are also from Ranger, pp. 1, 3, 2). The Resident Magistrate of Salisbury characterized them as "savages .... [w]th true kaffir deceit." A resident of Bulawayo jotted in his diary, "No one likes the Mashonas, dirty, cowardly lot. Matablele blood-thirsty devils but a fine type." Lord Grey, the third Administrator of the colony, wrote his wife that the Mashona "have the habits of a whipped cur and not infrequently bite through terror the hand outstretched to help them." But among the colonial civil servants a change occurred. The first Native Commissioner of Mrewa later said, "We had underrated the Mashonas. We knew nothing of their past history ... [and] none of us really understood the people or could follow their line of thought."

12. J. S. Furnivall, *Colonial Policy and Practice: A Comparative Study of Burma and Netherlands India* (N.Y.: N.Y.U. Press, 1956, c1948), pp. 6-7. While Furnivall [as cited, and also especially *Netherlands India: A Study of Plural Economy* (Cambridge: Cambridge University Press, 1944, c1939)] has been standard for scholars in Southeast Asia studies, he has not been so widely read by other social scientists, perhaps because of his career as administrator and advisor to governments rather than as historian or economist. Only Lord Hailey, *An African Survey, Revised 1956: A Study of Problems Arising in Africa South of the Sahara* (London/N.Y./Toronto: Oxford University Press, 1957) might be considered competitive, but its 1,670 pages should be treated as an encyclopedic reference.

13. See Hla Myint, *The Economics of the Developing Countries*, 4th (rev.) ed. (London: Hutchison & Co., 1973), pp. 42-46. Myint could hardly be described as unsympathetic to the people who made up the migrant labor forces that worked the European-managed mines and plantations. Myint's model of the colonial mining and plantation economy (pp. 41-53) presents a general model, in more economistic terms, of the phenomena described in this section. Myint (pp. 29-40) also presents the processes of peasant adaptation to colonial rule in an analogous model—but without, in either case, strongly emphasizing the roles of cultural perceptions or of the different groups and interests involved.

14. Both Godfrey Wilson, *An Essay on the Economics of Detribalization in Northern Rhodesia*, Part 1 (Livingston, Northern Rhodesia: The Rhodes-Livingston Institute, 1941), chapter 3, and Margaret Read, "Migrant Labour in Africa and its Effects on Tribal Life," *International Labour Review* 45 (June 1942): 615-31 make these points.

15. Ibid.

16. Barber, *The Economy of British Central Africa*, p. 197.

17. That the companies were not devoted to the system was evidenced by their change of policy as it became clear that independence would soon come to Northern Rhodesia (Zambia). The companies were willing to change fast enough when the political situation changed, and they do not seem to have suffered over much by upgrading black Zambians. Myint cites Robert E. Baldwin ("A Study in Dual Economy—the Case of Copper Mining in Northern Rhodesia," *Race* 4 [November 1962]: 73-87) to the effect that the rapid increase in wages for Bantu may have halved

the numbers of unskilled employed. Whatever the merits or demerits of the new policy of increasing wages, the results show that at appreciably higher wages the companies preferred to reorganize the system of production in order to eliminate unskilled labor—further evidence that the unskilled were not worthwhile at much higher wages. Speaking of the gold-mining industry of Southern Rhodesia in the 1950s, Barber (*The Economy of British Central Africa*, pp. 249-51) says, "Rising money costs of African labour have encouraged a shift to higher techniques. . . . The gold mines which relied on labour-intensive techniques have gone out of production; meanwhile the larger properties have apparently introduced methods more capital intensive than those they found it profitable to employ when African labour was cheaper." The argument here is not that, at an earlier time, the mining companies were paying "all they could," but that, within the system as it had evolved, they could not pay wages so much higher that the effects upon Bantu would have been significantly different.

22

Global Corporations
and National Stabilization Policy:
The Need for Social Planning

Ronald Müller

A conclusion reached by this article is that there is a clear-cut need for explicit public sector social planning in the United States. This conclusion is derived from a diagnostic on the *systemic* impacts arising out of contemporary worldwide conglomerate competition between global corporations, both U.S. and foreign based. The need for planning, however, currently is recognized by two different groups of advocates, each having different reasons and goals and, therefore, advocating different planning models. One group proposes transnational public institutions and planning for the international harmonization of nation-states' macroeconomic policies. The other group recognizes this need, but only as a derivative part of a national social development plan for the United States. The latter plan places a major emphasis on the social control and accountability of large corporations; the former does not.

Before examining these alternative views on planning, it is necessary to review the systemic impacts which result from the new competitive operating characteristics of global corporations. More specifically, the analysis focuses on whether the global interdependence of individual economies resulting from the globalization of their largest private corporations does not have a direct bearing on the growing inefficacy of national macroeconomic stabilization policy to maintain full employment, price stability, and balance-of-payments equilibrium. This review derives a number of testable propositions which, taken together, lead to the conclusion that since the mid-1960s macroeconomic monetary and fiscal policy for regulating the U.S. economy has had increasingly ineffective and at times perverse results. A direct causal connection is seen to hold between this policy inefficacy and the emergence of global corporations as the dominant actors of the U.S. political economy. It is this growing policy inefficacy which is an important reason for the need for planning. In proceeding the reader is warned that what follows is a highly condensed and abstracted summary of a rather vast literature and complex topic. Space constraints, for example, have necessitated the exclusion of instability in U.S. income distribution, although it is an important symptom of U.S. corporate globalization and its accompanying twin force, domestic corporate concentration.

A major contention of this article is that the globalization of the world's largest private enterprises, industrial and financial alike, represents a structural transformation in the location of their activities and the manner in which they behave as institutions. In turn, this structural transformation now has increased significantly the invalidity of the behavioral assumptions in the orthodox microeconomic theory of the firm, the underlying basis for modern Keynesian macroeconomic theory, and therefore policy. Because these corporations account for the dominant share of economic transactions within and between nation-states, it is hypothesized that their own transformation has brought about a structural transformation of the national and international economy. This change in the behavior of the U.S. economy, including its foreign sector, means that it no longer responds in the fashion predicted by the theoretical models underlying policy making. The major part of this article will present a range of empirical examples for the verification of this hypothesis. First, however, we turn to the meaning of structural transformation as it relates to our knowledge of how an economy changes its behavior over time.

Structural Change and the
Nature of Transformation

This is not the first time that the U.S. political economy has undergone a structural transformation. With the development of a nationwide communications infrastructure after the Civil War, the United States went from a set of regionally based economies to that of a nationally integrated economy. This transformation was led by that of the local-regional firm into the large nationwide corporation. Other institutions, however, lagged in this transformation process. Nationwide labor units lagged in their evolution, not receiving final legal recognition until after the beginning of the Great Depression. Public sector regulatory institutions were also slow in responding. Only in the very late nineteenth century, notably in the field of antitrust after the post–Civil War surge in industrial and financial concentration, was there a significant change in the regulatory functions of government over private business. Yet, it was not until the depths of the Great Depression that the public sector completed its own transformation into performing the regulatory and macro management functions of the national economy as they are known today. This "structural lag" in public sector institutions also mirrored a lag in economic theory. Again, only when the depression was well underway did economic theory experience its own transformation in the form of the Keynesian "synthesis." This was the last transformation of the U.S. political economy until that of the post–World War II period.

The Present Transformation

The present structural transformation can be identified by two sets of empirical indicators representing the *interrelated* forces of change which have been at work. The first, taking place via the largest banks and industrial enterprises, is the globalization of the economy. Stated otherwise, the U.S. economy has undergone an historic increase in its foreign dependency. The second set is the historic upsurge in the industrial and financial concentration of the domestic private sector.

The true extent of the U.S. economy's dependence on foreign operations cannot be gleaned by focusing on exports and imports as a percentage of GNP. Note, rather, that in 1960 the proportion of *total* corporate U.S. profits derived overseas was only 7 percent, with exponential increases commencing around 1967.[1] Today, an estimated 30 percent of total U.S. corporate profits are derived from overseas. Another indicator of the new global dependence of the U.S. economy is the amount of total U.S. corporate investment which goes overseas versus that which stays at home. In 1957, foreign investment in new plant and equipment was 9 percent of *total* U.S. corporate domestic plant and equipment expenditures; by 1970, it had reached a figure of some 25 percent. Again, exponential increases occurred, starting in the years 1965–1967. In 1961, the sales of all U.S. manufacturing abroad represented only 7 percent of total U.S. sales; by 1965, the figure had crept up to 8.5 percent; but by 1970, foreign sales were more than 13 percent of total sales of *all* U.S. manufacturing corporations. For the U.S. banking sector, current foreign dollar deposits of the nation's largest global banks are estimated at more than 65 percent of their domestic deposit holdings, up from 8.5 percent in 1960.

With a time lag, the corporate globalization process has led to an acceleration in the rate of increase in industrial and financial concentration of the U.S. *domestic* sector. Between 1955 and 1970, *Fortune*'s 500 industrial corporations increased their share of total manufacturing and mining employment, profits, and assets from slightly more than 40 percent to over 70 percent. Whereas during the 1950s the largest 200 were increasing their share of total industrial assets by an annual average of one percent, by the 1960s this annual rate of increased concentration had doubled. For 1947–1966, the largest 50 U.S. corporations increased their share of total value-added in manufacturing from 17 to 25 percent; the largest 200, from 30 to 42 percent.

The momentum of cumulative concentration is in part reflected by the corporate merger movement. Of the 14,000 individual mergers during 1953–1968, the top 100 firms accounted for only 333, but acquired 35 percent of all merged assets. In the mid-1960s the merger movement accelerated at an exponential rate: almost 60 percent of the $66 billion of total merged assets between 1953 and 1968 were acquired in the last four years of that period. In 1965, for example, the 1,496 mergers were the highest annual increase in the history of the United States.

Increases in banking concentration started somewhat later than in the industrial sector, but by 1970 the top 50 of a total of some 13,000 banks had over 48 percent of all bank assets. From 1965 to 1970 the top 50 were increasing their share of total assets at more than double their expansion rate during the previous ten years. Federal Reserve Board studies show that almost all foreign deposits of U.S. banks are in the hands of the top 20 U.S. global banks, with four holding 38 percent of these deposits, and 12 having 83 percent of all foreign banking assets. On the lending side, the 220 largest banks account for virtually all of industrial bank loans. Nine of the largest global banks account, for example, for more than 26 percent of all total commercial and industrial lending by U.S. banks. In addition, these same nine hold 90 percent of the entire indebtedness in the U.S. petroleum and natural gas industry,

66 percent in machinery and metal products, and 75 percent in the chemical and rubber industries.

These indicators are presented as evidence of the structural transformation of the economy itself. Globalization and concentration, however, are not the only indicators. Others, to be discussed shortly, include money flows and the use of credit. Of significance here is that an analysis of these various indicators shows that they broke their historical trend paths sometime during the mid-1960s. This suggests that the turning point in the structural transformation of the economy occurred somewhere between 1965 and 1967, which correlates well with the beginning of the "stagflation" phenomenon, an occurrence unaccounted for by economic theory and thus far defying governmental policy-making corrections.

Global Corporations and Global Corporate Competition: Policy Implications

To understand the transformed behavior of the economy, in contrast to the assumptions about its behavior embedded in policy making, it is necessary to review the institutional characteristics of actual corporate behavior, since, as already noted, global corporations account for the majority of the economy's transactions. If in the aggregate we understand the dynamics of the corporate sector of the economy, then we have gone a long way toward understanding the behavior of the national economy and the problems of current policy. We shall focus on the transformed goals and the actual operational means (corporate operating techniques) by which global enterprises accomplish these goals. This analysis, however, is only illuminating if done in the context of the global competitive forces that, to a certain extent, both constrain and determine the individual enterprise's behavior. Finally, our review of global corporate institutional characteristics can explain other aspects of the structural transformation of the national economy not yet discussed.

Global Maximization and National Welfare

When a national corporation evolves into a global one, the basic change in goals is that of maximizing the long-run profits of the parent's total global system. There is now abundant empirical evidence to demonstrate that global system profit maximization does not necessarily mean the maximization of each subsidiary's profits, at least in the sense of profits as recorded by national statistics. For example, transfer pricing permits cost minimization for the global system by shifting profits earned, but not reported, in one nation to another nation with a lower tax rate. The outcome is global tax minimization, one of the key requisites for global profit maximization. A second outcome is negation of the classical and neoclassical theoretical proposition which underlies much of current policy: A national production unit will be operated to maximize profits earned, declared, and accruing to the nation-state within which it is located. At the very least, therefore, the operational techniques of managing the multinational economic system of a global corporation make uncertain whether a parent's operation of any given subsidiary will be in harmony with a given country's national welfare. This uncertainty can be attached to the national welfare implications of both host and home nations alike, since the emphasis is on global system profit maximization, which need not be the same as home country profit maximization.

National Policy:
Concentration and Globalization

Two major and empirically well-established characteristics of global corporations are that (1) most of them are conglomerates and (2) that in the many different product groups or industries in which they operate, they compete as oligopolies, not as perfectly competitive firms. In turn, oligopoly competition, as orthodox economics correctly teaches, is characterized not only by nonprice forms of competitive behavior, but also, and more important for our present purposes, by a particular short-run management goal for assessing the stability of the corporations' long-term profit stream. This short-run goal of the oligopoly is minimally the maintenance, or preferably the increase, in its market shares vis-à-vis its other competitors. When an oligopoly, competing to maintain or increase its market share in one industry, is in fact a subsidiary of a parent conglomerate operating in many industries, the parent can choose to "cross-subsidize" the subsidiary with one or more of its three basic resources: technology (including mechanical, managerial, and accounting), finance capital, and marketing resources. If the subsidiary is competing with other oligopoly firms that are not subsidiaries of conglomerates, then the likely systemic outcome is that these nonconglomerate firms eventually will experience a decline in their market shares,[2] go out of business, or be absorbed by conglomerate enterprises. This is true because, compared to the single industry firm, the conglomerate's sheer size allows it to generate internal economies of scale which over time give it an inherent competitive advantage over smaller concerns. Such internal economies include, for example, easier and usually cheaper sources of external finance, lower effective corporate tax rates, lower input costs (for example, advertising) due to quantity discounts and/or greater expertise, greater financial leverage to sustain cyclical periods of profit decline, and/or more easily sustained losses during short-run price competition at times of initial entry to new industries. If, in addition, the oligopoly competition just described is between the subsidiary of a global corporation, that is, a global conglomerate and a single industry, strictly national, oligopoly, then the systemic outcome of increasing concentration is even more likely to occur.

In the 1930s orthodox economics accepted into its fold the field of industrial organization. Since that time this subdiscipline has produced a rich empirical literature to demonstrate that cross-subsidization between subsidiaries of conglomerates is a basic practice of modern corporate life. It is also well known that wherever global corporations expand, an increase in concentration usually occurs. This takes place first in both the more and less developed host countries into which global companies expand through cross-subsidizing their initial foreign entries with the resources of the parent's home network. Later, there is a feedback to increased concentration in the home country. After a wave of foreign expansion, the global corporation can use the added internal economies of scale from its now increased size to supplement its competitiveness at home. That is, globalization leads, with a time lag, to increasing domestic concentration in the home nation. That this proposition on the systemic outcome of global oligopoly competition should be taken seriously is confirmed by recent empirical studies of the changing nature of industrial/financial organization and concentration in the countries of the European community.[3] These studies show that the only way European firms could stop and/or regain declining market shares, lost during the 1950s to U.S. global corporations, was through a duplication of their U.S. counterparts' expansion pattern of globalization and domestic mergers and acquisitions. Thus, by the early 1960s, after recovery from World War II, the European response to the "American Challenge" was to expand, first, globally and later through mergers and acquisitions in the home territory of the European community. The timing of the historical concentration increases in the U.S. economy of the 1960s also would appear to be explained by this proposition on the systemic outcome of global oligopoly competition.[4] This concentration spurt occurred after the initial global expansions by U.S. corporations into Europe and the underdeveloped countries in the 1950s. It is in this sense that we can understand why increasing global interdependence and concentration are interrelated aspects of the U.S. economy's structural transformation in the post–World War II period: interrelated and to be directly associated with the globalization of its largest corporations, mostly conglomerates, increasingly engaged in a new form of oligopoly competition, across nations and industries, with competitors who are more and more themselves conglomerates. In short, there is a *systemic and cumulative* process toward increasing global interdependence and concentration of the national economy.

Given this transformation, one notes some significant structural lags in governmental regulatory institutions and policies. For example, antitrust laws primarily emphasize horizontal and, secondarily, vertical integration, with a relative neglect of conglomerate mergers. (Of the 14,000 mergers between 1953 and 1968, the government challenged 199 cases, won 90, and required divesture in 48.) In addition, as concentration proceeded over this period, there became apparent a set of "vicious circles" arising out of the impacts of Keynesian monetary and fiscal policy and leading to increasing policy inefficacy. A recent quantitative analysis by Professor John Blair of actual policy impacts verifies the mounting evidence of other econometric investigations.[5] During the boom phase, stabilization policy is aimed at reducing inflation via a reduction in aggregate demand. The findings of Blair and others are revealing, however: The more concentrated the industry, the greater has been the occurrence of continuing relative price increases, that is, the opposite of intended policy impacts.

Examining the vicious circles inherent in fiscal and monetary policy is helpful in understanding these unintended impacts. For fiscal policy, it has been shown that tax reductions to stimulate the economy are disproportionately absorbed by the largest firms.[6] (Internal economies of scale can explain much of this result.) On the expenditure side, studies also reveal disproportionate amounts going to the largest firms. In both cases, the effect is to give large corporations a greater expansion capacity than smaller firms, thereby promoting further concentration. In the next round, the increased concentration leads to policy's increased ineffectiveness. The vicious circle is complete. A similar phenomenon takes place with monetary policy. On the borrowing side, during periods of credit restriction, the largest industrial firms do not (or only with a long time delay) respond to higher financing costs since their oligopoly positions permit them to pass on increased credit costs to their buyers. Smaller firms, because of their relatively weaker oligopoly power, must respond immediately and lower their investment demands. As in the case of taxes and expenditures, these differential structural impacts of aggregate policy promote further concentration. On the lending side, vicious circles also are at work. For example, George Budzeika recently published findings on the behavior of the large New York City banks:[7] "Bank behavior in the past two decades has shown that it is very difficult to control large banks whenever the demand for credit is heavy." The reasons for this again turn out to be the internal economies, unique to the large but not the smaller banks, which because of a "lack of information and skills prevent [the smaller] from adjusting quickly to changing levels of monetary restriction." For large banks, "the only way to restrain efficiently is to reduce the overall liquidity of the banking system." But since the costs in unemployment of such a strong measure are politically unacceptable, only mild monetary restraint has been pursued. This leads to further bank concentration and makes the next phase of policy restraint that much more ineffective.

Market Policy in a Postmarket Economy

The conglomerate characteristic of global corporations and the nature of global oligopoly competition explain a third category of structural transformation: More and more of the private sector's total domestic and international transactions are between subsidiaries of the same parent corporation. Thus the global corporation is largely a *postmarket enterprise,* since a significant share of its total transactions are not with independent buyers and sellers dealing at arms' length through the market. Given the dominance of aggregate global corporate transactions in the domestic and foreign sector, and given the systemic outcome of increasing concentration which results from global corporate competition, it is an empirically verifiable fact that our contemporary national and world economy is becoming increasingly a *postmarket economic system.*

What is meant by a postmarket economy? It is one in which there has occurred the negation of the social *function* of the market as an institution for equilibrating the economy. There are markets in the sense of a commodity space indicating the total number of goods produced or consumed, but in the functional sense just defined, which is the meaning of the concept as used in classical and neoclassical economics, the market largely has been negated. The function of the market as a social institution is to generate price signals through the forces of supply and demand as carried out by independent buyers and sellers. In the Keynesian synthesis, these signals are relied upon by private business people, unions, and public policy makers as the information for guiding their decisions governing the allocation of resources and the distribution of income. Where the market is operative, these decisions theoretically should result in full employment, price stability, and balance-of-payments equilibrium. *Systemically,* that is, neither by intent nor design, but by the outcome of modern corporate competition, global corporations are a chief source of market negation. First, the increasing concentration which accompanies their expansion, as orthodox theory correctly teaches, increasingly distorts price signals. Second, intracorporate transactions negate the market's social function, by definition, because they completely bypass the market. Market negation is another significant aspect of the post–World War II structural transformation of the U.S. political economy. This transformation, however, is still incomplete, for there is a notable structural lag in public sector regulatory institutions and decisions underlying economic policy making, which still assume that the market is as healthy as it was, say, 20 years ago.

One ironic episode of the public sector's lag involves the price controls used at one point during the Nixon administration's NEP. Whatever the arguments for or against controls, if a government employs them, the chief question becomes whether they can contain inflation in the short run. It is now a matter of record that controls worked both during World War II and the Korean War. They did not succeed in 1971. One reason for this failure was the simple fact that the administration chose to enforce price controls over a vast number of transactions with a miniscule staff of 300 people, less than 10 percent of whom were trained economists.[8] A second reason deals with the current large degree of intracorporate, nonmarket transactions of U.S. exports and imports compared to the earlier periods of price controls. The Nixon controls did not take this structural change into account. Not controlled was the phenomenon of domestically produced goods transacted on paper as exports to foreign subsidiaries and then again transacted on paper as imports into the United States. Since controls did not extend to imports, there were in effect no controls over these types of goods produced and consumed at home. The evidence suggests the phenomenon was widespread in important "linkage" industries such as construction materials, semi- and processed metals, fertilizers, and agribusiness.[9]

National Policy and Financial Structures

Another major characteristic of the post–World War II large corporation is the change in the manner by which it finances its expansion across industries and nations. The sheer pace and quantitative magnitude of expansion has necessitated that global enterprises shift significantly their basis of financing from internal to external sources.[10] This shift was accelerated by governmental capital restrictions such as the U.S. voluntary and mandatory balance-of-payments program. The latter, of course, was a catalyst in the development of the Euro-currency market, a further important structural characteristic of the new pattern of corporate financing to be discussed immediately below. In addition, the growth of output from this rapid expansion could not be absorbed given actual increases in consumer incomes. Corporations reacted, particularly in consumer durables, by establishing ancillary credit mechanisms and advertising, emphasizing the use of credit, a marketing strategy pointedly and successfully aimed at changing the psychology and propensities of consumers to incur record-breaking debt increases over increases in current income. National governments correspondingly have provided the liquidity to meet the financing needs of this form of expansion, bringing about historic increases in the money supply. This took place at a time when other new structural characteristics of finance (for example, credit cards, "checking-plus," and leasing) have contributed further to unprecedented increases in debt and the velocity of money.

From the perspective of current short-run stabilization policy, however, the Euro-currency market is one of the most important structural innovations of the post–World War II period. Global banks' justifiable and understandable creation of the Euro-currency market to meet the needs of global corporate expansion nevertheless was permitted by national governments to evolve without normal public regulatory control. The latter is perhaps one of the most notable indicators of the structural lag between the public sector's regulatory function and a now transformed private corporate sector. The lack of deposit reserve requirements, particularly, has made this $110 billion-plus pool of deposits an incalculable and unpredictable source of further increases to the world money supply. A second characteristic of the Euro-currency market is that U.S. and other global banks operating within its domain regularly violate the first principle of sound banking: Never borrow short to lend long. These aspects of the Euro-currency market have led observers such as Harvard professor H.S. Houthakker to note its impact as a "huge creation of private international liquidity." In his view, it "almost certainly contributes powerfully to the inflationary pressures that no nation has succeeded in keeping under control."[11]

Finally, the intracorporate, nonmarket basis of much cross-nation financial flows and the development of an accounting technology for global optimization of firms' liquid assets, combined with the sheer magnitude and rapidity (relative to the past) of these financial transfers, has eroded the autonomy or sovereignty of a nation's money supply, implying the increasing inability of national authorities to control it. "Leads and lags," for example, is a standard tool of business, invented long before the age of global companies to preserve the value of liquid assets during periods of foreign exchange instability. Central bank procedures to account for the effect of leads and lags on the domestic money supply are also ages old. But today, given systemic increases in global concentration and improved accounting technology, these same procedures cannot match the more massive and more rapid liquid transfers by many fewer actors than could have been foreseen a few short years ago.

Leads and lags immediately affect the money supply of a country, yet, since they are unrecorded transactions, reflected only in the "errors and omissions" component of a nation's balance-of-payments account, their actual impact on changing the money stock is discovered by central bankers only after considerable delay. The German experience of the late 1960s and early 1970s illustrates the problem and adds a further reason why current monetary policy has become an unreliable tool for regulating the economy. Studies of the German Bundesbank have found that although its policy led to "complete neutralization of the liquidity inflows to domestic banks . . . it does not curb the expansive effects exerted by the inflows of funds from abroad to non-banks on the money stock."[12] Additional work on these nonbank inflows by Michael Porter showed that the Bundesbank's required reserves policies to control the money supply "were substantially and rapidly offset in their effect on bank liquidity by capital inflows recorded mainly in errors and omissions . . . within one month and by some 80 percent."[13]

This example of the loss of sovereignty over the money supply by national governments is also reflected in the 1968–1969 episode involving the Federal Reserve System, U.S. global banks, and the Euro-currency market. The latter two, in combination with U.S. global firms, have fostered what IMF consultant Frank Tamanga has called the "convergence of U.S. multinational corporations and multinational banks into an integrated U.S. economy in exile."[14] This episode involved the attempt to constrain money supply growth by lowering interest rates on certificates of deposit (CDs) with the hope of absorbing these released monies into treasury bills. Instead, these monies were drawn to the higher interest rates of the Euro-currency market. Overnight these liquid assets were brought back into the United States by the intrabank borrowings of global banks from their overseas branches. The U.S.-based parent banks, in turn, used these borrowed deposits to create additional loans to their largest industrial clients, which, for reasons mentioned earlier, were not deterred by the significantly higher interest costs involved. The then low fractional reserve requirements on borrowed Euro-deposits yielded an actual expansion in the U.S. money supply, the exact opposite of the CD interest policy's intended result. Here we see how the twin forces of globalization and concentration structurally erode the efficacy of the nation-state's aggregate stabilization tools. Although in late 1969 (and again in early 1971) fractional reserve requirements were increased, the inflationary damage already had been done.[15]

Mobility versus Immobility:
The Information Crisis

The capstone characteristic of what Professor Scott Gordon has called "one of the most momentous facts of the modern age, the emergence of the corporation as a primary *social* institution,"[16] is the structural mobility of this social institution as compared to other primary ones in our society. As the classical economists from Adam Smith to Joseph Schumpeter used the term, *structure* refers not only to the physical but also to the behavioral aspects of institutions. What distinguishes the global corporation of today from its pre–World War II predecessor is its heightened structural mobility, that is, its increased capacity to change rapidly where and what it produces and an accelerating change in its managerial techniques for controlling that production. What distinguishes the global corporation from other social institutions is that the latter are relatively immobile in the physical sense and much slower to adapt or change in the behavioral sense. For example, government, national business firms, and organized labor are globally immobile, being largely constrained in their institutional jurisdiction to the home nation.

This mobility versus immobility characterizing the structural lag of the noncorporate institutions of the economy has as a major symptom a "crisis in information." That is, information once provided via the workings of the market is today increasingly either missing or un-reliable. For the foreign sector, large-scale corporate sampling surveys reveal over 50 percent of total trade transactions are now of the non-market intracorporate variety. Yet, official governmental corporate disclosure information requirements can account for only about half this number.[17] The use of intraconglomerate transfers and the advent of such substitute financing as leasing, combined with the growth men-tality of the 1960s, has led Leonard Spacek, former chairman of Arthur Andersen & Co., to comment that the words "generally accepted ac-counting principles" on corporate consolidated balance sheets are a "fiction." "My profession appears to regard a set of financial statements as a roulette wheel." David Norr, of the American Institute of Certified Public Accounting, agrees: "Accounting today permits a shaping of results to attain a desired end. Accounting as a mirror of [economic] activity is dead."[18] Whatever legitimate corporate reasons consolidated balance sheets may serve, from the objective of social purposes they now hide more than they reveal. For example, a growing number of university studies now are documenting the frustration of unions to make, as a basis of their wage demands, an accurate assessment of the profitability of the particular subsidiary with which they are negotiating, since profits may have been shifted to another part of the parent con-glomerate's system.[19] For government policy making, reported corporate trade flows, profits, and debt burdens are the basis of decisions for managing employment, price, and balance-of-payments stability. But when the statistical basis of these decisions is unreliable and/or mis-leading, then the outcome of policy is, at best, uncertain, and at worst, perverse.

These behavioral aspects are not the only characteristics of the new corporate mobility. There is also the physical dimension. In the 1960s the pace of global oligopoly competition accelerated with the full-fledged entry of European and Japanese enterprises. Driven by interna-tional comparative cost differences in, first, labor and, later, the over-valued U.S. exchange rate and tax and antipollution costs, U.S. com-panies offset declining domestic and export market shares by displaying a remarkable mobility in transferring their production facilities to "export platform" facilities in underdeveloped countries. What Boston University's Peter Gabriel, Dean of Business, has termed the "herd instinct" of global corporations showed itself dramatically as the late-comer Japanese and Europeans began to duplicate export platform foreign investments of the pioneer U.S. companies. This pattern, starting in labor-intensive industries and quickly shifting to more capital-intensive sectors, further reinforced the global interdependence of nations, while it added new forms of structural lags and tensions in the home countries. Unions found another aspect of their countervailing power eroded as the threat of strike was effectively offset by the threat of production transfer overseas.[20] Smaller domestic subcontracting firms also felt the impacts of these transfers. In addition, government adjustment assistance programs, designed for times past, are ineffective in correcting the significant regional and industry dislocations in employment and small businesses. While no economist has yet to demonstrate the overall net domestic short-term employment impacts, positive or negative, of the new patterns of foreign investment, the results of structural long-term trend analysis are more pessimistic.

In the static theoretical market world of orthodox economics, changes in international comparative costs, dictating changes in the composition of national output and world trade, should lead to a new equilibrium situation via a path of smooth and rapid adjustments. This model underlying our current policies, of course, must assume that factors such as labor are domestically mobile and that basic economic institutions such as the market and the corporation never significantly change their behavioral characteristics. The real world of imperfect and nonexistent markets, global profit maximization and oligopoly competition and labor and governmental immobility, compounded by rapid changes in certain institutions and none in others, all make for an actual conclusion far removed from that of orthodox theory.

The Dilemma of National Policy Making:
The Need for Planning

On the eve of 1975, as this article is being written, the depths of structural lag in national stabilization policies are profound. Policy makers have yet to comprehend the many interrelated and intersecting forces arising out of the globalization and concentration processes of the corporate private sector. The worldwide complementary planning decisions of global banks and industrial companies have brought with them a convergence or harmonization in the business cycles of advanced nations. The upshot is that the United States no longer can rely, through foreign trade and finance multipliers, on Europe's upswing toward a boom to help bring us out of the declining phase of our own cycle, and vice versa. Today, one nation's deflationary or inflationary surges cumulatively help to bring about and accelerate those of other countries.

The rise of the global bank now finds its impacts in the global interdependence between national financial systems and money supplies, with this web of interdependence feeding unregulated banking transactions of a Euro-currency market. The structural lag accompanying the rise of the first and pioneering postmarket global corporations, those of the petroleum sector, as well as their bargaining power as a buyer's cartel to determine terms of trade, finally has been "overcome" on the supply side by a structural phenomenon called OPEC. Yet the lag persists in the failure to develop the financial structure to recycle the dramatic new distribution of worldwide liquid assets resulting from the rapid shift in bargaining power and accompanying changes in *real* terms of trade arising out of OPEC and similar phenomena.[21] Within this matrix of interdependence stands the obvious lack of a global central bank of last resort to stem the (now recognized) threat of an international spiral of debt liquidation crises triggered through the Euro-currency market.

For those who have been studying the interdependent *structural* changes arising out of the globalization of that "primary social institution," the large corporation, the current economic instability was predictable. For orthodox economists (and, unfortunately, the managers and government policy makers they advise), because of their preoccupation with *functional* studies of changes in aggregate data and their use of a model which assumes that primary institutions are static, the current events of the day have come as a surprise. The former group analyzes changes in *terms of trade* within and between national economies based on changing power relations arising out of the diffusion of new "knowledge" and as functionally constrained at the limits by aggregate supply and demand conditions. The latter group attempts to analyze terms of trade by a functional focus on supply and demand with little regard for changing power relations between primary institutions. The structuralist model incorporates the functional approach.[22] The functionalist model sees as unnecessary, and thereby assumes away, the study of structural changes. During a period of structural transformation the current functional model breaks down, as does the efficacy of its policy prescriptions. At this point the model needs "updating" to bring it closer to the structural reality which it seeks to predict. So it was with Keynes, who, in the midst of the crisis in economics of the 1930s, built upon the work of the Swedish structuralism-functionalism school of Knut Wicksell and Gunnar Myrdal to derive a new model for policy-making purposes, operative until the next, and in this case our current, period of structural transformation. The present crisis in economics was well summarized by George Shultz, former secretary of the treasury: "We have come into a very unusual period, where we more or less cast loose from beliefs that we once held to be unarguable. We have cast off from a large number of these old moorings and we have not yet found new ones."[23]

This is not the place for detailed proposals dealing with the inefficacy of current national stabilization policies. However, we may point to the chief parameters which will govern policy approaches to the problems of contemporary economic instability. In general, the traditionally accepted public sector regulatory institutions for managing the economy are structurally lagging behind the revolution in a basic institution of the private sector. The most notable symptom of this structural lag is an information crisis due to the mutually and systemically reinforcing processes of corporate globalization and concentration as they negate the market's social *function* for providing a reliable guide to policy making. An additional aspect of this conclusion is that the ultimate result of corporate globalization has been the obviously greatly increased degree of interdependence between nation-states. But the political implications of this interdependence are yet to be sufficiently understood.

On the one hand, there is a clear need in the United States to ask fundamental questions about the adequacy of current public regulatory institutions: antitrust laws and enforcement mechanisms, corporate disclosure laws, accounting conventions, banking and labor relations legislation, and the capacity of the government itself to maintain its corporate tax base. On the other hand, such seemingly national political issues have unpredictable economic impacts in a time of global interdependence. Thus the modification by only one nation-state of the public sector's regulatory function is severely limited unless such modifications are harmonized among all advanced countries. This is true because of the nature of global oligopoly competition and the extent to which national income is now dependent upon the competitiveness of home nation global corporations in their overseas operations. If the regulatory institutions of only one country, for example, the United States, are modified in an attempt to provide more reliable stabilization policies, there is a distinct probability that this nation's national income will suffer. In this case competitive oligopoly advantages could well accrue to the global corporations of other nations. Thus the age-old dilemma of the oligopolist, "if I do not take advantage of an opportunity my competitors will," becomes, in an era of global interdependence and corporations, the dilemma of the national policy maker and the underlying rationale for planned international harmonization. Yet, the parameters of planning obviously are never solely determined by the dictates of economic (in this case, global) efficiency, but equally by those of politics. This is so if for no other reason than because nation-states have different comparative resource endowments, different levels of development and developmental goals, and, therefore, different national interests.

It is within this context that the politics of international harmonization will have to deal with what, in the opinion of this writer, undoubtedly will be basic institutional modifications if world economic stability is to be regained. From this view of the necessity of planning, two central questions emerge: (1) Is global harmonization politically feasible? (2) If it is, for whom will it be economically desirable? These are the prime issues of the national and international "econopolitics" of the years ahead,[24] even when one looks at an alternative, structuralist, view of the need for planning, stemming from the works of such writers as Walter Adams, J.K. Galbraith, John Blair, Barry Commoner, Gunnar Myrdal, and others. Their view brings into focus additional considerations, such as the social as opposed to the private efficiency of the current size of large global corporations; the lack of local community input into the private conglomerate's centralized planning on the use and/or discontinuance of a given local subsidiary; and the desirability, let alone feasibility, of maintaining the present *composition* of national output.

Those who advocate planning only the international harmonization of nation-state economic policies assume the social desirability of the competitive dynamics of the present conglomerate system of private control of production. Stated otherwise, their philosophy of jurisprudence assumes the modern conglomerate to be a private, not a social, institution. The structuralist view challenges this assumption, and thus advocates different planning parameters. Similarly, the first view recognizes global interdependence while officially believing that the market's function as social regulator is still operative. Those of the alternative persuasion correctly recognize the negation of the market's social function and emphasize the heightened technological interdependence of society, but, in my opinion, they have yet to grasp fully the depths of global interdependence. Again the differences between the two groups mean different planning parameters and therefore different institutions for plan implementation.

Should those advocating planning for international harmonization of national economic policy emerge from the econopolitical process as the dominant group, one can derive "positivistically" some hypotheses as to what plan implementation for this purpose would entail: significant replacement of national public sector regulatory institutions by transnational institutions, particularly in the domain of finance, taxes, corporate disclosure, and antitrust. Such an outcome suggests an even further removal of productive forces from local and national social control. To the extent these hypotheses are predictively correct,[25] this writer, as an adherent of the normative tradition of classical political economy, must "normatively" judge them as unacceptable. He therefore turns to an alternative set of planning parameters: a social development plan for the United States, a basic purpose of which is to increase the degree of local community and national social control over the economic system.

The purpose of this article has been to diagnose current international and domestic economic and political forces and to suggest the need for an explicit public sector planning process, not to detail the plan basis and components of that process. Some suggestions should serve, however, to facilitate the discussion. First, a major objective of a social development plan is to take advantage of our current knowledge and afford to the U.S. polity the opportunity to decide what type of nation it wishes to be in the future. Second, the necessity for such a step is to avoid what the polity decides are the negative social consequences which can occur out of unplanned development in a nation and world which has become so obviously technologically and globally interdependent. Third, plan objectives, targets, and strategies, if they are to uphold personal freedom, must be explicitly decided upon through the political process and therefore should form an official part of each political party's electoral platform. The respective parties' social development plans thereby become a significant criterion by which the electorate determines for whom to vote. Fourth, major components of the social development plan should include a set of objectives covering the desired degree of income equality, a definition of full employment, the composition of national output, and thus the degree of foreign dependency these objectives necessitate. Fifth, because of the problematic aspects of current global interdependence diagnosed above, it is necessary to implement transitional planning phases of, for example, four years each, with initial plan objectives targeted for the twelfth year.

Finally, these transitional phases would lay the groundwork for the realization of subsequent planning processes and plan objectives. For example, there will be the need to pursue a foreign policy supportive of the plan's objectives, taking into account current levels of global interdependence and pushing for certain types of international harmonization derived from the plan itself. During the transition phases major legislative decisions should be undertaken, foremost of which could be the legal redefinition of large corporations as social rather than private institutions. From this follows the need to overcome the aforementioned corporate information crisis, through such measures as "deconsolidation of consolidated balance sheets" and a recomposition of boards of directors to include elected representatives from the various constituencies which large corporations as social institutions employ and serve. Suggestive of other major legislative questions is that of nationalization, including its definition, costs and benefits, and to which corporations (not necessarily industries), if any, it should apply, and so forth. Finally, by way of example, there is the question of whether or not the spatial definition of *local community* necessitates the redrawing of state boundaries into economic, political, and administratively functional regions so as to allow a feasible intermesh between community and national objectives.

These suggestions are admittedly incomplete, crudely formulated, and undoubtedly will shock many who read them. The shock will be of two types. There will be those whose dismay is of a political nature and who perceive the idea of a social development plan as a threat to personal freedom, initiative and enterprise. They are, however, mistaken; as shown above, the current lack of social planning would seem to negate the pursuit of individual freedoms for all but the most powerful. Still others will be dismayed on feasibility grounds, perceiving the tasks of plan design and implementation as overwhelming. I believe they, too, are mistaken, but their reservations are to be taken quite seriously. To restore stability in a world of instability is indeed an enormous task, but it is also a challenging one. For much too long our most basic human resource, new knowledge, has been focused largely on our material domain, on a public-private spectrum that extends from the Manhattan Project, to the factory production line, to the managerial and accounting technology for global maximization of private profits. Does not the drift of history suggest it is time to bring science and ethics back together again,[26] to commence, perhaps through a number of Manhattan-type projects, the refocusing of our new knowledge on the idea-task of an equitable and stable social organization?

Notes

1. All data on globalization and concentration indicators are taken from official government statistics and reports as well as studies of Business International Incorporated. Detailed documentation of these figures is found, for globalization, in chapter 10 and, for concentration, in chapter 9 of this writer's book, coauthored with Richard J. Barnet, *Global Reach: The Power of the Multinational Corporations* (New York: Simon and Schuster, 1974).

2. By "systemic outcome" is meant the inherent result from the interaction of various institutions with each other within the context of a given socioeconomic system. *Systemic* here is being used in the same sense as in the works of the classical economists such as Adam Smith and Joseph Schumpeter.

3. See the papers of H.W. de Jong, K.D. George and A. Silverston, Helmut Arndt, S.J. Prais and C. Reid, and Ronald Müller given at the Nijenrode International Conference on Industrial Organization, Holland, 12–17 August 1974, to be published in H.W. de Jong and A.P. Jacquemin, *International Aspects of Industrial Organization* (Amsterdam: North Holland Publishing Co., 1975).

4. The feedback of U.S. firms' foreign investment on increasing domestic investment concentration has been verified econometrically in Tom Horst's study for the Brookings Institution, "American Investment Abroad and Domestic Market Power," preliminary draft (Washington, D.C.: December 1974).

5. John Blair, "Market Power and Inflation: A Short-Run Target Return Model," *Journal of Economic Issues* 8 (June 1974): 453–77. See also the findings of Otto Eckstein and David Wyss, "Industry Price Equations," paper presented at the Conference on Econometrics of Price Determination, Washington, D.C., 30–31 October 1973; Otto Eckstein and Gary Fromm, "The Price Equation," *American Economic Review* 58 (December 1968): 1159–83; and Nancy S. Barrett, Geraldine Gerardi, and Thomas P. Hart, *Prices and Wages in U.S. Manufacturing: A Factor Analysis* (Lexington: D.C. Heath, 1973).

6. See Charles Vanik, "Corporate Federal Tax Payments and Federal Subsidies to Corporations for 1972," *Congressional Record,* House of Representatives, 1 August 1973, and also his "On 1971 Corporate Income Tax," in *Tax Subsidies and Tax Reform,* Hearings before the Joint Economic Committee, 92nd Cong., 2d sess. (Washington, D.C.: 1973), p. 17; and Peggy Musgrave, "Tax Preference to Foreign Investment," Congress of the United States, Joint Economic Committee, *The Economics of Federal Subsidy Programs, Part II—International Subsidies* (Washington, D.C.: 1972), "International Tax Base Division and the Multinational Corporation," *Public Finance* 27 (1972): 394–411, and her *Direct Investments Abroad and the Multinationals: Effects on the United States' Economy,* prepared for and to be published by the Senate Foreign Relation's Subcommittee on Multinationals (Washington, D.C.: 1975). For data on the expenditure side, see Barry Bluestone's review

of the literature presented in *Testimony,* Joint Economic Committee, 91st Cong., 2d sess. (Washington, D.C.: 1972).

7. George Budzeika, "Lending to Business by New York City Banks," *The Bulletin,* New York University, Graduate School of Business Administration, Institute of Finance, nos. 76–77 (September 1971).

8. Robert F. Lanzillotti, "Industrial Structure and Inflation Control: The U.S. Experience," paper presented to the Nijenrode International Conference on Industrial Organization, Holland, 12–17 August 1974.

9. For the role of foreign-based global corporations and their oligopoly pricing in the U.S. import sector as it made ineffective the 1971 dollar devaluation and led to an "overdevaluation" in 1973, see footnotes to, and text pages 287–90, chapter 10, Barnet and Müller, *Global Reach.* The impact on price controls is an example of negation of the market's social function via intracorporate transactions. The impact on devaluation policy is an example of market negation via oligopoly distortion effects. Important in the devaluation example is the policy's ineffectiveness in reducing imports, but effectiveness in "overstimulating" agricultural exports and the accompanying inflationary impacts of the latter.

10. See footnotes to, and pages 270–71, of Barnet and Müller, *Global Reach,* for a detailed breakdown on the various financial and monetary indicators discussed in the text.

11. H.S. Houthakker, "Policy Issues in the International Economy of the 1970's," *American Economic Review* 64 (May 1974): 139.

12. *Monthly Report of the Deutsche Bundesbank,* March 1973, p. 3. See also Samuel Katz, "Imported Inflation and the Balance of Payments," *The Bulletin,* New York University, Graduate School of Business Administration, Institute of Finance, nos. 91–92 (October 1973).

13. Michael G. Porter, "Commercial Flows as an Offset to Monetary Policy: The German Experience," *IMF Staff Papers,* July 1972, pp. 395 & 415.

14. Frank Tamagna, "Commercial Banking in Transition: From the Sixties to the Seventies," in *Banking in a Changing World,* papers of the 24th International Banking Conference of the Italian Bankers Association, Chianciano, Italy, May 1971.

15. Even in 1973 after further adjustments by the Federal Reserve, financial analysts were still worried about the gap in, and therefore uncertainty of, monetary policy fully "to integrate into its decision-making apparatus the most dynamic and expanding aspect of American banking, the foreign branch operations." See Frank Mastrapasqua, "U.S. Bank Expansion via Foreign Branching: Monetary Policy Implications," *The Bulletin,* New York University, Graduate School of Business Administration, Institute of Finance, nos. 87–88 (January 1973).

16. Scott Gordon, "The Close of the Galbraithian System," *Journal of Political Economy* 76 (1968): 635–44 (emphasis mine).

17. See text pages and the footnotes thereto of Barnet and Müller, *Global Reach,* pp. 259–61.

18. Leonard Spacek and David Norr as quoted in Adam Smith, *Super Money* (New York: Random House, 1972), pp. 197, 205, 206.

19. See the various studies in section 5 of chapter 10 and sections 1 and 2 of chapter 11 in Barnet and Müller, *Global Reach.*

20. On the export platform and the herd instinct of global oligopoly competition, see Ronald Müller, "National Instability and Global Corporations: Must They Grow Together?" *Business and Society Review,* no. 11 (Autumn 1974): 61–72. For examples of production transfers to offset unions' strike threats, see Barnet and Müller, *Global Reach,* chapters 10 and 11.

21. For the methodology and theory of bargaining power as a component of economics to analyze changing terms of trade occurring not only in petroleum, but also other raw materials, manufacturing, and financial sectors of underdeveloped countries, see Ronald Müller, "The Developed and Underdeveloped: Power and the Potential for Change," paper presented at the International Sociological Association, Toronto, Canada, August 1974, to be published in *World Congress of Sociology, Papers and Proceedings* (forthcoming). Also see C. Fred Bergsten, "Coming Investment Wars?" *Foreign Affairs* (October 1974), and "The Threat from the Third World," *Foreign Policy* (Summer 1973).

22. Ronald Müller, "Structuralism-Functionalism in the Study of Social Change," Department of Economics Study Paper, American University, January 1970, with an addendum by Professor Jiri Nehnevjasa, Department of Sociology, University of Pittsburgh, February 1970. See also V. V. Bhatt, "Sterility of Equilibrium Economics: An Aspect of Sociology of Knowledge," Economic Development Institute, International Bank for Reconstruction and Development, Seminar Paper No. 9, February 1974.

23. George Shultz, as quoted in *Fortune,* January 1974, p. 61.

24. The term *econopolitics* was first coined by Peter Peterson, former secretary of commerce, in a similar context.

25. The derivation of these hypotheses is outlined in Barnet and Müller, *Global Reach,* chapter 13.

26. On the relationships between new knowledge, science, and ethics see ibid.; Müller, "Structuralism-Functionalism"; and Bhatt, "Sterility."

23

The Industrial Economy
and International Price Shocks

Milton D. Lower

In the closing chapter of *The Industrial Economy,* in 1952, Clarence Ayres wrote: "The rise of the industrial economy signalized a turning point in the evolution of mankind; but the corner has not yet been turned."[1]

In the span of twenty-one pages, Ayres proceeded to define within this global evolutionary context the key domestic and international policy issues which would confront the industrial and the industrializing countries in the postwar era. The chapter is a model of how evolutionary theory can be employed to unify and illuminate policy problems which are widely perceived in non-evolutionary terms, and often quite wrongly.

The very organization of the chapter reflected Ayres's view that what orthodox economists and policymakers tend to see as separate "economic" and "political," or "positive" and "normative," or even microeconomic, macroeconomic and "inscrutable" technological issues, are in fact joined questions which arise in an evolutionary process. The first and last sub-headings of the chapter combine to read: "The Cultural Incidence ... of the Machine Process," echoing Thorstein Veblen's phrase from *The Theory of Business Enterprise*.

In these sections Ayres explored and extended Veblen's concept of the manner in which habituation to matter-of-fact technological processes attenuates ceremonial modes of thought and valuation. For the proximate future, Ayres projected a continuing worldwide technological revolution, in cultural conflict with the tribal traditions, including the conventional economic wisdom, of Western as well as emerging nations.

Sandwiched between these first and last sections—and linking this global process to the national policy challenges of industrial societies—were sub-chapters entitled "Abundance," "Stability," and "Peace." These postwar policy ends-in-view, Ayres noted, emerged as an indissociable "concert of values" from the industrial process itself and were the joint conditions of its continuance. But the corner would be turned only if and when the cultural incidence of industrialism was extended "throughout the social structure and throughout the world."[2]

The Challenges Posed Today

The conception of the industrial economy as a universalistic process—which is however *instituted* within a world of national, largely market-oriented or pre-industrial societies—is the broadest point of reference for my title and these remarks. While my principal focus will be the industrial economy of the United States in recent years, the international price shocks to which I refer have disrupted the industrial process and the achievement of industrial potential in developing countries as well as in "mature" industrial economies.

In the 1960s, at least prior to the Vietnam War, an institutional economist viewing the U.S. economy or other advanced industrial economies might reasonably have concluded that the Ayresian "concert of values" was progressively being realized. Abundance, stability, and at least plausible hopes for peace had been advanced or maintained in the postwar period. Those of us who were then concerned with the theory and policy of economic development—the cultural incidence of the machine process in less-developed countries—perhaps felt more the crushing weight of ceremonial impediments, in the "center" as well as the "periphery."

A major impediment, then as now, to "center" country policies that might have aided the development of less-developed countries was the fundamental misconception by economists and policymakers of the nature of the foreign investment process—of how it might and might not make a contribution to development. Had more people outside this room become familiar with Wendell Gordon's definitive works, showing that no *capital* contribution—as distinct from a possible contribution of technical knowledge—had ever been or was ever likely to be forthcoming from the foreign investment process, much of the world's current misery might have been avoided.[3]

Specifically, bank lending to Latin American countries at usurious interest rates might, as a matter of policy, not have been allowed to overwhelm or displace direct investment on terms acceptable to sovereign recipient nations as well as to foreign investors. We would not then have the "debt crisis" and the straitjacket it imposes on domestic and international policy in lending as well as in borrowing countries. At the other extreme, had the process of technology-transfer to newly industrializing Pacific rim countries yielded there a more widespread cultural incidence of the machine process instead of low-wage enclaves—sometimes owned by U.S. multinationals—the industrial economy of the United States would be able to afford a more charitable and long-term view of less-developed-country exports and economic growth today.

The policy challenges confronting a divided world order in the mid-1980s evolved from events of the 1970s—and more dramatically from the events of the past five years. And while these challenges are properly characterized as challenges to the future evolution of industrialism on a world scale, they cannot of course be understood in industrial or technological terms alone. The consequences of past national economic policies—affecting domestic stability and growth, international trade, investment, and payments—must be assessed. To do this one must also speak, as orthodox economists invariably do, and as institutionalists "dichotomously" do, of the pecuniary side of the evolved industrial economy.

The Investigation of Price

Prices are pecuniary pheonomena simply, contrary to the beliefs of either medievalists or classical economists that they express or measure ulterior qualities of justice or value. Also, contrary to the still-prevailing textbook model of prices determined in an equilibrium supply-demand mechanism, institutional economists from Veblen on have identified specific power centers and instituted decision-making processes in modern economies by which prices have been set, manipulated, negotiated, or administered.

It is in this investigatory spirit, certainly not in reference to a presumed departure from equilibrium, that I here refer to "international price shocks" as having afflicted industrial economies in the 1970s, and again, though quite differently, in the 1980s. The shocks of the 1970s are proximately understandable by extension of previous institutional analyses of pricing behavior, since they flowed rather directly from price-fixing by an international oil cartel.

The international prices shocks of the 1980s stem from considerably more complex pecuniary behavior and have had more complex and uneven industrial consequences as between national economies. Hence, before taking these up and before exploring the consequences of the two kinds of shocks, it would be well to recount in general outline how the industrial process interrelates with the pecuniary system in which it is instituted.

The Dual Character of the Industrial Capitalist Economy

If an orthodox economist were asked for three keys to understanding the contemporary U.S. economy, he might posit Robinson Crusoe, some wild berries, and a trading partner endowed with corn. An institutionalist, hearing a different question, might refer the questioner to Veblen's *Theory of Business Enterprise,* the Fed's Flow of Funds, and the most recent input-output table. With the latter two sources, one could passably update Veblen's theoretical account of the dual pecuniary and industrial character of our economy. These sources would also reveal the enormous expansion of government, not only as militaristic waste of industrial substance, which Veblen explored at length, but in the totality of its pecuniary and industrial impacts.

Veblen carried in his head a dynamic input-output model of the United States and perhaps several other national economies:

> The whole concert of industrial operations is to be taken as a machine process, made up of interlocking detail processes, rather than as a multiplicity of mechanical appliances each doing its particular work in severality. This comprehensive industrial process draws into its scope and turns to account all branches of knowledge that have to do with the material sciences, and the whole makes a more or less delicately balanced complex of sub-processes.[4]

This concatenation of interdependent processes reaches beyond the machine industry itself, through requirements for specialized auxiliary services:

> The resulting concatenation of industries . . . is commonly discussed under the head of the division of labor. Evidently the prevalent standardiza-

tion of industrial means, methods, and products greatly increased the reach of this concatenation of industries, at the same time that it enforces a close conformity in point of time, volume, and character of the product, whether the product is goods or services.[5]

By virtue of all this, Veblen noted, "the modern industrial system at large bears the character of a comprehensive, balanced mechanical process."[6] This poses a constant "requirement of interstitial adjustment" and, equally, the possibility of severe and cumulative derangement of the system by disturbances from without.

It is here of course that Veblen and later institutionalists introduce the role of pecuniary institutions and behavior, carried over to the new industrial situation from the commercial activity of early modern times. While the industrial system is a concatenation of productive processes, it is by buying and selling, by pecuniary investment, by "the larger use of credit," by financial consolidation, and by the differential advantage of increasingly large and diversified business enterprises that the working parts of industry are linked. But since business proceeds in terms of pecuniary advantage rather than industrial efficacy, it is as likely that the decisive differential advantage will come from derangement of the system as from benign interstitial adjustment.

Subsequent institutionalist research has built upon this basic dichotomy to extend Veblen's analysis of the detailed workings of an industrial capitalist economy. Starting with Veblen, institutional economists pioneered the theory of business cycles, the study of industrial organization, the study of the modern corporation and organized labor, the concept and measurement of national income and product, the role of credit and the evolution of financial institutions, and a host of other real-world questions and issues.

The Evolving Role of Government

As we suggested earlier, the contemporary role of government as a factor in the growth and stability of national economies had barely evolved in Veblen's time. In the absence of such possibilities, Veblen's own prognosis for the inordinately productive industrial economy was one of chronic and deepening depression, relievable only by massive "waste" in the form of war expenditures, or the growth of monopolies capable of preventing the derangement of the parts of industry by the unremitting struggle for differential pecuniary advantage.[7] Veblen died in 1929, just before his worst prognoses were verified in depression followed by war, but also before the Keynesian revolution in theory and policy created new possibilities for a peaceful national government role.

Those possibilities reached their highest level of implementation and success to date in the early to mid-1960s. The alleged "failure of Keynesianism" in the 1970s has been celebrated rather widely in recent years by those who prefer things the way they were in some golden age of unbridled capitalism that Veblen must have lived through but, even as history's most acute observer, somehow overlooked. The failures of government have been equally lamented, on the other hand, by those who live in the present and know that the next time around, policymakers must "choose the right wrench" if the machines are to be kept running, both in the industrial democracies and in countries struggling to industrialize.

The Search for Explanations

In any case, we come back to the search for explanations, so that successful policies for abundance, stability, and peace may be framed for the future. What did go wrong in the 1970s and 1980s? Is it the case that the Keynesian possibilities simply played out, or was the model misunderstood and/or misapplied? What new pecuniary mischief has evolved while monetarists and rational expectationists were perfecting their models of exogenous money and "natural" unemployment? And what manner of mythical economy is it in which tax forgiveness for the leisure class stimulates the "supply side"?

The present effort to interpret the difficulties of the industrial economy of the 1970s and 1980s in terms of "international price shocks" is not intended as a full explanation of events. Nor does it review the growing literature that touches these same concerns. It is, rather, a perspective on these events, which may owe as much to the vantage point from which I have viewed them as to the institutionalist theoretical lens I have used. I believe a full accounting of these events and their significance for policy will require the efforts of many specialties and methodological perspectives different from my own.

I have watched many of these events unfold as a Congressional staff economist. Since 1977, when I arrived in Washington and became an "instant policy expert" on whatever was before the Committee, my principal areas of responsibility have been: through 1980, energy; and then, in a Democratic House under Ronald Reagan's presidency, "industrial policy" and "trade policy." Given the policy alternatives I have seen adopted and not adopted, it will *not* be my contention that price shocks, including international ones, are "exogenous" to the system considered broadly—only that they are shocks.

Further, I do not mean, by calling these "international" shocks, when my focus is the U.S. economy, to imply that they necessarily have been shocks originating elsewhere that have been visited upon the industrial economy of the United States. On the contrary, a point I will want to emphasize is that the sheer weight and influence of the U.S. economy and the U.S. dollar mean that significant economic events occurring anywhere in the world will reverberate between the United States and other countries regardless of where the event occurs.

The 1970s Oil Price Shocks

The oil shocks of the 1970s appear to be rather straightforward price shocks imposed on the United States as well as on other countries by the OPEC cartel. In some sense this is no doubt true, but the fact that oil is priced in dollars leads to differential impacts that may alter the intuitive picture of even-handed misery this presents. Thus, a rising dollar has meant that the oil shocks have continued for many countries, despite declining prices. So has OPEC's gain, if reckoned in the goods of non-dollar countries.

That these were price shocks, however, is beyond doubt. More precisely, they were "relative price shocks" which resulted first in severe derangement of the industries which used significant quantities of petroleum as inputs. In the United States, sudden and dramatic increases in the relative price of oil, followed by other energy prices rising, as it is said in "sympathy," forced many industries to utilize existing capital equipment, energy-intensive in its design, at a sub-optimal rate and to make ad hoc substitution of labor for both energy and equipment. The resulting input mix, which was inconsistent with the design of existing plant and equipment, took its toll on the growth of productivity and output.[8]

In effect, large shifts in relative prices rendered much of the capital stock of the United States obsolete. At the same time, shifts of income from energy-using to energy-producing sectors in the United States and abroad deprived the former of the wherewithal to substitute new energy-efficient equipment, let alone to expand. As a measure of the sectoral derangement occurring between 1978 and 1980, we may consider the redistribution of profits between energy and non-energy corporations listed in the Fortune 500. Of the total increase in profits for

the Fortune industrials between those two annual periods, 97.9 percent
went to 56 oil and gas companies.[9]

As this suggests, for the United States with its substantial domestic
oil industry, transfers of purchasing power did not go exclusively
abroad. The purchasing power drain *for the nation* due to price increases (on a shrinking volume of imported crude oil) was $49.5 billion
in 1979 and 1980. However, the redistribution of purchasing power
within the country, through the combined effects of rising market prices
and the release to market prices by the Carter Administration of nearly
all the domestic production still under price controls in mid-1979,
came to almost $55 billion for the two years, on a nearly constant
domestic crude oil supply.[10] All of this ignores transfers due to price increases on imported petroleum products or on refiners' and distribu-
tors' margins in the United States.

Finally, as in other countries beset with energy shocks in the 1970s,
the *general* price level rose sharply in the United States during both the
1973–1974 and the 1979–1980 crises. During the more severe shock of
1979–1980, the direct and indirect contribution of energy price increases to the *acceleration* in the consumer price index exceeded 5½
points between 1978 and the first half of 1980, accounting for most of
the increase in the overall inflation rate from 9.0 percent to a 15.9 percent peak annual rate.[11]

In an important sense, macroeconomic policy in the 1970s was
captive—or was perceived to be—to energy-induced changes in relative prices and the general inflation rate. It is widely held that efforts to
control the energy inflation by means of restrictive monetary policy
caused, or at least seriously aggravated, the deep ill-timed recessions of
the decade. In any case the impact of stop-and-go macroeconomic policies, or of restrictive monetary policy simply, accentuated the damage
to industries and sectors weakened by energy shocks.

The Relative Magnitude of Two Import Shocks

Viewed in the context of international trade, the energy price shocks
of the 1970s were for the United States and other oil-importing countries also "import shocks." The cumulative consequences of rising oil
prices are clearly reflected in the U.S. balance of trade between
1972—the year before the Arab Embargo—and 1980 when the U.S. energy trade deficit reached its maximum.

During this time the U.S. "energy trade balance"—energy exports
minus energy imports—went from a $3.5 billion annual deficit to a

$76.1 billion deficit. This negative swing of $72.6 billion encompasses the cumulative balance-of-trade impact of the energy shocks of the 1970s, though it can hardly be said to measure the more complex, ongoing industrial impacts.

This balance-of-trade measure of the impact of oil price shocks suggests, however, a parallel with events in the 1980s and a means of approaching the question of more recent and more complex "international price shocks." For the case of the United States, I have elsewhere posed the recent, vastly larger shock to the balance of trade and payments—and to the U.S. industrial economy—as "industrial import shock."

To establish the relative magnitudes of the two shocks, we compare the above-described swing in the energy trade balance to the subsequent swing, from 1980 to mid-1985, in the U.S. "non-energy" trade balance. Over this period, the U.S. *non-energy* balance deteriorated from net *exports* of $50.6 billion to a net *import* balance in last year's second quarter of $81.4 billion (at an annual rate). This represents a negative swing of $132 billion.

Thus, in these current-dollar terms, industrial import shock has in just four and a half years exceeded the balance-of-trade impact of the combined oil shocks of the 1970s by more than eighty percent. However, it is a point of crucial importance, if the recent import shock is to be seen as an "international price shock," that when all of these current-dollar values are deflated and expressed in constant-dollar terms, the relative magnitude of the present shock soars in the comparison.

Indeed, the constant-dollar magnitude of the *oil* shocks was quite small, and the drastic swing in the balance virtually disappears when converted to real terms. The crisis in the 1970s consisted not in the United States being flooded with foreign oil, but in steep price increases for a quantity of imports (in barrels and in constant dollars) which fluctuated within a comparatively narrow range.

By contrast, the recent flood of industrial imports into the United States, induced by their low and even *declining* prices in dollars, is very "real" and tangible. Hence, when industrial import shock is examined in constant dollar terms, the precipitous drop in the balance of trade from net exports to net imports is even steeper than in current dollars. For many categories of industrial goods, current-dollar imports must be sharply *inflated* to be expressed in 1980 equivalents.

As in the 1970s, the price shock which has afflicted the U.S. industrial sector in recent years has been a *relative* price shock. Instead of originating in massive price increases for a single commodity input, however, the current shock has responded to relative (and absolute) price *deflation* for imported goods generally and relative price increases for all U.S. exports. U.S. agricultural and industrial producers have found their *output* decisions disrupted by a progressive decline in their ability to compete in their own markets.

The prime source of this massive, across-the-board shift in relative prices was the increase in the exchange value of the dollar, which rose by 88.5 percent from its 1980 trade-weighted value before it peaked in the last week of February 1985. The competitive effect of changes in the value of the dollar from 1980 to mid-1985 was that of a seventy percent increase in U.S. export prices and a forty percent decline in the price of imports. The last figure represents the margin within which foreign producers aiming at the U.S. market have been "free to choose" whether to lower prices or to increase profit margins, solely on the basis of changes in exchange rates.

Recent Price Shocks in Systemic Context: Pecuniary and Industrial Policies

This brings us to a fuller consideration of the origin and the consequences of these new "international price shocks." Both are extremely complex questions to which I will mercifully give brief and sketchy answers. The general answer is that they are of pecuniary origin in a broader sense than ordinary price fixing; specifically they are of policy origin. But they have consequences for the industrial sectors of the United States and other economies such as may always be expected when pecuniary institutions intrude upon the industrial process. That is to say, the pecuniary intent and the competitive outcomes are at best tenuously related to the technological character—what some might call the comparative costs—of the underlying productive base. But if sustained, such intrusions may seriously derange national industries and whatever productive relationships between industrial economies may have preceded the shock.

In the most immediate sense, the problem as seen from the perspective of the U.S. industrial economy is the "overvalued" dollar and price deflation for tradeable goods, which have made the ordinary conduct of industry by business progressively infeasible. But the overvalued dollar is itself one link in a circular system of pecuniary causes and effects which was set in motion by the "fiscal revolution of 1981."[17] This revolution, comprising the decision to cut taxes drastically while carrying out a massive military buildup, may in turn be seen as Ronald Reagan's demand-side alternative to needed supply-side industrial policy. In the recovery from Reagan's record recession of 1982, this pecuniary alternative has worked out, through the combination of exploding demand and massive price distortions in favor of imported goods, to a policy of U.S. de-industrialization.

This latter result, while perhaps not precisely intended, has nonetheless been part and parcel of the circular system of causation proceeding from the Reagan fiscal revolution; and the circle has nonetheless been regarded as, in the main, "virtuous." To say that it proceeds from the fiscal revolution of 1981 is to say that the best place to break into the circle is by examining the course of the *structural* or full-employment deficit.

Since the structural deficit is the federal budget deficit net of any cyclically induced expenditures or revenue shortfalls, it is commonly taken as a measure of the purely discretionary component of the deficit and of fiscal policy. At more than 2.5 percent of potential GNP since 1983, and 4 percent by early this year, the structural deficit has become a significant factor in the U.S. economy for the first time since the decision was made to finance World War II by the sale of war bonds.[18]

Recent structural deficits, then, measure the annual deferred costs, over and above such taxes as the government is willing to collect, to pay for Ronald Reagan's preference set. Insofar as the latter reflects the notorious Reagan predilection to dismantle all non-dynastic functions of government and to exalt the ancient pecuniary virtues at any cost, one may fairly characterize this preference as a penchant for "borrowing from the future to live in the past."

From the structural budget deficit and its larger pecuniary ramifications have been derived the other linkages in the once self-sustaining "virtuous circle." The main sequence—subject to the proviso that such circularity often involves reverse causation and mutual adaptation of the parts—is widely understood to have developed as follows: the expanding budget deficit, and Treasury borrowing to finance it, pushed up relative U.S. interest rates, which increased the value of the dollar. This cumulatively discouraged exports, encouraged imports, and created a second exploding deficit—the deficit in the balance of trade and more broadly in the U.S. current account.

The current account deficit has been financed by capital inflows occurring in response to the high U.S. interest rates and to other desires of foreigners or repatriating Americans to hold dollar-denominated assets. Some prefer to say that the capital inflows were the "tail that wagged the dog," forcing the United States to incur the trade deficits; but such a distinction is not crucial to the present argument.[19] These capital inflows, closing the circle, directly and indirectly financed 54.3 percent of the federal budget deficit in 1984.[20]

It will be admitted that all along there were linkages in this circular system which might not have been chosen as policy instruments—such as exorbitant real interest rates—but for the fact that they were essential to sustain the whole and to keep the pecuniary recovery going. It is just as evident that the cumulative direction of the whole was all along unsustainable.

There are reasons for believing that this virtuous circle may have already begun to turn vicious by the third quarter of 1984, when the growth in net imports of goods and services first exceeded the growth in U.S. final demand. In the ensuing economic slowdown there has been time to focus on the trillion dollars added to the national debt, and on the fact that the United States crossed over to net international debtor status early this year or before. Even the administration was recently required to abandon the posture that the high value of the dollar was an unmitigated cause for pecuniary national pride.

Similarly, the other "debtor country problem"—that of the less-developed countries, especially in Latin America—refuses to go away. This problem also may be viewed in the context of the "virtuous circle" of recent years. While the problems of LDC debtors no doubt had their origins in the U.S. bank lending of the 1970s, and owed something to the oil shocks, the problem only became intractable after 1982, in face of escalating real U.S. interest rates on floating rate loans.

In the context of the circular causation described, moreover, this very intractability reflects the conditions for sustaining "virtue." Without the high domestic interest rates which made the international problem intractable, and without the massive capital flight from the LDCs entailed by the continuing crisis, it would have been more difficult to sustain and finance the dual U.S. deficits. And if the LDCs did not have to export or die (or perhaps export *and* die) to pay their interest bills, there might be less of a U.S. trade deficit to finance. But LDCs might then be tempted to squander their freed-up resources on dangerously impecunious policies to improve the domestic standard of living. Where is the virtue in that?

Within the U.S. economy, the industrial consequences of the Reagan policy model are most clearly seen in the capital goods sector. Insofar as orthodox economists are able to distinguish between the pecuniary and the industrial concepts of "capital," they might agree with institutional economists that the sector which produces the tools, machinery, and equipment for other industrial (and even commercial and service) sectors is somehow basic to the functioning of an "industrial capitalist" economy. In any case, "capital formation" has always been an American preoccupation and was a central shibboleth of the Reagan "supply-side" revolution. While perhaps no one ever said so, this might have been presumed to mean that advocates of capital formation and supply-side policies had in mind the continued and even substantially increased production of capital goods in the United States.

It is important to note that when the Reagan fiscal revolution was launched, the position of the United States in this regard was strong indeed, most visibly so in terms of U.S. international trade. Calculated in 1972 dollars, the United States in 1980 had a net merchandise export balance of $18.4 billion. This was more than entirely accounted for by the U.S. net export balance in capital goods (excluding autos), which stood at an all-time high of $19.3 billion in 1980. To get ahead of the story just a little, by 1984 the real capital goods balance of the United States was in *deficit*. By the second quarter of 1985 this deficit had grown to $6.3 billion in 1972 dollars.

The trouble, at least before the slowing of the recovery, was not on the "demand side." It was common through the middle of last year for those who believed the virtuous circle might be sustained to celebrate the "capital spending boom" which had been created by the Reagan business tax policies. Indeed, from 1981 through 1984 more than half of the increased cash flows of corporations had in fact been due to increased tax depreciation benefits alone. And between the first quarter of 1981 and the fourth quarter of 1984, real final demand for capital goods (excluding autos) did increase by $20.9 billion net, despite its dramatic decline in the recession of 1982.

The problem was that only $1.1 billion of this net increase in demand across the cycle was met by real increases in domestic *supply,* or U.S. production of capital goods. The remaining $19.8 billion, or 9.46 percent of the increased demand for producers durable equipment in the United States, was met by the net swing mentioned above, from massive real net exports to real net imports of capital goods.

Nor does this trouble on the supply side of the U.S. "capital formation process" merely signal a natural transition of the U.S. economy from a "low-tech" past to some "high-tech" future of which we might catch a glimpse in some other segment of U.S. industry and trade. The capital goods sector *contains* the most important U.S. "high-tech" industries. Moreover, within this sector it is not the old-line producers who have suffered most, but as one writer put it:

> producers of state-of-the-art high-technology items—the area in which the U.S. is supposed to enjoy a strong competitive advantage and which many economists regard as the leading edge in the structural transformation of the U.S. economy.[25]

Conclusion

As I said I would at the beginning, I have focused mainly upon the United States to illustrate the impact on the industrial economy of what I have called "international price shocks." For the case of the United States, or any single national economy, some doubt might legitimately remain as to whether what is bad for that economy might not be just "too bad"—especially when the case has been put rather strongly that the country's own policies account for most of the trouble. Perhaps, after all, U.S. industry has simply lost the competitive struggle in an increasingly internationalized economy.

The broader point I have tried to make, however, is that such a view not only misconstrues the facts with respect to the current "competitive" posture of the United States, but also misconceives entirely what is at stake for all industrial economies in the mid-1980s. The increasing internationalization of the United States and the world economy about which we hear so much in recent years is a fact. But to date it is a pecuniary internationalization, which bears the same relation to the productive economy of the United States and of other nations as Veblen's "captain of finance" to the machine process. Thus far it is a matter of derangement.

If there have always been grounds for skepticism that what orthodox economists called the "international division of labor" was really based on differing, relatively fixed resource endowments, that skepticism can only grow in face of shifts in relative prices that clearly exceed any international cost differences. Such skepticism has always been, or should always have been, an important part of the equipment for any economist who does not see the world as divided between industrial and nonindustrial peoples. Such skepticism should also be applied today to the notion that any industrial economy can, will, or should actually deindustrialize in the name of "free trade" or pecuniary competition.

In the 1960s, it was possible for *some* development economists to conceive of a less-developed country circumventing the pecuniary institutions by the expedient of technology transfer, perhaps attached to direct foreign investment or, less likely, as a matter of international agreement. The key concept was one of the cultural incidence of the machine process, occurring within the domestic economy of the recipient country, increasingly under its own control, and increasingly narrowing the technological gap.

The other side of this conception, clearly, was that what would benefit the less-developed country would not threaten the industrial economy of the country providing the new technology. There was a common interest because knowledge increases in the degree that it is used, and the more widely it is used in a less-developed country, the greater its cultural incidence.

If development thus preceded any substantial degree of pecuniary competition between the two economies, such competition would occur between relative equals and would not involve what has come to be known as the "race to the bottom." The latter is the situation in which borrowed technology, encapsulated in low-wage economies, eschewing safety and environmental standards, may threaten a way of life which is itself the highest cultural incidence of the machine process.

What is thus at stake today is not whether, but how, the industrial economy is to be internationalized. The internationalization of the economy in the industrial sense would mean a worldwide cultural incidence of the machine process, with Veblen's "interstitial adjustments" of the parts carried out largely in international technical agreements, with limits on ruinous short-term competition in price. But we are very much further from such a pattern today, and especially in the past five years, than we were under the still largely bi-lateral arrangements for financial flows, and occasional flows of technical knowledge in the 1960s.

Notes

1. C.E. Ayres, *The Industrial Economy* (Cambridge, Mass.: The Riverside Press, 1952), p. 415.
2. Ibid., p. 418.
3. See, for example, Wendell C. Gordon, "Foreign Investments," *University of Houston Business Review* 9 (Fall 1962): entire issue.
4. Thorstein Veblen, *The Theory of Business Enterprise* (1904; reprint. New York: Charles Scribner's Sons, 1936), p. 7.
5. Ibid., pp. 15–16.
6. Ibid., p. 16.

7. Ibid., pp. 177–267.
8. Congressional Budget Office, "The Productivity Slowdown: Causes and Policy Responses," in *Capital Formation and Industrial Policy* (Part 1), Hearings before the Subcommittee on Oversight and Investigations of the Committee on Energy and Commerce, 97th Congress, 1st Session, Serial No. 97–13 (April-June, 1981): 281–322.
9. "The Changing Distribution of Industrial Profits: The Oil and Gas Industry Within the Fortune 500, 1978–80," Staff Report of the Subcommittee on Oversight and Investigations, reprinted in *Capital Formation and Industrial Policy* (Part 2): *The Impact of Energy,* Hearing before the Subcommittee on Oversight and Investigations of the Committee on Energy and Commerce, 97th Congress, 1st Session, Serial No. 97–162 (20 November 1981): 10–11.
10. Ibid., pp. 1–2.
11. "The Energy Inflation Crisis: Sources, Consequences, and Policy Options," Report by the Subcommittee on Oversight and Investigations of the Committee on Interstate and Foreign Commerce, 96th Congress, 2nd Session, Committee Print 96-IFC 61 (December 1980): 13.
12. U.S. trade data on a "balance of payments" basis from the U.S. Department of Commerce, *Survey of Current Business* (June 1983; June 1984).
13. "Industrial Import Shock: Policy Challenge of the 1980's," Staff Report, Subcommittee on Oversight and Investigations of the Committee on Energy and Commerce, 99th Congress, 1st Session, Committee Print 99-T (August 1985).
14. U.S. Department of Commerce, *Survey of Current Business* (June and September 1985).
15. For further discussion and graphic representations of these two import shocks in current and constant dollars, see "Industrial Import Shock," pp. 16–19, 33–36.
16. Calculated changes are for the Federal Reserve Board's "Index of the Weighted-Average Exchange Value of the Dollar," published in the *Federal Reserve Bulletin,* monthly, Table 3.28.
17. James Tobin, "The Fiscal Revolution: Disturbing Prospects," *Challenge* (January-February 1985): 12–16.
18. "Industrial Import Shock," pp. 64–70.
19. Henry C. Wallich, "Capital Movements—The Tail That Wags the Dog," Remarks at the Bretton Woods II Conference, Federal Reserve Bank of Boston, Bretton Woods, New Hampshire, 19 May 1984.
20. "Industrial Import Shock," pp. 89–90.
21. U.S. Department of Commerce, *Survey of Current Business,* September 1985.
22. Calculated by the author from U.S. Department of Commerce data.
23. "Industrial Import Shock," pp. 57–59.
24. Ibid.
25. Stephen S. Roach of Morgan Stanley and Company, quoted in "The Bad News Behind the Capital Investment Surge," *Business Week,* 4 March 1985, p. 20.

24

The Information Society: Implications for Economic Institutions and Market Theory

William H. Melody

I am honored to be selected by the Association for Evolutionary Economics as the Ayres Visiting Scholar. The writings of C. E. Ayres have provided me with much food for thought since my graduate student days. I can pay him no greater tribute than returning to his work as part of my preparation of this article. The stamp of his influence will be recognizable throughout.

The central theme for my analysis is drawn from the work of a Canadian contemporary of Ayres's, Harold Innis, who observed in his book *Empire and Communications* (1950) that "the subject of communication offers possibilities in that it occupies a crucial position in the organization and administration of government and in turn of empires and of Western civilization."[1]

An ever more popular theme in the social sciences, as well as in the general literature over the past decade, has been that technologically advanced economies are in the process of moving beyond industrial capitalism to information-based economies that will bring profound changes in the form and structure of the economic system.[2] Rapid advances in computer and telecommunication technologies are making it possible to generate information that was heretofore unattainable, transmit it instantaneously around the globe, and—in a rapidly growing number of instances—sell it in information markets. Some authors claim that the United States already devotes the majority of its economic resources to information-related activities.[3] The computer, telecommunication, and information content industries are among the most rapidly growing global industries, and are expected to remain so for the next decade. Many national governments are counting on these industries to provide the primary stimulus to their future growth.

Economists recognized long ago that the most important resource determining the economic efficiency of any economy, industry, productive process, or household is information and its effective communication. The characteristics of information define the state of knowledge that underlies all economic processes and decision-making structures. Fundamental changes in the characteristics of information, and in its role in the economy, should be central to the study of economics. The state of information in the economy has pervasive effects on the workings of the economy generally. It has intensified impacts on those sectors that provide information products or services, for example, press, television, radio, film, mail, libraries, banks, credit bureaus, data banks, and other "information providers," as they are now called.[4] And the establishment of information markets brings about changing conceptions of public and private information, as well as the property rights associated with marketable information.[5] In this article I am able to examine only a portion of the significant implications of the changing role of information for economic institutions generally as well as market theory.

Technical Efficiency and Market Extension

An expansion of available information, together with enhanced and improved telecommunication, should permit more efficient decision making and the extension of markets across geographical and industry boundaries. It should increase competition. It should allow resources to be allocated more rapidly and efficiently. The conditions of real markets should approximate more closely the assumptions of theory, where markets are frictionless and operate under conditions of perfect information. Indeed much of the literature on the information economy considers these developments to provide unmitigated benefits to society.[6]

But closer examination indicates that the benefits of these technologies will not be distributed uniformly across markets, that certain segments of society will be made poorer both in absolute as well as relative terms, and that the structure of markets in many industries will be affected in fundamental ways.[7] These new technologies permit markets to be extended to the international and global level. But only the largest national and transnational corporations (TNCs) and government agencies have the need for, and the ability to, take full advantage of these new opportunities. For them the geographic boundaries of markets are extended globally, and their ability to administer and control global markets efficiently and effectively from a central point is enhanced.

The manner in which these technological developments are being implemented creates a significant barrier to entry for all but the largest firms, thereby accelerating tendencies toward concentration.[8] In fact smaller firms are likely to find themselves disadvantaged because of the new technological developments. For example, the telecommunication systems in the United States and other technologically advanced countries are being redesigned to meet the technically sophisticated digital data requirements of high volume, multiple purpose, global users. For traditional, simpler communication requirements, such as basic telephone service, the new upgraded system will serve quite well, but at substantially increased cost to smaller users.[9] The telecommunication options available to small, localized, and even regionalized businesses do not reflect their unique needs. Rather, their range of choice is dictated by the national and global needs of the largest firms and government agencies. The most efficient telecommunication system for their needs has been cannibalized in the creation of the technologically advanced system.

In most industries the new competition is simply intensified oligopolistic rivalry among TNCs on a world wide basis. The firms that can now leap across market boundaries are already dominant firms in their respective product and geographic markets. Their entry has a major impact on the structure of the supply side of the market and prompts a strategic response from the established dominant firm(s). This is not atomistic competition responding to market forces that reflect consumer demand, but rather a type of medieval jousting for territorial control.

The focal point of this oligopolistic rivalry is on differentiated adaptations of particular technologies and product lines for sale to nation states. Major decisions involving multi-million-dollar commitments over many years are made relatively infrequently, for example, selecting a satellite system or a line of computer or telecommunication equipment. The rivalry is directed to obtaining a long-run position of market entrenchment and dominance in particular foreign national submarkets.

The rivalry among TNCs for entrenchment in new national markets differs fundamentally from traditional market theory in several respects. First, short-run market clearing prices are not the focal point of the rivalry. Rather, short-run pricing policy is simply one of many strategic tools for achieving the long-run objective. This rivalry stands far outside the short-run pricing behavior examined by traditional oligopoly theory.

Second, competitive advantage is obtained not primarily from the superiority of a product in the eyes of individual consumers exercising choice, but rather from effective persuasion of government leaders in foreign countries. The objective is to secure a position of special privilege in entering national markets. The privileged market position then is ensured by the national policy of the purchasing countries with respect to such matters as licensing, tax, tariff, currency exchange, capital repatriation, entry barriers imposed on rivals, etcetera.

In attempting to achieve these long-term dominant market positions, the TNCs are assisted by governments of their respective home-base countries. The home governments adopt policies and positions that will assist their respective TNCs, and sometimes they even participate in institutional marketing. Thus, the oligopolistic rivalry among TNCs involves a strong element of nationalism and direct government involvement on both the demand and supply sides of the market exchange.

Adoption of the new technologies tends to increase the significance of overhead costs, not only for the information and telecommunication activities, but also with respect to greater centralization of functions and capital/labor substitution, for example, robots. Thus, the inherent instability in oligopoly markets is magnified by the instability created by an increased and very significant proportion of overhead costs.

Taken collectively, these changes introduce new elements of risk. But they also provide new opportunities to shift these risks away from TNC investors and managers to the particular localities where production occurs, and the institutions that reside there, that is, local government, labor, and consumers. TNCs also can diversify their risks by expanding their absolute size and geographical coverage. The larger the TNC, the more resources at its command for allocation within the firm rather than through capital markets. The greater the geographical coverage, the more risks can be diversified by the TNC, although these risks could be disastrous for any particular production location dependent on the TNC. In addition, the enhanced market power strengthens the TNC's ability to exploit both resource and consumer markets.

Because the new technologies permit rapid transfer of new types of information, they permit more frequent short-run decision making by TNC managers. In global markets, the terms of trade, currency exchange rates, interest rates, and money movements are often as important to real profitability as the actual production of goods and services. With new opportunities for frequent, short-run decisions there is likely to be an increased emphasis on day-to-day financial transfers, if not ongoing speculative manipulation. This will create additional instability for any particular resource supplier or production location that might fall out of favor as a result of short-term shifts in financial and currency markets.

Historically, the current revolution in telecommunication technology can be compared in certain respects with the effect of the introduction of the telegraph upon the structure of markets in the United States over the period 1845 to 1890. In his study of these developments, Richard DuBoff concluded: "The telegraph improved the functioning of markets and enhanced competition, but it simultaneously strengthened forces making for monopolization. Larger scale business operations, secrecy and control, and spatial concentration were all increased as a result of telegraphic communications."[10] In fact, he says, "increasing market size helped 'empire builders' widen initial advantages which at first may have been modest."[11] DuBoff's assessment provides a useful benchmark for examining the current global developments that illustrate similar economic effects, but substantially magnified and modified as described in this article.

The Role of National Governments

For the TNCs, the domestic markets in their home countries provide a springboard to their activity in global markets. The home governments identify more directly with the international success of particular TNCs because they play an important role in the home country's domestic economy.

Home governments tend to exhibit greater tolerance for increased domestic monopoly power because it enhances the power of their resident TNCs in international markets. This can range from a reduced emphasis on the application of anti-trust and anti-combines laws to the actual encouragement of domestic cartels. In the United States, it will be recalled, the Webb-Pomerene Act has provided anti-trust immunity for foreign markets for almost seventy years. Some countries, for example, Canada and some Western European nations, have promoted domestic monopoly power in some industries for the purpose of creating a larger corporate presence that they hope will have the power to compete with the largest TNCs, mostly based in the United States.

Today, the U.S. government is extremely concerned about the access of U.S. based TNCs to foreign markets. Government advocacy of free trade is designed to open markets for some industries, particularly the computer, telecommunications, and information content industries. Restrictions on Japanese automobile imports illustrate a comparable defensive reaction.

As oligipolistic rivalry in global markets becomes more intense, national governments are more actively attempting to manipulate the terms of international rivalry to the advantage of "their" TNCs. Thus, the TNCs are becoming more direct instruments of macro-economic policy through R&D subsidies, tax concessions, tariff conditions, trade agreements, and other policies. This includes the assumption of market risk by home governments in the form of R&D funding, investment guarantees, government-industry joint ventures, and government assistance of home-based TNCs in international market negotiations through applying political pressure to foreign governments.

Today this kind of government involvement is labelled "industrial policy." For most nations, some kind of industrial policy has been a prerequisite for survival for a long time because their economies have been so dominated by foreign TNCs and larger, more powerful nations. The current interest in industrial policy in the United States is in part a reaction to this, but is also influenced by a decline in U.S. dominance in some global markets as well as a reaction to the prolonged recession in the U.S. domestic economy.

This new approach reflects a change in the role of government from adopting policies designed to stimulate the marketplace environment generally, toward adopting more focused policies designed to assist specific companies. As such, it reflects direct interference in the market. It identifies the economic prosperity of the nation with the financial success of the largest home-based TNCs. The role of government then becomes one of using its political power to manipulate the rules by which the market works to the advantage of the TNCs that it has chosen to support. In Canada, this is called "picking winners." These policies provide significant barriers to entry to those firms not selected, which includes all domestic firms not large enough to exploit international markets.

Under these conditions competition in the domestic market can be seen as potentially damaging to the ability of home-based TNCs to compete successfully in global markets. Anti-trust policies and pro-competitive domestic policies become less important, if not antiquated. Monopoly and cartel behavior are accepted as tolerable, if not promoted. Even monopolistic exploitation of domestic consumers becomes tolerable as providing the necessary strength, power, and resources to compete successfully in the global markets.¹² Politically it is much easier to provide subsidies by simply allowing a home-based TNC to exploit monopoly power in the domestic market rather than going through the cumbersome political process of first taxing and then granting subsidies.

In this new political economic environment, the conception of the public interest within a nation also changes. Traditional concerns about the prices and quality of public utility services and the universality of coverage of public service declines. For example, in the United States, basic telephone service as a priority of social policy is being questioned, if not yet abandoned, by the Federal Communications Commission (FCC). The international success of home-based TNCs, as measured by sales, profits, and a favorable balance of payments, becomes a primary objective of government public policy. This success is viewed as fueling domestic employment, productivity, and national wealth. Domestic consumers and social policies are seen to benefit from the trickling-down of benefits from successful TNCs. How social services will be funded from this wealth accumulated by TNCs, when government policy is directed to subsidizing their competitive efforts in global markets rather than taxing away their monopoly profit, remains a mystery.

The real change is a much closer identification of the national and public interests with the corporate interest of the dominant home-based TNCs. It is truly ironic that these industrial policies typically are justified by invoking the ghost of Adam Smith and free market competition. In fact, they represent a fundamental mistrust of the free market. We need not be reminded that, in fact, Smith argued that the wealth of nations would be enhanced if domestic competition were encouraged rather than sacrificed to the myopic criterion of mercantilistic success.¹³ One might question whether, under this approach, there is a significant difference between ITT, IBM, and Northern Telecom today, and the East India and Hudson Bay Companies of another era of colonial expansion.

In addition, national government policy designed to promote the power of TNCs in global markets may well be an exercise in gradual self-strangulation. The nature and direction of government policy intentions are always heavily constrained to some degree by market conditions and the power of corporations and other large economic units to prevent their effective implementation. Canada has been attempting to implement independent economic and cultural policies for generations. But it has neither the economic nor the political power to implement them effectively in the face of domination by U.S.-based TNCs. As national governments tie themselves more closely to the promotion of corporate power of their TNCs, they are at the same time reducing their own degrees of freedom to adopt domestic or international policies contrary to TNC interests.

The Role of Market Theory

Traditional market theory provides a perfect rationale for this expansion of TNC market power. By assuming that technology is autonomous and beneficial, that oligopolistic rivalry for long-term dominant positions in foreign national markets is competition, and that market-clearing prices maximizing short-run profit will yield optimal resource allocation, the theory simply reflects the short-run market power positions of the dominant firms. Such concepts as static equilibrium, marginal cost, and consumer surplus are perfectly pliable in their subjective application. Indeed, within this theoretical framework, nothing can be rejected that travels under the appropriate theoretical labels.

More recent theoretical developments such as Ramsey pricing, sustainability, and contestability move a step further away from reality into abstract metaphysics.[14] Under these new theoretical developments, one judges the effectiveness of competition in markets not by the existence of real competitors, but by the possibility that there might be. In keeping with most of neoclassical theory, alternatives not followed provide the sole basis for judging the efficiency of actual market conditions. It requires only a modest imagination to hypothesize an alternative set of conditions that would be worse (or better) than the reality experienced.[15] Either way, it is not very helpful in solving the problems of efficient resource allocation in the real world.

A current illustration of the abuse of market theory in the U.S. telecommunication industry is now unfolding in policy debates before the FCC, Congress, and more recently state regulatory commissions and legislative committees. The regulated telephone companies suddenly have discovered that the costs associated with the local loop facilities connecting telephones and other terminal devices to the central office, as well as certain central office functions, are not sensitive to variations in the volume of traffic—that is, they are short-run fixed costs. In addition, these costs are common to multiple services, including local, long distance, and specialized data services. It is argued that neoclassical theory does not permit the allocation of any short-run common costs to competitive (or contestable) long distance or data services. If high charges for accessing the system are imposed upon large business users, it is claimed that some will bypass the telecommunication network.

But these same fixed common costs apparently can be allocated to the monopoly basic telephone service. High access charges for local telephone service may force a good many poor people to give up telephone service. But that is tolerable because the estimated consumer surplus gains from increased long distance use by large-volume users will exceed the consumer surplus losses of disconnected customers with no alternatives they can afford.

The point here is that neoclassical market theory can justify equally well virtually any result. What it does tend to reflect in reality is the existing distribution of market power. The common interest among local telephone companies, long distance carriers, and large industrial users has permitted them to purchase a version of the theory that reflects that interest.

This version of the theory ignores the fact that the cause of increased costs of network access is upgrading the local exchange to meet the requirements of digital data and transcontinental communication, essential to enhanced data services and global networks, but unnecessary for local telephone service. It also ignores the fact that benefits to society do not decline when a business shifts some of its telecommunication traffic from a telephone company and begins using an alternate source of supply. However, societal benefits do decline, not only to that subscriber but also to others who would call that subscriber, when a subscriber is forced to disconnect service. Moreover, disconnected subscribers save the telephone company little, if any, costs. In the vast majority of instances, disconnections will be in the poorer parts of town where the telephone company has no alternative use for its loop investment. It will be stranded. In my view, a correct interpretation of neoclassical theory would require that no subscribers be permitted to disconnect unless they were unwilling to pay a price equal to their respective short-run social marginal costs. For users already connected, this must be close to zero, if not negative. However, local residential customers are not in a position to mount a competitive lobby advocating neoclassical theory interpreted from the perspective of their interest. Selection of the "appropriate" interpretation of neoclassical theory is not determined by an independent analysis of facts, but by the power of the interest groups in advocating rival interpretations.

Finally, it should be noted that one influential argument for reducing rates for long distance voice and data services at the expense of local telephone rates is to help domestic companies (in the United States and Canada, at least) compete more effectively in national and global markets. In the not-too-distant future local telephone rates may include a hidden cross-subsidy to give home-based TNCs an artificial competitive advantage in seeking foreign contracts.

The most relevant market model for examining the consequences of competition in the information age is one of indeterminate, unstable oligopoly wherein the TNCs deliberately employ short-run pricing strategy to achieve long-run entrenchment and monopoly power in national markets, foreign and domestic. For detailed analytical development of this type of market model, one must look at Joseph Schumpeter, Karl Marx, and other institutionalists following in the same tradition. Within this oligopoly model, the market provides ample room for negotiation to affect outcomes in both the short run and the long run, with a wide range of possibilities. Therefore attention must be paid to negotiate structures and criteria and alternatives, an area of analysis that has not been well developed.

The new oligopoly markets cannot be explained without reference to dependency theory. Incorporation of the possibility of dependent market relations simply recognizes that buyers and sellers are not part of a unified homogeneous market. The locational separation of economic functions may be total. The source of resources, production, consumption, profit recognition, and control over continuing reallocations of resources may each be in a different country. Many localities are dependent on a specialized production plant of a TNC used to serve markets on another continent. In fact, different economic, political, social, and cultural systems generally provide a basis either for significant specialized advantage to a TNC, or a significant barrier to production and marketing. In the "information age," dependency relations within global markets take on a new significance.

Implications

Dependency theories have some significant differences.[16] But they also are characterized by some common conditions.[17] Control is exercised at the market center. Peripheral or hinterland locations are developed primarily to serve the interests of the major centers of power by exploiting natural resources, low labor costs, or other elements of specialized, comparative advantage. Effective control over the type, the direction, and the rate of development rests at the center. Thus, the periphery is dependent on the centers of power. Apparent short-run efficiency and stability in the central markets is obtained at the expense of instability and distorted development in the outlying areas. The economy in the region bears the risk both of changes in short-run market conditions at the center and of the potential loss of its specialized comparative advantage to another region. But even this market arrangement cannot protect the center market from long-run instability, and under some circumstances may even accentuate it by requiring less frequent but more severe adjustments. Harold Innis concluded from his studies that "the economic history of Canada has been dominated by the discrepancy between the center and the margin of western civilization."[18]

As TNCs expand using the information technologies, they can reduce their dependency upon any single resource supply or production location, thereby enhancing their negotiating power with individual governments, unions, and other groups. A higher proportion of risk can be transferred to the resource supplier and producing regions. This can be done by means of pressure: (1) for subsidies, tax concessions, and regulations conferring special privileges or even government promotion of TNC interests; (2) for the maintenance of a labor force of specialized skills at low wages in the face of unstable employment; (3) for exemption from social controls such as health and environmental stadards; and/or (4) for a privileged position in the domestic market of the peripheral producing nations.

In addition, the TNCs may well be able to pass on an additional share of risk to their respective home countries by negotiating for the types of special privileges. Thus the information technologies become a major tool for TNCs to enhance both their market power and their autonomy in negotiating with all nation states, whether hinterland producers or home governments. Moreover, with direct broadcast satellites, and the massive spillover of television signals across national borders, TNC mass media advertising can severely weaken the effectiveness of formal government policies attempting to restrict TNC access to national markets and to limit the commercialization of their societies. New models of dependency may have to consider TNCs at the center, with all affected nations relating to them from different positions of dependency.

A significant separation of the incidence of risk from the beneficiaries of risk can have severe implications. It is an invitation for the TNCs to assume risks far beyond the level they would assume under normal market conditions or rational resource allocation. This may explain the willingness of U.S., Canadian, and European banks in 1981 to violate their own lending rules in loans to Third World nations in an attempt to exploit the very high short-term interest rates. Given the fact that oligopolistic rivalry for long-run entrenchment in national markets is a game with very large pay-offs, the incentive to overinvest both in production facilities and in market creation activities is great. When placed in a context of high overhead costs and fluctuating demand, the inherent instability in the economic system is likely to be magnified significantly.

Under these conditions, there is no reason to expect that the price system will work toward long-term efficiency in resource allocation. Short-term prices are likely to fluctuate significantly over wide ranges reflecting either excess capacity, short-term shortages, or opportunities for monopolistic exploitation. The market provides no constraint on over-investment. Indeed it would appear that the boom and bust cycles of investment in railroads and canals more than a century ago may provide the best historical reference point for analysis of the forthcoming surge in the computer, telecommunications, and information content industries.

After his study of the history of the megaproject investments of the past, Innis concluded: "As a result of the importance of overhead costs, in its effects on inelastic supply and especially joint supply, the price level has become an uncertain and far from delicate indicator in adjusting supply and demand."[19] Recent experiences with nuclear power, oil exploration, and international banking do not provide a basis for confidence that the economic system functions any better now in this respect than it did a century or two ago. Certainly a relevant model for the analysis of future global markets is the oil market, but with TNCs in the role of OPEC.

Clearly, if instability in the global economic system increases, it will affect all parties. Thus, the TNCs, by having the power to transfer the incidence of risk, may be stimulated to engage in investment and pricing behavior that will create more instability and risk than they are able to transfer. This is consistent with the standard explanations of instability from neoclassical oligopoly theory.

In this market environment neoclassical price theory is somewhat akin to a set of decision rules for optimizing the arrangement of the deck chairs on the *Titanic*.[20] The price signals tell us nothing about the speed and direction in which the economic ship is headed. Short-run prices are likely to be very misleading as guides to resource allocation. Here one cannot help recalling a passage from Ayres: "The time will come when we shall see that the root of all our economic confusion and the cause of the intellectual impotency which has brought economics into general disrepute is the obsession of our science with price theory—the virtual identification of economics with price analysis in almost total exclusion of what Veblen called the 'life process' of mankind."[21] The challenge for economic analysis is to address directly the problem of long-term resource allocation under conditions of unstable oligopoly, and the implications of policies designed to contain its worst possibilities.

These developments obviously do not bode well for the maintenance of traditional notions of public or consumer interests in domestic markets. Existing government regulatory agencies are likely to become even less effective in the future than they are now. Yet, the need for advocacy of consumer interests will be greater. Public interest advocates will have to seek other avenues of representation through the legislative and judicial process.

Countries such as Canada find themselves ambivalent with regard to these developments in the information industries. Canada has spent most of its history striving to maintain a small degree of independence in the shadow of first Britain and then the United States. But Canada is at the forefront of telecommunication technology and sees a window of opportunity to exploit global information and telecommunication markets.

Canada's major entry into the global information market sweepstakes —as policy makers sometimes call it—is Bell Canada Enterprises (BCE), most frequently through its equipment manufacturing subsidiary, Northern Telecom. Bell Canada recently undertook a corporate reorganization in which it created the holding company, BCE, and moved all of its activities except domestic telephone service out from under government regulation. This was necessary, according to the company, to position itself for competing in global markets against larger TNCs like ITT, ATT, Siemens, Phillips, IBM, etcetera. BCE has won lucrative contracts in Saudi Arabia and other developing countries, and is currently concentrating on China. The government has yet to get around to passing legislation that will give its regulatory agency, the Canadian Radio-Television and Telecommunications Commission (CRTC), effective power to investigate possible cross-subsidies between Bell Canada's regulated and unregulated activities. Recently Bell Canada announced that it will be seeking to rebalance its rates, following the access charge pattern already begun in the United States. It appears that success in the global market has taken priority over domestic social policy.

BCE has been sufficiently successful in the global telecommunication market that it has opened plants throughout the world. BCE employment in Canada has declined in recent years and rumors persist that the company may shift the headquarters of its successful equipment subsidiary to the United States. The Canadian government undoubtedly is seeking ways to keep BCE as a purely Canadian successful TNC. But BCE's interest seems to be shifting further and further from that of the Canadian domestic economy for any purpose other than exploitation.

It would appear that Third World nations will bear the brunt of the risk and instability associated with the exploitation of information industry technologies and markets. As producers in the periphery, they will have little, if any control over the product or profit from their labor and other resources. Moreover, successful global marketing by the TNCs requires that Third World leaders be convinced to import the latest computer/telecommunication systems. The Third World represents an extremely significant part of the potential market. But if they buy into these technologies, most will be committed to a long-run dependence that will contribute to continuing short-term balance of payments, and virtually permanent constraints on their domestic economies.

For nations with a 50 percent literacy rate, a 5 percent telephone penetration rate, and an average annual per capita income less than the cost of a computer terminal, one might question the priority of new technologies that provide instant access to data banks in New York and London, except of course that they facilitate TNC control in the region. In the future Third World nations desperately need to establish effective negotiating strategies to resist the technological salesmanship of the TNCs and their home governments, and to attempt to assert their own priorities. In a global market of oligopolistic rivalry, there is negotiating room for smaller countries to establish a variety of new cooperative and competitive market relations. In some areas the non-aligned nations have already begun to take modest steps in this direction. The relative negotiating positions may be unequal, because of differences in economic and political power, but they are not dictated by market structure. The inherent instability of rivalrous oligopoly behavior provides a soft underbelly to the power of dominant TNCs. If, for example, the Third World decided not to buy into the new information technologies, there would be at least instability, and possibly a short-run collapse in these industries at the TNC centers.

Conclusion

Although this analysis of some of the implications of the information economy is not comforting, neither is it entirely bleak. The developments outlined in this article will bring to the foreground and accentuate, perhaps as never before, the oligopolistic character of most national and global markets. In making the reality more visible, the problems may be addressed more directly. Perhaps it will provide a stimulus to reorient market theory from abstract notions of atomistic competition to the challenging reality of indeterminate, unstable oligopolisic rivalry.

Whereas the competitive model invites the abdication of analysis of real markets, the oligopoly model demands it. Significant progress will be made only when economics examines more deeply such matters as: (1) the characteristics of equal and unequal exchange; (2) the dimensions of oligopostic negotiation; (3) criteria for determining long-run balanced growth; (4) the specific causes of market instability; (5) the real world opportunity cost characteristics of overhead functions; (6) long-run efficiency criteria for sharing common costs in multi-product firms; (7) the rules and regulations essential to the efficient functioning of different kinds of markets; (8) mechanisms for accountability with respect to actual resource allocation in real markets; (9) comparisons between market and non-market systems of resource allocation; (10) methods for incorporating externality and public interest considerations in long-run resource allocation decisions. There are unlimited opportunities for institutional analysis and theoretical developments to make complementary contributions. Perhaps the changes unfolding in the information economy will provide the catalyst.

Notes

1. Harold A. Innis, *Empire and Communications* (revised by Mary Q. Innis), (Toronto: University of Toronto Press, 1972 [1950]), p. 5.
2. See for example: Daniel Bell, *The Coming of Post-Industrial Society: A Venture in Social Forecasting* (New York: Basic Books, 1973); M. Porat, "Global Implications of the Information Society," *Journal of Communication* 28 (Winter 1978): 70-80.
3. Fritz Machlup, *Knowledge: Its Creation, Distribution, and Economic Significance*, 3 vols. (Princeton, N.J.: Princeton University Press, 1980-84); Porat, "Global Implications."
4. See for example, Dallas W. Smythe, *Dependency Road: Communications, Capitalism, Consciousness, and Canada* (Norwood, N.J.: Ablex, 1981); and William H. Melody, "Direct Broadcast Satellites: The Canadian Experience" (1982), published in German in *Satelliten-Kommunikation: Nationale Mediensysteme und Internationale Kommunikationspolitik* (Hamburg: Hans Bredow Institute, 1983).
5. Herbert I. Schiller, *Who Knows: Information in the Age of the Fortune 500* (Norwood, N.J.: Ablex, 1981); and Rohan Samarajiwa, "Information and Property Rights: The Case of the News Agency Industry" (Paper presented at 14th Conference of the International Association for Mass Communication Research, Prague, Czechoslavakia, August 1984).
6. See, for example, Ithiel de Sola Pool, *Technologies of Freedom* (Cambridge, Mass.: Harvard University Press, 1983).
7. William H. Melody, "Development of the Communication and Information Industries: Impact on Social Structures" (Paper prepared for the *Symposium on the Cultural, Social, and Economic Impact of Communication Technology*, sponsored by UNESCO and Instituto della Enciclopedia Italiana, Rome, Italy, 12-16 December 1983).
8. Edward S. Herman, *Corporate Control, Corporate Power: A Twentieth Century Fund Study* (New York: Cambridge University Press, 1981).
9. William H. Melody, "Cost Standards for Judging Local Exchange Rates," in *Diversification, Deregulation, and Increased Uncertainty in the Public*

Utility Industries, ed. H. M. Trebing (East Lansing, Mich.: Michigan State University, MSU Public Utilities Papers, 1983), pp. 474-95; "Efficient Rate Regulation in the Competitive Era," in *New Directions: State Regulation of Telecommunications* (Symposium Proceedings, Washington State Legislature, Joint Select Committee on Telecommunications, and University of Washington Graduate School of Public Affairs, Seattle, 11-12 July 1984, Sect. VI, pp. 1-18).

10. Richard B. DuBoff, "The Telegraph and the Structure of Markets in the United States, 1845-1890," *Research in Economic History* 8 (1983): 253-277.

11. Ibid., p. 270, footnote omitted.

12. See, for example, Robin E. Mansell, "Industrial Strategies and the Communication/Information Sector: An Analysis of Contradictions in Canadian Policy and Performance" (Ph.D. diss., Simon Fraser University, 1984); and "Contradictions in National Communication/Information Policies: The Canadian Experience," *Media Culture and Society* (Spring 1985): 33-53.

13. See Adam Smith, *An Inquiry into the Nature and Causes of the Wealth of Nations*, 5th ed. (New York: Modern Library, 1977 [1776]).

14. See, for example, William J. Baumol, "Contestable Markets: An Uprising in the Theory of Industry Structure," *American Economic Review* 72 (March 1982): 1-15; for a critique, see William G. Shepherd, " 'Contestability' vs. Competition," *American Economic Review* 74 (September 1984): 572-85.

15. See William H. Melody, "The Marginal Utility of Marginal Analysis in Public Policy Formulation," *Journal of Economic Issues* 8 (June 1974): 287-300.

16. Gabriel Palma, "Dependency: A Formal Theory of Underdevelopment or a Methodology for the Analysis of Concrete Situations of Underdevelopment," *World Development* 6 (July/August 1978): 881-924.

17. See, for example, Harold A. Innis, *Empire and Communications* (rev. by Mary Q. Innis) (Toronto: University of Toronto Press, 1972 [1950]); Harold A. Innis, *Essays in Canadian Economic History* (Toronto: University of Toronto Press, 1956); and I. Wallerstein, *The Modern World System: Capitalist Agriculture and the Origins of the European World Economy in the Sixteenth Century* (New York: Academic Press, 1976).

18. Innis, *Essays*.

19. Ibid., p. 130.

20. The analogy is not mine. Source unknown.

21. C. F. Ayres, *The Theory of Economic Progress: A Study of the Fundamentals of Economic Development and Cultural Change* (Michigan: New Issues Press, Western Michigan University, 1978 [1944]), p. xxxv.

References

Ayres, C. E. 1962. *The Theory of Economic Progress: A Study of the Fundamentals of Economic Development and Cultural Change*. Michigan: New Issues Press, Western Michigan University (1944).

Baumol, William J. 1982. "Contestable Markets: An Uprising in the Theory of Industry Structure." *American Economic Review* 72 (March): 1-15.

Bell, Daniel. 1973. *The Coming of Post-Industrial Society: A Venture in Social Forecasting.* New York: Basic Books.

Caves, Richard E. 1982. *Multinational Enterprise and Economic Analysis. Cambridge Surveys of English Literature.* New York: Cambridge University Press.

Clark, J. Maurice. 1923. *Studies in the Economics of Overhead Costs.* Chicago: The University of Chicago Press.

Hymer, Stephen Herbert. 1979. *The Multinational Corporation: A Radical Approach.* Edited by Robert B. Cohen, et al. New York: Cambridge University Press.

Innis, Harold A. 1972. *Empire and Communications.* Revised by Mary Q. Innis. Toronto: University of Toronto Press [1950].

Machlup, Fritz. 1980-84. *Knowledge: Its Creation, Distribution, and Economic Significance.* 3 vols. Princeton, N.J.: Princeton University Press.

Melody, William H., L. Salter, and P. Heyer. 1981. *Culture, Communication, and Dependency: The Tradition of H. A. Innis.* Norwood, N.J.: Ablex.

Mitchell, Wesley C. 1964. *What Veblen Taught: Selected Writings of Thorstein Veblen.* New York: Sentry Press Reprints of Economics Classics [1936].

O'Brien, Rita Cruise, ed. 1983. *Information, Economics, and Power.* London: Hodder and Stoughton.

Palma, Gabriel. 1978. "Dependency: A Formal Theory of Underdevelopment or a Methodology for the Analysis of Concrete Situations of Underdevelopment." *World Development* 6 (July/August): 881-924.

Penrose, Edith T. 1968. *The Theory of the Growth of the Firm.* Oxford: Basil Blackwell.

Robinson, Joan. 1962. *Essays in the Theory of Economic Growth.* London: The Macmillan Press.

Robinson, Joan. 1978. *Contributions to Modern Economics.* Oxford: Basil Blackwell.

Robinson, Joan. 1980. *Further Contributions to Modern Economics.* Oxford: Basil Blackwell.

Schumpeter, Joseph A. 1954. *A History of Economic Analysis.* Edited by Elizabeth Boody Schumpeter. New York: Oxford University Press.

Shepherd, William G. 1984. " 'Contestability' vs. Competition." *American Economic Review* 74 (September): 572-85.

Smith, Adam. 1977. *An Inquiry into the Nature and Causes of the Wealth of Nations.* 5th ed. New York: Modern Library.

Smythe, Dallas W. 1981. *Dependency Road: Communications, Capitalism, Consciousness, and Canada.* Norwood, N.J.: Ablex.

Wallerstein, I. 1976. *The Modern World System: Capitalist Agriculture and the Origins of the European World Economy in the Sixteenth Century.* New York: Academic Press.